Vāc

The SUNY Series in the Shaiva Traditions of Kashmir
Harvey P. Alper, Editor

Vāc

The CONCEPT OF THE WORD *in Selected Hindu Tantras*

André Padoux

Translated by Jacques Gontier

State University of New York Press

Published by
State University of New York Press, Albany

Printed in the United States of America

For information, address State University of New York
Press, State University Plaza, Albany, N.Y., 12246

Library of Congress Cataloging-in-Publication Data

Padoux, André.
Vāc, the concept of the word in selected Hindu Tantras/André Padoux.
p. cm.—(The SUNY series in the Shaiva traditions of Kashmir)
Bibliography: p. .
Includes index.
ISBN 0-7914-0257-6. — ISBN 0-7914-0258-4 (pbk.)
1. Tantras—Criticism, interpretation, etc. 2. Sanskrit language—Religious aspects—Tantrism. 3. Tantrism—Doctrines. 4. Kashmir Śaivism—Doctrines. I. Title. II. Title: Word in selected Hindu Tantras. III. Series.
BL1141.27.P33 1990
294.5′95—dc20 89-11436
CIP

10 9 8 7 6 5 4 3 2 1

Contents

Preface

This book is a complete revision of my main doctoral thesis, *Recherches sur la symbolique et l'énergie de la parole dans certains textes tantriques*, presented at the University of Paris in 1964. One of the few merits of that thesis, begun some thirty years ago, was that it was one of the first attempts at a systematic study of the subject. It was, however, very far from perfect. There were inaccuracies, mistakes and an inordinate number of misprints. In those days very little had as yet been written concerning the Word—*vāc*—and the Indian cosmogonies related to it. A number of Sanskrit texts which are easy to consult nowadays were not accessible then. Such was the case with the manuscripts from Nepal, which have now been microfilmed under the Nepal-German Manuscript Preservation Project.

In spite of its many shortcomings the original version was approved by some colleagues and deemed useful as a (somewhat heavy) introduction to the subject. A second edition, cleansed of most of the misprints and incorporating a number of minor emendations, was issued in 1975. But despite such corrections I still found the work very unsatisfactory, and would gladly have forgotten it, together with other sins of my youth. It so happened however that some Indologists and historians of religion (including Harvey P. Alper, of Southern Methodist University, Dallas) thought it was not all that bad and suggested I should make it available to a wider audience by having it translated into English. With some misgivings I gave in to this suggestion, on condition that the text be entirely revised, corrected and expanded where necessary. This book is the result.

As the original title was both imprecise and too long, I have adopted one suggested by H. P. Alper but I have kept to the overall pattern of the original text. Chapters 1, 3, 4 and 5 have been reworked and supplemented, but incorporate no major changes: the plan is the same and some pages have been translated or transposed more or less directly into English. On the other hand, I have entirely rewritten chapters 2, 6 and 7. The reason for all these changes lies not only in the imperfections of the original but also, and sometimes mainly, in the progress made during the last thirty years in the field of tantric studies. My views on a number of points have been modified by these advances. Not only did I go on working on the subject, but Alexis Sanderson and Teun Goudriaan, to mention but two scholars, have opened up entirely new vistas in some of these fields. For example, no one could write nowadays what I wrote in the early sixties on the subject of tantrism or Kashmirian Śaivism. On certain topics, also, new and reliable studies are now available, and there would have been no point in restating here what I or others have written elsewhere. Finally, on the assumption that some readers of this book might have read the original in either the 1963 or the 1975 edition, I have sometimes rewritten a passage, not to correct it, but simply to include new material or quotations. Generally speaking, I quote more Sanskrit texts now than before.

Since Harvey P. Alper was the first person to suggest this English translation—he also suggested that the SUNY Press might publish it—it is only fair that I should dedicate the present volume to the memory of this greatly missed friend. My thanks also go to William D. Eastman, director of SUNY Press, for undertaking to publish a work which has proved far from easy to translate and edit, and which is hardly likely to sell like hot cakes.

It goes without saying that the bibliography and the footnote references have been updated and adapted as far as possible for the use of English readers.

Introduction

My purpose in this work was to examine the speculations relating to the Word—*vāc*—such as found in various Sanskrit texts of Tantric character, with special emphasis on those relating to the power or the energy (*śakti*) of the Word. It is therefore a study concerned with Tantric conceptions about the Word and its powers. It cannot claim to be a general review. It deals only with a very limited sphere of the Indian religious and philosophical literature, and must necessarily leave aside various conceptions, however interesting. Since in this culture so much emphasis has been placed on the Word for over three thousand years, it was not of course possible to consider the subject in its entirety. It was not even possible to study all the available tantric scriptures in Sanskrit dealing with this topic. Therefore the work (as the title of my 1963 dissertation implied) is restricted to "selected Tantras," that is, chiefly to scriptures belonging to the nondualistic Śaivism as it arose in Kashmir, probably in the early part of the ninth century A.D., and developed there before rapidly spreading throughout India. The reason for such a selection is understandable in that these traditions provide what is perhaps the most interesting and sometimes the most subtle, articulated, and reasoned developments on the subject. However, other non-Śaiva or non-"Kashmirian"[1] works have also been consulted and will be cited occasionally. Resorting to

1. I write "Kashmirian" because in the Kashmirian nondualistic Śaiva tradition, the texts quite often do not originate from Kashmir but from elsewhere, particularly from South India.

other traditions was desirable not only to broaden the scope of our investigation, but also because there have been interactions between Vaiṣṇavism and (dualistic or nondualistic) Śaivism in Kashmir itself, and probably longstanding contacts and exchanges of ideas between Kashmir and other areas of the Indian subcontinent. Similar developments in ideas also took place in Buddhism, which, however, has not been included as part of our investigation.

Indian speculations about the word obviously embrace those on language. They cover phonetics and grammar, both well developed in India even before our era, and whose basic notions are often to be met with in Tantric texts. As for Śaivism, it was often the religion of grammarians or grammarian-philosophers, some of whose conceptions are borrowed from Tantrism. There is a very close interrelation between Tantrism and the speculations about the Word. Although originating from two different backgrounds, both, however, have very ancient Indian sources.

This being so, to show how the present research fits into the general framework of Indian thought (Vedic/Brahmanic, and then Hindu), it seemed useful to outline, in an initial chapter, the antiquity of Indian speculations about the Word—*vāc*. The latter was conceived from the very beginnings as a creative power, the "mother of the gods." On the other hand—at least as far as its forms unrelated to current speech are concerned—the Word was very early regarded as a symbol of the Godhead, or more exactly as revealing the divine presence within the cosmos, as the force that creates, maintains, and upholds the universe. Those ancient notions, while subjected to transformations, have never been obliterated: change in continuity, as is well known, is a characteristic feature of India, whose culture has always succeeded in remaining unmovable in its essence, while following a constant process of evolution and adjustment. The ancient notions about *vāc* were restated and developed in Tantric Hinduism, a tentative definition of which will be given in the second chapter, where we shall also attempt to delineate a picture of the Kashmirian Śaiva schools or traditions, whose scriptures have been selected for our study. Both chapters will emphasize the continuity and the developments of the notion, present from the very outset, that the Word is an energy, and that the latter may be tapped and used by anyone who is able to penetrate its secret nature and mysteries. To the Indian mind indeed, in the beginning was the Word; but here the Word is a force: it is active and can be used for action.

Chapters 3 to 7, which form the core of the book, will be devoted to a description of the various aspects of this energy of the Word, according to selected Tantras. This exposition will, I believe, show a constant ambivalence, a continuous shift in the descriptions from the human to the cosmic and vice-versa, which is a distinctive feature not only of the Tantric mind, but more generally of the Indian mind, to which, as early as Vedism, the knowledge of the supreme reality, the highest understanding, was founded on the knowledge of anthropocosmic correlations. The energy (*śakti*), as we shall see, is at the same time Word (*vāc*), consciousness (*cit, saṃvid*), breath, and vital or vibrative energy (*prāṇa*): there are no absolute distinctions, no discontinuity between the human and the cosmic, the vital, the psychic, or the spiritual. All the developments of the Word which will be described can occur homologously within man or the cosmos. Such is the case with the evolution of the primal sound-vibration and the movement of the *kuṇḍalinī* as a form of phonic energy (chap. 3). Thus this ambivalence originates from the very premises of a system that views the creative act as an utterance which is a human act, but chooses to reverse the order and to see in this act nothing but the reproduction at the human level of an archetypal, divine act or process. So we shall see (chap. 4) how the universe emerges within divine consciousness, through the four stages or levels of speech, just as language or explicit thought does within human consciousness, while the process in its cosmic transposition will serve to account for the human process, and more especially for the cognitive validity of speech. Similarly (in chap. 5), we shall see how the categories (*tattva*) of the cosmic manifestation arise concurrently with the Sanskrit phonemes (*varṇa*) arranged in their grammatical order, while grammar—as well as traditional phonetics—will serve to account for the cosmogony. Of course, Sanskrit, the language of revelation, is divine; whereas grammar—"the gateway to salvation," "close to *brahman*, and the ascesis of ascesis" (according to Bhartṛhari: *tapasām uttamaṃ tapaḥ . . . vyākaraṇam -Vākyapadīya,* 1.11)—provides one of the chief supports of all reasoning to anyone using Sanskrit.

We shall see, again with respect to the aforesaid ambivalence, how the Word is also and above all used as a means for liberation. In the last portion of this study, it will no longer appear so much as the energy that brings gods and worlds into existence as the substance wherein they are resorbed, and more especially as a means for human beings to progress toward liberation (chap. 6), or still more as a means to take hold, through mantras (chap. 7), of the primal energy which is Speech or Word, and thereby not only to make use of it, but to go back to its very source, and therefore to be freed from the chains of the becoming. Is not freedom or more exactly absolute autonomy (*svātantrya*) precisely one of the main characteristics of the supreme Word as spiritual energy, as identical with the primal principle? *Svātantrya* is a recurrent term with our authors, and Abhinavagupta even held it as such a fundamental notion that he sometimes referred to his Trika as *Svātantryavāda*, the doctrine of freedom or autonomy. The primordial principle is indeed pure, creative spontaneity, the flashing forth of the uninhibited power and overflowing bounty of the divine. Absolute autonomy is the attribute of the highest aspect of the Godhead. With the cosmic flow of emanation this freedom gradually diminishes until creatures, in our world, are bound to the becoming. The Word, simultaneously, losing its absolute autonomy, its nature of a pure and free act, becomes the human language, subject to "conventions," and the source of bondage for human beings. However, if the free source, the pure foundation of this language is "recognized" behind the appearances, if human beings know how to probe into and use such forms of speech (the mantras) as are free from the limitations of language, they reconnect with that source and, as liberated while still alive, they identify with the spontaneity, the creative autonomy, of the source of the Word.

This return to the source of the Word will appear indeed not only as an identification with the Word *in statu nascendi*, but also as a merging with that wherefrom the Word arises, which is a Beyond beyond the Word, a still, silent area, a pure transcendence, a notion which, in Tantrism, keeps up the view, which occurs from the very beginnings of Indian thought, that the Word is subordinate to Silence, the uttered to the unuttered.

One may be inclined to consider this approach as an over-simplification, especially in its endeavor to bring together several traditional systems under one general theoretical framework. Of course there are differences and distinctions, and we won't fail to point them out occasionally. However, the mind cannot grasp the diversity of the facts unless it organizes them somewhat into a system. Above all, while acknowledging the plurality of Indian views and interpretations, we feel that the framework adopted here is not too unfaithful a reflection of the basic orientation—underlying their diversity—of the Tantric-inspired speculations about the Word, whether in nondualistic Śaivism or in other theologico-metaphysical traditions.

It may not be out of place to explain here why the Sanskrit *vāc* has been rendered by *word*, a term also referring to the central theme of this work. Here we are confronted with a problem of translation, no translation ever being totally satisfactory. *Vāc*, from *VAC*—to speak, to say—means voice, speech, word; it may also refer to utterance and language. It is also the embodied, divinized Word: the Goddess who is Word, and this latter aspect will be the most frequent here. As *vāc* is both what is said, uttered, and that which says or utters—One who is said and is saying—its translation as *word* (or *Word*) seems to us the least inappropriate of all. But it should not be confused with the *logos*, the status of which is by no means that of *vāc* (we shall deal with this later). *Language* would have been a totally inadequate translation, if only because *vāc*, at the stages described in the following pages, is prior to any language, and in its most obvious Tantric use, that of mantras—chiefly *bījamantra*—has no connection whatever with language. The translation of *vāc* as speech or Speech, which is used by some authors, is, however, also possible: we have sometimes resorted to it.

Finally, two further points must be outlined, one which relates directly to our subject, the other to its position within Indian reality as a whole.

First, a major feature of the Word, as conceived of in India and as it will be considered here, is its strictly verbal or aural—unwritten—character. The Revelation is the *Śruti*, the Word heard by the sages, the *ṛṣi*s, the seers-poets of the Vedic hymns. The earliest of those hymns were composed at a time when Aryan India did not know about writing. May not this early, purely verbal stage account for the subsequent depreciation of written texts? That is a moot point. However, the fact remains that henceforth Brahmanic-Hindu India has always proved to be suspicious of the written aspect of the word. The Veda, as is well known, should not be written down; when written down, a mantra is truly a "dead letter"; it should only be imparted by word of mouth during initiation. So here our primary concern will be with the spoken, speaking Word or Speech, with sound, and not with (written) scriptures.[2] This is not to say that the rule has no exceptions: written works have, in time, become a part of the Hindu religious tradition. Tantras have been committed to writing. Making copies of them came to be held as a pious task. We shall see that some mantric practices involve either writing or visualization of written signs.[3] Let us also mention that diagrams (*maṇḍala, yantra, cakra*) play a part in rituals and have contributed to create a link, even an isomorphism between the visual and the aural.[4] Furthermore, it is well known that Vedic mantras (and the other ones as well) are supposed to have first been "seen" by the *ṛṣi*s. Vision, or beholding (*dṛṣṭi*) often plays an important part in the ritual. Finally, we shall see the importance of visual metaphors in nondualistic Kashmir Śaivism. Still the fact is that here, utterance, the verbal, the audible (or inaudible), explicitly or implicitly, will be placed on the front line.[5]

---

2. About the verbal-aural character, not only of the Revelation but of Indian scriptures in general, cf. for instance: C. Mackenzie Brown, "Purāṇa as Scripture: From Sound to Image of the Holy Word in Hindu Tradition," *History of Religion* 16/1 (1986): 1-33.
3. As in the "placing" (*nyāsa*) of mantras. See also the "demons' writing," *bhūtalipi*.
4. On this point refer to Padoux (ed.) *Mantras et diagrammes rituels dans l'hindouisme* (Paris: CNRS, 1986): introduction.
5. There would be much to say about the role of sound in ritualistic action and, more generally, in human experience, especially that of the sacred. But this is too vast a subject to be pursued here.

The primacy of the oral over writing—and this is the second point I wished to emphasize—appears as somewhat paradoxical, considering that the only language to which we shall refer here is Sanskrit. Now, it is likely that in India, Sanskrit never really existed as a spoken, current language. It may have been spoken in certain circumstances, no doubt: it is still so to this day. But it has always been a learned, liturgical language: the language of the gods, not of men, and especially not of ordinary people. In their daily life, Indians used to speak "popular" Indo-Aryan or Dravidian languages, those through which were spontaneously expressed their experiences of everyday life, their feelings, their emotions, Sanskrit being used only, when at all, for a scholarly, learned or literary purpose, as well of course in connection with religious or liturgical matters.[6] Sanskrit, indeed, has been the vehicle for the literary, religious, philosophical, and scientific culture of India, insofar as this culture is Vedic-Brahmanic, and subsequently Hindu. But it does not reflect all that has been said or written in India, and since it developed very largely in a non-Sanskritic milieu, it necessarily always interacted with it. We cannot, however, deal here with this issue which others have treated elsewhere.[7] I think it had to be pointed out at the outset of this book: here, when dealing with the Sanskrit tradition, we shall consider the most sophisticated and elaborate teachings of India about the Word, though not all that India may have said or thought on this matter.

---

6. Here may be mentioned the distinction made by Fr. Walter J. Ong (*Interfaces of the Word*) between "father language" and "mother tongue." "Unlike the mother tongue," remarks R. K. Ramanujan, "Sanskrit is the language of the fathers."
7. Especially R. K. Ramanujan in the Postface of *Hymns for the Drowning; Poems for Viṣṇu by Nammāḻvār* (Princeton: 1981), from whom I quoted in the above footnote.

1

Early Speculations about the Significance and the Powers of the Word

The Tantric speculations and practices that will be considered in the following chapters are not, in India, something outlandish or strange, however unexpected or excessive they may appear to us in some respects. They emerged in a rich and ancient culture where, from the outset, so it seems, the Word was given a prominent position. Thus, before studying these speculations, the ancient notions on the subject should be first of all briefly reviewed. This preliminary survey may appear somewhat hurried and incomplete. But a deeper investigation would fill a whole volume, while this is meant only as a short preface to, or a kind of basic framework of, what will follow.

India seems indeed, of all the countries in the world, one—or even the one—best exemplifying an ageless, unbroken tradition of speculations about the Word; of elaborations, and therefore experiences, of myths where the primordial Word, Speech, plays a vital part; of speculations about the cosmogonic or magic power of certain forms of the Word; of reflections on the value and nature of language, together with the elaboration, from a remote past, of phonetics and grammar. This is a land where grammar went so far as to be considered as one of the *darśana*s—"views" on the world, which are at the same time paths to salvation—since it helps to preserve and understand a primeval revelation which embodies the whole Truth and is given in the form of sacred formulas (mantras), pregnant with riddles and correlations, which express—and through which expresses itself—the *brahman*, which is both transcendent

Reality and supreme Word. Finally, India also is a country where throughout the ages a "linguistic theology" has evolved, elements of which are to be traced, at different periods in time, in most of the thought systems that arose there.

Providing a general overview covering the whole range of this extensive body of myths and speculations is no easy task, and such an attempt would be an unwise, because superficial, approach. We may point out, however, the antiquity of these notions, which are therefore Vedic (and this does not necessarily mean Aryan), since we have only Vedic documents concerning the earliest developments of Indian thought. Let us also now note that a historical survey cannot be contemplated here, both because there is no relevant material for a history of ideas in India and because the Indians themselves—even though they may have disputed against each other—have always been inclined to expound their various systems *sub specie aeternitatis*, and not according to their historical unfolding. It is obvious, though, that such an unfolding did take place, and we shall have some opportunities to point it out. But there is hardly any hint about how it progressed, hence the temptation of what may be termed a structural approach through which, rather than how conceptions did evolve, we could grasp the different aspects of the Vedic-Brahmanic, then Hindu, vision of the universe, including the position of human beings therein, as well of course as the nature and significance given therein to the Word.

To give a clearer picture of this extensive body of ancient speculations, one might be inclined to make a tentative distinction, at least as a heuristic procedure, between two aspects. One[1] that may be said to be more specifically Brahmanic is chiefly based on the exegesis of the Veda, which, to the orthodoxy, represents the Revelation itself, the epitome of sacred knowledge. Considering the mantras and the *brāhmaṇas* of the Vedic ritual, the authors of these schools—those of the

1. Cf. L. Renou in *L'Inde classique*, vol. 1, paragraphs 1508ff., vol. 2, pp. 79ff.; and D. S. Ruegg, *Contributions à l'histoire de la philosophie indienne* (Paris, 1959). For these ancient notions dealing with the Word one may refer to K. Madhava Sarma's article, "Vāk before Bhartṛhari," *Poona Orientalist* VIII (1943): 21-36.

Mīmāṃsā—seek to justify the eternal existence of the Veda, and to this end will have to establish that *śabda*—a term that means both "sound" and "word," that is, the phonic signs making up the Veda—is eternal (*nitya*). With this hermeneutic of the Veda, with grammar, and even more with grammatical philosophy, this body of speculations about how sounds, words, or sentences may be a valid means of knowledge (*pramāṇa*) evolved an epistemology of speech, a philosophy of knowledge as relating to language, and a metaphysics of language or sound. Poetics and aesthetics are connected with this current, which includes a number of outstanding authors, of whom one at least should be mentioned here: Bhartṛhari, not only because of the value of his great work the *Vākyapadīya* ("[Treatise] about sentences and words"), but also because he is held as a master—much discussed but even moreso quoted—by the authors of the Trika, and more especially by the foremost among them, Abhinavagupta. The latter, who was indeed one of the leading Indian poeticians, refers repeatedly, in his Tantric works, to these speculations about the Vedic origins of the word and the validity of knowledge. He very naturally resorts thereto in his philosophico-linguistic approach since, like that of all Sanskrit authors, it is based upon the traditional treatises, the *śāstra*s.

But Abhinavagupta's conceptions about the word, like those of the other Sanskrit authors with whom we shall deal, while retaining Mīmāṃsaka elements,[2] are at the same time fully involved with myth. They are part of a mythic vision of the cosmos, some aspects of which go back to the Vedic cosmogonic myths; most of them, however, are taken from the visionary and ritualistic theologico-metaphysical system of the Tantras, where the individual self ultimately merges, through complex, ritualistic, theological and yogic representations, into the absolute of the divine Self.

2. The Mīmāṃsā and its "realism" surely had a strong influence in Kashmir, as evidenced by a number of textual references. Indeed, the prevailing conception in India is that speech—language—operates as a relationship between words and things, the speaker's subjectivity playing no important part in the process: this is, perhaps, a legacy from the Mīmāṃsā.

That is the aspect we may distinguish, another side, of the speculations about the Word, an outlook or a way of thinking, according to which the Word, uttered at the origin of time (and sometimes personified), is a creative and efficient power, an energy (*śakti*) both cosmic and human, of which humans can take hold through the formulas (mantras) which express it (those formulas also have a magical value and are normally used in a ritual context), thereby becoming the equal of gods or of the primal creative principle itself. This is a type of thought for which any form of speech somehow partakes of this magical potency.

Those myths, those speculations about the powers of the Word, occur as early as the *Ṛg Veda.* They are also found later in the *Atharva Veda*, replete as it is with prayers and magical formulas, as well as in the *Yajur Veda* (where one finds, for instance, such a series of names of gods as the *śatarudrīya* of the *Taittirīya Saṃhitā*). In those works an important part is also assigned to syllables or words with no apparent meaning but pregnant with a transcendental or magical import. Those speculations, where myth and verbal magic intermingle, continue in the Brāhmaṇas, which, with their numerical divisions of the cosmos and the vital functions, their magical identifications, the part assigned to the vital breaths, formulas and syllables, and "etymologies," may be the source of many Tantric speculations. All this material appears next in the Āraṇyakas and the earliest Upaniṣads, where cosmogony is sometimes related to the Word, or where cosmogony and a physiology based on "breaths" (*prāṇa*) are closely interrelated. This appears too in some later Upaniṣads.

But it is with Tantrism that these considerations about the powers of the Word, which is henceforth identified with the divine energy itself (*śakti*), will come to their full development, and that sacred or magic formulas (mantras) will be most widely used (to such an extent in fact that the *mantraśāstra*, the science of Mantras, will come to be held as the most important portion of Tantric teachings). However, the oldest Tantras are later by several centuries than the Vedic Upaniṣads: When did those texts appear first? Where? To what can they relate? Are they a renewed form of the Vedic and Upaniṣadic speculations, or did they appear as a result of foreign influences or as issuing from an "autochthonous" background? Those are questions that arise and that will be briefly discussed later on. For the time being, let us simply note the antiquity and importance of these speculations, and the fact that grammar-phonetics and hermeneutics constantly mix with ritual and magic.[3]

In this initial chapter therefore we shall simply point out some ancient notions about the nature and power of the Word, and record a few ideas or terms occurring in Vedism and Brahmanism, which will reappear later on, with identical or very close meanings, in Kashmirian Śaiva scriptures or, more generally, in Tantric works. Such is the case, for instance, with the speculations about *oṃ* or about the breaths (*prāṇa*). The notion of Tantrism will be discussed in the next chapter, where we shall further examine the complex and sometimes difficult to assess relationship that may be traced between Tantric Hinduism and Vedism and orthodox Brahmanism; finally, we shall take up the study of the mythic architecture of the Word and the speculations about its powers as elaborated, more especially, in some nondualistic Śaiva works.

As early as the *Ṛg Veda*[4] much emphasis is placed on the

3. Here as elsewhere in this book, the term *magic* is used as a convenient way of referring to the manipulations of the powers of the Word or speech (or of any "force") for a specific purpose, whether worldly or otherworldly, together with their attendant rites (or the rites they consist in), and the speculations that seek to support and explain them; granted that in India (and elsewhere too probably) the sphere of "magic" can never be considered as totally apart from that of the "religious." All the *mantra-śāstra* scriptures and all speculative works on the subject clearly reveal this interconnection. About modern aspects of the inseparability of the "magic" and the "religious," one may refer to C. G. Diehl's study, *Instrument and Purpose* (Lund: Gleerups, 1958).

4. On this point one should refer to L. Renou, "Les pouvoirs de la Parole dans le Ṛgveda," in *E*(tudes) *V*(édiques) et *P*(aninéennes) I, pp. 1-27. For the Indian speculations about the Word in Vedism, one may also refer to earlier studies, such as: O. Strauss, "Altindische Spekulationen über die Sprache und ihre Problemen," *Z.D.M.G.* 82 (1927). For the theory of the Vedic ritualistic word, the works of F. Staal are of special interest (Cf. Bibliography).

For the *Ṛg Veda*, I have used Geldner's translation and notes, *Der Ṛgveda aus dem Sanskrit ins Deutsch Übersetzt* (Cambridge, Mass., 1951).

significance of the Word: it is referred to by various terms, and in several places it appears as a primordial principle, a creative force bringing forth the universe. So much so that it has been said that "the Vedic speculations, as expressed in the hymns, are based upon a kind of primacy of the word."[5]

First let us dwell for a while—though without overemphasis—on a term referring to a form of the Word, destined to be remarkable, since it will eventually be used, more than any other, to refer to the supreme Reality, the Absolute: *brahman.* This term has enjoyed an extraordinary and perhaps unexpected good fortune. As early as the *Ṛg Veda*, the word *brahman*[6] (neuter) refers to a major aspect of the Word: the ritualistic word, the "formula" par excellence, the supreme Word. This word, however, is also subject to the strict rules of poetics, but in a system of thought where the poet (*kavi*)[7] establishes an order in the universe as he celebrates it with the help of the Word. Finally *brahman* appears as a mysterious, most cryptic word.[8] This mysterious and arcane quality of the original Word will be found later on several occasions, together with those correspondences that were instituted by the *brahman* and are a major feature of Indian metaphysics (as of any mythic thought).

Among the terms referring to the Word in the Veda, we shall first consider *vāc*, the one which will be found again, with the same meaning of *word*, in a number of texts that will be discussed subsequently.

---

5. Renou, "Les Pouvoirs de la Parole dans le Ṛgveda," p. 1, and O. Strauss, "Hier finden wir auch die Verknüpfung von Sprachlichen und Religiösem, welche die spezifisch indische Farbung jener Problem ausmacht" (*op. cit.*).
6. About this term, see L. Renou (and L. Silburn), "Sur la notion de brahman" (*J.As.*, 1949, pp. 7ff.); Gonda, *Notes on Brahman* (Utrecht, 1950); P. Thieme, *Brahman* (*Z.D.M.G.* 102, 1952).
7. Cf. Renou, *E.V.P.* 2, p. 66, note: "In fact, the creation of the cosmos is similar to that of a work of art, either being the *kavi*'s deed," and L. Silburn, *Instant et Cause*, p. 21: *kavi*, the poet of measurement.
8. Cf. L. Renou, "Sur la notion de brahman" (p. 13): *brahman* is "this form of cryptic thought consisting in establishing a correlation, an explanatory identification, that which the Brāhmaṇas will refer to as *nidāna* or *bandhu*, and finally as Upaniṣad."

Vāc (a feminine word!) occurs in a number of isolated stanzas in various books of the *Ṛg Veda*, including those held as the oldest ones: the creative role of the Word seems therefore a notion present from the greatest antiquity. However, to find a hymn exclusively devoted to *vāc* one must turn to Book X, of later origin (hymns 71 and 125). In the first of them, dedicated to Bṛhaspati, the lord of the sacred formula, the knowledge (*jñāna*) of the origin and secrets of the sacred Word are expounded upon. According to tradition it begins: "O Bṛhaspati, that was the first unfoldment of the Word, when they stirred into action, giving a name [to things]," a formulation that from the outset points to a major role of the Word (which will be greatly emphasized in Tantrism), that of the placing of names, *nāmadheya*; and giving a name, in mythic thought (not only in India), is giving being. For the word, the name, as early as the *Ṛg Veda*, is the very being of what is named, it is immortal (*amṛta*; cf. 10.139.6, where the immortal [names] of the cows are the cows themselves). This hymn also outlines the association of word and sacrifice, a fundamental one in a context where sacrifice, always including as its central feature the utterance of the sacred formulas, assumes a cosmic significance: "They have walked along the path of the Word through sacrifice" (ibid., stanza 3). It also stresses the fact that the Word is not disclosed to all: "Many a one who have eyes have not seen the Word, many a one who have ears do not hear it" (stanza 4). It is as mysterious as *brahman*, even though this hymn only refers to the poetic word, but *brahman* itself is poetic word. It is also noteworthy that in the second stanza the sages "create the Word through the help of thought," which may appear as a prefiguration of the theories we shall examine later, and according to which the Word is subordinated to consciousness.

In the second hymn (10.125) the Word (which is made to speak) is glorified as a supreme power: " . . . I support both Varuṇa and Mitra, I bear both Indra and Agni (stanza 1) . . . I am the ruler (*rāṣṭrī*),[9] who brings treasures together, who understands; of those who receive worship, I am foremost

9. Just as is the sacred formula, *brahman;* cf. *AV* 4.1.2.

(stanza 3) . . . Whomever I love, him I make powerful, a receiver of formulas, a seer, a sage (stanza 5) . . . I pervade heaven and earth. It is I who give birth to the Father, on the summit of this [world] (stanzas 6-7)." Here the Word is truly placed above everything else, even giving birth to the godhead who creates the various forms in the world. True, such hyperbolic praise is particular to this type of hymn; there is however another hymn mentioning "the Word that speaks and is the harmonious ruler of the gods" (8.100.10); but it further states that "the gods did create the Goddess Word, whom all kinds of animal speak" (ibid., 11); still it is to this Word "listened to by the gods" (10.98.7) that the latter owe their power: "Thou, Indra, become great owing to the Sacred Word" (10.50.5).[10] This *vāc* is related to *brahman* as well, which is not a mere sacred formula, but supreme Word, and also powerful activity. In hymn 10.114.8, *vāc* appears as co-extensive with it: *yā́vad bráhma viṣṭhitaṃ tā́vatī vā́k*, "as much as *brahman* did expand, as large is the Word." This formula—implying a subordination of the Word to *brahman*, wherefrom the former would have sprung (cf. Geldner, *op. cit.*: "*brahman* ist hier die Grundlage der *vāc*")—would rather suggest that *brahman* is not the Word,[11] but the Word exists at different stages, and *brahman* itself is Word. This formula will indeed be eventually interpreted as identifying *brahman* with Word: *brahma vai vāk* (*Aitareya Brāhmaṇa* 4.21.1).[12]

The Word is extolled and identified with *brahman* in the

---

10. *Bhuvastvam-indra brahmaṇā mahān.* Cf. *RV* 8.6 and 14.11, where through the chanting of a song of praise Indra's power is increased: "Denn, dir sind, o Indra, die Lobgesänge, die Lobgedichte eine Stärkung" (Geldner, vol. 2, p. 314).
11. Cf. L. Renou, *E.V.P.* 1, p. 12.
12. The subordination of the Word to *brahman* remains nevertheless significant, insofar as it corresponds to a subordination of the expressed to the unexpressed, of the manifest to the unmanifest.

    The poetic word is a creation of inspiration, of thought. This is not apparent in hymn 10.125, and yet more often than not, the Word, although superior to the gods, nonetheless arises from something that was prior to it (cf. *infra* p. 12). One should not, however, be too categorical here, for from this extensive body of scriptures no system emerges.

Atharva Veda as well. The latter, composed mostly of magical prayers and incantations, resorts of course to the efficacy of the Word; but it also contains a few cosmosgonic or speculative hymns, some of them stating the preeminence of *vāc*. Thus hymn 4.1, praising "the sacred Formula (*brahman*) that was first born in the East, the seer discovered it, from the glorious summit (of the worlds) . . . [There he saw] the womb of the existent and the non-existent. Let it lead the way, to the primal generation, this age-old sovereign who dwells in beings!"[13] This sovereign, who is divinized as Bṛhaspati (ibid., 5), is the *vāc*. This is also, probably, the one whom the seer of hymn 2.1 has seen "secretly"—this "supreme [abode] where everything becomes of one form, and which is the milk yielded to us by the mottled [Cow],"[14] (for the cosmic Cow is the Word). In hymn 19.9.3, again *vāc* is called "supreme Goddess, sharpened by *brahman*": *iyám yā parameṣṭhinī vā́g devī́ bráhmasáṃśitā*. It is again exalted in other hymns with similar images, and, of special interest to us, in the form of one of the Vedic meters, *virāj*,[15] which is the subject of hymns 9 and 10 of Book 8. There *virāj* appears as the cosmic cow, identical with *vāc*, whose calf is Indra and who is once described—becoming masculine for the occasion—as "the father of *brahman*" (8.9; also 9.10.24: *virā́d vā́g virā́ṭ pṛthivī́ virā́ḍ antárikṣaṃ virā́ṭ prajā́patiḥ*). "Verily she was this [Universe] at the beginning. Of her, when born, everything was afraid, [thinking:] this one indeed will become this [Universe]" (8.10.1). Herbs, space, and waters did the gods milk from her (ibid., 14ff.). *Virāj*, therefore, is identified with *vāc*. Moreover (in accordance with its etymology, *vi* plus the root *RĀJ*), she appears as an active principle, ruling, luminous, nourishing,[16] and feminine, as a creative energy[17]

13. and 14. About these two hymns, cf. L. Renou, "Etudes sur quelques hymnes spéculatifs" (*E.V.P.* 2, pp. 55ff.).

15. Cf. L. Renou, *Virāj* (*J. As.* [1952]: 141ff.).

16. The Brāhmaṇas identify *virāj* with *śrī:* both are shining and nourishing (*ŚBr.*, 8.3.2.13; *GBr.*, 1.5.4: *annaṃ vai śrīr virāḍ annādyam*; etc. . . .). Cf. J. Gonda, *Aspects of Early Viṣṇuism* (Utrecht, 1954), p. 187.

17. Thus in the hymn to the Puruṣa (*RV* 10.90.5): "From it is born the [creative] Energy, from the creative Energy man (or the Puruṣa) is born." Geldner (op. cit., vol. 3) p. 287, notes: "Der Urpuruṣa lässt aus sich heraus

which might already, because of this aspect and role, prefigure the *śakti* of the later periods (and furthermore, this is an energy which is Word).

Actually, although we already see, as early as the *Ṛg Veda*, a Word that is a female creative energy, it is not, however, known as *śakti*. The latter term, although appearing as early as the *Ṛg Veda*,[18] does not in that text carry the meaning it will assume later. There is also *śacī*, acting as a companion to certain gods (*RV* 1.139.5, or in 10.134.3, where she is Indra's inherent power); or there are the Gnās (*RV* 5.46.7-8), the consorts of the gods. However, those feminine entities play but a limited part, by no means comparable to that which *śakti* eventually will have.

This is also to be found elsewhere, more especially in the Brāhmaṇas; and in some cases, being the consort of a god is a function assumed by *vāc*, which then gives rise to the creation as a result of union with the god Prajāpati, the father of creatures. Thus in the *Yajur Veda:* "Prajāpati was there; *vāc* was his companion. He united with her. Then she parted from him and bore all these creatures. Afterwards she came back into Prajāpati." (*Kāth.S.* 12.5).[19] The relationship between *vāc* and Prajāpati is not indeed always of that type. Much the same as in the *Atharva Veda*, it is sometimes associated with him, at others, assimilated into him. It is indeed noteworthy that in the passage just quoted, *vāc* returns into him after uniting with him, and therefore it is both distinct and nondistinct from him. In this way, it is described as the greatness or the inherent power of Prajāpati (*asya mahimā, ŚBr,* 2.2.4.4). Or else the latter—sometimes described as the Lord of the Word, Vācaspati

---

die Virāj, das weibliche Schöpfungsprinzip, geboren werden und lässt dann sich von ihr als Welt gebären."

In the *BĀUp.* (4., 22-23), *virāj*, as a human form appearing in the left eye, is the consort of Indra (*asya patnī virāṭ*), and both unite in the heart; cf. *infra* p. 28).

18. *RV* 3.57.3; 7.68.8; or 10.88.10, where she is the power of Agni.
19. Cf. similarly the union of Mṛtyu with *vāc* in *BĀUp.* 1.2.1-5. Or *ŚBr.* 3.2.1.25ff., where sacrifice (*yagna*) desires Vāc and unites with her, Indra then entering the embryo.

(*ŚBr.* 5.1.1.16)[20]—expresses his creative power by means of the Word, when, for instance, he creates the worlds by naming their parts: "He said *bhūḥ*, and the earth was."[21] (ibid., 11.1.6.3). "He created the waters by means of the Word" (ibid., 6.1.1.9).[22] Or Prajāpati himself is assimilated into *vāc* (5.1.5.6: "Prajāpati is the Word; this, assuredly, is the supreme Word"). In a somewhat different, although closely related, perspective, it is noteworthy that in the Brāhmaṇas *vāc* is identified with Sarasvatī.[23] Now this goddess, who eventually will become the goddess of eloquence and learning, appears as early as the *Ṛg Veda* (where she is first of all the river of that name), endowed with a motherly ("the best of mothers," *ambitamā*, *RV* 2.41.16), protective nature, taking care that the sacrificial prayers bear fruit (*RV* 2.3.8), a nature that she shares with the Word, and still retains in the Brāhmaṇas, the latter asserting her identity with *vāc* (*ŚBr.* 3.9.1.7; or *AitBr.* 3.1.10). Therefore Sarasvatī appears as being at once word, motherly, and creative power,

---

20. *Prajāpatir vai vācaspatir.* *Vāc* is also exalted for its own sake, as, for instance, in *TaitBr.* 2.8.8.4-5: "There is no end to the Word, it is beyond the entire creation, immeasurable. All the gods, the *gandharvas*, human beings, and animals live within it. Within the Word do human beings reside. The Word is the firstborn syllable of the Order, the mother of the Veda, the navel of immortality."
21. Which may be compared to *RV* 3.30.4: "Auf dein Gebot (Indra) standen Himmel und Erde" (Geldner, 2, p. 364).
22. Similarly: *PañcBr.* 20.142: "Prajāpati alone was this [universe]. He had only the Word as his own. The Word was the second [thing that was in existence]. He wished: "Let me now put forth this Word; she will fill up all this [universe]. He put forth the Word, and she filled up the universe." He then cut it into three: *ā*, which forms the earth; *ka*, the intermediate space; and *ho*, the sky (in the same way, *JaimBr.* 2.244 and *PañcBr.* 20.147 mention *a*, *kṣa*, and *ra*—that is the *akṣara*—as the three original sounds).
23. About Sarasvatī, cf. Bergaigne, *Religion Védique* 1, p. 327 and 2, p. 491; also Macdonell, *Vedic Mythology* (Grundriss . . . , Strasbourg, 1897), p. 86; and first and foremost H. Lommel, "Anāhita-Sarasvatī," in *Asiatica, Festschrift Friedrich Weller* (Leipzig, 1954), pp. 405-413, according to whom the association of Sarasvatī with the Word is very old (*"urarisch"*), Sarasvatī and the Avestic Anāhitā representing two aspects of the same Aryan goddess.

qualities that will be, much later, those ascribed to the Goddess, who will also be Word.[24]

One point should perhaps be stressed here, that we shall have the opportunity to discuss again elsewhere in this work: insofar as the Word is conceived of as the consort of a god, as a power that belongs to him or of which he makes use—even though it appears at the same time or in other passages as identified with him—it is therefore subordinate to him. The "primacy of the Word," of *vāc*, although indisputable, should not be asserted without these reservations. *Brahman*, even though being Word, Speech or Formula par excellence, is also mysterious, and owes its power to all of its unexpressed content, to its silence. Is not the concealed portion of the Word its best one (*RV* 8.100.10)? And yet this portion remains unexpressed: Word, perhaps, but silent.

There is another term in the Veda, referring both to an aspect of the Absolute, or to the sacred word as the imperishable basis of speech or creation, a term that subsequently (while nonetheless retaining its grammatical sense of "syllable") came to refer to the primal, imperishable principle, more especially when symbolized by the monosyllabic mantra *oṃ*, and that is *akṣara.* It is well worth discussing here, if only briefly, as much for its relation, as early as the *Ṛg Veda*, to the speculations about the powers of the Word, as for the prominence of the speculations about *oṃ* as early as the Brāhmaṇas: this was a prominence that was retained henceforward. It is also worth discussing due to the role that will be played, in Tantric lore, by the *bījamantra*s and the phonemes; and finally, because of the connecting link that existed from the outset between *akṣara, pada*, and the fourfold partition of the Word.[25]

---

24. Cf. Maryla Falk, *Il mito psicologico nell' India antica* (Reprint. Milan, 1986).

25. About the term *akṣara*, cf. L. Renou, "Rituel et grammaire", *J. As.* (1941-42): 150-52; Ibid., *E.V.P.* 1.9-10; J. A. B. Van Buitenen, "Notes on Akṣara," *Bulletin of the Deccan College Research Institute* 17, 3; and also, "Akṣara," *JAOS* 79 (1959): 176-87. One may also refer, for more recent meanings of the term, to P. M. Modi, *Akṣara, a Forgotten Chapter in the History of Indian Philosophy* (Baroda, 1932).

Akṣara, according to the traditional etymology—*na kṣarati* or *na kṣīyate*—is that which does not flow out or perish, hence the imperishable, the indestructible, the eternal[26]; it is also the "syllable."[27] Indeed, *akṣara* appears as early as the *Ṛg Veda*, as related to speech, and to the sacred, original, all-powerful Word, that which is at the beginning of the world: "When the first dawns were gleaming, the great [thing], the Word (*akṣaram*) came into being in the footsteps of the Cow.[28] It strengthens further the vows of the gods [since indeed] great [must be] the singular asuric power of [these] gods" (3.55.1). Similarly in hymn 1.164.41-42: "The Cow-Buffalo bellowed, creating lakes, one foot, two feet, four feet, eight feet, nine feet in size, a thousand syllables in the supreme space. From her flow down the oceans, by her exist the four regions of the world: from her [place] flows the imperishable [Word], who nourishes the whole universe." The cow or cosmic buffalo, mother and nourisher

---

26. "Das Unvergangliche": Geldner, *ad RV* 1.164.42 (vol. 1, p. 253).
27. Cf. Geldner, ibid. (vol. 1, p. 399): "*akṣaram* eigentlich das Element der Sprache, Laut, Silbe, hier für die sakrale Rede, die eine Erfindung jener ersten Ṛṣi's ist."
28. *padé góḥ:* the footprints, the track of the Cow, which is also that of the Word, followed by the sages (*RV* 10.71.3), which is secret, mysterious, and leads to the transcendental, the latter being the hidden Word. Cf. L. Renou, *E.V.P.* 4, p. 51: "The Great Word is born in the abode of the Cow," or in modern rendering: "The great syllable is born in the realm of the transcendental language." Cf. also Renou, *Etudes sur le vocabulaire du Ṛgveda*, pp. 21-22 (s.v. *pada*), and *E.V.P.* 1, pp. 9-10.

There is a variant of the term *akṣára*, which is *ákṣarā*, which is both cow and word: *RV* 1.34.4; cf. Geldner's note, *op. cit.* (vol. 1, p. 41), who remarks that Sāyana sometimes ascribes to *ákṣarā* the meaning of word, at others, that of cow.

The Word, *vā́c*, is also assimilated with a cow in *RV* 8.100.10. One should bear in mind that the Word is cow: *dhenúr vā́g*. We have already seen, *supra* p. 9, the same assimilation with regard to *virāj*.

The reason for the Vedic identification word-cow may possibly lie both in that the term *gaúh*, cow, is given as related to *GĀ*, to sing, and in the fact that the hymns assimilate prayers with cows; this assimilation arose due to the fact that through the utterance of the sacrificial Word the utterer would obtain a cow as *dakṣiṇa*. For this, see B. Oguibenine, *Essais sur la culture védique et indo-européenne* (Pisa: Giardini, 1986), in particular p. 129.

of the universe, is the sacred Word, the thousand-syllabled word, and also the imperishable syllable, the *akṣara* which, as the smallest division of the word, is taken as its basic element ("die Ursilbe," Geldner),[29] that to which it can be reduced and, it may be assumed, from which it emerges. It is, at the same time, for priests and poets of *bráhman*, which is a measured word, the element by which it is measured, hence its twofold significance: as a basic element of the Word, and as a measure of the sacred Word. Is it not said, in the same hymn of the *Ṛg Veda*, in the two stanzas preceding that we just quoted: "To him who does not know the syllable, which is the abode of all the gods in the supreme space, of what avail will be the hymn?" (1.164.39); and in stanza 24: "With the syllable are constructed the seven voices," i.e., the Vedic meters. As to hymn 6.16.35-36, it shows how both the *akṣara* and the sacrificial fire are born from the cosmic and ritual order (*ṛta*).[30] All this clearly shows why priests and poets could sense power in the sacrificial, poetical, and creative word, foundation of the universal order (even though it also appears as born thereof) or helping to maintain it; one can understand why the syllabic element, which measures the Word and that to which it can be reduced, may be considered as the phonetic or metric seed of the cosmos.

Indeed, the Brāhmaṇas, and subsequently the Upaniṣads, leave no uncertainty as to the transcendence of this *akṣara.* The latter, to be more precise, will come to be identified with the syllable *oṃ*, which will appear clearly, as early as the Vedic Upaniṣads, as the main symbol, the phonic expression par excellence of the *brahman*, and then as the basic mantra, the primordial sound, to which all mantras as well as any form of speech can be reduced, as the very source of the Word.[31]

One may wonder why the syllable *oṃ* has been given such an exalted position. It was used, so it seems, as early as the

29. "Die Silbe is das Element der Rede (*vā́c*), die Ursilbe, vielleicht schon die Silbe *OṂ*" (note, *ad. RV* 1.164.39, vol. 1, p. 234).

30. Cf. *TaitBr.* 2.8.8.5, quoted *supra* p. 11, n. 20: "The word is the firstborn syllable of the Order, the mother of the Veda, the navel of immortality."

31. For the Tantric conception of *oṃ* as found in some Śaiva scriptures, cf. chap. 7, pp. 402ff.

Yajur Veda, where it is not yet divinized.[32] (The *Yajur Veda* contains other syllables used for ritualistic purposes: *him, hum, svāhā, vaṣat, veṭ*, but which will not have a comparable destiny.) The *praṇava*—as *oṃ* will be called—is originally nothing but the interjection *o*, lengthened by the *pluti* up to three morae and ending with the nasal sound *m* (marked *ṃ*). It is used in the Vedic ritual by the *hotṛ*, who utters it loudly at the end of the *anuvākya*, but it came soon to be regarded as an utterance of vital importance, as the syllable par excellence.[33] In some texts it is described as a kind of assent; thus *AitBr.* (7.18) ascribes to *oṃ* the same meaning, in the language of the gods, as to what, in the language of humans, is expressed by *tathā:* "All right, yes"; and similarly in the *ChUp.* (1.1.8), which however goes on to say: "For whenever one assents to anything, this indeed is fulfillment. He becomes a fulfiller of the desires who, with this knowledge, becomes aware that the syllable [*oṃ*] is the *udgītha*": at this stage, the deification of the syllable *oṃ* has been achieved.

At the beginning of the *Jaiminīya Upaniṣad Brāhmaṇa*[34] (1.1), Prajāpati conquers the universe by means of the three Vedas, then, afraid lest the gods steal it from him by means of the same threefold science, he decides to take the sap or essence (*rasa*) away from it by means of the triple utterance: *bhūr bhuvaḥ svar*,[35] thereby creating the earth, the intermediate

---

32. We may mention, by the way, Winternitz's opinion about this type of speculation: "There is," he writes in this connection, "yet another kind of 'prayers,' as we cannot help calling them, with which we meet already in the Yajurveda, and with which also, at later periods, much mischief was done . . ." (*History of Indian Literature*, vol. 1, p. 185).

33. J. A. B. van Buitenen (*JAOS*, vol. 79), thinks that the prominent position of *oṃ* may be due to how certain ritual recitations are performed. Cf. also L. Silburn, *Instant et Cause*, p. 92: "It is likely that the syllable *oṃ*, the instigator, was also, as early as the Brāhmaṇas, the continuous humming sound it will become at a later date in the Upaniṣads. Though imperceptible, it would underlay the whole ceremony and would thus appear like *brahman* as the upholder of the sacrifice" (J. G.'s translation).

34. Cf. *The Jaiminīya or Talavakāra Upaniṣad Brāhmaṇa*, text and translation by Hanns Oertel (*JAOS* 16 [1894]: 79ff.).

35. These are the *vyāhṛti*, the three "utterances" par excellence, which are

space, and the sky: "Somehow it happened that of one syllable (*kasyai 'vā' kṣarasya*) he could not take the essence: of *oṃ*, just of *oṃ*. This [syllable] became this speech, and this [speech], namely *oṃ*, breath is the essence thereof." The text now brings together *oṃ* with the *gāyatrī;* next (1.2) we are told that it is fire, wind, and sun, and that speech is earth, intermediate space, and sky: *oṃ* therefore sums up the whole universe. Further on (1.10),[36] the immortal, celestial Cow, who sends forth her thousand streams in all directions unto all this world (*RV* 1.164), is this "true syllable" that is *oṃ:* "In it the waters are firmly set, in the waters the earth, in the earth these worlds. As leaves might be stuck together with a pin, so these worlds are stuck together by this syllable." Then again, this Brāhmaṇa (1.23)[37] places at the beginning (*agre*) the space or "ether" (*ākāśa*), which is Word (*sa ya ākāśo vāg eva sā*). Prajāpati presses this Word; of its being pressed, the essence streamed forth. That became the worlds; these, being then also pressed, became the gods Agni, Vāyu, and the Sun, which, pressed, became the three Vedas, which became *bhūr buvaḥ svar*, and those finally became the *akṣara* which is *oṃ*.[38]

There is a very similar passage in the *Chāndogya Upaniṣad:* "Prajāpati brooded over the worlds. From the worlds issued forth the threefold Veda; he brooded over it. Therefrom arose the syllables (*akṣarāṇi*): *bhūr, bhuvaḥ, svar.* He brooded over them; therefrom arose the name *oṃ* (*oṃkāra*). As leaves are

---

chanted in the course of the Vedic ritual. For the interrelation between the cosmos and the *vyāhṛti*, cf. also *TaitUp.* 1.5-6.

36. *JaiUpBr.* p. 89.
37. Ibid., pp. 100-101.
38. The *JaiUpBr.* explains that *akṣara* can be the essence by interpreting it as that which flowed out (*akṣarat*), and also that which does not become exhausted (*na kṣīyate*), and states that the true name of *oṃ* is *akṣaya* while *akṣara* is a term used to keep it secret. And it further states that the *akṣara* should be chanted neither "*o*" or "*om*", but *oṃ*, for in this way only does this sound merge with the essence. Why does it place such emphasis on the *anusvāra*? At the time of the *JaiUpBr.* speculations about the *bindu* (which later on will be considered as the concentrated energy, and therefore the very essence of the mantras as well as of the universe), as far as we know, had not yet come into existence.

held together by a spike, so all the worlds merge into the sound *oṃ*. The sound *oṃ* is the whole universe."[39] In its previous section (2.22) the same Upaniṣad—dealing with the seven musical modes (*gāna*) and noting how the phonemes making up words should be pronounced (as is well known, pronouncing Vedic mantras with absolute accuracy is a prerequisite to their efficacity)—further says that the innermost nature (*ātman*) of all vowels (*svara*) is Indra, while that of the spirants (*ūṣman*) is Prajāpati and of the consonants (*sparśa*) Mṛtyu; the Upaniṣad goes on to say that vowels should be pronounced strong and sonant, with the thought: "To Indra let me give strength,"[40] and so forth. This is interesting if we refer to the later speculations: each of the three groups of phonemes is correlated with a deity, while that of the consonants is not associated with a potent and creative god but with death, and occupies a markedly lower position. Does this not look like an embryo of the Tantric speculations about the phonemes?[41]

Coming back to *oṃ*, it is worth noting that the Upaniṣad itself opens with lines in praise of the *akṣara* (1.1.1-10), identified in this case with the most important portion of the *sāman*, the *udgītha*, which is itself "the foremost of all essences, the supreme essence, the most excellent one." There is no mention of *oṃ* in the *Bṛhadāraṇyaka Upaniṣad*, which, however, contains an

---

39. *ChUp.* 2.23.3-4.
40. Cf. above, p. 8, n. 10, cit. *RV.*, 8.14.11: the performance of a laudatory hymn increases Indra's potency.
41. A still more marked prefiguration of Tantric elaborations is the passage in *AitĀr.* 3.2.5, which associates the three groups of phonemes with the three portions of the cosmos: consonants being the "form" (*rūpa*) of the earth, that is to say that of which it is made, spirants the "form" of the intermediate space, and vowels that of the sky; here again a progression can be observed: consonants are associated with the lowest and vowels with the highest. Similarly phonemes are also correlated with fire, wind, and sun: *pṛthivyā rūpaṃ sparśā antarīkṣasyoṣmāno divaḥ svarāḥ / agne rūpaṃ sparśā vayor uṣmānaḥ ādityasya svarāḥ //*

    This distribution might simply be the consequence of the phonetic nature of the various phonemes such as defined by the Prātiśākhyas, phonetic findings being thereafter taken up by myth: this mixing up of phonetics and myth later appears very clearly in the speculations of Abhinavagupta on the subject (cf. chap. 5).

elaboration on *akṣara*, no longer appearing as a syllable, but as the absolute, the imperishable, the unconditioned, the foundation and basis of everything.[42] In some other early Upaniṣads, on the other hand, *oṃ* is exalted above all. Thus in *Taittirīya Upaniṣad* 1.8 (the first section of which is mainly devoted to a phonetic teaching or a teaching relating to the ritual words): "*oṃ* is *brahman*", and so forth. The *Māṇḍūkya Upaniṣad* also deals primarily with *oṃ*; it begins: "Hari is *oṃ*. This syllable is this whole. The past, the present, the future—everything is just the phoneme *oṃ*";[43] or again, *Praśna* 5.6 or *Kaṭha* 2.15-16: "The word which all the Vedas rehearse, that is said [to be equal to] all the austerities, desiring which men live the life of brahmanical studentship, that Word to thee I briefly declare: that is *oṃ*! That syllable truly is *brahman*, that syllable indeed is the Supreme. Knowing that syllable, indeed, whatsoever one desires, is his."[44] Also in the *Maitri Upaniṣad*, which, it is true, is of later date: "*oṃ* is the greatness of *brahman*" (4.4); "*oṃ* has three morae. By means of these is woven the whole world, warp and woof" (6.3), and so forth. All those texts clearly show the unrivaled value attributed to *oṃ*—the fact that it was taken as symbolizing adequately, and therefore as being, the Absolute. It should also be noted, on the evidence of the quotation from the *Kaṭha Upaniṣad*, that it is not necessary to wait until Tantrism to find texts asserting that there is nothing which cannot be achieved by an adept through the sole means of a mantra, through the sole knowledge (that is to say, of course, through a gnosis, a comprehensive intuition) of an apparently meaningless syllable, yet standing as a symbol of the divine.

It may be worth noting that this extolling of *oṃ*, as containing the very essence of the Vedas, shows how in Indian thought, as early as Vedic times, the condensed, the concentrated, has always been given primacy over the extended, the

42. *BĀUp.* 3.8.7-11: "Verily, O Gārgī, at the command of that Imperishable, the sun and the moon stand apart. Verily, O Gārgī, at the command of that Imperishable, sky and earth stand apart," and so forth.
43. *MāṇḍUp.* 1.1.
44. *KaṭhUp.* 2.15-16.

diluted. There is nothing more powerful than *oṃ*, for within this one syllable (which should always be uttered at the beginning of any Vedic text) is encapsulated the whole of the Veda. The monosyllabic, the indivisible (*akṣara*)—and later the dot or drop, *bindu*—being dimensionless and extensionless, is therefore beyond all extension, and thereby illimitable.

Upaniṣadic as well as Vedic speculations about *oṃ* sometimes have one more feature which will appear afterwards in Hinduism and is elaborated upon extensively in Tantric texts: the breaking up of *oṃ* into its constituent phonemes, to which are ascribed theological or cosmic meanings. *Oṃ* is thus considered as breakable into its three morae (*mātrā*), or into its three phonemes (*a, u, m*), which are viewed as a replica (*pratinidhi*) of the threefold Veda and of the three worlds as well. It may also be considered as made up of four elements (*a* + *u* + *m* + *oṃ*—about this type of division into 3 + 1, cf. *infra* p. 21, n. 49), or of three and one-half elements.[45] As the phoneme *a*, in such cases, stands at the head of the *praṇava*, the Āraṇyakas sometimes claim, on the strength thereof, that it is its essence. It may then appear as forming the totality of the Word,[46] a condition which we shall find again later (chap. 5)

---

45. Thus in two Atharvanic Upaniṣads, the *Atharvaśikhā* and the *Atharvaśiras*, to *a*, *u* and *m* is added an "elided *m*" (*luptamakāra*), correlated with the fourth Veda, the Puruṣa, *virāj*, and so forth.

One finds *oṃ* split according to the *mātra*, with its extolling, in one of the *Atharva Veda*'s latest Brahmaṇas, the *Gopatha*, which contains one Upaniṣad: the *Praṇava Upaniṣad*, devoted to *oṃ* (*GoBr.* 1.1.16-20). In this Upaniṣad *brahman* creates the god Brahmā, to whom *oṃ* is revealed as comprised of two letters, or four morae, through which he perceives the whole universe, because of the interrelation between those elements of *oṃ* and the different parts of the cosmos, of the sacrifice, and so forth (Cf. Bloomfield, *The Atharva Veda*, p. 108).

46. Thus *AitĀ.* 2.3.6: *akāro vai saiva vāk saiṣa sparśoṣmabhir vyajamānā bhavī nānārūpa bhavati:* "Truly, the vowel *A* is the whole Word. The latter becomes manifold and varied when specified by the consonants and the fricatives."

For those early divisions of *oṃ*, see Charles Malamoud, *Le Svādhyāya, récitation personnelle du Veda. Taittirīya Āraṇayaka, Livre II* (Paris: Institut de Civilisation Indienne, 1977, pp. 85-87), from which I take the above quotation.

with extensive elaborations when dealing with the phonematic emanation.

This division of *oṃ* is found neither in the *Bṛhadāraṇyaka* nor in the *Chāndogya.* The latter, however, after asserting the identity of *oṃ* and the *udgītha,* correlates the three syllables of this word with the three Vedas, three divinities, the three worlds, and the three vital functions (ibid., 1.3.6-7).[47] And so do other Upaniṣads with regard to *oṃ.* Thus *Praśna Upaniṣad* 5.1.5: "Verily, O Satyakāma, that which is the syllable *oṃ* is both the lower and higher *brahman* . . . If he meditates on one element (namely *a*), having been instructed by that alone, he comes swiftly into the earth . . . Now if he is united in mind with two elements (*a* + *u*), he is led by the Yajus formulas to the intermediate world . . . He who meditates on the highest Person (Puruṣa) with the three elements of the syllable *oṃ* is united with brilliance in the sun," and so forth. In the *Maitri Upaniṣad* (6.3-6) the threefold division of *oṃ* is compared with that of the *udgītha* and is correlated with the three genders; with fire, air, and sun; Brahmā, Rudra, and Viṣṇu; the three breaths, and so forth. In the *MāṇḍUp., a, u,* and *ṃ* are equated with the three states (*vaiśvānara, taijasa,* and *prājña*) through which passes the individual soul when moving from its ordinary condition to the fusion in its own essence, *brahman.* Here, therefore, it is no longer a question of vital breaths and cosmic divisions, but of levels of consciousness. Furthermore, the Upaniṣad states that *brahman* has four quarters (or *pāda*). Similarly there are four states of the soul or modalities of consciousness (the three previous ones and the "fourth" one, *caturtha* or *turīya*), and therefore *oṃ* is also divided into four quarters by adding *oṃ* itself to *a, u,* and *ṃ,* as it is considered to be at the same time made up of its three constituents and transcending them.[48] But why do we have such a fourfold division of *oṃ* (which indeed is

---

47. For the speculations, and the macro-microcosmic correspondences concerning the *udgītha,* cf. for instance *JaiUpBr.* 1.57ff. (Oertel, ed., *JAOS* 16, p. 135ff.).

48. "Now this *ātman,* with regard to the syllable, is the *oṃkāra;* the elements are the fourths of *oṃ,* with regard to the syllabic elements, and the fourths are the elements, namely the letter *a,* the letter *u,* and the letter *ṃ.*

not an actual division into four, since in fact there are only three distinct elements, which the fourth one encapsulates and transcends)? Precisely because of the fourfold division of *brahman*, established on the authority of an even older tradition. *ChUp.* 3.18.2 had already made the assertion that *brahman* has four quarters, the first of which is the Word, and correlated those four quarters with fire, air, sun, and the intermediate regions. Thus it accepted both a tripartition (1.3.6-7) and a quadripartition of the universe (and indeed other divisions also, notably a fivefold and a sixteen-fold).[49] Similarly, *BĀUp.* 5.14, indulging in the same sort of speculations about the *gāyatrī*—an eminent mantra that the *Yajur Veda* and the Brāhmaṇas had earlier described as *tejas*, or effulgence (*TaiS.* 6.4.7); as

---

"*Vaiśvānara*, the waking state, is the letter *a;* it is the first mora, so called because it is primacy (*ādimatvāt*) and attainment (*āpter*). He that knows it for such attains indeed all his desires and becomes first.

"The second instant, *taijasa*, the dream state, is the letter *u*, so called because of its exaltation (*utkarṣāt*) and ambivalence (*ubhayatvāt*). He that knows it for such exalts indeed the continuity of his knowledge; he becomes balanced . . .

"The third instant, *prājña*, the deep sleep state, is the letter *m*. It is so called because of its being erection and absorption.

"And the fourth state, without any constituents, with which there can be no dealing, bringing diversity to an end, possessed of the blissful nonduality, is the *oṃkāra*, the Self. He that knows it for such enters the Self" (*MāṇḍUp.* 8-12).

The following passage in a much later Upaniṣad, the *Brahmabindu*, might be interpreted in a similar way: "Let him meditate in yoga with the help of the vowel; (next) let him contemplate the voiceless supreme; through silent contemplation one attains being and not non-being": *svareṇa saṃdhayed yogam asvaraṃ bhāvayet param asvareṇa hi bhāvena bhāvo nābhāva īṣyate.* It should be noted that here again one seems to shift (presumably with the help of the resonance, the *anusvāra*) from the word to the silence that lies beyond it.

49. Such a practice—adding to an already accepted division of a whole one more division, which both encapsulates and transcends the former ones—occurs elsewhere too and seems to correspond to an inclination of Indian thought. This we shall see again in the course of this work, when dealing with the four stages of the Word and the energies of Śiva (3 + 1), with the *kalā*s (15 + 1 or 16 + 1), with the four modalities of consciousness (4 + 1), and with the *tattva*s as well (36 + 1).

power (*KausBr.* 7.10); and as giving life to the other Vedic meters and taking them to the gods (*ŚBr.* 1.3.4.6), therefore in terms similar to those used elsewhere in relation to *vāc* or *akṣara*—this Upaniṣad also distinguishes in the *gāyatrī* four *pāda*s, of which the first three correspond to the three worlds, the three Vedas, and the three "breaths," while the fourth one (*caturtha*, also *turīya*) is resplendent, shines beyond the worlds, and is the support, the foundation of the *gāyatrī* itself and of the universe.[50]

However, the fourfold partition of *brahman*, of the Word or the universe occurs even earlier than the Upaniṣad. The *Ṛg Veda* mentions on one occasion (4.40.6) the existence of a fourth *brahman* through which Atri was supposed to have discovered the hidden sun, and so it may be assumed that there are three further ones.[51] But the cosmic fourfold partition had yet a stronger support in the *Ṛg Veda*'s hymn to the Puruṣa (10.90), according to which the primordial Giant divided into four: "All beings are a quarter of him: the Immortal, in heaven, the [remaining] three quarters" (although in this case what remains transcendent is three quarters of the Puruṣa, and not the fourth one). Moreover, this hymn lays down those correlations, which are so important in the history of Indian thought, between human beings, the cosmos, and the sacrifice. Last, but not least, was the famous stanza 45 of hymn 1.164: *catvā́ri vā́k párimitā padā́ni*, . . . "The Word is measured in four quarters which are known to those brahmans endowed

50. *Pada* means foot as well as quarter or abode, and also (as in the case of the three steps—*pāda*s—of Viṣṇu, which cover the whole universe: *RV* 1.154.1) trace of the gods or of the Cow, and therefore of speech—hence "word." For this term, cf. L. Renou (*Etudes sur le vocabulaire du Ṛgveda*, lère série, pp. 21-22), who observes that only occasionally does *pada* actually mean "foot."

51. While not intending to make a somewhat unsafe comparison, one may note that the *PT* (*śloka* 9) mentions a "third *brahman*" which is, according to Abhinavagupta (and Jayaratha, commentator of the *TĀ*), the universe as resting within the energy united with Śiva. So a fourth *brahman* could be accepted, which would be pure transcendence (as far, of course, as one can refer to transcendence in the case of a system such as the Trika. Cf. chap. 5, p. 235, n. 25.).

with intelligence. Three remain concealed and motionless; human beings speak the fourth quarter of the Word," a stanza which was later to be discussed extensively and variously interpreted, and which was to be used, notably, to vindicate the theory of the four stages of the Word. Here again only one quarter is manifest. There was also stanza 10 of hymn 8.100, where from the speaking Word, the celestial Cow, springs forth a fourfold stream,[52] which is milk and food; and of which the poet asks where has gone the best part; a part that might be precisely the hidden and transcendent quarter of the Word. Those speculations about the interrelations between cosmos and Word continue elsewhere, as for instance in the *MaitrS.* (1.11.5) or in the *KāthS.* (14.5) of the *Yajur Veda*, where the four quarters of the Word are divided among heaven, the intermediate space, the earth and animals, and human beings and gods; or in the *JaiUpBr.* (1.40), where they are divided among mind, sight, hearing, and empirical speech, and where it is also stated that all that is on this side of *brahman* is Word, the rest being *brahman* itself (which means that everything does indeed stem from the Word, while nonetheless a part remains transcendental and beyond words).

One sees thus how firmly established, by Vedic times, is this fourfold partition of the Word and its ritualistic, human, and cosmic correspondences, and how abundant are speculations about the symbolic meaning of certain words or syllables and about their interrelations and the creative power of the Word.[53] The frequent recurrence of all those interconnections—which are indeed greatly diversified and by no means comprising

52. It is clear that any cow, whether European or Indian, contemporary or Vedic, has four udders as well as four legs or feet (*pada*). If the Word is a cow, it will have naturally four *pada*s and the milk will necessarily flow in a fourfold stream.

53. Such speculations are in no way limited to *oṃ* and the *udgītha*. Some of them, as we have seen, deal with the *gāyatrī* and the three *vyāhṛti*. Also with other syllables of the liturgical chant, such as, for instance, the *stobha*s *haü, haï, atha*, and so forth in the *ChUp.* (1.13.13). Again in *PañcBr.* 20.143, with *a, ka, ha*, and ibid. 147, where Prajāpati creates various parts of the universe through the utterance of the sounds *a*, then *kṣa*, then *ra*—which makes *akṣara*, the primeval syllable.

a consistent system—is one of the usual features of the Brāhmaṇas and the Upaniṣads, those Upaniṣads whose very name seems to evoke the correlations that are at the root of their teaching. These correspondences are of special interest to us, for one of the characteristics of Tantrism lies precisely in the constant establishment of correspondences between humans, rites, and the cosmos, and in the cosmic as well as human aspect of energy. Now those correspondences, as may be seen, are not peculiar to Tantrism, but on the contrary very ancient: "For all deities are seated in humans as cows in a cow-stall. Therefore one who knows human beings thinks: 'this is *brahman*,'" said the *Atharva Veda* (11.8.32); the powers that give life to the cosmos are identical with those that make human beings alive. This cosmic and human energy will be symbolized in Tantrism especially by the *kuṇḍalinī*, which will appear as life-force, breath, and speech at the same time. The term used from the earliest times to denote the life-force stands also for the vital breath, *prāṇa*. It is also used to refer not only to a particular breath, but also to the five "breaths" taken as a whole, which are usually acknowledged (and mentioned as early as the *Atharva Veda*), and which obviously are not respiratory breaths but vital "winds" (*vāyu*). Furthermore, *prāṇa* is the breath of the cosmic Giant (*RV* 10.90.13) and therefore an aspect of the energy that animates the cosmos.[54] Whether Vedic thought intended to explain the body with the help of the cosmos or the cosmos with the help of the body,[55] the correspondence between microcosm and macrocosm is in any case undisputable. Undisputable as well is the association of breath and Word. As early as the *Ṛg Veda vāc* was compared

---

For Vedic mantras and the shift from *stobha* to Tantric *bījamantra*, cf. Frits Staal, "Vedic Mantras" in H. P. Alper, ed., *Understanding Mantras* (Albany: SUNY Press, 1988), pp. 48ff.

54. In this connection one should refer to the works of J. Filliozat: *La doctrine classique de la médecine indienne* (2nd ed.; Paris, E.F.E.O., 1975); "Taoisme et Yoga," *J.As.* (1969): 41-87, and above all "La force organique et la force cosmique dans la philosophie médicale de l'Inde et dans le Véda," *Revue Philosophique* (1933).

55. For the former way, cf. Filliozat, op. cit.; for a consideration of both explanations, cf. P. Mus, *Barabudur*, especially pp. 440-447.

with the wind: "I blow like the wind" (*RV* 10.125.8). In the *Atharva Veda* there is a hymn (11.4) extolling the breath (*prāṇa*)—"who has been lord of all, in whom all stands firm." The hymn describes the wind which "with thunder roars at the herbs" as the human breath, and also as the *virāj*, this Vedic meter which, as we have seen, is a form of the Word and a creative energy.[56] The *ŚB* (1.3.5.15), observing that the sacrificer cannot recite the formulas without breathing, states that the reason for the sacrificer's breathing is that the *gāyatrī* itself is breath; the association of breath and speech is obviously, like the inseparability of breath and life, a fact of elementary observation, even though it is perhaps not from such observations that the correlations and mythic developments of Vedism originate.[57] The same is found in the Upaniṣads. In *BĀUp.* 1.3.19ff., "breath" is the essence of the limbs (*aṅgānāṃ rasaḥ*), "and also it is Bṛhaspati: The *bṛhatī* is speech. He is her lord and is therefore Bṛhaspati" (20). "It is also Brahmaṇaspati; *brahman* indeed is speech. He is her lord and is therefore Brahmaṇaspati" (21). It is also the *sāman* and the *udgītha:* "It was indeed with speech and breath that he sang the *udgītha*" (24). The *ChUp.* (1.1.5-6) also asserts: "The *ṛc* is speech; the *sāman* is breath; the *udgītha* is this syllable *oṃ*. This verily is a pair, namely, speech and breath, and also the *ṛc* and the *sāman*. This pair is joined together in this syllable *oṃ*." It is this union[58] of speech and breath that explains why *oṃ* can fulfill all desires. Now, we shall see further on that in Tantrism any practice designed to empower the mantra will consist in

---

56. As seen above (*supra*, p. 16), according to the *JaiUpBr.* (1.1), breath is the essence (*rasa*) of *oṃ* (this could, however, also simply refer to the presence of the *anusvāra* in *oṃ*).

57. Hauer (*Der Yoga*, p. 26) ascribes the origin of yogic *prāṇāyāma* to breathing exercises, to which Vedic poets would have been submitted. Whatever the origin of the methods of breath control in yoga, some early considerations about breath and speech may indeed have come about due to the major role of breath in chanting.

58. *Mithuna*: this is a sexual union. Similarly in *ŚBr.* 1.4.12: *vāc ca vai prāṇaśca mithunam.* Later, the *bindu* in *OṂ* will be supposed to be a symbol of the union of Śiva and Śakti, and thereby will to some extent account for the potency, the fruitfulness of mantras (cf. chap. 3, p. 112).

associating the sound-energy of the mantra with the human and cosmic energy of *prāṇa*, which is life force and, to some extent, breathing:[59] those are indeed very ancient notions.

As might be expected, the later Upaniṣads, so far as they touch upon this subject, are even more explicit. Thus the *Praśna Upaniṣad*, which is devoted to the five "breaths" and expounds upon their role within human beings and the cosmos, devotes a section (the fifth) to the meditation upon *oṃ*. Although it does not explicitly link this meditation with the breaths, the fact that four sections are devoted to breath and one appended section is devoted to *oṃ* may not be entirely fortuitous. Much more typical on those questions is the *Maitri Upaniṣad*, and we would like to conclude therewith this short survey from ancient texts related to speech and breath. The *Maitri* is held as the most recent among the earlier Upaniṣads. Some of its sections (those to which we shall now refer, the sixth and seventh *prapāṭhaka*s) are probably much later than the other Vedic Upaniṣads and were presumably composed at a time when yoga was being systematized and perhaps even included

---

59. Cf. chap. 7, p. 399ff. Breath is also regarded, as early as Vedic times, as having a ritualistic significance, which will emerge again later. The *KauṣUp.* (2.5) describes the inner *agnihotra*, which consists of offering breath as an oblation in speech (when one is speaking) and speech in breath (when one falls silent, for "as long as a person is breathing, he is not able to speak; then he is sacrificing speech in breath"); that is to say that it considers both functions as ongoing oblations. In this, of course, the body is assimilated to the sacrificial altar, and the adept's life itself becomes a sacrifice.

This tendency appears earlier than the *Kauṣītaki:* for example, in *BĀUp.* 1.5.23, *ChUp.* 5.19-24, *Śbr.* 11.3.1, and so forth. Eventually the inner sacrifice will even come to be held as superior to the outer, because it is mental (*mānasa*), and mental action, being unexpressed (*avyakta*), belongs to a higher level than that of external action, which is manifest (*vyakta*). This is asserted especially in a later Upaniṣad devoted to the inner *agnihotra*, the *Prāṇāgnihotra Upaniṣad* (edited and translated by J. Varenne, together with the *Mahānārāyaṇa Upaniṣad*, vol. 2, pp. 95ff.; cf. also ibid., pp. 53ff. for the mental sacrifice). This will be stressed even moreso in Tantrism, where the interiorization of rites, ensuring and expressing the correspondences between human beings and the cosmos, is a prominent feature; cf. chap. 2, p. 38ff.

some Tantric elements. It is precisely because some passages in the *Maitri* seem to announce some of the speculations found in Tantras that it will be briefly examined here.

The sixth *prapāṭhaka* contains some considerations about *oṃ* (6.3-5), the *vyāhṛti*s (6.6), and the *gāyatrī* (6.7), which we have already mentioned and which are not unexpected. On the other hand, sections 18 to 20 describe as means of union with *brahman* some processes—breath control (*prāṇāyāma*), withdrawal of the senses (*pratyāhāra*), meditation (*dhyāna, samādhi*), and so forth—which are yogic and form "a six-limbed yoga" (*ṣaḍaṅga ity ucyate yogaḥ*).[60] Moreover, section 21 tells us that the artery leading upwards, called *suṣumṇā*, conveys the breath and pierces through the palate, and that through this artery—by joining together the breath, the syllable *oṃ*, and *manas*—is released the upgoing "breath" (which of course is not a breathing process but a form of the vital energy); when this process comes to an end, the breath stands still, complete oneness with the unlimited is achieved. The description given by the Trika texts of the *uccāra* of the mantras[61] will go into further details but will not differ essentially from this. Similarly section 22 describes various sounds heard "within the heart," when the ears are closed with the thumbs:[62] this sound was already mentioned in the *ChUp.* and the *BĀUp.*, but here the enumeration is strongly reminiscent of the various types of *nāda*s listed in the Tantras or the yogic Upaniṣads, such as the *Haṃsa Upaniṣad* (section 16), rather than of those of the two Vedic Upaniṣads.

The seven *prapāṭhaka*s, finally, end with a section dealing with *oṃ* and breath (section 11) which, not unexpectedly, is somewhat similar both to some speculations—which we just examined—found in Vedic Upaniṣads and to Tantric descriptions of the origin of the Word. According to this section the innermost or essential nature of the ether (*nabhas*) pervading

---

60. For this yoga, cf. A-Z. Cerba, "The ṣaḍaṅgayoga," *History of Religions* (1963) 1.27ff.
61. For the *uccāra* of the *bījamantra SAUḤ*, cf. for instance chap. 7, p. 421.
62. Cf. chap. 3, pp. 99-100, n. 41 and 119-122, n. 100.

the inner space of the heart (*kha*)[63] is the effulgence or supreme fiery energy (*paraṃ tejas*). This energy has a threefold manifestation: in fire, sun, and breath (therefore it is clear that "breath"—*prāṇa*—is both luminous and vital, human and cosmic: it is an energy). The essential nature of this ether is the *akṣara oṃ*, which enables this luminous energy to emerge from the heart, to appear and breathe (therefore the syllable *oṃ* is that which brings forth the vital energy, and wherein, so it seems, vital energy and breath commingle). Within the body, this fiery energy is associated with *prāṇa*, the ascendant "breath," and is comparable to a flash of lightning. Then, taking up an image or a myth from the *BĀUp.* (4.2), the *Maitri* says that Indra dwells in the right eye, his consort (who, according to the *BĀUp.*, is *virāj*) in the left, both joining within an artery located in the heart[64] and arising therefrom, and which is both single and twofold. At that moment, thought (*manas*) is supposed to stir up the bodily fire (which would be, then, the vital energy, the human counterpart of the cosmic energy) and set in motion the wind (*marut*) which, as it moves within the chest, gives rise to a deep or gentle (*mandra*) sound (*svara*). This sound, when stirred up within the heart through its contact with a fire kindled by friction or churning (*khajāgni*),[65] appears then as extremely subtle, as one tiny atom. This atom of sound becomes doubled when rising next to the throat region, and

---

63. *Kha* means a hole, a cavity, a cave, the central hole in the hub of a wheel, and also void, hence space, sky. This is also the void at the center of the heart (*hṛd*), which is itself a secret place, a cave, as well as the abode of the supreme *brahman*, a place full of peace and light. Hence the equivalence between *kha* and *hṛdaya* (which occurs repeatedly in the Trika).

64. On the physiological as well as psychic function of the heart in the Upaniṣads as well as in some texts of the Far East, one may refer to Maryla Falk and Jean Przyluski's article, "Aspects d'une psycho-physiologie dans l'Inde et en Extrême-Orient," *Bull. of the School of Oriental Studies* 9, part 3, pp. 723-28), or to J. Gonda, *The Vision of the Vedic Poets* (The Hague: Mouton & Co. 1963), chap. 12, "Some Notes on the Function of the Heart."

65. The Upaniṣad does not explain the nature of this churning. The term used suggests the ignition of the ritualistic fire through churning. It might also be assumed that this churning or rubbing is performed by Indra and his consort, since the Upaniṣad just mentioned their union in the heart; however, this may be an unduly Tantric interpretation.

is tripled when reaching the tip of the tongue; then the sound flows out of the body as the mother (*mātṛkā*) [of the phonemes]. He who sees all this, the Upaniṣad concludes, sees only the All, obtains the All, and has therefore nothing to fear anymore.[66]

We chose to analyze this whole section of the *Maitri Upaniṣad* because it is strangely similar to the description by some Tantric texts of the arising of the phonemes and of the stages of the Word, when linked to the ascent of the *kuṇḍalinī* which, in the Tantras, is a fiery energy associated with the breaths and with mantras. Thus, if one refers to a section of the *Tantrasadbhāva* cited by Kṣemarāja in the *Śiva Sūtra Vimarśinī* (2.3)—a section that we cite and analyze below[67]—it will be seen that the *kuṇḍalinī* (which is often compared to a flash of lightning), awakened through a churning due to the union of Śiva and Śakti, stretches out while emitting sparks, and that she is possessed of one atom on reaching the heart, of two when at the throat level, and of three when reaching the tip of the tongue, for that is the place, says the Tantra, where the phonemes are brought forth, that is, empirical speech is produced. This is how, adds Kṣemarāja, the mother-energy of the phonemes (*mātṛkā*) arises. The similarity is quite striking. Would that mean, then, that the *Maitri Upaniṣad*, in its later sections, includes Tantric elements? This is not impossible. But when did what we call Tantrism begin? And after all, what indeed is Tantrism? This is what we are going to examine in brief in the next chapter. Our purpose here was simply to point out, in one Upaniṣad presumably pertaining to the earlier series of such texts, the presence of elements that were the harbingers, so to speak, of a new age. The Upaniṣadic speculations about *oṃ* and about the breaths—and not only those just mentioned in this chapter—may lead one to think that there had been no gap, insofar as the notions about the Word are concerned, between the earlier elements and the later Tantric elaborations.

---

66. For this particular passage of the *Maitri* as well as for the creative and liberating role of *vāc* and the micro-macrocosmic correlations, one may refer to Maryla Falk's work *Nāmarūpa and Dharmarūpa* (Calcutta, 1943), as well as to her *Mito Psicologico*.

67. Chap. 3, pp. 128ff.

2

Tantrism—The Texts of Kashmirian Śaivism

Since this work is based on "selected Hindu Tantras," it is necessary to elucidate what the terms *Tantric* or *Tantrism* are generally understood to mean (or at least what *I* understand them to mean). A perfectly clear and thorough elucidation would in fact be somewhat difficult to provide. However, this is not my purpose here, where I shall simply offer a few remarks or observations about the problem of Tantrism, and no in-depth study thereof. Those few considerations, as they will help to form a clearer picture of the problem, will perhaps be instrumental, if not in providing us with its solution, at least in progressing toward a temporary solution. (Let us further state that only Hindu Tantrism will be discussed here, Buddhism remaining outside the scope of our research.)

As mentioned above, it is hardly possible, in the present state of scholarship, to put into historical perspective, or even to follow the evolution of the post-Vedic—and notably Tantric—developments of the speculations about the Word. One can hardly go beyond recording the presence, and even for some of them, the omnipresence, of those speculations from a certain period in time, the beginning of which is also hardly datable. Furthermore, some elements—as mentioned earlier—just seem to be there from the origin. Thus if ritualistic notions and customs are found as early as ancient Brahmanism, and if identical or quite similar concepts or practices emerge once again ten centuries later in Tantric lore, must we view them rather as a more or less accountable reappearance of a vanished material? Or shouldn't it rather be assumed that those elements that revealed their presence to us from a certain period in time have in fact never ceased to exist locally, but were simply not mentioned in the texts as long as another ideology prevailed? I believe the latter view could all the more be admitted since we do not by far know all the texts that might have been in existence, and we are very far also from being able to date precisely those texts that we do happen to know. There are so many gaps in this field of research that all definite assertions must be avoided. Such being the case, and with all due reservations, the viewpoint that might be called evolutionist seems to me, for the time being, more convincing, and indeed the case for it is stronger than for a, so to speak, "transformist" standpoint.[1] Thus Tantric Hinduism would have emerged progressively through a process of ongoing evolution over an extended period of time, granted, however, that we know nothing as to the nature and modalities of the process, and that we do not know how and when it started.[2]

Defining Tantrism proves difficult because of the wide range of variegated material that must be put under this term (and also because some of the elements thus brought together are found, whether separately or not, in cases not relevant to Tantrism). This difficulty arises also from the term itself, for the notion of Tantrism comes from the West.[3] This word was in fact coined in the previous century to refer to practices and notions discovered in the Tantras (hence that name), and which were then considered as both bizarre and exceptional:

---

1. Cf. for instance Frits Staal's remarks in *Understanding Mantras* (Albany: SUNY Press, 1988, p. 65) on the "reappearance" of the Vedic monosyllabic mantras: there is indeed no evidence whatever as to their disappearance. It may be that we just cannot trace them in between Vedism and the Tantras.
2. Keeping nevertheless L. Renou's remark in mind: "In India, developments are as easy to follow as breaking points are difficult to discern," *EVP* 6, p. 11.
3. As A. Avalon wrote as early as 1922: "The adjective *Tantric* is largely a Western term." The adjective, in fact, is thoroughly Indian, but the substantive is not. Avalon was, however, aware of the problem, which in itself was praiseworthy.

they were believed to form but a small space of abnormality within the Indian, Buddhist or Brahmanic norm, to be a phenomenon limited in scope and therefore easy to grasp and characterize. But the progress of research brought the realization that, far from being exceptional, Tantrism was in fact very widespread and indeed the common property of all the religions of India: Hinduism, Mahāyāna Buddhism, and even Jainism. "Tantrism becomes, from the fifth century A.D. onward, a pan-Indian 'religious fashion'," Mircea Eliade wrote in 1948.[4] Henceforth it became difficult to state what Tantrism was actually supposed to mean. Still more difficult—since it was almost all-pervading—was to establish what was relevant thereto and what was not.[5]

Although of great interest, and precisely because of its importance, this question will not be discussed here, for that would demand lengthy developments. And indeed it has already been treated elsewhere.[6] Let us add that, owing to the magnitude of the Tantric phenomenon, there is a very extensive body of

---

4. M. Eliade, *Techniques du Yoga* (Paris: Gallimard, 1948, p. 176). And in addition to that, this remark by L. Renou: "Tantrism partly obliterates the earlier practices and partly accommodates them while altering them. Henceforth the Purāṇic religion—and consequently the underlying Vedism—somehow receded into the background. All the later literary evidence, which appears free from Tantrism (or Āgamism), may only reflect the almost archaeological will to regenerate ancient Hinduism" ("Le destin du Veda dans l'Inde," *EVP* 6, p. 10).
5. Cf. L. Renou's remark quoted above. Let us add that this becomes all the more difficult in that Tantrism is comprised of many different levels, from the Kāpālika or the most extreme Kaula to those, notably Śaivasiddānta or Pāñcarātra, which are quite close to the Vedic orthodoxy—which happens occasionally to reconcile itself with a few practices of Tantric nature or origin (*bījamantra, nyāsa*, etc.).
6. For example, S. Gupta, D. J. Hoens, and T. Goudriaan, *Hindu Tantrism* (Leiden: Brill, 1979); and T. Goudriaan and S. Gupta, *Hindu Tantric and Śākta Literature* (Wiesbaden: O. Harrassowitz, 1981), hereafter abbreviated as *HTSL*.

   Interesting information and comments will be found in M. Eliade's two studies, *Techniques du Yoga, op. cit., supra* n. 4, and *Le Yoga* (Paris: Payot, 1968). The sections by L. Renou *et al.* in *L'Inde classique* (2nd ed.; Paris: A. Maisonneuve, 1985), vol. 1, §841ff. and vol. 2, §217ff. are still worth reading. See also the entries "Tantrism: An Overview,"

literature which may be considered as relevant thereto (if one takes into account all of its different aspects and currents), and which is still quite unexplored. A number of Tantras, Āgamas, Saṃhitās, Sūtras, and other texts have yet, if not to be discovered, at least to be studied, and also to be situated in time and space: this is a world whose systematic exploration has yet to be done. Hence general assertions about Tantrism as a whole are, for the time being, necessarily relative and temporary. Here, we shall simply concern ourselves with a few general remarks and the enumeration of a few facts or features, which, we believe, may be regarded as more specifically Tantric, with a view not to provide a solution to the problem, but simply help toward locating and dating the texts upon which this work is based.

There is probably no need to remind the reader that, notwithstanding the term *Tantrism*, any text called Tantra is not necessarily Tantric. Neither is it necessary to say surely that a Tantric text is not always called a Tantra. Moreover, one cannot regard as rigorously valid the usual division of those texts into three categories: the Tantras, considered, as a rule, as primarily "Śākta" or "Śāktaśaiva,"[7] more often than not nondualistic, and chiefly referring to private worship (*ātmārthapūjā*); the Āgamas, Śaiva and generally dualistic, and mostly dealing with temple life and worship (*parārthapūjā*); and finally the Saṃhitās, usually Vaiṣṇava, belonging to dualism or qualified nondualism (*viśiṣṭādvaita*), and considered as the treatises of

---

"Hindu Tantrism," and "Hindu Tantric Literature," in M. Eliade, ed., *Encyclopedia of Religion* (New York: Macmillan, 1986).

For the position of Tantrism in the Hindu world, and especially its situation in contrast with *bhakti*, one should read M. Biardeau's penetrating remarks in *L'hindouisme, anthropologie d'une civilisation* (Paris: Flammarion, 1981). As will be seen later, my position on those questions is largely inspired by M. Biardeau's ideas.

Finally, it is only fair to cite the works of A. Avalon (Sir John Woodroffe), who was the first pioneer in Tantric lore, with the texts he published in the "Tantrik Texts" series, and with his studies, especially *Shakti and Shakta*, and *The Garland of Letters* (Madras: Ganesh & Co.), both works being regularly reprinted. (cf. Bibliography.)

7. For those two terms, see *infra*, p. 52.

the Pāñcarātra;[8] and that, if only because the term *Āgama* is used with reference to the texts of the three traditions. One should also take care, in this textual field, not to ascribe over-systematically—as I did in 1963[9]—the Tantric lore to North India and the Āgamic to South India: although this is often the case, those texts (and even moreso their commentaries) are of various, and indeed sometimes uncertain, geographical origin. Therefore it is not absolutely correct to speak of a Northern (nondualistic) Śaivism as opposed to a Southern (dualistic) one; we shall take up this point again later on.

While the substantive term *Tantrism* is not Indian, the adjective *tāntrika* exists in Sanskrit, generally in contrast with *vaidika.* Thus Kullūka Bhaṭṭa (fifteenth century) states in his commentary on the *Mānavadharmaśāstra* (2.1) that Revelation is twofold—Vedic and Tantric (*śrutiś ca dvividhā vaidikī tāntrikī ca*). This formula distinguishing between two forms of revelation introduces an initial aspect of the Tantric tradition, which indeed is usually held as different from the Vedic, as revealed by the divinity without referring to the Veda, and as being more adapted than the Vedic revelation to the present age of mankind. In fact, the relationship between the two traditions is complex.[10] Notwithstanding what some have written, there is obviously nothing Tantric in Vedic literature. However, a number of Vedic elements (notably those related to the Word) have survived in Tantric texts (some of them have been mentioned in the previous chapter). Moreover it seems that from a certain

---

8. For those latter texts, see for example, H. Daniel Smith's two volumes, *A Descriptive Catalogue of the Printed Texts of the Pāñcarātrāgama* (Baroda: Oriental Institute, 1975 and 1980. G. O. S., nn. 158 and 168). V. Varadachari's study, *Āgamas and South-Indian Vaiṣṇavism* (Madras: M. Rangacharya Memorial Trust, 1982), is well in the traditional line but contains a wealth of information. The Vaikhānasa scriptures, which are "Vedic", are also discussed therein.
9. And as still do some eminent authors in this field, such as H. Brunner. This division is not entirely unfounded, and it is convenient. But still I maintain that it ought to be qualified.
10. For this relationship, cf. in particular L. Renou's study, "Le destin du Véda dans l'Inde," *EVP* 6, pp. 8-12, which includes a comprehensive bibliography, and also M. Biardeau's remarks in *L'hindouisme.*

period onward Vedic elements have been introduced or added in Tantric works—Tantras or Āgamas—so that they may look more respectable, more acceptable within Brahmanic circles.[11] (Indeed, perhaps as early as the ninth century A.D., a twofold movement of tantricization of the Brahmanic milieu, and of "brahmanization" or "vedantization" of Tantrism, is apparent in Kashmir[12] as well as in South India, with the Śrīvidyā.) Hence an ambiguous, intricate situation, likely to generate misunderstandings, especially about the so-called Tantrism of the Veda. Actually, if Tantrism is opposed to Vedism, it is partly because of its being altogether different from it, and also partly (and maybe above all) because it gives a different, a new interpretation and usage of Vedic elements. This is clearly apparent, for instance, with the Tantric *mantraśāstra*, where there remain a number of Vedic elements (in various arrangements and degrees depending on the sects); some of them we shall see later on.[13]

One important distinction between Tantrism and Vedism (or orthodox Brahmanism) is that, contrary to the Veda, the Tantric revelation is supposed to be available to all, irrespective of caste or sex. This is something new, in contrast with the religion of the Vedas and the Upaniṣads. This has sometimes been considered as a result (and an evidence) of the Brahmanic-Hindu religion expanding into new social strata or groups, and it may be so. But *bhakti* too, although it remained "Vedic," has proclaimed over and over again the same egalitarianism before the divinity.[14] It has also often been said that social

---

11. The most extreme or esoteric among those "left" (*vāma*) Tantric sects sometimes mark themselves off (such as the Kaula) from the others by referring to the latter as *tāntrika*, which would then refer to exoteric, public Tantrism.
12. On this point see A. Sanderson's study, "Purity and Power among the Brahmans of Kashmir," in M. Carrithers, S. Collins, and S. Lukes, eds., *The Category of the Person* (Cambridge University Press, 1985), hereafter abbreviated as "Purity and Power."
13. See above p. 31, n. 1.
14. This egalitarianism does not, however, extend to the social field. Even though Tantrism is especially notable for certain transgressive practices in violation of the regulations about caste and ritual purity, it does not

groups that were outside the Brahmanic fold and/or of lower caste, or above all "non-Aryan," "aboriginal" elements, must have played a decisive role in the advent of Tantrism.[15] I shall not investigate here this interesting issue, but simply say that while there is no evidence against such a role, neither is there any clear evidence in support of it. It is no doubt quite possible that, in particular, the spread of the cult of the female deities, above all when endowed with fearsome and domineering qualities, should be ascribed to an autochthonous background: the Goddess, then, would be of local origin. However one should not forget that, whatever the role of this autochthonous fund, Brahmanism itself developed in India, and therefore within the local milieu, where there were surely "non-Aryan" elements, some of which it may well have absorbed quite early. But in this matter one is at present reduced to conjecture.[16]

Furthermore, although Tantrism rejects the authority of the Vedas, it has retained some Vedic elements and sometimes developed them intensely. Rather than denying the import of the Veda, Tantrism contrasted itself from it, rejecting some of its elements while preserving, developing, and above all reinterpreting others. In this respect, it appears somehow as

---

appear at all as socially egalitarian, and still less as revolutionary. Transgression indeed owes its efficacity to the force of the transgressed norm.

For the "social" aspect of Tantrism, see T. Goudriaan, *Hindu Tantrism*, p. 32. For its "transgressive" aspect, cf. A. Sanderson's study mentioned above.

15. Due to the fact that Tantrism has had important and ancient centers on the boundaries of India, from Kashmir (or Swāt) to Assam, and in areas close to Tibet (where it has remained very much alive) and China, some of its practices have sometimes been thought as possibly originating from Central Asia and from shamanic cults. Some Tantric texts say that their doctrine comes from Mahācīna, that is, Tibet, or describe their practices as *cīnācāra* (cf. Tucci, "Tracce di culto lunare in India," *Riv. Stud. Or.* 12 [1929]). Chinese Tantrism being very mild in contrast with India's, it is unlikely that China should have played a seminal role.
16. But one should certainly not overlook the contribution of non-Sanskritic traditions to the developments of Hindu thought and practices. These traditions, embodied in the vernacular mother-tongues of the peoples of India, surely never ceased to provide the living, real, and daily background of Indian lives. Cf. *supra*, introduction, p. xv.

preserving and reviving that which was most alive in Vedism.[17] Such is the case, for instance, with regard to the relationship between macrocosm and microcosm, to the correlations—which are actually identifications—that Tantrism establishes between man and the cosmos, gods and rites. These ancient correspondences are further elaborated and organized into a system where all is interconnected, where there is an interplay between the different levels in each field, where energy is both cosmic and human, and therefore where microcosm, reenacting macrocosm, becomes identified with it and, by means of symbolic efficacy, is able to influence it (or comes to believe that he does, which is all the same). In such a perspective, the cosmic manifestation and man's bondage in the world, cosmic resorption and deliverance from the cycle of births, are both perfectly homologous processes: going through one, one goes through the other as well, because those are two movements of the same energy.[18]

The spirit permeating Tantrism is quite close to that of the Veda insofar as it reacts against the spirit of renunciation which settles in India with the Upaniṣads and early Buddhism. Tantrism, however, is also a continuation of the Upaniṣads

---

17. Cf. M. Biardeau, *L'hindouisme* (on the tantric speculations about the Word): "Le tantrisme, sur ce point encore, n'aurait fait qu'amplifier jusqu'au délire une direction de pensée authentiquement brahmanique." ("Tantrism, here again, would have but elaborated to a paroxysm a genuinely brahmanical way of thinking," ibid., p. 168).

18. We shall see this in chap. 3, when dealing with the *kuṇḍalinī*, and in chap. 5, with the *varṇa-parāmarśa*, a cosmic action, the work of Śiva, but whose movement the yogin has to assimilate in order to attain salvation.

Of course systems vary in their scope and practices, depending on traditions and sects. Śāktaśaiva nondualistic Tantras are more inclusive in their structure than the Saiddhāntikā Āgamas or the Pāñcarātra. Abhinava's Trika, which we shall see here, provides an especially comprehensive example. However, those systems of anthropocosmic representation are always quite similar in their orientation, in their atmosphere: there is a certain unity in the Tantric vision.

In an early but still interesting study, H. von Glasenapp very aptly defined Tantrism as "eine universale Weltanschauung sakraler Magie" ("Tantrismus und Saktismus," *Ostasiatische Zeitschrift*, neue Folge, b. 12, 1936, pp. 120-33).

in that it is essentially—at least from a certain period in time—a gnosis based on micro-macrocosmic correlations; in that it conceives deliverance (*mokṣa*) not only as related to rites, but also as the result of the intuitive knowledge of a primary spiritual or vital principle. Tantrism, however, unlike the Upaniṣads, does not always require that one should renounce the world in order to engage in the search for deliverance; on the contrary, it endeavors to reconcile deliverance (*mokṣa*) with enjoyment (*bhoga*). The Tantric adept does not pursue the sole emancipating knowledge, but autonomy[19] and power as well. He stays in the world[20] and controls it. He becomes one with the Transcendental. But the Transcendental is the primary creative and destructive principle, holding within itself the paradigm of the cosmos and pervading it: united or identified with this principle, with this primeval energy, the liberated-while-living of Tantrism attains not only self-mastery but mastery over the universe; he is a man-god. No doubt this will to achieve control over the universe, this quest for power together with (or sometimes rather than) liberation, must have been very strong to have prevailed not only in Hinduism but even in Buddhism (with Tantric Buddhism) which, in its very principle, was so utterly averse to it.

So this attitude of renunciation of early Buddhism and of the Upaniṣads appears as corresponding to a limited period in time, or rather to one only of the two faces of Indian thought, which seems basically always to have focused on the magical

---

19. Tantrism, wrote P. Masson-Oursel, is "a pursuit, not of knowledge, but of autonomy." In fact both are generally interrelated, the adept's pursuit culminating in autonomy through the merging with a primary principle which, notably in the case of nondualistic Śāktaśaiva systems, is described as essentially free, autonomous, and which is awareness, cognition. This holds true even though, on the practical level, the adept's pursuit and its fruit may appear of little "intellectual" value: this is because it takes place within a system where the physical and spiritual are associated in the concept of energy, which is indivisibly life, force, and consciousness.

20. Cf. for instance *PTV*, p. 18, which states that liberation, according to a text like the *PT*, is a condition where a person remains in the world while being transformed through his/her merging with energy.

control over the universe. This, I believe, is an ever-present or even underlying component of Tantric or tantricized Hinduism: even for escaping the cycle of births its follower practices rites that give him supernatural powers (*siddhi*s), or at least goes through a stage where those powers are offered him by the deities he must propitiate in order to attain liberation.[21] I, for one, am tempted to see at play, in this search for liberation and powers, two tendencies—antagonistic in some respects, complementary in some others, but above all fundamental—of the Indian soul. This is one of the inner tensions (rather than conflicting elements) of Tantric Hinduism—where there are others too, as we shall see, notably one, of general character, between the householder and the renunciate.

For Tantrism too, notwithstanding its quest for powers, does have its renunciates, and even to the highest degree. Whence would have emerged Tantric sects, with their initiatory lineages, if not from groups of renunciates first gathered around a master, then transmitting the teaching from master to disciple (*guruparamparā*)? Tantric sects have always been first of all small groups of initiated ascetics,[22] even though, with time, becoming more respectable, more "brahmanized," they did accommodate *gṛhastha*s.[23] However, whether renunciate or *gṛhastha*, the *tāntrika* need not necessarily renounce powers. It is clear indeed that Tantric texts—Āgamas, Tantras, and Saṃhitās—were written first of all for the use of *sādhaka*s,[24] a class of initiated adepts, who by definition are *bubhukṣu*, "desirous of enjoyment" (*bhukti*), and therefore of supernatural powers, rather than *mumukṣu*, who aspire to liberation (*mokṣa*).

---

21. See, for exmple, *PT, śl.* 12-18; or *YH*, 3-152, and so forth. Examples could be multiplied.
22. One of the characteristics of Tantrism, indeed, is that it is made up of sects—closed initiatory groups—each claiming its superiority to the others. It is often asserted that one cannot be initiated in two different Tantric traditions, Tantric affiliation on the other hand being no obstacle to the observance of non-Tantric Hindu rules and practices.
23. Cf. *infra*, p. 73.
24. For the *sādhaka*, see H. Brunner's study "Le *sādhaka*, personnage oublié du śivaïsme du sud," *J.AS.*, CCLXIII, 1975, pp. 411-443.

Even though in certain texts the latter class of adepts are held as superior, since their aim is the highest, they still tend to be considered, if not as secondary to others, at least as the unmarked category of adepts, and this is, I believe, something very typically Tantric. We shall see later on, when dealing with mantras, not only the powers of the Word and their transcendental, liberating role, but also the various types of powers—sometimes very worldly—that may be granted by certain forms of speech.

This will to rule over the world, so important here, brings us to another aspect of Tantrism, which in itself and because of its consequences is probably its cardinal feature. And that is the prominent position of the world as a means to salvation (to powers and/or deliverance), and as the place where this salvation is achieved and experienced—this liberation-while-living (*jīvanmukti*), the ultimate state for the Tantric adept. If indeed, as has often been said since Louis Dumont first propounded this idea in 1959, Hindu religious concepts are dominated by the opposition between the householder and the renunciate, Tantrism—although not free from the tensions and inconsistencies inherent in Hinduism—can be understood as an attempt to overcome at least the main one. This it seeks to achieve, as Madeleine Biardeau has put it excellently, through "harnessing *kāma*—desire—(in every sense of the word) and all of its related values to the service of deliverance." It seems to me that it is in this ideology, where desire holds a preeminent position, that the truly distinctive feature of Tantrism lies. There is, no doubt, an equally Tantric trait in the very peculiar, invading ritualism. But in its most typical forms (notably

---

As a rule, only he is a *tāntrika* who is a member of a sect, an initiated disciple of a master, and who puts the teaching into practice. A. Wayman's formulation, although designed for Buddhist Tantrism, stands generally true: "Understanding a Tantra is being able to do it" (*The Buddhist Tantras*. London: Routledge & Kegan Paul, 1973, p. 62).

Despite its extensive literature and its major role in rites, arts, and so forth, Tantrism has probably never been practiced but by small groups. Cf. A. Padoux, review article in *History of Religions* quoted *infra*, n. 28.

sexual practices[25]) this ritualism makes use of *kāma* to reach the divine, to experience it within. Of course there are many other characteristic features besides those: the proliferation of mantras and related material, the swarming pantheon with its fearsome deities, the transgressive practices where immersion in impurity means gaining access to power. However, all this and much more, all those features (of which a long list[26] could be made) become significant, relevant to the Tantric system I would say, only to the extent that they are structured, organized, orientated, by a specific ideology, a general purpose, which is not to be found—at least not explicitly—in Hinduism generally. This ideology or purpose is—to quote again M. Biardeau—"not to sacrifice this world to deliverance, but to reintegrate it somehow in the perspective of salvation." And all the moreso, I would add, since this salvation is not a merging of the individual self into a transpersonal and immutable absolute, but the Godhead's taking possession of the adept (in the early Tantras), an implosion of the individual self within the Self of the deity, a fusion into cosmic energy, therefore an identification with the force that moves the universe.[27]

Related to this, and equally characteristic, is the concept of the Godhead as being sexually polarized in male and female —the female pole being that of energy—and acting through the expansion of energy, man and the universe being equally pervaded by this energy which gives them life and sustenance. This being so, the pursuit of deliverance will in the main consist of tapping and using (not to say manipulating) this energy. Some such notions with their related practices may indeed be

---

25. Other instincts are used as well: fear, anger, and so forth. For such practices, see, for example, *VBh.* There is in Buddhism the interesting example of *krodhāveśa*, described for instance in Nāḍapāda's *Sekoddeśaṭīkā*, a text of the Kālacakrayāna (Baroda: Gaekwad Oriental Series, 1941).
26. T. Goudriaan, *Hindu Tantrism*, pp. 7-9, lists eighteen of them.
27. What I write here is above all relevant to the nondualistic Śaiva texts which will be examined in this study. Liberation, in dualistic Āgamas, or for the Pāñcarātra, does not involve any such identification with the Godhead. Yet the role of energy, the assimilation of its power, remains there of paramount importance.

found also in non-Tantric schools. But when these notions and practices are organized within the ideological pattern we have just described, then Tantrism is there. Those distinctive features of Tantric practice and discourse will be found time and again throughout this book.

Believing as I do in the primary importance of the Tantric *Weltanschauung*,[28] I do not share the view that Tantrism is only "the ritual and technical aspect of religion," as J. Filliozat put it.[29] For such an aspect is also encountered in texts which are by no means Tantric (for instance the Vaikhānasa's *Marīcisaṃhitā*). Conversely, various Tantric works prescribe to the most advanced initiates (such as those of the *śāktopāya* or the *śāmbhavopāya* of the *Tantrāloka*) to renounce all rites: when he abides by this rule the adept does not cease to be a *tāntrika*, and that not only because, to reach this point he, as a rule, practiced Tantric rites and had a kind of intuitive inner vision of the ritual's meaning, but also and above all because his outlook on the world, on how he should act and fit into it, are wholly Tantric.[30]

---

28. I stressed this point (and a few others) in a review article on Gupta's, Hoens's & Goudriaan's *Hindu Tantrism*, in *History of Religions* (1981): 345-60: "A survey of Tantric Hinduism for the historian of religions."
29. In a review published in *J.As.* in 1968, p. 237. Also J. N. Banerjee, *Pauranic and Tantric Religion* (University of Calcutta, 1965): "Tantrism in its general sense of systematized ritualism of a particular sort."
30. The fact that Āgamas theoretically open with a *jñānapada* also shows the at least theoretical significance of doctrine in Āgamic thought. Like all initiatory traditions, Tantric traditions are gnoses: deliverance or powers come through knowledge and not through the sole ritual (even though the latter is held as essential), and that knowledge is always that of some secret doctrine, which, whether original or not, is the base upon which the tradition rests.

    I wish to add that there is no rite or cult which is not grounded in, explained and justified by a system of beliefs. Similarly if "at the beginning was action," action, subsequently, cannot be apprehended, cannot survive except within a system of representation, within a doctrinal pattern.

    Finally, the simple fact that the present work, where the speculations about speech are dealt with at great length, could be written, shows the primary significance of ideology.

Thus a whole body of doctrines and practices has been elaborated in the Tantras, Āgamas, Saṃhitās, and so forth, and in their commentaries. Notwithstanding its diversity and its variants (which are sometimes very important), this body appears to me as forming a whole, even a system, I should say, or several similar, Tantric, systems. Assuredly this is an invasive system since, generally or in some of its aspects, it more or less permeates the religious life of most Hindus. This, however, does not mean that it is the all-in-all in Hinduism. Some areas are free from it. Neither is it only the ritual aspect of Hinduism, even though Tantric texts deal mostly with practices.[31] Tantrism should rather be seen as a specific system within the more general system of Hinduism (even though it occupies a very large part of it). True, its doctrines or its practices (or at least some of them) are also present outside Tantrism, so that any doctrinal originality may be understandably denied to it, or even any other form of existence other than being one (essentially ritual) aspect of Hinduism. But precisely, the originality of Tantrism lies, rather than in its components themselves, in the way in which it organizes them into a visionary pattern.

Concerning some of the features that seem characteristic of Tantric Hinduism, it may be useful to return to the polarized concept of the Godhead, and to dwell on its female pole and on the role played, in Tantric texts, by the *śakti*, divine and cosmic energy, as well as cosmic, vital, and spiritual force. Here is indeed an element of primary importance in the Tantric conception of the Godhead and of the world—at least in those texts with which we shall deal hereafter, and which are mainly those of nondualistic Śaivism.[32] The supreme, male Godhead

---

31. Cf. A. Wayman's quotation above, p. 40, n. 24.

32. Which, like others (such as T. Goudriaan, *Hindu Tantrism*), I feel inclined to regard as more specifically Tantric, as it is the vehicle of the most typical or topical ideology and practices. Yet, as I said earlier, Tantric tradition extends outside Śaktism and Śāktaśaiva texts. It also includes Āgamic Śaivism, where Śiva's power, *śakti*, plays an important part, although altogether different from the above described. Tantrism includes also (within Hinduism) the Pāñcarātra, where the role of *śakti*, though limited, is also apparent; it is more apparent however in the Pāñcarātra texts of the Kashmirian tradition, such as the

(Śiva, Viṣṇu, or one of their forms), does not act by himself, but only as inseparably associated with—and through—his energy, his *śakti*, the dynamic power that manifests, animates, sustains, and finally reabsorbs the cosmic manifestation. This power is infinite, all-powerful, since it is the Godhead: theologically, it is the Goddess, in her various names and aspects.[33]

Ahirbudhnya or *JayākhyaS.*, or above all the *Lakṣmītantra*—which, however, has surely been subject to Śaiva influences: cf. *infra*, p. 68).

Śākti and sexual speculations and practices are on the other hand much in evidence in Sahajiyā Vaiṣṇavism (for this, cf. Edward C. Dimock's study *The Place of the Hidden Moon* (Chicago University Press, 1966).

33. Much could be said about the Goddess. First, can one speak of *the* Goddess (or even of "Goddess" as one says God)? The Goddess, which is commonly looked upon as Śaiva—Pārvatī, Durgā, the consort of Śiva—is a sister to Viṣṇu (and his consort as well), as Śrī or Lakṣmī. Could she be primarily Vaiṣṇava? She is the primal energy, which we shall find here again as the *kuṇḍalinī, parāvāc*, the Trika's threefold goddess Parā, Parāparā and Aparā, and as the life of Consciousness (*vimarśa*) as well, unfolding—against the background of the Absolute, Śiva, who is motionless (or rather who would be so but for her)—all the cosmic activity, a reminiscence in Hinduism of the old dichotomy *puruṣa-prakṛti*. One may well wonder how those various aspects of the Goddess (or those various goddesses) and their interrelations can be apprehended as a whole.

Next comes up, in the Śaiva field with which we are here primarily concerned, the question of the relationship between the Goddess and the God—between Śākti and Śiva. Though inseparably united (*vāgarthāviva saṃpṛktau*, as Kālidāsa would say), they are (like the word and the object) metaphysically hierarchized: Śiva comes first. Yet in various sects, and even more in temples, often the Goddess appears as the supreme Godhead. Many "Śaiva" sects are distinguished according to the Goddess they worship. This is why one may speak of Śāktism, not a very felicitous word however, since it tends to distinguish between Śāktism and Tantrism, as if those two could be opposed. There is, I believe, no Tantrism without Śakti, therefore without "Śāktism," even though there are some Tantric texts where the *śakti* does not have a major role. Above all, there is no "Śākta" text or practice that is not Tantric. One should probably make a distinction between metaphysics, which ontologically subordinate Śakti to Śiva (who is the first of the 36 *tattva*s), and the religious field (that of the cult, of the temple, and sometimes of theology) where the Goddess may be preeminent.

Although limitless, this divinity is also very near: the Goddess of Hinduism is generally experienced as closer to her devotees, more concerned with their daily problems than the masculine Godhead. But *śakti*, above all, is manifold and of infinite aspects, for it is she who acts on all levels of the cosmos. Out of the supreme Energy flow forth countless subordinate hierarchized energies, which are aspects of this original Power, higher divinized energies, as well as lesser divinities, ranging from major goddesses to lower forms, being at the lowest level hardly more than some kinds of demonesses or fairies. All those energies have a role in the unfolding of cosmic cycles as well as in the economy of deliverance, or in the bondage of human beings. The yogin learns how they can be propitiated and subdued, and they are one of the means (or obstacles) to his spiritual progress and his mastery over the universe.[34]

Emanating from the primal Energy, those divinized energies are each, like her, associated (and more often than not metaphysically subordinated) to a male partner of whom she is the consort.[35] Cosmically, all that comes forth, whether material

---

There are some "Śaiva" texts or sects where the whole set of practices is "Śākta," in that it focuses on the Goddess as the principal form of the deity, while retaining a metaphysics where Śiva remains the supreme aspect of the Godhead. I thought it fit to call those traditions, with which we shall often deal later, "Śāktaśaiva," for they represent an important aspect of nondualistic—notably Kashmirian—Tantric traditions.

For the question of the Goddess—covered by an extensive literature —I refer once again to M. Biardeau's remarks in *L'hindouisme* (esp. p. 142ff.) and to the volume edited by M. Biardeau, *Autour de la Déesse Hindoue* (Paris: Editions de l'EHESS, 1981, Collection "Puruṣārtha," vol. 5); cf. also Th. B. Coburn, *Devīmāhatmya, the Crystallization of the Goddess Tradition* (Delhi: Motilal Banarsidass, 1984); J. S. Hawley and D. M. Wulff, eds., *The Divine Consort: Rādhā and the Goddess of India* (Delhi: Motilal Banarsidass, 1984). For the relationship between Śāktism and Tantrism, see T. Goudriaan's views in *HT*, pp. 5-12, as well as Brunner's criticisms on this matter in *Indo-Iranian Journal* 23/2 (1981), especially pp. 140-42.

34. As stated for instance in the *PT*, *śl.* 9-18 (pp. 231ff.) or in *ŚS*, 3.19 (p. 100), in both cases with regard to the phonemes taken as energies.
35. Sometimes referred to as *dūti* (the [female] "messenger"), which clearly places the male Godhead in the dominant position. Whenever the

or immaterial, is conceived of as resulting from the sexual union or conjunction, of two complementary—male and female—principles. This is a fundamental element both of the Tantric conception of the Word and of its ritual practices, as will be seen in this study. In those systems of representation—and even outside of "Śākta" Tantrism—we find or feel, at every level, the explicit or underlying presence of sexual values and symbolism. Such symbolism is indeed ancient: nowhere is it more apparent than in some Brāhmaṇas. But only in Tantrism—and especially in the Śāktaśaiva context—does it unfold and pervade fully. Nonetheless one must beware not to look upon Tantrism as a pan-sexualism: whatever some may have written about it, Tantrism, even Śāktaśaiva or Sahajiyā Vaiṣṇava, is not "divinized eroticism." However, the sexual polarity of the divine not only necessarily permeates all levels of the cosmos, but, being a cosmic paradigm, it is the source of the play, of the work, of the microcosm. Hence the sexual symbolism of certain rites. Hence the *kuṇḍalinī*, a female cosmic energy within man where she unites with Śiva: a symbolic realization of androgyny. Hence, finally, the ritualistic sexual yogic practices, where the union of the yogin and his partner mirrors, at the human level, that of the male Godhead and his energy, and will be used to participate mystically thereto.[36] The Tantric pantheon is characterized both by those sexual, divine couples and by the endless proliferation of deities forming the retinue of the great divinities or their attendant hierarchical circles ("surrounding" them, *āvaraṇa*).

Also relevant to micro-macrocosmic correlations is the Tantric ritual, an outstanding element, since all Tantras, Āgamas, and so forth, in all traditions are essentially ritualistic texts, and since this ritual is abundant. Let us simply mention here the cult, the *pūjā*, which, altogether different from the Vedic sacrifice, is a worship, often very complex, performed

---

energy is the main aspect of the deity, her male partner will be a [male] "messenger," *dūta*.

36. Magic eroticism appears in fact as early as certain Vedic rites, and as we have seen (chap. 1, p. 10), cosmic creation, in the Brāhmaṇas and the Āraṇyakas, is sometimes considered as the result of a sexual union.

with the help of an image (*mūrti, bera, arcana*), whose shape is that of the deity, or with that of a symbolic support of the deity's presence, to which the worshiper pays obeisance. This cult, which indeed became the common cult for Hinduism, achieves, however, a particular dimension in that it implies an initial "divinization" of the worshiper, who, before he is able to pay his obeisance to the divinity, must identify with it. As expressed by the traditional phrase *nādevo devam arcayet*, he cannot worship a deity who has not become god. Hence various ritualistic practices, mental and physical—meditation, "visualization,"[37] placing (*nyāsa*) of mantras on the body, *mūdra*—all aiming at securing this identification.[38] Hence the cosmic dimension of the cult,[39] more or less prominent depend-

---

37. These are the two meanings of the word *dhyāna:* both meditation—notably of a deity—and a clear-cut mental picture created by meditation of the deity's form, according to its scriptural description (in *dhyāna-śloka*).

38. The most comprehensive (and most annotated) exposition of the Śaiva cult is that of the *Śomasambhupaddhati* (*SP*), edited and translated by H. Brunner-Lachaux (3 vols., Pondicherry: I.F.I., 1963-1977).

The *Śrīcakrapūjā*, the cult of the Śrīvidyā deities in the Śrīcakra, is described in the third chapter of the *Yoginīhṛdaya*, the cosmic and metaphysical implications of which are developed by Amṛtānanda in his commentary (cf. *infra*, pp. 63-64). For this same cult, see also the *Nityotsava* and the *Paraśurāmakalpasūtra.* A descriptive study of the contemporary tantric *pūjā* (according to the *PRKS*) by S. Gupta will be found in S. Gupta, J. D. Hoens, and T. Goudriaan, *Hindu Tantrism* (Leiden: Brill, 1979), pp. 121-62, and still better in Madhu Khanna's unpublished Ph.D. thesis (Oxford, 1987).

For the use of ritualistic diagrams (*maṇḍala, yantra, cakra*) in worship, besides the comparatively ancient studies of H. Zimmer, *Kunstform und Yoga im indischen Kultbild* (new ed.; Frankfurt: Surhkamp, 1976), of Tucci, *Teoria e practica del mandala* (Rome, 1949), and of P. A. Pott, *Yoga and Yantra* (The Hague: M. Nijhoff, 1966), one may refer to Padoux, ed., *Mantras et diagrammes rituels dans l'hindouisme* (Paris: CNRS, 1986).

For the placing (*nyāsa*), cf. A. Padoux, "Contributions à l'étude du *mantraśāstra*, II: *nyāsa*, L'imposition rituelle des mantra," *BEFEO* 67 (1981), pp. 59-102.

39. For this see vol. 2 of J. Varenne's edition of the *Mahānārāyāṇa Upaniṣad*, pp. 53ff. Cf. also *ChUp.* 5.34.1-2 and the *Prāṇagnihotra Upaniṣad*, translated and annotated by J. Varenne, with the *MNUp.*, vol. 2.

ing on the sects, but ever present. In a Śāktaśaiva context, the *pūjā* offerings include also liquor and pieces of meat or fish.[40] Finally, the cult may include a ritual sexual union (or consist essentially thereof). This is a very characteristic practice, a

---

The Vedic *svādhyāya*, similarly, preceded the Hindu and Tantric *japa*. Cf. C. Malamoud, *Le svādhyāya, récitation personnelle du Veda, Taitt. Ār, Livre II* quoted *supra*, p. 19, n. 46.

40. Some cults may even require an offering of human flesh (thus SvT. 8.14-15). It is noteworthy that in the early Śaiva Tantras, the worship of certain deities implied their possessing (*āveśa*) the adept. Those cults, notably Kāpālika, were sometimes performed during the night in cremation grounds (*śmaśāna*), occasionally making use of a corpse: those awesome, impure elements enhance the transgressive aspect of these practices, where gaining access to the divinity's power was attempted through a plunge into impurity.

In some Āgamas there are still traces of those sexual practices, for instance the *MatPār*, Kp. 11.40-53, where occurs a description of the *asidhārāvrata* (pp. 203-05 of R. N. Bhatt's edition, Pondicherry, 1982, where this rite is referred to as *saṃdigdhavrata*).

It must be emphasized that while in Tantrism sexual practices, images, and symbolism often denote a transgression, such is not the case in the Brahmanic tradition, where references to sexual activity and its representations are justified rather by their auspiciousness. That such should also be their purpose in the Tantric sphere is far from impossible, much to the contrary. Transgression would thus be confined to cases where impurity is sought as a path toward a sacrality that transcends social norms, and as a means of conquering the supernatural powers that are associated with anomic deities. The transgressing of usual norms of conduct (ritual or otherwise) should however not always be taken as expressive of some kind of "transgressive sacrality." It rather expresses the absolute transcendence of the supreme Godhead, who is above human norms, but is also their source. Abhinavagupta—the Kāpālikas—are not to be confused with the Marquis de Sade.

For the role of auspiciousness, see Frédérique Apffel Marglin's study, *Wives of the God-King. The Rituals of the Devadasis of Puri* (Delhi: Oxford University Press, 1985), part 3: "Time, Auspiciousness, and Inauspiciousness"; and John B. Carman and Frédérique A. Marglin, eds., *Purity and Auspiciousness in Indian Society* (Leiden: E. J. Brill, 1985). For a similar approach in connection with the sculptures of the Khajuraho, Konarak, and other such temples, see Devangana Desai, *Erotic Sculptures of India, A Socio-cultural Study* (New Delhi, 1979), or Thomas E. Donaldson, "Erotic Rituals on Orissan Temples," *East and West*, vol. 36, nn. 1-3, 1986, pp. 137-182.

typically Tantric one, and therefore, "central" to Tantrism. Nonetheless it has probably never been widespread, being restricted to highly advanced adepts, and indeed prescribed only by a few texts of the most "extreme" sects: sex, actually, was probably more often a symbol than practiced "in the flesh."[41]

Finally, foremost among the characteristic features of Tantrism, in all its forms and tendencies, is the material related to speech and its powers. There is no need to dwell on this point here, since all this work is devoted thereto. Suffice it to say, as a general remark, that while from Vedic times speech had a divine quality and a central role, the same is even more true in Tantrism, of which all the speculations about the Word are based upon the identity established between the latter and the divine energy, an energy which, in its innermost nature, is speech and is acting through speech; thereby everything related to articulate sound and language is endowed with an exceptional position and power. Since the energy is all-pervading and since everything springs from it, thus will it be with speech; and since efficacy and power are the main concerns of Tantrism, which seeks to tap and use this energy, speech will permeate everything. Such is the case in ritual, every act of which will be accompanied by formulas (mantras), and more specially syllabic formulas (*bīja:* the phonic "seeds," which will almost entirely supersede the Vedic-type mantra), sometimes endlessly repeated loudly or softly, or only mentally,[42] and which are used for the worship of the deity, for vivifying its image, for identifying the adept with the deity, for purifying him, and so forth. Indeed, such is the power of mantras that they can be, at least theoretically, fully operative outside any ritual performance, the mere enunciation (*uccāra*) of certain mantras—provided they are duly performed, that is, associated with a spiritual purpose and proper yogic practices—being

---

41. For these practices, cf. for instance J. A. Schoterman, *The Yonitantra* (New Delhi: Manohar, 1980). Abhinavagupta gives a description of a secret Kaula ritual, the "great sacrifice" (*mahāyāga*) in chapter 29 of the *TĀ;* it was studied (and partly translated) by L. Silburn, *Kuṇḍalinī, the Energy of the Depths* (Albany: SUNY Press, 1988).
42. Cf. chap. 7, p. 399.

likely to impart to the adept the highest knowledge (therefore any power) and liberation.[43] It is the same with magical practices, as well as with yoga, of which every moment, every practice is linked to the utterance of mantras. These are deemed to be as much, if not more, important as the adept's physical and spiritual efforts (as far as they can be differentiated therefrom[44]), and are thus necessary means for his progress. All mantras being phonic aspects of the universal energy, they correspond to specific levels of consciousness,[45] and therefore also to specific stages or planes of the cosmic process. To assimilate a mantra means therefore reaching this plane, both on the human and on the cosmic level.

For mantras indeed proceed from the divine energy: they encapsulate it. That is why it is said that each mantra is "that which expresses" (*vācaka*) that is, it is the phonic form, the energy, the very essence of one aspect of the deity. Some mantras are envisaged as symbols not of a particular deity but of the divine absolute, of the primal energy itself—such is the case, for instance, of *OṂ*, or in the Trika of *AHAṂ* or *SAUḤ*, and so forth.[46] In this perspective, the original Word, inseparable from the transcendental Godhead, will itself come to be considered as a mantra.

This original Word, identical to the primal divine Energy, is envisaged in this Tantric perspective as phonic energy (*vākśakti*), eternal,[47] indestructible, and all-pervading, which however unfolds and evolves, bringing forth all the various aspects and stages of the cosmos. This word, this sound, is endowed with a creative force. Being "that which expresses" (*vācaka*), it must be prior to the object that is to be "enunciated" or "formulated" (*vācya*), which comes from it and is therefore inferior to it: the Word precedes the object, it brings it forth,

---

43. Cf. *PT., śl.* 18-25.
44. Cf. chap. 7, p. 390ff.
45. Ibid.
46. See *infra*, chap. 7, p. 401ff.
47. Tantric scriptures generally acknowledge, like the Mīmāṃsa, the eternal (*nitya*) nature of the Word, but they place it in an altogether different perspective: that, before all cosmologic, of the divine energy.

it is the energy that upholds it, its innermost nature, that into which it will dissolve at the time of the cosmic resorption. The process of emanation, related to speech, is variously described depending upon texts and schools; however, it appears generally as unfolding from an initial luminous vibration or sound (*nāda*), which is an extremely subtle state of pure phonic energy, which through a series of transformations and condensations will become less subtle, forming a concentrate or a drop (*bindu*) of sound-energy, from which, when it divides itself, worlds, humans, and language will come forth. This creative evolution of the Word is also described as occurring through four successive stages, or else through the gradual emergence of fifty phonemes (*varṇa*), the mother-energies (*mātṛkā*) of creation. All this, of course, being valid both on the cosmic and on the human level, and animated with a double movement: the outward movement of emanation, converting itself into a movement of return to the source. This being so, the energy of speech moves through stages that correspond to those of cosmic creation and resorption, as well as to those of ordinary life and of deliverance;[48] similarly the levels of the Word are at the same time cosmic levels, levels of consciousness, and stages in the development of language and of thought, or conversely phases through which thought and speech go back to the source of the universe. While in this connection

48. There is a difference, however, between cosmic resorption and deliverance (which will be seen in the next chapter with regard to the *kuṇḍalinī*) in that the cosmic movement is automatic, spontaneous, natural, whereas the pursuit of deliverance is deliberate; moreover, unlike the cosmic cycles, it is not endlessly repeated: the liberated-in-life does not fall back into bondage. This fact should however be qualified by the following one: when identified with Śiva, the Tantric adept can identify with all of his activities; therefore, as a man-god he can reactualize the cosmic cycles, reexperience them within himself; this however he does from the standpoint of Śiva, who presides over those cycles, and not from that of those who are subject to them. The passages in this work that deal with the micro-macrocosmic correlations of the double movement (*sṛṣṭi-saṃhāra, saṃkoca-vikāsa, unmeṣa-nimeṣa*) animating the universe should be read with those reservations in mind. It goes without saying, surely, that the cosmic experiences of an adept are only of a symbolic, or imaginative, kind.

Tantrism accommodates early Vedic notions about the powers of the Word, it has extensively elaborated upon and gone far beyond their data, developing into a complete and impressive system (albeit not free from inconsistencies) that which was but in seed-form and scattered in the preceding age. It is not a mere carrying-on from former times: it establishes in its place something new.

After stating some of the main features of Tantric works, we shall next briefly mention those texts that will be discussed hereafter, as well as how they may be interrelated.

The texts we shall see here are, in the main, Śaiva or—to use the current expression—Śaiva or Śākta. This latter distinction should not be taken, however, as opposing two particular sects, but only as distinguishing related forms of a revelation traditionally ascribed somehow or other to Śiva, and whose followers may be either worshipers of a form of Śiva or of a form of the Goddess. Moreover, the views of certain texts with regard to the theological or metaphysical preeminence of the masculine or the feminine aspect of the Godhead are sometimes rather ambiguous, thereby making it difficult to ascertain into which category they fall. This is what induced me to call such texts "Śāktaśaiva," an epithet which may be discussed, but which, if nothing more, underlines the fact that it is not at all unnatural for a Śākta to be a Śaiva as well (and vice-versa, as for instance in the Trika). It is not possible here to treat this subject in any detail,[49] but this is a point that should be borne in mind.

Those are the texts, then, Śaiva in the broad sense, which will command our attention. They were chosen for they appeared to us as more specially Tantric in their ideology, and as particularly abounding in characteristically Tantric speculations and practices.[50] Moreover they are also the works where

49. On this point see for instance A. Sanderson, "Śaivism and the Tantric Tradition," in S. Sutherland et al. (eds.), *The World's Religions* (London: Routledge, 1988, pp. 660-704).

50. The question may be raised as to whether it was speculations or rites that appeared first in the Āgamas, Tantras, and other such texts. One

the speculations about speech have been elaborated upon most extensively (at least in judging from what has come down to us from this literature). And it so happens that the most interesting, the most penetrating of those works often relate to what is usually, but not very felicitously, called "Kashmir Śaivism,"[51] that is to say, in fact, to the various nondualistic Śaiva (or "Śāktaśaiva") traditions, which emerged, developed, and flourished most brilliantly in Kashmir, or which are traditionally associated with this region. Therefore our main concern here will be with works—not necessarily from Kashmir, for many originate from South India—but related to the Kashmirian tradition. This tradition, all the same, cannot be set apart from the other forms of the Śaiva tradition, which is very ancient and of great importance. Its historical background is quite obscure, and in the present stage of scholarship[52] very little can be said about it with certainty. Here we shall not even attempt to outline it.[53] Suffice it to say that one may assume

---

may presume it was rites: such is H. Brunner's opinion with respect to the Āgamas. Leaving aside the very beginnings, of which nothing can be said, let us note however, as far as Tantras are concerned, that the earliest among them are already equipped with an elaborate and sometimes very subtle metaphysics or doctrine. And as I remarked above (p. 42ff.), there is no religious or "magic" practice that does not reflect an ideology, that does not correspond to a system of representation. This obviously does not prevent a subsequent development of speculations on the basis of the existing ritual, in order to elucidate, or justify, it (and sometimes to induce new elaborations thereof) for instance, in Kashmir Śaivism, Abhinava's theological-cum-metaphysical developments in the *TĀ*, on the basis of the Svacchanda-Bhairava cult or of various other practices (which have probably been but little affected by these theoretical developments. Cf. *infra*, p. 73, n. 112).

51. The publication, generally of a good standard, between 1911 and 1947, of the principal of these works in the Kashmir Series of Texts and Studies (*KSTS*), in making them accessible, was somewhat instrumental in determining our selection. Most of the volumes in this series are now out of print and nowhere available. Some of them however are being reprinted elsewhere in India: I have mentioned these new editions in the Bibliography whenever they were known to me.
52. I write this in 1987.
53. K. C. Pandey published in 1954, along with his translation of the *ĪPV* in the light of the *Bhāskarī* (*Bhāskarī*, vol. 3; Lucknow: U. P. Govt.

that the earliest form of "philosophical" Śaivism (but not of the Śaiva cult, which is surely earlier) is that of the Pāśupatas, and next, that of the earliest Āgamas, which themselves preceded the Bhairavāgamas as well as other Kāpālika systems. However, neither the *Pāśupatasūtra* nor the beginnings of the āgamic literature can be dated; nonetheless it is very likely that they date as far back as the very first centuries A.D.

The Kashmirian authors that will be seen here, and especially Abhinavagupta and Jayaratha,[54] take the Śaiva teachings, which to them are the divinely revealed tradition, as comprised of three sets of texts: ten dualistic, eighteen nondualistic (which corresponds to the usual list of the twenty-eight principal Āgamas, "Kāmika, etc."), and finally sixty-four nondualistic, sixty-four being the traditional (and quite theoretical as well) number of Tantras.[55] Over those three sets of texts are supposed to preside respectively Śiva, Rudra, and

---

Publications) an "Outline of the History of Śaiva Philosophy," a work which has recently been edited by R. C. Dvidvedi (Delhi: Motilal Banarsidass, 1986). One may also, in this respect, refer to J. Gonda's *Die Religionen Indiens*, vol. 2 (Stuttgart: Kohlhammer, 1963).

However, the latest in this field is to be looked for in A. Sanderson's works, some elements of which will be found in the two studies cited here in notes 12 and 49 of this chapter, above all in the article "Śaivism and the Tantric Traditions" where he brings together the final conclusions drawn from all his various inquiries into Śaivism which, following a traditional distinction in India, he divides between *atimarga* (where the Pāśupata and the Lākula are placed), and *mantramarga* (bringing together, roughly, Saiddhāntika "Āgamic" Śaivism and the Bhairavāgamas).

54. Cf. *TĀ* 1.18:

daśāṣṭādaśavasvaṣṭabhinnaṃ yacchāsanaṃ vibhoḥ/
tatsāraṃ trikaśāstraṃ hi tatsāraṃ mālinīmataṃ//

This is a *śloka* commented upon by Jayaratha (ibid., vol. 1, pp. 36-49) while expounding upon the mythical process of manifestation through the five faces of Śiva—Īśana, and so forth, and giving a list of the Tantras according to the *Śrīkaṇṭhīyasaṃhitā*.

55. For the classification of the Āgamas and Tantras into 10 + 18 + 64, cf. H. Brunner, "On the threefold classification of Śaiva Tantras," in *Proceedings of the Fifth World Sanskrit Conference* (New Delhi: Rashtriya Sanskrit Sansthan, 1985), pp. 464-74.

Bhairava, here again a wholly theoretical distribution, whose aim is probably only to establish the superiority of Bhairava over the other forms of Śiva, and of Bhairavāgamas over the other Śaiva texts. All this has no historical value. However, this classification holds some interest insofar as it reflects, translating them in terms of myth, both the interrelations that may have occurred historically between the various forms of Śaivism and the hierarchical position that Abhinavagupta wished to assign to his own system among these various forms. (His system is thus viewed as the secret, esoteric teaching—*viśeṣaśāstra*—in contrast with the basic, exoteric teaching—*sāmānyaśāstra*—of the Śaivasiddhānta.)

When Kṣemarāja (eleventh century) asserts in his *Vimarśinī* on the *Śivasūtra*[56] that these *sūtras* were revealed to restore the true Śaiva teachings and set them over against dualists, it clearly shows that (absolute or qualified) dualism prevailed in Kashmir from ancient times and was probably anterior to nondualism. The Āgamas—as evidenced by quotations in the works of Abhinava and others—were present in Kashmir. It may even be that some of them originated in North India.[57] The *Kāmika* (*Kā*), the *Mṛgendra* (*Mṛg*) or *Mṛgendratantra;* or the *Mataṅgapārameśvarāgama* (*Matpār*), are often cited by nondualistic authors. Dualistic works were still produced in Kashmir after the "revelation" of the *Śivasūtra.* Such is the case, for instance, with the works of Nārāyaṇakaṇṭha (tenth century?), the author of the *Mṛg*'s *Vṛtti*, or with the works of his son Rāmakaṇṭha,[58] who commented upon several Āgamas (*Kiraṇa, Kalottara, Matpār*) and wrote the *Nādakārikā*, to which we shall have the opportunity to refer subsequently. There is evidently, notwithstanding many differences, an important set of doctrines and practices shared by Āgamic Śaivism—

56. *ŚSV*, p. 3: *tatra prathamaṃ nareśvarabhedavādipratipakṣyeṇa caitanya-paramārthataḥ śiva eva viśvasya ātmā ity ādiśati.*

57. Or may it be that there were different recensions of the same Āgama in South and North India.

58. Not to be confused with Rāmakaṇṭha, the author of the commentary (*Vivṛti*) on the *SpK.*

Siddhānta[59]—and the various nondualistic Śaiva and Śākta streams, which is all the less surprising since those traditions existed side by side at the same places and times, in North and South India as well. While nondualistic authors cite the Āgamas, the (dualistic) commentators of these texts do not fail to cite nondualistic Tantras, particularly the *SvT*,[60] and even (for instance, Nārāyaṇakaṇṭha in his commentary on the *Mṛg*) a text so typically in the Bhairavian tradition—though not characteristically nondualist—as the *MVT*. Those borrowings reveal the existence of this common background of Tantric notions and practices (notably those relevant to the Word) which we mentioned earlier.

However we should now turn to this other, bhairavāgamic, Śaiva tradition. It is a very important one, for it is precisely its contribution to the speculations and practices of the texts studied hereafter that distinguish these texts from those of Āgamic Śaivism, and which, in particular, is responsible for their specific overtones, their occasional strangeness, and above all their cosmic dimension. Jayaratha refers to this tradition on *TĀ* 1.18, when he enumerates, citing the *Srīkaṇṭīyasaṃhitā*, the sixty-four Bhairavāgamas, divided among eight groups of eight texts. This list, which at first looks somewhat arbitrary, as is the case with any list of this type,[61] includes several texts that contributed to a large extent—one could even say centrally—to the elaboration notably of Abhinavagupta's Trika doctrine. It is a very extensive literature, of which a number of works have been lost, while the surviving ones are yet quite unexplored. We will not attempt to describe it here.[62] However we shall

---

59. This is the name that Abhinavagupta, notably, uses for Āgamic Śaivism. This Siddhānta should not be confused with the Tamil Śaivasiddhānta, which comes later (thirteenth century).

60. Whose nondualism, it is true, is not clearly apparent. Cf. *infra*, notes 66, 86.

61. For instance, the list of the sixty-four Tantras "of the Mothers" given in *NṢA*, 1.13-21 (pp. 42-45). For these lists see T. Goudriaan's exposition and views in *HTSL*, pp. 13-14.

62. This literature has been dealt with in detail in *HTSL*, to which I refer the reader. For the relationship between some of those texts and Abhinava's Trika, see A. Sanderson, "Maṇḍala and Āgamic identity in

often have to refer to some of its texts,[63] for several of the speculations with which we shall deal are based upon them.

In his Tantric works, however, not only does Abhinava refer to the sixty-four Bhairavāgamas, or to any of them in particular,[64] but he also lists occasionally the various Śaiva or Śāktaśaiva traditions (including the Bhairavāgamas), in hierarchical sequences of growing perfection or esoterism, from what seems to him the lowest one up to the highest; this, for him, is the Trika such as expounded in certain texts, and above all such as formulated by him. Such a list can be found in the *TĀ* (13.300-01), running thus:

kramikaḥ śaktipātaś ca siddhānte vāmake tataḥ//300//
dakṣe mate kule kaule ṣaḍardhe hṛdaye tataḥ/
(vol. 8, p. 181)

and in the *PTV* (p. 92), where Abhinava quotes the following stanza:

vedācchaivaṃ tato vāmaṃ tato dakṣaṃ tataḥ kulam/
tato mataṃ tataś cāpi trikaṃ sarvottamaṃ param//

supporting it with two quotations (from the *Niśācāra* and the *Sarvācāratantra*), and a reference to (probably) Somānanda.

---

the Trika of Kashmir," in *Mantras et diagrammes rituels dans l'hindouisme* (Paris: CNRS, 1986), hereafter abbreviated as "Maṇḍala." Of the same, see also the above-cited study "Śaivism and the Tantric Traditions."

63. My references will be almost exclusively to the published texts. However there are very important works in manuscript form, notably in Nepal, now accessible on microfilms. A large number thereof have been studied by T. Goudriaan for his *HTSL.* Alexis Sanderson went through some of them, of which he made use for his published articles: to him I owe the references I shall give here to such works. Sanderson also lectured on the Bhairavāgamas in Oxford: his teaching has been extensively used (but hardly acknowledged) in Mark Dyczkowski's *The Canon of the Śaivāgama and the Kubjikā Tantras of the Western Kaula Tradition* (Albany: SUNY Press, 1988).

64. As does of course not only Jayaratha, the commentator of the *TĀ*, but also the various authors who will be cited here, notably Kṣemarāja.

Abhinava (roughly) takes up this classification again in the last *āhnika* of the *TĀ* (37.25b-28).[65] The initiatory progression into the esoteric gnosis therefore begins (if one leaves aside the "Veda," which may refer to orthodox or non-Śaiva sectarian Hinduism) with the Saiddhāntika, Āgamic Śaivism. Next come Vāma, then Dakṣiṇa, representing two streams (*srotas*) within the Bhairava tradition, to which a number of texts cited by Abhinavagupta, Kṣemarāja, and others[66] are relevant. Next comes the Mata, then the Kula (or vice-versa:

---

65. This is the passage:

uktaṃ śrīratnamālāyām etac ca parameśinā//25
aśeṣatantrasāraṃ tu vāmadakṣiṇam āśritam/
ekatra militaṃ kaulaṃ śrīṣaḍardhaśāsane//26//
siddhānte karma bahulaṃ malamāyādirūṣitam/
dakṣiṇaṃ raudrakarmāḍhyaṃ vāmaṃ siddhisamākulam//27//
svalpapuṇyaṃ bahukleśaṃ svapratītivivarjitam/
mokṣavidyāvihīnaṃ ca vinayaṃ tyaja dūrataḥ//28//

(vol. 12, pp. 400-01)

"This the supreme Lord declared in the *Ratnamālā* (*Tantra*): the essence of all Tantras, present in the right and left traditions, and which has been unified in the Kaula (is to be discovered) in the Trika. The ritual is overemphasized in the Siddhānta, which moreover is not free from the taint of *māyā*, and other things. The right tradition abounds in awesome rites, whereas in the left one supernatural powers are predominant. Keep far away from those disciplinarian texts, which bring little merit and much affliction, which no personal intuition illuminates, and which are lacking in wisdom and liberation."

66. For the Vāma and Dakṣiṇa streams (*srotas*), see A. Sanderson, "Maṇḍala," p. 182.

Of the Vāma nothing has survived to this day but the *Vīṇāśikhatantra*, which has been edited and translated by T. Goudriaan (Delhi: Motilal Banarsidass, 1985). There the principal divinity is Tumburu, a form of Bhairava. "The Dakṣiṇa," writes Sanderson in the aforesaid article, "though here also much has been lost, has survived in its principal tradition, the cult of (Lalita) Svacchandabhairava and it is clear that in Abhinavagupta's time it was this more than any other cult which stood for the Trika elite between themselves and the Siddhānta." The *SvT* (also called *Sv-Bhairavatantra*) appears as its most well-known text. It deals essentially with the *dīkṣā* rites. The cult of Svacchandabhairava has remained alive in Nepal as well as in Kashmir where he is the form of the divinity in the Brahmans' daily worship.

the order varies). Finally the Trika, held as the highest of them all: *kulāt parataraṃ trikam* (*PTV*, p. 91).

I am leaving the Mata aside, of which very little is known:[67] Abhinava (*TĀ* 4.262-69) and Kṣemarāja (*NTU*, vol. 1, p. 274) refer to it without further explanations. Let us mention however that this system appears as one of those relevant to Kula, forming, it seems, its *uttarāmnāya*. It is a tradition devoted to the worship of Kālī (or the twelve Kālīs): the Kālīkrama and of other fearsome, often theriomorphic goddesses. The Mata seems related to another Śākta tradition, relevant to the same Kula *amnāya*, the Krama. We shall see this tradition again later, for its doctrines are found in the *TĀ* and in Jayaratha's commentary. It is characterized by a pantheon and cultic and spiritual practices, organized in fixed sequences or phases (*krama*)—hence its name. The deities worshiped, which are female, are the sixty-four Yoginīs and the twelve Kālīs. Krama is traditionally said to have emerged in Oḍḍiyāna, the Northern *pīṭha* (*uttarapīṭha*), that is, in Swāt. This location, which may be mythical, is interesting, for it is also found in other Hindu or Buddhist Tantric traditions.

One should, with respect to the classification of the Śaiva doctrines as proposed by Abhinava, point out how the Kula permeates the texts we shall see hereafter. The Kula, or Kaula tradition,[68] which mythically goes back to Matsyendranātha (also called Macchanda) seems indeed to have been of considerable influence—notably in North India (and therefore with those authors from the south of Kashmirian affiliation)—and from a rather early age, an influence extending outside not only Śaivism but even Hinduism. Kula is also mentioned

---

67. Sanderson seems to be the only scholar to have studied the Mata, on which he delivered lectures in Oxford, but he has not published anything on the subject other than a few paragraphs in the article "Śaivism and the Tantric Religion," cited *supra*, p. 52, n. 49.

68. Both terms are usually employed to refer to one and the same thing. Yet they may also be understood to refer to two different traditions, such as in the *TĀ* (*śl.* 13.301) quoted above. The difference between Kula and Kaula seems to be of a ritual sort. For this, cf. A. Sanderson, "Purity and Power," n. 110, and (giving another explanation) my introduction to the *YH*'s French translation (forthcoming).

in Buddhist texts. Abhinava, initiated into the Kula by his master Śambhunātha, refers to it time and again, notably in the *TĀ*, as an authoritative tradition: we just saw (cf. p. 58, n. 65) that he took it as combining the Vāma and Dakṣiṇa streams into a higher or more profound synthesis, second only to the Trika. The practices of mystical eroticism of the sexual *ādiyāga* in the *TĀ* (chap. 29) are presented as stemming from the Kaula tradition. The latter probably owes its name to the fact that the female deities, Mothers or Yoginīs, worshiped in the Kaula sects, where their cult is an essential feature, were divided among groups or "families" (*kula*). Therefrom probably arose the custom to refer to the Absolute, or the highest divine/cosmic plane, by the name *kula*, or (apophatically) of *akula;* to name *kaulikā/ī* the energy of this Kula; *kaulikasiddhi* the perfection and supernatural powers which may be attained by the Kaula adept; and *kaulācāra* the practice to be followed by the latter.

Through Abhinava, the Kula appears rather as Śaiva, despite the three goddesses Parā, Parāparā, and Aparā being placed above everything else. However, some purely Śākta traditions (such as Mata or Krama), or those of Kubjikā and Tripurā, are also forms of Kaulism. The Kula may not be one of the earliest Tantric traditions in the Śaiva field, yet it certainly is one of its most important. It is related to the old Kāpālika background, of which it has kept, with various nuances, transgressive practices and the cult of fearsome deities. It has been passed on down the ages by initiatory sects or transmissions, which, whatever their diversity, assert their relevance thereto, Kaula teachings, rites, and *dīkṣā* making up their esoteric kernel.[69] Thus the Kula appears as a unifying element—both inner, secret, and external, on the surface—of traditions that are otherwise quite different: more extreme and Śākta in the case of the Mata (so I understand) and the Krama, more Śaiva (and, with Abhinava, more "intellectual") with the Trika,

---

69. This is what Jayaratha seems to mean when (*ad TĀ* 4.24, vol. 3, pp. 27, and 278 *ad TĀ* 4.251) he quotes the formula: *antaḥ kaulo bahiḥ śaivo lokācāre tu vaidikaḥ*, which sums up the behavior of the *gṛhastha* Brahman following the Trika.

"Śāktaśaiva" finally with the Kubjikā tradition, and the probably later (and gentler) Tripurā tradition. Kaula systems have each evolved through time, generally emerging, so it seems, from obscure origins within small groups of renunciate ascetics, of "heroes" (*vīra*), practicing strange, transgressive rites, possession cults (*āveśa*), and developing into more brahmanized, more "orthodox" forms, acceptable to householders of pure caste. The Trika, in the form Abhinava gave it on the basis of the *ŚS* and of the Pratyabhijñā, or the Śrīvidyā, which itself quite early bore the stamp of the Pratyabhijñā philosophy and was finally utterly brahmanized (and even vedantized), provide two very characteristic examples of this evolution of the Kula.

The Kula-related schools are generally divided into four main systems, or "transmissions" (*āmnāya*), named according to the four cardinal points (therefore likely to correspond to the four faces of Śiva). The Pūrvāmnāya (The Oriental, and also the Foremost)[70] appears as being the basic one, from which all the others would derive. It was devoted to the worship of the deity in the form of Kuleśvara in union with Kuleśvarī, surrounded by the eight Mothers (Brahmī, etc.). Its esoteric teaching was imparted to humans by a line of spiritual masters who, along with their consorts (*dūtī*), ensured its continuity. The initiates, divided into initiatory lineages (*ovalli*), recognized each other by various practices, signs, and secret formulas. The *yoginī* played a very significant role therein, together with —at the ritual level—the *dūtī*s, as partners in sexual rites[71] and necessary mediums for uniting with the deity.[72] The Trika is directly related to this transmission, adding little to its basic teachings, emphasizing intensity of immersion (*samāveśa*) into the divinity rather than elaborate ritual, which remains,

70. East is the direction of Śiva, faced by the performer of the cult. Also, any *pradakṣiṇa*, any oriented counting, starts off from the East.

71. In a number of texts *yoginīvaktra*, "mouth of the *yoginī*," refers to the female sexual organ—through which indeed, in sexual rites, illumination is achieved. Cf. *TĀV*, vol. 2, p. 104, which refers to the Kula.

72. Cf. *TĀV*, vol. 1, p. 35: "*strīmukhe nikṣipet prajñaḥ strīmukhād grāhayet punaḥ ity ādy ukteḥ kulaprakriyāyāṃ dūtīmukhenaiva śiṣyasya jñānapratipadanāmnāyāt*," etc.

however—above all in the early period—complex and manifold.[73]

To the *uttarāmnāya* (the Northern transmission) are related the mysterious Mata and the Krama. Some of their texts have survived in manuscript form, such as the *Jayadratha-yāmala*,[74] the *Ciñcinimatasārasamuccaya*, the *Devīpañcaśataka* or the *Kramasadbhāva*. The ancient *Kramastotra* has been published. Above all, Abhinava, who adopted certain Krama notions (and so does Jayaratha), has devoted several works (*Kramastotra* and various hymns[75]) to this doctrine, as did also Śivānanda (*Śrīkālīstotra*), then Maheśvarānanda, from whose *Mahārthamañjarī* and its commentary, *Parimala*,[76] we shall quote occasionally.

The Paścimāmnāya (Western transmission) has as its main deity a particular form of Kālī: Kubjikā, a hunchbacked or stooped goddess, hence the name Kubjikāmata of this doctrine, also called Śrīmata, or Kulalikāmnāya. Therefrom we shall quote here the *Ṣaṭsāhasrasaṃhitā*,[77] when dealing notably with the *mālinī*, which plays there a certain part. There is also a

73. K. C. Pandey, in *Abhinavagupta: An Historical and Philosophical Study* (Varanasi: Chowkhamba, 1963, ch. 7), expounds his views about the Kula. R. Gnoli, in the appendix to his translation of the *TĀ* (Torino: U.T.E.T., 1972), makes a concise but clear and useful exposition of the main features of the Kaula system. This is also, but more interestingly, summed up by A. Sanderson in "Śaivism and the Tantric Tradition," *op. cit.*

74. M. Dyczkowski has given a résumé of the canon of the Jayadratha-yāmala in appendix C of his book on *The Canon of the Śaivāgamas* (cited above, p. 57, n. 63), using the elements given him by A. Sanderson who has edited (but not published) this text and has lectured on it at Oxford.

75. They will be found along with a French translation in L. Silburn, *Hymnes de Abhinavagupta* (Paris: I.C.I., 1970).

76. Translated or commented upon by L. Silburn, *La Mahārthamañjarī de Maheśvarānanda, avec des extraits du Parimala* (Paris: De Boccard, 1968). For the Sanskrit text, I refer to Vrajvallabha Dviveda's edition (Banaras: Sanskrit Viśvavidyālāya, 1982, Yogatantra-granthamālā, 5).

77. This extended version (with 6,000 *śloka*s, as indicated by its name) of the *Kubjikāmatatantra* has been partially edited and translated by J. Schoterman, *The Ṣaṭsāhasrasaṃhitā*, ch. 1-5 (Leiden: Brill, 1982).

Śaiva (or Śāmbhava) form of the Paścimāmnāya where the deity is Śambhu (Śiva) in the form of Navātma.[78]

Finally, the "Southern" transmission, the Dakṣiṇāmnāya, places at the top of its pantheon the goddess Tripurasundarī (also called Kāmeśvarī), worshipped with a diagram, the *Śrīcakra*, a symbol of her cosmic dynamism, and whose *mūlamantra* is the *Śrīvidyā*—hence the name Śrīvidyā often given to this tradition. Its two most important and best-known surviving texts are the *Vāmakeśvarīmata* (*VMT*) or *Nityāṣoḍaśikārṇava* (*NṢA*) and the *Yoginīhṛdaya*.[79] The Traipuradarśana is probably the latest of the Kaula transmissions (tenth-twelfth century?). However, it holds an important position in Tantrism as a whole, due to the literary quality of its texts, to its expansion all over India (notably in the South), and to its continuity. The *VMT* has been commented upon by Jayaratha as well as by Śivānanda and Vidyānanda (authors of other works of note in this school) and, later (eighteenth century), by Bhāskararāya. There is a commentary on the *YH* by Amṛtānanda (late thirteenth-early fourteenth century) much in the line of Kṣemarāja's *Pratyabhijñā*. Relevant to this tradition is another work

---

It was to be continued shortly. The *Kubjikāmata* has recently been edited by T. Goudriaan and J. A. Schoterman: *The Kubjikāmatatantra, Kulalikāmnāya Version* (Leiden: Brill, 1988). Possibly emerging earlier than the Śrīvidyā, this tradition, some works of which still exist in manuscript form in Nepal (*HTSL*, pp. 52ff.), seems to have survived there to this day. See T. Goudriaan, *op. cit.*, and "Kubjikā's Samayamantra and its Manipulation in the Kubjikāmata," in *Mantras et diagrammes rituels dans l'hindouisme*, and the discussion on the subject, ibid., pp. 161-67.

78. Cf. A. Sanderson, "Śaivism," quoted *supra*, n. 73.

79. There is a good edition of the *NṢA*, with the commentaries of Śivānanda and Vidyānanda, appended to which are a few shorter works of this tradition, by Vrajvallabha Dviveda (Banaras: Yogatantragranthamālā, n. 1, 1968). We shall refer to it here. The *MVT*, with Jayaratha's commentary (*Vivaraṇa*) has been edited in the *KSTS*, n. 45. There is an English translation of the same by L. Finn (Wiesbaden: Otto Harrassowitz, 1986). The *YH* with Amṛtānanda's *Dīpikā* and Bhāskararāya's *Setubandha*, has been edited by Gopinath Kaviraj in 1963 (Sarasvatibhavana-Granthamālā, n. 7). A new and much improved critical edition of the *YH* and the *Dīpikā*, with Hindi translation and commentaries, by V. V. Dviveda has just appeared (Delhi: Motilal Banarsidass, 1987).

(among others, for there is a wealth of them), the *Kāmakalā-vilāsa*, ascribed to Puṇyānanda, a short yet important text, to which we shall turn in the next chapter. Those works are usually considered as Kashmirian. If however the *VMT/NṢA* comes probably from Kashmir (or from that region), the same is not at all certain for the *YH*, and such authors as Puṇyānanda, Śivānanda, Vidyānanda and Amṛtānanda, although belonging to a Kashmirian tradition, were from South India.[80] From this school we shall also quote the *Gandharvatantra*.[81]

We must now come back to the hierarchical classification, by Abhinavagupta, of the Śaiva traditions that culminate with the Trika, and point out that he considered the latter to have included, in the course of time, several important texts. The first phase in the history of the Trika would have included such tantras as the *Siddhayogeśvarīmata*, the *Mālinīvijayottara-tantra* (*MVT*) and the *Tantrasadbhāva*. In a second phase such texts as the *Devyāyāmala*, the *Trikasadbhāva* and the *Trika-hṛdaya*.[82] Of these the *MVT* only is still extant: it is on the basis of this tantra that Abhinava expounds the doctrine and ritual of the Trika in his *TĀ*. It was published as volume 37 of the *KSTS*. We shall quote it often. Abhinava considered it as of fundamental importance. "Of the teaching of the Lord" (*śāsanaṃ vibhoḥ*), he writes in the *TĀ* (1.18), "the essence is

---

80. Although originating in all likelihood from north India, the Śrīvidyā is to be found very early in south India also. There, it was influenced by Abhinavagupta's Trika (and by that of his followers) and, stripped of its more Tantric elements, it was adopted in that purified form by the Śaṅkarācāryas of Sṛṅgeri and Kañcipuram and became thus a dominant form of nondualist śaivism. The commentary of Lakṣmīdhara (sixteenth century) on the *Saundaryalaharī*, a classical text of southern Śrīvidyā, is typical of this exegetical tradition.

81. The edition by R. C. Kak and H. B. Shastri (Srinagar, 1934-KSTS, n. 62) has long been out of print. It is reprinted in the *Tantrasaṅgraha, tṛtīyo bhāgaḥ* (Banaras: Yogatantra-Granthamālā, n. 6, 1979; pp. 1-340). It is probably not an ancient work. Usually considered as from Kashmir, it may in fact have originated elsewhere.

82. The distinguishing of three main phases in the historical development of the Trika is due to A. Sanderson: he describes this in "Śaivism" (previously quoted. See note 49, p. 52).

the Trika doctrine, and of this the essence is the teaching of the Mālinī" (cf. n. 54, p. 54 above). This Tantra, also called *Pūrvaśāstra*, "the primal teaching," appears as one of the Trika's most venerable, if not the most venerable. Its third and fourth chapters show how the manifestation of the cosmos and the phonemes (of the *mātṛkā* and of the *mālinī*) are linked, while the deities, *yoginī*s, and so forth are associated with the various phonemes or groups of phonemes. The *MVT* is essentially a ritualistic text. We still have Abhinava's commentary (1470 *śloka*s) on the beginning of this Tantra. This work, the *Mālinīvijayavārttikā*[83] (*MVV*), deals on several occasions with questions concerning *vāc* from the specific viewpoint of its author. The *MVV* is of great interest, but often rather abstruse.

Among the texts forming the Tantric Śaiva tradition (sometimes called the Āgamaśāstra, and including Āgamas as well as Tantras), as this tradition came down to the authors we shall consider, should also be mentioned the *Parātriṃśikā* (*PT*), thirty-six *śloka*s supposedly from the *Rudrayāmalatantra*, of which Abhinava's two commentaries, the *Vivaraṇa* (*PTV*) and the *Laghuvṛtti* (*PTLv*) are part of the basic texts of the Kashmirian metaphysics of speech or the Word.[84] Another important work that Abhinava does not mention, but which was, like the *SvT*, commented upon by Kṣemarāja, is the

83. *KSTS*, n. 31.

84. *KSTS*, n. 18 (*PTV*), and n. 68 (*PTLv*). The *PTV* is a very abstruse text, and the *KSTS* edition was far from satisfactory. It has now been scientifically edited (and translated into Italian) by R. Gnoli, *Il Commento di Abhinavagupta alla Parātriṃśikā* (Rome: ISMEO, 1985): This is the edition to which I shall refer here. An English translation by Jaideva Singh is now available (SUNY Press, 1990). For the *PTLv*, see *infra*, Bibliography.

On the *Rudrayāmalatantra*, the two texts of which, published in India, seem to be of a later period and do not contain the thirty-six *śloka*s commented upon by Abhinava, cf. *HTSL*, pp. 40, 47. Abhinava's *PTV* makes up *KSTS* n. 18; its *PTLv*, published along with Lakṣmīrāma's *Vivṛti*, makes up nn. 68-69. There is another commentary, versified and not devoid of interest, the *PT-Tātparyadīpikā* (*KSTS*, n. 74).

Netratantra (*NT*),[85] devoted to the *netra* mantra or *mṛtyujit*. We shall quote some passages from this text in the next chapters, when dealing with mantras, on which we shall also quote extensively from another text, a vast one, providing a wealth of information on mantras and rites, the *Svacchanda Tantra*.[86]

Shorter and yet of great interest with regard to practices, notably mantric, is the *Vijñānabhairava* (*VBh*),[87] probably a Kashmirian text, known to Abhinava, and commented upon by Kṣemarāja and subsequently by Śivopādhyāya. The authors belonging to the Pratyabhijñā consider it as very authoritative. Another short Kashmirian work, akin to the Krama, the *Vātūlanāthasūtra*,[88] should also be mentioned, for it will be cited later on.

There are still other Śaiva or Śāktaśaiva Tantras, of a later period as a rule, but which should also be mentioned, for we shall refer to them occasionally. Such are, for instance, the *Kulārṇavatantra* (of the Kula), the *Tantrarājatantra* (a Śrīvidyā text), or a Śākta work with no marked sectarian affiliation, the *Prapañcasāratantra*, ascribable to Vidyāśaṅkara (thirteenth century). Many additional, more or less authoritative Tantras could also be mentioned, not to speak of commentaries which developed between the thirteenth and the nineteenth centuries. We shall cite some of them in passing, and so shall we do with some Purāṇas (notably the *Agni*

---

85. *The Netratantram, with Commentary by Kṣemarāja, KSTS*, nn. 46 and 61 (Bombay: 1926 and 1939). This text has been reissued in a one-volume edition by V. V. Dvideva, *Netratantram* (*Mṛtyuñjaya Bhaṭṭārakaḥ*), *with Commentary Udyota by Kṣemarāja* (Delhi: Parimal Publications, 1985). This work has been analyzed by H. Brunner, "Un tantra du Nord, le Netratantra," *BEFEO* 61 (1974): 125-97.

86. Cf. *supra*, p. 58, n. 66. For the dualistic or nondualistic nature of this text, cf. A. Sanderson's and H. Brunner's opinion in *Mantras et Diagrammes rituels dans l'Hindouisme*, pp. 208-09. The *SvT* has been edited in the *KSTS*, of which it comprises nn. 31, 38, 44, 51, 53 and 60.

87. *KSTS*, n. 8; French translation by L. Silburn, *Le Vijñānabhairava* (Paris: de Boccard, 1961). English edition and translation by Jaideva Singh, *Vijñānabhairava or Divine Consciousness* (Delhi: Motilal Banarsidass, 1979). Edition with Hindi translation by V. V. Dvivedi (Delhi: Motilal Banarsidass, 1984).

88. *KSTS*, n. 55.

Purāṇa), which are often tantricized[89] and sometimes include interesting material about speech or mantras: here again one finds the common fund (Śaiva as well as Vaiṣṇava) of practices and speculations of the *mantraśāstra*.

The Śaiva tradition, indeed, is not the only one worth mentioning: there is also the Vaiṣṇava. Śaivism and Vaiṣṇavism are not two separate worlds: the exclusivism of Tantric sects always went side by side with "inclusivism," which is one of the characteristics of Indian thought.[90] To be more precise, according to the *Rājataraṅginī*, and also as evidenced by archeology, Vaiṣṇavism flourished very early in Kashmir, notably in the Tantric form of the Pāñcarātra. Judging by the Vedic mantras they quote and by their iconographic descriptions, it does seem that some of the earliest Saṃhitās originated from Northwestern India. Such seems to be the case with the *Sātvatta*, the *Jayākhya*, and possibly the *Ahirbudhnya* Saṃhitās.[91] In Kashmir, surely, the Pāñcarātra predated the Śaiva systems based upon the *Śivasūtra*, whose authors, in fact, sometimes refer to the Saṃhitās or to Vaiṣṇava authors. One of the earliest references of this type may be the one occurring in the *Spandapradīpikā* of Utpalavaiṣṇava,[92] who probably lived in the same period as Abhinava, and who, in view notably of his name, was probably a Vaiṣṇava. Utpalavaiṣṇava mentions several Saṃhitās, and among his citations appears a *śloka* which may come from the *ABS*.[93] As to Abhinava, he knew the Vaiṣṇava authors (and surely the Saṃhitās also). Besides, he wrote a study on the *Bhagavadgītā* and his *Paramārthasāra* is

89. However, making a clear distinction between Paurāṇic Hinduism and Tantric Hinduism is far from easy.

90. For this "characteristic feature," according to P. Hacker, cf. G. Oberhammer (ed.), *Inklusivismus, eine indische Denkform* (Vienna: Gerold & Co., 1983).

91. Such was already Schrader's opinion, *Introduction to the Pāñcarātra and the Ahirbudhnya-Saṃhitā* (Adyar, 1916). Sanderson's recent works confirm and further elucidate this view (personal communication).

92. Not to be confused with Utpaladeva, the author of the *Īśvarapratyabhijñākārikā*, Somānanda's son and disciple, and therefore earlier than Abhinava, who wrote a commentary on his work.

93. Schrader, *op. cit.*, pp. 18-19.

an adaptation, along the lines of the Trika doctrine, of an earlier text, the *Ādhārakārikā* of Śeṣamuni, which, as far as can be ascertained, was a work of Vaiṣṇava bent.

This being so, we shall have to cite Saṃhitās now and then, to substantiate our assertions or to show how certain notions or practices extend outside the Śaiva field. Thus the Pāñcarātra may have played a part in the development of Śaiva esotericism.[94] But, in point of fact, those were not one-way interactions: Śaivism and the cults of the Goddess which existed in Kashmir side by side with the Pāñcarātra, and which, like it, probably spread very early to South India, could not fail to affect the latter. This is reflected in the texts. Such is the case, for instance, with the *Lakṣmītantra*,[95] where elements from nondualistic Śaivism are clearly apparent. Those contacts and interchanges occurred and went on in South India (where, as stated above, the Kashmir Śaiva tradition, especially as it evolved from Kṣemarāja's teachings, was long very much alive). All this makes it sometimes difficult to decide whether a notion, present both in the Pāñcarātra and in nondualistic Śaivism, stems from Vaiṣṇavism or Śaivism, and whether it is from North or South India.

For instance, there appears in chapter 16 of the *ABS*[96] (a text generally held to be earlier than the tenth century[97])

---

94. This information again I owe to A. Sanderson, who plans to publish a study on the history of the Pāñcarātra, and especially on its earliest Kashmirian developments: the emanationist, nondualistic concepts of Kashmir Śaivism were indeed quite close to Pāñcarātra theism.

95. *Lakṣmītantram* (Adyar: the Adyar Library and Research Centre, 1959). English translation by S. Gupta, *Lakṣmī Tantra, a Pāñcarātra Text* (Leiden: Brill, 1972).

96. *Ahirbudhnya-Saṃhitā of the Pāñcarātrāgama*, 2 vols. 2nd ed., revised by Pandit V. Krishnamacharya (Adyar: The Adyar Library and Research Centre, 1966).

For the phonematic cosmogony of the *ABS*, see *infra* chap. 5, pp. 223ff.

97. Sanderson, however, thinks that he can give sufficient evidence of the *ABS* (and of the *LT*) having been composed in south India, most probably during the twelfth century (personal communication, June, 1987). May, then, the *ABS* have taken over elements from the Trika?

a description of how Sanskrit phonemes arose, which sometimes, and notably in the terms used for vowels (*anuttara, icchā,* etc.), is very similar to that given by Abhinava in the third *āhnika* of the *TĀ* as well as in the *PTV*. The manifestation of the phonemes by the Godhead begins with *nāda* and is linked with the *kuṇḍalinī*. It is therefore also akin to what we shall see in the next chapter concerning the evolution of sound. Of course, one finds in the Pāñcarātra texts, and notably in the *ABS*, a number of notions and practices similar to those of the nondualistic Kashmir Śaiva tradition, but they are elements of sometimes very ancient origin, which are the common property of Tantric thought; such are, for instance, the notions of *bindu*, of *nāda*, of the three or four levels of speech, of mantras, and so forth. However, there are so many other similarities between chapter 16 of the *ABS* and what appears in the Śaiva texts, notably in Abhinavagupta, that one may ask oneself whether the two traditions were interrelated: could it be that one had drawn at least part of its theory from the other? Or could it be that both would have drawn from yet another—earlier—source? And would this source be Śaiva or Vaiṣṇava? It seems difficult, at present, to answer those questions. There is undoubtedly, in early Śaiva and Śākta texts, a tradition of speculations about speech, with cosmogonies where phonemes and *tattva*s are interrelated: such is the case with the *Siddhayogeśvarīmata* or with chapter 3 of the *MVT* —also, I am told, in the *Jayadrathayāmala* (*JRY*), sources from which Abhinava had drawn. Yet, strangely enough, if he refers to such texts in the *TĀ* and the *PTV*, he rarely does it to substantiate his system of phonematic emanation, or else he does it so briefly that we remain in doubt about the original source, which might be either Vaiṣṇava or Śaiva.

We have yet to mention, in addition to the anonymous "revealed" texts and the works ascribed to various authors, those works more specially related to the various tendencies of Kashmirian nondualistic Śaivism, which are the main basis for this whole book. Those works are of special importance to us, for they contain the most comprehensive and systematic exposition of the theories (and practices) that we shall describe. They are generally of a high literary and philosophical standard, which accounts for—if it does not justify—the "Kashmirian bias" of our work.

The early Śaiva teachings of these tendencies, the Āgamaśāstra, come to an end with Vasugupta's (early ninth century) *Śivasūtra* (*ŚS*), several of which deal with the Word. These terse and abstruse aphorisms are elucidated in two commentaries, the *Vārttika* of Bhāskara (tenth century) and the *Vimarśinī* of Kṣemarāja (first half of the eleventh century), whose interpretation draws its inspiration from Abhinavagupta's Trika.[98]

Ascribed like the *ŚS* to Vasugupta, next come the *Spandakārikā* (*SpK*), which further develop some of their teachings. *kārikā*s 2.10-11 identify the power of mantras to the incipient energy, which is a luminous "vibration" (*spanda*). The *SpK* have been commented upon by Rāmakaṇṭha, whose dates might be 950 to 1000 A.D. (*SpK-Vivṛtti*),[99] and by Kṣemarāja (*Sp-Nirṇaya*).[100] We shall have to refer to both commentaries, notably when they deal with mantras.

Next must be mentioned the *Śivadṛṣṭi* (*ŚD*), the only surviving work of importance by Somānanda, who is the originator of the so-called Recognition tradition (Pratyabhijñā), and whose dates might be about 900 to 950. He seems to have been a Kaula and well acquainted with the Krama.[101] The

---

98. The *ŚS* and the *Vimarśinī* make up vol. 1 of the *KSTS*. Bhāskara's *Vārtika* with the anonymous *Vṛtti* and Varadarāja's *Vārtika* (two later commentaries of little interest) make up vols. 4 and 5 of the *KSTS*; Italian translation by R. Torella, *Śivasūtra col il commento di Kṣemarāja* (Rome: Ubaldini, 1979); French translation by L. Silburn, *Śivasūtra et Vimarśinī de Kṣemarāja* (Paris: I.C.I., 1980); English edition and translation by Jaideva Singh, *Śiva Sūtras: The Yoga of Supreme Identity* (Delhi: Motilal Banarsidass, 1979).

99. *KSTS*, n. 42.

100. *KSTS*, n. 6, with a rather poor English translation. English edition and translation by Jaideva Singh, *Spanda-Kārikās: The Divine Creative Pulsation* (Delhi: Motilal Banarsidass, 1980). Mark Dyczkowski has written a comprehensive work on the Spanda: *The Doctrine of Vibration* (Albany: SUNY Press, 1987).

101. He wrote a commentary, now lost, on the *PT*, to which Abhinava refers time and again in his *Vivaraṇa* (cf. *PTV*, p. 16). See also *TĀV* (*ad TĀ* 4.193, vol. 3, especially p. 194).

second *āhnika* of the *ŚD* is to us of special interest, because therein Somānanda refutes the conception of the grammatical philosophers—that is, especially, of Bhartṛhari—on *brahman* in the form of speech (*śabdabrahman*), which they identify to *paśyanti vāc.* Against this theory Somānanda sets up the doctrine of the four levels of speech, common in Tantrism, from which Bhartṛhari had deviated.[102] A short commentary (*Vṛtti*) on the *ŚD* was composed by Utpaladeva.[103]

Mention should be made of the *Īśvarapratyabhijñākārikā* (*ĪPK*) and its brief commentary (*Vṛtti*)[104] by Utpaladeva, believed to have been the son and disciple of Somānanda. It is not directly concerned with the Word (except *ĪPK* 1.5.13), but mainly with the supreme Consciousness as the source and substratum of everything, and with its modalities (*vimarśa, pratyavamarśa*), with memory (*smaraṇa*), with the experiencer or the knower (*pramātṛ*), all of which are concepts central to nondualistic Śaivism. Abhinavagupta, in his two commentaries, the *Īśvarapratyabhijñāvimarśinī* and the *Īśvarapratyabhijñā-vivṛtivimarśinī* (*ĪPV* and *ĪPVV*), further expands on their teachings, notably with regard to certain aspects of the theory of the four levels or stages of the Word. It is indeed above all for those two commentaries, remarkable works, that the *ĪPK* is famous. Of Utpaladeva let us mention in passing the *Siddhi-trayī*,[105] of which the first one, the *Ajaḍapramātṛsiddhi*, is frequently cited by Abhinavagupta in some of the texts we shall study.

We come now to Abhinavagupta (late tenth-early eleventh century), who, as a metaphysician, aesthetician, and Tantric initiate, was to devise a formulation, which one may be tempted to term as final, of the nondualistic Śaiva philosophy of the

---

102. On this point, see M. Biardeau's introduction to her translation of the first book of the *VP:* Bhartṛhari, *Vākyapadīya Brahmakāṇḍa, avec la Vṛtti de Harivṛṣabha,* (Paris: Ed. de Boccard, 1964).

103. *ŚD* and *Vṛtti: KSTS*, n. 54. Its first *āhnika* has been translated by R. Gnoli into English (*East and West* 1957, pp. 16-22) and Italian (*Riv. d. Stud. Or.* 43, 1959, pp. 55-75).

104. *KSTS*, n. 34.

105. *KSTS*, n. 34 (which includes also the *Pratyabhijñākārikā Vṛtti*).

Word. For it is above all with him, and to a lesser extent with his disciples and commentators Kṣemarāja and Jayaratha, that we find the most comprehensive, often profound, exposition of this doctrine. His major work on the various aspects of the Word is the *Parātriṃśikāvivaraṇa* (*PTV*), a lengthy commentary (drawing upon, he tells us, Somānanda's now-lost commentary) on the thirty-six *śloka*s of the *PT*. Therein are treated more or less extensively most of the aspects of the Word—metaphysical, cosmogonic, psychological, and epistemological—from mantras and phonemes (*varṇa*) to speech.[106] The short *Laghuvṛtti* (*PTlv*) he wrote on the same *śloka*s examines above all their relevance to the ritual.[107] The other text of Abhinavagupta of importance to us is his great Tantric work, the *Tantrāloka* (*TĀ*),[108] which expounds the Trika teachings such as he developed them in particular along the lines of the *MVT*. It is divided into thirty-seven chapters (*āhnika*: "day's work"); the third one gives a systematic exposition of the phonematic emanation (*varṇaparāmarśa*), while the other ones also include passages concerned with various aspects of the Word, notably how it operates in *dīkṣā*. Of course

---

106. *KSTS*, n. 18. A critical edition with an annotated Italian translation, by R. Gnoli, *Il Commento di Abhinavagupta alla Parātrimśikā* (*Parātrimśikā vivaraṇam*), has been published (Rome: ISMEO, 1985). It is to this text—a significant improvement on the *KSTS* one—that we shall refer and shall translate here, while retaining however the *KSTS* pagination given also by R. Gnoli in his edition. English version: *Parātrīṃśikā Vivaraṇa: The Secret of Tantric Mysticism* (Delhi: Motilal Banarsidass, 1988), by Jaideva Singh.

107. *KSTS*, n. 68. French translation by André Padoux (Paris: de Boccard, 1975). Italian translation by R. Gnoli, *La Trentina della Supreme* (Torino: Boringhieri, 1965). A new edition of the text, with a translation into Italian by R. Torella, is in progress.

A study of this text, by Paul Müller-Ortega, was recently published: *The Triadic Heart of Śiva* (Albany: SUNY Press, 1989), p. 000.

108. The *TĀ*, with Jayaratha's commentary, *Viveka*, comprises twelve volumes of the *KSTS*, published between 1918 and 1938 (nn. 23, 28, 30, 36, 35, 29, 41, 47, 59, 52, 57, 58). It has been translated into Italian by R. Gnoli, *Luce delle Sacre Scritture* (Torino: *UTET*, 1972). It has been reissued in eight volumes by R. C. Dvivedi and N. Rastogi (Delhi: Motilal Banarsidass, 1986).

the same questions are treated again, more succinctly, in the *Tantrasāra*, a summary of the *TĀ* made by Abhinavagupta himself.[109] Finally, as we just said, elaborations on the Word are also to be found in his two commentaries of Utpaladeva's *ĪPK*[110] and in the *Mālinīvijayavārttika*. Some more or less brief indications are also to be found in some of his other works.[111] The very "intellectual" work of Abhinava seems to have contributed more than any other to the shift of nondualistic Śaivism from the visionary traditions of the Bhairavāgamas meant for renunciate ascetics, to a symbolic, metaphysical system, acceptable to *gṛhastha* brahmans, the form in which it has survived to this day.[112]

Among the authors who came after Abhinava, we have already mentioned most of the works (commentaries on the *NT, SvT, SpK, VBh*) of his disciple Kṣemarāja, who, like him, was both a *tāntrika* and an aesthetician. A staunch follower of the Trika's *saṃvidadvāya*, he seems to have played, through his work, a major role in the expansion of the nondualistic Śaiva doctrines in South India. Of his works let us mention the *Pratyabhijñāhṛdaya*,[113] an excellent compendium of his doctrine, containing several interesting passages about the

---

109. *KSTS*, n. 17. Italian translation by R. Gnoli, *Essenza dei tantra* (Torino: Boringhieri, 1960).

110. *IPV*, edited by K. A. Subramanya Iyer and K. C. Pandey, 2 vols. (Allahabad, 1938-1950); also *KSTS*, nn. 32-33. *IPVV*: *KSTS* nn. 40, 42, 45.

111. The *Paramārthasāra*, for instance (*KSTS*, n. 7), edited and translated by L. Silburn (Paris: de Boccard, 1959); or the *Paryantapañcāśikā*, edited by V. Raghavan (Madras); or again various hymns: L. Silburn, *Hymnes de Abhinavagupta*, translated with commentaries (Paris: I.C.I., 1970).

112. The prominence given here to Abhinavagupta's work should not however unduly enhance his actual role. Although this role was very significant as concerns ideas, it does not seem outstanding with regard to ritual practices, namely religion as experienced and practised in Kashmir, where rites have probably been little affected by speculations, even by those speculations that were directly based on them.

113. *KSTS*, n. 3. English edition and translation by Jaideva Singh, *Pratyabhijñāhṛdayam: The Secret of Self-Recognition* (Delhi: Motilal Banarsidass, 1963). This is the edition to which we shall refer.

Word, and also a short treatise, the *Parāpraveśikā*,[114] close in its spirit and exposition (based upon the *bījamantra SAUḤ*) to the *PTV*.

One should not forget, of course, the *Viveka*, Jayaratha's commentary on the *TĀ*, providing additional material and further elucidation on its teachings and citing some of its sources. This wealth of information makes it necessary to refer again and again to the twelve volumes of the *TĀ* (with the *Viveka*) whenever one deals with the Trika, or even more generally with nondualistic Tantric Śaivism, for it is one of its greatest texts. In this commentary, where he cites numerous Tantras, Jayaratha provides on various points further details on the Kula and Krama teachings also, two traditions with which Abhinava had a strong connection,[115] and which he used together with the Trika Tantras, to build up his own synthesis.

The Krama (which is yet to be thoroughly investigated) has certainly played a central part in Tantric practices, of which its cult is one of the most typical aspects. Among the surviving works belonging to this tradition, one of the most interesting (which we shall quote) is the *Mahārthamañjarī* and its commentary, the *Parimala*, both written by Maheśvarānanda (twelfth-thirteenth century).[116] Also related to it is the *Cidgaganacandrikā*.[117] One of the masters who came before Maheśvarānanda is Śivānanda (twelfth century), the author notably of the *Ṛjuvimarśinī*, a commentary on the *NṢA*, also commented upon in the *Artharatnāvalī*[118] by his contemporary

114. *KSTS*, n. 15.

115. Two works by Abhinavagupta, the *Kramakeli*, now lost, and the *Kramastotra*, are related to the Krama. The *Kramastotra* has been edited and translated into French, along with an early *Kramastotra*, Śivānanda's *Śrīkālīstotra* and the *Pañcadaśikā*, by L. Silburn, *Hymnes aux Kālī, la roue des énergies divines* (Paris: I.C.I., 1975).

116. Edited by V. V. Dviveda in the *Yogatantra-Granthamālā*, n. 5 (Banaras, 1972). French translation by L. Silburn, *La Mahārthamañjarī de Maheśvarānanda avec des extraits du Parimala* (Paris: de Boccard, 1968).

117. This *kāvya*-style commentary on the *Mahānayaprakāśa* ascribed to Arṇasiṃha (eleventh century) is probably a work from south India.

118. Edited with the *NṢA* by V. V. Dviveda, along with the *Subhagodaya*, the *Subhagodayavāsanā*, and the *Saubhāgyahṛdayastotra* of the same

Vidyānanda. From Vidyānanda's work may be mentioned a text as yet unpublished on the Tripurasundarī cult, the *Jñānadīpavimarśinī.* Those latter texts obviously belong to the Śrīvidyā, to which belongs also Amṛtānanda, an author we have already mentioned (*supra*, pp. 63-64), whose *Dīpikā* on the *YH* is a work of great interest, deeply influenced by Kṣemarāja's Trika-based *Pratyabhijñā.* As I stated above, the Śrīvidyā had outstanding exponents throughout the ages, to whom one is often to refer on the subject of mantric speculations and practices as well as on rituals in general.

Finally we ought to mention some "nonsectarian" Tantric works, which we shall cite occasionally, such as, for instance, the *Śāradātilaka* (*ŚT*) ascribed to Lakṣmaṇa Deśika (eleventh century?), which, along with Rāghavabhaṭṭa's commentary (dated 1484), contains many interesting remarks on the *mantraśāstra;* or such as Kṛṣṇānanda's (fifteenth-sixteenth century) *Tantrasāra.* We cannot, however, review here all the Tantric materials related to the Word, not even its main works: for this I refer to the *HTSL*, already cited on several occasions. Our inquiry, indeed, is deliberately restricted to selected texts, chiefly those of the Kashmirian tradition, for therein, I believe, are to be found the works most relevant to our purpose. The other texts to which I alluded here, or some others, will be quoted only occasionally. In addition, the references given in the preceding and following pages—all quoted or mentioned materials—will be found in the Bibliography at the end of this work.

Turning to our subject itself, it should be noted that, elaborated from the ninth century onward on the basis of various traditions, as we mentioned above, the theories related to the Word which shall be studied here, do not appear, in the literature, as a coherent and consistent whole. It has been systematized above all by Abhinavagupta, who dealt with all its aspects and combined in a comparatively original structure

---

author, and Amṛtānanda's *Saubhāgyasubhodaya* and *Cidvilāsastava.* Cf. above, p. 63, n. 79.

the teachings of early texts with those of the *Śivasūtra*s, the Spanda and the Pratyabhijñā. In spite of this, however, he did not design a perfectly consistent and comprehensive system concerning the Word. While some of its points receive extensive treatment, some others are merely touched upon or left aside. Like any other Indian master, Abhinava dealt exclusively with topics that seemed important to him, or above all useful for the spiritual growth of his disciples, as there is no significant or useful theory that is not related to a *sādhana*, and meant as an instrument for some purpose, be it supernatural powers and/or liberation. Moreover, Abhinava and the other authors whom we shall study belonged to a particular tradition, therefore to a system of representations and rules of conduct generally acknowledged, a background to which they refer explicitly or implicitly in their developments, and which contributed to the overall harmony of their teachings. That is why we may here resort to different works to expound the theories of cosmic or human evolution of sound, the stages of the Word, the arising of phonemes, or those dealing with mantras: in so doing, we are not making an arbitrary, unjustifiable mixture. We believe that we are expounding explicitly that which, for Abhinava, Jayaratha or others, was implicitly admitted, giving the virtual meaning, and in no way one of our own devising, and which indeed, more often than not, clearly appears from their very words, or from hints in their works. Abhinavagupta's work, supplemented by Jayaratha's and Kṣemarāja's, will therefore serve as the main basis for this study, which however will also resort, following their example, to all the surviving works acknowledged by the nondualistic Śaiva tradition. In so doing one is liable to being censured for having produced a personal synthesis in completing here and there the teachings of one author with another's, thus bringing together materials scattered in the texts and extending over several centuries. But quite often differences are confined to minor points: they will always be duly mentioned. Further they are more important in the sphere of theology (of the pantheons) and of practices than in the very structure of the metaphysical system, which is precisely our main concern here—together with mantras, but the *mantraśāstra* too is remarkably consistent in its general pattern. On many other points also the speculations on the Word are generally in agreement, whether those doctrines are explicitly put forward by Abhinava, Kṣemarāja, or others, or appear self-evidently when one goes through and compares several texts.

This being so, we must now, before proceeding with the principal aspects of those speculations about the powers of the Word, give the outlines of the cosmology and metaphysics accepted by the various streams of the nondualistic Śaiva (or Śāktaśaiva) tradition. Thus we shall have the framework, the general pattern, wherein the theories and the specific facts subsequently examined are fitted.

For those traditions the first principle, Śiva (referring in that case to his supreme plane, Paramaśiva), is Consciousness (*cit, saṃvid*), which is both pure light-consciousness (*prakāśa*) and self-awareness or active-consciousness (*vimarśa*) of this light: it is *prakāśavimarśamaya*, that is to say light and/or transcendent-and-immanent consciousness, a consciousness which, far from being a still, inactive absolute, is on the contrary a luminous throbbing (*sphurattā*), a luminous vibration (*spanda*), a power or energy (*śakti*), all these aspects expressing its *vimarśa* nature.[119] The notion of *vimarśa* is peculiar to nondualistic Śaivism of Kashmirian tradition. It is an essential feature of the "doctrine of nondual Consciousness" (*saṃvidadvāyavāda*), elaborated by Abhinavagupta and his disciples, especially Kṣemarāja. From the standpoint of the categories or hypostases of cosmic manifestation (the *tattva*s), which in Tantric systems are usually thirty-six in number, *prakāśa* is Śiva and *vimarśa* is *śakti*, both, however, being utterly inseparable.[120] Now the aspect of energy, of life, of active awareness, of freedom or autonomy (*svātantrya*) of the first principle, is also its aspect of Word (*vāc*).

---

119. *Vimarśa* is difficult to translate. We shall see in the course of this work the different meanings of this term: Cf. the index. Cf. also my translation of the *PTLv*, especially nn. 33 and 87. Also see M. Hulin's remarks in *Le principe de l'ego dans la pensée indienne classique* (Paris: Collège de France, 1978), pp. 296ff.

120. *na hi śaktiḥ śivād bhedam āmarśayet* (*PTV*, p. 3).

Vāc, the female energy principle,[121] is therefore the life of Consciousness, the very energy of Śiva. She is, within Śiva, the Power, or the Word, better still the Energy-Word taken at its source, the power through which he creates, maintains and withdraws in himself the universe. Thus the Word, right from the first principle, appears as an aspect of Consciousness. Consciousness is inseparable from the Word because it is alive; just as in this world (according to Bhartṛhari's aphorism, taken up by Abhinavagupta), there is no reflectiveness, no idea, that is not accompanied by speech.[122] However, just as one may somehow consider the sole *prakāśa* aspect of the primary principle, just as Śiva may be considered as exclusively transcendent, aloof from the universe,[123] in the same way may be assumed a primary stage where pure Consciousness would not yet be Word, a realm beyond the Word, an inconceivable point where the Word would emerge from or be reabsorbed into silence. But the highest level of the Word, the supreme Word (*paravāc*) is somewhat already so close to silence, whereas the primary principle is so difficult to conceive as separate from its energy, that there seems scarcely to be any scope for such a stage at all. This meeting point of the highest Word with the pure transcendence beyond even the supreme Word is sometimes called *unmanā*.[124] Retaining this supreme stage, a pure, silent transcendence, allows the maintenance of a transcendent absolute in a system naturally averse to it. For Abhinavagupta, acknowledging the existence of the *unmanā* level and the possibility for the adept to gain access to it is the distinctive feature of the Trika; it is a feature that makes it superior to the other systems such as the Kula and others.[125] Finally it is

---

121. Cf. chap. 1, p. 7.
122. Cf. chap. 4, p. 178. As we shall indicate further on, the theory seems to be a transfer on the cosmic plane of psychological observations. Śaiva cosmogony often appears as a "cosmization" of psychological experiences and vice-versa. Anthropocosmism, so important in Tantrism, dates back, as is well known, to the Veda.
123. It is then called Paramaśiva and may be considered as a thirty-seventh *tattva*. Cf. chap. 3, p. 96, n. 29.
124. Cf. chap. 6, p. 348 and chap. 7, p. 405.
125. Cf. A. Sanderson, "Maṇḍala," p. 169ff.

worth noting that this distinction which—at least in theory—admits that there is a plane beyond the supreme Word (a plane of totally pure Consciousness, or *cit*) perpetuates in the Trika the age-old concept asserting the subordination of speech to silence or to thought, of *vāc* to *brahman*, that we saw previously when dealing with the Veda.[126]

The aspect of the primary principle stressed by our texts (and more especially of course by those dealing with the Word), is that where Śiva is united with Śakti, where Consciousness is with the Word. For this is the aspect where the first Principle is endowed with the fullness of his emanative power (a limiting, binding, power, but also a liberating one), often symbolized by the sixteen *kalā*s of Śiva.[127] United with this creative, resorbing energy, and made alive by her, Śiva is also considered, at this stage, to contain in himself the whole cosmic manifestation, which dwells within him (or more exactly within his energy in union with him), just as in the yolk of the peacock's egg all the colors of that bird[128] are in a latent, indistinct state (to use a comparison occurring now and then in the Trika), or as the banyan tree is contained potentially or in essence (*sāra*) in its seed.[129] Tantric thought, indeed, and not only non-dualistic Śaivism, seems averse (like any mythic thought probably) to the idea of an *ex nihilo* creation, of an absolute *fiat*, of a shift from the state of nothingness or pure being to that of the phenomenal world. Accordingly, the universe is not considered as created but as emanated, projected, by the primary principle which is able to manifest it only insofar as it was already implicit within himself: what is not inside the primary principle cannot exist outside thereof.[130] That is an application of the *satkāryavāda* of the Sāṃkhya, for which any effect whatsoever preexists in its cause, which, therefore, does not bring forth but what was already preformed within it. The entire manifestation will therefore appear first within the

126. Chap. 1, pp. 8 and 12.
127. Cf. chap. 3, pp. 89-91.
128. *mayūrāṇḍarasavat.*
129. *PT, śl.* 24; *PTV*, pp. 258-59.
130. *PTV*, p. 102, quoted and translated in chap. 5, p. 306.

primary principle, within its energy, as a paradigm, as a kind of undifferentiated manifestation of what is to be.[131] From there it is emitted (*visṛj*) as a throbbing, radiating light (*sphurattā, ullāsa*), as a shining forth or a luminous projection, which is then reflected (*pratibimba*) on ever lower levels, where, gradually losing its initial power and radiance, it will gradually reveal all the cosmic levels down to the lowest one. But while in the course of the process the manifestation condenses, becomes solid, dense,[132] progressively losing its initial freedom and light, it does not, however (in the perspective of the "idealist realism" of the *ābhāsa* system of nondualistic Śaivism), cease to share in the effulgence, the consciousness and life of the primary principle, that by which it is energized, enlivened and sustained. The light is just obscured, never does it cease to be present, for otherwise the world would be inert (*jaḍa*)[133] and lifeless; it would not even have any existence at all, being unconnected to the source of all existence. Thus manifestation exists first as an archetype, potentially, as pure energy, in the Power united with Śiva; and at the same time this energy (which is consciousness, energy, or Word: it is all the same) is ever-present and all-pervading[134] in the manifestation. It is its essence (*sāra*). It is also its ground or substratum, that upon which the world rests, by which it is permeated (*vyāpyate*), (just as oil permeates the sesame seed, according to the traditional analogy[135]) and thanks to which it becomes real. For the world is not, according to those traditions, a pure, non-

---

131. Or as its essence (*sāra*), its essential nature.

132. As expressed by terms like *ghanatā, śyānatā, āśyānatā, styānibhāva*, and so forth, which suggest the idea of thickening, coagulation, drying, or hardening.

133. Cf. for instance *PTV*, p. 5 and the *ĪPV*. 1.5.11 (vol. 1, pp. 241-44). The inert state of things (*jaḍatā*) is also referred to by the word *aprakāśatā:* being without lustre, not shining. For this cf. *PTV*, ibid., and above all *ĪPK* 1.5.3: "The nature of a manifest object is light, but for which nothing exists," and 1.5.10, along with Abhinavagupta's commentary on those two aphorisms (*ĪPV*., vol. 1, pp. 204-08, 236-41).

134. Referred to in Abhinavagupta by such a word as *satatodita* (*PTV*, pp. 13, 14, 35, 45, etc.). For this term, cf. *infra* p. 172, n. 12.

135. Cf. chap. 3, p. 103, n. 51.

existent appearance, but a real creation,[136] which owes its reality to its emergence from the primary being (*sat*)[137] through an actual transformation of the latter from the condition of cause to that of effect.[138] This being remains however unaffected by this transformation brought about as a kind of sport (*līlā*) by its overflowing bounty, its free and boundless spontaneity (*svātantrya*), the workings of which cannot affect its radiant and unchanging pure essence. Not only does manifestation derive its reality from this origin—and indeed as a consequence thereof—but also from its permanent grounding in being.

Thus it appears that the primary principle, as inseparable from its energy, is immanent to the manifestation which is entirely contained within it.[139] However, the various non-dualistic Śaiva traditions maintain at the same time that Śiva ever transcends his cosmic manifestation since the latter does not affect his pure state and since he may always be looked upon—at least logically—at an initial stage as pure luminous Consciousness (*prakāśa*) separated from energy.[140]

---

136. Cf. *ŚD* 2.79, and Utpaladeva's commentary: the universe emanating from Śiva in conformity with this god's own nature (*śivānurūpyeṇa*) is but one aspect of Śiva and therefore its existence is real (*śivarūpam eva ata eva ca satyarūpam*, pp. 88-89); cf. chap. 3, p. 152 and chap. 4, p. 168).
137. In some cases *sat* will indeed refer to the universe, the existent, but to the extent that it partakes of the original being and derives its reality therefrom; see chap. 7.
138. Nondualistic Śaivism, for which the manifestation is a projection of light, a reflection of what exists in the light of the primary principle, is akin to the *pariṇāmavāda*, the doctrine of the actual transformation of cause into effect, and thus rejects the *vivartavāda*, according to which this transformation is illusory.
139. It is, according to a verse of the *Yogavāsiṣṭha*, commented upon by Abhinavagupta in the *PTV* (pp. 85-92), the one "within whom everything [dwells], from whom everything [is issued], who is everything and everywhere, who is omnipresent and eternal." This idea that everything springs from the Absolute (*anuttara*), and actually remains immersed therein, is the main theme of the *PTV*, part I.
140. Śiva then will be called *paramaśiva*, the supreme Śiva. He will also sometimes be referred to as the thirty-seventh or even thirty-eighth *tattva*. This role of Śiva as the transcendent absolute is clearly apparent in the Śāktaśaiva systems, such as that of the Śrīvidyā, which thus main-

This being so, the energy of Consciousness, or of the Word, which is, like Śiva, vibration (*spanda*), flashing forth (*sphurattā*), appears as a creative pulsation, a continuous movement of contraction and expansion (*saṅkoca-vikāsa*). At the highest level, this movement is the extremely subtle one that is the very life of the primary principle, the pure act, the first stirring (*spanda*). Somewhat lower, it is that of the cosmic emanation and resorption, bringing about the ever renewed cycles of the cosmic periods.[141] And this cosmic movement, in a Tantric system of thought, has its microcosmic counterpart, both being linked through constant correspondences and interrelations, so that the movement toward creation appears as that which creates human bondage, and the movement of withdrawal as that of deliverance. This quasi-identity of both movements, cosmic and human, is symbolized, as previously stated, by the *kuṇḍalinī*,[142] who is both vital and spiritual energy, present both within human beings and in the cosmos. Hence any description of the levels and aspects of the Word, of their emergence and resorption, will be not only the description of a cosmic event, but also that of a process which may be experienced by the adept, and through which, tracing the Word back to its source, this adept will gain access to liberation. Each of the following chapters, describing various aspects of the creative and destructive movement of the Word, will be not only cosmogonic expositions, but also as many methods, as many roads toward deliverance.[143]

This surging forth of the Word, of the sound-energy, may appear as assuming three aspects. These are interrelated since

---

tain his ontological superiority to the Goddess, although she is the highest form of the Godhead.

141. The same movement is also indicated by the two terms *unmeṣa* and *nimeṣa*, used in particular in the Spanda's first *kārikā* (*SpK.* 1.1); cf. chap. 5, p. 250, n. 72. The same process is sometimes also evoked by the term *haṃsa*, taken as Śiva's creative and destructive breath (*SvT.* 7.27; cf. chap. 3, p. 140). It may be noted in this respect that Śaṅkara, commenting upon the *Brahma-Sūtra* (2.1.33), which defines the activity of the Lord, also compares it with the breathing process.

142. For the *kuṇḍalinī*, cf. next chapter, pp. 124ff.

143. Cf. *supra*, p. 51, n. 48.

they describe the same process from different points of view:

• Either (chap. 3) as a gradual externalization, or as a condensation of the energy of the Word taken as being mainly a phonic energy. This power, Śiva's energy (*śakti*), a primal sound-vibration, gradually condenses, and passing through an initial "resonance" (*nāda*), becomes a drop (*bindu*) of phonic energy, divides, and subsequently gives birth to the matrix of the phonemes (*mātṛkā*), then to the phonemes themselves (*varṇa*), and to words. This sound process is "that which expresses" (*vācaka*), and induces thereby the emergence of "that which is expressed" (*vācya*),[144] namely the world of objects (*artha*) or of the meanings that it expresses. The phonic energy is symbolized by the *kuṇḍalinī*, in her twin aspect, human and cosmic, connected with "breath" (*prāṇa*). This description, which emphasizes the human, bodily aspect of the process, the yogic breathing techniques, and which therefore stresses its practical effects and aspects, is frequently encountered in the Tantras of the various schools: those are indeed generally accepted Tantric notions. They are to be found in the texts of the Āgamaśāstra rather than in the Spanda, the Pratyabhijñā or the Trika, but their being frequently referred to in those systems clearly shows that the latter took these speculations for granted, that they implicitly acknowledged them.

• Manifestation may also be taken (chap. 4) as occurring through the unfolding of the Word through four levels or stages of the Word, from the supreme Word (*parāvāc*)—identical to the primal energy in union with Śiva, who is the starting and ending point, and is the basis for the next stages. These are the "seeing" or "visionary" word (*paśyantī*), the first dawn of differentiation; the "intermediate" (*madhyamā*), where duality

---

144. Translating *vācaka* as significans and *vācya* as signification should be avoided, for the meaning of those two Sanskrit words is altogether different from that which is conveyed in modern linguistics by the terms *significans* and *signification*. *Vācya*, indeed, the expressed, is not the concept but the object referred to by the word: the referrent. This being so, it is *vācaka* which, from the Indian point of view, is related to consciousness, to the *logos*, whereas our linguistics relates the *logos* to what is signified: to the idea, not, as in India, to the thing.

appears; down to the lowest empirical level of speech called *vaikharī*, the "corporeal," the level of sounds as perceived through the ear, as well as that of the world of objects. Although these stages of the Word correspond to levels of sound condensation and to the rising of the *kuṇḍalinī*, and though the concept of these four stages goes back to the earliest antiquity and was elaborated more especially, as it seems, within Tantric circles,[145] its exposition, notably by Abhinavagupta, is much more philosophical than the previous one, farther from myth, less directly related to yoga (even though, as it may be assumed, we have here a metaphysical translation of yogic experiences). It gives Abhinavagupta an opportunity to outline an ontology and an epistemology of the Word. Not only shall we see there how the universe gradually emerges along with the various levels of the Word, but also how those levels are ontologically rooted in the supreme transcendental Word, and how the latter is at the very source of speech, which it establishes as an instrument of knowledge. This theory permits Abhinavagupta to propound a fine and subtle study of the simultaneous emergence in man of speech and of explicit thought.

- Finally (chap. 5), the cosmogonic process of the Word may be examined in its relation to the Sanskrit phonemes (*varṇa*), which are supposed to arise successively following the order of the "enumerative transmission" (*varṇasamāmṇāya*), that is, as enumerated in traditional grammar. In that case, the arising of each phoneme is looked upon as the result of a synthetic realization (*parāmarśa*)[146] of Śiva, each realization and each phoneme corresponding to the emergence either of one aspect of Śiva's energy (for the first sixteen phonemes), or of one of the thirty-four other *tattva*s, which form the entire cosmic manifestation. In this way the universe comes forth together with the four levels of the Word, the various aspects of the phonic energy, and the awakening of the *kuṇḍalinī*.

Thus will have been examined three aspects of the self-manifestation of the Word, and thereby of its manifesting the

145. Cf. chap. 1, pp. 20-23.
146. For this term, cf. chap. 5, pp. 228ff.

universe, though this process, again, may be followed the other way around: It is reversible, and serves the purpose—for the authors with whom we shall deal—of revealing ways of salvation. However, the description we give in these three chapters is mainly that of the process of manifestation. Now, the reverse movement should also be considered: the process which, from the manifested universe, from the empirical world where human beings live, will ultimately result in the Word's returning to its source, and thereby, for human beings, in their liberation.

This flow of the energy of the Word back to its source will be shown (chap. 6) with the theory of the sixfold path, or the six ways (*ṣaḍadhvan*), which may be considered as six aspects of the progress toward liberation (corresponding, of course, to cosmic resorption). The first three aspects are expressly related to aspects of the Word (these are the "paths of time," those of *varṇa*s, mantras, and *pada*s). The other three (those "of space," as they are called) are those of *kalā*s, *tattva*s, and *bhuvana*s); they are associated with and subordinated to the former three, and more especially related to the use of mantras.

With these latter will this study come to a close (chap. 7). Mantras, indeed, being major means to deliverance, appear as privileged instruments for the return to the source of the energy of the Word. More than that, a mantra is often itself a symbol or, rather, a form of this primal energy. It detains this preeminently in a most effective and practical form. But it is also alive with an inner force tending intensely toward the primal source of all speech, toward the Power which is the Word. Mantra, therefore, brings together both the practically effective and creative, and the transcendental and liberating, powers of the Word.

3

The Manifestation of Sound

The activity of divine consciousness which brings the universe into existence, and which, at the highest level, is, as we have seen, pure light, *prakāśa*, is often described, especially in the Trika, as a flashing forth, a radiance, a luminous vibration. This is conveyed by such terms as *sphurattā, ullāsa,*[1] and others. This vibrating effulgence, as much as that of consciousness, is that of the Word at its ultimate stage: we shall see later (p. 174) how *parāvāc* is defined as consciousness (*cit*) and glittering light (*sphurattā*). Manifestation, as it is born out of the Word and along with it, may thus be understood as a flashing forth which gradually becomes obfuscated. This occurs through a series of transformations and condensations of sound or phonic primal energy, which gradually brings forth (but in a never-ending process, for it takes place beyond time) the manifested universe, a process that takes place analogously in human beings, within whom sound (and then speech) will develop following a process corresponding to that of the cosmogony, and where the phonetic symbols appear as closely related to visual metaphors referring to the Word's aspect of light.

---

1. *Ul-LAS* means to shine forth, to radiate, to become revealed or perceptible, to appear. It also means to reverberate, to move, to sport, to dance, to be happy or cheerful. In the causative, *ullāsayati* means to bring out, to move, etc. Therefore this word conveys very aptly the quality of light projection, of uninhibited manifestation, of sport, of a living, luminous principle, which is that of the manifestation, according to the traditions considered here.

To follow this evolution of sound from its source, a few stanzas from Lakṣmanadeśika's *Śāradātilaka* may be taken as a guideline, for they reflect a generally acknowledged outlook.[2] After describing the Absolute, which is permeated (*vyāpta*) by the Word, this text reads thus: "Out of the supreme Lord, overflowing with existence, consciousness, and bliss, endowed with *kalā*, was born the [phonic] energy. Out of that came forth *nāda* and out of *nāda, bindu*, which is a manifestation of the supreme energy, and which itself divides into three. Its three portions are called: *bindu, nāda*, and *bīja*."[3] Out of this threefold division, adds the *Śāradātilaka, śabdabrahman* now comes into existence and assumes the form of the *kuṇḍalinī*. Therefrom arise the phonemes (*varṇa*), then speech; the gods, then the elements and the empirical world.

This is, in a nutshell, how this sound-energy moves on, bringing the whole emanation into existence, from the primary principle, transcendent and yet endowed with an urge toward manifestation (*sakala*). Although the process occurs mostly (down to *śabdabrahman*) within Śiva's energy, it is nonetheless described in rather concrete terms. It is a cosmogonic process, and yet, with the *kuṇḍalinī*, it occurs within the human body, which indeed is considered as identical with the cosmos, the swan (*haṃsa*) being the vital breath as well as the flashing forth of the supreme energy.

Such a cosmogony, on the whole, is commonly to be found in Śaivism and Tantrism. Kashmirian authors, however, notably those of the Trika, have usually looked at the emanation related to sound and the Word from different perspectives: that of

---

2. *Sāraṃ vakṣyāmi tantrāṇām* (Ibid., 1.4). Rāghavabhaṭṭa's comprehensive commentary on the *ŚT* (dated 1484), is interesting both because of its elucidations and its references to numerous texts. The *ŚT* has been published by A. Avalon in *Tantric Texts*, vols. 16 and 17 (Calcutta, 1933); this is the edition used here.

3. *ŚT* 1.7-8 (vol. 1, pp. 16-17):

saccidānandavibhavāt sakalāt parameśvarāt /
asīcchaktis tato nādo nadād bindusaṃbhavaḥ //
paraśaktimayaḥ sākṣāt tridhā 'sau bhidyate punaḥ /
bindur nādo bījam iti tasya bhedāḥ samīritāḥ //

the four stages of the Word and that of the "phonematic emanation"; these will be examined in the next chapters. These authors, however, are in no way unfamiliar with the cosmogony examined in the present chapter. For it contains various elements common to all traditions relevant to Tantrism: *nāda*, *bindu* and the triads arising therefrom, *kuṇḍalinī*, and *mātṛkā*, are very widespread notions. Thus the *Svacchanda Tantra* (and Kṣemarāja's commentary thereon) deals at length with the stages of the resorption of the *praṇava* sound-energy, which, from the *bindu* to the supreme Śiva, scarcely differs from the process described by the *Śāradātilaka*. Another text, the *Netra Tantra*, (which Kṣemarāja also commented upon) follows the same process in the reverse order with the movement of the energy of *OṂ*. The *Kāmakalāvilāsa* also, a Śrīvidyā work, offers a much similar description of the emergence and the division of the *bindu;* and other works of this tradition do the same (*VMT-NṢA*, *YH*, and so forth). The present chapter, then, in resorting to a great extent to materials belonging to various traditions, shows how much the concepts of which it gives a synthetic account, are part of a common background of Tantric notions related to the Word.

Śiva-Śakti

It is, of course, from the primary principle, Parameśvara, Paramaśiva, the Supreme Lord, the transcendent Śiva, that the process herein examined originates. But Śiva assumes two aspects. First, that of the pure, eternal, utterly transcendent principle; it is, according to nondualistic Śaivism, pure consciousness, (*saṃvid, cit*) or pure light-consciousness (*prakāśa*), and in this case, it is beyond manifestation, to which it is totally transcendent (*viśvottīrṇa*), as nothing can affect its purity and its absolute limpidity. It may, however, also be looked at as turned toward manifestation, keeping it concealed within itself in a state of primal undifferentiation and then projecting it outside, yet within itself. Śiva is then immanent (*viśvamaya*) and is inseparably united with his energy, Śakti, who is, strictly speaking, the cause and source of the entire manifestation.[4] As already stated,[5] the energy corresponds to the Word aspect of the primary principle; it is the self-awareness (*vimarśa*) of the light of consciousness, and that self-awareness gives it life.[6] That is the aspect of Śiva considered here, as indicated by the epithet *sakala* appended to it in *śloka* 7 of the *ŚT* cited at the beginning of this chapter.[7]

The term *sakala* refers to the immanent aspect of the Godhead, who assumes the form of the universe, the salient feature of which is its being comprised of parts (*kalā*); it also implies that Parameśvara is considered as associated with the energy, as awareness (*vimarśa*), and more especially as being endowed with a dynamism which, while corresponding to the highest level of energy, tends toward division and limitation. Owing to this dynamism, he brings forth the universe. Originally *kalā* refers to a portion, and more especially one-sixteenth of the moon's diameter, which is the additional portion it takes on each day of the fortnight, the whole of them forming the full

4. Those two aspects of the first principle will be found again when dealing with *a* in the phonematic emanation; cf. chap. 5, pp. 235ff. The same distinction is expressed by the two terms *kula* and *akula* (Ibid., p. 240). For this, see also Amṛtānanda's *Dī* on the *YH* 2.74, p. 203.
5. Chap. 2, p. 78.
6. Cf. *ĪPV* 1.5.20 (vol. 1, p. 294): *sa prakāśajīvitasvabhāvo vimarśaḥ.*
7. This distinction between both aspects of Śiva appears from the outset in the passage of the *ŚT* quoted above, for it reads thus: "One should be aware that Śiva is twofold: with and without qualities. Without qualities, he is eternal and separate from Nature. He is known as with qualities when endowed with the *kalā*." *Nirguṇaḥ saguṇaśceti śivo jñeyaḥ sanātanaḥ/ nirguṇaḥ prakṛter anyaḥ saguṇaḥ sakalaḥ smṛtaḥ//* (*ŚT* 1.6, vol. 1, p. 15).

   Therefore, here *kalā* should be understood as the dynamism peculiar to nature (*prakṛti*); not that *prakṛti* exists at the level of Śiva, but Śiva, when envisaged in union with the energy, is eminently endowed with the creative dynamism that nature will exhibit at her own stage of differentiation (*kalā-prakṛtiḥ*, according to the commentary on the *ŚT*. Ibid., p. 15).

   This *niṣkala/sakala* or *nirguṇa/saguṇa* distinction also occurs in Vaiṣṇavism, and even with the Vaikhānasa. Cf. G. Colas, "La vision de la divinité dans le diagramme selon le viṣṇouisme vaikhānasa," in *Mantras et Diagrammes rituels dans l'hindouisme* (Paris, CNRS, 1986), pp. 84ff.

moon. This lunar simile has been translated in the concept of the sixteen *kalās* of Śiva. The sixteen vowels associated with Śiva in the phonematic emanation[8] are, as a matter of fact, called *kalā*[9]—and indeed they are the portions into which he divides, while being also the various aspects of his creative dynamism. The sixteenth *kalā*, however, is different from the other fifteen. In the case of the moon, in fact, it is that which exists during the night of the new moon (when sun and moon are supposed to live together, hence the name *amāvāsya*[10] of this night and the term *amākalā* referring to this *kalā*), when the moon is invisible. The sixteenth lunar *kalā* is then regarded as an invisible and yet immortal *kalā*, which makes possible the subsequent reappearance of the moon. Similarly, the sixteenth *kalā* of Śiva will be regarded as that wherein both his solar and lunar aspects coincide and reach their culmination, as that which enables him, not to come into being again, but to emit the manifestation.[11] This *kalā* can then be regarded

---

8. Cf. *infra*, pp. 148ff., and more exhaustively chap. 5, pp. 233ff.
9. Or *tithi*, which also indicates any day of the lunar "fortnight."
10. Cf. Maryla Falk's article *Amāvāsyā in Mythical and Philosophic Thought* in *I.H.Q.* 18 (1942): 26-45.
11. This division of the supreme being into sixteen *kalās* is not peculiar to Śaiva Tantras, and is much earlier than them. As a matter of fact, Prajāpati appears as divided into sixteen in a mantra of the *Yajur Veda* (*Vāj.Sam.* 8.36), and the *Śatapatha Brāhmaṇa* 7.2.2.17 and 9.2.2.2 mentions *ṣoḍaśakalaḥ prajāpatiḥ*. In the same text (1.2.2.3) is even mentioned a division of Prajāpati into seventeen. Similarly, *BĀUp.* 1.5.14-15 states that Prajāpati has sixteen parts:

    "He is composed of sixteen parts. His nights, truly, are fifteen parts. His sixteenth part is steadfast. He is increased and diminished by his nights alone. Having, on the new moon night, entered that sixteenth part into everything that has breath, he is born thence on the following morning. . . . The person who knows this is himself that Prajāpati with the sixteen parts who is the year. The fifteen parts are his wealth. The sixteenth is his *ātman*."

    For the Upaniṣads, therefore, the sixteenth *kalā* was the highest, immortal one, the hub around which everything revolves.

    For this division, cf. H. Lüders, *Die Ṣoḍaśakalāvidyā* (*Phil. Ind.*, pp. 509ff.); Maryla Falk's above-mentioned article; and foremost

as summing up the whole creative and limitative dynamism of Śiva, while standing for his emitting aspect (the sixteenth *kalā* of Śiva is also in fact the sixteenth phoneme, the *visarga*, following which consonants, then the entire manifestation, are emitted). However, when referring to Śiva in his transcendent aspect, beyond all the aspects of his emitting and limiting power, the Trika will also use the term *kalā*, and say that there exists a seventeenth *kalā*. This will be the transcendent, immortal *kalā* (*anuttara-* or *amṛtakalā*), which is the energy of pure consciousness (*citkalā*), transcendent and yet endowed with a determinative tendency containing in seed-form all the other energies and the entire manifestation. This, says Abhinavagupta in the *Tantrāloka* (*TĀ* 3.137-40; vol. 2, pp. 140-41), is the supreme *kuṇḍalinī*, the supreme *brahman*, the heaven of Śiva (*śivavyoman*).[12] In the same way the Trika sometimes states that there is a thirty-seventh *tattva*, meaning Paramaśiva, the supreme Śiva, who is none other than Śiva, the thirty-sixth *tattva*, but regarded as absolutely transcendent.[13]

In addition to these sixteen (or seventeen) *kalā*s, there are of course, those of the consonants, which makes fifty in all. But it is said also that the *kalā*s are innumerable, and so they are indeed, since they are aspects—and those are infinite—of Śiva, who divides, or tends toward division, in order to manifest the infinite diversity of the universe born of this division.

Such being the meanings of this term, and to distinguish *kalā* from *śakti*, the energy, we translate it by limitative dynamism or energy, or energy tending toward limitation.[14]

J. Gonda, *Change and Continuity in Indian Religion* 4, "The Number Sixteen," pp. 115-30 (The Hague: Mouton & Co., 1965). For the solar and lunar aspect of Śiva and the energy, cf. *infra*, p. 157ff., n. 204-206.

12. Cf. also *PTV*, p. 27 (cited in chap. 5, p. 193) and p. 244: "Next to [the *visarga*] is the seventeenth *kalā*, the unequalled (*anuttara*), who is united with the heart." Some texts, says Abhinavagupta, even recognize an eighteenth *kalā*, which would be the transcendent, higher than Śiva; which means that, notwithstanding its original sense, *kalā* may come to indicate that which is beyond all differentiation.

13. *TĀ* 11.21-28 (vol. 7, part 2, pp. 13-23).

14. *Kalā*'s aspect of limitating energy is also apparent through its referring to one of the five "cuirasses" (*kañcuka*) which, together with *māyā*, restrict the universal experiencer to a limited being. Finally, *kalā* may

This same *śloka* of the *ŚT.*, when giving to Parameśvara not only the epithet *sakala* but also *saccidānandavibhava*, stresses a vital point, which is that even when turning toward manifestation and uniting with the energy, the primary principle does not lose anything of its own nature, that of the pure, transcendental Śiva.[15] One should be careful, in this respect, not to be mistaken by the mere phrasing of this text, which seems to hint that the energy is flowing out of Parameśvara (*parameśvarāt asīcchaktiḥ . . .*).[16] The energy is logically born of Śiva, since each *tattva* emerges from the preceding one, but is also potentially contained in it.[17] However, in the case of the energy, one goes a step further, for it is actually inseparable from Śiva.[18] Energy may be taken as coming from him, no

---

be one of the five portions into which the cosmic manifestation is divided (cf. chap. 6, pp. 356ff.), in which case the aspect, not only of part but of spatial division of the term *kalā* is more perceptible. The five *kalā*, in the sixfold course, are indeed included in the "path of space," *deśādhvan.*

15. Emanation has been well defined as "a process whereby, while the products come into manifestation, their source remains entirely unaffected and exists as it ever was": J. C. Chatterjee, *Kashmir Shaivism*, p. 58.

16. This objection came to Rāghavabhaṭṭa's mind, who, in his commentary on this Tantra (Ibid., p. 16), adds as an explanation that the energy remains merged within the Principle in a subtle form of pure consciousness (*caitanya*), and that subsequently it swells (*ucchūna*), so to say, toward manifestation. Cf. *PTV:* "The body (or aspect) of energy [of the Lord] is none other than the "I" (*aham*) of Parameśvara, who grows through his own *camatkāra*": *parameśvarasya hi svacamatkāravṛṃhitaṃ yad aham iti tad eva śāktaṃ vapuḥ* (p. 69, 1.8).

17. That is a consequence of the *ābhāsavāda*—for which objective appearances are fundamentally grounded in consciousness, which causes them to "shine forth"—and of the theory of causality acknowledged by the Trika (*satkāryavāda*): everything exists potentially in that which precedes it and of which it is the effect. Abhinavagupta, in the *PTV*, applied this theory to the *tattva*s, and infers therefrom the important consequence that all the *tattva*s are present in each single one: *PTV*, pp. 47, 63, 139, 151; in the same text, p. 138, he clearly states that this conception of the *tattva*s is relevant to the *satkāryavāda.* For this, see also Amṛtānanda, *Dī, ad YH* 2.34-35, p. 149. The Trika authors also stress the nonseparability of the four levels of the Word: on this point, cf. next chapter.

18. As proclaimed from the very first sentence of the *PTV*: "The energy, indeed, cannot be conceived as different from Śiva": *na hi śaktiḥ śivāt bhedam āmarśayet* (p. 3).

doubt, when one considers the emanation and its thirty-six *tattvas*, of which Śakti is the second one, but that is a relative view, which should not overlook the absolute inseparability of the first two *tattvas*.[19] Similarly, it will be seen that the next stages in the evolution of sound, those of *nāda* and *bindu*, are in fact nothing but aspects of the energy and cannot be separated. Their identity with Śiva and Śakti will be more or less categorically asserted according to the various expositions of this process, which differ, indeed, but the principle itself of this essential identity is never questioned.

It is indeed noteworthy that the sound emanation, from Śiva down to *bindu*, occurs (except in the case considered in the *Netra Tantra*) with *śakti-* and *Śiva tattvas*, at the level of the supreme Word (*paravāc*).

As a matter of fact, the texts do not state simply that *śakti* stands for the highest level of the sonic energy, that of the highest and purest sound vibration.[20] They distinguish stages therein, in order to describe the most subtle phases of the emergence or subsiding of sound.

The Śaiva or Śāktaśaiva texts—the *Svacchanda* and *Netra*

---

19. The Trika asserts this nonseparability when pointing to that of *prakāśa* and *vimarśa*. Cf. *ĪPV* 1.5.11 (vol. I, p. 241): *svabhāvam avabhāsasya vimarśam*, where Abhinavagupta explains *avabhāsasya* as *prakāśasya*.

20. The Principle, as living consciousness and source of the becoming, is, as one knows, described by certain texts as *spanda*, a term which may be rendered by *vibration;* but one must be aware that such a translation does not perfectly convey that which is not a perceptible movement, but the pulsating radiance (*sphurattā*) of the light of consciousness, the first stirring, the source of all life, the pure act *in statu nascendi*. Cf. chap. 2, p. 77.

Concerning the vibratory nature of speech one is tempted to remark that for the *Ṛg Veda*, trembling (*víp*) is a particular feature of thought and speech; "this 'trembling,' of which the poets are the cause is indeed the urge to speak, sacred inspiration" (L. Renou, *Etudes sur le vocabulaire Ṛgveda* [Pondicherry: IFI, 1958], p. 30. This "concrete or figurative vibration" as being not only the function but the nature of speech appears therefore as an ancient simile—as noted by J. Gonda (*The Vision of Vedic Poets*, pp. 38-39). That another meaning of *víp* is "spear-headed formula" (*RV* 10.99.6) directed against the enemy is also noteworthy, bearing in mind the Tantric conception of the nature of mantras (cf. *infra*, chap. 7).

Tantras, *Tantrāloka*, *Yoginīhṛdaya*, and others—usually describe these levels when dealing with the utterance (*uccāra*)[21] of the *praṇava*: the mantra *OṂ*—or of some other *bīja* ending with the nasal *ṃ* (*HAUṂ*, *HRĪṂ*, etc.). They show how the "gross" sound vibration of the phonemes making up the *bījamantra* arises, becomes subtler, then merges into the pure transcendent energy identical with Śiva, where sound and breath are reabsorbed and wherefrom they originate.[22] It is to this upward movement of the phonic energy that the yogin identifies in order to merge into the energy. However, this process has of course a twin aspect, human and cosmic, the yogin attaining liberation as a result precisely of his identification with increasingly higher levels of energy. This moving back to the source of the energy is therefore not only that of the yogin toward liberation, but also of the cosmic resorption (*saṃhāra*), and taken the other way around, of the emanation (*sṛṣṭi*). This is indeed how it is described in the *Netra Tantra*,[23] chapter 21, to which we shall refer time and again in the following pages.

In the course of this gradual resorption of the *bījamantra* sound vibration, the resonance (*nāda*), ending in *nādānta*, merges from *bindu* into the energy, *śakti*, which is its source and which therefore is still endowed with a certain form of sonic vibration. Then the dissolution of this vibration goes on within the energy itself, and three ascending levels are again distinguished therein: *vyāpinī, samanā*, and *unmanā*.

If viewed in the order of the cosmic emanation, *unmanā* appears first; this is the "Transmental" or "Superconscious," the supreme transcendent energy one with Śiva and virtually identical with him.[24] Next comes *samanā*, the "Conscious,"

---

21. For the meaning of this term, cf. *infra*, p. 142, and more importantly, chap. 7, pp. 399ff.
22. For the *uccāra* of *oṃ*, cf. chap. 7, pp. 402ff.
23. *NT.* 21.60-70 (vol. 2, pp. 285-95).
24. Ibid., 21.60 (p. 285): *Sā śaktiḥ paramā sūkṣmā unmanā śivarūpinī*; it is, says the commentary, pure essence, which could not allow the emergence of the universe within itself. It may be assumed that *unmanā* is a state almost prior to the Word, a point where it is still unmanifest, or is about to arise within supreme consciousness. This is the borderline where the primeval Word, utterly inexpressible, emerges from silence or becomes lost therein; although this is a very high stage, it is still—at least for

which is still transcendent, but wherein occurs the first stirring bringing the universe into existence. It holds it within itself in a latent state at the time of the cosmic withdrawal and projects it at the time of emanation.[25] As for *vyāpinī*, the Pervading, it is the energy immanent to the manifestation, which it pervades (*vyāpyate*) and to which it gives life. These three energies are of course forms of the sonic energy. Sound, it is said, right from the level of *vyāpinī*, fades away and becomes one with the energy,[26] although it obviously still exists in *samanā* and *unmanā*, for these energies are the very source of manifestation, which comes into being as a result of a sound vibration. This vibration, although in an extremely subtle state, exists however from the beginning. This is evidenced by the fact that for the yogin the "utterance" (*uccāra*) of the mantra, linked to this upward movement of the breath energy called *haṃsa*,[27] reaches *unmanā*, and subsides only beyond the *śakti tattva*, in Śiva.[28] The sound vibration, thus, appears already on the level of energy. *Unmanā* is also described as a state of extreme subtlety and as transcendent void. The higher planes of spiritual reality (as well as their being experienced) are sometimes described as void or emptiness (*śūnya*).[29] Finally it is noteworthy that the

---

Abhinavagupta and *SvT* 11.312—subordinated to that of the supreme Śiva. Cf. *infra*, n. 29. For *unmanā*, cf. chap. 7, pp. 405ff.

25. "It radiates," says Kṣemarāja, "in the form of the energy which brings forth the transcendental emanation that is the expansion of the countless cosmic emanations and withdrawals it holds within itself": *garbhīkṛtā-śeṣaviśvasṛṣṭisaṃhāraprapañca mahāsṛṣṭiśaktirūpatayā sphurati. NT.*, 21.61, comm. (p. 286). For *mahāsṛṣṭi* cf. ch. 5, pp. 306ff.

    (2) *Aśeṣabhāvāsūtraṇarūpam*, *Sv.T.*, 4.269, comm. (vol. 2, p. 172, line 3). For the term *vyāpti*, cf. *infra*, p. 103, n. 51.

26. *Praśāntaśabdavyāptikatva. Sv.T.*, 4.384, comm. (vol. 2, p. 241 *in fine*).
27. For *haṃsa*, see *infra*, pp. 140-42.
28. *Sv.T.*, 4.262: *Śivatattvagato haṃso na caret vyāpako bhavet*: "having reached the Śiva *tattva, haṃsa* subsides and becomes all-pervading (vol. 2, p. 166).
29. It does not, of course, refer to an ontological void, but, quite to the contrary, to the fullness of the pure being, who is void but of the imperfection of the manifested world, and who, in order to bring it into existence, shines forth in this void (cf. *PHr.*, 4, comm. p. 30; cf. also *PTV.*, p. 20: *sarvavedyaprakṣayātmaśūnyapada*, and p. 87, where different levels are discerned.

movement animating the energy from *samanā* and *vyāpinī* onward is that of the union of Śiva and Śakti, manifestation being the fruit of this union. Such movement brings about the awakening of the *kuṇḍalinī*.

Nāda

"From the Śakti [level] emerges [that of] *nāda*,"[30] with which it may be said that the condensation of the primeval sound vibration begins; this condensation is indeed hardly

---

Thus the *SvT* (4.289-94, vol. 2, pp. 184-89) enumerates six successive *śūnya*s, from the stage of the energy immanent to the manifestation, to that of *unmanā*, which is ultimate, unconditioned and changeless reality. Finally there is a seventh "void" in addition to the six others, which it absorbs within itself; it is known as the "nonvoid" (*aśūnya*), it is the supreme, transcendent Śiva: Paramaśiva, a compact mass of consciousness and bliss, pure being (*sattāmātra*), luminous, transcendent, and yet holding everything within itself.

The *YH*, 3.174ff. describes the meditation of the six voids (which the *Dī*, ibid., p. 364, correlates with the *kalā*s of the *bīja HRĪṂ* up to *unmanā*) beyond which is the great void (*mahāśūnya*), which is the supreme level (*paraṃ tattvam*).

The *TĀ* 11.21 (vol. 7, part 2, p. 13) refers to the supreme level as that of the transcendent Śiva, who may be taken as a thirty-seventh *tattva* ruling over the thirty-six others, called *śūnyātiśūnya*—the "void beyond the void" (a term that Kṣemarāja, in his commentary upon *NT.* 21.61, seems rather to apply to *unmanā* or even *samanā*, the level of the all-pervading energy: *śūnyātiśūnyātmavyāpinī bhūr uktā*). All this is nothing but a negative way of describing the highest reality. For *śūnya* in the phonematic emanation, cf. chap. 5, pp. 259-61.

30. *Nāda:* resonance, sound, or voice. The term, used in the Veda for a loud sound, is interpreted in traditional Indian phonetics as "force of voiced breath," as a characteristic feature of vowels and voiced consonants, which are described as "having voice as their main cause" (*nādānupradāna*), whereas the voiceless letters have *śvāsa*, voiceless breath as their characteristic (*Taittirīyaprātiśākhya*, 1.12-13: *śvāso 'ghoṣeṣvanupradānaḥ nādo ghoṣavat svareṣu. Ṛkprātiśākhya*, 13.4-5: *śvāso 'ghoṣanāṃ itareṣāṃ tu nādaḥ* ("breath is emitted for the voiceless sounds, and voice for the others").

The transition from this phonetic meaning to that found later in yoga and Tantrism is easy to understand since these systems give a prominent place to cosmic or inner sound, using *nāda* to indicate a

perceptible, for if *nāda* is a form of sound, it remains however imperceptible, at least when taken at the cosmological level:[31] it is the first resonance (*nāda*) of the Supreme Word (*parāvāc*), of the vibration (*spanda*) which gives life to the primary principle. It is, says the *Netra Tantra*, the *sphoṭa*,[32] which is a sound form pervading the universe.[33] Kṣemarāja explains that

---

particularly subtle form of sound, a form that appears more akin to the resonance following a sound than to the sound itself; this is felt as too closely connected with the physical means wherefrom it arose to be considered as subtle. The term occurs in this sense, for instance, in Yoga Upaniṣads such as the *Dhyānabindu* or the *Nādabindu*, where *nāda* is important in the meditation of *OṂ* associated with the arousal of the *kuṇḍalinī*.

We shall see that in certain systems pertaining to the Āgamas and Tantras, *nāda* appears twice: first at the level here considered, then at a lower stage as a result of the division of *bindu*. In dualistic Śaivism, *nāda* is a mere offshoot of *bindu*, but there *bindu* does not have the same role as in nondualistic systems. On this point, cf. *infra*, p. 119, n. 100).

31. When the emergence of sound is looked at on the microcosmic level, that of yoga, with the awakening and ascent of the *kuṇḍalinī*, *nāda* can be a somewhat perceptible sound. Thus the *Haṃsopaniṣad* describes the ten types of *nāda* heard by the yogin who performs the *japa* of *haṃsa*. According to this Upaniṣad, when the upward-flowing breath energy (*haṃsa*) merges into *nāda*, and the breath of the yogin comes to a stop, the latter perceives ten varieties of *nāda*: the first one is called *cini*, the second *ciñcini*, the third sounds like a ringing bell, and so forth; and on perceiving the tenth, the yogin's mind merges into the energy. Jayaratha (*TĀ* 5.99, comm. vol. 3, p. 410) cites a text which also enumerates ten *nāda*s, of which the tenth grants liberation.

Those sounds, that must be perceived by the yogin who performs certain exercises designed to arouse the *kuṇḍalinī*, are variously described in a number of texts; cf. for instance, *Gheraṇḍa Saṃhitā* 5.81-82, *Hathayogapradīpikā* 4.65-102, *VBh.*, 38, or *NādabinduUp.*, 31-41.

32. For this term, so important in Indian grammarian philosophy, one may refer to Ruegg, *Contributions à l'histoire de la philosophie linguistique indienne* (Paris, 1959), who cites the main texts and studies devoted to the *sphoṭa*. See also M. Biardeau's edition and translation of Maṇḍana Miśra's *Sphoṭa Siddhi*.

33. *NT* 21.61-63 (vol. 2, pp. 287-88):

dhvanirūpo yadā sphoṭas tvadṛṣṭāc chivavigrahāt//
prasaraty ativegena dhvaninā̄pūrayañ jagat/
sa nādo devadeveśaḥ proktaś caiva sadāśivaḥ//

when the energy (in *unmanā*, and on lower levels of sound) wishes to bring forth the universe, which is nothing but itself in the form of "that which expresses" and of "that which has to be expressed" (the universe being made up of a collection of significant sounds and words—*vācaka*—and of what they express—*vācya*—namely, the objects that they bring into existence), it retains within itself the vibration (*spanda*) which will form the "expressed," and manifests first the "expressing" vibration in the form of the particularized *nāda*.[34] *Nāda* being "that which expresses" is therefore that which manifests or reveals (*sphuṭati*) the universe—hence the epithet *sphoṭa* given to it by the Tantra; it is the totality of sonic energy (*śabdagrāma*) bringing forth universes, or *śabdabrahman*,[35] that is, *brahman*, the supreme reality as assuming the form and nature of sound (*dhvanirūpa, śabdanasvabhāva*).[36]

If *nāda* is viewed from an opposite perspective, that of the return of the energy to its source, then it is the resonance that follows the *bindu*, which itself condenses the power of the mantra, which, through *nāda*, merges into Śiva's energy. When describing the return of the differentiated consciousness to pure consciousness, Abhinavagupta and Jayaratha similarly define *nāda* as that which is left of the experiencer's synthetic self-awareness when all differentiating thought disappears.[37]

"When, from the invisible form of Śiva the *sphoṭa*, which is a form of sound, expands, impetuously filling the world with sound, it is called *nāda*, O Master of the Gods, and Sadāśiva." For the term *dhvani*, cf. *infra*, p. 138, n. 143.

34. *NT* 21.62-63, comm. p. 287: *saiva vācyavācakātmaśāktarūpaṃ viśvaṃ avabibhāsayiṣuḥ kroḍīkṛtavācyaspanda vācakasāmānyanādarūpatayā prathamaṃ spandate.*

35. This important term, indicating the supreme reality for the grammarian philosophers, does not occur frequently in Kashmirian nondualistic Śaivism, for which as for various Tantras, it is an epithet, not of the highest reality, but of an already condensed form of sound, quite close to the differentiated emanation. Cf. *infra*, pp. 122-24.

36. Ibid., p. 288: *sphuṭati abhivyajyate asmāt viśvaḥ śabdagrāmaḥ iti sphoṭaḥ śabdabrahma, ata eva dhvanirūpaḥ śabdanasvabhāvaḥ.*

37. *TĀ* 4.175 (vol. 3, pp. 204-05): *nādaḥ svātmaparāmarśaśeṣatā tadvilopanāt*; comm.: *tadvilopanād iti—teṣāṃ vikalpajñānādīnāṃ vilopanāt.*

Here we are at the junction of the energy (which is Word) united with Śiva and of the manifestation of this sonic energy; or, when the process is reversed, at the point where the manifested Word or sound, and differentiated thought—and therefore, cosmically, manifestation—finally dissolve within the energy.[38]

Jayaratha, in the commentary on the *TĀ*,[39] describes the level of *nāda* as consciousness transcending the universe and self-awareness. *Nāda*, he goes on to say,[40] is an "unstruck" (*anāhata*),[41] almost unmanifest, sound (*dhvani*), for there the phonemes are not differentiated. It is, however, sometimes referred to by the term *phoneme* (*varṇa*), for it is both the

38. We say "finally" because the differentiating thought and the differentiated manifestation do not exist, strictly speaking, until *māyā* "intervenes" at a much lower level than *nāda*. But the first lineaments of differentiation may appear in *nāda*, and therein also, thus, during the reversed process, they will finally disappear.

39. *TĀ* 5.75; comm. (vol. 3, p. 384): *vimarśātmikāṃ viśvottīrṇāṃ saṃvidaṃ.*

40. Ibid., 5.131, comm. (vol. 3, p. 444): *sarvavarṇāvibhāgasvabhāvatvād avyaktaprāyo yo 'sāvanāhatarūpo nādaḥ sa varṇotpattinimittatvād varṇa ucyate varṇaśabdābhidheyo bhavet.*

41. The term *nāda*, while generally indicative of a subtle sonic (or rather phonic, for it is inaudible) vibration on a very high level, may also be used for any form of sound, even a perceptible, "gross" one. This explains why various types of *nāda* have been distinguished, from the most subtle to the most audible. One of those classifications is to be found in Anantaśaktipada's commentary on the *Vātūlanāthasūtras*; although probably an author of a later period (sixteenth century?), he follows nonetheless a generally recognized tradition. He distinguishes four levels of *nāda:*

    1. *Anāhahatottīrṇa:* beyond the "struck" and "unstruck" sound, which he describes as a slight throb, the first stirring of the great vibrating act (*iṣaccalatātmakamahāspandaprathamakoṭi*). Jayaratha (*TĀV*, vol. 2, p. 76) applies the term to the Absolute (*anuttara*), the phoneme *a*.
    2. *Anāhatahata:* the "struck-and-unstruck sound"; not very different from the previous one. It is the basis for the sixteen vowels.
    3. *Anāhata:* the "unstruck" sound. It occurs at the *nāda* level. As said above, Abhinava (*TĀ* 6.217) describes it as an element common to all the phonemes, and Jayaratha (*TĀV*, vol. 3, p. 444, *ad TĀ* 5.131) as the efficient cause of the arising of the phonemes.
    4. *Hata:* the "struck" sound, caused by physical or material means. This is the audible sound.

instrumental cause of the arising of the phonemes and the underlying element to each of them; he quotes a *śloka* from the *TĀ*: "The single phoneme, made up of resonance (*nāda*), inseparable from all the other phonemes, is termed herein "unstruck," for never can it disappear." (*TĀ* 6.217).[42] Thus it is a perpetual sound vibration, and this is why it may be termed "unstruck," for only a sound that is not caused by a "shock," that is to say a material means, can be everlasting.

Jayaratha uses,[43] in his exposition of the phonematic emanation,[44] the term *nāda* to define the *visarga*, which is, he says, *nādamātra* and *avyaktahakālā*,[45] that is, unmanifest

---

I refer, for this fourfold *nāda*, the description of which is linked with the writing of the letter *a*, to the commentary on the *VS*, and for French readers to L. Silburn's annotated translation with commentaries of the *VS* (Paris: Editions de Boccard, 1959), notably pp. 31-34 and 66-73).

There are still further distinctions in the *nāda*s, more concerned with the various types of audible sound. Some are to be found, in particular, with certain authors of the Śrīvidyā, for instance Amṛtānanda's *Dī* on *YH* 3.142-43 (p. 334-35), and in Vidyānanda's *Artharatnāvali* on *NṢA* 1.12 (pp. 33-37), where *nāda* is divided into sixty-seven, with eight *nāda*s falling into *anāhata*, forty-seven into *hata*, and twelve said to be *hatottīrṇa*, three levels which may correspond to the *paśyantī*, *madhyamā* and *vaikharī* stages. This strange classification of the *nāda*s is given by these authors according to the *Saṅketapaddhati*, a *Śrīvidyā* text now lost.

42. *eko nadātmako varṇaḥ sarvarṇāvibhagavān/*
*so 'nastamitarūpatvād anāhata ihoditaḥ//*217//
(vol. 4, p. 178).

Vidyānanda (*Ṛjuvimarśinī ad NṢA*), cited by Maheśvarānanda (*MM-parimala*, p. 124 *ad MM*, 50), defines *anāhata* as supreme Word: *paravāgātmā*.

43. *TĀ* 3.146 (vol. 2, p. 147).
44. Cf. chap. 5, p. 282-85.
45. The *kalā* (which may be understood as dynamism or more simply as part) of the phoneme *ha*, is unmanifest. It is the *visarga*, which, being the final aspiration in a word (or rather the emission of breath at the end of a word), is viewed as a concealed *h* and at the same time as the "emitting" phoneme, Śiva's emitting power (*TĀ* 3.146). The same conception appears also in various texts, such as the *Jñānārṇavatantra* 10.8 (p. 31) or the *YH-Dī*, p. 19, where *nāda* is half of *ha* (*hārdha*, or *hārdhakalā*), that is, precisely the *visarga*.

emitting dynamism. Now, the *visarga* arises just when the energy united with Śiva is about to project the emanation within him or herself: here too it is a point of junction or transition. For the *Netra Tantra*, indeed, *nāda*, from the perspective of the *tattva* hierarchy, is at the level of *sadāśiva:* the ontic level where the phonematic emanation is projected into the energy and where consonants begin to arise. However, even if looked at from the perspective where *nāda* is still at the level of the energy united with Śiva, it retains the same nature, that of a point where the manifestation dwells within Śiva's energy, where Śiva both attains awareness of himself as "I" (*ahantā*) and becomes aware of the objective world which will be manifested (*idantā*) as dwelling in the substratum he provides for it:[46] a point of junction of the energy connected with the transcendent and of the manifestation which is concealed within it and which it is about to externalize. The same term appears therefore to be used for states in several respects similar, but for quite different levels, of the Word. There is, in fact, no synthetic and consistent theory of *nāda*, except in that *nāda* usually signifies, whatever its level, a subtle sound form.

In the course of this gradual condensation of the primal sound vibration which took us down to *nāda*, some stages are still distinguished. From Śakti, in effect, the sound energy becomes first *nādānta*, then *nāda*, then *nirodhinī*; next comes *bindu*, itself preceding *ardhacandra*.

Nādānta is, as the name suggests, the end of *nāda*, the very point where the resonance ultimately merges into energy.

---

46. *NT.* 21.63. comm. (vol. 2, p. 288): *saiva nādabhaṭṭārako 'kṛtakāhantedantāsāmānādhikaraṇyavimarśātmakaparacitprakāśarūpaḥ iti nādaḥ sadāśivaḥ iti sāmānādhikaraṇyokter āśayaḥ:*

"This blessed *nāda* is the pure light of the supreme consciousness when it becomes aware both of itself as the repository of objectivity and of this objectivity which dwells within itself, as being uncreated, of identical nature and as dwelling in the same substratum (which is itself). Such is *nāda*. And it is *sadāśiva*, namely the receptacle for the utterance of this identity in nature and substratum (or relating to the same object and residing in the same subject: *sāmānyādhikaraṇya*)."

Kṣemarāja, in the above-mentioned passage of his *udyota* on the *Netra Tantra*, compares it to the echo, or the last vibration (*anuraṇana*) of a ringing bell, when its sound fades away. This, he writes, is the moment when Śiva, the eternal knower, a solid mass of consciousness and bliss, becomes aware, in an all-inclusive and undivided way (*āmarśa*), of the supreme *nāda* (*paranāda*),[47] the sound of which may be compared to the indistinct murmur of a brook.[48] He becomes intensely aware (*parāmarśa*) at the same time of the universe as being within himself and permeated with the sound vibration of *nādānta*. The latter then starts to radiate forth in order to bring the universe into manifestation, being replete with the energy of the supreme Word wherefrom it originates.[49]

---

47. This term, together with *mahānāda*, is sometimes used for *nādānta*. It is also used at times in order to differentiate between a higher *nāda*, that which is here described, and a lower *nāda*, *aparanāda*, which is the outcome of the *bindu*'s triple division. Similarly are contrasted *parabindu*, or *mahābindu*, that is, *bindu* itself, issued from *nāda*, and *aparabindu*, the outcome—with (*apara*)-*nāda* and *bīja*—of its triple division.
48. Comparing it to the indistinct sound of a brook suggests both the quietness and the indistinctness of the continuous sound vibration in *nāda* and *nādānta*; however, no actual sound, obviously, arises at this cosmic level. Such comparison takes on a more precise sense when the sound vibration occurs at the microcosmic level, with the rising of the *kuṇḍalinī* (cf. *supra*, p. 97, n. 31): this is how *VBh*, 38 uses it (on which one may consult pp. 88-89 of L. Silburn's French translation).
49. *NT*. 21.63, comm. (vol. 2, p. 288): *sphuṭati abhivyajyate asmāt viśvaḥ śabdagrāmaḥ iti sphoṭaḥ śabdabrahma, ata eva dhvanirūpaḥ śabdanasvabhāvaḥ, adṛṣṭād iti anākṛter draṣṭrekarūpāt paranādāmarśātmanaḥ prakāśānandaghanāt śivasvarūpād ativegena avyucchinnadrutanadīghoṣavat prasarati/ kīdṛk/ dhvaninā ghaṇṭānuraṇanarūpeṇa nādāntena jagat viśvam āpūrayan āmarśanena ātmasātkurvan . . . prasarīty uktyā paravākśaktir eva parameśvarī iyaṃ sphuratīti ādiśati//*

    Issuing from *parā vāk*, *nādānta* should therefore, according to the *NT*, be placed at the subsequent level of speech: *paśyantī*. Abhinava, in the *PTV* (p. 128), referring to the *MVT*'s (chap. 8) description of the throne of the three goddesses Parā, and so forth, describes *nādānta* as that level where the "Great Preta" Sadāśiva rests (*sadāśivāntam āsanaṃ nādāntapakṣaniviṣṭam*). The next level of the trident throne is in fact *śakti*. Cf. also *TĀ* 15.339-42 (vol. 9, p. 170-71).

    However, establishing a complete and consistent system of correspondences between the various expositions of the sound emanation, of

Next we are in *nāda*, which, as sound moves on toward manifestation, becomes *nirodhinī* or *nirodhikā*. The sound energy is then termed by that name, because, we are told, this is the level beyond which the gods, such as Brahmā and the others do not go, unable to move higher because they have not the capacity to grasp the pure undifferentiation of the supreme Śiva. They remain at this stage, where the diversity of the gods is firmly established instead of the complete undifferentiation of the one transcendent principle.[50] "When this blessed, all-pervading, unconquerable, 'unstruck' *nāda* proceeds toward manifestation, it reaches a state of rest, in which, by merging into its own all-pervasiveness (*vyāpti*),[51] it brings forth the

---

the Word or of the phonemes, is no easy task. The chart on pp. 120-21 brings out the differences between the *ŚT* and *KKV* expositions and that of the *NT*.

50. *NT.* 21.64-65 and comm. (vol. 2, pp. 288-89):

> *dhvanir adhvagato yatra viśrāmyaty anirodhitaḥ/*
> *nirodhinīti vikhyātā sarvadevanirodhikā//*
> . . . *paramaśivābhedākhyātir eva brahmāder nirodha ity āha*
> *niruddhasya maheśatvamahimā na pravartate/*
> *ataś ca abhedākhyātyaiva tatrasthānāṃ nānātvam.*

The term employed by Kṣemarāja to indicate that Brahmā and the others are not aware of the supreme Śiva is *akhyāti*, a term denoting in the Trika the nonperception (*khyāti*), the non-intuition of the true nature of Consciousness, which is linked to the appearance of the first lineaments of the differentiation: once this begins to dawn, the pure supreme consciousness cannot be apprehended any longer. Kṣemarāja, in the *PHṛ.*, 4, comm. (p. 43), assimilates it to *anāśritaśiva* (*cidaikyākhyātimayānāśrita-śivaḥ*, which means that it would appear when the transcendent primary principle's primeval fullness begins to fade. Abhinava (*ĪPV*, 15.13) has it arise from *paśyantī*, which, in this text, he places at the level of Sadāśiva, but of which the furthest point (*paramakoṭi*) would correspond to *anāśritaśakti* (*PTV*, p. 147). The theory of *akhyāti*, of the nonapprehension of the real nature of things, occurred already in the Mīmāṃsā as well as in the Sāṃkhya.

51. *Vyāpti* is a term that denotes an all-pervasiveness, a permeating (just as, in the traditional simile, oil permeates the sesame seed) of a state of being by an energy or by a mantra, as well as the ability for this energy to freely pervade this state. For the meanings of this term, cf. Renou, *Terminologie grammaticale*, p. 301, s.v. *vyāp*.

pervasion [by this phonic energy] of its receptacle. Then it is called *nirodhikā*, also named *mantrakalā*."[52]

Thus Nirodhinī, for the *Netra Tantra*, is also that level where appears the dynamism peculiar to mantras (*mantrakalā*). The energy to which they owe their potency (*mantravīrya*) is of course that of Śiva united with Śakti;[53] however it seems there is a level, *nirodhinī*, where their dynamism would be more particularly marked, or to put it another way, where the energy would appear more especially in the form of the dynamism peculiar to mantras. For the *Netra Tantra*, all the same, *nirodhinī* is situated, with respect to the *tattvas*, between *sadāśiva* and *īśvara*, at the level of which arise, according to the Trika, those aspects of the knower, or agent of cognition, named *mantramaheśvara* (or *mantramaheśa*) and *mantreśvara* (or *mantreśa*): great lords, and lords, of the mantras.[54] If we

---

52. *Adhvagato 'śeṣavyāpako 'nirodhito 'nāhato nādabhaṭṭārako yatra viśrāmyati svavyāptinimajjanena adharavyāptim unmajjayati, sā nirodhikākhyā mantrakalā vikhyātā* (*NT.* 21.64, comm., vol. 2, p. 289).

The *SvT* 10.1229 (vol. 5, p. 524) ascribes to *nirodhinī*, "because it causes obstruction," three energies called Rundhanī, Rodhanī, that is, Obstructing, and Raudrī, Fearsome. It goes on saying, however, that the awakened yogin finds there two additional energies, Jñānabodhā, Consciousness of Wisdom, and Tamopahā, Destroyer of Darkness, which help to his upward progression. There are then five energies.

53. Cf. chap. 7, pp. 386-89.

54. The Trika distinguishes seven levels of agents of cognition (*pramātṛ*), that is, forms of consciousness more or less subject to limitation. Those are: Śiva, the highest, unlimited one; next *mantramaheśvaras*, which can rise up to the Sadāśiva level (*PHṛ.*, 3); then *mantreśvaras*, which can reach the level of Īśvara: both these terms are employed in the plural, since from this point onward consciousness is already divided: we just saw that the gods exist in *nirodhinī*. Next come the mantras, in infinite number, on the level of the *śuddhavidyā tattva*. Next the *vijñānākalās*, viz., beings who, owing to their discrimination (*vijñāna*), are free of *kalā*, that is, not fettered by the *tattvas*, *kalā*, and so forth, of the world of *māyā*, and which are subjected to the first only of the three impurities which Śaivism distinguishes and which are instrumental in the limitation of consciousness: the "atomic" impurity (*āṇavamala*), that which reduces the soul to the state of *aṇu*, separate consciousness. Next come the *pralayākalas*, "deprived of *kalā* because of the *pralaya*": those are beings who survive a cosmic dissolution because their *karma* is not exhausted; besides, they

consider that *nāda* and *bindu*, the sound and resonance at the end of the mantras, are that which permit their fusion with the energy and more especially empower them, it is natural that their dynamism (*kalā*) and their rulers (the *mantreśvaras*) should appear at the time of this fusion. But let us now deal with the *bindu*.

Bindu

"From *nāda bindu* originates," says the *ŚT.*[55] "It is nothing but the supreme energy. Then it divides into three, and its subdivisions are called *bindu*, *nāda*, and *bīja*."

Bindu is one of the most significant terms in the Indian speculations about energy and the Word. It refers to an essential stage in the process we are now considering. It is also encountered in the phonematic emanation[56] and in a number of Tantras and Yoga scriptures. *Bindu* is the "drop" of energy, that is, the energy as collected within a single drop or point, concentrated upon itself, and therefore endowed with special potency. At the same time, it is, graphically, the dot above the line marking the *anusvāra*, the nasalization and lengthening of

---

are subject to the impurity of action (*karmamala*). Finally, the *sakalas*, which are subject to *kalā* and to all the lower *tattvas*, and who are the individual knowers subject to one additional impurity, that of *māyā* (*māyīyamala*).

These various levels of consciousness are, with respect to cosmic manifestation, those which universal and undifferentiated consciousness passes through in order to assume progressive self-limitations and thus create the universe. They stand also for the more or less evolved levels of consciousness in creatures, and therefore, in ascending order, for the planes of consciousness reached by the yogin as he progresses toward divine consciousness, planes that are of course both micro- and macrocosmic states of consciousness.

For the various *pramātṛs* according to the Trika, cf. *TS*, chap. 9 (pp. 92-108), or *TĀ* 15.339-42, where they are described as arranged in tiers so as to form Śiva's *āsana;* or *ĪPV*, 3.2 and *PTV*, pp. 59, 117-19, which refers to *MVT*, 1.15ff., and 132-33. See also *PHṛ*, *passim.*

55. *ŚT*, 1, *śl.* 7-8; cf. *supra* p. 86, n. 2.

56. This is the fifteenth phoneme, the *anusvāra;* cf. chap. 5, pp. 272ff.

the vowel over which it is written, and especially (and more importantly), the nasalization that prolongs the sound of the mantra *OṂ* and is charged with its whole divine energy.[57] The notion of a drop—that is, a concentrate—of energy and that of resonance come together, therefore, in that of a phonic expression of an essential stage of the energy which is Word or sound. In addition to its phonic aspects, *bindu* assumes some other ones: we shall see that it is luminous, that it plays a role in the awakening of the *kuṇḍalinī.* One should not equate all these aspects to the particular aspect it assumes with respect to the phonematic emanation; however, it will be seen that these notions are interrelated: their various meanings are somehow always related to the notion of a pinpoint mass of energy.

In the emanation, *bindu* is the concentrated energy prior to its creating of diversity[58] through its own division. Now the energy owes its power to the fact that it is not alone but united with Śiva, the emanation being nothing else than the outcome of this union. This union, as is well known, is eternally accomplished right from the transcendent level, otherwise nothing could ever be brought into existence. However, just prior to the bringing forth of the universe, it is not out of place to mention once more the existence of this union: such is one of the roles of *bindu.* More than that, if the energy gathers and summons all its power before starting its activity, how could it summon up more creative power than through its union with Śiva? This, then, is how *bindu* appears: "a mass formed by the union of Śiva and Śakti."[59] Moreover, the differentiated

57. Cf. chap. 7, p. 394.
58. Cf. *PST* 1.41:

> *sā tattvasaṃjñā cinmātrā jyotiṣaḥ sannidhes tadā/*
> *vicikīrṣur ghanībhūtā kvaccid abhyeti bindutām//* (vol. 1, p. 16).

> "Such a one, known as the [energy] *tattva,* and which is but pure consciousness, coming now into contact with light, and having, so to speak, condensed owing to its wish to send forth [the emanation], assumes the state of *bindu.*"

59. *"Śivaśāktimithunapiṇḍa," KKV,* 5.

emanation arises out of the division of *bindu*, in other words, out of the division of its two constituent principles. Even if a third term brings them at once together again, their division remains nevertheless an established fact. Now *bindu* offers both the two principles and their coexistence: a reminder, at the threshold of differentiation, of all dichotomy as well as of all fusion. At the time of cosmic resorption *bindu* is of course the point within which the universe is reabsorbed as it merges into the energy gathered upon itself.

This is how *bindu* is described in the Trika texts and in those of other Tantric systems as well. When we meet it again, in a later chapter, in the form of the *anusvāra*, the fifteenth moment of the phonematic emanation, it will be seen that, notwithstanding some important differences, it still retains, due to its place in the alphabet, to its graphic representation and to its name, the same main characteristics as in the present context.

In the foregoing pages we saw how the phonic energy condensed by stages, ranging from *unmanā* to *nirodhinī*, according to chapter twenty-one of the *Netra Tantra*. Let us then first take up again this text, which describes the "creation of the mantras" (*mantrasṛṣṭi*), viz., the condensation of Śiva's energy, from *unmanā* down to the phonemes, of which the mantra is comprised. Coming to *bindu*, the *NT* associates it with the *īśvara tattva*,[60] where the power of activity (*kriyāśakti*) predominates. According to Kṣemarāja's commentary, there arises now—by contrast with the total awareness (*āmarśa*) of the undifferentiation of all that expresses (*vācaka*), which characterizes *nāda*[61]—a differentiating—in some respects—awareness (*vimarśa*)[62] of the objective world (*idantā*) as already manifest,

---

60. *NT.* 21.66 (vol. 2, p. 290): *sa binduś ceśvaraḥ smṛtaḥ.*
61. Cf. *supra*, p. 101, n. 46.
62. *Vimarśa*, as we have seen, being the free activity of consciousness, is inseparable from *prakāśa*, and appears right from the transcendent primary principle. Therefore it is not a form of thought subject to duality (*vikalpa*). But it is nonetheless different from *amarśa*, a term that Kṣemarāja had used thus far—for he was dealing then with a synthetic and all-inclusive consciousness—and to which he now substitutes *vimarśa*

although inseparably united with the supreme ipseity or I-ness (*ahantā*): this is an awareness that illumines undifferentiatedly all that has to be expressed (*vācya*).[63] Therefore it is no longer the aspect of the energy corresponding to the Word or to the sound which will bring the world into existence, no longer the "expressive" vibration, *vācaka*, which is emphasized, but that aspect—subordinated to the previous one—of the energy, which is the seed-form of what will be expressed, *vācya*, through this Word. We are thus one step further down, one stage further toward manifestation, or, for the *NT*, at a level of the mantra closer to its audible form.

It is known, however, that the *NT*, like all the texts dealing with the stages of the *uccāra* of a *bījamantra*, distinguishes different levels of enunciation. So, just as *nāda* was preceded by *nādānta* and followed by *nirodhinī*, *bindu* is preceded by *ardhacandra*. These subdivisions in themselves may not be of much import to us for the moment, but they are worth considering since they help to follow more closely the movement of consciousness and sound toward emanation: in the present case they contribute to further elucidate the nature of *bindu*.

The *ardhacandra*, the "half-moon," is the sign ँ, which looks, if not like a half-moon, at least like a crescent with a dot above it, and is commonly used in the graphic form of the mantra *OṂ*, where the nasalization is habitually noted, not by means of the *anusvāra*, but of the *anunāsika*.[64] When the energy

---

because he wishes to stress, more than *āmarśa* would allow, the consciousness aware of the difference between subject and object (here between *ahantā* and *idantā*), a difference experienced as immersed in and inseparable from the supreme "I." *Bindu* is awareness of *ahantā* and *idantā* as different and yet one, the emphasis being placed, however, on *idantā* (predominence of the "expressed").

63. *NT* 21.66, comm. (p. 290): *paraiva śaktir icchāśaktivyāptyā samanātaḥ śaktyantaṃ padam unmīlya jñānaśaktivyāptyā śaktiprādhānyam unmīlayanti samastavācakābhedinādāmarśamayatāṃ dhvanimātrātmanādāntavyāptyābhāsitāṃ nirudhya samagravācyābhedaprakāśarūpāṃ sphuṭedantāhantaikyavimarśātmeśvararūpabindvātmatāṃ gṛhṇāti.*

64. In spite of their purely phonic nature, all the *bīja kalā*s, from *bindu* to *unmanā*, have a "form," a visual symbol, to be used in meditation (cf. the chart appended to Bhāskararāya's *Varivasyārahasya*, edited by Subramanya Sastri [Adyar: The Adyar Library, 1948]).

of the sound vibration, states Kṣemarāja in his commentary upon the *NT* 21.66, wishes to manifest the stage of *bindu*, where lies the undifferentiated knowledge of all that "has to be expressed," it first reaches to the state of *ardhacandra*, where this *vācya* comes to the fore, but still in a hardly emergent stage. Then the nectar of Śiva, looked upon as *nāda* and lord of *sadāśiva*, this nectar, which is both potency and the seed of the manifestation (*sṛṣṭivīrya*), and which serves the purpose of bringing objectivity into distinct manifestation, falls upon the head of the *bindu*, which has to be manifested and which is the essence of the universe.[65] The initial emergence of *bindu* is called *ardhacandra*, which then becomes full, and next arises that form of energy called power of activity (*kriyāśakti*), which is *bindu*: *bindu* in effect, emits the manifestation, a role that is especially devolved to the power of activity, and it has the form of the full moon.[66] Such being the case, *ardhacandra* rather than *bindu* should be held as the immediate cause of the undifferentiated emanation, or conversely, of its withdrawal.[67]

Such is the process expounded in the *NT*. It comes to an end, after *bindu*, with the three phonemes *m*, *u*, and *a* of the mantra *OṂ*, with which the mantra or—if one considers this process at the cosmic level—the manifestation, is fully un-

---

65. This passage underlines some other aspects of *nāda*: as energy and semen giving birth to the universe, as well as of *bindu*: as an energy which is the essence, the true nature (*sattā*) of the manifestation. (In the Tantric texts, *bindu* may have among other meanings that of menstrual blood, cf. *infra*, p. 112, n. 80).

66. *Bindu* may in effect be considered as the full moon, that is, the totality of the emitting and limitating energy of Śiva, insofar as it is given the role and nature, which, in the phonematic emanation, are those of *bindu* and of the *visarga*.

67. *NT* 21.66, comm. (vol. 2, p. 291): *vimarśapravaṇanādakalāvācyasaṃhāra-pradhānā svasattānirodhena nirodhinīpadaṃ śritvā samastavācyābheda-vedanātmabindudaśāṃ sisṛkṣuḥ prathamaṃ kiṃcid unmajjad vācya-pradhānām ardhacandradaśāṃ śrayatīti tātparyam/ padārthas tu śivasya nādātmanaḥ sadāśivanāthasya sambandhi amṛtaṃ sphuṭedantābhāsātma sṛṣṭivīryaṃ sraṣṭavyasya viśvasattātmano bindor mūrdhni patati bindū-dayāt prathamam unmiṣati yadā, tadā sa mantrāvayavo 'rdhacandra ity ucyate, yatas tena āpyāyo bhavet tadbhūmikārūḍhasya pūrṇacandrākārā sraṣṭrī bindvātmā kriyaśāktidaśā udayate.*

folded.[68] We shall not follow its developments here, and will stop at *bindu*.[69]

Bindu, it should be noted, is luminous. It is a concentrated sound vibration, a drop not only of energy but also of light. Sound and the Word eminently partake, in effect, of the luminous nature of consciousness, according to various Tantric traditions:[70] the energy of the Word manifests, emits, the universe through a pulsating, radiant light, *sphurattā, prakāśa.*[71] Kṣemarāja, in his commentary on the *Śivasūtras*, defines *bindu* as supreme light: *binduḥ paraprakāśaḥ.*[72] More precisely, the *Kāmakalāvilāsa* describes *bindu* as a luminous point arising from the reflection of the radiance of the sun that is Śiva upon

---

68. This process will be examined in chap. 6 with respect to the resorption of the five *kalās*, and in chap. 7, with respect to the overall movement of the energy of *OṂ*.
69. It should be noted, however, that, according to the *ŚT.* 1.25-26 (vol. 1, pp. 26-27), the five *kalās*, from *śāntātītā* to *nivṛtti*, arise from the body of *nāda*, that is (according to Rāghavabhaṭṭa), from *bindu*.
70. Cf. *supra*, pp. 86-88. The luminous nature of *bindu* is a common view in Tantrism. Thus it can be equated with the ultimate reality, which, from the Vedic Upaniṣads onward is held to be of the nature of light, the sun being the visible symbol of the *brahman*, whose symbol is also the mantra *OṂ* (which *ChUp.* 1.5.1, equates to the sun) and the essential part of which is considered as formed by the *bindu*. Thus, for instance, for the *Tejobindu Up.*, the ultimate reality dwells, as a drop of light, within the heart of the supreme being.
71. Cf. for instance *PTV*, pp. 5-6: "this [supreme Word], wonderment of the Self, rests within itself, which is radiant, pulsating light, this pulsating radiance being the highest reality, the absolute "I" (*ahaṃ*): *yad iyaṃ svacamatkṛtimayī svātmany eva prakāśanamaye viśramya sphurati, tad evaṃ sphuritam avicchinnatāparamārtham aham iti.*
72. *ŚSV* 2.2, pp. 49-50. The luminous nature of *bindu* is clearly apparent in connection with the arousal of the *kuṇḍalinī* (notably in *ŚSV* 2.3). Cf. *infra*, pp. 128ff. In the *VBh, śl.* 36-37, (also *ŚSV.* 2.4, p. 57), *bindu* indicates a luminous dot and a one-pointedness of thought appearing during certain meditations. But the human level considered in the *VBh* is not separate from the cosmic level considered here. *Bindu*, in meditation, is light, thought and sound, because such are the characteristics of the cosmic *mahābindu*; the symbolism of the *bindu* is valid on both those levels, which its role as a symbol is precisely to identify. The interrelation of the two levels is still more apparent in the description of the arousal of the *kuṇḍalinī;* cf. *infra*, p. 134ff.

the mirror of his energy (*vimarśa*).[73]

Abhinavagupta's description of the *bindu*, in connection with the phonematic emanation,[74] corroborates the present analysis. There *bindu* is in Śiva, no doubt, and not as for the *NT* at the level of *īśvara;* but we are then in a different cosmogony, where the manifestation emerges first in Śiva; and this is also why *bindu*, there, comes after the vowels and before the *visarga.* The symbol, however, is the same, and therefore assumes its various meanings, related to those we have seen here: just like here, it is the sound energy gathering itself, prior to its division and its moving down to a less subtle stage of manifestation. Assuredly the division that comes after *bindu*, in that case, is a division into two—the two points of the *visarga* —and not into three as in the *ŚT.* But this makes little difference; for the division of *bindu* into three may in many respects be considered as a division into two, that is, in *visarga*, to which is added a third dot, combining the two others.[75] Moreover, some of the triads which here will appear in *bindu* are also met with in the phonematic emanation,[76] where it is seen as being above them, as pure light,[77] made of consciousness or cognition,[78] and characterized by the predominance of the power of action (*kriyāśakti*).

---

73. *KKV*, 4 (p. 15):

paraśivaravikaranikare pratiphalati vimarśadarpaṇe viśade/
pratirucirucire kuḍye cittamaye niviśate mahābinduḥ//

The Sanskrit commentary on the text clarifies the simile, remarking that it occurs just as in the ordinary world, where a mirror focuses the rays of the sun upon a wall in the form of a luminous dot, *tejobindu.*

We have seen previously that the *KKV* is a Śrīvidyā text.

74. Cf. chap. 5, pp. 272-77.
75. This is seen in the *KKV.* More explicitly, *KKV*, *śl.* 18 mentions three *bindu*s, which are precisely the *anusvāra* and the *visarga.*
76. *TĀ* 3.111 (vol. 2, p. 117).
77. *TĀ* 3.133 (vol. 2, p. 136):

atra prakāśamātraṃ yat sthite dhāmatraye sati//
uktaṃ bindutayā śāstre śivabindur asau mataḥ/

78. Jayaratha, *TĀ* 3.110, comm. (vol. 2, p. 117) quotes a widespread traditional etymology of *bindu* (corresponding to the frequent spelling *vindu*),

For the *KKV*, which, as we have just seen, defines *mahābindu* as a luminous dot produced by the rays of the sun of Śiva, this *mahābindu* is also a mass born of the union of Śiva and Śakti, which holds within itself all the phonemes from *a* to *ha*, and which is thus *aham*[79] (*a* + *ha* + the *bindu ṃ*, which transcends and unites them), which is a symbol for the emitting power of Śiva and of the energy who both conceals within herself the archetype of the universe and emits it, and is the source of the power of mantras.

The supreme "I," which is the *mahābindu*, is thus made up of two *bindus*, a white one and a red one,[80] pulsating in unending expansion and contraction, which are Śiva and Śakti in their creative union, the cause for the emergence of the Word (*vāc*) and objects.[81] The *KKV* is a Śrīvidyā text and describes

---

which he derives from the root *VID*, to know: *vettīti vinduḥ vidikriyāyām svatantraḥ pramātā*. Abhinavagupta, in the *PTV*, says of *bindu* that it is *pūrṇavedanāmātra* (p. 176, line 11).

79. The fifty phonemes in Tantric texts extend in fact to *kṣa* (and not *ha*). But *ha*—grammatically the last letter of the alphabet—is often used as a symbol for the whole collection of consonants, for Śakti and *vimarśa*, whereas *a* stands as a symbol for the vowels, for Śiva and *prakāśa*. We have thus the totality of the phonemes, of Śiva-Śakti, and of consciousness. *Bindu* comes in addition, symbolizing the union of *a* and *ha* into a single, homogeneous and dynamic mass. This makes *aham* or rather *AHAṂ*. For the role of *bindu* in *ahaṃ*, cf. *PTV*, pp. 87 and 196; on *ahaṃ*, see chap. 5, pp. 286-89.

80. Red and white are held as bright, radiant, colors. Red, moreover, is especially an attribute of the Goddess, who is energy. It is the color of blood (notably of menstrual blood, *śoṇita*). Śiva is of a corpse-like pallor, having no power by himself but only through Śakti. White, however, is also the color of sperm; that of Śiva is burning hot. Cf. A. Padoux, "Le Monde hindou et le sexe," *Cahiers Internationaux de Sociologie* XXVI (1984): 29-49.

81. *KKV*, *śl.* 6-7 (18-20):

sitaśoṇabinduyugalaṃ viviktaśivaśaktisaṅkucatprasaram/
vāgarthasṛṣṭihetuḥ parasparānupraviṣṭavispaṣṭam//
bindur ahaṃkārātmā ravir etan mithunasamarasākāraḥ/
kāmaḥ kamanīyatayā kalā ca dehanenduvigrahau bindū//

Cf. also the Sanskrit commentary to these two *ślokas* in A. Avalon's edition (pp. 18-25).

cosmogony as manifesting through the *śrīcakra* and *śrīvidyā*, the diagram and the mantra, which both symbolize and constitute the cosmic activity of the Goddess Tripurasundarī. It describes this *bindu* as the "phoneme I" (*ahaṃkāra*)—born of the union of these two poles—and as the sun, as giving birth to two more *bindus*, that are moon and fire (*somāgni*), which makes three in all. Thus appears the triangular diagram of the *kāmakalā*, a symbolic form of the Goddess,[82] after which the diversification of the phonic energy will go on.

In coming to this phase of the process, it may be pointed out once again how, in order to describe a phonic or sound process, the texts we are studying make use not only of luminous metaphors, but of visual and spatial ones as well: *bindu*—and its double or treble division—and even more the *kuṇḍalinī*—with its "bodily" course from *cakra* to *cakra*—and the *kāmakalā*, involve mental pictures, inner visions. Even the most subtle levels of sound vibration have their visual symbolism.[83] This is a common feature of Tantrism, where adepts, through the practice of *dhyāna* or *bhāvanā*, must, in numerous rites, resort to visualizations and identify with them: the symbol turns into experience (as Mircea Eliade would say).[84] Another characteristic feature is the shift from a phonic to a spatial

---

82. The *kāmakalā* appears in the text as identified both with *haṃsa/so'ham*, and with a diagram having a triangular base containing the three *bindus*, *a, ha/visarga*, and the phoneme *ī* (in ancient pictorial representation, with three dots as the three *bindus*), which gives the *bīja IṂ*.

    For the *kāmakalā*, besides the *KKV* and its commentary, which are not very explicit, see the *YH* 2.21 with Amṛtānanda's *Dī*, p. 130-32 (and the notes of my translation), along with *Gandharvatantra*, chap. 30, which is more detailed if not clearer, or Purṇānandagiri's *Śāktakrama*, chap. 5.

83. Cf. *supra*, p. 108, n. 64.

84. *Techniques du yoga* (Paris: Gallimard, 1948, p. 184-85). In a Tantric context, in the Āgamas and Tantras as well—and in Buddhism (even more than in Hinduism)—*dhyāna* is not the meditation of classical yoga but the clear visualization of a divine or other entity such as described in a text. It is, one might say, a technique of controlled hallucination. We may note in this respect that the meaning of "inner vision of a deity" given to the word *dhyāna* is related to the primary sense of the verbal root *DHĪ*: to see.

symbolism (or vice-versa), an isomorphism exemplified notably by the *bindu*, the symbolism of which pertains equally to both domains. Thus sound may sometimes appear as a subtle form of an image.[85] But let us come back to this *bindu*, which is precisely at the same time supermundane phonic energy, intense radiance, and a geometrical point.

The Division of Bindu

From this twin-natured *bindu*, the polarized energy of the Word proceeds with its manifestating movement through further division, thus coming gradually nearer to the multiplicity of letters (then speech), and of the objective world.

The *KKV* goes on with its description of this sonic evolution, in relation to the drawing up of the *śrīcakra*, the symbol of the cosmic creative impulse of the Goddess (united with Śiva) residing at its center, in the *bindu*, wherefrom will evolve an initial energic and phonic triad, and from this triad the rest of the universe. "The flashing forth of this red *bindu*," says this text, "generates a sound (*rava*) that is *nādabrahman*, which is the sprout from which are born ether, air, fire, water and earth (that is, the five *mahābhūtas*, "gross" elements, the lowest cosmic categories, or *tattvas*, of the cosmos) and the phonemes[86] (which, of course, precede the elements)." The

---

85. Thus the description of the Śrīcakra in *YH*, chap. 1, where the phonic *kalās*, from *bindu* to *unmanā*, continue the structure of the *śrīcakra* from the outer square to the central *bindu* (precisely!) on the subtle plane. For the interplay of the spatial and phonetic symbolism, see *Mantras et diagrammes rituels dans l'hindouisme* (Paris: CNRS, 1987).

For *bhāvanā*, see F. Chenet's study "*Bhāvanā* et créativité de la Conscience," *Numen* 34: 1 (1987).

86. *KKV*, 9:

sphuṭitād aruṇād bindor nādabrahmāṅkuro ravo vyaktaḥ|
tasmād gaganasamīraṇadahanodakabhūmivarṇasaṃbhūtiḥ

"From the swelling and throbbing red *bindu* arises a sound (*rava*) which is the sprout of the *nādabrahman*. From this come ether, air, fire, water, and earth."

white *bindu*, inseparable from the former, since both in fact make but one single unit, naturally has the same role.[87] These two *bindu*s are, as we have seen, Śiva and Śakti, but also the creative word (*vāk*) and the objects (*artha*) it creates (or at least their archetype). Thus we have the original seed or germ (*bīja*), made of the three *bindu*s, and which, in order to bring forth the subsequent phases of the emanation, produces various triads, such as those of sun, moon, and fire, of knower, knowing, and known, of the threefold cosmic activity (emanation, maintenance, and resorption), of the three *bījas*[88] or of the three fundamental powers for which those *bīja*s stand, and so forth.[89] Further on, the same text describes again the drawing of the diagram, but in relation to the levels of Speech: "The *bindu* in the center of the *śrīcakra* is the supreme (*parā*: the Goddess as well as the Word). Being swollen, bloated (*ucchūna*), that is, ready to evolve, it transforms and manifests itself as a triangle,[90] which is the source of the successive three planes of Speech, *paśyantī*, *madhyamā*, and *vaikharī*, and is also the three *bīja*s (and therefore the three parts of the *śrī-*

---

87. Ibid., 10:

atha viśadād api bindor gaganānilavahnivāribhūmijaniḥ/
etat pañcakavikṛtir jagad idam aṇvādyajāṇḍaparyantam//

"From the white *bindu* come also ether, air, fire, water and earth. This universe, from the atom to the sphere of the unborn is made of these five evolutes."

88. The three *bīja*s are the three portions of the *mūlamantra* of Tripurasundarī: the *śrīvidyā*, which arises together with the *śrīcakra*.
89. *KKV*, 12-14:

vāgarthau nityayutau parasparaṃ śivaśaktimayāv etau/
sṛṣṭisthitilayabhedau tridhā vibhaktau tribījarūpeṇa//
mātā mānaṃ meyaṃ bindutrayabhinnabījarūpāṇi/
dhāmatrayapīṭhatrayaśaktirayabhedabhāvitāny api ca//
teśu krameṇa liṅgatritayaṃ tadvac ca mātṛkātritayam/
itthaṃ tritayapurī yā turīyapīṭhādibhedinī vidyā//

90. The Sanskrit commentary on these verses of the *KKV* identifies this triangle with the phoneme *e*, since *e* is made up of the three energies: the Absolute (*a*), Bliss (*ā*), and Will (*i*): *a* or *ā* + *i* = *e*. On *e*, see chap. 5, pp. 263-67.

vidyā). Vāmā, Jyeṣṭhā, Raudrī, and Ambikā, on the other hand, form the higher (or first) part (of the *śrīcakra*), whereas *icchā, jñāna, kriyā*, and *śāntā* constitute its other part. The two phonemes (*a* and *hā*) taken together or separately (and added to the preceding elements) make up the elevenfold *paśyantī*," which is to say that all the phonemes, from *a* to *ha* also appear.[91]

If one refers now to the passage in the *ŚT* already partially quoted at the beginning of the present section and of the previous sections of this chapter, one will find a description of the division of *bindu* very similar to what we have just seen. The *ŚT* clearly distinguishes, by contrast with the *KKV*, between an initial, higher, state of *bindu* and its division into three; yet, for it as for the *KKV* (and contrary to the *NT*), the division of *bindu* takes place within the energy united with Śiva. *Bindu* being thus placed, as we already remarked above, at the same level as in the phonematic emanation, it is clear that *bindu* and its division are therefore, for the *ŚT* and the *KKV*, the same gathering up and then dividing movement of Śiva's energy, which occurs, in the phonematic emanation, with *bindu* and *visarga*.[92]

"The three subdivisions of *bindu*," says the *ŚT*, are called *bindu, nāda*, and *bīja*. This [lower] *bindu* is of the nature of Śiva, *bīja* of that of Śakti, and *nāda* is the union, the mutual

---

91. *KKV, śl.* 22-24:

madhyaṃ cakrasya syāt parāmayaṃ bindutattvaṃ evedam/
ucchūnaṃ tacca yadā trikoṇarūpeṇa pariṇataṃ spaṣṭam/
etat paśyantyāditritayanidānaṃ tribījarūpaṃ ca/
vāmā jyeṣṭhā raudrī cāmbikayānuttarāṃśabhūtāḥ syuḥ//
icchājñānakriyāśāntaścaitaccottarāvayavāḥ/
vyastāvyastaṃ tadarṇadvayam idam ekādaśātma paśyantī//

The eleven divisions of *paśyantī* alluded to in this passage are the eleven energies: *vāmā, jyeṣṭhā, raudrī, ambikā*, presided over by *parā*, then *icchā, jñāna* and *kriyā*, to whom are added the two phonemes (*arṇadvayam*) *a* and *ha*, which sum up the whole phonetic energy.

92. In the phonematic emanation, however, there occur, prior to *bindu* and *visarga*, threefold divisions of the emanative power. This is notably the case with the triangular seed *trikoṇabīja, e,* and even with the phoneme *a*; cf. chap. 5, pp. 242, 263-67.

relation, between these two, so say those who are learned in the Āgamas."[93] Thus here again the energy of sound first focuses and concentrates, then divides itself into three units which dissociate its elements, and it then recombines them: the luminous *bindu* represents the Śiva aspect, and *bīja* the Śakti aspect, which is kinetic; *nāda* combines both in its creative resonance.[94] This division into three brings about a succession of triads which will generate the differentiated manifestation:

"From the [lower] *bindu*," the *ŚT* goes on to say, "comes Raudrī, from *nāda* Jyeṣṭhā, and from *bīja* Vāmā.[95] From these [three divinized energies] come forth [the three gods:] Rudra, Brahmā, and the Lord of Rāma (Viṣṇu). Their [respective] natures are [those of the three powers of] knowledge, will, and

---

93. *ŚT* 1.8-9.

94. As stated *supra* (pp. 99-100, n. 41), *nāda*, which appears here once again, retains, in all the systems of the cosmogony of sound or Speech, a general sense besides its more particular one, namely that of a very subtle and very pure phonic vibration, as a very high form of the energy of Speech: in the phonematic emanation, *nāda* is applied notably to *bindu* and *visarga*. Even *a* is *anāhatanāda*.

95. These three divinized energies are found in a number of Tantric texts. Their attributes are held to be Śiva's three main activities or powers. The *TĀ* 6.56-57 (vol. 4, pp. 49-50) describes their role: Vāmā, controller of the creatures who wander helplessly in *saṃsāra*, is the one who manifests, who vomits (*vāmana*) the universe; Jyeṣṭhā, controller of those who have attained wisdom, is endowed with Śivahood, and as such is the eldest (*Jyeṣṭhā*) of the three; Raudrī rules over those who pursue wisdom, destroys suffering, and brings to an end the karmic consequences of all actions. Similarly, *Jñānārṇava Tantra* 1.14-15.

The *Yoginīhṛdaya* mentions four goddesses, adding Ambikā, the Mother who rules over the other three (as does also the *KKV*, 23, and many other texts); *YH* further correlates them with the four levels of Speech: Ambikā is *parāvāc*. When she is moved to bring forth the universe, held within herself in seed form, she brings forth Vāmā, who vomits the universe, who is the power of will (*icchāśakti*), and abides in *paśyantī*. The power of knowledge (*jñānaśakti*) is in *madhyamā* and is known as Jyeṣṭhā, and Raudrī, the power of action (*kriyāśakti*), is in *vaikharī* (Ibid., 1.36-40). This process, which is also that of the drawing of the inner triangle of the *śrīcakra*, comes to an end with Ambikā, in the central *bindu*, the starting and returning point of the whole cosmic manifestation.

action: they are fire, moon, and sun.[96] Through this division of the supreme *bindu* springs forth the unmanifest sound (*rava*) called *śabdabrahman* by those who are learned in all the Āgamas."[97]

The evolution of sound as expounded so far, from Śiva down to the division of *bindu*, could be summarized in a comparative chart. We have, in effect, examined three accounts thereof, which are somewhat at variance: those of the *ŚT* (and of the *PST*) and of the *KKV*, which are almost identical, and that of the *NT*, which is more exhaustive, and which underscores aspects (notably of the awareness of sound) not men-

96. Rāghavabhaṭṭa, in his commentary on this passage of the *ŚT*, correlates these three powers, these three deities, and these three luminous elements with the three phonemes *a*, *u*, and *ṃ* of the mantra *OṂ*, thus coming close to the exposition given in *NT*, chapter 21, which we have seen. For the polarity *soma/sūrya* cf. *infra*, pp. 157-59.

97. *ŚT* 1.10-12 (pp. 17-18):

raudrī bindos tato nādāj jyeṣṭhā bijād ajāyata/
vāmā tābhyaḥ samutpannā rudrabrahmarāmādhipaḥ//
saṃjñānecchākriyātmano vahnīndvarkasvarūpiṇaḥ/
bhidyamānāt parād bindor avyaktātmā ravo 'bhavat//
śabdabrahman taṃ prahuḥ sarvāgamaviśaradāḥ/

In the *TĀ* also similar aspects and triads, in connection with *bindu*, are to be found: *bindu* is, Abhinavagupta says, moon, sun, and fire (*TĀ* 3.111). It is of two aspects, white and red, associated respectively with moon and sun, and brought together in fire (Ibid., 114).

In a passage of his commentary on the *TĀ*, Jayaratha quotes, with respect to the phoneme *a* (*TĀ* 3.67), a passage of the *Tantrasadbhāva* and of the *VM*, about which more will be said later when we deal with the *kuṇḍalinī*, and where *bindu* arouses Raudrī, and the other energies together with all the phonemes.

The *Jñānarṇava Tantra* (1.14-15), a Śrīvidyā text, also correlates Vāmā, Jyeṣṭha, and Raudrī with the threefold *bindu*, which consists of the *anusvāra* and the *visarga* (Ibid., 4-5); *visarga* and the fourteen vowels forms the circle of the *kalā*s (*kalāmaṇḍala*). This threefold *bindu* is made of the three powers of will, cognition, and action, associated with the three *guṇa*s and with the three states of the self: waking, dreaming, and deep sleep. Beyond lies the fourth state (associated with Ambikā), which is the pulsating radiance of the plenitude of being, pure consciousness, beyond the phonemes, and so forth, and which appears as the resonance (*nāda*) of the threefold *bindu* (Ibid., 1.16-27, pp. 2-3).

tioned by the other two. As we have observed, it also correlates the levels of sound condensation with the levels of speech, or with the *tattvas*, somewhat differently from the other two expositions. The reason for it is that the *NT* describes the stages not of the emanation in general, but as related to the creative enunciation of the mantra *OṂ* (*mantrasṛṣṭi*). Now, a mantra can be uttered. The three phonemes *a*, *u*, and *ṃ*, comprising *oṃ*, are therefore necessarily situated at the level of empirical speech, *vaikharī*, and of the *tattvas* of the impure manifestation,[98] hence the inconsistencies between the exposition of the *NT* and that of the other two texts. This, however, does not detract from the value of the *NT*'s elucidations for our purpose, and the symbolic meaning of the main stages: *śakti*, *nāda*, *bindu* remains the same. This is why this text could be used here. In chapter 7[99] the stages of the *uccāra* of *OṂ* will be found again. Here they occupy the right section of the chart.[100]

---

98. In the *NT* the *mātṛkā* does not appear until later on (Ibid., *śl.* 71-72), in spite of its being the mother-energy of the phonemes and therefore normally prior to the mantras. But mantras are sometimes described as being the very highest level of Speech, as we shall see later on.

    Dualistic Āgamas (for instance *Mṛg, Kp.* 1.2, p. 2, N. R. Bhatt's edition; Pondicherry, 1962), usually describe the evolution of sound in the following order: *śakti*, *nāda*, *bindu*, *akṣara* (or *praṇava*), and *mātṛkā*, which corresponds to the description given by the *NT* and which, as regards the general structure of the system, does not differ much from what we have seen here.

99. Chap. 7, pp. 402ff.

100. It may be worth noting, incidentally, the description of the emanation of sound and the Word as proposed by a later (eighteenth century) writer and grammarian philosopher, Nageśa, in his *Vaiyākaraṇasiddhāntalaghumañjuṣā*, which is quite close to what we just saw. For him, when there arises in Parameśvara the modality of *māyā* (here of course *karaṇamāyā*, the causal *māyā*, a transcendental principle of illusion and emanation: such is the doctrine, notably, of the Śaivasiddhānta, not of the Trika), which is his movement toward creation, there emerges a threefold *bindu*, which is energy. The three parts of this *bindu* are: *bindu*, which is consciousness (*cit*), *bīja*, the nonconscious (*acit*), and *nāda*, which is both (*cidacit*). From this *bindu* arises what is known as *śabdabrahman*, where the particularized phonemes are not yet in existence, where knowledge predominates, which is an awareness free

Śāradā Tilaka	Kāmakalāvilāsa	*tattva, kalā* Levels of Speech
Parameśvara ↓	*Paraśiva* (*prakāśa*) ↓	Śiva
śakti ↓	śakti	
	nāda	*parā-vāk*
nāda ↓		*śāntatītākalā*
bindu ↓	*mahābindu* (*aham*) 	
bindu (śiva) fire Raudrī Rudra *jñānaśakti* 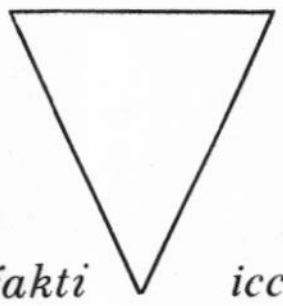 *bindu* (śakti) moon Vāmā Viṣṇu *icchāśakti*	*kāma* (sun) *A* 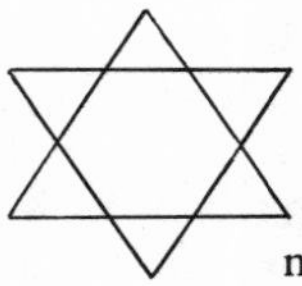 *kalā* fire; *kalā* moon; *HA*	
nāda (śiva/śakti) sun *kriyāśakti* ↓	↓	Śakti
Rava-śabdabrahman	*nādabrahman*	sadāśiva (*śāntakalā*)

Netra Tantra *mantrasṛṣṭi*	*tattva, kalā*	Levels of Speech
Paramaśiva	Śiva	
unmanā	(*śāntātītākalā*)	
samanā		*parā*
vyāpinī		
śakti	Śakti	
nādānta		
nāda	*sadāśiva*	*paśyantī*
śabdabrahman	*śāntakalā*	
nirodhinī	*īśvara*	*madhyamā*
ardhacandra	*śuddhavidyā*	
bindu		
M	*māyā-puruṣa*	
U	*vidyākalā*	
A		*vaikharī*

Śabdabrahman

According to the *ŚT* (and to the *Prapañcasāratantra*)[101] as well as for the *KKV*, the division of *bindu* brings about an unmanifest humming or sound (*rava*) which, according to the *ŚT*, is the element of consciousness existing in all living creatures.[102] The *NT* applies the term *śabdabrahman* to *nāda*.

---

of particularization, and yet a state conducive to the emergence of creation, and which is nothing but *nāda*. It is the material cause of the world and is called sound (*rava*), supreme Word, and so forth (*VSLM*, pp. 171, 175). In the early eighteenth century, Bhāskararāya, in his commentary on the *Lalitāsahasranāma*, where he draws from many different sources, offers practically the same exposition of the emanation of sound (*LSN*, 132, pp. 98-99).

In our description, we have totally left aside dualistic Śaivism: that of the Āgamas or of Śrīkaṇṭha, whose theories are at variance on several points with those of the nondualistic works studied here. For the *Ratnatraya* of Śrīkaṇṭha, for instance, emanation originates from the primal *bindu*, known as *paranāda*, from which arise successively *nāda*, *bindu*, and the phonemes (*RT*, 22). The primal *bindu* resides within Śiva, and together with him and Śakti it forms the three jewels: *ratnatraya*. *Nāda*, which comes from it, corresponds to the subtle state (*sūkṣma*) of Speech, namely to what the Trika calls *parāvāc*. *Bindu*, termed *akṣarabindu*—because all the phonemes are there in the primeval state of undifferentiation, like the colors of the peacock's feathers within the egg of that bird: *mayūrāṇḍarasavat* (Aghoraśiva's comm.)—corresponds to *paśyantī*. Next come the manifested and differentiated phonemes. A brief summary of the theories of these schools will be found in Ruegg, *op. cit.* above, p. 97, n. 32, pp. 101ff., and somewhat more extensively in K. C. Pandey's introduction to his translation of Abhinavagupta's *ĪPV: Bhāskarī*, vol. 3, pp. lxviff.

Rāmakaṇṭha's *Nādakārikā*, a Kashmirian text, whose doctrine is that of dualistic Śaivism, offers an original theory on *nāda:* arising from the primal *bindu*, *nāda* plays, with regard to knowledge, a role similar to that of the *sphoṭa* for the grammarians (or in much the same way, to that of *paśyantī* and *madhyamā* for the Trika): this *nāda*, the support for the "inner word" and the meaning, is that which enables the intellect to grasp what is meant (*NK*, *śl.* 10-13, pp. 8-9).

101. *PST* 1.44 (p. 17):

bindos tasmād bhidyamānād ravo 'vyaktātmako bhavet/
sa ravaḥ śrutisampannaiḥ śabdabrahmeti kathyate//

102. *caitanyaṃ sarvabhūtānām* (*ŚT* 1.13).

This term is not used very frequently in Tantric Śaivism. And when it occurs it does not indicate (as for example in Bhartṛhari[103] and Puṇyarāja) the ultimate reality as sound, the first principle, but something lesser. We just saw that this holds true in the *ŚT* and the *PST*. The *NT*, when applying this term to *nāda*,[104] places it therefore at the level of *sadāśiva*, precisely where *śabdabrahman* appears in the *ŚT*. For Bhartṛhari, as is well known, the supreme level of Speech is *paśyantī*; now, nondualistic Kashmirian Śaivism has, with Somānanda, positively refuted this view: for him, *paśyantī*, being already affected by differentiation in its early stage, is by no means the supreme level of Speech;[105] it is placed at the level of *sadāśiva*, that is, precisely where *śabdabrahman* has just been found to appear.

This being so, *śabdabrahman* appears as a very high sound-form with *nāda* and *bindu* for substance, as the root cause of the phonemes, yet prior to them, an unmanifest, "unstruck" (*anāhata*), and therefore inaudible sound. It is, according to Rāghavabhaṭṭa,[106] the first coming forth (*prathamollāsa*) of the supreme Śiva when he becomes intent on creation. The *ŚT* (and Rāghavabhaṭṭa) maintain that it should not be confused with empirical speech or with the senses or objects (*artha*) connected with it, for it is of a much higher nature, sharing in the nature of Śiva.

With all these characteristics *śabdabrahman* is yet a lower form of sound-energy than those existing prior to the division

---

103. Cf. *VP* 1.1: *anādinidhanaṃ brahma śabdatattvaṃ yad akṣaraṃ*. For the Upaniṣads, see for instance the *MaitriUp.* 6.22, for which *śabdabrahman* is the supreme, and is identified with *oṃ*. The Upaniṣad also mentions seven audible forms of *śabda*, which may be perceived "in the heart" when the ears are stopped; (these are yogic speculations similar to those mentioned above, p. 97, n. 31, with respect to *nāda*). Beyond these sounds, which have distinct characteristics, the *Maitri* places the unmanifest *brahman*, the supreme sound. However, it subordinates *śabdabrahman* to *parabrahman*, for the latter, it says, is attained through awareness of the former: *śabdabrahmaṇi niṣṇātaḥ paraṃ brahmādhigacchati*.
104. Cf. *supra* p. 99, n. 31.
105. Cf. chap. 4, pp. 191-93.
106. *ŚT* 1.12-13, comm. (vol. 1, pp. 19-20).

of *bindu.* This is evidenced by the term *rava*, by which it is defined and which, while here by no means taken in the early sense of the root *RU*, to roar, to rumble, however denotes more clearly than *nāda* a sound, a humming; whereas *nāda*, used almost down to the level of *bindu*, is nothing but the resonance which follows a sound. *Rava* qualifies the rather abstract term *śabdabrahman*, to which it gives, one could say, a more concrete, nearly audible[107] character.

This *śabdabrahman*, whose phonic energy gives life to all living creatures, assumes, according to the *ŚT*,[108] the aspect of the *kuṇḍalinī*, the energy lying at the center of the body in all animate beings, and which appears then in the form of the phonemes, giving rise to the manifest, audible, and intelligible sound, of which empirical speech is made. Thus we come, through the agency of the *kuṇḍalinī*, to the "gross" sound, and thereby to the increasingly lower stages of manifestation: gods, elements, and so forth, down to the earthly and inanimate world.

This arising of the phonemes in relation to the awakening of the *kuṇḍalinī* is what must next be examined.

Kuṇḍalinī

The form of power called the *kuṇḍalinī*, "the coiled one"—for she is compared to a serpent which, while at rest, lies curled up, and which, when awakened, rises—plays a part of paramount importance in Yoga and Tantrism. She is the cosmic energy, the divine creative impetus, present in and giving life to the human body. When awakened through appropriate

---

107. In the *VBh*, 38, *śabdabrahman* is the "unstruck," unbroken, sound moving as swift as a river and located in the receptacle of the ear, which the yogin can perceive under certain conditions, and which enables him to gain access to the supreme *brahman;* this is in agreement with the doctrine of the *MaitriUp*. (cf. above footnote 103).

108. *ŚT* 1.14 (p. 20):

tat prāpya kuṇḍalinīrūpaṃ prāṇināṃ dehamadhyagam/
varṇātmanā 'virbhavati gadyapadyādibheditaḥ//

practices, she brings the yogin to the state of liberation by uniting the individualized energy and consciousness with the universal consciousness.

The *kuṇḍalinī*, as a latent energy lying coiled up at the base of the spine in the *mūlādhāra* (the "basic support"), which, when awakened, rises up the median canal, the *suṣumnā nāḍī*, and forces its way step by step through the different centers (*cakra*s—"wheels" or "circles") of the subtle body, situated one above the other along the spine and in the brain, up to the ultimate one, the *sahasrāra* ("thousand-petalled"), and sometimes even beyond, is part of an ancient "mystical physiology," wherein arteries (*nāḍī*s), breaths or winds (*prāṇa*s), *cakra*s, *ādhāra*s, *sthāna*s, and other centers, "places," or "supports" play a central part. The origins of the *kuṇḍalinī* are probably to be found in cosmogonic notions (the cosmic serpent), and in the idea—also very ancient and related to the cosmogonic symbolism (to be found outside India as well)—according to which the soul's progress results from an ascendant movement, as also in the conception of the body as a replica of the cosmic pattern.[109] This being so, the *kuṇḍalinī* has an essential symbolic role—as an energy that is both universal and present within human beings—in the correspondences between the human and the cosmic levels. Tantrism asserts this again and again, and the purpose of its teaching and practices is precisely to enable the adept to realize it. The adept, indeed, when he awakens his *kuṇḍalinī* and is able to follow her movement, repeats within himself the various phases of cosmic emanation and resorption.[110] It may therefore be said that the arousal of the *kuṇḍalinī* (as well as her becoming dormant) always takes place at two levels simultaneously: cosmic and human. It seems necessary, however, to distinguish between two movements of the *kuṇḍalinī*: one where the cosmic and emanative aspect is

109. We have seen in chap. 1 (pp. 23ff.) that these concepts were of very ancient origin.

110. For the *kuṇḍalinī* one may refer especially to A. Avalon, *The Serpent Power, Being the Shat-Chakra-Nirupana & Paduka-Panchaka, Two Works on Laya-Yoga* (5th edition; Madras: Ganesh & Co., 1953), with its extensive introduction (315 pages).

predominant, and another where the human and resorption aspect predominates.

First occurs the movement that brings the universe into existence, that of the supreme *kuṇḍalinī* (*parakuṇḍalinī*). It is the same movement as that of the process of emanation, from Śiva downward, of the universal phonic energy. We just saw this process going from *śakti* to *bindu.* After *bindu*, it pursues its emanative course downward so as to bring the manifestation of the universe to completion. An analogous movement takes place within every human being where occurs a spontaneous ascent of the *kuṇḍalinī*, generally unnoticed by the subject, as a result of which every human being is endowed with not only the faculty of speech, but also with all the four levels of Speech and sound—of which however he remains unaware but which are always there since these levels are the underlying basis of human language. Owing to this spontaneous movement of the *kuṇḍalinī*, all the stages—even the higher ones—of the phonic energy are present in the human body, which is a true microcosm. At its every stage this movement is spontaneous and universal, since it is the unfolding of the emanation.

But there is also an ascent of the *kuṇḍalinī* that results from a deliberate endeavor. Such an ascent takes place in the yogin who seeks liberation. The movement of the *kuṇḍalinī*, which is then consciously perceived, now brings about a gradual removal of the obstacles to liberation due to human nature. No longer a universal movement, it is suited to each seeker. However, because of the micro-macrocosmic correspondences, this movement is analogous with the cosmic process—that of resorption—and has thus a cosmic aspect as well.[111]

In this chapter only one movement of the *kuṇḍalinī* will be considered, that of emanation. One might add, however,

111. A similar process, which includes the rising of the *kuṇḍalinī* from the *mūlādhāra* to the *brahmarandhra* or to the *dvādaśānta*, is *bhūtaśuddhi*, a ritual process preceding the *pūjā*, where the elements and the *tattva*s making up the physical and subtle bodies dissolve within each other up to the highest one. Cf. *SP*, 1, pp. 104-07, *AjitĀ.*, 1.20.51ff., or in the *Pāñcarātra*, *LT*, chaps. 35 and 54.

that such a movement—although usually spontaneous and universal, since it is through its agency that emanation starts and reaches completion—can also be consciously repeated and experienced by the adept who, in this way, will experience the cosmic process of emanation. In both cases the human and cosmic levels are constantly not only analogous, but also correlated and experienced as such by the adept. We have here an indivisible whole.

The *Śāradā Tilaka*—turning now once again to the passage already used on several occasions as a convenient guide to this description—states, as we have seen, that with the division of *bindu* the phonic energy assumes the form of *śabdabrahman*. Out of this same *bindu* the energy acting through the *kalā*s—those forms of energy functioning as a dividing, limiting power[112]—brings forth the *sadāśiva tattva*, and then the rest of the *tattva*s and the manifestation.[113] The phonic energy is of course present in this creation since it is the creative energy itself: phonic energy, says the *ŚT*, is "the *kuṇḍalinī* dwelling in the center of the body in all animate beings,"[114] and it is also the supreme cosmic energy.

That the phonic energy may be termed *kuṇḍalinī* right from the highest, transcendent stage is clearly apparent in a passage of Jayaratha's commentary on the *TĀ*, where he describes movements of the *kuṇḍalinī* resulting in the written shape of the letter *a* in the *devanāgarī* script.[115] Now *a*, in the phonematic emanation as described in the third chapter of the *TĀ*, is the highest level of Śiva's energy. On this occasion Jayaratha quotes a passage from the *Tantrasadbhāva* which sums up the evolution of the phonic energy, viewed as *kuṇḍalinī*-

112. Cf. *supra*, pp. 89-91.
113. *ŚT* 1.15-25.
114. Ibid., 14; cf. *supra*, n. 108.
115. *TĀ* 3.67 (vol. 2, p. 77). This passage, with my comments, will be found in chap. 5, here p. 241-43, and pp. 73-74 in L. Silburn's edition of the *VS*, where she also gives the pictorial representation of the letter *a*. While drawing this letter, the *kuṇḍalinī* brings forth from *anuttara* the three powers of will, cognition, and action, and from Ambikā the three goddesses Vāmā, Jyeṣṭhā, and Raudrī, whom we have seen (*supra*, pp. 116ff.), when arising from the division of *bindu*.

śakti, from the emergence of this energy down to empirical speech. This passage[116] deserves to be quoted in full. It reads as follows:

> This energy is called supreme, subtle, transcending all norm or practice (*nirācāra*). Enclosing within herself the *bindu* of the heart,[117] her aspect is that of a snake lying in deep sleep. Sleeping there, O Illustrious Goddess, she is not conscious of anything, O Umā! Having cast within her womb the moon, the fire, the sun, the planets and the fourteen worlds,[118] this goddess becomes as if made senseless by poison. Then, O Fair One, she is awakened by the supreme sound[119] whose nature is knowledge, being churned[120] by the *bindu* resting in her womb. This whirling

---

116. It is also quoted, more extensively, by Kṣemarāja in his commentary upon the *Śivasūtra* (*ŚSV* 2.3, pp. 52-54). This is the text we have translated here. The commentator on the *Kāmakalāvilāsa* (*KKV*, 27) also quotes it, but with some variants. The *Tantrasadbhāva* is known to us only through quotations. Cf. above, p. 64.
117. This is Śiva. The "heart" is, for the Trika, the resting place of the Lord, the flashing forth of consciousness prior to all manifestation; cf. *ĪPV*, 1.5.14, where the "heart," moreover, is assimilated with *parāvāc*, the source and foundation of the power of Speech. For the "heart," cf. also *PTV*, pp. 61 and 86-88, and also the *PTLv*, on which see P. Muller-Ortega's study, *The Triadic Heart of Śiva* (Albany: SUNY Press, 1988).
118. The fourteen "worlds" are infernal, terrestrial, and celestial. Their list is given in the *MVT* (5.1-9, p. 27). The text may also refer here to the first fourteen phonemes, from *a* to *au*, which precede *bindu*. But whatever the fourteen elements may be, they express the cosmic manifestation as a whole, held up within the energy prior to its being projected outside. The term *bhuvana*—although the number of *bhuvana*s varies according to different classifications (extending to 224)—is sometimes used to indicate the number fourteen; see, for instance, *KKV*, 43.
119. *Ninādа:* sound or resonance. This is a first, infinitely subtle stirring of sound, the initial movement of the phonic energy.
120. *Mathitā*. The root *MATH* or *MANTH* means to stir or whirl around, to rub or cause friction, a movement such as the rotation of one stick on another (*araṇi*) to produce fire by friction. (It is an ancient notion; cf. *RV* 3.29.) It is therefore understandable that sparks can be produced in this way. The term also denotes churning, as well as the movement of sexual union: it indicates any recurring and generative movement. *Bindu* is Śiva; by uniting with Śakti, he arouses her and thus the manifestation is brought into existence.

churning goes on moving in the body of Śakti and this cleaving [in herself] results first in very brillant light-drops (*bindu*). Awakened by this [luminous throbbing], the subtle force (*kalā*), Kuṇḍalī, is aroused. The sovereign *bindu* (Śiva), who is in the womb of Śakti, is possessed of a fourfold force (*kalā*).[121] By the union of the Churner and of She that is being churned[122] this [Kuṇḍalinī] becomes straight. This [Śakti], when she abides between two *bindus*, is called Jyeṣṭhā. Being agitated by the *bindu*, this straightened *amṛtakuṇḍalī* is then known as Rekhinī, having a *bindu* at each of her two ends. She is also known as Tripathā ("the threefold path") and is celebrated under the name of Raudrī. She is [also] called Rodhinī because she obstructs the path to liberation. Ambikā, whose shape is that of the crescent moon, is the "half moon" (*ardhacandrikā*).[123] The supreme Śakti, who is one, thus assumes three forms.

Through the conjunction and disjunction of these [energies], all nine classes of phonemes[124] are produced. She is called ninefold when considered as made up of these nine classes. When, O Goddess, she resides successively in the five mantras, *sadya* etc.,[125] she is called fivefold, O Mistress of all gods! Staying in the twelve vowels,[126] she is called twelvefold. Divided in fifty, she abides in [all] the phonemes from *a* to *kṣa*.

In the heart, she is said to be of one atom. In the throat she is of two atoms. She is known as being of three atoms when

---

121. This limiting fourfold power appears in the energy with the arising of the divine energies, Ambikā, Jyeṣṭhā, and the others. On this subject, see Bhāskara's commentary (*Vārttika*) on *Śivasūtra* 1.3 (*ŚSVrt.*, p. 6-7).
122. That is, Śiva and Śakti.
123. This passage describes the movements of the *kuṇḍalinī* that bring about the written form of the letter *a*; cf. preceding page and chap. 5, p. 242.
124. The nine classes (*varga*) are those where the fifty phonemes are arranged in their traditional serial order: sixteen "vowels," five groups of consonants, the semivowels, the fricatives, and *kṣa*; cf. *infra*, p. 154-55.
125. The mantras *sadyojāta, vāmadeva, aghora, tatpuruṣa*, and *īśāna*, which correspond to the five faces of Śivabhairava. For these mantras, cf. *PTV*, *śl.* 26, pp. 161-63, and more especially *SvT* 1.45-58. A Śaiva Upaniṣad, the *Pañcabrahmopaniṣad*, is devoted to these five mantras, which are sometimes called the five "*brahmans*" (*pañcabrahman*) or Brahmamantras.
126. That is, the sixteen "vowels," from *a* to *visarga*, minus the four "barren" phonemes (*ṣaṇḍhavarṇa*): *ṛ, ṝ, ḷ, ḹ*; on this point, cf. chap. 5, p. 262.

permanently abiding on the tip of the tongue:[127] without any doubt, the birth of the phonemes is accomplished at the tip of the tongue. In this way is described the going forth of the sound (*śabda*) by which the [whole universe] moving and unmoving is pervaded.

"This passage," adds Kṣemarāja in his *Vimarśinī*, "shows that the nature of the energy of the phonemes (*mātṛkā*) is none other than that of the supreme Word (*parāvākśakti*) of the supreme Bhairava, and it establishes that the birth of all the phonemes is due to the diversity resulting from the expansion of the energies called Jyeṣṭhā, Raudrī, and Ambikā".[128] We

---

127. At the heart level the phonic energy is that of *paśyantī;* it is said to be of one atom only because no division occurs there. At the throat level is *madhyamā*, where the dichotomy expressive/expressed is established, hence two atoms. In the *cakra* of the palate is *vaikharī*, empirical speech born of three elements: the organ of phonation, the utterance of the phonemes, and the effort to produce sound, hence three atoms. For the *kuṇḍalinī* and the levels of Speech, see the following pages. *Jihvāgra*, the tip of the tongue, is the place of articulation of the cerebrals.

128. *ŚSV* 2.3 (pp. 52-55):

yā sā śaktiḥ parā sūkṣmā nirācāreti kīrtitā//
hṛdbinduṃ viṣṭayitvāntaḥ suṣuptabhujagākṛtiḥ/
tatra suptā mahābhāge na kiñcin manyate ume//
candrāgniravinakṣatrair bhuvanāni caturdaśa/
kṣiptvodare tu yā devī viṣamūḍheva sā gatā/
prabuddhā sā ninādena pareṇa jñānarūpiṇā/
mathitā codarasthena vindunā varavarṇini//
tāvad vai brahmavegena mathanaṃ śaktivigrahe/
bhedāt tu prathamotpannā vindavas te 'tivarcasaḥ//
utthitā tu yadā tena kalā sūkṣmā tu kuṇḍalī/
catuṣkalamayo vinduḥ śakter udaragaḥ prabhuḥ//
mathyamanthanayogena ṛjutvaṃ jāyate priye/
jyeṣṭhāśaktiḥ smṛtā sā tu vindudvayasumadhyagā//
bindunā kṣobhamāyātā rekhaivāmṛtakuṇḍalī/
rekhiṇī nāma sā jñeyā ubhau bindū yadantagau//
tripathā sā samākhyātā raudrī nāmnā tu gīyate/
rodhinī sā samuddiṣṭā mokṣamārganirodhanāt//
śaśāṅkaśakalākārā ambikā cārdhacandrikā/
ekaivetthaṃ parā śaktis tridhā sā tu prajāyate//
ābhyo yuktaviyuktābhyaḥ saṃjāto navavargakaḥ/
navadhā ca smṛtā sā tu navavargopalakṣitā//

have thus followed the movement of the phonic energy in its highest form, that of the supreme energy *kuṇḍalinī*, first motionless, united with Śiva, the *bindu*; then arousing with the emergence of the primal sound vibration, which generates the division of *bindu* and the limiting power of the *kalā*s, then the three powers that go by various names, and thence the phonemes; the exposition closing with the fundamental notion that the whole universe is pervaded (*vyāpta*)[129] by sound.[130]

The description of the role of the *kuṇḍalinī* in the *ŚT* agrees completely with what we have just seen, while also further

---

pañcamantragatā devi sadyādir anukramāt/
tena pañcavidhā proktā jñātavyā suranāyike//
svaradvādaśagā devi dvādaśasthā udāhṛtā/
akārādikṣakārāntā sthitā pañcaśatā bhidā//
hṛtsthā ekāṇavā proktā kaṇṭhe proktā dvitīyakā/
trirāṇavā tu jñātavyā jihvamūle sadā sthitā//
jihvāgre varṇaniṣpattir bhavaty atra na saṃśayaḥ/
evaṃ śabdasya niṣpattiḥ śabdavyāptaṃ carācaraṃ//

ity ādinā granthena parabhairavīyaparāvākśaktyātmakamātṛkā, ata eva jyeṣṭhāraudryambikākhyaśaktiprasarasaṃbhedavaicitryeṇa sarvavarṇodayasya uktatvāt.

129. Cf. *supra*, p. 103, n. 51.

130. There is a very similar description of the role of the *kuṇḍalinī* as phonic energy in the *ABS* (16.54ff., pp. 150ff.). According to this *saṃhitā*, Viṣṇu's primal energy, which is *kuṇḍalinī*, in its unfolding, brings forth the manifestation. She is the power of action, the great Being (*mahāsattā*), unutterable (*anākhya*). Being in the nature of *śabda* and wishing to express herself, she evolves to the emanative state. Creation is the flow (*sarga*) which she emits. She thus rises from the *mūlādhāra*, at first pure, spotless (*nirañjana*); and then, as *samskāra*s progressively appear, she evolves and assumes the twin aspects of speech and objects (*śabda* and *artha*). In the region of the navel she produces *paśyantī;* then, in that of the heart, *madhyamā*, where exists the duality of expressive/expressed; lastly, in the throat, all the phonemes are actually produced.

This description of how speech and then objects appear may show an influence of Śaiva ideas on the *ABS*. The origin of such notions is, however, ancient (cf. the passage in the *Maitri Up.* quoted previously, chap. 1, p. 26ff). The similarities of the description of the *Tantrasadbhāva* as quoted by Kṣemarāja and J. and of that of the *ABS* are nevertheless quite remarkable.

elaborating on some of its aspects. This supreme energy, it says, is verily the omnipresent consciousness assuming the form of the universe. One with Śiva, beyond space and time, she is present in her pristine purity within all beings and is therefore both supreme and nonsupreme. Especially present in the heart of yogins, she is also present, eternally, in the entire universe where she lies coiled up inside the *mūlādhāra* of all living creatures, dazzling like a flash of lightning. Folded upon herself, this Goddess is Kuṇḍalinī, the Coiled One, serpent-like, holding within herself all the gods, all the mantras, all the *tattvas*. All-pervading, more subtle than the subtle, she generates the triadic energy of moon, sun, and fire. Made up of sound, she assumes the form of the forty-two phonemes of the *bhūtalipi* as well as that of the fifty phonemes of the *mātṛkā.* Supreme Goddess, all-pervading, she is the creative energy immanent to the universe (of a universe, it should be noted, which is itself *mantramayam*, "made of mantra," that is, whose deepest nature is that of the Word).[131]

It is to be noted that like the *Tantrasadbhāva*, this text underlines the twin aspects, cosmic and microcosmic, of the *kuṇḍalinī*, and that it shifts from one aspect to the other without any transition. While it distinguishes both aspects of the *kuṇḍalinī*, it stresses at the same time that the energy dwelling within human beings is the energy of the cosmos itself; thus

131. *ŚT* 1.51-57 (vol. 1, pp. 43-45):

tataś caitanyarūpā sā sarvagā viśvarūpiṇī/
śivasannidhim āsādya nityānandaguṇodayā//
dikkālādyanavacchinnā sarvadehānugā śubhā/
parāparavibhāgena paraśaktir iyaṃ smṛtā//
yogināṃ hṛdayāṃbhoje nṛtyantau nityam añjasā/
ādhāre sarvabhūtānāṃ sphurantī vidyudākṛtiḥ//
śaṅkhāvarttakramād devī sarvam āvṛtya tiṣṭhati/
kuṇḍalībhūtā sarpāṇām aṅgaśriyam upeyuṣi//
sarvadevamayī devī sarvamantramayī śivā/
sarvatattvamayī sākṣāt sūkṣmāt sūkṣmatarā vibhuḥ/
tridhāmajananī devī śabdabrahmasvarūpiṇī/
dvicatvariṃśadvarṇātmā pañcaśadvarṇarūpiṇī/
guṇitā sarvagātreṣu kuṇḍalī paradevatā/
viśvātmanā prabuddhā sā sūte mantramayaṃ jagat//

the awakening of the phonemes it describes may be that which endows human beings with speech as well as that which brings the universe into existence. This coalescence of the two aspects appears, for instance, when the *ŚT* says that the *kuṇḍalinī*, depending upon the characteristics it assumes, creates all the gods, the mantras, the *bīja*s and the *tattva*s, and then adds that she dwells in the *mūlādhāra*, therefore within human beings,[132] and that, identified with the subtle energy of the phonemes, she is immanent to the universe, therefore playing a cosmic role.[133]

The same ambiguity continues as the text goes on: "This *kuṇḍalinī*," it says later, "all-pervading, made of *śabdabrahman*, generates *śakti*, then *dhvani*, out of which proceeds *nāda*, out of which comes *nirodhikā*; from the latter come *ardhendu*, then *bindu*, then the [four] levels of Speech: *parā*, *paśyantī*, *madhyamā*, and *vaikharī*, the stage where language is produced. She is made of [the three powers] of will, cognition, and action, effulgent, endowed with the properties of created things (*guṇātmikā*). Through this process *kuṇḍalī* creates the garland of letters divided into forty-two,[134] ranging from *a* to *sa*, and when she divides into fifty, the garland of the fifty phonemes, and with these phonemes, being undifferentiated [but animated with] a limiting force, she brings forth in succession [the gods such as] Rudra and the others [and the rest of the cosmos]."[135]

---

132. But this may as well be taken as: at the source of the manifestation: *infra*, p. 135, n. 137.
133. Ibid., *śl.* 58-108 (46-59).
134. The *bhūtalipi*; cf. *infra*, p. 149, n. 174.
135. *ŚT* 1.108-11 (vol. 1, pp. 59-61):

sā prasūte kuṇḍalinī śabdabrahmamayī vibhuḥ/
śaktiṃ tato dhvanis tasmān nādas tasmān nirodhikā//
tato 'rdhendus tato bindus tasmād āsīt parā tataḥ/
paśyantī madhyamā vāci vaikharī śabdajanmabhūḥ/
icchājñānakriyātmanā 'sau tejorūpā guṇātmikā//
krameṇānena sṛjati kuṇḍalī varṇamālikām/
akārādisakārāntāṃ dvicatvariṃśadātmikām//
pañcaśadvāraguṇitā pañcaśadvarṇamālikām/
sūte tadvarṇato 'bhinnā kalā rudrādikān kramāt//

In this passage the *kuṇḍalinī* is seen to go again (with but one variant: *dhvani* instead of *nādānta*) through the stages of the emanation of the sound energy, from *śakti* to *bindu.* Now these have already been produced. Therefore what is considered here cannot be but the repetition of these stages by the *kuṇḍalinī* at the microcosmic level: it is the continuation in a human being of the emanative movement, which endows him with all the levels of the phonic energy, which, however, is both human and cosmic; and indeed the passage ends with the creation of the gods, that is, with a cosmic process which may be reenacted by the adept if he has the capacity, thus bringing the human being and the universe at one.

This being so, we will now try to see in further details the last stages of the phonic emanation in relation to the awakening of the *kuṇḍalinī*, through which, on both the human and the cosmic levels, will be manifested the stages of Speech and the whole collection of the phonemes.

The evolution from *śiva-śakti* down to the division of *bindu* and the emergence of *śabdabrahman*, which may be looked at as the cosmic evolution of the supreme *kuṇḍalinī*, brings the phonic energy to a state where, as we have seen, it divides into a series of triads. At this juncture the *kuṇḍalinī* within a person lies in the lower *cakra*, the *mūlādhāra*, located at the base of the spinal column. There she lies dormant, a static energy, curled around the *śivabindu;* there she awakens through the agency of this same *bindu*;[136] and thence she stretches out and rises along the central channel, the *suṣumnā*, in order to reach the other "wheels."

As we have seen, *bindu*, which is *śiva* and *śakti*, divided into three and produced the triangle *kāmakalā*. When the same process is looked at with respect to the *kuṇḍalinī*, she is

136. In this respect, the seven stages, from *śakti* to *bindu*, enumerated in the passage of the *ŚT* quoted previously, may be regarded as taking place in the *mūlādhāra*. In this case the division of *bindu* into three is the triangle in which it is enclosed. The *kuṇḍalinī* goes beyond the *mūlādhāra* only with *paśyantī vāc*.

represented similarly as being united with Śiva, at the center of a triangle. From the standpoint of the stages of Speech, we are there in the *mūlādhāra*, at the level of the supreme Word (*parāvāc*),[137] who holds within herself, in the primeval state of undifferentiation, the archetype of the whole cosmos, and therefore also the essence of all the phonemes.[138] *Parāvāc* exists,

---

137. Cf. *PST* 2.42 (vol. 1, p. 33): "The state (of Speech) which arises first from the *mūlādhāra* is known as *parā*." Or: "The highest resonance known as *parā* [*vāc*] arises in the *mūlādhāra*; it is made of "breath" (*prāṇa*) and of wind (*vāyu*); it exists when the power of will is not yet in existence" (*Kādimatatantra*, quoted by Rāghavabhaṭṭa in his commentary on the *ŚT* 1.109, vol. 1, p. 60). We should note the use of the term *nāda* to indicate *parāvāc* and the presence of "breath" right from this level.

The commentary on this *śloka* from the *PST* states that the *mūlādhāra* is the receptacle (*ādhāra*) made of pure consciousness (*cit*) of the illusion which is at the root (*mūla*) of the universe. At this level there is no vibration whatsoever (*niḥspanda*). Those are characteristics of *parāvāc* (cf. chap. 4, pp. 172ff.).

138. In the Yoga scriptures and in various Tantras the *cakra*s are represented with phonemes written on the petals of the lotuses which form these "wheels." The *mūlādhāra*, in such a case, has four petals, usually with the letters *sa*, *ṣa*, *śa*, and *va* upon them. The next wheel has six, and so forth up to the *ājñācakra*, with two petals only. Thus all the fifty phonemes are in the lotuses.

In fact this allotment of phonemes to the *cakra*s differs from text to text, if only because these do not always admit the same number of *cakra*s. However, the principle remains that there is a link between the phonemes and the centers acknowledged by yogic physiology, and this will account for a particular *bījamantra* supposedly affecting particular centers, thus being instrumental in bringing about the ascent of the *kuṇḍalinī*. We do not deal in this chapter with all of this material, despite its great practical import, because it concerns the conscious rising of the *kuṇḍalinī*, that is, cosmic resorption, and not the cosmic manifestation we are studying here. In this yogic ascent of the *kuṇḍalinī*, the four phonemes of the *mūlādhāra* stand for the gross elements, which are first to be dissolved, and so forth up to the highest *tattva*s, in the *ājñācakra*. Then all the phonemes will reappear in the *sahasrāra* (multiplied by twenty, according to some texts, so that there are as many phonemes as petals) from *a* to *kṣa*, and no longer in the reversed order. The *sahasrāra cakra* thus contains the pure energy prior to the resorption, identical to the energy which lies at the center of the *mūlādhāra*. This process is identical to the cosmic one with which we deal here, but in the reversed order.

only at a much earlier and higher level than the plane where humans live. This particular stage is therefore primarily cosmic. And yet it is also within each individual, in the *mūlādhāra*, for, *parāvāc* being the root of the other levels of Speech, were human beings not endowed with this level neither would they be endowed with the others.[139]

Issuing from the *mūlādhāra*, the *kuṇḍalinī* then flows up within the *suṣumṇā* and reaches the other *cakras*. She is self-propelled, as the sound vibration produced by the division of *bindu*, identical with *śabdabrahman*, keeps on evolving spontaneously at the human and cosmic levels. This sound energy or energy of Speech is regarded as partaking of the nature of "breath" (*prāṇa*). *Prāṇa*, indeed, when taken in its more general meaning, is the vital energy and the life-force of animate beings.[140] At the cosmic level it is the movement of conscious-

---

The particulars of this subtle pattern and of the phonic stages that fit into it vary from text to text, but the general structure and the spirit always remain the same and are to be found in all the texts of Kuṇḍalinī-yoga.

The phonemes forming a triangle around the *kuṇḍalinī* in the *mūlādhāra* are sometimes described as forming a triangle called *akatha*, a triangular line with its three sides supposedly formed by the letters *a* to *aḥ*, *ka* to *ta*, and *tha* to *sa* (hence its name), to which are added, in the angles, *ha*, *kṣa*, and the "Vedic" *ḷ* (ळ), which makes fifty-one. Generally situated in one of the higher *cakra*s of the subtle body, and notably in the center of the *sahasrāra*, pierced by the *kuṇḍalinī*, this triangle is described in various texts, notably, as it seems, in those related to the Kula. It is found in the *YH* 2.63, in the *Pādukāpañcaka, śl.* 2—whose commentary mentions in this connection the *Kālīkulāmnāya* and *Svatantratantra.* The three divine energies Vāmā, Jyeṣṭhā, and Raudrī are on the three lines of this triangle, which, defined by three *bindu*s, is identified by this commentary on the *Pādukāpañcaka* with the *kāmakalā* (*kāmakalārūpam*).

139. Cf. chap. 4, pp. 178ff.

140. *Prāṇa*, taken in its restricted sense, is the ascendant breath (flowing through the *iḍā* channel). It is one of the five vital airs, or winds, which give life to the body. In addition to *prāṇa* are *apāna*, the descendant breath, which flows through the *piṅgalā* channel; *udāna*, which is also an ascendant breath but produced through the union of the former two and flowing through the *suṣumṇā* channel; and finally *samāna* and *vyāna*, two breaths flowing through and infusing life into the body. The

ness that brings forth the universe.[141] Since the term *prāṇa* indicates also that breathing which, empirically, helps to produce the phonemes, it will be taken metaphysically as the cause of their emergence.[142]

Such is the meaning, for instance, of the *Svacchanda Tantra* when it states that the soul of phonemes is sound (*śabda*), which

---

precise meaning of these terms is not the same in all schools and traditions. For their meaning in traditional medicine, see J. Filliozat's contribution to *L'Inde classique*, 1622, 1652, and 1672 (on yogic physiology).

These breaths are sometimes held as corresponding both to aspects of the manifestation and to states of consciousness of the yogin whose meditation identifies him with these various levels of the manifestation. Abhinavagupta writes about this in the fifth chapter (part 2, dealing with *uccāra*) of the *TS* (pp. 38-39) as follows:

"When one wants to emit breath (*prāṇam uccicārayiṣuḥ*), he first rests in the void in the heart. Then he does the same outside with the ascending breath (*prāṇa*). Then, with the moon becoming full, that is, with the descending breath (*apāna*), he sees himself identified with the whole external world and thus becomes indifferent to everything. When, thereafter, the equalizing breath (*samāna*) appears, he experiences a rest (*viśrānti*) in the friction and fusion [of the whole manifestation]. When the fire of the ascending breath (*udāna*) appears, all distinctions between knower, known, and so forth, are devoured. Finally, when the pervading breath (*vyāna*) comes and this devouring fire subsides, he shines, free of all limitations. We are taught that these [six] reposes (*viśrānti*), from that in the void to the pervading breath, are called the six lands of felicity (*ṣaṭ ānandabhu*): *nijānanda, nirānanda, parānanda, brahmānanda, mahānanda*, and *cidānanda*."

141. See, for instance, the beginning of chapter 6 of the *TĀ*, according to which consciousness takes on the form of *prāṇa* in order to bring forth the universe (*śl.* 8). It is the energy of this breath—which is primal vibration (*spanda*), pulsating radiance (*sphurattā*)—which, when the wish toward creative effort arises, radiates within the heart of all living creatures and makes them conscious (*śl.* 13-14).

142. This identification of phonic energy and breath is not surprising. As we have seen, the older speculations about the breaths are much earlier than the texts which, later on, organized the cosmogony of Speech into a system. It did not take long for phonetics—namely, the description of how breath affects the speech organs—and cosmogony to become mixed: we shall see them again and again further in this book either being intermingled or leading to each other.

is produced by breath (*prāṇa*), which, in turn, gives life to the phonemes.[143] The same text, in another passage, when enumerating the ten arteries (*nāḍī*s) and the ten breaths flowing through them, mentions three arteries and three breaths as more important than the others. These are the *prāṇa, apāna* and *udāna* breaths, and the *iḍā, piṅgalā*, and *suṣumnā* arteries.[144]

Bhartṛhari quotes as representing the point of view of the Śikṣās a description of the manifestation of Speech where the role of breath is most concrete. Sound (*śabda*), in the text, arises from the subtle level of Speech (*sūkṣmā vāk*), then, on reaching the level of the mind (*manas*) and on being "ripened" by the inner fire, it enters the wind called breath, which lifts it up. This wind, wherein speech resides, is identified with the internal organ and transforms itself into the word. Then, cutting off the knots that are within itself into a variety of audible sounds, this breath eventually manifests all the phonemes and merges into them (*VP* 1.113-16). The description, using concrete elements to such a degree and being imbued with mythic conceptions, looks very awkward when compared to that given in Trika texts.

143. *SvT* 4.248 (vol. 2, p. 156). Kṣemarāja comments that sound (*śabda*) is breath associated with *dhvani*, and out of this *dhvani* the phonemes are produced. When breath, which is made of *śabda*, subsides, the phonemes also vanish.

Here *dhvani* is the sound element that converts the rather abstract form of sound which is *śabda* into phonemes. It will be remembered that, for Patañjali, *dhvani* is that which qualifies *śabda*. This is a variable element (unlike *sphoṭa*) which manifests the word: *dhvaniḥ śabdaguṇaḥ* (*MBh*, vol. 1, p. 181, ed. by Kielhorn). *Dhvani*, as we have seen, may also be viewed as a level of sound corresponding to *nādānta* (cf. above, p. 134). The term is also used at times as meaning *nāda*, as for instance, in *SvT* 6.5, comm.: *haṃso 'nāhatadhvaniḥ* and *supra*, p. 99).

The meanings ascribed to *dhvani* in these Tantric texts (and also by Abhinavagupta when he comments upon such texts, such as the *PTV*, pp. 70 and 189) are utterly different from what it means in the poetic theory of *dhvani* such as formulated by Ānandavardhana in his *Dhvanyāloka*, a meaning also given to it by Abhinavagupta in his aesthetic works, for instance the *Dhvanyālokalocana*. *Dhvani*, in this case, means then the suggested meaning, the unexpressed but essential element evoked through words by the best poets.

144. *SvT* 7.15-20 (vol. 3, pp. 179-81). The same lists of *nāḍī*s and breaths are found, with variants, in most Tantras. Similarly the *ABS* (32, *śl.* 20-30) enumerates fourteen *nāḍī*s, some of which are those of the *SvT*, and ten breaths, which are exactly the same: *prāṇa*, *apāna*, *samāna*,

The importance of these three breaths is due to the fact that the conjunction of the two lateral breaths, the ascendant and the descendant, into a single median and upgoing breath, is what causes the rising of the *kuṇḍalinī:* one sees how energy and breath are equated. The *SvT* further equates *prāṇa* and *bindu*, and *apāna* and *nāda;* so both of these breaths are equated with two important aspects of the phonic energy. The conjunction of the two breaths, corresponding to that of *nāda* and *bindu*, is of the nature of energy: the *kuṇḍalinī*, as we have seen, is the Power itself.[145]

This movement of the breath, which goes on day in and day out within human beings and which gives them life,[146] is the cosmic breath, responsible, at the human and at the universal level as well, for the emergence of the phonemes,[147] those seeds

---

udāna, *vyāna*, *nāga*, *kūrma*, *kṛkara*, *devadatta*, and *dhanañjana*. These breaths are the ten "vital winds" perceived by the yogins, from whom the Tantras borrowed them (cf. *Inde classique*, § 1672).

145. Ibid., *śl.* 19-20. This assimilation of *prāṇa* and *apāna* with *nāda* and *bindu* is also found in the *ŚD* 2.42 (pp. 63-64) and in Jayaratha's commentary on *TĀ* 6.239 (vol. 4, p. 195). It is also held (*SvT* 7.19-20, comm.) that *prāṇa* corresponds to the power of knowledge and *apāna* to that of action. Thus we have a series of polarities harmonized and transcended by a third element:

prāṇa	/ *apāna*→	*udāna*
bindu	/ *nāda*→	*śakti*
sun	/ moon→	fire
knowledge	/ object→	knower

and so forth, which play an important role, notably in the Trika thought. Some aspects of this polarity, or tripartition, will be seen *infra*, pp. 157-59.

146. Ibid., *śl.* 21 (vol. 3, p. 182).

147. Ibid., *śl.* 23, p. 183. See also Abhinavagupta, *TS*, chap. 5, part 3:

"The phoneme is a somehow unmanifest form of sound (*avyaktānukṛtiprāyo dhvaniḥ*) which shines in the rising of the breath (*uccāre*) [we have just seen]. Its nature is mainly that of the seed of emanation and of resorption. By repeated exercise [on it] one enjoys supreme consciousness."

of speech and of the manifestation. This movement of the breath, when looked at in its highest aspect as phonic energy which creates and reabsorbs, is known as *haṃsa.* We should dwell awhile on this term before we proceed with the rising of the *kuṇḍalinī.*

Haṃsa is the migratory bird—the swan, as is usually said—a symbol since the Vedas for the supreme entity,[148] a symbol also for the individual soul, one with *brahman.* As early as the *Katha Up.*, it seems to be somehow identified with breath, going either up or down (ibid., 5.3). This term, rich with symbolic meanings, was to be used again in later texts, notably in the so-called Yoga Upaniṣads as well as in the Tantras, which gave it new meanings. For them it still represents the supreme reality: Śiva. But they also break it up into its two syllables *haṃ* and *sa*, the former associated with drawing in, the latter with breathing out air or vice-versa.[149] Therefore it came to symbolize quite naturally the movement of the breath which gives life to all creatures and, more especially, the supreme reality as giver of life and present in breath, or breath taken as supreme energy.[150] "Śiva," says the *SvT*, "is by his own nature *haṃsa.* The

---

148. *RV* 4.40.5: "*Haṃsa* is the god whose seat is pure sky, space." Cf. *Bāṣkala-mantra Upaniṣad* (24): "The swan, free of care, ancient, walking (straight), this is truly I."

149. Kṣemarāja, in *ŚSV* 3.27 (p. 114), quotes the following *śloka* from the *Dhyānabindu Upaniṣad* (*śl.* 62): "With the letter *sa* [the breath] goes out. With the letter *ha* it goes in. Thus does the living creature utter a continuous vocal prayer (*japa*) with the *haṃsa-haṃsa* mantra." It may be noted that this Upaniṣad as edited (or compiled) by Upaniṣad Brahmayogin (Adyar, 1920), gives the two letters in the reversed order: *ha* for exhalation, *sa* for inhalation, but the principle remains the same. This same *japa* is to be found in the *Haṃsopaniṣad* (10-13) which, like Sāyana, equates *haṃsa* with the mantra *so'ham:* "*Ham,*" says the *Haṃsopaniṣad*, "is the seed (that is, Śiva), and *sa* is the Power (Śakti). *So'ham* is the wedge (*kīlaka*) [of the mantra]." (Here again we have one of those polarities mentioned in the preceding page.) For the *haṃsa japa,* see A. Padoux, "Contributions à l'étude du *mantraśāstra*, III: Le *japa*," *BEFEO*, vol. lxxvi, 1987.

150. Cf. *Haṃsopaniṣad*, where *haṃsa* pervades the bodies of all beings even as fire pervades fuel and oil permeates sesame seeds (5). It is the innermost individual soul identical with the universal soul (*paramahaṃsa*).

dazzling sun is *haṃsa*. The Self is also called *haṃsa*, and breath goes along with *haṃsa*."[151] Kṣemarāja, in his commentary, explaining *haṃsa* as *hāna*, forsaking, and *samādāna*, taking back, says that Śiva, indeed, gives out and takes back the universe in his cosmic activity of emanation and resorption, that the sun gives out and takes back its life-giving warmth, that the Self is in the nature of Śiva, and finally that breath gives and takes back air through respiration, and that it is an aspect of Śiva in the form of his unlimited energy identical with the "unstruck" sound (*anāhata*).[152] This shows that *haṃsa* is not the breath itself but the energy of breath. Later on, precisely, the same text declares that "*haṃsa* can neither be emitted nor held back, it is self-uttered and dwells within the heart of all creatures";[153] Jayaratha, in the *TĀ*,[154] applies this *śloka* to the phoneme *a*, that is, to the highest stage of the phonematic emanation; and Kṣemarāja, in the *SvT*, explains in his commentary that *haṃsa* is the supreme Śiva, that it is the spontaneous sound corresponding to the penetration of breath into the central channel of *suṣumnā*, ceaselessly shining and pulsating, indestructible, eternal, higher than the phonemes, and dwelling in the heart of all living creatures to which it gives life.[155]

"All the *śāstra*s," the *SvT* further says, "are made of sound (*śabda*), and sound is called *haṃsa*."[156] What should be understood thereby, says Kṣemarāja, is that ultimately all that the scriptures are comprised of is the mass or totality of sounds (*śabdarāsī*),[157] that is, the fifty phonemes as present in Śiva.

---

151. *SvT* 7.29 (vol. 3, p. 188): *śivo dharmena haṃsas tu sūryo haṃsaḥ prabhanvitaḥ*, and so forth.
152. *SvT* 6.5, comm. (vol. 3, p. 107, line 2): *haṃso'nāhatadhvanir iti nirṇītam.*
153. *Sv.T* 7.59 (pp. 207-08): *nāsyoccārayitā kaścit pratihantā na vidyate/ svayam uccārate haṃsaḥ prāṇinām urasi sthitaḥ.*
154. *TĀ* 3.67 comm. (vol. 2, p. 76); cf. chap. 5, pp. 000-00.
155. *SvT*, ibid., (p. 208); also *SvT* 4.260 (vol. 2, p. 164).
156. *SvT* 4.341 (vol. 2, p. 215, line 1), *śāstraṃ śabdātmakaṃ sarvaṃ śabdo haṃsaḥ prakīrtitaḥ.*
157. This expression usually indicates, in the Trika, the collection of the fifty phonemes existing as archetypes in the energy united with Śiva; chap. 5, pp. 306ff.

The sound they are comprised of is *haṃsoccāra, uccāra* being, he tells us, in essence an expansion (*sphāra*) experienced by the supreme energy.[158] It is, therefore, the spontaneous creative movement of this energy.

Rising in this way, the *kuṇḍalinī* successively reaches the other *cakra*s. From the *mūlādhāra* she moves up to the *nābhi*, often called *maṇipūra*, the center located in the umbilical region. This is when the second level of the Word arises, the "Visionary," *paśyantī vāc.* At this level the sound vibration becomes more perceptible, without being yet particularized (*sāmānya spanda*). This means that differentiation there begins to dawn, however faintly, and that the phonemes are present, not as differentiated and utterable, but in the form of the energies which generate them and which are inseparable from the overall phonic energy.[159] This state of Speech is equated by the *ST*'s commentary with the state of *bindu* and by the *PST*'s commentary with that of *nāda.* It corresponds to the expansion of the power of will or to the power of cognition,[160] and as such it is sometimes associated with Vāmā,[161] the

158. *SvT* 4.341 (vol. 2, p. 215). Elsewhere in his commentary on the same *paṭala* (*śl.* 257, ibid., pp. 161-62), Kṣemarāja describes *haṃsa* as the self-propelled breath, *nāda.* According to this passage, the supreme energy, which is the supreme *kuṇḍalinī*, holding in herself the universe, shines and pulsates in the form of *varṇakuṇḍalikā*, viz., the *kuṇḍalinī* with all the phonemes, she being *nāda* and *vimarśa*, and manifesting herself in the form of *prāṇakuṇḍalinī*, that is, as life-giving breath, the ascendant and descendant movement of which is *haṃsa.*

Similarly, in *SvT* 6.5, comm. (vol. 3, p. 107), *haṃsa* is described as "unstruck" sound (*anāhatadhvani*), moving by itself, uncreated, the pulsating shining forth of the median breath. Additionally, in ibid., *śl.* 25, comm. (p. 126), *haṃsa* is self-uttered (*svayamuccaradrūpa*), that is, it appears as an impulse of Śiva's energy (animating, in the present case, the *uccāra* of the *praṇava*, which for Kṣemarāja is *OṂ*.

Uccāra (a term that originally means to go upward, ascend, rise) is thus used to designate breath as a means to liberation (hence this aspect of ascending energy); for *uccāra* see chap. 5, part 2, of the *TS*, p. 38: *atha uccāraḥ*, and so forth; cf. chap. 7.

159. Cf. *infra*, pp. 150.

160. The next chapter, pp. 188ff., will provide a more extensive description of *paśyantī*.

161. *KKV*, 23; *Yoginīhṛdaya*, 1.38-40; cf. *supra*, p. 117, n. 95.

divinized energy that "vomits" the universe. With respect to the modalities of consciousness, while *parāvāc* is that of *turya* or *turyātīta, paśyantī* is deep sleep, *suṣupti.*[162]

When the *kuṇḍalinī* passes beyond the umbilical region and rises to the next center, that of the heart (*hṛdaya*), the "intermediate" word, *madhyamā vāc*, is produced. The sound vibration at this level becomes particularized (*viśeṣaspanda*), for there the distinctive features of the phonemes, and even of speech, appear, though still hardly emerging out of the undivided phonic energy.[163] This is the level of inner speech, of thought.[164] Therefore *madhyamā* is associated with the inner organ (*manas*) and with the intellect (*buddhi*).[165] The commentary on the *PST* equates it with *bindu* and the *ŚT*'s commentary with *nāda-bindu*, namely the division of *bindu*. There, the power of cognition predominates, it is associated with Jyeṣṭhā. It corresponds to the modality of *svapna*, the dream state.

Finally the *kuṇḍalinī* reaches the region of the face, where are the organs of speech. Then she touches the throat *cakra* (*kaṇṭha*). She mingles with the breath and produces the phonemes, the syllables, and the words of empirical speech.[166] The sound vibration, then, is as fully manifest and distinct (*spaṣṭatara spanda*) as it possibly can be. This is the final stage

---

162. *Turyātīta* is the state of the supreme Śiva, and *turya* that of *īśvara* and *sadāśiva*. *Parā*, then, should rather be related to *turyātīta*. In *suṣupti* consciousness rests in the breath or in the void (*ĪPV* 3.2.15), which is beyond the intellect (*buddhi*); *buddhi*, together with the inner organ (*manas*), corresponds to the modality of dream (*svapna*) which, like *madhyamā*, is a state where differentiation is present and yet not outwardly manifested as it is in *jāgrat*, the waking state, or in *vaikharī*.

163. As will be seen *infra*, p. 209, and in chap. 5, pp. 320ff., there appears in *madhyamā*, according to Abhinavagupta, a form of the manifestation of the phonemes especially replete with energy: the *mālinī*.

164. Cf. chap. 4, pp. 205ff.

165. *ŚT* 1.109, comm. (pp. 60-61).

166. *ŚT* 2.1-2 (vol. 1, p. 65): "I shall tell now of the manifestation of the phonemes in human beings, which is due to the strength of the wind (*marut*) flowing through the [two higher] "wheels" of the *suṣumnā*. They arise owing to [the air striking the] organs of speech situated in the throat, and so forth."

of Speech: *vaikharī.* Its nature, says the *ŚT*'s commentary, is that of *bīja.*[167] It is the power of action associated with Raudrī and corresponding to the lowest modality of consciousness, the waking state, *jāgrat.* The phonic emanation is henceforth made complete, the universe fully manifested, and human beings endowed with speech.

There are further *cakra*s in addition to these four: that of the eyebrows (*bhrūmadhya*) and, at the top, the *brahmarandhra*, the opening of Brahmā. To this is sometimes added, in certain texts, especially those of the Kula tradition, the *dvādaśānta.*[168] In the last *cakra* occurs the merging of the

---

167. These correspondances between the stages of speech and *nāda, bindu* and *bīja* do not mean anything in themselves; they simply reflect the wish to connect the three levels of the Word with the three divisions of *bindu* together with all the triads which then appear. It serves the purpose of reminding us that the emanation comes from a threefold division of the primeval energy. We saw, in fact, previously (*supra*, p. 116) that the *KKV*, 22-24, describes the three levels of Speech, *paśyantī*, and so forth, as resulting from the division of the supreme *bindu.*

With respect to the interrelations between the bodily *cakra*s and the levels of sound, we may note that the heart center (*hṛdaya*) is often called *anāhata*, as the dwelling-place of this subtle form of sound. Let us underline once more the fact that, within a common pattern and general scheme, the various descriptions of the evolution of sound may differ in their particulars.

168. The *dvādaśānta* is a center of the subtle body (which the *SvT* says is *vyomastha*, therefore in the "inner space"), generally considered to be twelve fingerbreadths above the top of the head, hence its name. It is the highest of the *cakra*s. (Except in systems that admit a still higher one, the *ṣoḍaśānta.*) Abhinava sometimes mentions two *dvādaśānta*s, and "inner" and an "outer" one: cf. chap. 7, p. 420.

The *cakra*s enumerated above are those usually mentioned in the Śaiva scriptures. They are not those of the Yoga texts which, after the *mūlādhāra*, enumerate generally the *svādhisthāna*, the *maṇipūra* (in the umbilical region), the *anāhata* (in the heart region), the *viṣuddha* (in the throat region), and the *ājñā* (in the palate region), above which is the thousand-petalled "circle," the *sahasrāra.* Some texts, however, number nine, twelve, or even sixteen *cakra*s, and more are sometimes mentioned (see, for instance, the *Kumbharipava* manuscript, translated and studied by T. Michaël in *Corps subtil et corps causal*, pp. 317ff.).

individual energy into Śiva's energy and the achievement of liberation. Therefore only the yogins reach it at the final stage of the induced rising of *kuṇḍalinī*; and this corresponds to the final merging of the universe into the energy. It is the end of the cosmic process of resorption. But here we deal, on the contrary, with the process of manifestation which brings forth the successive lower stages of the cosmos and of consciousness; thus for us *kuṇḍalinī* does not move beyond the center of the throat.

The following chart sums up what has just been said about the four levels of the Word and their interrelations with the *cakra*s, the powers, the modalities of consciousness, and so forth.[169]

On this subject one may refer to F. Novoty, *Eine durch Miniaturen erläuterte Doctrina Mystica aus Srinagar* (The Hague: Mouton & Co., 1958). See also H. Brunner's remarks in her analysis of the *NT*, *BEFEO* vol. LXI, 1974 (pp. 125-97).

The number of *cakra*s tiered along the *suṣumnā* varies according to need. Thus *YH* 2.8 lists nine of them when they are to be related with the nine *cakra*s of the Śrīcakra, but elsewhere only six are mentioned (3.30). In addition to the *cakra*s there are also centers of the subtle body called *ādhāra*, *sthāna*, *granthi*, *śūnya*, and so forth: the structure of the subtle body, though offering on the whole a consistent picture, differs to some extent in its particulars.

169. Among the descriptions of the emanation of sound as related to the *kuṇḍalinī*, one of the best known is that given by Bhāskararāya in his commentary on *Lalitasahasranāma*, *śloka* 132 (pp. 98-100). It is lucid and quite interesting. But this is a later work (*circa* 1725), highly "brahmanized," which makes a synthesis of various systems: Āgamas, Trika, and others. Further, A. Avalon drew largely from it in his *Garland of Letters*, and has quoted it profusely in *The Serpent Power* (especially pp. 167ff.). Therefore it seems unnecessary to reproduce it here.

It would have been interesting to look at other descriptions of the human/cosmic rising of the *kuṇḍalinī* as connected with the emergence of the sound of the phonemes, notably those of the Vaiṣṇava tradition. However, this would have been beyond the scope of the present study. Let us note nonetheless that similar systems are also to be found in Vaiṣṇavism. Thus, for instance, the *SātS*, 260ff., where the adept, through the worship (*upāsana*) of the deity, forces upward the *śabdabrahman*, which is *nāda* and made up of the letters from *a* to *ha*, from its seat in the heart where it shines forth—this is the "bee of Speech" (*vāgbhramarī*) —to the *brahmarandhra*. The *LT*, too (for instance, 50.38-40), connects

Cakra	*Levels of the Word*	*States of Energy and of the Word*	*Powers*	*Divinized Energies*	*Spanda*	*Modalities of Consciousness*	*Stages of the Phonematic Emanation*
mūlādhāra	*parā*	*parā*	*cid-ānanda* or *śāntā*	*Ambikā* or *Śāntā*	*niḥspanda*	*turyātīta turya*	*śabdarāśi*
nābhi	*paśyantī*	*parāparā*	*icchā*	*Vāmā*	*sāmānya spanda*	*suṣupti*	*mātṛkā*
hṛdaya	*madhyamā*		*jñāna*	*Jyeṣṭhā*	*viśeṣa spanda*	*svapna*	*mālinī*
kaṇṭha	*vaikharī*	*aparā*	*kriyā*	*Raudrī*	*spaṣṭatara spanda*	*jāgrat*	*bhūtalipi, sthūlavarṇa*

Mātṛkā Varṇa[170]

We have mentioned in the foregoing pages the various ways in which phonemes appear in relation to the various stages of the manifestation of sound and Speech. We should now deal with these phonemes before proceeding, in the next chapter, to a more comprehensive study of the four levels of the Word, and then (chap. 5) studying again more extensively the phonemes with the theory of the phonematic emanation (*varṇaparāmarśa*) such as expounded by Abhinavagupta and his disciples.

---

the four stages of Speech (*śantā, paśyā, madhyā, vaikharī*) with the rising of the *kuṇḍalinī*, etc. (But the *LT* includes whole passages taken from Śaiva texts).

On the other hand, the Tantric texts about the *kuṇḍalinī* mention almost always that the fifty phonemes, or certain groups of letters, are placed upon the chalices or on the petals of the "lotuses" (*padma*) forming the centers of the subtle body through which flows the *kuṇḍalinī*. Whatever the actual distribution of the letters, the system is an expression of the idea that there is an essential link between these phonic energies (and the deities of whom they are the "seed") and the cosmic and human stages of the rising of the *kuṇḍalinī*. Such a notion, *mutatis mutandis*, accounts for the presence and the distribution of phonemes (or of *bīja*) in the various parts of the ritual diagrams used for worship or meditation—more especially in the rather special cases when such diagrams are symbols of the cosmic activity of the deity, a role assumed particularly by the *śrīcakra* of the goddess Tripurasundarī. The matter is of importance in religious and yogic practice, which is not our main concern here; few are the original theoretical developments it inspired (those of the Śrīvidyā, for instance, draw much from the Pratyabhijñā and the Trika). Therefore we shall not deal with them here.

170. *Varṇa* (which first of all refers to "color"), is the term usually employed in Tantras and by Kashmirian Śaiva authors to indicate the Sanskrit phonemes, about which they have so extensively speculated. With Pāṇini this term is used with respect to the phonemes only for the short vowels. However, it came later on (in fact, starting as far back as the Brāhmaṇas) to be applied to all phonemes. In the Tantras or in various works is sometimes found *arṇa* instead of *varṇa*, with the same meaning.

Another term also indicates phonemes, *akṣara*, the origin of which we have seen previously (chap. 1, pp. 12ff.). Originally applied to the vowels, or to consonants, it came later on to mean a syllable. In our texts it means the phoneme or the syllable, as a phonic unit, as an unbreakable

Phonemes are encountered from the beginning, or nearly so, of the emanation of sound. In this system, where manifestation is a shining forth, a projection of light, where nothing can exist on a lower level that is not already present somehow at the preceding level, phonemes, of necessity, appear archetypally as paradigms, in the first principle. We have seen, in

---

sound element. It is used less frequently than *varṇa* by Abhinavagupta.

The various phonemes are, as is well known, usually referred to by joining the suffix *-kāra* (lit., "making") to the relevant letter, for example, *akāra, ukāra*, and so on. A phoneme plus *kāra* then constitutes the name of that phoneme. Generally Sanskrit phonemes have indeed no particular names, except for those secondary phonemes which cannot be pronounced alone. The only exception to this rule is that of the phoneme *r*, called *repha.* The term *kāra* is also used, as far back as the *Yajur* and the *Atharva* Vedas to note the ritual interjections: *hiṅkāra, oṃkāra*; the Tantras proceed in the same way with regard to their own interjections. It should be noted, however, that the rule according to which Sanskrit phonemes have no name applies only to grammar and phonetics. This rule is also usually followed by Abhinavagupta, Kṣemarāja, and others. But in some Tantric works it so happens that they are given names. Thus we find lists of names of phonemes in the Saṃhitās (*Jayākhya*, VI, *śl.* 4-20; *Sanatkumāra*, 3.2.1ff.), in Bhāskararāya, and in others. Phonemes also have names inasmuch as they appear as deities. Grierson (*The Śarada Alphabet*, *JRAS*, 1916, pp. 677-708) mentions names he found in use in Kashmir, which are not Sanskrit, but apply to Sanskrit phonemes in relation to local speculations about Speech.

Finally the texts relevant to our purpose also apply to phonemes the term *mātṛkā.* This word is sometimes used in the general sense of phonemes, in the way of *varṇa* (for instance *PTV*, pp. 188-89, 192); but in fact this term stresses more than *varṇa* the nature of energy, of generative power, both fearsome and benevolent, the aspect of divinized energies, of phonemes. This is clearly apparent in the passages where this term is used (for instance *ŚSV*, 2.7, where the description of the phonematic emanation distinctly shows the power of phonemes). *Mātṛkā* is indeed, in some cases, specifically used to indicate the mother-energy of phonemes by contrast to phonemes themselves (cf. *infra*, 151-53). *Mātṛkā* is the term generally used for the ritual placing (*nyāsa*) of the fifty phonemes.

For the terms *varṇa, akṣara*, and *karā*, cf. Renou, *Terminologie grammaticale;* Ibid., *Connexions entre le rituel et la grammaire en sanskrit* (*JAS*, CCXXXIII, 1941-42); Allen, *Phonetics in Ancient India* (Oxford: Oxford University Press, 1953), or K. V. Abhyankar, *A Dictionnary of Sanskrit Grammar* (Baroda: Oriental Institute, 1961).

point of fact, that the first resonance, *nāda*,[171] was regarded by Abhinavagupta and Jayaratha as a phoneme underlying all the others, and as such, in the phonematic emanation, to be equated with *a* (which includes, as will be seen, insofar as it is *ahaṃ*, all the other phonemes).[172] With yet stronger reason all the phonemes will be present in *bindu* (which is also *ahaṃ*)[173] and in the triangle of energies evolving from it.

The *kuṇḍalinī*, says the *ŚT*—which here again puts forth a somewhat general viewpoint—when lying coiled around the *bindu*, in the *mūlādhāra*, though universal and all-pervading, assumes the form of the fifty phonemes.[174] According to some

---

171. Cf. *supra*, p. 98.
172. Chap. 5, pp. 235-38. It is indeed in connection with *a* that Jayaratha, in his commentary on *TĀ*, 3.67, quotes the passage we have translated: pp. 128ff. of the *Tantrasadbhāva*, where the *kuṇḍalinī* is described as arising through the action of *bindu*, drawing the letter *a* and producing all the phonemes.
173. *KKV*, 5, *supra*, p. 112.
174. *ŚT* 1.53-57 (vol. 1, pp. 45-47) and 107-11 (pp. 59-61). The *ŚT*, in fact, emphasizes another collection of phonemes: the forty-two letters, from *a* to *sa*, making up the *bhūtalipi* ("demon-writing" or "writing of the elements"?), regarded as a mantra containing the most essential aspect of all phonemes. The *kuṇḍalinī* is indeed described by the *ŚT* as *dvicatvariṃsadvarṇātmikā pañcāsadvarṇarūpiṇī*. From this *bhūtalipi* (*śl.* 107-10) the *kuṇḍalinī* (*dvicatvariṃśātmikām*) brings forth the four stages of Speech (*parā*, and so forth), the three powers (*icchā*, and so forth), and then (*śl.* 111), by dividing itself into fifty, the "garland of the fifty phonemes" and then the fifty Rudras. (The context, it is true, is about the emergence of various mantras).

    The *bhūtalipi* is described in *ŚT*, chap. 4, where it is said to be very secret and not to be known easily. It consists of the following phonemes, classified in nine *vargas*: (1) the five short vowels, *a*, *i*, *u*, *ṛ*, *ḷ*; (2) the four diphtongs, *e*, *ai*, *o*, *au*; *ha* and the semi-vowels arranged in this order: *ya*, *ra*, *va*, *la*; and finally (*vargas* four to eight) the five classes of consonants, given, however, in an irregular order, beginning with the nasal (thus *na*, *ka*, *gha*, *ga*); finally (9): the sibilants *sa*, *ṣa*, *śa*.

    The *bhūtalipi* plays a particular part in the worship of the *śrīcakra* deities such as described in the *YH*. Amṛtānanda explains in his commentary that *bhūtalipi* appears when the *kuṇḍalinī*, rising from the *mūlādhāra*, pierces the *granthis* and *cakras* tiered along the *suṣumṇā* (ibid., pp. 328, 335, 344). *KKV*, 27 mentions it, but as a gross, manifested (*bhūta*) form of the phonemes.

    It is also found in the *Phetkāriṇītantra*, chap. 18 (*Tantrasaṅgraha*,

interpretations, the coiled *kuṇḍalinī* forms as many rings around the *bindu* as there are phonemes; other texts, as we have seen,[175] describe them as placed on the petals of the *cakra*s or on the triangle enclosing the *bindu*: those are details of secondary importance. Most important is that phonemes are present right from the beginning—and this view is held by all the texts (including Vaiṣṇava works such as the *ABS*—which may, however, have borrowed the notions from the Śaiva)—and that they participate in the nature of the supreme energy, viz., of Śiva and Śakti, or of Viṣṇu and his Energy, a notion that is equally admitted although expressed in various ways. The *ŚT*[176] does it, stating that since the *bindu* is solar in nature, that is, produced by the conjunction of a fiery and a lunar element, phonemes also participate in this threefold nature since they evolve from *bindu*. Now, this threefold nature is also that of the three main powers of will, cognition, and action, and also that of Śiva, Śakti, and their conjunction: that, in fact, of all the triads. Of course this threefold nature will also be present in the phonemes that make up the words of ordinary language, in *vaikharī*.[177] Abhinavagupta and his commentators will give a more philosophical (and more grammatical) expression to the idea, in the theory of the phonematic

---

vol. 2, p. 214). I do not know the origin of the *bhūtalipi*. One may note, however, as regards the number of its phonemes, that the *akṣarasamāmnāya* of Pāṇini is comprised of fourteen groups of letters totaling forty-two.

175. Cf. *supra*, pp. 133ff.

176. *ŚT* 1.112-13 (vol. 1, p. 64):

nirodhikā bhaved vahnir ardhenduḥ syān niśākaraḥ/
arkaḥ syād ubhayor yoge bindvātmā tejasāṃ nidhiḥ/
jātā varṇā yato bindo śivaśaktimayād ataḥ/
agnīṣomātmakās te syuḥ śivaśaktimayād raveḥ/
yena saṃbhavam āpannāḥ somasūryāgnirūpiṇaḥ//

(*Nirodhikā*, *ardhendu*, and *bindu*, in this passage correspond, at the human level, to the threefold division of *bindu* into *nāda*, *bīja*, and *bindu*); cf. *supra*, pp. 116-17.

177. *Infra*, p. 157.

emanation, by positing the presence of *a*, Śiva's threefold energy, in all the other phonemes.[178]

The phonemes thus appearing in the *mūlādhāra*, that is, at the cosmic level of the *śiva* and *śakti tattvas*, are there in the most subtle form. They appear first, as we have said,[179] in the form of what is sometimes called the mass or totality of sounds: *śabdarāśi*. Once they have progressed beyond the initial movement,[180] the phonemes, prior to their distinct emergence, and when being yet but energy, are termed as mother-energy, "little mother"—*mātṛkā*—of Speech and of the universe. "The mother unknown[181] [to those who are

---

178. Cf. chap. 5, p. 236; cf. also *TĀ* 3.220 (vol. 2, p. 207), which quotes the *Siddhayogeśvarīmata* as saying: "The *kuṇḍalinī* is the seed [the emanation], she is alive and in the nature of Consciousness. Of her is born the triad of the Absolute (*anuttara*), of will, and of unfolding, and hence the phonemes." (Abhinavagupta chooses the triad *anuttara*, *icchā*, and *unmeṣa* (=*jñāna*) rather than *icchā*, *jñāna*, and *kriya*, on phonetical grounds, these three powers having *a*, *i* and *u*, the first three vowels, as their initials). This triple energy, he further states, (Ibid., *śl.* 221-22) generates the phoneme *a* from which all the others are issued.

The *ABS*, chap. 16, also relates the emergence of the phonemes to the awakening of the *kuṇḍalinī*, described as *kriyāśakti*, made of *śabdabrahman*, and rising from the *mūlādhāra* toward the higher *cakras*; the only mentioned stage of Speech is *paśyantī* (*ABS* 16.54ff., vol. 1, pp. 147ff.). For the *ABS*, *a* is somehow also present in all the phonemes.

179. *Supra*, p. 135.

180. *Śloka* 199 of the eleventh *patala* of the *SvT* (vol. 6, p. 112) says: "There is no higher wisdom than that of the *mātṛkā*'s." Commenting on this, Kṣemarāja states that energy as *mātṛkā* is, in the highest sense, the conscious self-awareness (*vimarśa*) of the totality of sounds (*śabdarāśi*), which is in the nature of the unalloyed rapture (*camatkāra*) experienced by Śiva when looking at the universe contained within himself in the countless forms, "expressing" and "expressed," of which *śabdarāśi* is the archetype. Therefore *mātṛkā* is indeed the moment of self-awareness (*vimarśa*), which is Śakti and which logically follows the initial movement of light (*prakāśa*) and rapture or wonderment that are Śiva.

181. Kṣemarāja uses much the same expression in his commentary on *SvT* 1.31 (vol. 1, p. 26): *mātṛkāṃ paśunām ajñānāṃ viśvamātaraṃ sarvamantratantrajananīm*. "*Mātṛkā*, the mother of the universe, unknown to the bound creatures, begetter of all the mantras and Tantras." Mother of the universe issued from sound or from the Word, the *mātṛkā* binds

fettered by the triple impurity], writes Kṣemarāja in his commentary on the *Śivasūtra*, is *mātṛkā*, the begetter of the universe, who assumes the form of the phonemes from *a* to *kṣa*."[182] As such, while being one of the highest stages of Speech, she is the root of its lowest forms, those of the various scriptures of the tradition, as well as those of the limiting powers of cognition and of the various activities of human beings.[183] In the commentary on another *sūtra* of the same work, Kṣemarāja states again, referring to the *Mālinīvijayottaratantra*, that the supreme energy, having divided itself into the three powers of will, cognition, and action, and assuming the forms of vowels and consonants, becomes *mātṛkā*, the mother of the phonemes from *a* to *kṣa* expressive of Śiva, Śakti, Maheśvarī, and so forth. She permeates all the levels of thought or perception, whether discursive or undivided, in all knowers, supporting by inner awareness all sounds, gross or subtle. By presiding over the deities that reign on the different phonemes or groups of phonemes, she gives rise variously to wonder, joy, fear, attachment, aversion, and so on, and, by concealing the real, unfettered nature of consciousness, she brings about the limited, dependent nature of embodied creatures.[184] But *mātṛkā* can be known: to put it in the very words of the *Śivasūtra*: "The perfect knowledge of the wheel of *mātṛkā* [can be attained by the disciple]."[185] The knowledge of the true nature of the

---

those beings who are engulfed and fettered by the flood of *saṃsāra*. As the mother-energy of the phonemes making up the words of language, she enslaves those who, for want of the necessary knowledge, are bound by the net of words or blinded by the false glamour of words. To know her is to return to the source of Speech and of the universe; it is the liberation of the human being and the cosmic resorption.

182. *ŚSV* 1.4 (p. 16): *tasya ādikṣāntarūpā ajñātā mātā mātṛkā viśvajananī.*

183. Cf. ibid., p. 17.

184. *ŚSV* 3.19 (pp. 101-02): *pārameśvarī parāvāk prasarantī icchājñānakriyārūpatāṃ śritvā bījayonivargavargyādirūpā śivaśaktimaheśvaryādivācakādikṣāntarūpāṃ mātṛkātmatāṃ śritvā, sarvapramātṛṣu avikalpakasavikalpakatattatsaṃvedanadaśāsu, antaḥ parāmarśātmanā sthūlaśūkṣmaśabdānuvedhanaṃ vidadhānā, vargavargyādidevatādhiṣṭhānādidvāreṇa smayaharṣabhayarāgadveṣādiprapañcaṃ prapañcayantī, asaṃkucitasvatantracidghanasvasvarūpam āvṛṇvānā saṃkucitaparatantradehādimayatvam āpādayati.*

185. *ŚS* 2.7: *mātṛkācakrasaṃbodhaḥ.*

mother-energy of the phonemes is, finally, the knowledge of energy itself, whose nature, truly, is not different from that of Śiva.[186] This knowledge, according to Kṣemarāja, is obtained through the science of the phonematic emanation such as expounded by Abhinavagupta in the *TĀ* and the *PTV*. This science had probably never been expounded as exhaustively as by the latter at the time when Śiva disclosed the *Śivasūtra*s to Vasugupta. Yet its scheme, based on ancient cosmogonic notions and traditional phonetics, was, as we have seen, already accepted and found in various Tantric schools. As far as the Trika is concerned, they occur notably in the *Mālinīvijayottara-tantra*, a text held by the writers of this school as highly authoritative.[187] We shall see later (chap. 5) the exposition of Abhinavagupta and his disciples. Here let us simply see how phonemes issue from the *kuṇḍalinī* and, to this end, the best course is probably to turn to the *MVT*.

Siva's energy, according to this Tantra, first assumes the form of the three powers of will, cognition, and action (which corresponds to the tripartition of the *bindu*). "And then," the *MVT* says, "this leader [of the gods], though she be of only two aspects, reaches down, by means of further divisions and

---

186. Cf. Kṣemarāja's quotation of the *Tantrasadbhāva* in *ŚSV* 2.3 (p. 51): "All mantras consist of phonemes whose nature is energy, O dear One. But Śakti should be known as being *mātṛkā*, whose nature is Śiva." This precedes the quotation translated *supra*, pp. 128ff., which describes the arousal of the *kuṇḍalinī* and the emergence of phonemes, following which Kṣemarāja again states that the *mātṛkā* has for its nature the energy of the supreme word of the supreme Bhairava: *parabhairavīya-parāvākśaktyātmakamātṛkā*.

Bhāskara, in his commentary on the same *sūtra* (*ŚS Vart*., 2.7), defines the *mātṛkā* as the Lord's self-luminous supreme power of action. Her circle consists of all the *kalā*s. She comes from Śiva's power of will, when he desires to manifest his power. She is the vivifying breath of the whole manifestation, She is to be equated with the "unstruck" sound (*anāhatanāda*), and is the Word as containing the fifty phonemes (Ibid., pp. 35-37).

Cf. *NT* 21.38: "When dividing into eight and assuming the form of the phonemes, the Supreme Goddess is power of action and called *mātṛkā;* then she is in the form of sound (*dhvani*), *sphoṭa*, and so forth."

187. Cf. chap. 2, p. 64. See also *SvT* (first *paṭala*), a text referred to both by the commentators on the Āgamas and by the followers of the Trika.

because of the condition peculiar to created objects, to the multiplicity, like the miraculous wish-fulfilling jewel. Assuming the nature of Mother (*mātṛbhāvam*), she divides herself into two, nine, and fifty, [forming thus] the garland of letters (*mālinī*). She is twofold because she splits into germ (*bījā*) and womb (*yoni*). The germs are the vowels, the womb is the consonants *ka*, and so forth. She is ninefold when, divided into phonemes, she irradiates fifty rays. The germ, here, is Śiva; Śakti is known as the *yoni.* The energy of Śambhu thus divides herself into [divisions forming] his expressive (*vācaka*)[188] aspect. The eight groups of phonemes must also be known as corresponding respectively to Aghora and the others, and to the eight [Mothers], Maheśvarī and the others."[189]

The main interest of this passage is that it expounds the most widely accepted divisions of the *mātṛkā* and the phonemes.[190] The initial twofold division—seed (*bījā*) and womb (*yoni*)—is the basic one, for it corresponds to that of Śiva and Śakti: creation comes into being through their conjunction. Vowels (*svara*), which are aspects of Śiva, are the seeds or germs. Consonants (*vyañjana*) are energy and womb;[191] as such they are held as inferior to vowels, which come before them and give them birth. They are, in fact, enumerated after the vowels in the *varṇasamāmnāya.* With respect to the *tattva*s, the vowels are held as corresponding to Śiva, whereas consonants correspond to energy and to all of its contents, namely to all of the other *tattva*s from *śakti* down to the earth.

The division into *varga*s is that of the groups of phonemes. There are either nine or eight *varga*s: the former is comprised

---

188. Which is to say that Śiva brings about the various classifications of the phonemes, which are the sound-energy that precedes and gives rise to the objective world forming "that which is to be expressed" (*vācya*). Cf. *supr*, p. 98.
189. *MVT* 3.8-13 (p. 15).
190. Bhāskara's commentary on *Śivasūtra* 3.19 (*ŚS Vārt.* 3.19, pp. 60-61) gives an entirely similar exposition.
191. The *MVT* (śl. 25ff.) adds: "From the particular interaction of these energies of the phonemes arise the countless sound combinations of which the scriptures consist and which pervade the cosmos."

of the vowels (*avarga*); the five classes of consonants, arranged in their articulatory order; the semi-vowels; the spirants or fricatives; and finally *kṣa*, which makes a class of its own. The latter, with eight *varga*s only,[192] counts *kṣa* (which is actually a combination of two phonemes) with the spirants.[193] Each of these eight groups is presided over by a goddess or divinized energy (*adhiṣṭhātṛdevatā*); the *MV* mentions Maheśī, Brāhmaṇī, Kaumārī, Vaiṣṇavī, Aindrī, Yāmyā, Cāmuṇḍā, and Yogīśī.[194]

The division into fifty phonemes is the usual one: that of the *varṇasamāmnāya*, where the fifty phonemes are arranged as follows: sixteen vowels (*svara*), being: the nine short and long vowels with *ḷ* in addition (the existence of which accepted on grounds of symmetry by some grammarians, is purely theoretical), the *anusvāra* and the *visarga*;[195] then the twenty-

192. For instance, *SvT* 1.33-36; *NT* 21.38.

193. Strictly speaking, the term *varga* is to be applied only to the twenty-five consonants from *k* to *m*, arranged in five classes: gutturals, palatals, cerebrals, dentals, and labials, in their articulatory order.

194. The lists differ. *SvT*, 1.33-36 gives: Mahālakṣmī (*avarga*), Kamalodbhavā (*ka*), Maheśanī (*ca*), Kumārikā (*ṭa*), Nārāyaṇī (*ta*), Vārāhī (*pa*), Aindrī (*antaḥsthā*), and Cāmuṇḍā (*ūṣman*). The *varga* group of *adhiṣṭhātṛdevata*s is quite similar to that of the seven Mothers, or Great Mothers (*saptamātṛ, mahāmātṛ*), who govern the *indriya*s. In the commentary on *SvT* 1.33-36, Kṣemarāja assimilates the seven Mothers with those who govern the *varga*s of the consonants.

When eight in number, as Aṣṭamātṛkā or Aṣṭamātaraḥ, they are often known as mistresses of the eight *mahāsiddhi*s, the main supernatural powers achieved through the practice of Tantric yoga or ritual: thus *NṢA* 1.11 and 156-57 (pp. 28 and 126) or *YH* 3.115-124 (p. 314-15), where the Mothers abide in the *śrīcakra* and bestow supernatural powers upon those who worship them there. For the *mātṛkā*s found in the pantheons of various sects, which differ in names and numbers, cf. Th. Coburn's study, *Devīmāhātmya: The Crystallization of the Goddess Tradition* (Delhi: Motilal Banarsidass, 1984), appendix A, pp. 313ff.

195. The *anusvāra* is not a vowel, but since, as its name indicates, it is pronounced after a vowel, it was probably destined to follow the vowels in the enumeration of the phonemes. Moreover its written form (that of the *bindu*) made it somehow necessary that it should be placed in Śiva. As to the *visarga*, its written form being a splitting of the *bindu* into two, it naturally follows it, and precedes the consonants that it "projects" (*vi-sṛj*). Cf. chap. 5, pp. 272 and 277.

five consonants (*sparśa*), the four semi-vowels (*antaḥsthā*), the four spirants (*ūṣman*),[196] and finally the compound phoneme *kṣa*, the addition of which is sometimes justified on theoretical grounds because it logically fits in a given metaphysical system; but the real reason of its being placed there is difficult to ascertain,[197] except perhaps as a means to have fifty phonemes[198] rather than forty-nine. Naturally, since each phoneme is a form of energy, it is correlated with a deity. There are several texts[199] giving differing lists of these fifty divinized energies. Finally, another and much less known arrangement of the phonemes is to be found in works of the Kubjikā and the Trika tradition, for instance the *MVT*: it intermingles consonants and vowels and is called *uttaramālinī* or simply *mālinī*. We shall see it later on (chap. 5),[200] when studying the phonematic emanation (*varṇaparāmarśa*). In that phonetic cosmogony,

---

196. For the terms *antaḥsthā* and *ūṣman*, cf. chap. 5, pp. 300-301.

197. Some texts, usually later ones, list fifty-one phonemes instead of fifty, by adding the "vedic *l*" (ळ), a sign long fallen into disuse. For instance, the Pādukāpañcaka (for the *akatha* triangle), or Bhāskararāya who, commenting on *LSN* (p. 207) that calls the Goddess *pañcāśatpīṭharūpiṇī*, explains that this is to be understood as meaning "having the form of fifty-one *pīṭha*s corresponding to fifty-one phonemes" . . . ळ is also to be found in the *ABS* 16.95.

198. The case of the sequence stop + fricative, *k* + *s*, is in fact a peculiar one. *kṣa* has been described by Indian phoneticians as a single and indivisible unit; the evolution in prākrit of this group differs from that of other comparable groups; *kṣa*, also, was written with a single, particular sign in older Indian scripts (Gāndhārī, Karoṣṭhī). The presence of *kṣa* among the phonemes as a specific phonetic unit may thus well be less fortuitous than one may be tempted to believe. Cf. W. S. Allen, *Phonetics in Ancient India*, p. 78-79.

199. For instance, *MVT* 3.17-23, enumerating the sixteen energies issuing from Rudra (for the vowels), and the thirty-four from Yoni (for the consonants). The *ŚT* 2.29, gives a list of fifty Rudras, then of fifty energies, then of fifty aspects of Viṣṇu with their fifty energies, all of them related to the phonemes.

200. It will be found in *MVT* 3.35-40, where it is described as an arrangement of Śiva's power helping primarily to achieve a purpose, and, in particular, as having to be used for the assignation (*nyāsa*).
    MVT 3.13 assimilates the fifty phonemes with the fifty Rudras. The

as described by Abhinavagupta and Jayaratha, the *mālinī* appears at a lower level of the Word than the *mātṛkā*, which, issuing from *parāvāc*, is in *paśyantī*,[201] whereas *mālinī* is in *madhyamā*. On a still lower level appear the phonemes of manifested and articulated speech, *vaikharī*. However, these phonemes retain the features received from the phonic energy that produced them. Thus we find that the *ŚT*—which at the close of the first chapter restated the triple character, solar, lunar and fiery, of all the phonemes—says at the beginning of its second chapter (*śl.* 8), dealing with the phonemes empirically manifested through the contact of breath with the speech organs, that these phonemes are all, in their essence, Śiva and Śakti, that is, in the nature of the highest energy. Then it enumerates several classifications which mention precisely their supreme nature, and then enumerates[202] all the deities related to them.

Vowels, according to the *ŚT* in this passage,[203] are lunar, consonants solar, and the rest of the phonemes (described as "those covering all cases": *vyāpaka*), that is, semi-vowels, spirants, and *kṣa*, are fiery.[204] Among the vowels themselves,

---

ritual assignation of the fifty Rudras (the first one being Śrīkaṇṭha) with their consorts, termed *śrīkaṇṭhādinyāsa*, is found in various texts of the Kaula tradition, and also in the *Agni Purāṇa*, chaps. 145 and 293. This relationship between the Rudras and the *mātṛkā*s is also mentioned in *ABS* 16.104.

Abhinava (*TĀ* 15.129-31) says that there exist a number of divisions of the phonemes—the Kulaputtalikā (?) for instance—of which the *mālinī* is the chief one:

śāstreṣu bahudhā kulaputtalikādibhir//
bhedair gītā hi mukhyeyaṃ nādiphānteti mālinī/.

He relates the *mālinī* with the Rudras: *mālinī mālitā rudrair* (Ibid.).

201. Cf. chap. 5, pp. 312-320.
202. Cf. preceding page, n. 199.
203. *ŚT* 2.3-6 (vol. 1, pp. 65-66).
204. This distribution is found again in a number of works. Thus *YH Dī*, p. 199: it is the rule with the Śrīvidyā. The *ŚT* correlates this triple division with a distribution of Śiva's limiting powers (*kalā*) into thirty-eight (*ŚT* 2.12-16, vol. 1, pp. 72-73) in the following way: There are first the sixteen lunar *kalā*s of the vowels, then the twelve solar *kalā*s for the twenty-four consonants from *ka* to *bha*, which are arranged in pairs taking

the short ones (*hrasva*) and *bindu* are solar and male; the long ones (*dīrgha*)[205] and the *visarga* are lunar and female;[206] the four retroflex are neuter;[207] this twofold classification may

---

letters from both extremities of the list (*ka-bha*, *kha-ba*, *ga-pha*, etc.); finally, ten fiery *kalā*s for the *vyāpaka*. *Ma* is not included in the list, but this is because it is considered as representing Śiva, namely the whole collection of *kalā*s. The division of Śiva into thirty-eight *kalā*s is accepted by the Śaivāgamas. See, for instance, the chart of the thirty-eight *kalā*s, related to the five "faces" of Śiva (Sadyojāta, and so forth), according to eight Āgamas or commentaries in N. R. Bhatt's edition of the *Rau*, *Vp*, vol. 1, p. 28 (Pondicherry: IFI, 1961).

This same division is related by the commentator on the *ŚT* (Ibid., p. 72) to the division into three of the *praṇava oṃ: a* is the emission (*visarga*) and lunar: the sixteen vowels; *u*, the emission of energy, stands for the consonants; and *ma* for the *vyāpaka*. Jayaratha's commentary on a passage of the *Tantrāloka* (*TĀ* 3.221-22, vol. 2, p. 210) about the threefold and fivefold *visarga* (for those, cf. chap. 5, pp. 289-93), alludes to this division into thirty-eight *kalā*s, then called *bindumālā*, the garland of *bindu*s which, we are told, pervades the entire universe. There is, in this case, a coalescence of the notions of the energy of the *praṇava*, of that of *bindu* and *visarga*, and of that of all the phonemes—for those are all symbols of the various dividing forces existing in the energy of the Word.

205. The short vowels are *i*, *u*, (*ṛ* and *ḷ*), *e*, and *o*; the long are *ā*, *ī*, *ū*, (*ṝ* and *ḹ*), *ai*, and *au*.

206. It may be noted that the *ŚT*, in its previous chapter (cf. *supra*, pp. 114-19) when discussing the division of *bindu*, related the Śiva aspect and *aparabindu* with fire and not sun, and Śakti and *bīja* with the moon: because the lunar, female character of the energy—*śakti*—is in no way questionable. Sun and fire, on the other hand, are interchangeable: in *TĀ* 3.114, comm., sun + moon = fire, whereas according to *TĀ* 3.67, comm., the sun is placed between moon and fire. A confirmation of this classification is to be found in *ŚT* 2.7, for which short vowels are in *piṅgalā* and long ones in *iḍā;* now *piṅgalā* is the channel through which flows the *prāṇa* corresponding, as we have seen, to *bindu*, therefore to Śiva and sun, whereas through *iḍā* flows *apāna*, corresponding to *nāda*, energy and moon. In the diagram of the Kāmakalā, Kāma is *bindu*, sun—male and *prakāśa;* Kalā is *visarga*, moon (and fire)—female and *vimarśa* (that is, energy). Similarly, in *ABS* 16.79 (vol. 1, p. 150), the seven short vowels are called "sunbeams" (*sūryakiranāḥ*) and the long ones "moonbeams," the short flowing during daytime through *piṅgalā* and the long at night through *iḍā*, while Viṣṇu's supreme energy flows through the *suṣumnā*.

207. *ŚT* 2.9-10 gives one more classification of the phonemes, into five groups correlated with the five elements.

appear inconsistent, for if the sixteen vowels are connected with the lunar aspect, how could some of them be connected with the solar aspect as well? As it is, those are inseparable aspects since the whole and indivisible nature of Śiva and Śakti is present in every phoneme. Also, vowels are necessarily lunar inasmuch as they are sixteen in number, a figure, as we have seen above (p. 90), symbolically related to the moon. This combination of the solar and the lunar, using the numbers twelve and sixteen, occurs also in Abhinavagupta, in connection with the emergence of the vowels. Thus, when describing the "utterance" (*uccāra*) of the phonemes by consciousness, the *TĀ* (5.63-67), along with Jayaratha's commentary, gives as appearing first the twelve vowels from *a* to *visarga* minus the four "liquids" *ṛ*, *ṝ*, *ḷ*, and *ḹ*. These, named *amṛtavarṇa*, "ambrosial phonemes"[208] and therefore lunar and full or plentiful (*pūrṇa*) in nature, appear after the first twelve, thus completing the collection of sixteen vowels: the sixteen *kalā*s of the full moon, together with the three powers of will, cognition, and action. This mass of phonic energy is then "disturbed" (*kṣubdha*) and gives rise to all the consonants from *ka* to *kṣa*. Henceforth there is thus both consciousness and all that can be known by it: the knower and the knowable. The same solar and lunar nature of the movement and stages of consciousness (and of speech) is found also in *TĀ* chaps. 3 (120ff.) and 4 (23ff.), as well as in the *PTV*, which distinguishes between twelve and sixteen *kalā*s.[209]

---

208. Cf. *infra*, chap. 5, p. 254ff.

209. The speculations of Abhinavagupta and Jayaratha in this passage are based upon notions that are distinctive of the Krama tradition, for which, among the wheels of energy which connect the knower with the world and the Absolute (a typical concept of this system), there is a wheel of light (*prakāśacakra*) with twelve rays—twelve *kalā*s—where abide the sun—corresponding to the knower and the means of knowledge—and the twelve vowels (minus *ṛ*, *ṝ*, *ḷ*, and *ḹ*); and a wheel of bliss (*ānandacakra*), with sixteen rays—sixteen *kalā*s—containing the whole of the sixteen vowels, which is lunar, full (owing to the *amṛtakalā*s), and where the knowable predominates. Thus there are two moments of consciousness: first, one of self-awareness, then one of awakening to the world. In chap. 4 (127ff., vol. 3, p. 136ff.), dealing with the wheels of consciousness (*saṃviccakra*), Abhinavagupta describes two such wheels, with

As the reader may have noticed, the cosmic and human manifestation of Speech, the condensation of the sound of *brahman* leading toward language, occurs not only through the emergence of the phonemes but also through that of mantras which, notably in the hierarchy of knowers (cf. *supra*, p. 104, n. 54), form a very high and sometimes even a supreme form of Speech. Like speech itself, these mantras are sometimes described as emerging with the cosmic rising of the *kuṇḍalinī*. For instance, describing the latter when she assumes the form of the *bhūtalipi* and of the fifty phonemes, *ŚT* 1.56-57 (p. 45) says that she thereby generates a universe "made of mantras" (*mantramayaṃ jagat*). And Rāghavabhaṭṭa, when commenting on this passage, says of the *kuṇḍalinī* that she is *bhūtalipimantra-mayīm* prior to her being, with the fifty phonemes of the *mātṛkā*, *mātṛkāmayīm*. Chapter 7 of the *ŚT* itself expressly describes the *bhūtalipi* as a mantra. The texts describing the rising of the *kuṇḍalinī* always relate her (in various ways) to mantras and phonemes as well, at both cosmic and individual levels. Moreover, we know that the manifestation of Speech, at the highest level, often assumes the form of either *OṂ* or *AHAṂ* (or of *haṃsa*; cf. *supra*, p. 142, n. 158), or else of *SAUḤ*, the "heart *bīja*," or of any other *mūlamantra*. Mantras, in this respect, though consisting of phonemes, are looked upon as their source: as the supreme Word. In such a perspective, the utterance of a mantra is identical with that of the Word which creates the world.[210]

Coming back to the traditional divisions of the Sanskrit phonemes and thus to terminate with the manifestation of

---

twelve and sixteen rays, with reference to the *Yogasaṃcāratantra*, probably a Kula text (cf. *HTSL*, p. 49).

On this subject, see *TĀ* 5.63-67 (vol. 3, pp. 367ff.); *PTV* pp. 205-06 (and R. Gnoli's very helpful note, pp. 130-31 of his translation of this text); and *MM* and *Parimala*, 36-38, pp. 93ff. (pp. 123ff. of L. Silburn's French translation).

210. Cf. *infra*, chap. 7, p. 380. The *Sanatkumārasaṃhitā, Indrarātra*, 2.1-15, describing how the phonemes arise from each other, from *a* to *kṣa*, says of this process: *mantroddhāraṃ pravakṣyāmi.* It then enumerates the fifty *devatā*s of the phonemes, then sixty-four *puṭa*s, which are probably *bījamantra*s (Ibid., *śl.* 30ff).

sound—since with phonemes we come to the constituents of articulate speech (whether these phonemes emerge with the rising of the *kuṇḍalinī* or in some other way)—it may be worth mentioning before closing this chapter that the fiftyfold division is not the only one to be found in Indian thought and to be used phonetically and metaphysically, notably in the Trika. This division is of course the most frequent one; it is the norm, since it is that of the forty-nine phonemes (plus *kṣa*) of the Sanskrit alphabet. Two additional divisions are also in use in our texts, though never to the extent of those based on the "garland" (*mālā*) of the fifty phonemes. They, too, rest upon the analyses of Indian phoneticians, used so as to support the notions current in the Śaiva or Śakta traditions and taken up notably by the Trika. One numbers sixty-four phonemes (*varṇa*), the other eighty-one *pada*s.

In the *PTV* (pp. 191-92) Abhinavagupta quotes a verse from the *Trikaratnakula*: "This *mātṛkā*, considered as divided in eight times eight, is the wheel of the Kula, pervading the universe," and explains that the *jihvāmūliya* and the *upadhmānīya* can be added to the sixteen phonemes from *a* to *visarga*, the five nasal phonemes, the *yama*s,[211] to the nasals, and that the seven phonemes *ḍa, ḍha, ya, ra, la, va*, and *kṣa* may be uttered in two ways: in the usual way or with less effort (*laghuprayatnatara*),[212] which makes sixty-four *varṇa*s in all.

---

211. The *jihvāmūliya* ("formed at the root of the tongue") is the element into which the *visarga* is changed before a guttural; the *upadhmānīya* is substituted for the *visarga* before a labial. The *yama*s ("twins") are nasal phonemes—with no written forms but discerned by Indian phoneticians—which are a transitional sound intervening between a consonant and a nasal. All these phonetic elements (with *anusvāra* and *visarga*) are known as *ayogavāha*. For these terms see L. Renou, *Terminologie grammaticale du sanskrit* (Paris: Champion, 1957); W. S. Allen, *op. cit.*, pp. 75-78; and K. V. Abhyankar, *op. cit.*

It should be noted that Indian grammarians usually mention only four *yama*s. But then there would be only sixty-three phonemes, a non-significant figure, whereas sixty-four is a traditionally meaningful number, hence the fifth *yama*.

212. *PĀ* 8.3.18 mentions this utterance only for *ya* and *va*. Cf. Renou, ibid., p. 262, *s.v. laghu*. V. S. Abhyankar, *op. cit. s.v. laghu prayatna*. More explict on this subject is W. S. Allen, *op. cit.*, pp. 67-69.

The sixty-four *varṇa*s are distributed as follows:

vowels	16
jihvāmūlīya and *upadhmānīya*	2
5 groups of consonants from *ka* to *ma*	25
5 *yama*s	5
ḍa, ḍha, ya, ra, la, va, kṣa shorter	7
semi-vowels	4
spirants	4
kṣa	1
Total	64

The use by such authors as Abhinavagupta of this distribution into sixty-four is obviously due to the symbolic significance of this number in the Śaiva or Śāktaśaiva systems. Sixty-four is eight times eight. It is the number of the Bhairavāgamas (or of the groups of Tantras). The figure eight is especially related to the Bhairava cult of the *aṣṭabhairava*s) and to the Goddess (the *aṣṭamātṛkā*s), and so forth. Since Abhinavagupta refers in this connection to the *Trikaratnakula*, this distribution of the phonemes may be held as a Kaula feature. However, descriptions of the phonetic process by Indian phoneticians based on Pāṇini to which Tantric works refer, are obviously much earlier than these works. These, therefore, in this particular case as well as in all their esoteric phonetic speculations, have adapted phonetics to suit their purpose, with myth and theology giving them new colors and above all their own interpretations. Sixty-four, in fact, had been holding from a remote past, a prominent place in Indian cosmology and ritual. The *Bṛhatsaṃhitā* of Varāhamihira (sixth century), for instance, to mention but this one text, prescribes two types of diagrams for the building of temples: with sixty-four and eighty-one squares (*pada*s),[213] a formula found also in the Āgamas. Sixty-four is also four times sixteen, the number of parts into which Puruṣa is divided. A number of other instances of the impor-

213. See, for instance, S. Kramrisch, *The Hindu Temple* (Delhi: Motilal Banarsidass, 1976), vol. 1, pp. 46ff.

tance placed on numbers six, sixteen (thirty-two), and sixty-four could be cited.[214]

As the number eighty-one too occurs in ancient cosmogonic and ritualistic speculations (the *vastumaṇḍala* numbers either sixty-four or eighty-one *pada*s), it is not surprising that it should occur also in the *mantraśāstra*, notably in connection with the basic elements of all sacred texts and mantras: the *varṇa*s, which, while remaining forty-nine or fifty in number, may be considered as arranged into eighty-one *pada*s or *ardhamātrā*s, half-morae.[215]

---

214. The distribution of *varṇa*s into sixty-three or sixty-four occurs in *AgniPur.*, chap. 336, a section dealing with phonetics and prosody: *triśaṣṭiḥ syur varṇa vā caturadhikāḥ.*

We also find sixty-three *varṇa*s, but in a different arrangement, in Kṣemarāja's commentary on the fourth stanza of the *Sāmbapañcāśikā*, which reads: "Word arising from the dwelling place of Mitra and Varuna! I bow before the visionary (*paśyantī*), the first-uttered, and next before the intermediate seated in the intellect, and last before the corporeal (*vaikharī*) born in the mouth, through the speech organs which, once they came to be, are struck by breath and give birth to the sixty-three phonemes (*triśaṣṭiṃ varṇān*)."

Kṣemarāja, referring to Bhartṛhari (placing *parā vāc*, however, on the summit), comments on this stanza by first giving a brief outline of the emanation of Speech. Then he gives the following arrangement of the phonemes:

a, i, u, and *ṛ* have three forms, short, long, protracted, numbering therefore as	12
ḷ has only two forms, short and protracted, hence	2
e, ai, o, and *au* have two forms (long and protracted), hence 4 × 2 =	8
25 consonants, from *ka to ma*, have but one *mātrā* each, hence	25
4 semivowels and 4 spirants with one *mātrā*, hence	8
4 *yama*s, *jihvāmūlīya, visarga, anunāsika*, and *upadhmānīya*, all with one *mātrā* each	8
Total	63

This results from counting the morae (*mātrā*) thus: short phonemes (*hrasva*) as having one mora; long (*dīrgha*), with two; and protracted (*pluta*), with three.

215. Cf. *TĀV*, vol. 2, p. 190: *ardhamātragaṇanākrameṇa ekāśītipadāpi devī varṇapañcāśatyevāntarbhavayiṣyate, ity āha: ekāśitipadā devī hy atrāntarbhavayiṣyate*//197//

Abhinavagupta describes this division of the *varṇas* in *TĀ*, sixth *āhnika*, where he explains, among other things, how to conquer time through the control of *prāṇa*; this can be achieved notably by lengthening the breathing process more and more, up to the duration of cosmic cycles. An operation such as this is also both human and divine, or rather it is a human practice having its foundation in the Godhead; for the breathing movement is also the vital-cosmic movement of *prāṇa* and *apāna*—which are themselves assimilated with dyads that we have already seen: sun-moon, *bindu-nāda*, and so forth, the phonic energy flowing during this practice from the heart center to the *dvādaśānta*. There again we see how the power of Speech evolves from the highest stage, the *anāhata nāda*, down to the "subtle," then "gross" phonemes, and finally to words and syllables (*pada*s) of which a mantra consists.

The relevant passage of the *TĀ* (6.216-28, vol. 4, pp. 177-86), describes how, with the movements of the "breath," arise in succession short and long vowels, diphthongs and liquids, followed by the consonants from *ka* to *ṣa*, and finally *sa*, with *bindu* and *ha*. This is a spontaneous (*ayatnaja*) arising, since it is the very movement of the Godhead toward the manifestation of speech. Such speech, in the event, is not language, but a particular mantra, the *vyomavyāpin*, a long formula consisting of eighty-one *pada*s, each of which being (depending on the type of mantra being described) either a syllable, a word, or a short sentence.[216] As for the phonemes

---

"Though the Goddess has 81 *padas*, if the half moras are reckoned [these] are to be included in the 50 phonemes. Therefore he says: "The Goddess with 81 *padas* shall be here included in [the 50 *varṇas*]."

Cf. also *TS*, chap. 1, p. 17:

. . . *ekaikaparāmarśaprādhānye pañcāśadātmakatā/ tatrāpi sambhavadbhāgabhedaparāmarśane ekāśītirūpatvam/*:

"When [within the Lord] separate and successive awarenesses [of the phonemes] predominate, He divides into fifty. If, moreover, there occurs an awareness where all the different [possible phonematic] divisions are contained, [He takes on] a form [divided into] eighty-one."

216. *Cf. Mataṅgapārameśvarāgama (Kriyāpāda, Yogapāda, and Caryāpāda)*, critically edited by N. R. Bhatt (Pondicherry: IFI, 1982), introduction,

of the *varṇasamāmnāya*, one gets eighty-one *pada*s (which, in fact, are half-morae—*ardhamātra*s—normally half a short syllable in length) by dividing the *varṇa*s as follows (*TĀ* 6.225-26):

5 short vowels: *a, i, u, ṛ*, and *ḷ*, hence 5 × 2 =	10
8 long vowels: *ā, ī, ū, ṝ, e, ai, o*, and *au*, hence 8 × 4 =	32
ḷ has but a protracted form with three morae, hence 3 × 2 =	6
33 consonants, from *ka* to *ha*, each with half a *mātrā*	33
Total	81

From this division the yogin goes on to the words and sentences of the mantra *vyomavyāpin.* This mantra, while thus seemingly derived from the phonemes, is nonetheless said by Abhinavagupta to be the root of these eighty-one *pada*s: Śiva himself, he says, (*śl.* 227-28), taught it in the *Mataṅgatantra.* As it is, the *MatPār*, *Kp* 1.60ff., elaborates on this mantra extensively. Here again this is a case where the hierarchy *varṇa*-mantra is reversed, but this does not go against the essential nature of mantras.

After having thus seen the cosmic evolution of sound down to the phonemes and nearly to language, we must now go into further details as to the meaning and significance of the four levels of the Word, of which so far we had but just a glimpse.

---

pp. 11-16 and text pp. 16ff., with a chart of this mantra, pp. 25-26, giving the number of *pada*s and *varṇa*s. The *vyomavyāpin* occurs in other Āgamas as well: *Raurava, Vp.*, chap. 10; *Uttarakāmika*, and so forth.

The *SvT* (chaps. 4 and 5) also describes a mantra with eighty-one *pada*s which it calls *vidyārāja*, but this is something different: the *pada*s form one of the six *adhvan*s (cf. infra, chap. 6).

4

The Levels of the Word

The evolution of sound-energy may also, as we have seen, be described considering the Word as passing through four successive stages or levels, or more exactly, through three stages, from one primal, supreme condition somehow retained in subsequent stages. Such evolution is parallel and analogous to the evolution we have just described, and it will be found again in connection with the phonematic emanation. But it may be examined separately so as to bring out its characteristic features. The theory of the four levels or stages of Speech, in addition to its main aspect, which is cosmological, (for it is also a description of how the universe emerges from and through the Word) has another, very valuable, aspect related to the philosophy of language.

In fact, it is with one of the most eminent representatives of this philosophy, Bhartṛhari (presumably about the middle of the fifth century A.D.),[1] in the first book of the *Vākyapadīya* (*VP*), that one of the earliest formulations of the theory of the three stages of Speech (*trayī vāc*) is to be found. This notion of the stages of Speech, and their names—*paśyantī*, the "visionary" speech, *madhyamā*, the "intermediate," and *vaikharī*, the "corporeal," which is articulated speech and sound as perceived by the ear—may possibly be earlier than Bhartṛhari,

1. For the date of Bhartṛhari, long considered as belonging to the sixth-seventh century, cf. notably: Hajime Nakamura, Tibetan Citations of Bhartṛhari's Verses and the Problem of His Date, in *Prof. Susumu Yamaguchi Presentation Volume* (Kyoto: 1955), pp. 122-36.

but there are, as far as I know, no actual elements to prove conclusively how ancient the theory can be.

We saw, however, that, much earlier than Bhartṛhari, the much quoted hymn of the *Ṛg Veda* (1.164.45), had already distinguished four forms of *vāc*, and that speculations about correlative quadripartitions of speech and the universe occured even in the Upaniṣads.[2] But if, according to grammarian philosophers, the theory of the four stages of speech can be related to these ancient speculations, such speculations, in their days, had of course nothing to do with the philosophy of speech; and to this day no text has been found that would shed some light on the origins of this theory such as expounded in Bhartṛhari and his commentator Harivṛsabha (who, oddly enough, propounds another quadripartition of Speech, by distinguishing between *vaikharī* and empirical, concrete speech, *Vṛtti ad VP* 143, pp. 181-82 in M. Biardeau's French translation). In addition, no older texts have been found explaining this theory as it is later described by Kashmirian Śaivite authors, and upon its possible connection with the earliest speculations about Speech.

Whatever the origins of this theory, it is maintained chiefly in Tantrism, and notably in nondualistic Śaivism, where it appears in its clearest exposition and further developments. While Bhartṛhari and the author of the *Vṛtti* on the *Vākyapadīya* provided a more specifically philosophical formulation, from the standpoint of a kind of psychology of language, in Tantrism, on the other hand, it assumes its original relation to myth, and appears as linked with cosmology and mystical physiology.[3] This does not mean that it was not at times envisaged from the standpoint of the philosophy of language, as will be seen when dealing with Somānanda's expositions, or those of Abhinavagupta, whose thought on this subject largely draws from the *Vākyapadīya*. Tantrism, however, whether dualistic or nondualistic, whether in the Bhairavāgamas, the Trika, or the Śaiva-

2. Cf. chap. 1, pp. 20-23.
3. It may be assumed that Bhartṛhari, whatever his religion, knew of Tantric speculations about speech, but there is no specific information available on this point.

siddhānta, generally acknowledges not three but four stages of Speech, adding to *vaikharī*, *madhyamā*, and *paśyantī* a fourth (or rather a first) level which is above them and contains them: *parāvāc*, the Supreme Word.[4]

The existence of this supreme stage of Speech is variously justified. In nondualistic Śaivism it is justified notably because it was found desirable to have, as concerns Speech—and similarly to what occurs with consciousness (in this system both are inseparable)—a level both transcendent and immanent, free of all objectivity, and yet providing its root and substratum. Furthermore this form of Śaivism being *ābhāsavādin*, the stages of Speech are held here as real,[5] for they are aspects of the supreme consciousness which becomes manifested as one moves away from the first principle that, nevertheless, never ceases to permeate and to underlie them. Consequently all the forms of Speech are eternally present, in the primordial state of nondifferentiation, in such a principle, for the principle can project, as the cosmic manifestation, only that which is within itself.[6] Yet while such considerations may be used by philosophers such as Somānanda and Abhinavagupta to substantiate their refutation of Bhartṛhari's theory of the three stages, it may be assumed, however, that the philosophical justification of the quadripartition of Speech is not central, and if the notion is maintained, it is primarily because of its ancient origin. Thus Abhinava's Trika combined the analysis of the stages of

---

4. The evolution of Speech, from *parā* to *vaikharī*, is used also, sometimes, to account for the advent of revealed scriptures, described as coming down to us through a gradual condensation of the primal, supreme (*parā*) Word.

5. Utpaladeva, commenting on *ŚD* 2.78-79 (p. 88-89), explains that the universe is born from Śiva, according to his nature. Since it is inseparable from his energies, it is a form of that God. It is therefore real.

   jagad api tataḥ śivarūpāt śivarūpānurūpyeṇa tathā sarvaśaktiyogāt yadā prasūtaṃ tadā śivarūpam eva, ata eva ca satyarūpam. Cf. also *supra*, ch. 2, p. 79, and ch. 2, p. 92.

6. Despite the differences regarding *parā vāk* or other points that may arise between Bhartṛhari and the Trika, Abhinavagupta, all the same, refers to him as an authority and with the respectful appellation *tatrabhavant*.

speech such as found notably in the *Vākyapadīya* with the Tantric speculations about the division of the Word, which, as we have seen, are very early and originate in Vedic thought.

The doctrine discussed in this chapter will be that of the Trika, for this is the one that affords the most systematic and valuable exposition of the theory of the four levels of the Word. This theory is to be found in Kṣemarāja, then through him, in a number of nondualistic Śaiva writers of Kashmirian tradition, from the thirteenth century almost to this day—hence its importance. It should be remembered, however, that it has also been expressed elsewhere. Such accounts are no doubt less significant because much less elaborated. However, they remain interesting in that they show how this notion of the four stages of Speech—or levels of the Word—is generally accepted by, and a common feature of, various traditions.

Thus, regarding Vaiṣṇava Tantrism, one may cite the *SātS* (12.153, p. 245), where the *vāgmaṇḍala* divides into three: "*paśyantī* and what comes after" (*tridhā paśyanti-pūrvakam*). The *ABS* (chaps. 16 and 17), on the other hand, after the supreme Word, does not mention anything but *paśyantī*. These are relatively ancient texts. Other works are more explicit. Such is the case notably with the *LT*, which, it is true, is in this matter surely subject to Śaiva influences. The *LT* distinguishes four stages of Speech: *śāntā*, *sūkṣmā* or *paśyantī*, *madhyā*, and *vaikharī*. This is how chapter 51 deals with the subject:

> Made of pure consciousness (*śuddhasaṃvid*), I first evolve (*vivarte*)[7] into *prāṇa*, then, going through several planes, I evolve into sound (*śabda*), then into *śāntā*, *sūkṣmā*, *madhyā* and *vaikharī*, the discriminator. Evolving by these four forms into what expresses and what is expressed, from *śāntā* I become *sūkṣmā*. This subtle state is twofold: *śakti* and *nāda*. Being *sūkṣmā*, I evolve and arrive at the state of *madhyā*, which is *bindu* in which the totality of the phonemes (*akṣara*) and the corres-

7. This is not the terminology of nondualistic Śaivism, for here there is no *pariṇāmavāda* or *ābhāsa*.

> ponding aspects [of creation] are assembled. Evolving from *madhyā*, I enter the state of *vaikharī*, where, dividing into fifty, and so forth, I manifest myself as the phonemes and as the corresponding phenomena. He who, knowing *śabdabrahman*, meditates unceasingly on this process of ascension and descent (that is, dissolution and creation) enters a condition that is beyond all sound (*śabdātītam*).[8]

This is, briefly expressed, a less intellectually elaborate description than that of Abhinava, yet it is quite similar to it.

Now we shall begin with a short account of these stages of Speech such as found in *TĀ*, chap. 3, devoted to the *śāmbhavopāya*, in which the disciple must become one with the precognitive impulse (*icchā*) of Śiva manifesting the universe through *vāc*:

> When manifesting differentiation she is said [to assume] a threefold body known as *paśyanti*, *madhyamā*, and *vaikharī*, which is gross. //236//

This is how Jayaratha comments upon this verse of Abhinavagupta:

> "She," that is, the synthetic awareness (*parāmarśa*) whose nature is the [absolute] I (*aham*) and whose form is that of the supreme Word. [*Vaikharī*] is said to be "gross" so as to show that the other two states [of *vāc*] are [respectively] subtle and supreme. The supreme Word refers to nothing else but itself (*anyānapekṣaṃ paratvam*). When this supreme sovereign, due to her innate and total autonomy (*svasvātantryāt*), wishes to appear externally yet without producing the multiplicity associated with the process of what expresses and what is expressed (*vācyavācakakrama*), since the light of pure consciousness (*cit*) still prevails there, she is called the Seeing or the Visionary (*paśyantī*) since she is a form of the Subject who sees (*drastṛ*). After this, the level of the intermediate Word (*madhyamāpada*)

---

8. *LT* 51.24-32, p. 218. See also *LT*, chap. 57, 1-18, which again describes the unfolding of the energy of Speech through successive stages, distinguishing notably three forms of sound at every stage. Cf. *infra*, pp. 203-04.

is expressed when that which predominates is the sight, or view (*darśana*), intermediate between the Subject who sees and the object to be seen (*dṛśya*). This is a plane where, although the process [inherent in any discourse] made of what expresses and what is expressed begins to unfold in outline, the [Word] nevertheless remains grounded in the intellect (*buddhimātraniṣṭha*) in a form that is both manifest and unmanifest. After that, when the objective world predominates—and the clear manifestation of the multiplicity resulting from the fact that henceforth the process of the phonemes together with the speech organs, the places of articulation, and the articulatory process are present—[the Word] becomes completely solid, bodily and extended, and we have the [level of speech] called corporeal (*vaikharī*). Such is the threefoldness of the manifestation of the universe (*viśvarūpatāvabhāsane traividhyam*).[9]

---

9. *TĀ* 3, *śl.* 236 and comm. (vol. 2, pp. 225-26). Cf. also *PTV*, notably pp. 3-6, or the following passage on p. 13:

> "The supreme Lord, the Absolute, is the very reality of consciousness. Everything that shines in Him without any differentiation is, on the plane of *paśyantī*, the object of an awareness (*parāmṛṣṭam*) marked by a tendency towards differentiation into phonemes, words, and sentences. Then, in *madhyamā*, differentiations appear and the objects tend to be produced, whereas in *vaikharī* there is the differentiation in various words and sentences of the plane of *māyā*."

A short and clear exposition of the four levels of Speech is also to be found in Rāmakaṇṭha's commentary upon *SpK* 4.18 (pp. 149-51). Similarly, in Ānantaśaktipada's commentary upon *sūtra* 7 of the *Vātūlanātha* (pp. 8-10; L. Silburn's translation, pp. 24-25).

Maheśvarānanda, however, following the pentadic system of the Krama, distinguishes five stages of Speech in the *MM*, commenting upon stanza 50:

vaikharikā nāma kriyā jñānamayī bhavati madhyamā vāk/
icchā punaḥ paśyantī sūkṣmā sarvāsāṃ samarasā vṛttiḥ//

"The corporeal Speech is activity, the intermediate consists of knowledge, the visionary, then, is will, the subtle is the common essence to all [of them]." He further states in the *Parimala* (pp. 123-25) that *vaikharī*, the power of action, is ordinary speech, or language. The intermediate, a power of knowledge, is situated at the level of the intellect; this is inner speech. The visionary is the power of will (*icchā*), for it corresponds to a movement toward the manifestation of speech. Then comes the subtle, a power of

We should now further examine the characters of each of these four stages or levels of the Word, for which we shall refer mostly to Somānanda, Abhinavagupta, and Utpaladeva (and his disciple Kṣemarāja).

Parāvāc

If we turn to the work of Abhinavagupta or Kṣemarāja,[10] *parāvāc* appears as the primordial, uncreated Word, the very essence of the highest reality,[11] ever-present and all-pervading.[12] She is identical with the luminous, pure consciousness (*cit*), which, for the Trika or for the Pratyabhijñā, is the ultimate reality.[13] Like this consciousness, she is conceived of as a luminous throbbing (*sphurattā*),[14] which is not only the throb

---

bliss (*ānandaśakti*); this is the level where the various elements appearing in the former three merge and become one, like the different colors of the peacock's tail within its egg. This is the exertion (*udyoga*) of the supreme Lord ready to perceive (that is, to bring forth) the universe. Finally the supreme (*parā*) is of the very nature of the supreme Godhead: *parameśvarasya svarūpam*. Maheśvarānanda quotes on this occasion the *YH*, Śivānanda's *Ṛjuvimarśinī* on the *NṢA*, the Saṃvitstotra; the *TĀ*, and even Bhartṛhari, thus bringing together works which differ in their doctrines.

The *YH*, for its part, (1.36-40, *Dī*, pp. 54-57) paradigmatically establishes *paśyantī*, *madhyamā*, and *vaikharī* as arising with the archetypal "drawing" of the three lines of the inner triangle of the *śrīcakra*, *parā* being in *bindu*. Descriptions, as can be seen, may vary depending on traditions or circumstances, but the pattern, the principle, of a process going from *parā* to *vaikharī*, from the divine level of the Word to that of the ordinary world, remains the same.

10. Notably *PTV*, *TĀ*, *ĪPV*, *PHṛ*, and *ŚSV*.
11. *PTV*, p. 5.
12. *Satatodita* (ibid., p. 13), which means that nothing can destroy her, that manifestation, which comes from her and rests in her, cannot conceal her. This term could be rendered as "eternally present," "ever acting." Masson and Patwardhan (*Śāntarasa and Abhinavagupta's Philosophy of Aesthetics*, Poona, 1963) translate it as "which is eternally in creative motion." Cf. above, chap. 2, p. 80 and *infra*, p. 181.
13. *PTV*, p. 13; *PHr*, p. 67: *citprakāśād avyatiriktā*. We shall see shortly that *parāvāc* corresponds in fact more especially to the *vimarśa* aspect of consciousness.
14. *PTV*, pp. 6, 13.

of pure consciousness itself, but also that of the whole cosmic manifestation shining—that is, existing—within her, undifferentiatedly. She contains, therefore, in the state of primordial undifferentiation, not only all the stages of the Word or Speech, all the phonemes, but also all the words, actions, and objects which will be produced to form the universe.[15] Thus she is the receptacle and the original source of all. She is the seminal Word (wherein the "vibration" of consciousness (*spanda*) is but hardly perceptible) while containing nonetheless all that will come to be. The undifferentiated presence of the manifestation in *parāvāc* and its emerging from her is sometimes expressed by equating this with the absolute "I," *aham*, and therefore with its three phonemes (*a* + *ha* + *ṃ*) as a symbol, precisely, of the condensed form (the *bindu: ṃ*) of the energy or of the manifestation (*ha*) in the absolute (*a*).[16] Similarly, as will be seen in connection with the phonematic emanation, the latter first takes place as a whole in *parāvāc*, in Śiva (what is known as *mahāsṛṣṭi*), before it is projected and reflected onto the next levels of the energy and of Speech.[17]

But *parāvāc* is more than the starting point of manifestation. She is more than the source and primal receptacle of all. And this is because of the very nature of the *ābhāsa*. In effect, for words or objects to exist, it is not only necessary that they should be first, undifferentiatedly, in *parā*, but also that *parā* should actually be present in them. Abhinavagupta clearly states this: "She is actually present at the levels of *paśyantī*, and so forth, for without her, darkness, and therefore unconsciousness, would prevail."[18] How life and consciousness permeate the various levels of the cosmos is therefore due to their essence being the Supreme Word, who is the luminous and living pure consciousness, to their being identical in their innermost nature, and to this Word being, though transcendent,

---

15. Ibid., pp. 15, 184-88.
16. *PTV*, p. 6, and the above-translated passage of *TĀ* 3.236. For *aham* see the following chapter (pp. 286-89).
17. See the following chapter, pp. 305ff.
18. *PTV*, p. 5: . . . *taduttaraṃ paśyantyādidaśasvapi vastuto vyavasthitā tayā vinā paśyantyādiṣu aprakāśatāpattyā jaḍatāprasaṅgāt.*

immanent to the whole manifestation. "Everything," continues Abhinavagupta, "stones, trees, birds, human beings, gods, demons, and so on, is but the venerable Supreme [Word] present in and consisting of everything, in the form of (that is, identical with) the supreme Lord."[19]

Parāvāc, we said, is identified with the supreme consciousness, which for the Trika is *prakāśavimarśamaya*, that is both undifferentiated light or pure consciousness (*prakāśa*), and awareness, realization of this pure light (*vimarśa*).[20]

These two aspects can never be separated and are therefore to be found in *parāvāc*, although the latter corresponds more particularly to the awareness aspect. This is first evidenced in Abhinavagupta's statement that *parāvāc* is characterized by *camatkāra*,[21] wonder, thrill of joy, wonderment, and ecstatic rapture, experienced by consciousness at its self-revelation and its self-awareness, or when contemplating the manifestation that it holds within itself.[22]

---

19. *PTV*, p. 188: *ata eva sarve pāśāṇatarutiryaṅmanuṣyadevarudrakevalimantra tadīśatanmaheśādikā ekaiva parābhaṭṭārikābhūmiḥ sarvasarvātmanaiva parameśvararūpeṇāste iti.* (R. Gnoli emends *sarvātmanaiva* to *sarvātmaiva*).
20. Cf. chap. 2, p. 77; also L. Silburn, *PS*, introduction, pp. 21-23. On *vimarśa*, see also M. Hulin, *La notion d'ahamkāra dans la pensée classique indienne* (Paris: Collège de France, 1979), who suggests "resaisissement" as a rendering for *vimarśa*. In English, one might perhaps suggest "representation" or "self-representation."
21. *PTV*, pp. 6, 12. For *camatkāra* one may refer to numerous passages in the *PTV*. Abhinava defines it, in the *Abhinavabharatī*, as "possession by enjoyment, unbroken and devoid of any dissatisfaction": *atṛptivyatirekeṇāvicchinno bhogāveśaḥ.* A. Sanderson once suggested to translate *camatkāra* by "an act of undifferentiated subjective experience" which is precise but more in the manner of a gloss than of a translation. Cf. *infra*, p. 179 and 257.
22. The presence of the manifestation within the Absolute is, as we just mentioned, symbolized by *aham*, the perfect and full I-consciousness. Now, *aham*, insofar as it is regarded as identical with the "heart" (*hṛdaya*), that is, with consciousness as the source of the energy, and notably of the potency of mantras (*mantravīrya*), is *vimarśa*. So *parāvāc* would also appear as *vimarśa* insofar as it is identical with *aham;* cf. *PHṛ*, p. 67: *parā vāk śakti* is *pūrṇāhaṃvimarśamayī;* cf. also *PTV*, 166 and 193.

Such wonderment is said to permeate the supreme Word. Now, *camatkāra* is also a characteristic feature of *pratyavamarśa*,[23] the reflective awareness or representation of the Self, a notion that is close to that of *vimarśa* since it is, according to Abhinavagupta, the essence of, or that which gives life to, or the soul of *prakāśa*.[24] And *parāvāc* is also expressly assimilated with *pratyavamarśa* by Utpaladeva and Abhinavagupta, who thus underscore an important aspect of the supreme Word according to the Trika: that of the source and foundation of speech.

"Active consciousness (*citi*)," writes Utpaladeva, "is 'representation' (or reflective self awareness). It is the supreme Word, self produced and manifested. It is essentially total freedom. It is the Sovereignty of the absolute Self."[25] Here is a passage from Abhinava's commentary on this:

> 'Representation' (*pratyavamarśa*) is by nature a verbalising (*śabdana*) that is a [purely] internal enunciation or expression (*antarabhilāpa*). This verbalizing indeed has nothing to do with [ordinary] 'conventional' [language] (*saṃketa*).[26] It is an act of undifferentiated subjective experience (*camatkāra*) comparable to an internal nod of the head [pointing out or indicating assent]. It is this which gives life to the letters *a* and all the others that are the constituents of conventional language on the plane of *māyā* (*māyīyasāṃketikaśabda*) for it is the basis of all the other 'representations' (*pratyavamarśāntara*) such as "I am Caitra' or 'This is blue' [that is, of both reflexive and nonreflexive mental representations]. [This Word is called] *parā*, [that is, 'supreme'

---

23. *ĪPV* 1.5.13; *PS*, *śl.* 6.
24. *ĪPV*, 1.6.1.
25. Ibid., 1.5.13. (vol. 1, p. 250):

citiḥ pratyavamarśātmā parā vāk svarasoditā/
svātantryam etan mukhyaṃ tadaiśvaryaṃ paramātmanaḥ//

26. Abhinavagupta admits, with the Nyāya, that the meaning of words results from a convention (*saṃketa*) derived from divine will. This explains how the same things can go by different names in various languages. Such conventions of course prevail only at the level of human languages, and therefore of *māyā*.

> but understood as 'full'] because it is fullness,[27] and *vāc* (Word) because it speaks (*vakti*), that is, it expresses (*abhilāpati*) the universe thanks to this 'representation' (*pratyavamarśena*). For this reason [Utpala says of this Word that] it is produced and manifested (*udita*) by itself, because it is consciousness (*cidrūpatayā*), [which is to say that] it rests in its own self, [being] the ever existent eternal 'I'.[28]

It could not be put more explicitly than by this passage that the universe exists but insofar as the Word gave it birth, that prior to its being manifested it is internally expressed or enunciated, and that it emerges through this enunciation. Before it emerges it therefore exists as Word. But what may seem strange is that this Word which creates universes appears not only as the primal state of sound, as the Word before words, a level much higher and earlier than speech, where there is no such thing as any constituent part of language—and all this it is indeed—but also as already associated with something which heralds the language of which this Word is the source and basis. From this standpoint *parāvāc* is regarded as *pratyavamarśa.* In fact, when consciousness turns back upon itself, recognizes itself (*pratyabhijñā*), and becomes not only aware of itself but also of all that exists paradigmatically in it (what is expressed by *aham*—*parāvāc*, as we just saw, is *pūrṇāhaṃvimarśamayī*),[29] then it is supreme Word. And in this *parāvāc*, though prior to all expression, there arises, however, a kind of expression (*abhilāpa*), similar in its movement to speech, a sort of unmanifest inner whisper, perhaps. Of course, as indeed Utpaladeva and Abhinavagupta

27. To give this interpretation, Abhinava derives *parā* from the verb root *PṚ:* to bring out, promote, excel.
28. *ĪPV* 1.5.13 (vol. 1, pp. 252-54): *pratyavamarśaś ca antarabhilāpātmakaśabdanasvabhāvaḥ, tac ca śabdanaṃ saṅketanirapekṣam eva avicchinnacamatkārātmakam antarmukhaśironirdeśaprakhyam akārādimāyīyasāṅketikaśabdajīvitabhūtaṃ—nīlam idaṃ caitro 'ham ity ādipratyavamarśāntarbhittibhūtatvāt, pūrṇatvāt, parā, vakti viśvam abhilāpati pratyavamarśena iti ca vāk, ata eva sā svarasena cidrūpatayā svātmaviśrāntivapuṣā uditā sadānastamitā nityā aham ity eva.* Similarly *PTV*, pp. 5-6.
29. *PHr*, p. 67.

do not fail to state, this inner "speech" should by no means be mistaken for the language connected with dualistic thought-construction (*vikalpa*), the ordinary state of the human mind corresponding to the level of *vaikharī*. "The reflective awareness of the Self (*ahaṃpratyavamarśa*)," says Utpaladeva, "being light of consciousness and being embodied in the supreme Word, is not thought-construction, because [any thought-construction] is a decision or ascertainment, which [implies always] a choice between two [possibilities]".[30] Abhinava comments upon this as follows: "The [supreme] Word is an expression (*abhilāpa*) that is a verbalizing (*śabdana*) still immersed in consciousness, shining within it, and completely different from the sounds or words that can be heard and are of the nature of objects."[31]

Thus we see the role played by the supreme level of the

---

30. *ĪPK* 1.6.1:

ahaṃpratyavamarśo yaḥ prakāśātmāpi vāgvapuḥ/
nāsau vikalpaḥ sa hy ukto dvayākṣepī viniścayaḥ//

31. *ĪPV* 1.6.1 (vol. 1, p. 303): *viṣayarūpāt śrotragrāhyāt śabdād anya eva antaravabhāsamānaḥ saṃvidrūpāveśī śabdanātmābhilāpo vāk.* Abhinavagupta pursues: "The Word (*vāc*) is so-called because it expresses (*vakti*) objects by superimposing itself on them by the unification [brought about between word and object by such phrases as]: "That is this" (ibid., 1.6.1, p. 303). (Such identification between two elements is precisely what *pratyavamarśa* achieves.) But can this really occur prior to all differentiation?—Yes, it can, says Abhinavagupta, for only two things alike in nature can be exactly superimposed; here object and word should be of one nature, that is, no different at all from the pure light of consciousness where there is no duality; a similar twin aspect subsequently appears in the manifestation: word and object, *śabda* and *artha*, or expressing and expressed, *vācaka* and *vācya*, respectively connected with *vimarśa* and *prakāśa*. Objects, indeed, in the *ābhāsa* system—an appearing brought about by the Absolute, *prakāśa*, which holds them within itself, which sees them within itself just as we see objects in a dream—are, like it, *prakāśa*, "appearances" or appearings (*ābhāsa*), each "shining" (that is, existing) at its own level. Cf. K. C. Pandey, *Abhinavagupta*, pp. 319ff.: "*Ābhāsa* or 'realistic idealism'."

"*Ābhāsa* is the objective aspect of every cognitive event", writes H. P. Alper, in "Śiva and the Ubiquity of Consciousness," *Journal of Indian Philosophy* 7 (1979).

Word in this conception of the supreme consciousness. The latter is pure light, but in it the cosmos exists archetypically and undifferentiatedly prior to all manifestation: this results from its twin aspect of *prakāśa* and of *vimarśa* (or *pratyavamarśa*), that is, from its being both consciousness or light, and Word or, to say it differently, both pure, luminous (*prakāśa*), changeless consciousness and consciousness holding the paradigm of the cosmos in this Word which, as it were, whispers it to and within consciousness, and therefore makes it reflectively and introspectively aware—or brings about a representation—(*pratyavamarśa*) of the cosmos.

This identification of the archetype of the cosmos with the supreme Word is easily understandable: the Word represents the energy, or *vimarśa*, aspect of consciousness: the Word is basically energy, it creates the cosmos. But why is it identified more especially to *pratyavamarśa*? Here we may see the influence of Bhartṛhari, for whom any conception or notion (*pratyaya*) is inseparable from speech (*śabda*),[32] which itself cannot be without a kind of inner awareness or representation: *pratyavamarśa*. Abhinavagupta mentions thus that differentiated or discursive knowledge is, in all its forms, always associated with some form of verbalizing (*śabdana*), which is expression (*abhilāpa*) and inner murmur or muttering (*saṃjalpa*),[33] both being precisely the characteristics of *pratyavamarśa*.[34]

Therefore for the Trika, the Pratyabhijñā, and so forth, there is no knowledge, no awareness, which is not connected with a form of speech. But this is first of all, notwithstanding

---

32. Abhinavagupta used to quote *kārikā* 123 of the *Vākyapadīya*, Brahmakāṇḍa:

na so 'sti pratyayo loke yaś śabdānugamād ṛte/
anuviddham iva jñānaṃ sarvaṃ śabdena bhāsate//

"In this world, there is no conception [or notion] that is not accompanied by speech. Any form of knowledge appears as if penetrated by speech."

33. *ĪPV* 1.2, 1-2 (vol. 1, p. 87).
34. In *ĪPV* 1.5.19 (vol. 1, p. 289), the knowable is said to be *abhilāpamaya* because it is *vimarśa*.

a term such as *abhilāpa*, a wordless speech or thought, which appears moreover on the highest level, prior to any interference, not only of language, but even of an utterer, since it exists in *parāvāc*, that is, at the level of supreme consciousness. And yet this highest plane of the Word is also present in the limited knowers, since it is at the root of their thoughts, of their words, which are grounded in this underlying layer (*antarbhitti*). Any conscious act is, indeed, grounded in the supreme consciousness, in the absolute "I," which is, finally, the sole cognizing subject and the sole cognized object.[35] Abhinavagupta, in the above-quoted passage, said of this inner expression (*antarabhilāpa*) that it is undifferentiated wonderment, an act of pure undifferentiated experience (*camatkāra*); now *camatkāra* excludes all discursive thought. In the *ĪPVV*,[36] Abhinavagupta defines it as consciousness resting within, without any reference to anything outside of it (*svātmani ananyāpekṣe viśramaṇam*); as a verbal act (*śabda*) which is conscious synthetic self-awareness (*parāmarśa*), born of the inner "vibration" of consciousness; or else as a state when something is to be enjoyed (*bhuñjānatārūpam*), which is precisely the state of the supreme consciousness, or *aham*, when it becomes aware of—and is about to enjoy—the still undifferentiated universe paradigmatically enclosed within it. The same term *camatkāra* is used by Abhinavagupta to describe the culmination of aesthetic experience,[37] which is considered as very close and almost identical to mystical experience. We have here, most probably, a transfer on the metaphysical level of psychological experiences by yogins, who on reaching certain states of consciousness

35. Ibid., 1, fifth and sixth *āhnika*.

36. *ĪPVV* 2.4.19 (vol. 3, p. 251).

37. *Abhinavabhārati*, 1, p. 281: *sa cāvighnā saṃviccamatkāraḥ;* cf. R. Gnoli, *The Aesthetic Experience according to Abhinavagupta*, pp. 71-72. "This [form of] unimpeded consciousness (that is, which is but pure aesthetic enjoyment) is wonder, ecstatic amazement (*camat*)." Abhinava further states in the cited passage of the *ĪPVV* (vol. 3, p. 251) that *camat* is "the undeveloped expression (*avyaktā*) of a verbal act (*śabdana*), which is synthetic self-awareness (*paramarśa*) of the pulsation of the inner vibration (*āntaraspandāndola*) [of being]": speech (or rather, word) and inner experience are one.

have felt that at a certain point thought is pure consciousness resting within itself, a condition where speech does not function any more, but is, nonetheless, still present somehow. The characteristic of the human being is that it is a being that speaks. Therefore for him speech can never be entirely absent, even in the depth of utter spiritual silence. But then of course words are no longer those of "conventional" language. There is, to use Abhinavagupta's phrase, "a kind of inner nod," namely, a state of consciousness that could be expressed in words but does not go that far, which only indicates, suggests, a movement of thought, and therefore an expression through language, of which the intention, the pattern would somehow be felt, but which, however, still remains unexpressed. This is the primal seed of language which will gradually evolve into *paśyantī*, then emerge in *madhyamā*, whereas the same movement will bring the universe, present in *parāvāc* in the undifferentiation of the pure Knower, to appear progressively through the other two levels of the Word.

This role as the source and ground of language played by the supreme Word is also justified by Abhinavagupta, from a logical, and no longer psychological standpoint: *parāvāc* is the timeless and absolute foundation upon which are based all the meanings of "conventional" language. It is even the basis of its phonetic system, since, for our authors, phonetics and meaning cannot be separated.

One knows that the thought of such authors as Abhinavagupta was strongly influenced by Buddhist logic. For Abhinavagupta, for instance, dualistic thought (*vikalpa*) is a mental construct which follows and is based upon an initial moment of thought devoid of all thought-construction (*nirvikalpa*), which is pure thought, direct perception (*pratyakṣa*) of the supreme reality. For him, *parāvāc* represents with respect to the next levels of the Word, the first level, the primary purely intuitive and undifferentiated moment. And this is also what is experienced in *camatkāra*. Thus we have here a moment logically and ontologically preceding all the other stages of speech and thought, a moment that can also be experienced by one who seeks liberation by rising back to the source of the Word. The following, in fact, is what Abhinavagupta writes in the *PTV* regarding the emergence of the Sanskrit phonemes:

> The plane of the supreme Word (*paravāgbhūmiḥ*) of these phonemes is the one described [here], where these [phonemes] exist in the form of pure consciousness, uncreated, eternal. In such a condition of pure consciousness there are no separate forms of existence (*sarvasarvātmakatā*): all is perpetually and actually produced (*satatodita*). This supreme Goddess, [the Word] supremely venerable, whilst remaining in this state of unequalled nonduality, takes into herself the [planes of] *paśyantī*, and so forth, which are the expansion of the venerable [goddesses] Parāparā and [Aparā], and is thus the womb of their infinite varieties. . . . Do consider this divine primordial consciousness (*saṃvid*), free from all traces of the impurity of contraction (*saṅkoca*), which is called illuminating intuition (*pratibhā*)![38]

This supreme Consciousness-Word, the root of every form of speech, is for Abhinavagupta inseparable from these forms: they rest in her as on their bedrock, their essential and ever-present underlying layer, a substratum that not only is always there, but may be apprehended by the seeker in the interstices, as it were, of discursive thought. "This consciousness," says Abhinavagupta later on in the same text, "which the Āgamas celebrate under the name of insight (*pratibhā*), unfolding (*unmeṣa*), and so forth, abides in the interval between two dualistic cognitions, when one ceases and the other appears.

38. *PTV* p. 102: *tathāhy amīṣāṃ varṇānāṃ parāvāgbhūmir iyam iha nirṇīyate yatraivaiṣām asāmayikaṃ nityam akṛtrimaṃ saṃvinmayam eva rūpaṃ saṃvinmaye ca vapuṣi sarvasarvātmakatā satatoditaiva/ sā ca parameśvarī parābhaṭṭārikā tathāvidhaniratiśayābhedabhāginy api paśyantyādikāḥ parāparābhattārikādisphārarūpā antaḥkṛtya tattadananta-vaicitryagarbhamayī/ . . . / parāmṛśata ca prathamāṃ pratibhābhidhānāṃ saṃkocakalaṅkakāluṣyaleśaśūnyāṃ bhagavatīṃ saṃvidam/*

One should note the use of the term *pratibhā*—which may perhaps be rendered also as "insight" (or "vision")—to indicate both the supreme reality which is Word and its apprehension by the yogin. This term is probably taken from Bhartṛhari, for whom *pratibhā* means the intuition through which is fully grasped the meaning of a sentence through (and beyond) the discrete elements of which it consists.

This insight, however, not only flashes forth when one comes to understand the meaning of a word or sentence, but, more generally and more profoundly, dwells within every sentient being, simply because, latent within each, are all the stages, and thus all the powers, of the Word. Cf. *infra*, p. 185-87.

It is undifferentiated [or devoid of thought-construct: *avikalpakam*]. It precedes as such all differentiated thought-construct such as the notion of blue, and so forth, which are mutually exclusive [since linked to duality]. As such, it is inseparable from the infinite diversity of appearances [constituting the world]. That there is such an interval between two cognitions cannot be denied, because [cognitions] cannot but be different; and this interval is made of pure consciousness. . . ."[39]

To regard cognitive thought as founded on the bedrock of absolute consciousness, the "conventional" meanings of human language as based on the "nonconventional" foundation of the absolute Word, is for Abhinavagupta a logical necessity, for to him what is related to the manifestation of duality, concept or discourse, cannot be justified in itself, for relativity cannot but produce relativity. Now, an absolute starting point, or basis, is a necessity. If human thought is to be of any value and if language is to be meaningful and therefore a valid means of knowledge and communication, they must be grounded in

---

39. *PTV*, p. 106: *bhavati cedam astamitodeṣyadubhayavikalpajñānāntaralāvarty unmeṣapratibhādiśabdāgamagītaṃ nirvikalpakaṃ sasaṃvādaviruddhābhimatanīlādivikalpapūrvabhāvi/ tasmāt tad anantāvabhāsāvibhāgamayam eveti/ ubhayoś ca jñānayor antarālam anapahvanīyaṃ jñānayor bhedād eva/ tac ca saṃvidātmakam eva . . .*

Concentration upon this interstitial void between two thoughts, where may be grasped the absolute reality behind cognitive thought, is mentioned in *VBh*, 61 and 62. One cannot say for certain that Abhinavagupta has drawn from this text for his theory, for which he is much indebted, as we just said, to Bhartṛhari. Yet he quotes *VBh* 61 in *ĪPVV* 3.2, 19 (vol. 3, p. 346). Both stanzas are also quoted by Kṣemarāja in *SpN* 3.9, where he comments upon the *kārikā* saying that "that should be known as *unmeṣa* whence another thought arises in the mind of a person who is already engaged in one thought." Kṣemarāja states that the yogin who leaves one object and does not move mentally toward another, but remains in the middle between those two thoughts, is able to gain access to the *spanda*, the original "vibration" of consciousness. This background of pure consciousness which is the underlying layer and pervading essence of two successive thoughts (*cintādvayavyāpakaviśuddhamātrasvarūpaḥ*), according to Rāmakaṇṭha in his commentary upon *SpK* (*SpK-Vivṛtti*, 4.11, p. 117), is the root of everything: this is the substratum of the universe.

On *unmeṣa*, see chap. 5, p. 250-51.

some absolute; they need an unconditioned, transcendental basis which be not merely an initial stage of thought or speech—for such an initial stage would have also to be justified, which would lead to a *regressio ad infinitum*—but the transcendental absolute, and all-pervading consciousness or Word. This is why *parāvāc*, from the standpoint of language as well as of the manifestation, should not be regarded as an initial stage of speech but as the basis of *paśyantī*, *madhyamā*, and *vaikharī*, which alone are actual stages.

In the *TĀ*, answering the question as to how the phonemic energies which make up language and which can in principle express anything may have but a limited activity, that is, only a particular meaning, Abhinavagupta says that this is due to the fact that they rest on pure consciousness, the basis and bedrock of all verbal meanings: "Insofar as the conventions [of ordinary language] rest on this eternal and uncreated phonematic consciousness (*varṇasaṃvidi*)," he writes, "they also participate in the nonconventional [aspect of the Word]. If it were not so, all the various conventions [on which ordinary speech is based], having no final locus on which to rest, one would be confronted by a *regressio ad infinitum* and there would be no other possibility [to explain the meaning of a word] than to have recourse to other words, and so forth, indefinitely. To a child who wishes to be taught, one could indeed be content with showing him [the object that the word he ignores denotes]. But this would not suffice to create in him a nondiscursive [therefore, a valid form, of knowledge]. Now, dualistic cognition (*vikalpa*) is based on language, and language, in turn, is based on the conventions [fixing the meanings of the words]. This is why it is necessary to admit that there exists an ensemble of all the phonemes[40] such as [have been described, that is], not submitted to *māyā*, infinite, inseparable from the *vimarśa* aspect of consciousness and which never cease to spread out [giving their basis to words as well as to objects]. There and

40. *Varṇagrāma:* the term is akin to that of *śabdarāśi*, meaning the collection of the fifty phonemes manifested in Śiva, that is, in *parāvāc*, to form the "great emanation," *mahāsṛṣṭi;* cf. chap. 5, pp. 306ff.

nowhere else do all phonemes of the realm of *māyā* find their base and origin."[41]

One might well be tempted to ask how it is possible that the Word, at so exalted a level, prior to all differentiation, can be the root of a dualistic cognitive knowledge, had we not seen that *parāvāc*, so far as it is defined as *pratyavamarśa*, can, for Abhinavagupta, take the form of a kind of inner expression (*abhilalāpa*). Here indeed it is not so much a question for *parāvāc* to conceal within herself the archetype of discursive thought or speech (the first lineaments of thought-construction are, as we shall see, in *paśyantī*) as to provide speech with its ontological grounding and its vivifying principle.

Abhinavagupta goes a step further in a passage of the *PTV* where he shows how *parāvāc* is the foundation of phonemes and sounds as conveying specific meanings: "Although the condensed state [of the Word]," he writes, "appears manifestedly in *vaikharī* only, it exists however [already] in essence in the body of *parāvāc*, where there are no separate forms of existence. The speech organs as well as the places of articulation [of the phonemes]—throat, lips, and so forth—[are also there] without any separate form.[42] This is our own view. It is,

---

41. *TĀ* 11.67-71 (vol. 7/2, pp. 54-56):

asyāṃ cākṛtrimānantavarṇasaṃvidi rūḍhatām//
saṃketā yānti cet te 'pi yānty asaṃketavṛttitām/
anayā tu vinā sarve saṃketā bahuśaḥ kṛtāḥ//
aviśrāntatayā kuryur anavasthāṃ duruttarām/
bālo vyutpādyate yena tatra saṃketamārgaṇāt//
aṅgulyādeśane 'py asya nāvikalpā tathā matiḥ/
vikalpaḥ śabdamūlaś ca śabdaḥ saṃketajīvitaḥ//
tenānanto hy amāyīyo yo varṇagrāma īdṛśaḥ/
saṃvidvimarśasacivaḥ sadaiva sa hi jṛmbhate//

42. If the differentiation of the phonemes is held to originate in *parā*, the organs of speech, the points of articulation, and so forth must also be there. As will be seen in the next chapter, the various groups of consonants arise in *parā*, not from the play of the vocal organs, but from the "condensation" of vowels, which are energies. But this they do following the order of the Sanskrit "alphabet," that is, that of the phonetic processes as established by the Indian phoneticians who described them according to a certain order of the articulatory processes. Insofar as this

however, a matter of experience that one can speak or see inwardly. The difference [between the phonemes] is due to their [different] places of articulation and so forth, for the phonemes are animated by [that is, made of] sound only. What reason is there for saying more?"[43] We find here again the idea expressed in the passage of the *TĀ* quoted previously, regarding the role assumed by *parāvāc* as the root and bedrock of knowledge.

Abhinavagupta goes on to say that the supreme Word is also the basis of the differentiation not only between phonemes, but also between the various cognitive concepts, the moments of time, and so forth. Everything, as it is, is rooted in *parāvāc*. The sounds of musical instruments, the cries of animals, if we understand what they mean (which we can do by yoga),[44] and, similarly, the diversity of opinions in phoneticians regarding the points of articulation or the divisions of phonemes, if all these things are of little import, this is because all of this, which pertains to *māyā*, "abides in the great effulgence (*mahasi*) of the mantra of *parāvāc*,[45] which is pure conscious awareness (*śuddhavimarśa*), subject neither to *māyā* nor to the conventions [of ordinary speech]. This plane is recognized by all as being

---

order is supposed to exist from the very beginning, it is necessarily from the first plane of the Word that the speech-organs and the places of articulation of the phonemes can be said to preexist in *parā*. The passage quoted above actually follows another one in the *PTV* that describes how the consonants appear in *parāvāc*.

43. *PTV*, pp. 184-85: *evaṃ ca ghanībhāvo 'pi vaikharīrūpe yady api sphuṭībhavati tathāpi sarvasarvātmani parāvāgvapuṣi mukhyatayāvatiṣṭhate/ tatra paraṃ kaṇṭhoṣṭhasthānakaraṇāny api sarvasarvātmakam eveti viśeṣaḥ/ tathāhy antar api saṃjalpet paśyed iti sphuṭa evānubhavo bhedaś ca sthānādikṛta eva, śrutyekaprāṇatvāt varṇānāṃ/ kim bahunā.*

   The passage shows clearly that *parāvāc* is not only the ontological foundation, but also the epistemological background of language, since in *parā* objects and speech exist archetypally and in the primal state of indivision.

44. *Yoga Sūtra* 3.17.

45. Here and in the passages of the texts quoted further should be noted the use of the term *mantra* to indicate *parāvāc*. Here the mantra is *ahaṃ*: mantra, a symbol of the supreme reality as the source of Speech; cf. chap. 7, pp. 385-86.

devoid of thought-constructs. Thus, on this earth and other [places], it is the effulgence of the supreme mantra [that is, *parāvāc*] which takes on the forms of the phonemes *ka* and so forth, that, isolated or in combination, make up the *bīja-* or *piṇḍa-*[mantras] as well as everything else. If it were otherwise,[46] all nondiscursive forms of cognition, be it of Mount Meru or of a jujube tree, of water or of fire, of being or of nonbeing, of a jug or of something pleasant, would be all one, and such would then be the case with thought-constructs also, since, being born from this [original supreme nondiscursive plane], they could not behave differently from it in their nature. Thus the sages see that the nonconventional body of the [supreme] mantra (*asāṃketikaṃ mantravapuḥ*) takes on mutually differing forms and they teach that it must be revered since it is that which brings about the conventions [of ordinary speech]. It is indeed in the effulgence of the Word (*vāṅmahasi*) transcending all conventions that the [linguistic] conventions of the realm of *māyā* fall and then become one in nature with the [supreme] mantra that is nonconventional and not subject to *māyā*. Therefore the fact that [words] are expressive is simply that they come back to their own inner nature[47] (*svarūpapratipattir eva*). The clear knowledge [of this truth can be obtained] by repeated exercise only. The consciousness of what the word *cow* [for instance] expresses, which is part of the world of [linguistic] conventions, whether the knowledge of the meaning of the word comes from a previous experience, or is acquired through the convention when seeing the cow, falls in any case equally in the glory (*dhāmani*) of that other consciousness that is free from all conventions and not subject to *māyā*. This essence [of the Word], free from all conventions, is to be found at the origin of the consciousness of a child even admitting that [such notions may] arise from his previous births, for if it were not so, one would be confronted by a *regressio ad infinitum*. It

46. That is, if cognition and the differentiation of phonemes did not have their paradigm in *parāvāc*.

47. Which is *parāvāc*.

is thus only, and not otherwise, that one can explain satisfactorily the apprehension of the [linguistic] conventions."[48]

So this is indeed *parāvāc*—this supreme essence of Speech, divine in nature, wherein are grounded ontologically, logically, and (as we shall see) archetypally, all that expresses and all that is to be expressed—that provides the basis both for the reality of the universe and the validity of its cognizance through speech. It is an entirely justified standpoint from the perspective of the Trika "idealist realism," where all that is manifested by the Godhead is but the appearing (*ābhāsa*) of Consciousness-Word. Everything is born out of her, in her everything has its root. Words and things, springing from and remaining immersed in the Absolute, are but the brilliant game, the pulsating radiance, of the uninhibited light-consciousness, of the Word, of the first principle. Although set in the context of Tantric Śaivism (as appears from the mention by Abhinava of some forms of the Goddess) this theory also reminds one—as we said previously—of Bhartṛhari's views, for whom *pratibhā* (a term used by Abhinava as we have seen), the intuition through which the meaning of words and sentences is grasped, is due to a capacity innate in all human beings, to a power which is that of the original, primordial Word, the very substance of everything.

48. *PTV*, pp. 193-95: *tad evam . . . amāyīyāsāṃketikasvarūpabhūtaśuddhavimarśātmaparavaṅmantramahāmahasi tāvat pratiṣṭhāṃ bhajate, yatra sarvavādibhir avikalpā daśā gīyate, tat ca paramamantramahaḥ pṛthivyādau śuddhavyāmiśrādipāramārthikabījapiṇḍarūpakādivarṇātmakam eva, anyathā merubadarajalajvalanabhāvābhāvaghaṭasukhanirvikalpajñānānīty ekam eva sarvaṃ syāt/ vikalpo 'pi tatprasādotthaḥ tām eva saraṇim anusaret, na tu pratyuta tatsvarūpaṃ bhindyāt/ tathā ca yad eva tad asāṃketikaṃ mantravapus tad eva anyonyavicitrarūpaṃ paśyadbhiḥ sarvajñaiḥ saṃketopāyam upāsyatayā upadiśyate/ tatraiva cāsāṃketike vāṅmahasi tathā khalu māyīyāḥ saṃketāḥ patanti yathā ta evāmāyīyāsāṃketitamantratādātmyaṃ pratipadyante/ tathāsvarūpapratipattir eva hi teṣāṃ vācakatābhāvo nānyaḥ kaścit/ atra ca sphutam abhijñānam abhyāsavaśād/ sāṃketikatām āpanno ciratarapūrvavṛttagośabdaparāmarśas tathaiva saṃketakāle goparāmarśo 'py anyo 'māyīyāsāṃketikaparāmarśadhāmany eva nipatati/ yāvat bālasyāpi janmāntarānusaraṇe 'pi citsvabhāvasyādau sthitaivāsaṃketikī sattā, anyathānavasthānāt/ evam eva khalu saṃketagrahaṇopapattir nānyathā. . . .*

As it is said in the initial stanzas of the *VP*:[49] "This *brahman* without beginning or end, sound principle, imperishable syllable, transforms itself into objectivity, from which appear the animate world . . . From this One, that holds everything in germ, that appears in various forms: those of the enjoyer, of the enjoyed and of enjoyment, from Him [all proceeds] . . ."

Thus we saw how the universe, meaning, and language take their root in the supreme Word, and exist there undifferentiatedly, in seed-form, endowed with the full kinetic force peculiar to a seed. Such a force will assert itself and these seeds will start to grow in the next stage of Speech, *paśyantī*, the "Visionary" Word.

Paśyantī

When a tendency toward manifestation arises in *parāvāc*, there appears *paśyantī*, which is, properly called, the first stage of Speech. It is born from[50] and is identical in nature[51] to the supreme Word, yet—and this is why it is but a stage—it does not possess the transcendence and the all-pervasiveness of *parā*. Nondualistic Śaivites, Somānanda, and then Abhinava and his followers severely criticize indeed those who see in *paśyantī* the primordial and highest level of Speech.

It is called *paśyantī*, "the Visionary," because at this level there emerges in consciousness a kind of desire to see and a sort of initial vision of what will be manifested with the gradual

---

49. *VP* 1.1:

anādhinidhanaṃ brahma śabdatattvam yad akṣaram/
vivartate 'rthabhāvena prakriyā jagato yataḥ//1//
ekasya sarvabījasya yasya ceyam anekadhā/
bhoktṛbhoktavyarūpeṇa bhogarūpeṇa ca sthitiḥ//4//

The commentary (*Vṛtti*) on this text is curiously similar to what Abhinava said in the foregoing passage, although the absence, in Bhartṛhari (and in the *Vṛtti*), of *parāvāc*, that is, of the supreme stage where Speech is absolute Consciousness, alters the perspective.

50. Ibid., p. 58: *parābhaṭṭārikāyāśca paśyantyāditādātmyaṃ nirṇītam.*

51. *PTV*, pp. 82-83: *paśyantyā api parābhaṭṭārikāyāḥ prathamaprasaratvāt. . .*

emergence of the universe during the development of the next stages of Speech.[52] There is in *paśyantī* only a tendency toward, but not any, objectivity, since the pure subjectivity of consciousness still prevails here. In the *PTV* Abhinavagupta writes that therein dawn the first lineaments of differentiation: *bhedāṃśasya āsūtraṇam*;[53] or that there occurs a synthetic and intense awareness (*parāmarśa*) of all that is inwardly and undifferentiatedly in the consciousness of the supreme Lord (that is, an awareness of the manifestation archetypally contained in *parāvāc*), such awareness being characterized by a desire for the differentiation of speech into phonemes, words, and sentences,[54] that is, a tendency, a movement toward the forms of language such as they appear in *madhyamā* and *vaikharī* (and toward the objective aspects of the manifestation which are derived from this evolution of Speech).

But although different from *parāvāc*, the Visionary is very close to her. Here is how Abhinavagupta describes its emergence, in an aforementioned passage (p. 173) at the beginning of the *PTV*, to which we shall return (p. 193): "This Energy, which is a self-representation filled with grace for [all creatures of] the world, at first is not separated from the hundreds of energies appearing in outline within the intense form of consciousness that is the Visionary. It rests, however, in this very

---

52. Cf. *supra*, p. 170, the quotation of *TĀ* 3.236; also *SD*, 2.83 (p. 91):

paśyantī hi kriyā tasyā bhāgau pūrvāparau sthitau/
etad draṣṭavyam ity etad vimarśaḥ pūrvato bhavet//83//

"The visionary is [the power of] action. She is of two parts. The first part consists in the act of consciousness: "this should be seen."

53. *PTV*, pp. 6, 15: *bhedāsūtraṇarūpāyāṃ paśyantyām kramabhūjuṣi* . . . and p. 143: *paśyantīdaśāyāś cārabhya bhedāsūtraṇātmāṃśāṃśollāsaḥ.*

54. *PTV*, p. 13: *evaṃparamārthamayatvāt parameśvarasya cittattvasya yad evāvibhāgenāntarvastu sphuritaṃ, tad eva paśyantībhuvi varṇapadavākyavibibhājayiṣayā parāmṛṣṭam.*

"The consciousness of the supreme Lord being thus in its supreme condition and essence, that which shines there internally and free from all distinction is the object, on the level of the Visionary [Word], of an act of consciousness in which the phonemes, words, and phrases tend to appear."

first moment, in a consciousness that is not limited by time and space and whose nature is that of the Supreme Great Mantra [*ahaṃ* = *parāvāc*], a consciousness [still] entirely devoid of the divisions into questions and answers that are to appear in *paśyantī*. This [supreme Energy] is made of the nonduality of consciousness of all the agents of cognition and is ever present. Then comes the Visionary . . ."[55]

Paśyantī, says Abhinavagupta, is the first moment of cognition, the moment where one is still wishing to know rather than truly knowing. More exactly, in view of the Trika theory of knowledge, this is the initial, undifferentiated moment of consciousness which precedes dualistic cognitive awareness, a moment—when what expresses and what is expressed are not yet divided.[56] We just saw that this initial moment is in *parāvāc*. It may, however, be considered as still going on in *paśyantī* (and in a perhaps more actual way for the individual consciousness than for that of the Godhead). Here indeed we do not see the emergence of objectivity and of the thought constructs associated with it: we see them dawning only within a still prevalent—although assuredly no longer complete—undifferentiation. That of *paśyantī*, then, is an ambiguous condition, since it represents a transition between complete undifferentiation and the commencement of differentiation. It corresponds, in effect, to the supreme-nonsupreme state (*parāparā*) of the Word and of the Energy, where subjectivity (*ahantā*) and objectivity (*idantā*) coincide; however, in *paśyantī*, the *aham* aspect is still prevalent; only in *madhyamā* will both of them be in equilibrium or will the emphasis be placed on *idam*. This

55. *PTV*, pp. 4-5: *sā ca śaktiḥ lokānugrahavimarśamayī prathamataḥ parāmarśamayapaśyantyāsūtrayiṣyamānānantaśaktiśatāvibhinnā prathamataraṃ paramahāmantramayyāṃ adeśakālakalitāyāṃ saṃvidi nirūḍhā tāvatpaśyantyudbhaviṣyaduktipratyuktyavibhāgenaiva vartate/ saiva ca sakalapramātṛsaṃvidadvayamayī satatam eva vartamānarūpā/ tatas tu paśyantī . . .*

56. *PTV*, pp. 4-5: *na hi prathamajñānakāle bhedo 'trāsphurat, yatra vācyavācakaviśeṣayor abhedaḥ . . .*
Cf. also *ĪPVV* 1.5.13 (vol. 2, p. 190, line 19). *IPK* 1.5.13 deals precisely with *parāvāc*.

ambiguous nature of *paśyantī* is pointed out in a passage of the *Vṛtti* on the *Vākyapadīya* (1.142) quoted—approvingly, it seems—by Abhinavagupta in the *ĪPVV:*

> *Paśyantī*, although the sequentiality [proper to language] is entirely resorbed in her, possesses however the energy [that animates sequentiality]. She is both mobile and immovable and is attained by mental concentration. The forms of the objects of knowledge appear in her as immersed in consciousness, their forms being either resorbed, or absent. All this appears in her in a variety of discrete aspects or as forms fused into each other, or it may appear as having lost all form.[57]

Paśyantī, as we can see, does not manifest objectivity, but only the principle that gives life to this first obfuscation of the complete awareness of Reality, known as *akhyāti*,[58] and which will make consciousness perceive itself as different from objectivity. This condition of *paśyantī*, very close to that of the Supreme, is underscored by Abhinavagupta when he mentions (in the *PTV*, p. 147), with regard to the phonematic emanation, that at its highest point *paśyantī* is identical to *anāśritaśakti* (*anāśritaśaktyātmakapaśyantīparamakoṭi*).[59]

Paśyantī, then, though close to *parā vāk*, should not be confused with it: in chapter 2 of the *Śivadṛṣṭi* Somānanda strongly refutes Bhartṛhari's view according to which *paśyantī* is the supreme plane of the Word. But it should be noted that

---

57. *ĪPVV* 1.5.19 (vol. 2, p. 226): *pratisaṃhṛtakramāntaḥ satyapyabhede samāviṣṭakramaśaktiḥ paśyantī / sā acalā ca calā pratilabdhāsamādhānā ca / saṃvinniṣṭhajñeyākārā pratilīnākārānirākārā ca, paricchinnārthapratyavabhāsā saṃsṛṣṭārthapratyavabhāsā ca sarvārthapratyavabhāsā praśāntapratyavabhāsā ca iti.*

    The text quoted here, following the *KSTS* edition of the *ĪPVV*, is somewhat different from that known to us through the *Vṛtti* on the *VP* (cf., for instance, *VP*, edited by M. Biardeau, pp. 176-78).

58. *Akhyāti* is the nonperception of the true nature of the all-containing Self. For this term, see chap. 3, p. 103, n. 50.

59. For *anāśritaśakti*, cf. *supra*, ibid., and *infra*, chap. 5, p. 312-317ff, where we shall see how Abhinava further elucidates the role of *paśyantī* in the emanation.

Abhinavagupta (and Utpaladeva as it seems),[60] accepts almost all that Bhartṛhari[61] wrote about *paśyantī:* he quotes from him extensively in the *ĪPVV.* As it is, the objection raised by these authors to Bhartṛhari is based on logical grounds and derived from the *ābhāsavāda.* Once it had been established that *paśyantī* is rooted in an original state of the Word, *parā*, and accepted that the three levels of Speech do not constitute separate and illusory planes or stages of each act of consciousness and speech (at the cosmic or individual level)—and this makes, assuredly, a very great difference—there was nothing against accepting Bhartṛhari's or the *Vṛtti*'s description of the actual content of each stage, the meaning of which being reinterpreted from this new perspective.

In the same passage of the *ĪPV* (1.5.13),[62] the term *pratyavamarśa* is applied to *parāvāc* and *paśyantī*, but in the former case it refers to the reflective representation of the absolute "I": *ahaṃpratyavamarśa*; and in the latter case to the condition peculiar to objectivity: *idaṃbhāvarūpasya pratyavamarśa*, which "rests" precisely in the state or condition of the absolute "I" (*ahaṃbhāvaviśrānti*). For these nondualist Śaiva authors, a state or a category "rests" only in what is above it and wherein, by definition, it preexists in essence; and the ultimate "rest" is the rest of everything in the supreme consciousness or in *parāvāc.* The differences between *parā* and *paśyantī*, and their hierarchy, are thus clearly indicated. Abhinavagupta further

60. This was probably evidenced by his now lost commentary on the *Īśvara Pratyabhijñāsūtra*, upon which Abhinavagupta wrote the *ĪPVV.* Bhartṛhari is also quoted by Rāmakaṇṭha regarding *paśyantī* when he expounds the four stages of the Word in his commentary on *SpK* 4.18 (pp. 147ff.); he sums up his statement by giving a *śloka* (from the *MhBh*?) quoted in the *Vṛtti* on *Vākyapadīya*, 1.144:

avibhāgā tu paśyantī sarvataḥ saṃhṛtakramā/
svarūpajyotir evāntaḥ sūkṣmā vāg anapāyinī//:

"*Paśyantī* is undifferentiated, all process is entirely withdrawn within it. It is in essence nothing but light. It is, inwardly, subtle and indestructible speech."

61. Or the author of the *VP*'s *Vṛtti.*

62. Vol. 1, pp. 251-54.

clarifies this difference when he writes in the *PTV*: "*Paśyantī* becomes aware through the sole movement of consciousness of anything which, desired [by it], is specifically awakened by a definite cause."[63] This means that in *parāvāc* everything was contained in absolute undifferentiation and without any limit, whereas here the power of will, insofar as it is intent on the manifestation of the universe, limits the supreme consciousness and brings forth in *paśyantī* only that which serves its limited purpose—the manifestation of the universe. Such a limitation is brought about by the appearance of the lineaments of objectivity, which restrict the original freedom and utter plenitude of consciousness. Abhinavagupta compares on this occasion the Visionary to memory (*smṛti*), where images only arise when evoked by a particular cause.

Paśyantī is placed, as we have seen, at the level of the *tattva* of *sadāśiva*, which is, in Śaiva cosmogonies, the third *tattva*, following those of *śiva* and *śakti*, which cannot be separated and which correspond to *parāvāc*. It is also identified by Abhinavagupta with *icchāśakti*,[64] the power of will (or precognitive impulse) which, precisely, is said to be more specifically manifested at the *sadāśiva* level.[65]

In this interplay of Śiva's energies, which brings the universe

---

63. *PTV*, p. 4: *tatas tu paśyantī yad yad abhipsitaṃ tat tad eva samucitakaraṇaniyamaprabodhitaṃ bodhasūtraṇamātreṇa vimṛśati.*
64. The identification of *paśyantī* with the power of will is found above all in Abhinavagupta's and Utpaladeva's works; cf. the passage of the *PTV*, p. 4 quoted above, p. 190, or *ĪPV* 1.5.13 (vol. 2, p. 189, line 13): *iyaṃ eva ca icchāśaktirūpa.* Somānanda, on the other hand (*ŚD* 2.1), equates it with the power of cognition (and also with *sadāśiva*).
65. Each of the five energies of Śiva are ever-present and active, but they become predominant, individually, in turn. Thus the first five ontic levels —*śiva, śakti, sadāśiva, īśvara,* and *śuddhavidyā*—each correspond to the successive predominence of the powers of consciousness (*cit*), bliss (*ānanda*), will or impulse (*icchā*), cognition (*jñāna*), and action (*kriyā*); cf. *PS*, *śl.* 14.

    However, *sadāśiva* is sometimes regarded as associated with the predominence of the power of cognition.

into being—or in the movement which, in the human mind, brings about the awareness of the objective world—the power of will, the first precognitive impulse, corresponds to the moment that follows immediately after that of the first complete and undifferentiated awareness. This moment is characterized by a subtle vibration (*parispanda*) of consciousness, wherein arises a movement toward manifestation—or toward the object or notion—which is first perceived as a whole, not divided from consciousness, pure subjectivity being still predominant and actually covering these first lineaments of objectivity. The latter appears not as the universe or as an object, but as a desire, or an intent, or a first nondiscursive stirring of the will toward this objectivity. This is, to take up Somānanda's comparison, what would be experienced by a potter when thinking, prior to all creative acts; prior even to any definite representation of the prospective pot he would think: "I would like to make a pot."[66]

This power of will is in fact quite similar to the power of cognition to which *paśyantī* may also be equated: Abhinavagupta writes (*PTV*, p. 4) that *paśyantī* is at the first moment of knowledge (and some texts also place *jñānaśakti* at the level of *sadāśiva*). Indeed, envisioning an action to be performed

---

66. *ŚD* 2.84-85 (p. 91):

yathā kartuḥ kulādāder ghaṭaḥ kārya itīdṛśaḥ/
vimarśa icchārūpeṇa tadvad atrāpi saṃsthitam//
sā sthitā pūrvatas tasyā icchāyāḥ prasaraḥ katham/
yāvan na sūkṣma ullāsaś citaḥ kāryonmukhaḥ sthitaḥ//

"Just as the agent, be it a potter [who is about to make a pot], or any other person, becomes aware, in the form of an act of will, that 'a pot should be made,' likewise here (in *paśyantī*), the same situation [occurs]. How could the will that thus precedes [action], develop if there was not [from the outset] a subtle expansion of consciousness intent on the prospective object?"

It should be noted that in the same passage (*śl.* 83 quoted above, p. 189 n. 52), Somānanda describes knowledge as an action (*kriyā*). This action is said to have two parts (*bhāga*): first the representation of an action to be performed; second, probably, the inner, nondiscursive, vision of the object. All this has Śiva as background.

or something to be done implies knowing already—at least in outline—what one would like to do. And in fact, if one refers to the *ĪPVV*, one sees that Abhinavagupta, commenting upon a passage where Utpaladeva assimilates *paśyantī* with the power of will, writes that the latter "has for its nature the desire to know the object which is to be known. This energy of will brings forth those of cognition and action. The desire to know is, in fact, nothing else in essence but knowledge itself, for there the [prospective] object is already revealed in the full light of manifestation".[67] Here, of course, is meant a manifestation within, and inseparable from, consciousness, on a level, as we have seen, which is hardly separated from the supreme Word. Hence cognition is nothing but this first, kinetic, representation, devoid of all thought-constructs, of the pursued object or goal, which is inseparable from any act of will.

We have already seen *paśyantī* (in chap. 3) when dealing with the arising of the *kuṇḍalinī*, the higher stages of which may be described as corresponding to the levels of the Word from *parā* down to *vaikharī* (cf. *supra*, pp. 133-36), those stages and their interrelations being indeed not always described in the same way. These fluctuating views, these apparent discrepancies, are due primarily to the fact that the levels of the Word and even more the stages in the rising of the *kuṇḍalinī* are not described in the same way in all traditions. They are also due to the fact that in the same tradition (and sometimes in the same text even, as we shall see) the levels of the Word are envisaged differently depending upon what is being described (cosmic or human level, phonetic speculations or yoga), the different elements being used, however, within the same general pattern, wherein cosmic, ritual, or yogic terms correspond, due to the symbolic meanings they retain within differing systems of representation or visualizations. Thus *parā*, *paśyantī*,

67. *ĪPVV* 1.5.13 (vol. 2, p. 189): *bodhyabubhutsāsvabhāvā api iyaṃ bhavati/ ataś ca evaṃ—yadicchāśaktir jñānakriyāśaktyor anugrāhikā—iti, kiṃtu bubhutsā api bodhasvabhāvaiva tasya vastunas tatra avabhāsaparipūrṇatayā prakāśanāt.*

madhyamā, and *vaikharī*, representing three stages of the Word—supreme, intermediate, and inferior—are correlated, in the description of the throne (*āsana*) of the deity (*PTV*, p. 129), with the three goddesses Parā, Parāparā and Aparā; now these three deities, in the Triśūlamaṇḍala[68] of the Trika, are beyond *unmanā*, above the Śiva *tattva*, on the supreme level. On the other hand, *paśyantī* is described in the same passage of the *PTV* as extending (with the *ūrdhvakuṇḍalinī*) no further than *parā*, taken then as being the support for the three goddesses, which marks its upper limit. The same text goes on (pp. 129-30) correlating *paśyantī*, supposedly resting in Sadāśiva's power of cognition with the individual intellect (*pratyagātmani buddhi*), having Rudra for its deity. *Madhyamā*, in this case, corresponds to *manas* while abiding in Sadāśiva's power of action, and has the god Brahmā as its deity. Finally, *vaikharī*, dwelling in Īśvara's power of action, corresponds to *ahaṃkāra* and has Viṣṇu for its deity. These are not the correspondences of the Triśūlamaṇḍala.[68] But they fit into the same general vertical pattern, in the same ascending movement of meditation, and are expressions of the same theological concerns: we remain, notwithstanding all the variations, in the same system of representation associated with the same meditative-ritual picture of the body.[69] Many other examples could be mentioned of these variations within the same structure.

Coming back to the Visionary, it should be added that the apprehension of the manifestation as undifferentiatedly contained within the "I" consciousness—or self-representation—(*ahaṃpratyavamarśa*), which takes place in *parāvāc*, where it already appeared as a kind of inner expression (*antarabhilāpa*), must necessarily proceed in *paśyantī*, and still more markedly since henceforth one progressively emerges from undifferentiation. Thus Abhinavagupta notes in the *ĪPPV* that *paśyantī* is made of such a subtle murmur (*sūkṣmasaṃjalpasvabhāva*).[70] That, of course, is a kind of inner formulation

68. For this *maṇḍala*, cf. A. Sanderson, *Maṇḍala, op. cit.*

69. On this issue see *Mantras et diagrammes rituels dans l'hindouisme, op. cit.*

70. *ĪPVV* 1.5.13 (vol. 2, p. 190), line 18.

that accompanies the desire for action, a kinetic ideation of the universe to be made manifest, or of the action to be performed, which is still steeped in subjectivity. This formulation is peculiar to the power of will, and therefore to *paśyantī*. It is not subject to temporality (*akramika*), or it is, at least, completely totally immediate (*kṣaṇamātra*). Thus, behind any action or any thought-construct, there seems to be, following the initial, nondiscursive and undifferentiated moment corresponding to *parāvāc*, an adumbration, an intent, something like a synthetic intuition of the act or thought that is to come. Or else, to use Abhinavagupta's phrase, an intuition or a creative and a synthetic (or more exactly, undeveloped, inceptive) apprehension of the words which will come to express such an act or thought (*saṃvartitaśabdabhāvanā*), and this occurs in *paśyantī*.[71] In the *ĪPV*, still commenting upon this same *sūtra* (1.5.19) of Utpaladeva, Abhinavagupta endeavors to clarify this direct and immediate apprehension, wherein lies, however, an actual awareness (*vimarśa*) of the subsequent act or thought. It is, he writes, like the thought of a person who rushes to attend to something or who races through a book: neither can he utter distinctly the words he is reading nor clearly state to what he is rushing, and yet he is fully aware of it and could express it if he had the time to. In such circumstances, he says, the mental and "gross" thought-construct which normally follows upon the first nondiscursive apprehension is not there. However, since the action is done at full speed there must occur a subtle reflective representation (*pratyavamarśa*) of what is to be done consisting in the synthetic apprehension of the words expressing the act which, when it eventually takes place and is outwardly displayed, will then be accompanied by a "gross" thought-construct.[72] Thus we see

71. *ĪPV* 1.5.19 (vol. 1, p. 293); cf. next footnote.

72. *ĪPV* 1.5.19 (vol. 1, pp. 290-93): *bhavatu vā kṣaṇamātrasvabhāvaḥ sākśātkāraḥ, tatrāpi asti vimarśaḥ/ avaśyaṃ ca etat, katham anyatha, iti/ yadi sa na syāt tat ekābhisaṃdhānena javāt gacchan, tvaritaṃ ca varṇān paṭhan, drutaṃ ca mantrapustakaṃ vācayan, na abhimatam eva gacchet, uccārayet, vācayet vā/ . . . atra ca yataḥ paścādbhāvisthūlavikalpakalpanā na saṃvedyate, tata eva tvaritvam iti sūkṣmeṇa pratyava-*

that the higher levels of the Word are intrinsically bound with any act of speech or thought (which indeed amounts to the same, since for anyone agreeing with Bhartṛhari, there is no thought or act without some form of speech); those are necessary moments of consciousness, whether individual consciousness or the supreme Consciousness manifesting and sustaining the universe—the latter, as conceived by the authors of the Trika, being indeed nothing but a transfer to the level of cosmogony of their notions about individual consciousness.

It should be added that *paśyantī* is not a mere stage prior to verbal expression and cognitive thought, or to the differentiated manifestation. Being the condition of consciousness and speech at a level where objectivity cannot be separated from subjectivity, where the world, "that" (*idam*), is inseparably united with the "I" (*aham*) and subordinated to it, *paśyantī* is at a junction point in the movement toward manifestation (this we saw with the gradual development of a thought tending to discursive verbal expression) and resorption as well.

Paśyantī is said to occur, as we have seen, at the level of *sadāśiva* which, cosmically, is the second stage of the manifestation as well as the next-to-last one of the resorption. Similarly, at the human level, *paśyantī* does not appear as a mere stage in the formulation of a thought-speech tending toward a discursive mental and verbal expression, but also in what the Trika conceives of as a return of diversity of thought-constructs to the unity of the thinking subject, namely in memory, *smaraṇa*. Abhinavagupta points out this twofold movement in the *ĪPVV*. In the passage we quoted above[73] where he describes *paśyantī* in the terms of the *Vṛtti* on *Vākyapadīya, kārika* 1.142, he describes the stages in the development of thought: first there is the stage of the "I"-consciousness (this is the self-awareness, *vimarśa*, proper to *parāvāc*; this, cosmically, is the stage of *śakti*); then comes, at the level of

---

marśena saṃvartitaśabdabhāvanāmayena bhāvyam eva, saṃvartitā hi śabdabhāvanā prasāraṇena vivartyamānā sthūlo vikalpaḥ.

73. *Supra*, p. 191.

sadāśiva, the form of consciousness that is indicated by the term *that*, but as inherent to, having the same substratum as the "I"-consciousness (*idam ity ahaṃbhāvasāmānādhikaraṇyena sadāśivabhūmyadhiṣṭhānam*). Next appears "that" alone, namely, objectivity perceived as distinct from the "I" (*tato'pi idam ity eva bhedamātreṇa*), with its infinite variety. When the knower, however, ceasing to become aware of fresh objects, turns back to what he previously perceived, then the awareness of the diversity of the objective world is replaced by a "subtler" (*sūkṣma*) state of consciousness which is memory (*smaraṇa*). *Smaraṇa*, says Abhinavagupta, belongs to *paśyantī* because in *paśyantī* (and here he quotes the *Vṛtti* of *VP* 1.142) there occurs precisely this resorption of the linguistic process, this inherence of objectivity in subjectivity, which is proper to a consciousness turning back upon itself when, desisting from the perception of fresh objects, it recalls those previously perceived and resting within it in a "subtle" form. "Thus, he concludes, when an agent of cognition (a person) walking along a path where he is conscious of the world around him ceases to [have this consciousness], memory [occurs. And this memory] can be said to be nondiscursive as compared with the preceding state because it consists in a synthetic apprehension of the words expressing what happened before from the point of view of what follows. In spite of which [memory] has also a discursive aspect since it is made up of particular representations [of things past]."[74] The western reader will perhaps be tempted here to mention Marcel Proust. Be that as it may, we shall see later on[75] that, according to this view, since memory permits one to grasp a particular occurrence as one with the knower, to apprehend diversity as rooted in consciousness and therefore to rise from the diversity of the empirical world to the unity of consciousness, it can be held as a means for one to grasp the essence of mantras. But let us come back to *paśyantī* considered

74. *ĪPVV* 1.5.19 (vol. 2, p. 226): *tathāca mārgagatāvidantāvimarśata eva pramātur uparama iti tāvati ca smaraṇam, uttarottarāpekṣayā ca pūrvapūrvasya saṃvartitaśabdabhāvanārūpatvād avikalpatvam ucyate saty-api vimarśaviśeṣātmakavikalparūpatve.*

75. Chap. 7, pp. 397ff.

as a movement toward the appearance of the world and that of language, with which we are primarily concerned in this chapter.

Paśyantī and consciousness as power of will being such as described above, they appear thus as the seat of the dynamic seeds of all prospective acts and thoughts, a plane where they exist only as a barely formulated Word, which is pure energy, ready to generate the whole multiplicity of diversity. But these seeds of knowledge, this subtle thought which precedes thought-constructs, which is a kind of subconscious thought, is it not the *ālayavijñāna* of Madhyamaka Buddhism? As a matter of fact, in the *ĪPVV* Abhinavagupta identifies the power of will with the "store Consciousness" (as *ālayavijñāna* is sometimes translated).[76] He compares it to the will of a person who sets in motion the chain-buckets of a waterwheel that brings water out of a well: in the same way, the energy as will (*icchā*), or as a first noncognitive impulse, first assents globally to all that will henceforth appear in a definite order as the empirical world.[77]

On several occasions in the *ĪPVV* Abhinavagupta returns to this role of vision of the act to be performed played by the Word at the level of *paśyantī*, or by the power of will by which it is characterized. He even goes so far as to introduce a kind of hierarchy in these representations, viewing an act of will, the implementation of which implies several operations, as a great *paśyantī* (*mahāpaśyantī*), to which are subordinated the *paśyantī*s antecedent to the performance of these secondary operations. "Thus," he says, "'I go to the village' is a great

---

76. *ĪPVV* 1.5.5 (vol. 2, p. 99, 1.7): *icchākhyālayavijñāna.*
77. Ibid., vol. 2, p. 98: *sā ca icchālayavijñānakalpāraghaṭṭaghaṭīyantravāhakecchā iva anantakālabhāviniyatakramakam ābhāsavaicitryam āgūryaiva uttiṣṭhatī/*

In the *PTV* (p. 108) Abhinavagupta refers also to the *ālayavijñāna*, following a passage we quoted above (p. 182) in connection with *parāvāc*, where he states that the "conventions" of language are based upon a nonconventional and nondiscursive background.

paśyantī as compared to the *paśyantī* 'I leave the house.' In the same way, one must consider the plane of *sadāśiva* as a great *paśyantī* in comparison with the innumerable *paśyantīs* of the individual knowers subject to *māyā*."[78] And this great *paśyantī* might itself be regarded as enclosed in a supremely great *paśyantī* (*paramahāpaśyantī*), which is nothing else but *parāvāc*; this assertion is not unexpected if one remembers that *parāvāc*[79] includes the seeds of discursive thought or empirical language, which will be encountered further on.

Let us add that the interplay between the stages of speech and other elements of the nondualistic Śaiva vision of the universe which we saw above, appears also in another light, which will remind us of what has been said in chap. 3 regarding *nāda*. There is in Abhinavagupta (and Jayaratha) a description of *paśyantī* where it assumes the form of an audible sound, and is more (or rather less) than an infinitely subtle and transcendent, therefore inaudible stage of the Word. In *TĀ*, third *āhnika* (3.234ff., vol. 2, pp. 223ff.), Abhinavagupta says that "the supreme consciousness, as the goddess Kālasaṃkarṣiṇī uniting with Bhairava, experiences a reflexive awareness—or representation—(*pratyavamarśa*) of the absolute "I," *aham*. As a result—owing to *ahaṃparamarśa*,[80] therefore to the absolute, intense assertion of this "I" encompassing the whole universe within itself—arise the three stages of the Word: *paśyantī*, *madhyamā*, and *vaikharī*, that are respectively (*śl.* 236) supreme, subtle, and gross,[81] in addition to which each of these three stages also has three aspects: supreme, subtle, and gross.

---

78. *ĪPVV* 1.5.13 (vol. 2, p. 195): *evaṃ grāmaṃ gacchāmīti mahāpaśyantī gṛhāt niḥsarāmīti paśyantīm apekṣya tāvat yāvat sadāśiveśvaradaśā mahāpaśyantī māyāpramātṛvartyaśeṣapaśyantyapekṣayeti mantavyaṃ.*

79. Ibid., vol. 2, p. 197: *yā 'sau mahāpaśyantīnāṃ pratyagātmarūpāṇām avibhāgātmikā paramahāpaśyantī tayā ca yo 'sāvānandamahimā para-svātantryātmā ullāsanīyaḥ, sā bhagavataḥ parā vāg iti darśitam.*

80. Note that there is here no very clear difference between *pratyavamarśa* and *parāmarśa*.

81. This *śloka* and Jayaratha's commentary have been quoted above, p. 171.

Thus regarding the Visionary, *sthūlapaśyantī* is a resonance as light and beautiful as a series of musical notes, not divided into phonemes, and so forth.[82] This is not an articulate sound, for articulation implies that air strikes the organs of phonation, which here cannot be, because it would be much too corporeal: such speech, Jayaratha explains "in its own nature, in its essence, is nothing but the primordial resonance" (*prathāmikanādamātrasvabhāvā*). However delicate and subtle, this *paśyantī* is, however, audible. But it should be remembered in this regard that *nāda*, the primordial phonic vibration or resonance, is classically compared to the ultimate, finest (although perceptible) vibration of a bell. Such a sound or the sound of a stringed instrument (therefore without perceptible striking of air against something) is apparently the case here,[83] and of such a sound Abhinavagupta (*śl.* 239) says it is "very near to consciousness" (*saṃvitsavidhavṛttitaḥ*).

Other gross forms of sounds (or speech) belong to *madhyamā* or *vaikharī.* The Visionary, however, and the other two levels as well, have, according to Abhinavagupta, a subtle and supreme aspect. Since an aiming at, an intention (*anusaṃdhāna*), he says, precedes any gross state of Speech, the intention to produce a sound will be the subtle stage of *paśyantī* (and of the other two *vāc* as well). This brings us back to the usual description of the Visionary as *icchāśakti.* Finally, both these stages are dominated by and included in a supreme stage: that is, the first unconditioned (*anupadhimant*) state of such an intention: this is the very reality of consciousness (*saṃvitattvam*), the highest point or limit (*pūrvakoṭi*) of will, a primal condition devoid of the "coloring" element that the mere wish to emit a sound would suffice to bring about (since a wish is always a wish for something).

All of this may appear surprising. It is, however, very understandable, for several reasons. First, because Abhinava, in this

---

82. *tatra yā svarasandarbhasubhagā nādarūpīṇī //236//*
sā sthūlā khalu paśyantī varṇādyapravibhāgataḥ/

83. We have also seen previously (p. 96, n. 30) that there are audible forms of the *nāda*. Cf. for instance the ten *nāda*s perceived by the yogin according to *Haṃsopaniṣad*, 16 (*Yoga Upaniṣad*, Adyar: 1920, p. 537).

passage, deals with the phonematic emanation as reflected in *paśyantī* (where all the phonemes are in the form of energy),[84] and because primarily he wishes to explain the paradoxical coincidence of a universe emanated out of the Godhead—and therefore, in some respects, extraneous to it—and of the supreme consciousness, which is one and absolute (*anuttarā*), the only reality which actually *is*.[85] Hence this presence of the gross in the supreme, and above all of the supreme Word in all the other stages of Speech and of consciousness. This passage looks at the emanation from the perspective of the Krama (as evidenced by the fact that *śl.* 234 mentions Kālasaṃkarṣiṇī, the highest of the Kālīs). Now, in this system, as a result of the workings of the "wheels of the energies" of consciousness, the Kālīs (with which Abhinavagupta deals in *śl.* 250ff.), there occur various successive permutations where each element of the system may take the place, dialectically, of any other one.[86] The whirling of the wheels both symbolizes and brings about the all-pervasiveness of the energy in all its forms.

Finally let us note that there is a similar threefold subdivision of the stages of the Word in the last chapter of the *LT* (57.1-18, p. 224). Sound (*śabda*) is here described as being of three possible types: *vyakta, vyaktasama*, and *avyakta*. In the case of *vaikharī*, *vyakta* is that sound which is "in the body of living beings and which begins and ends there": those are probably the sounds emitted by the organs of phonation: words,

---

84. Cf. *infra*, chap. 5, p. 313-14, quoting the *PTV*, pp. 144-45.
85. *Nanu* (says Jayaratha, vol. 2, p. 2) *ekaivānuttarā parā saṃvid asti, tadatiriktasya anyasya kasyacit saṃvedyamānatā yogāt?*
86. Many are the Tantric texts, usually marked by the categories of the Krama, where occur classifications or distribution of this type:

supreme-supreme	subtle-supreme	gross-supreme	
supreme-subtle	subtle-subtle	gross-subtle	
supreme-gross	subtle-gross	gross-gross	and so forth.

See, for instance, *YH* 1.74-78 and *Dī*, pp. 91-95, where *sṛṣṭi-sthiti-saṃhāra* are caught in a series of such permutations, thus establishing these three functions in the three portions (each divided into three) of the *śrīcakra*. See also ibid., pp. 120-22, *ad YH* 2.17.

cries, and so forth. "The sounds of the *vīṇā*, of a flute, of a drum, and so on, arising through some exertion, and the desire to produce them" are *vyaktasama.* The sound-energy (*śabda-śakti*), finally, "caused by the movement of air in oceans, rivers, mountain caves," is *avyakta.* Here again we have a hierarchical gradation of sounds into more or less manifest (hence more or less elevated or subtle) according to whether they are farther from or nearer to the spoken word, or to the phonemes of which words are made up. In each of these categories of sound, the *LT* goes on to say (*śl.* 15-16), may be distinguished the four levels from *śāntā* to *vaikharī* (or vice-versa), the same distinction holding good for what these sounds have to express (*vācyaṃ caturvidhaṃ jñeyaṃ śāntadipravibhāgavat*): "the objects denoted are also of four types corresponding to the classification of sound as *śānta*, and so forth" (S. Gupta's translation), which seems an awkward summary of what had been more clearly and above all more subtly expressed by Abhinavagupta.[87] But let us now come to the "intermediate" Word.

Madhyamā

Still resting in and arising from *parāvāc*,[88] resulting from the ongoing movement that already produced *paśyantī*, there emerges the next stage of Speech: the Intermediate, *madhyamā.* It is so called because it is in an intermediate position between the subtle and still undifferentiated Word, *paśyantī*, and the manifest and articulated "gross" speech, *vaikharī.*[89]

With *madhyamā* we come out of undifferentiation.[90] While

87. It has been already noted (above, chap. 2, p. 68) that the *LT* has probably come under strong Śaiva influences.
88. *PTV*, pp. 6, 11, and 16: *madhyā paśyanty atha parām adhyāsyābhedato bhṛśam*: "The Intermediate and the Visionary being assuredly inseparable from the Supreme."
89. The term *madhyamā* may be considered as confirming that there are in fact only three stages of the Word, from *paśyantī* to *vaikharī*—*parā* being not a stage but the original Word. Cf. Bhāskararāya's commentary on *Lalitasahasranāma śl.* 132 (p. 100).
90. *PTV*, p. 6, line 5: *yatra ca madhyamāyāṃ bhedāvabhāsaḥ.*

there was in *paśyantī* nothing but "a desire for the division of the Word into phonemes, words, and sentences,"[91] here this division is actually achieved: language appears at last. It is not, as we have seen, that language was totally missing in *paśyantī*, but it was not there in full. The complex—and, in some respects, somewhat contradictory—analysis of Abhinavagupta was meant precisely to help us grasp what may differentiate language itself from the initial vision of an act which, in a system where the Word is omnipresent, cannot but consist in Word, without, however, actually being language. The clue as to the difference between *paśyantī* and *madhyamā*, in this respect, probably lies in the phrase used by Abhinavagupta in the *ĪPV* and the *ĪPVV*,[92] *saṃvartitaśabdabhāvanā:* the undeveloped, enveloped (or inceptive) apprehension or realization[93]—not yet evolved into discursive, empirical, language—of the words expressing the action that will take place. Here, in *madhyamā*, linguistic consciousness appears: "phonemes, words, and sentences" are present, and consequently also the division in "expressing" and "expressed"[94] resulting from convention (*saṃketa*) that is proper to speech.

With language and speech being there, there appear now in the Word both the constituent sound materials of language, namely, that which expresses (*vācaka*), which is creative, and the whole creation, that which thereby has to be expressed (*vācya*). This is the plane on which objectivity (*idantā*), the universe (*viśva*), is born from the Word and within it. At the level of individual consciousness, of cognition, this is the plane where the mind moves on to an analytical stage of its own

---

91. *PTV*, p. 13, quoted *supra*, p. 189, n. 54.
92. Cf. *supra*, p. 197.
93. *Bhāvanā*, we may remark, in a Tantric context, is both vision, creative (√*BHU*) meditation, or intuitive realization, and identification with the object mentally created or intuited.
94. *PTV*, p. 5: *madhyamā punaḥ tayor eva vācyavācakayoḥ bhedam ādarśya sāmānādhikaraṇyena vimarśavyāpārā.*

 "The Intermediate, for its part, reveals the duality of the expressing and the expressed, which, however, owing to the reflective awareness attached thereto, [appears] as grounded in the same subject."

awareness of speech and becomes aware not only of the differentiation innate in cognitive thought and in language, but also of a differentiation between signs (*vācaka, śabda*) and what they mean or refer to (*vācya, artha*). One must add, however, that since *madhyamā* is not yet the level of empirical, "gross" manifestation, the signs, as well as that which they refer to or mean, have no physical existence: they are either mental (for the individual consciousness), or mere aspects or forms of the energy inseparable from divine consciousness (for the cosmogony). In *madhyamā*, Abhinavagupta writes, there occurs an awareness of the expressed and of what it expresses, as having the same nature and resting in the same mental stuff,[95] or as consisting of energy. Abhinavagupta states precisely that the level of the Intermediate is that of a form of consciousness where the objective world, though manifest, remains "covered"[96] by subjectivity. We shall see that this is due, at the cosmological level, to *madhyamā* normally appearing at the level of the *īśvara tattva*. For individual consciousness, *madhyamā* is said to be at the level of the intellect (*buddhi*),[97] the highest portion of the inner organ (*antaḥkaraṇa*), where consciousness is still

95. Ibid.

96. *Ācchādita, pracchādita*: objectivity is considered as covered by, overlaid with the supreme subjectivity that permeates it, holds it within itself, covers it, as it were, as with a cloth (but one made of light); cf. *PTV*, pp. 75, 114-15, 130, and 148.

97. Cf. *SpK* 4.8, p. 150 of Rāmakaṇṭha's commentary, which quotes the *Vṛtti* on the *Vākyapadīya:*

kevalaṃ buddhyupādānā kramarūpānupātinī/
prāṇavṛttim atikramya madhyamā vāk pravartate//

"Associated with the intellect, following a regular order, the intermediate Word stays beyond the activity of breath."

In *ĪPVV* 1.5.13 (vol. 2, p. 188, quoted *infra*, p. 208), Abhinavagupta extends the field of activity of *madhyamā* to *ahaṃkāra* and *manas*. This can be true only if one includes in *madhyamā* its extensions or its "grosser" forms, for its own place is the intellect.

See also Rāghavabhaṭṭa's commentary on *ŚT* 1.109 (vol. 1, p. 61): *bāhyāntaḥkaraṇātmakāṃ hiraṇyagarbharūpiṇīṃ nadabindumayīṃ nābhyādihṛdayāntābhivyaktisthānāṃ viśeṣasaṃkalpādisatattvāṃ madhyamām āha madhyameti/ madhye mā buddhir asyā iti vigrahaḥ.*

impersonal. So, although thought-constructs (*saṃkalpa*) and discursive thought (*vikalpa*) appear there, they retain, however, a somewhat nonempirical nature.

"Although at the plane of [*śuddha*] *vidyā*, on that of *māyā*," says Abhinava in the *PTV*, "manifestation remains undifferentiated, the reflective awareness [that takes place there] is of a different sort. At the plane of [*śuddha*] *vidyā*, indeed, the 'this' (*idam*), formed by the whole aggregate of the knowers and the subjects of knowledge, comes together as if it were one with the 'I' (*aham*). One therefore is aware of it as 'covered' (*ācchādita*) by the 'I,' [the result being] 'I-this.' This is to say that these two [factors: 'I-this'] are reflected in the same common subtratum of consciousness (*cit*). Being thus manifested undifferentiatedly, they are said to be grounded and to abide in the same substance of consciousness. This is why the venerable Utpaladeva has said, concerning the *īśvaratattva*, 'that which exists on this plane is of supreme-nonsupreme (*parāpara*) nature, and, analogously, on the plane of *māyā* [its nature is] nonsupreme (*apara*), but the energy of Śiva is neither supreme-nonsupreme nor nonsupreme.'"[98]

In the *ĪPVV*, Abhinava develops the same theme but from a more psychological point of view: "The intermediate [stage of the Word], he writes, is that energy of self-awareness (*vimarśa-śakti*) which activates the internal organ (*antaḥkaraṇa*), which is to say *manas*, *buddhi* and *ahaṃkāra* resting on the substratum of vital energy (*prāṇa*), the eightfold subtle body (*puryaṣṭaka*) in the central place between [the flow of the breaths: *madhya-bhūmau*]. When the internal organ has been thus activated by this [power], it engages in its proper function, that is, intentional thought activity (*saṃkalpa*), judgment (*niścaya*)

---

98. *PTV*, p. 130: *yady api hi vidyāpade māyāpade 'py abhedena bhāsanā sthitāpi tatra vimarśo 'nyathā/ vidyāpade hīdam iti pramātṛprameya-jātam ekato 'hamātmani saṃkrāmet tadācchāditaṃ vimṛśyate "aham idam" iti/ tad etat samāne cidātmany adhikaraṇe ubhayaṃ pratibimbitam abhedenaivāvabhāsamānaṃ sāmānādhikaraṇyam uktam/ ata eva "īśvara-sthāyāṃ parāparātmikāṃ daśāṃ bhāvā bhajante, yathaiva māyādhvany aparāṃ na tu saiva parāparaśaktir aparā vā" iti yad īśvaratattvam prati abhihitaṃ śrīmadutpaladevapadaiḥ.*

and self-reference (*abhimāna*), which constitute the process of dualistic thought (*vikalpana*). Then the representation embodying word (*vimarśamayī vāc*) can be described as 'thought' (*cintana*), because it 'fully enjoys' (*ābhuṅkte*), is entirely aware of both the 'grasped,' that is, what is intended by thought and so forth, and of 'that which grasps,' that is, the subject of the intentional thought, this being done with the diversity (*bhedena*) proper to it [namely] the distinct process of designation (*abhidhāna*) of such words which express something as 'I, Caitra, desire this pot.' Because this [stage of the Word], which is what is expressed by thought, comes between [*paśyantī* and *vaikharī*] it is [called] the Intermediate. Its nature is that of the [energy] of cognition (*jñānaśaktirūpā*)."[99]

These two quotations help to bring out the "intermediate" character of *madhyamā* as well as its role in the dialectics of the cosmic manifestation and of language.

From the standpoint of cosmology, *madhyamā* appears even more markedly than *paśyantī* to dwell at the level of the supreme-nonsupreme energy, namely at the juncture of the differentiated and the undifferentiated, of time and timelessness, of objectivity and subjectivity. This, writes Abhinavagupta,[100] is the level where the supreme-nonsupreme energy expands fully. Indeed, *madhyamā* is considered to be the level of the *īśvara* and *śuddhāvidyā tattva*s; now, *īśvara* is that level where objectivity distinctly emerges in the pure knower but where

---

99. *ĪPVV* 1.5.13 (vol. 2, p. 188): *antaḥkaraṇaṃ manobuddhyahaṃkāralakṣaṇaṃ madhyabhūmau puryaṣṭakātmani prāṇādhāre viśrāntaṃ yā vimarśaśaktiḥ prerayati sā madhyamā vāk/ tatpreritaṃ ca tadantaḥkaraṇaṃ saṃkalpane niścaye abhimanane ca svasmin vyāpāre vikalpanalakṣaṇe pravartate/ tatkāle sā vimarśamayī vāk saṃkalpyādikaṃ grāhyam saṃkalpayitrādirūpaṃ ca grāhakaṃ svena abhidhānasya imaṃ ghaṭam ahaṃ caitraḥ saṃkalpayāmītyader vācakasya śabdasya bhedena sphuṭena krameṇābhuṅkte gāḍham parāmṛśati yatas tataś cintanaśabdavācyā madhyabhavatvāt madhyamā jñānaśaktirūpā.*

The English translation of such passages of the *ĪPVV* as this (and others quoted in this chapter) is not easy. I wish to thank Alexis Sanderson for his help in the matter. The undoubtedly imperfect final result being of course my responsibility, not his. (A. Padoux)

100. *PTV*, p. 148, quoted *infra*, p. 210.

the subject is still predominant; whereas on the level of *śuddhā-vidyā* both tendencies are exactly balanced; after which the balance, under the action of *māyā*, tips in favor of objectivity.[101]

With regard to the energies or powers, here again we have the same relative uncertainty we have already seen in *paśyantī*: *madhyamā* can then be taken as corresponding either to the power of cognition or to that of action.[102] In fact, if one bears in mind what has been seen regarding *paśyantī*, it may be held that *madhyamā* consists of the power of cognition, insofar as the knowledge of objectivity or of the action to be accomplished is experienced, and since this objectivity or action are discursively formulated in consciousness or in the intellect. But it may also be regarded as consisting of the power of action, since the articulate language, which is action, already appears. The correspondence between *madhyamā* and both the *īśvara* and *śūddhāvidyā tattva*s could support this interpretation if one considers that the power of cognition is predominant in the former and that of action in the latter.[103]

The presence in the Intermediate of the expressing and the expressed is also mentioned by Abhinavagupta in a passage of the *PTV* where he points out that they are not only "covered" by the pure subjectivity, that is, resting on the bedrock of consciousness, but also closely and mutually superimposed. Therefore in the Intermediate, the Word and the universe which springs therefrom exactly coincide and intermingle in their form of pure energy. As a result, the presence of the energy in the manifested world, and the "rest" of the latter in the former, is strengthened, with the effect, notably, of making human speech more efficient. We shall see later on, when discussing the phonematic emanation, that it is in the Intermediate that appears the *uttaramālinī*—this arrangement of phonemes where vowels (which are precisely regarded as *vācaka*) and consonants (*vācya*) are mixed up—an arrangement considered as particularly powerful and efficacious, both because rooted

101. *PTV*, p. 11, and *ĪPVV* 1.5.13 (vol. 2, p. 188), previously quoted.
102. *PTV*, p. 148, as quoted on next page.
103. Cf. *supra*, p. 193, n. 65, and p. 195, n. 67.

in *madhyamā* and because of this mixing up of the phonemes.[104]

Here is the relevant passage of the *PTV*:

> The situation [which is that of the phonemes] of which one must be conscious on the plane of the Intermediate is that of the development of the venerable [goddess] Parāparā[105] [but] as residing in the supreme consciousness. The plane proper to *madhyamā* is on the level of *īśvara*, which is the power of action. It consists of a form of knowledge (*vedana*) that is a covering [by pure consciousness] of the clearly manifested object of cognition; just as in the expressed is the expressing, here the expressed also is superimposed [on the expressing]. Such an imposition, consisting of a reciprocal mixing and covering [of these two elements], can happen only if the expressing is entirely [superimposed] on the expressed, which is all the manifest, and if all the manifest [is imposed on the expressing], and not otherwise. A cloth cannot cover another one if it is three or four fingerbreadths shorter. And this omnipresence of all in all (*viśvātmakatvam*) is due to this mutual mixing up of the natures proper to [*vācya* and *vācaka*].[106]

"In the world of duality (*bhede 'pi*)," he adds further on, "that which expresses (*vācaka*) appears only as indissolubly linked with the subjectivity, be it under the form of the performer or in that of the performance" (*pratipādyapratipādakobhayarūpapramātṛsvarūpāvicchinna eva*) Or: "For us, the

---

104. Cf. chap. 5, pp. 320ff.

105. The three planes of energy (or of the Word)—supreme, supreme-nonsupreme, and nonsupreme (*parā, parāparā, aparā*)—are also seen as aspects of the three supreme goddesses of the Trika: Parā, Parāparā and Aparā. On these, see two papers by A. Sanderson, "Maṇḍala" and "Śaivism and the Tantric Tradition," cited previously.

106. *PTV*, pp. 147-48: *evaṃ ca parasaṃvidantarvartini madhyamāpade parāparābhaṭṭārikāvijṛmbhāspade sthitir vimṛśyate / madhyamā tāvat svādhikārapade kriyāśaktyātmany aiśvare pade sphuṭavedyapracchādaka-vedanarūpā vācye vācakaṃ tatrāpi ca vācyam adhyasyate / viśvatra vācye viśvātmanī vācakam api yadi viśvātmaiva tad evaṃ parasparācchādana-lolībhāvātmā nirvahed adhyāso na tv anyathā / na hi tricaturaṅgulanyūna-tāmātre 'pi paṭaḥ paṭāntarācchādakaḥ syāt / viśvātmakatvaṃ ca paras-parasvarūpavyāmiśratayā syāt.*

word (*gīḥ*: the voice) is a consciousness (*saṃvidātmakam*) that is both one and unique and containing within itself the infinite diversity of things. In ordinary life also, on the plane of *māyā*, the Word (*vāk*) is of the nature of light (*prakāśarūpa*), producing reflective awareness (*pratyavamarśakāriṇī*). It is indeed made up of the discrete elements linked up in succession by time that are the syllables and words of this world, but these have as their essence a one and single act of conscience (*ekaparāmarśasvabhāvaiva*)" (p. 150). "This is how," he concludes (p. 158), "the blessed venerable *parāparā*, possessed of the division into words, since this is the main role of the Intermediate, takes on the form of the venerable Mālinī, and none other. . . ."

Let us now examine, in light of these quotations, the role of *madhyamā* in the development of thought and language. It is because, in the Intermediate, the expressing and the expressed appear in a mental form and are exactly superimposable, that superimposition of the words of language to material objects—that is, two categories different in nature—is possible.[107] Differentiation, the dual aspect of empirical diversity, emerges from oneness or returns to it in *madhyamā*. If one looks at the whole process, there is first the undifferentiated oneness of a consciousness which is seminal speech (*parā*), then a synthetic awareness of the concept or of the act to be accomplished, through an undeveloped intuiting of the words that express it (*paśyantī*); thereafter appear discursive language and thought, immanent, however, to consciousness or to the intellect, and where the expressing and the expressed[108] are exactly superimposed (*madhyamā*). In *vaikharī* the two

---

107. It may be assumed that Abhinavagupta had in mind, when defining the levels of the Word, Bhartṛhari's views, whom he so frequently refers to on this occasion, on the "mental word" (*buddhisthāśabda*), to which corresponds a mental object (*bauddhārta*).

108. It is tempting to use here the Saussurean terminology: "signifiant" and "signifié," but it would be unwise, because misleading, to do so. One might, however, in the case of *madhyamā*, consider that what are superimposed there are the verbal form and the notion (not forgetting, however, that of these two the verbal form, the *vācaka*, is the highest).

elements are separate, yet since the earlier stages of speech are, as we have already said, ever present moments of thought and and language, the latter will never be cut off from thought or things. The underlying oneness remains, prevents an absolute and insuperable dualism, and stands as the basis for the validity of knowledge.

Abhinavagupta draws therefrom a practical application to the language of children, of which the gradual acquisition, while relevant to the Corporeal, is, he believes, a result of the characteristics of the Intermediate. If *parāvāc*, as we have seen, was not the root of any form of speech, the child would never develop the knowledge of significations, since these would lack their necessary grounding in the Absolute. But it is primarily because there exists in *madhyamā* an outwardly unexpressed language, where the expressive (*vācaka*) and the expressed (*vācya*) are exactly superimposed and intimately blended, and because *madhyamā* is the ground from which *vaikharī* emerges that the child will be able to coordinate words and objects which are given him separately in *vaikharī*, and that he will, at the empirical level, learn to speak.[109]

109. *PTV*, pp. 158-59: "Children, even though their places and organs of speech articulation are fully developed when they are only two or three years old, increase from day to day, from month to month, their ability to make use of language. Now, if the first features of the phonemes together with the places and organs of articulation from which they are inseparable and that are fully developed in *vaikharī* only, were not already there on the plane of *madhyamā*, there would be no difference in the development [of intelligence and use of language] between a child born on the previous day and one that is one month or one year old. [You might object] to this if it were so that this difference would be felt in *madhyamā* only. But what is the situation, in fact? Let us examine it: it is by hearing the words and seeing the objects [that they refer to] that [a child] increases [his intelligence and use of language]. The phonemes [making up the words] that he is aware of and that are audible pertain to the plane of *vaikharī*, in regard to which he is as if born blind [that is, he can hear but does not know to what the words refer]. It is therefore necessary that *vaikharī*, together with the places and organs of speech articulation which make it up, should already exist internally within *madhyamā*. This is so even for the mute": *tathā hi bālā dvitrair varṣair yady api sphuṭībhūtasthānakaraṇāḥ bhavanti tathāpi eṣāṃ māsānumāsa-*

Finally, as regards speech, and not knowledge, *madhyamā* appears as inner speech. This is why we are told that there one finds the places of articulation of the phonemes (*sthāna*) and the organs of phonation (*karaṇa*); if words can be uttered inwardly, there must also be some organs within to utter these inner speech-sounds. Thus when one speaks mentally to himself, or when one thinks very clearly in words and sentences, he is not in *vaikharī* but in *madhyamā*. This applies also to the repetition of mantras. Abhinavagupta may therefore write: "The supreme Lord himself, in the section on *japa* of the *Svacchandatantra*, explains that the [*japa*] that cannot be overheard is called [done] 'secretely' (*upāṃśu*) and it is so called because it takes place in the Intermediate [Word], where the self only hears, and none else."[110] Later in this same passage Abhinavagupta even seems to accept the idea that *madhyamā* can go beyond the stage of inner speech and develop nearly to a whisper, provided it is heard by none but its utterer.[111]

This point of view will perhaps appear as oversimplified and as detracting from the subtler and more penetrating analysis of speech developed above. The reason for this approach is, however, probably an intent to establish a correspondence between the three types of mantra repetition and

---

dinānudinaṃ eva vā hi vyutpattir adhikādhikarūpatām etiti tāvat sthitaṃ/ tatra yadi madhyamāpade tathāvidhavaikharīprasarasphuṭībhaviṣyat-sthānakaraṇāvibhāgavarṇāṃśasphuraṇaṃ na syāt tad aharjātasya bāla-kasya māsajātasya saṃvatsarajātasya vā vyutpattau na viśeṣaḥ syāt/ madhyamaiva sā vyutpattyā viśiṣyate iti cet, katham iti carcyatāṃ tāvat/ śṛṇvann eva tāñ śabdān paśyaṃś cārthān vyutpadyate varṇāṃś ca śrūyamāṇān eva parāmṛśec chrūyante ca vaikharīmayāḥ teśu ca asau rūpa va jātyandhavat/ tasmād antarmadhyamāniviṣṭasthānakaraṇādi-mayī asty eva vaikharī/ mūke 'pi evam eva.

110. *PTV*, p. 71: *tathāhi śrīparameśvara eva śrīsvacchandaśāstre japavibhāga-nirṇayāvasara evam eva nirūpitavān 'ātmanā śrūyate yas tu sa upāṃśur iti smṛtaḥ' atra hi madhyamāpade ātmaiva saṃsṛṇute nāpara ity uktam.*

It should be noted, however, that Kṣemarāja (*SvT* 2.148, comm.; vol. 1, 2nd part, p. 83) places mental *japa* in *madhyamā*, and *japa* "done secretly" in *vaikharī*.

For *japa*, cf. A. Padoux, "Contributions à l'étude du *mantraśāstra*, 3, le *japa*," *BEFEO* lxxvi (1988).

111. *PTV*, p. 72.

the three levels of the Word. Further, the stages of the Word are also stages of sound and, from this standpoint, a very faint sound or one endowed with certain characteristics may be considered as belonging to *madhyamā.* In this respect, we may note that Rāmakaṇṭha, in his commentary upon *SpK* 4.18, states that in *madhyamā* there is no "articulatory effort" (*prayatna*)—that is, no articulatory process—(necessarily) associated with breath, but that there is a great variety of sounds (*dhvani*) "without beginning or end," that is, spontaneous and accompanied by "breath" (*prāṇa*).[112] One finds there also the sequential aspect and the division of the phonemes. Nonetheless, he adds, the Intermediate retains its own domain, its nature being in the form of consciousness. And he quotes the following *śloka* from the Vṛtti on the *VP*: "Associated with the sole intellect, following a regular order, the Intermediate Word stays beyond the movement of breath" (*kevalaṃ buddhyupādānā kramarūpānupātinī/ prāṇavṛttim atikramya madhyamā vāk pravartate//*). *Prāṇa*, as we know, is not necessarily breathing. Thus, when Utpaladeva, commenting upon *ŚD*, chapter 2, associates the Intermediate to the unfolding of the *prāṇa* and *apāna* breaths (called *bindu* and *nāda*) to bring about the Corporeal, he mentions that the central, inner point between these two "breaths" is where the One, the supreme reality abides. So this is not a breathing process and thus *madhyamā* retains its nonmanifest quality.[113] Abhinavagupta, in the passage of the *TĀ*, third *āhnika* discussed above (*supra*, pp. 201-204) in relation to the Visionary and where he distinguishes

112. *SpK* 4.18, comm. (pp. 149-50): *yadā prāṇaprayatnavyatirekeṇa pratiprāṇi śarīrāntarasvoditānādinidhanadhvaniviśeṣātmakatayā kālādikramaṃ varṇādivibhāgaṃ bhāvinam anugacchantī prasaraṃ gṛhṇāti.*

113. *ŚD* 2.6, and comm. (pp. 41-42):

āste vijñānarūpatve sa śabdo 'rthavivakṣayā/
madhyamā kathyate saiva bindunādamarutkramāt//

comm.: *saiva ca madhyamā vāk kathyate krameṇa bindunādasaṃjñaprāṇāpānavāyūllāsāt, "prāṇāpānāntare nityam ekā sarvasya tiṣṭhati" iti.*

"When this sound reaches a plane of thought where the desire to express the objects appears, this is called the Intermediate. This [Intermediate] is due to the movement of *bindu* and *nāda*. . . ." Commentary:

three forms (supreme, subtle, gross) in each of the three planes of the Word, says that the gross aspect of *madhyamā* is "the sound (*dhvani*) produced by a drum or any other similar instrument, which is both distinct and indistinct"; owing to this characteristic, this aspect belongs to the Intermediate, wherein, says the *TĀ* (*śl.* 242), there is indeed an element of indistinctness, or nondistinction (*avibhāgāṃśa*). Abhinavagupta continues with considerations of an aesthetic order, mentioning that this aspect of indistinctness or of nondivision into distinct parts makes the Intermediate attractive (which is the case, according to him, with any uninterrupted succession of notes as well as with rhythm—which, precisely, is usually marked by drums), thereby differing from *vaikharī*. Such considerations are easily understandable when one bears in mind that there is a link between the supreme Word and *camatkāra*, the undifferentiated experience, the rapturous wonderment of the highest aesthetic enjoyment. As was said above (p. 202), this gross state of the Intermediate is ontologically and logically preceded by a subtle and a supreme state, whose presence is a necessary link for connecting any form of speech to the supreme Word, to consciousness, thereby giving it its reality, by grounding it in this absolute—an absolute that always permeates these *saṃvidadvaya* systems.

As we are going to see, the three same forms of the Word will be found again in relation to the Corporeal, *vaikharī*, the ordinary language which, when it is uttered, does not obliterate

---

"This Word is called the Intermediate. Due to the movement of *bindu* and *nāda* means due to the process/sequence of *prāṇa* and *apāna* breaths. It is said: 'The One that, of all the universe, is eternally in *prāṇa* and *apāna*.'"

(Note that Utpaladeva comments upon the words *bindunādamarutkramāt*, relating them to *madhyamā*, whereas these words are in fact to be connected with the next *śloka:* the movement of the breath gives rise to *vaikharī;* thus if *prāṇa* and *apāna* may here indicate breathing, this is in relation to *vaikharī*, not to *madhyamā*.) This view agrees with what we said above, chap. 3, pp. 136-37, regarding *dhvani* and the breaths. It is to be noted that Abhinavagupta (*ĪPVV* 1.5.13, quoted *supra*, p. 207) relates *madhyamā* to the "central point" of breath, where breath is present but is still: this, in fact, takes place in the subtle body (*puryaṣṭaka*).

the inner utterance, that of the Intermediate, by which it is preceded and, as it were, preordained; nor evidently does it obliterate the supreme Word, the unique fount of all multiplicity. In a very interesting passage of the *PTV* (pp. 184-93), the beginning of which has been quoted above (*supra*, pp. 184-85) and to which we shall return when discussing phonemes (*varṇa*) and mantras, Abhinavagupta expounds in further details this notion of how everything is permeated by the levels of the Word and most of all by its supreme plane, consciousness, of which any sound, any language, is but the outer manifestation, the appearing.

Vaikharī

Finally there arises, at the level of the nonsupreme energy (*aparā*),[114] the last stage of Speech, *vaikharī*,[115] that stage where differentiation is fully manifested,[116] and which is linked with time since with it the process of language becomes fully manifest. Here we are in the sphere of objectivity, of *māyā*,[117] in the empirical and limited world brought about through the agency of cosmic illusion. Everything that language consists

114. *PTV*, p. 13.

115. The texts give various explanations of this term. We have seen (*supra*, p. 171) Jayaratha's, on *TĀ* 3.236: *vaikharī* is what is in that which is *vikhara:* quite solid, viz., the body. Bhāskararāya's explanations in his commentary on the *Lalitasahasranāma* (132, p. 100) are different: for instance, *vaikharī* is what certainly (*vai*) enters (*rati* = *ri*) in the space (*kha*) of the ear; or else Rāghavabhaṭṭa in his commentary upon *ŚT* 1.19 (vol. 1, p. 61): *viśeṣena kharatvāt vaikharīty arthaḥ:* "*vaikharī* is so named because of the special strength (that of the "gross," earthly world), which is its specific quality"; M. Biardeau in her translation of the *Vākyapadīya* opted for the "Displayed," (l'Etalée), as I do when writing in French. R. Gnoli translates it into Italian with "la Corporea." In English, the corresponding translation, the Corporeal, is, I believe, not too unsatisfactory.

116. *PTV*, p. 5: *vaikharī tu tadubhaya* (*vācyavācakasya*) *bhedasphuṭatāmayy eva*

117. *ĪPV*, 1.5.13 (vol. 1, pp. 254-55): *aparaṃ tu idambhāvasyaiva nirūḍhau māyāgarbhādhikṛtānām eva viṣṇuviriñcendrādīnāṃ, tat tu teṣāṃ para-*

of has henceforth been produced: "phonemes, words, and sentences," breaths, organs of phonation and places of articulation of the phonemes[118] physically present in the body, the variety—right or wrong—of pronunciations, the sacred and secular texts,[119] and so forth, as well as everything that is thereby expressed and denoted.

To use the language of Rāmakaṇṭha in his commentary upon *SpK* (4.18): "What is born then is [a form of the Word] present in different parts of the body: in the breast, and so forth, with the wind called *prāṇa*, set in motion according to the will of the person who speaks. It is a form of sound common to all, having the form of the letters which are divided into vowels, consonants, and so forth, but it proceeds without being affected by the variety of those who speak it. This is how the aspect of the Word that is called the Corporeal, the receptacle of the breath manifested with the division of the phonemes, and so forth, expands. As has been said: "When the breath meets the places of articulation, the Corporeal Word [appears], comprised of the fully achieved phonemes and linked to the movement of the breath of those who speak."[120]

---

meśvaraprasādajam eva.

"The nonsupreme [Word] is placed where the world of objects predominates, dominated by Viṣṇu, Brahmā, and Indra, when they take in themselves *māyā* and the rest. This power, however, comes to them thanks to the grace only of the Supreme Lord."

118. *PTV*, p. 13: *vaikharyantam . . . bhinnamāyīyavarṇapadavākyacaraṇāntam*: "finally the Corporeal... where is found the complete expression in phonemes, words, and sentences of the differentiated world of *māyā*."

Ibid., p. 159: *evaṃ ca vaikharīpadam eva madhyamādhāmalabdhavijṛmbhaṃ svāṃśe parasparavaicitryaprathātmani sphuṭavācyavācakabhāvollāse jāle tattvajālam antaḥkṛtya yāvad āste tāvad aparābhaṭṭārikā*: "So, then appears the plane of *vaikharī* which develops from within the state of *madhyamā*. In her own portion [of the Word] is born the expansion of that which expresses and that which is expressed in a clearly manifested form, together with the variety of things which differ from each other. This [Corporeal] contains in herself the collection of all the *tattva*s and, in this state, is [a form of] the venerable Aparā."

119. Ibid., p. 89.

120. *Sp.K.* 4.18 (pp. 150-51): *yadā tu prayoktṛpuruṣecchānuvidhāyiprayatnaprerite prāṇābhidhāne maruti śarīroddeśeṣu uraḥprabhṛtiṣu jātābhidhāte/*

It should be noted that Rāmakaṇṭha underlines here that, however diversified language and speech may appear as social or individual facts, sound (*śabda*) or the level of the Word (*vāc*) remains one. The multiple and the empirical never cease to be grounded in an underlying unity, that of *vaikharī vāc*, which is itself connected with the preceding levels, and like them grounded in the one and undifferentiated supreme Word. The Corporeal, indeed, is nothing other than a "condensed" state of the Word:[121] in its deepest nature it is identical to and inseparable from the two preceding levels and from *pāra*.[122] "Although the condensed state [of the Word]," says Abhinavagupta, "does not appear until the level of the Corporeal, it is, in fact, especially present on the level of the all-pervading,

---

saiva sāmānyadhvanirūpā svaravyañjanādibhedavibhaktākārādiniyatavarṇarūpatāṃ prayoktṛbhede 'pi avyabhicarantī prasarati/ tadā varṇabhedādivyañjakaprāṇamātrāśrayā vaikharyabhidhānavāgrūpā vivṛttiḥ —ity uktam/ yaduktam

sthāneṣvabhihate vāyau kṛtavarṇāparigrahā/
vaikharī vāk prayoktṛṇāṃ prāṇavṛttinibandhanā//

This is a *śloka from the Vṛtti* on the *VP*.

The definition of *vaikharī* by the grammarian philosophers, as supported by Somānanda at the beginning of the *ŚD*, chaps. 7-8, could also be quoted:

saṃprāptā vaktrakuharaṃ kaṇṭhādisthānabhāgaśaḥ/
vaikharī kathyate saiva bahirvāsanayā kramāt//
ghaṭādirūpair vyāvṛttā gṛhyate cakṣurādinā/

"When [with the movement of the breath, the Word] reaches the cavity of the mouth and divides itself according to [the different] points of articulation [of the phonemes]—the throat and the rest—it is called the Corporeal. This [Word], due to the impressions of the external world, transforms itself into such objects as pots and the like and can thus be grasped by sight and the other [senses]."

The *LT* (20-30) characterizes *vaikharī* as *prayatnasthānabhedinī*, divided according to the various points on which the articulatory effort is exercised.

121. *PTV*, p. 184: *evaṃ ca ghanībhāvo 'pi vaikharīrūpe yady api sphuṭībhavati tathāpi sarvasarvātmani parāvāgvapuṣi mukhyatayāvatiṣṭhate.*

122. *PTV*, p. 158: *parābhaṭṭārikāsaṃvidantargataṃ tu vaikharīpadam.*

supreme Consciousness." *Vaikharī* is nothing but the completion of the process commencing with *paśyantī* and which goes on uninterruptedly, being thereby reversible. As already seen in relation to the other levels of the Word, the Corporeal is in essence present right from *parāvāc*: "Let us examine the stage of *vaikharī*, present in consciousness of the venerable Parā, for truly, even there, *vaikharī* is not missing," he again says in the *PTV* (p. 158).[123] This is a passage that continues with the lines quoted above, pp. 212-13, where he says that the acquisition of language by children can be understood only because *vaikharī* has its root in *madhyamā* and thus in *parāvāc*.

Thus the Corporeal is the final materialization of a continual, timeless, and unbroken process which, from *parā* and, metaphysically, without actually ever leaving her, starts with the Visionary and, through the Intermediate, results in the Corporeal. This is a basic concept in regard to the nature of the universe, which is nothing but the appearance, the *ābhāsa*, of consciousness, inseparable therefrom. It is essential also from the standpoint of liberation, which can be achieved through the same, but reversed, process, either by going back from words up to the source of speech or, as we have seen, by apprehending the background of undivided consciousness behind words, the nondiscursive, undifferentiated Absolute, lying in the space between two thoughts (*supra*, p. 181); or else, as in the *śāmbhavopāya* of *TĀ*, chapter 3, through identification with the prediscursive primal impulse (*icchā*) of consciousness which gives rise to all the phonemes. This soteriological concern explains why Abhinavagupta continues the above discussion (*PTV*, pp. 159-65) by dealing with purification (*śodhana*), through which all that belongs to a lower stage can return to the next higher stage, and so on up to the Absolute.[124]

It is in *vaikharī* that the division into expressing (*vācaka*) and expressed (*vācya*), begun in *madhyamā*, becomes marked

---

123. *tatparābhaṭṭārikāsaṃvidantargataṃ tu vaikharīpadaṃ vimṛśyate / na hi tatraiva vaikharyā asambhavaḥ /*

124. This process—where each *tattva*, element, or aspect of the manifestation is "purified" through its merging into its antecedent where it is present in essence—will be touched upon in chap. 6 dealing with *ṣaḍadhvan*.

and is finally established. These two complementary terms are henceforth totally distinct, though of course without being entirely disconnected; a connection, which, as we have seen, strengthened in *madhyamā*, makes it possible for words or sounds to have a meaning. *Vaikharī*, therefore, consists of all the elements of the "significans" empirically manifested and perceptible to the ear, namely of "gross" phonemes and speech. This is why it is said to be linked with breath—which here should be taken in the specific sense of respiratory breath—since it is through this breath, on its striking the organs of phonation, that the sounds of language are produced. But *vaikharī* also consists of all that has to be expressed (*vācya*), namely "gross" images and representations belonging to conceptual thought, and material objects which form the manifested universe, which the Word brings into existence and words denote. It is the level of language or speech, and of the world which can be known through speech. All this at first exists seminally in *parāvāc*, then in a more or less subtle form in *paśyantī* and *madhyamā*.[125]

Regarding the purely phonetic aspect of *vaikharī*, it should be noted that the texts mention only language and no other forms of sounds perceptible to the ear. Such forms do not belong to *vaikharī* but, as we have seen, to *paśyantī* or to *madhyamā*. They are regarded as less manifest (*sphuṭa*) or differentiated than language, because they lack the phonemes

---

125. Cf. *KKV*, *śl.* 32: "By *parā*, *paśyantī*, and *madhyamā* in her form of gross phonemes, by these is produced *vaikharī*, which consists of the fifty-one letters." The commentary adds that *vaikharī*, which has for its nature the totality of sounds, is the creator of the entire emanation which consists of all the letters, from *a* to *kṣa*, and that it is in the form of the universe:

parayā paśyantyāpi ca madhyamayā sthūlavarṇarūpiṇyā/
etābhir ekapañcāśadakṣarātmikā vaikharī jātā//

ādikṣāntākṣararāśimayākhilaprapañcanirmātrī sarvaśabdātmikā vaikharīti/ tathoktam "vaikharī viśvavigrahā" iti.

KKV, *śl.* 33, associates consonants with *vaikharī* in the *śrīcakra* where they are placed on the eight-petalled lotus, the vowels being on the sixteen-petalled lotus.

(*varṇa*) of which language consists. Phonemes, however, may exist right from the highest level of the words: vowels, notably, correspond, as we shall see, to the supreme Word,[126] and the first of them, *a*, is the Absolute itself. This bestows on phonemes a very high status, higher than the status of noises or the sound of musical instruments. Here, however, phonemes are looked at as uttered empirically; they are then linked to the breathing process and therefore to the body. Moreover, they represent a clearly defined and delimited form of sound, which phonetics endeavored to describe with accuracy. Finally they are the constituent elements of words, therefore of language, that is, of the empirical world. By contrast with the indetermination of musical sounds, for instance, they thus appear as a precise and distinct form of sound, related to a level of the Word where all distinction and delimitation become clearly apparent.

From the standpoint of the powers, *vaikharī*, being on the plane of *aparāśakti*, is made up of a lower form of energy, where the power of action predominates; but it is obviously at a much lower level than the level of the *tattva* where this power arises, since it comes into being only after the appearance of *māyā*, and at a level where the body and sense organs are in existence.

Finally, there should be recalled here the passage in the third chapter of the *TĀ*—already referred to in connection with *paśyantī* and *madhyamā*—which distinguishes, in the three levels of the Word, three aspects: gross, subtle, and supreme.

The gross aspect is the one we have just seen: "The cause of the phonemes in their manifest [form] is the gross Corporeal, whose work is mainly [to produce] sentences and so forth."[127] "Such sounds," comments J., "are those perceptible to the ear, that appear according to their own specific characteristics.

---

126. Infra, chap. 5.

127. *TĀ* 3.244 (vol. 2, p. 230):

> *yā tu sphuṭānāṃ varṇānāṃ utpattau kāraṇaṃ bhavet//*
> *sā sthūlā vaikharī yasyāḥ kāryaṃ vākyādi bhūyasā/*

They are full of 'hardness' (*paruṣya*) so that one does not feel attracted to them." By attraction or attachment (*āsakti*) one must understand the aesthetically pleasant, seducing, character of a sound—such as those we have seen before in the Visionary and the Intermediate.

Here again, Abhinavagupta reminds us that any spoken word or sentence arises from the will to speak and is ultimately grounded in absolute consciousness.

Thus we can see that, from the standpoint of the Trika, where "all is in all" (*sarvasarvātmaka*—that is, where there are no separate forms of existence since consciousness is all-pervasive), where the empiric arises from the Absolute, is rooted in it and can never move away from it, the lower one goes through the levels of the Word, the less is there to be said, since everything is there, seminally, right from the beginning. It is the Source, the supreme Word, Consciousness, which alone is of true import. As we shall see in the following chapters, the various stages as aspects of the Word can all bring the initiated yogin back to this origin, that is, if he exerts himself properly and if divine grace is bestowed upon him.

5

The Phonematic Emanation

The movement through which the Word evolves from an unconditioned, supreme state down to the "gross" sound vibration as perceived in this world and which thereby brings about the gradual emergence of the cosmos, may finally be envisaged from yet another perspective, directly related to the Sanskrit phonemes (*varṇa*s).[1] Each of these will then stand for a different moment in the gradual condensation and solidification of the energy of the Word, and will bring successively into existence each of the thirty-six ontic levels, the *tattva*s, of which the entire manifestation consists.

We have seen previously[2] that the Tantric texts of various tendencies contain cosmogonies where the emergence of the phonemes in the order of the *varṇasamāmnāya* is linked to the gradual manifestation of the stages of the emanation. I shall here consider again, briefly, one of these texts, the *ABS.* But our main concern will be the description of the stages as given by Abhinavagupta in the *TĀ* (commented upon by Jayaratha) and in the *PTV.* As far as I know, such extensive and systematic account on this theme as occurs in these two works is nowhere else to be found in the literature of the time: most of the third *āhnika* (*śl.* 66ff.) of the *TĀ* is devoted thereto, together with a considerable portion (pages 97-216) of the *PTV.* This system of emanation thus fits into the philosophical framework peculiar to Abhinavagupta—which A. Sanderson

1. For the various terms indicating the phonemes, cf. chap. 3, p. 147-48, n. 170.
2. Chap. 2, pp. 49ff. and chap. 3, pp. 147ff.

has called the "Trika-III"[3]—where material from the Spanda and the Pratyabhijñā (and notions from the Krama) are used to expand and develop into a system certain notions inherited from older texts. Some of Abhinavagupta's conceptions were subsequently taken over by his disciples, notably Kṣemarāja, and much has survived to this day, particularly in the Śrīvidyā, without, however, resulting in such a comprehensive and elaborate exposition. Now, whence did this system of phonematic emanation originate? Abhinavagupta, it is certain, did not invent it. More likely he merely systematized and elaborated upon earlier notions. But which ones and from which works? The teaching of the *TĀ* is based mostly, he tells us, upon the *MVT*, which itself is supposed to transmit the essential teachings of one earlier text of the Trika, the *Siddhayogeśvarīmata* (*MVT* 1.8), a text to which Abhinavagupta refers sometimes, for instance in *TĀ* 9.13, concerning the "alphabet-deities" Mātṛkā and Mālinī, described as identical to Parā, the supreme Word. The *MVT*, however, is mostly concerned with the *mālinī;* and moreover does not elaborate on its cosmogonic aspects. It may be assumed, on the other hand, that the *Siddhayogeśvarīmata* expounded, if not a comprehensive phonematic cosmogony, at least the successive appearance of the phonemes in the order of the *varṇasamāmnāya*, the phonemes emerging from one another, in relation to the movements of the *kuṇḍalinī*: this appears in some (too brief!) quotations from this text by Abhinavagupta in the *TĀ* (3.220-21) and by Jayaratha (Ibid., vol. 2, pp. 207ff.). This, therefore, is perhaps where we should look for the origin of the phonematic cosmogony we are going to discuss. Unfortunately, while its inception is presumably quite early, the earliest explicit formulations of the system are still to be discovered.

According to tradition, the earliest description of a phonematic emanation is that of the *Nandikeśvarakāśikā*, a short treatise in twenty-seven *sūtra*s ascribed to Nandikeśvara, a supposed contemporary of Patañjali; if it were so this would be a distinctly pre-Tantric work. However, Upamanyu's com-

3. Cf. A. Sanderson, "Maṇḍala," *op. cit.*

mentary on the *kāśikā* is surely not earlier than the twelfth century, that is, later than Abhinavagupta. Furthermore, the doctrine of the *kāśikā*, and especially its terminology, are so close to that found in Kashmirian nondualistic Śaivism, notably in Abhinavagupta, that it cannot be considered as an early work. For instance, *sūtra* 3 defines the phoneme *a* as the power of consciousness (*citkalā*) when assuming the form of the universe (*jagadrūpa*). *A* is the supreme Lord (*parameśvara*) who, as consisting of all the phonemes, is the absolute "I" (*aham, sūtra* 4), and so forth: all notions similar to those of the Trika. This Śaiva work appears as a metaphysical interpretation of the first fourteen *sūtra*s, the Pratyāhārasūtras, of Pāṇini's grammar, *sūtra*s said to have been revealed by Śiva-Naṭarāja through the beating of his drum. The cosmology of the *Nandikeśvarakāśikā* does not use the arrangement of the phonemes that we have already met with, from *a* to *kṣa*, nor that of the *Mālinī*, but that of the Pratyāhārasūtras.[4]

As we have remarked above (*supra*, chap. 2, p. 69), it is not impossible that the phonematic cosmogony of chap. 16 of the *ABS* be earlier than Abhinava's. But there is no certainty about this: influence may have operated the other way round.[5] Be that as it may, according to the *ABS* the awakening (*unmeṣa*) of Viṣṇu's power of action (*kriyāśakti*), his one-pointed and willful thought (*saṅkalpa*), which is also the "mantric condition" (*sthitiṃ mantramayīm*) of the Energy, assumes the form of the supreme *nāda*, "sounding like the deep, sustained vibration of a bell" (*dīrghagaṇṭhanādopamam*), which expands (*kvacid unmeṣaṃ gacchati*) and evolves into the "drop" of sound-energy, the *bindu*. The latter divides into two, its nature being

4. An outline of the *Nandikeśvarakāśikā* can be found in D. Ruegg, *Contributions à l'histoire de la philosophie linguistique indienne,* (pp. 108-09).

K. C. Pandey states, in the introduction to his translation of Abhinava's *ĪPV* (*Bhāskarī*, vol. 3, p. 57), that he has reasons to believe that Kashmirian nondualistic Śaivism originated from Nandikeśvara's Śaivism, which he considers earlier than the Christian era. This is, to say the least, unlikely. It is, furthermore, hardly possible to elaborate a metaphysical system on the basis of the twenty-seven *sūtra*s of *Nandikeśvara*.

5. Such is the opinion of A. Sanderson who considers that there is, in the *ABS*, a large scale incorporation of Pratyabhijñā material.

that of the name and of the named (*nāmanāmisvarūpeṇa*); this twofold aspect is, on the one hand, the aspect of the *śabdabrahman*, the Word, and on the other, of what exists (*bhūti*), the objective world (this is the dichotomy of *vācaka* and *vācya* that we have already seen). Out of the name aspect (*nāman*) of the energy and as a result of the latter's will (*svecchayā*) there arises first the phoneme *a*, the Absolute (*anuttara*);[6] this is the primordial awakening (*ādisamunmeṣa*), the totality of the Word, one and yet dividing into various forms (*sarva vāg ayam evaikas tattadākārabhedavān, śl.* 45). It is from this division that the rest of the phonemes, vowels (*svara*) and consonants (*vyañjana*), which it goes on permeating, will arise. When it desires (*icchan*), then awakens (*unmeṣan*), *i* and *u* are produced. Out of these three short vowels spring the three long ones (*ā, ī, ū*), the diphthongs, then the four liquids.[7] In this way Viṣṇu's supreme energy, says the *ABS*, takes on various aspects, then, evolving, it attains the emanating state (*sṛṣṭitām yāti*), which gives rise to the *visarga.* The phonic energy is then described as the *kuṇḍalinī* who, although ever pure, is now tinged with latent impressions (*saṃskāras*) and differentiates into *śabda* and *artha* as it rises from the *mūlādhāra* (58). This process is thus described as both a cosmic process, and the process of the emergence of speech in human beings, since the movement of creation and resorption (*sṛṣṭisaṃhāra*) of the phonic energy is linked to the ascent of the *kuṇḍalinī*, to the movement of *prāṇa* in the *īḍā, piṅgalā*, and *suṣumnā* channels. Then consonants arise, beginning with *ha*, then *śa, ṣa, sa*, and *kṣa*, out of which will come next the semi-vowels (*antaḥsthā*) *la, ra, ya* and *va*, called *dhāraṇa* in the *ABS*, and followed by *ma*, which has a particular and prominent position. Last comes the rest of the consonants, from labials to gutturals, an order which is the reverse of that of the *varṇasamāmnayā*, each phoneme corresponding, however, to a particular *tattva*, from

6. *sā hi bindumayī śaktiḥ svecchayā nāmatāṃ gatā/*
avarṇo 'py ekadhā pūrvam anuttaramayātmanā//41//

7. The *TĀ*, the *PTV*, and others give vowels in the order *a, ā, i, ī, u, ū*, and liquids as arising before diphthongs, which is in accordance with the *varṇasamāmnāya.*

puruṣa (*ma*) to *pṛthivi* (*ka*); these are the same as the correspondences given by Abhinava in the *TĀ* and the *PTV* for the emanation in Śiva (*mahāsṛṣṭi*; cf. *infra*, pp. 306ff.). In the following pages we shall refer in the footnotes to some details of this description, which fills almost the whole of chapter 16 of the *ABS*, (vol. 1, pp. 148-55). Chapter 17 of the same text enumerates all the phonemes, giving to each a different name. "Such is," it says, "the garland of phonemes in their aspect of mother-energy (*mātṛkāvarṇamālinī*): this is the great Goddess, the matrix of mantras" (*mantrayoni, śl.* 141). "Such is the essential nature of Viṣṇu's energy as the mother-energy of the phonemes" (*varṇamātṛkāvaiṣṇaviśakti, śl.* 142). As appears from these few quotations, the *ABS*, apart from references to Viṣṇu, uses the same terminology as the Trika texts.[8]

For Abhinavagupta the emergence of the fifty phonemes

---

8. There is in the same chapter (*śl.* 38-41) a description of a "lotus of the wheel of the phonemes" (*varṇacakrapadma*) together with (*śl.* 42-46) correspondences between phonemes and the bodily parts of the Goddess (for instance, to the hands correspond *ka* and *ca*, to the feet *ṭa* and *ta*, etc.). Such correspondences are used for the "placings" (*nyāsa*).

Chapters 18 to 20 of the *LT* give a description very similar to that of the *ABS*. Chapter 18, dealing with the arising of mantras, describes how the four levels (*śāntā*, *paśyantī*, *madhyamā*, and *vaikharī*) of the Word arise, followed by the phonemes. The process is described with more details in chapter 19 where, after the fifteen vowels from *a* to *bindu* in the regular order, come as in the *ABS* the four *dhāraṇa*s from *ya* to *va*, then the "fivefold" *brahman* (*pañcabrahman*): the fricatives from *śa* to *ha* and *kṣa* corresponding to the *vyūha*s and to the supreme energy, *satyā*. Thence occurs the emission (*visarga*)—according to a particular process involving all the phonemes and their various characteristics—of all the *tattva*s of the cosmic manifestation, with their corresponding *varṇa*s, enumerated, as in the *ABS*, starting from *ma*, that is, going from *ba* to *ka*.

Chapter 20 deals with what the *LT* calls the way of phonemes (*varṇādhvan:* one of the six "courses"), that is, with the twin process of manifestation and resorption of the phonemes and the cosmos, as connected with the movement of the *kuṇḍalinī* and linked to the four *vyūha*s (this is both a human and a cosmic process). Thereafter are enumerated the fifty energies presiding over all of these aspects of sound (*svarādhisthāyinī*). It should be noted, incidentally, that *śl.* 8 compares *śabdabrahman*, the primordial sound, the unmanifest *akṣara*, to the indistinct and soft sound of a stringed instrument (*tantrīśabdo yathā kalaḥ*).

(from *a* to *kṣa*) occurs through successive "phonematic awarenesses" (*varṇaparāmarśa*) of the supreme Śiva. The latter, as supreme consciousness (*parasaṃvid*), is, as we have said, both undifferentiated pure light or pure consciousness (*prakāśa*) and active awareness, self-representation, free activity of consciousness (*vimarśa*); and it is this free activity, this self-reflective actualization that gives life to the supreme consciousness. It also makes manifestation possible, for it is the state peculiar to the agent of cognition, the knower (*pramātṛ*) who perceives manifestation and, as such, is intent on it. Finally *vimarśa*, as we have seen, too,[9] characterizes the Word aspect of the supreme consciousness; now Word indeed is that which brings the universe into existence. This being so, within consciousness—thus defined as an undifferentiated radiance of consciousness or light, inseparable from an active, living self-awareness tending toward manifestation and which, moreover, is Word (*parāvāc*)—will arise a more clearly defined, more intent on creation, state of consciousness, referred to by the term *parāmarśa.* This word denotes a synthetic awareness, or consideration,[10] bringing together in a single act of consciousness the oneness of the agent of cognition (*pramātṛ*), that is, of the divine, absolute, consciousness which brings forth the universe, and the particularized forms of this universe, which, as we know, ever dwells in the knower. Thus the phonematic emanation will occur through a succession of fifty "phonematic awarenesses:" *varṇaparāmarśa*, through which the supreme Śiva will become aware, and thereby bring forth fifty different aspects of his own energy, that of the Word, which he will apprehend both as being all different and yet dwelling all within him.[11] *Parāmarśa* is thus the creative act itself. Through it

9. Chap. 2, p. 77, and chap. 4, p. 174.

10. For the Nyāya, *parāmarśa* is the mental act through which one goes from the premiss to the conclusion. This term, sometimes translated as "subsumptive reflection," describes a logical process of inferential judgment implying a reflective act of synthesis bringing together two elements. See, for instance, S. Kuppuswami Sastri: *A Primer of Indian Logic, According to Anambhaṭṭa's Tarkasaṃgraha* (Madras: 1951, pp. 188ff.).

11. This twin aspect of *parāmarśa*—as well as the wish to make it clear that the existence of fifty "phonematic awarenesses" does not in any way

Śiva brings into existence within himself what will be subsequently projected into the energy, which will reflect it, and thereby give birth to the worlds, for the fifty phonemes are associated (somewhat intricately, as we shall see) with the thirty-six *tattva*s of which the manifestation consists.

A study of the phonematic emanation according to Abhinavagupta and Jayaratha is not devoid of interest, not only because these authors describe on this occasion an aspect of the cosmogony of speech complementing what we have seen so far, but also because we are faced here with a metaphysical exposition based, in fact, upon notions elaborated by the Indian grammarians or phoneticians. Most of the speculations about the phonematic emanation are based upon such Indian traditional conceptions. This endeavor to translate phonetics into metaphysics may seem strange, but it is true to the spirit of the Indian culture where Sanskrit grammar, and grammatical reasoning, are fundamental.[12]

Here is first, in short, how this emanation occurs: In the supreme Godhead, the Absolute, prior even to the first phoneme (*avarṇa*: the nonphoneme) there arises the primordial sound-vibration, and through an initial *parāmarśa* the vowel *a* will appear, then out of the latter and through further *parāmarśa*s, the rest of the vowels: *a*, *i*, *ī*, and so on, then the diphthongs, and finally the *anusvāra* or *bindu*, and the *visarga*: sixteen phonemes altogether, all of them regarded as vowels (*svara*) and associated with the *śiva tattva*, wherein their birth brings about the emergence of different aspects of the divine energy.

---

bring any differentiation within the supreme consciousness—has led our authors, and notably Jayaratha, to describe also manifestation as resulting from one single (yet subdivided into fifty) *parāmarśa*. Abhinavagupta, similarly, contrasted the multiplicity of the *parāmarśa* with the oneness of the free reflective awareness (*vimarśa*) which both precedes and always underlies them; cf. *infra*, p. 285.

12. L. Renou's formula "Adhérer à la pensée indienne, c'est d'abord penser en grammairien" (*L'Inde classique*, 2, p. 86) should always be borne in mind when studying Indian philosophy or religion.

This divine energy finally focuses upon itself (this is *bindu*) and becomes thus ready for the emission (*visarga*), the emitting act, which sends forth the manifestation and also precedes the emergence of consonants.

Associated with Śiva, vowels have, among the phonemes, an outstanding position. They are regarded as seeds (*bījā*), just like Śiva himself. They bring into being the consonants (*vyañjana*), which are subordinated to and dependent upon them, whereas vowels, like Śiva—since they are identical to him—are self-existent. These are notions drawn from the grammarians. Patañjali,[13] indeed, glosses *svara* by *svayaṃ rājante*, "that shine by themselves" or are "self-luminous", a phrase thus commented upon by Dūrgasiṃha: "which are capable of having a meaning even though they be isolated."[14] Vowels, moreover, come first in the "assemblage of letters" (*varṇasamāmnāya*), the Sanskrit alphabet, even as *śiva* is the first *tattva*.

Of the vowels three stand out: the three short vowels *a*, *i*, and *u*. This is because, we are told, they correspond to the three fundamental energies of Śiva: the supreme or absolute energy of consciousness: *anuttara* (*a*), the power of will, *icchā* (*i*), and of cognition or awakening, *unmeṣa* (*u*).[15] But actually the grammarians already considered long vowels as equal to two short ones of the same kind, and diphthongs as a combination of two vowels, thus reducing ten phonemes to three. The role of the four liquids, *ṛ*, *ṝ*, *ḷ*, and *ḹ*, from this standpoint, was more difficult to justify.[16] *Bindu*, on the other hand, was well adapted to its role by its pictorial representation and to its position with its name (*anusvāra*), glossed in the *Pāṇinīyaśikṣā* by *svaram anubhavati*, "which follows a vowel"; and so was it with the *visarga*.

---

13. *Mahābhāṣya*, 1.2.40.

14. *Kātantra*, 1.1.2; cf. Renou, *Terminologie grammaticale*, pp. 345 and 533, *sv. svara.* This term derives in fact from the root *SVṚ*, to sound, or resound, and also to shine: *svaryante śabdyante iti svarāh*, "those which are sounded are *svaras*" (to quote Uvaṭa on *Ṛkprātiśākhya* 1.3).

15. Similarly in *ABS*, 16.46: "These three phonemes give rise to all the vowels": *eta eva trayo varṇāḥ sarvasvaravibhāvanāḥ.*

16. Cf. *infra*, pp. 254-62.

Self-luminous seeds, vowels are also described as limiting energies or portions (*kalās*) of Śiva, a term that is, in fact, also applied to consonants, as we have already seen,[17] but which is more specifically justified in the case of vowels, for theirs is the same number as the *kalās*, or lunar days. Vowels are indeed also sometimes called *tithi*,[18] a term that also means a lunar day.

These vowels will give birth to consonants. While the former are seeds or germs (*bīja*), the latter are wombs (*yoni*), like the energy with which they are associated. They arise, our texts tell us, from the limitation or "condensation" of vowels. They each appear thanks to a phonematic awareness (*varṇa-parāmarśa*) of Śiva; the connection of their various classes to certain vowels, and the order in which they arise, are based upon grammar. Thus will appear first the occlusives (*sparśa*) arranged in *varga*s, beginning with gutturals, then followed by the four semi-vowels and the four fricatives. The sequence ends, however, probably with a view to have fifty rather than forty-nine[19] phonemes, with a phoneme made up of two consonants but considered as a single phoneme, *kṣa*. Here again there is a shift from phonetics to cosmogony.

But the particular characteristic of the phonematic emanation, thus summarized, is that it does not occur directly and all at once from the primal principle down to earth. It goes through several phases, occurring through projection of light and reflection (*pratibimba*), which is in accordance with the tenets of Abhinavagupta's emanationist nondualism. So it is first entirely contained in Śiva: there, all the phonemes, and not only the sixteen vowels, are to be produced; this is called *śabdarāśi*, the mass or totality of sounds, as eminently and undifferentiatedly contained in the supreme level of the Word (*parāvāc*) or supreme Energy (*parāśakti*). Together with the phonemes arise also their corresponding *tattva*s; we shall thus have in Śiva the archetype of the whole manifestation: this is the "great emanation" (*mahāsṛṣṭi*).

---

17. Chap. 3, pp. 89-91.
18. *PT, śl.* 5 (*PTV*, p. 97).
19. Cf. chap. 3, p. 155-56.

This paradigm of the whole collection of phonemes and *tattva*s will then be projected by Śiva into the supreme-nonsupreme energy (*parāparā*), that is, in *paśyantī*, which will reflect it, thus giving rise to the emanation of the phonemes (and of the *tattva*s) as pure energy; this is the *pūrvamālinī* or *mātṛkā*, the mother-energy of the phonemes.

But even as this reflection occurs in *paśyantī*, the mass of sounds (*śabdarāśi*) appears, yet in a very different way, in *madhyamā*, and we have the *uttaramālinī*, or *mālinī*.

Finally the phonemes will emerge at the level of the lower energy (*aparā*), the level of *vaikharī*, and with them the *tattva*s, from the *māyā tattva* downwards, and they will bring the world into its final—and lowest—stage of existence.

It goes without saying that the phonematic emanation—just as the two emanative processes we saw previously—is not a purely cosmic occurrence. The third *āhnika* of the *TĀ* does in fact describe it as the emanation of the universe, but this is not the only aspect it considers. We have already seen, indeed, in chap. 3 of the present work, that the fifty phonemes arising right from the highest level of the energy are produced with the ascent of the *kuṇḍalinī*, who is both a human and a cosmic form of energy. Further, the *varṇaparāmarśa* is described by Abhinavagupta in connection with the *paropāya*, or *śāmbhavopāya*, which is one of the four ways toward or means for liberation advocated by the Trika. This shows that the *varṇaparāmarśa* can be used by the yogin for achieving liberation, either by going backward—toward resorption—through the process which gave rise to words and things, or by identifying with the initial precognitive impulse of the divine will (*icchā*) which brings forth the manifestation. We have seen, indeed (chap. 3, p. 152), that knowledge of the circle of the *mātṛkā* is, according to the *Śiva Sūtra* (2.7), a means toward liberation, for which, says Kṣemarāja, one should follow the teaching of Abhinavagupta such as given in the *PTV* and the *TĀ*, that is, the very texts we are going to study here more particularly. And we shall see again in the next chapter that the path of the *varṇa*s (*varṇadhvan*) may also constitute a way toward liberation in the system of the six paths (*ṣaḍadhvan*).

The validity, on the human level, of the process of the

phonematic emanation cannot therefore be questioned, and micro-macrocosmic correspondences will be encountered on various occasions in the following pages. Right from the start we shall have to deal again with a text that we have already discussed (chap. 3, pp. 128-30), where the arising of the phoneme *a* is described as resulting from the movement of the *kuṇḍalinī*. Similarly, the various aspects of the energy corresponding to the various phonemes will be considered at the same time by our authors as states than can be experienced by the yogin (for instance *au*, which is the *nirañjana* state, etc.). Finally, we shall again encounter, in connection with those of the emanation, the levels of the Word, the human and cosmic aspects of which we saw in the preceding chapter.

From A *to* AḤ: *Śiva*

Akārādivisargāntaṃ śivatattvam (*PTV*, p. 112): the sixteen phonemes from *a* to *visarga* arise in succession within the ontic level of *śiva*. But each emerges together with a different aspect of the divine energy: they are but aspects or moments of the supreme Godhead when, intent on creation, he goes through an inner evolution which will bring him, from a primal and eternal state of transcendent and changeless absolute—changeless but not lifeless, of course[20]—as symbolized by the phoneme *a*, to a state where all the energies are fully and intensely awake (*au*); then, after these energies have gathered, as it were, upon themselves, are focused on one point (*bindu*), to an aspect where Śiva will emit, through his energy, the manifestation archetypally contained within himself, this emission having indeed for its symbol the sixteenth phoneme: the *visarga*.

This inner evolution cannot be described but in terms of a process. It is, however, timeless. And it is not even an actual evolution (since it occurs within a principle which, being changeless, cannot evolve), but rather different aspects distinguished through reasoning, yet ever present within the Godhead

---

20. Cf. *supra*, p. 228.

who, as our authors emphasize time and again, is completely undifferentiated and beyond all duality. Śiva should therefore be described only as such, were it not for the theory of the *ābhāsa* and of the reflection (*pratibimba*), which demands that the paradigm of all differentiation should abide within the primal state of undifferentiation.

Beyond all differentiation, and even transcendent, such are the phonemes inasmuch as they are viewed as abiding within Śiva. No longer are they so when they are reflected in the energy, and even less so in ordinary speech. And yet they are not for all that ever deprived of their primal and supreme essential nature.

These sixteen *kalā*s,[21] says Abhinavagupta, manifestations of a mental movement which is sheer joy, are called vowels (*svara*) because they "vocalize" (*svarayanti*),[22] they produce a sound, because they denote or represent consciousness and reveal their own nature (*svaṃ svarūpaṃ rānti*); thus they take one into the supreme knower. They also reveal themselves, that is, they shine forth, as wombs, which are the consonants *ka* and so forth.[23] It is worth noting that in this respect the sixteen vowels are known not only as *kalā* and *tithi*, but also as *tuṭi*:[24] moments of breath or consciousness, and that they appear then as connected with the movement of breath (*prāṇa*) in the yogin; this movement divides into sixteen moments corresponding to the sixteen stages of the awareness of differentiation, from an initial movement of undifferentiated consciousness, devoid of all thought construct (*nirvikalpa*): here we come again to the twin human and cosmic aspect of the energy which is word and consciousness.

But first let us see these sixteen *svara*s as they emerge within Śiva.

---

21. Cf. above, p. 159.
22. That is, they possess the accent (*svara*) proper to vowels.
23. *PTV*, p. 202: *tad evam etāḥ kalā eva hlādanāmātracittavṛttyanubhāvakāḥ "svarā" ityuktāḥ, svarayanti śabdayanti sūcayanti cittaṃ svaṃ ca svarūpātmānaṃ rānty evam iti parapramātari saṃkrāmayantaḥ dadati svaṃ ca ātmīyaṃ kādiyonirūpaṃ rānti bahiḥ prakāśayanto dadatīti svarāḥ.*
24. *PTV*, pp. 200-01; *TĀ* 6.63ff., and *TS*, chap. 6. Cf. *infra*, p. 248, n. 65.

A

The first phoneme, the first sound that arises within the Word at its highest level, is *a*. It is the highest and purest form of Śiva's energy: *cit-śakti*, the energy of pure consciousness. It is the unexcelled, the peerless one: *anuttara*,[25] or the Absolute. *A* is the original phoneme, (*ādyavarṇa*)[26] which comes before all others, whence they all proceed and where all of them will return. This is the "supreme matrix of sound,"[27] says Abhinavagupta. Thus it is fullness (*pūrṇatā*). The fullness of the

---

25. We have not been able to find a satisfactory translation of *anuttara*. One could say unexcelled, or unsurpassed. R. Gnoli translates it by "Senza Superiore." Abhinava, at the beginning of the *PTV* (pp. 19-32), gives sixteen different interpretations, or sixteen possible ways of apprehending the senses and meanings of *anuttara*. The number of these interpretations is evidently not fortuitous but due to the fact that there are sixteen lunar "days" or *kalā*s, the sixteenth of which—the supreme one—being, like *anuttara* here, the supposed background for the rest of them and the cause of their renewal. *A*, indeed, as first among vowels, the root of all phonemes, is the supreme *kalā*.

    One could also be tempted to render *anuttara* as "transcendent," except that there is no such thing really as transcendence in nondualistic Śaivism. As we shall see later on, there is, for Abhinavagupta or Jayaratha, a particular interplay between transcendence and immanence. The primary principle, the *anuttara*, is both *viśvottīrṇa*, beyond manifestation, unimpeded pure consciousness, and *viśvamaya* or *viśvarūpa*, assuming the form of the universe, that is, pervading it, being its essence or substratum. It can be envisaged as either or both of them.

    Such a conception of the primary principle of the universe is not, of course, peculiar to Abhinavagupta and is much earlier than he. There is for instance, at the beginning of the *Mahānārāyaṇa Upaniṣad* (ed. Varenne, vol. 1, pp. 17-23), a cosmogonic poem exalting Prajāpati as the sole principle in the universe, both transcending the world and pervading it like a vital force, to the point of being its very soul. There is in all such cases a synthesis into a decidedly ambiguous concept of the old notion of the supreme lord of creatures, Prajāpati, who governs them, and of the conceptions of the Upaniṣads, for which *brahman* is the primary principle, impersonal, abstract and all-pervading.

    As for the translation of *anuttara*, we have chosen "the Absolute" not as a better translation, but because it sounds better in English.

26. *TĀ* 3.67 (vol. 2, p. 76).
27. *Citsvabhāvatāmātranāntarīyakaḥ paranādagarbhaḥ, TS* chap. 3, p. 12.

    Similarly the *ABS* (16.45-46, vol. 1, p. 149) says that *a* is the unex-

pure and absolute supreme consciousness (*pūrṇaparasaṃvit-tattva*), fullness also in that this consciousness is inclusive of all the worlds and that like it, the phoneme *a* is inclusive of the countless number of phonemes which will bring the worlds into existence, sustain them, and eventually dissolve them. Abhinava, in the *PTV*, gives of *a* (as the initial syllable of the word *anuttara*) the following definition:

> *A* is the [totality of the] limitating power (*kalā*) not submitted to *māyā*, beyond hearing, uncreated, wondering at its own [essence: that of the] waveless sea of consciousness resting in the great light [of the Absolute]. It spreads from the first to the last stage [of emanation], being the condition of the fullness of the supreme "I"[28] in its total awareness of the universe [as produced by] the effulgent spreading out of the Energy.[29]

A corresponds indeed to the first and therefore the highest synthetic awareness that is to manifest the universe: the *para-parāmarśa.*[30] Being pure consciousness it is, like this awareness, absolute light (*anuttaraprakāśa*) always shining with unsurpassed brilliance.[31] *A* is the nameless (*anākhya*), says Jayaratha,[32] which no limitating term, even that of Śiva or Śakti, or any other, can denote, for any name would put a limitation upon it, whereas it is beyond all limitation.

Although a phoneme, *a* corresponds to a level of the Word too elevated to be considered in terms of ordinary

---

celled (*anuttara*) which produces all the other phonemes in dividing into various shapes, for it is by itself the whole of speech: *sarvā vāg ayam evaikas tattadākārabhedavān.*

28. Or *pūrṇāhantā*, absolute subjectivity.
29. *PTV*, p. 27: *a iti ca yā iyam amāyīyāśrautanaisargikamahāprakāśa-viśrāntanistaraṅgacidudadhisvātmacamatkārarūpā śāktollāsamayaviśvā-marśanarūpaparipūrṇāhambhāvaprathamaparyavasānobhayabhūmigā kalā.*

   A is thus described as the collection of the *kalā*s of Śiva in their primal transcendence. This is sometimes described as the seventeenth *kalā:* cf. chap. 3, p. 91.
30. *TĀ* 3.67, comm., (vol. 2, p. 75).
31. Ibid., comm. (vol. 2, p. 76).
32. Ibid.

phonemes. It stands at the level of spontaneous sound, the phonic aspect of the supreme reality which is produced without any "striking", whether of a percussion or from the contact of the respiratory breath with the organs of phonation, and so forth. It is even beyond the "unstruck" (*anāhata*) sound. It is the root thereof, the initial stir of sound-vibration "beyond struck and unstruck [sound]" (*anāhatahatottīrṇa*):[33] "no one utters it, no one can possibly hold it in check. It is self-uttered, O Goddess, and dwells within the heart of all sentient beings."[34]

A is all-pervading.[35] Being pure energy of consciousness, on the transcendent plane of the Word, it is no doubt beyond all manifestation. But due to the interplay between immanence and transcendence in nondualistic Śaivism, *a* is looked upon, as it were, as twofold: first as beyond the universe, and in this case its being known as *avarṇa* should be understood in the sense of "non-phoneme" and not of phoneme *a* (*akāra*);[36]

---

33. Cf. chap. 3, p. 99, n. 41. Also comm. on *TĀ* 3.67 (vol. 2, p. 76):

anāhatahatottīrṇo mahāviṣamacidgatiḥ/
vīrahṛdghaṭṭanodyukto rāvo devyā vijṛmbhate//

"The song of the Goddess unfolds, born of a rubbing within the hero's heart, moving in the vast depth of consciousness, beyond the 'struck' and 'unstruck' sound."

34. Ibid.: *so'pi hi devaḥ*
nāsyoccārayitā kaścit pratihantā na vidyate
svayam uccarate devi prāṇinām urasi sthitaḥ//

ityādyuktasvarūpād anāhatāt sthānakaraṇābhighātotthāc ca hatāt śabdād uttīrṇatvena parāparāmarśaśālisitataraprakāśātmatayā sarvadaiva dyotamānaḥ.

"This god indeed of whom it is said: 'no one utters it, no one . . .'" and so forth, is always shining everywhere. His nature is that of the purest light endowed with supreme awareness and is beyond the struck sound produced by the striking of air on the points of articulation and on the organs of speech, and he is also beyond the unstruck sound."

The *śloka* here quoted by Jayaratha is from the *Svacchanda Tantra* (*SvT* 7.59), where it refers to *haṃsa*; on this point, cf. chap. 3, pp. 140ff.

35. *ABS* 16.45 defines *a* as the totality of the Word dividing into various forms. Cf. *supra*, p. 226.

36. *Avarṇa* has of course, in our texts as elsewhere, primarily the same meaning as *akāra:* the phoneme (or letter) *a*.

second, as the source of the energy, the origin of phonemes, the starting point of manifestation which is then within it in seed-form, *a* being in the manifestation as its essence, its background.

Actually *a* is one and whole in nature rather than twofold. Abhinavagupta points this out, for instance, in the *PTV* (p. 224), when he defines *brahman* as *anuttara*, as a fusion of knower and known, as "united with, inseparable from, the initial, still undifferentiated stage of the four [cosmic functions of the Godhead]: the creative outburst, and so forth."[37]

"The power of absolute freedom or autonomy (*svātantrya-śakti*)[38] of the Lord," he writes elsewhere (ibid., pp. 167-68), "is called '*a*'. In it the objectivity has not yet begun to develop and it is therefore essentially a reflective awareness whose inner nature is that of a pure interiorized mass of consciousness (*antarghanasaṃvid*). Such a state [can also] be called will (*icchā*), [but a will where] that which is willed has not yet appeared and which is thus only the synthetic awareness (*parāmarśa*) of the state of the Absolute (*anuttarasattā*). The supreme Lord thus never ceases to be conscious (*āmarśa*) of his own nature and it is whilst being conscious of the plane of *akulaśakti*, that he is conscious of the energy of *kula*, in spite

---

37. *Yad etad brahma sāmarasyaṃ vedyavedakayoḥ, catasṛṇāṃ daśānām udyogādīnāṃ samāhāro 'vibhāgabhūḥ.*

The creative outburst, *udyoga*, is the first of the four moments through which consciousness creates or apprehends the outer reality. The other three are *avabhāsa*, the manifestation of reality; *carvaṇa*, its "chewing up," sometimes named *samkrāma*; and finally its dissolution or rest, *viśrānti*, within the subject.

Those are notions from the Krama, for which *viśrānti* is normally preceded by *alaṃgrāsa*, the swallowing, since it is a pentadic system.

38. Absolute freedom, complete autonomy, is for Abhinavagupta the highest aspect of reality. It is the very root of its nature as active, living consciousness (*vimarśa*); cf. Kṣemarāja (*ŚSV* 1.1): *caitanyam . . . paripūrṇaṃ svātantryam ucyate.* This is stressed in this quotation. Freedom is such cardinal a notion in this system that the latter is sometimes known as *svātantryavāda:* the doctrine of the freedom [of consciousness]—it is notably on this point that the followers of Kashmirian nondualistic Śaivism contrast themselves to Śaṅkarian Vedānta, whose conception of *brahman* as a still and inactive pure Subject they disavow.

of the fact that the consciousness of *kula* is quite different from that of [*akula*]. This [state of *akula*, which is that of *a*] is thus the reflective awareness (*vimarśa*) of the Holder of the Power, Bhairava."[39]

Thus we can see how the emphasis is placed upon this notion, which may seem at first glance contradictory, of the awareness of objectivity, of diversity, being present within the divine, pure, and undifferentiated subjectivity: the Godhead, at the level of the phoneme *a*, is pure *anuttara, akula* consciousness, therefore an internally self-centered consciousness (*antarghanasaṃvid*). But it is at the same time vividly aware of *kula*—a term meaning "family" or "body"—that is, of the manifestation. Consciousness, then, which is *prakāśavimarśamaya*, is ever shining (*prakāśa*), never losing its self-awareness in this eternal self-representation that is *vimarśa*,[40] while having at the same time this powerful, synthetic, creative consciousness of the manifestation, *parāmarśa*: Not only does *parāmarśa* cause Śiva to produce the constituent parts (phonemes and

---

39. *PTV*, pp. 167-68: *evaṃ parameśvarasya svātmanīcchātmikā svātantryaśaktir anunmīlitabhāvavikāsā tathāvidhāntarghanasaṃvitsvabhāvavimarśasārā "a" ity ucyate/ sa cāvasthā iccheti vyapadeśyā īśyamānānudrekā tata evānuttarasattāparāmarśātmikaiva eṣā/ parameśvaraḥ satataṃ svasvarūpāmarśako 'kulaśaktipadātmakam api rūpam āmṛśan yady api kulaśaktir anuyātu tathāpi kulaparāmarśato 'sya syād eva viśeṣa bhairavaśaktimadvimarśasatteyam.*

See also *TS*, chap. 3, p. 12, where Abhinava says that since the whole world is reflected in consciousness, it is of the very nature of the Lord to be made of all the world (*viśvātmakam*). It is therefore not possible that He should not be aware of the universe. "It would indeed be absurd to say that He whose nature is consciousness (*citsvabhāva*) is not consciously aware of his own nature [that is, of Himself]. Verily, if such reflective consciousness of [the Principle's] own essence did not exist, all would be inert (*jaḍatā syāt*). This consciousness (*āmarśa*) is nonconventional (*na sāṃketika*). However, being inseparable from the very essence of consciousness, it is called the supreme womb of [all] sound (*paranādagarbha*)."

40. For *āmarśa, vimarśa, parāmarśa*, and so forth, cf. *supra*, pp. 174-75. See also my translation of the *PTlv*, notes. Cf. also M. Hulin, op. cit. *supra*, p. 174, n. 20.

tattvas) of the universe, but it also maintains them perpetually in existence, such existence being indeed nothing but the existence of consciousness "assuming the form of the universe" (*jagadviśvarūpa*).

This same condition, paradoxically one and twofold, one and inclusive of diversity, of the Absolute, *anuttara*, *a*, is expounded in *TĀ*, *āhnika* 3, *śl.* 67.

"The supreme energy of this God, *akula*, is *kaulikī*, through which *kula* arises, and from which the Lord cannot be divided."[41] Commenting upon this rather obscure stanza and referring to the *PTV*, pp. 61-62, Jayaratha (*TĀV*, p. 75) states that *a*, the *kaulikī* energy, is that energy of which the self, the essence, is the *akula*, the supreme deity, while belonging to and abiding in *kula*, the manifested universe. *Kula*, he says, is the body (*śarīra*) of the Godhead, and its characteristic is the phoneme *a* (*akāralakṣanaṃ kulaṃ śarīram asya* [*akulasya*]): this asserts the immanence, in the manifestation, of the Supreme, which remains at the same time transcendent. In fact, further amplifying this notion of the germinal presence in *a*, as their source and essence, of all that is to follow, Jayaratha, in the commentary on this *śloka* of the *TĀ*, considers not only the energy in the form it will assume in *ā* as also present in *a*, but he goes on to say that since Śiva and Śakti cannot be separated—and they are indeed united even in *a* since the Word in its

---

41. *Akulasyāsya devasya kulaprathanaśālinī/*
kaulikī sā parā śaktir aviyukto yayā prabhuḥ//67//

For *kula* and *akula*, cf. *PTV*, pp. 32-34, where *kula* is described as nothing else but a condensed, hardened, state of consciousness: *bhodasyaiva āśyānarūpa.* Or pp. 61-62 where, referring to *SpK* 1.8 and 2.1, Abhinavagupta remarks notably that *kula* as such exists only insofar as it is grounded in the light of *akula*, *kulaṃ hi akulaprakāśarūḍham eva tathā bhavati.* Or ibid., pp. 164-65: "*Akula* is understood as being of the nature of Bhairava. So *akula* holds within itself the creative impulse [notably of time], because the energy of *kula* [that of the manifested universe] abides within it. The energy of reflective awareness indeed, *is* impulse. But for it, even *akula*, [also] known as [the modality of] *turyātīta*, would not be . . ."

. . . *akulaṃ bhaivavātma parāmṛśyate/ tenākulam evāntargṛhītakalanākaṃ kulaśakter atraiva niveśāt/ kalanātmikā hi vimarśaśaktiḥ tām antareṇākulam api turyātītaṃ nāma na kaṃcit. . . .*

highest form is, fundamentally, energy—there the phonemes *a* and *ha* are also united, for they cannot be separated any more than air from the sky.[42] Now, while *a* is the first, *ha* is the last phoneme.[43] It represents the energy in and through which the principle, Śiva, will be actively reflected. Here it should therefore be taken as a symbol of the emanation as a whole, which takes place between *a* and *ha*. Thus once again is established the basic principle of the presence within the Absolute of the whole emanation.[44]

Finally, there are, with reference to *a*, speculations of a type less common in the Trika, found almost exclusively in relation to the phonemes *a* and *e*, and concerning the written form of this phoneme in the *devanāgarī* script.[45] Such speculations are not irrelevant to what has just been said about the energies present in the first principle. They occur, like the

---

42. *TĀ* 3.67, comm. (vol. 2, p. 80): *tad uktam*
akāraś ca hakāraś ca dvāv etau yugapat sthitau/
vibhaktir nānayor asti mārutāmbarayor iva//

iti, evam avibhāge 'py anayor ekaikaprādhānyena svarūpamātraviśrānter ekavīratvaṃ cicchaktirūpatvaṃ ca.

43. *Ha* comes last in the alphabet and is often taken as a symbol for its termination, although the Trika (and other traditions), in order to have fifty phonemes, add *kṣa* to it. It is to be noted that *ha* is a symbol of *śakti* only with respect to the emanation within *parāvāc*, and even this is not always the case; on this point, cf. *infra*, p. 312.

44. Similarly Kṣemarāja in *ŚSV* 2.7 (p. 60) defines *a* as *ahaṃvimarśaprathamakalā anuttarākulasvarūpa*: "the initial dynamism (or the original portion) of the active awareness of the [absolute] "I," which is in the nature of the unsurpassed—*akula*." *Ahaṃ* is indeed the manifestation as archetypally dwelling in consciousness; on this point, see *infra*, pp. 286ff.

45. Such speculations are also to be found in Vaiṣṇava Tantrism, in the *Jayākhyasaṃhitā*, for instance, where every letter has a secret name deemed to evoke its form in a more ancient alphabet; cf. *JS* 6.32ff. (pp. 43-44) and the introduction to this work (pp. 30-34) in the G.O.S., vol. liv. One may also refer for additional references—and hypotheses—on this subject to R. Shamashastri, *The Origins of the Devanāgarī Alphabet* (*Indian Antiquary* 1906, vol. xxv, pp. 253ff.); there the author lists (pp. 314-5) fifty names of the Goddess, each having as its initial letter one of the fifty phonemes, from *a* (Amṛtā) to *kṣa* (Kṣamāvatī); this list is taken from a Tantric work, the *Pūrvāṣoḍhānyasa*. A list of

Outline of the Letter *A*

1: Raudrī
2: Ambikā
3: Jyeṣṭhā
4: straight line with *kālāgni*

former ones, in Jayaratha's commentary on *TĀ*, Book 3, *śloka* 67. The body of the phoneme, Jayaratha tells us, is manifested as follows by the energy of the supreme known as *kaulikīśakti*: "When the supreme subtle energy, *kuṇḍalinī*, fuses with Śiva as a result of their mutual embrace, she rises up and takes the form of the [powers of] will, cognition, and action. Opening the seal of Raudrī, she becomes Ambikā, of triangular shape. Then, entering the state of Jyeṣṭhā, shaped like a digit of the moon that is the letter *u*, she brings about the apparition of the shape of a clear straight line where lies the *bindu ra*,[46] the fire of time (*kālāgni*) born from the *bindu* of the moon. Thus she displays the body of the primordial phoneme" (*TĀV*, vol. 2, p. 77).[47] Jyeṣṭhā is given the shape of

---

the various "names" given to the fifty phonemes by some *saṃhitā*s is appended to the edition of the *Lakṣmī Tantra* (Adyar, 1959), pp. 227-31.

Metaphysical and yogic speculations related to the form of the letter *ī*, either in *devanāgarī* or in *brahmī* script, where it is represented by three dots, are to be found in the *kāmakalā* diagram of the Śrīvidyā: Jayaratha refers precisely to a Śrividyā text, the *NṢA*, in connection with the above-mentioned division of *a* into three elements.

46. *Ra* (or *RAṂ*) is the seed of fire, *agnibījā*.

47. Jayaratha then quotes the passage in the *Tantrasadbhāva* about the rising of the *kuṇḍalinī*, which we have seen *supra*, pp. 128-30, thus stressing the twofold—cosmic and microcosmic—nature of the process of the phonematic emanation.

the letter *u* in *devanāgarī* and represents the left part of the letter *a;* the two other energies make its right part. There is an alternative interpretation by Jayaratha three pages further where four energies instead of three are mentioned, Vāmā being added to the other three.

However, what matters to us here is that right from the highest transcendent stage, three energies have been considered which were not *a priori* expected to be met with until later on, and which are held as forming the body (*śarīra*) of the transcendental sound that is *a.* This kinetic body is the primal energy known as Tripurā, since it is threefold and will give rise to the "three worlds."[48] This same energy will also bring about their resorption, for the destructive aspect of the energy is also present in the triad: Raudrī is the destructive energy, Rudra's energy, and *kālāgni*[49] is also the energy of Rudra, which dissolves the universe into fire.

Ā

While two aspects—*akula* and *kula*—may be distinguished in the first, supreme stage of the Word, they are there inseparably united. Now, at a second stage, they will be distinguished,

48. Such triplicity was brought in also because here (*TĀv*, p. 78) Jayaratha refers to the *VMT/NṢA* (4.5cd, then 9cd-11), a Śrīvidyā text where the Goddess is Tripurasundarī (or Tripurā). Referring to another text, whose name is not given, Jayaratha also calls these three functions *dhāman*, that is, luminous form, effulgent manifestation. The passage quoted connects these three cosmic functions with the three luminous forms (*dhāman*) that are moon, fire, and sun. For *dhāman*, cf. J. Gonda, "The Meaning of the Sanskrit Term *Dhāman*" (Amsterdam, 1979).

49. Ibid. (pp. 78-80). For *kālāgni*, cf. also *TĀ* 4.167 and comm. (vol. 3, pp. 180-83). Kālāgni is the last and lowest *bhuvana*; therefore it is from it that the resorption of the universe starts. Śiva and the Goddess in their destructive aspect are thus called sometimes Kālāgnirudra and Kālāgnirudrakālī. They are then in the form of the primordial fire, or the "great time," *mahākāla*, wherein the whole universe dissolves, going back to the absolute "I" (*ahaṃ*). *VBh* 52 mentions a meditation on *kālāgni*, as a fire that swallows up the body of the yogin (cf. also *ŚSV* 3.4, pp. 76-79).

There is a Śaiva *Kālāgnirudra Upaniṣad* which deals with the application of ashes over the body to form various marks. There Kālāgnirudra is Śiva in his destructive aspect.

although not completely differentiated, for until one goes beyond the sixteen phonemes from *a* to *aḥ* one remains in Śiva, namely at the level of the absolute nonduality of the first principle. Jayaratha states this once again before proceeding with the description of the *a* stage, quoting the following stanza: "Neither Śiva without Śakti. Nor Śakti without Śiva. The cosmic flow [is issued from] their couple (*yāmalam*)." "Their union," he adds, "consists in that they are mutually intently turned toward each other" (*parasparaunmukhyātmakaṃ yāmalaṃ rūpaṃ syāt*) and this produces the flow of the cosmos "born of the fusion (or unifying friction) of the two Absolutes" (*anuttarayor eva saṃghaṭṭāt*). "Here," he says, "Śiva and Śakti appear as separate for they are [respectively] transcendent (*viśvottīrṇa*) and made of the world (*viśvamaya*), but though made of the world [the deity] remains beyond it in its total fullness, for [on such a plane] there can be no division or limitation" (ibid., p. 81).

A therefore divides into two: *a* + *a*, which produces the second phoneme: the long vowel *ā*. The Absolute, *anuttara*, divides into Śiva and his energy, denoted by the terms *akula* and *kaulikīśakti*. "The state of union of these two," says *TĀ*, third *āhnika*, *śloka* 68 (p. 81), "is called unifying friction (*saṃghaṭṭa*). It is known as the energy of bliss (*ānanda*), from which the universe will be emitted."[50] Taking place during this stirring up, this unitive friction denoted by the term *saṃghaṭṭa*, this energy of bliss, Jayaratha tells us (ibid., p. 81), is a stir (*calana*), a springing forth (*ucchalattā*), or a "vibration" (*spanda*): all this makes the principle alive and creative. Any generative act is accompanied by bliss. This is why the energy of Śiva which is now manifested is the energy of pure happiness or bliss: *ānanda* = *ā* (it was necessary now to have an energy denoted by a term beginning with a long *ā*). This energy, says Abhinavagupta in the *PTV*,[51] arises with the phoneme *ā* when Bhairava, the holder of the energy, becomes aware (*vimarśa*) at once of his *akula* aspect and of the *kula* energies. At this point, then,

50. *Tayor yad yāmalaṃ rūpaṃ sa saṃghaṭṭa iti smṛtaḥ/ ānandaśaktiḥ saivoktā yato viśvaṃ visṛjyate//*

51. Pp. 167-68.

not only are those two aspects, *kula* and *akula*, more in evidence, but there appears a reflective awareness in consciousness, which is full of bliss.[52] *A*, the Absolute, pure consciousness (*cit*), is nothing but pulsating light (*prakāśa*); with *ā* there is an awareness (*vimarśa*) of this radiance, yet without the interference of duality, and without *vimarśa* prevailing over *prakāśa*.

TĀ śloka 69 further states that this is a "reality" (*tattva*) beyond the supreme and nonsupreme, known as Goddess. This is the essence, the heart, the emission, the supreme Lord,"[53] all which should be understood to mean, Jayaratha explains (ibid., p. 82), that it is beyond both the immanent aspect of the reality related to *śakti* (*viśvarūpāt śāktāt*), and its transcendent, Śiva aspect (*viśvottīrṇāt śaivād rūpāt*). The heart (*hṛdaya*) denotes indeed, for Abhinavagupta, the supreme reality, the Absolute,[54] the very generative center of consciousness. The *TS* (chap. 3, p. 12) describes *ā* as rest within the Absolute (*anuttara eva viśrāntir ānandaḥ*). The term *rest* (*viśrānti*) in no way implies the absence of energy or dynamism. On the one hand, indeed, it may be held that a long vowel, as it corresponds to two short ones, is a kind of pause, of resting, in this vowel, that, as it were, spreads out (*prasaranti*: *PTV*, p. 168). On the other hand, and more markedly, bliss, *ānanda*, notably as aesthetic enjoyment, is rest, repose (*viśrānti*), in the sense of absorption, of peaceful immersion within itself of the consciousness which is merged with the object of contemplation.[55] We must also note that Abhinavagupta (*TS*,

52. Cf. also *ŚSV* 2.7 (p. 60): *ahaṃvimarśaprathamakalā anuttarākulasvarūpa sati.* Bliss is defined by Abhinavagupta in *ĪPVV* 1.5 (vol. 2, p. 177, in fine): *svarūpasya svātmanaḥ paripūrṇanijasvabhāvaprakāśanam eva parāmarśamayatāṃ dadhad ānanda it ucyate:* "that is known as bliss which is but the fullness of the self-revelation of one's own nature, accompanied with a reflective awareness, a self-representation of one's own nature."

53. *Tat sāraṃ tac ca hṛdayaṃ sa visargaḥ paraḥ prabhuḥ//69//*

54. Cf. *PTV*, p. 31, quoting the *Tantrasāra*—or, still better, see Abhinavagupta's developments in the *PTlv*.

55. Such enjoyment, says Abhinava (*Abhinavabharatī*, 1, p. 179), is *ānandamayanijasaṃvid viśrāntilakṣana.* The state of the absolute "I," as we shall see, is defined by Utpaladeva in *APS*, 22 as "rest within itself of

chap. 1, p. 6) defines the energy of bliss as freedom: *svātantryam ānandaśaktiḥ*, which amounts to placing it on the supreme level.[56] This exalted position vouchsafed on the energy of bliss is clearly apparent, finally, in *TĀ*, *śloka* 70 (and in Jayaratha's commentary, p. 81), quoting the *Devyāyāmalatantra*, which describes the Goddess "beyond the supreme" (*parātītā*) as higher than the three goddesses of the Trika, Parā, Parāparā, and Aparā, placed on the three prongs of the trident.[57]

Finally, one may notice that Abhinavagupta returns later on in the *TĀ* (3.160-61) to the conjunction of the two *anuttaras*, saying that it may give rise either to a disturbed energy (*kṣobhātmaka*), in which case bliss (*ānanda*) will be generated, or to an undisturbed energy, in which case the outcome will be in the nature of the Absolute (*anuttarātmakatā*). This may sound surprising, but as appears from Jayaratha's commentary on this point (p. 161), Abhinavagupta only meant to take up a rule of internal *sandhi* where the merging of two *a*'s may result in *a* and not in *ā* (thus *sima* + *anta* makes *simanta*). Here again we can see how a rule of phonetics may be given a metaphysical interpretation: cosmogony and grammar should not be at variance!

Although with *ā* we are in the eternal and immovable supreme, the latter pursues, however, its inner evolution, which gives rise to the third vowel, *i*.

I

The third phoneme, *i*, corresponds to *icchāśakti*, a term which may be tentatively translated as power of will. *Icchā*, in fact, is rather indicative of an impulsion, a strong wish, a drive or an urge toward some desired object, or else an intention

---

the light of consciousness" (cf. *infra*, p. 287). The entire manifestation, similarly, "rests" within consciousness, wherefrom it springs forth, or originates: cf. *TĀV*, p. 182 (*ad TĀ* 3.186-87): *vastutaḥ sarvavastunāṃ pramātary eva viśrānteḥ*, "for truly everything rests in the knower."

56. Cf. *supra*, p. 174.

57. For this trident, cf. A. Sanderson, *Maṇḍala* (*op. cit.*), notably the figure, p. 187.

or intentness. Abhinavagupta, in the *Tantrasāra*,[58] interprets *icchā* as *abhyupagama*, that is, an assent, a move forward or nearer to what is going to occur. *Icchā* is therefore not so much the divine creative will as the movement of the divine, which, from that bliss consisting in the recognition of, and the rest in, the transcendent, enters a phase which brings it a little closer to the emanation and where it assents to it, where a creative intent or impulsion unveils itself in Śiva. This creative intent, says the *Tantrasāra*, rests in the energy of bliss. It is the wonder (*camatkāra*) experienced by the principle at its own freedom.[59] As we have seen, according to Abhinavagupta, bliss is freedom (*svātantrya*). When pure consciousness[60] spreads out (*prasaranti*), he adds, this is the perfect fullness of the power of will. It corresponds to a more condensed form of consciousness (*saṃvidghana*)[61] where the primordial freedom tends, but without limiting itself, toward what will subsequently curtail its original spontaneity.

In the *Tantrāloka*,[62] Abhinavagupta gives the following description of *icchāśakti* and of the phoneme *ī*: "In this unifying friction, owing to its being consciousness,[63] [there arises] a reflective awareness (*pratyavamarśa*): the power of will, the supreme sovereign of the nonfearsome energies."[64]

Jayaratha explains this reflexive awareness or re-presen-

---

58. *TS*, chap. 8 (p. 74): "The power of will has indeed for nature a balanced movement, without specification, toward knowledge and activity" (*jñāna-kriyayoḥ sāmyarūpābhyupagamātmakatvāt*). There is a similar definition in Utpaladeva's commentary on *SD* 1.3 (p. 7).
59. *TS*, chap. 1, p. 6: *taccamatkāra icchāśaktiḥ*.
60. *PTV*, pp. 168-70.
61. For the meanings of the term *ghana, ghanatā*, cf. *PTV*, pp. 64, 66, 166-67, and 170.
62. 3.71 (p. 83).
63. That is, says Jayaratha, because it predominates.
64. *saṃghaṭṭe 'smiñcidātmatvād yattatpratyavamarśanam/*
icchāśaktir aghorāṇāṃ śaktīnāṃ sā parā prabhuḥ//

As we have seen (chap. 4, pp. 175-76 and 192), *pratyavamarśa* is a characteristic feature of *parā* and *paśyantī vāc*.

tation as an act of synthetic awareness (*parāmarśa*) of the supreme knower, which is a desire to project the emanation (*sisṛkṣātman*). There is no emanation there, but only a drive toward, an intentness on emanation, a thought oriented toward what will eventually evolve as the emanation, and which is pervaded by joy at all that is surging forth within consciousness; this is why there appears the first element (*prathamatuṭi*),[65] the highest one of the energy of will, not yet affected, still undisturbed by what will be created subsequently.

It should be noted here that *icchā* is of paramount importance in the *śāmbhavopāya*, the way toward liberation that is "of Śambhu": Śiva—described precisely in the *TĀ*, third *āhnika;* and this both because the entire manifestation through phonemes is the very act of this divine will and because emancipation, according to this path, consists in the yogin's identifying with this will, this primal noncognitive impulse (existing in human beings and the Godhead as well) prior to all knowledge. Abhinavagupta states this in the first chapter of the *TĀ* (1.146) when he says, "What is clearly revealed in the first moment of self-awareness free of all thought-construct is what is known as will."[66]

The other, lower, aspect of the emanative intention which, according to Jayaratha (ibid., p. 84) begins to emerge from *i*, will be manifested with the fourth phoneme: *ī*.

Ī

Ī is *īśāna*,[67] the power of lordship, of mastering or ruling, also called the sovereign. Phonetically, *ī* is *i* + *i*. From the standpoint of Śiva's energies, it is a more marked form of the power of will. It is in *icchā*, says the *TS*, that *īśāna* rests: *icchāyām eva*

---

65. *Tuṭi* or *truti* denotes a moment, a division in the flow of breath (*prāṇa*) and in the awareness of the universe. There are sixteen *tuṭi*s. The first one is the initial movement of consciousness, free of duality (*nirvikalpa*). Cf. *TĀ* 6.63ff., and *TS*, chap. 6.

66. *tatrādye svaparāmarśe nirvikalpaikadhāmani/*
*yat sphuret prakaṭaṃ sākṣāt tad icchākhyaṃ prakīrttitam//*146//
(vol. 1, p. 185).

67. A term which, like *icchā*, occurs already in *ABS*, 16.47.

viśrāntiḥ īśānam. And the *TĀ*: "When this [power of will] is disturbed (*prakṣubdharūpa*), it appears as the sovereign. Then arise the supreme and nonfearsome goddesses, who are guides on the path of Śiva."[68]

Such a disturbance or stirring of the power of will, which does not exist in *i*, is due to the fact that the emanative intent becomes more marked and tends to cloud the perfect purity of the original consciousness. Here, says Abhinavagupta in the *PTV*,[69] will, in its freedom, begins to wish to perceive what will appear as power of cognition. It wishes to see objectivity appear.[70] Sovereignty, or lordship, says Jayaratha in his commentary,[71] consists in an external manifestation (yet of course beyond duality) in the form of Śiva's countless energies. Those are the energies mentioned in *śloka*s 72-73 quoted above. They are auspicious and guide the disciple upon the path toward liberation. (Let us mention again as regards *ī* (cf. *supra*, p. 116) that in the Śrīvidyā, whose metaphysical doctrines owe much to the Trika-based Pratyabhijñā, there is an ancient written representation of the *bīja ĪṂ* (.:.) in the visualizing meditation of the *kāmakalā*).

U

With the fifth phoneme, *u*, the desire to manifest the universe, which appeared with *i* as a reflective awareness (*pratyavamarśa*) of the supreme knower, takes the form of an awakening, an unfolding, a revelation, or a coming forth

---

68. *TĀ* 3.72-73 (p. 84):

saiva prakṣubdharūpā ced īśitrī samprajāyate//72
tadā ghorāḥ parā devyo jātāḥ śaivādhvadaiśikāḥ/

69. *PTV*, p. 168.
70. Regarding the shift from the perceptible object to pure consciousness, Abhinavagupta notes (*PTV*, p. 170) that there may be a conscious awareness of the supreme energy (*svasaṃvitpramāṇalabdhaḥ*), since it is in the nature of that moment when consciousness, which is freedom (*svātantryam*), is anticipating cognition of an object to surge forth from within itself (*bhāvojjigamiṣātmakam*).
71. *TĀ*, ibid., (85).

(*unmeṣa*),[72] within this consciousness, of the cosmos as an object toward which will be directed the power of cognition of the supreme.[73]

For now appears the power of cognition (*jñānaśakti*). What was yet but emanative intent (with *icchā*), then desire to perceive the manifestation (with *īśāna*), evolves into the knowlege of the manifestation. It is a knowledge however purely ideal, for at this level there is no form, no object to be known. It is, says Jayaratha, the awakening, the revelation, of the cosmos upon which is directed the intentness toward manifestation, due to a desire arising within consciousness to know it inwardly. This is the primal subtle vibration (*ādyaḥ parispanda*),[74] that is, the initial, infinitely subtle movement which is at the root of any movement, of the entire universe.

---

72. *Unmeṣa*, properly speaking, is the opening of the eyes, the blossoming of a flower; by contrast *nimeṣa* denotes their becoming closed, folded. It is therefore understandable that these two words be used to denote the emergence of the manifestation, then its dissolution, within the supreme consciousness. Here is how divine activity is described in the first verse of the *Spanda Kārikā*: "We laud that Śaṅkara, who is the source of the power of the wheel of the energies, by whose opening and closing of the eyes there is the appearance and dissolution of the world: *yasyonmeṣa nimeṣabhyāṃ jagataḥ pralayodayau*." But as pointed out by the commentators (Rāmakaṇṭha in his *Vivṛtti* on *SpK*, and Kṣemarāja in the *SpN* and *SpS*), the coming forth (*unmeṣa*) of the universe is correlative with the disappearance (*nimeṣa*) of the pure undifferentiated consciousness; and conversely the revelation of the latter entails the closing down or disappearing (*nimeṣa*) of the empirical world and consciousness. Thus there is a constant interplay between *unmeṣa* and *nimeṣa*, each taking in turn the sense of the other, depending upon whether they are viewed from the perspective of the emanation or of the resorption.

    We have seen previously (chap. 4, p. 181) that *unmeṣa*, as an awakening to the supreme reality, indicates also the background free of all thought construct (*nirvikalpa*), of any form of discursive thought.
73. *TĀ* 3, *śl.* 73-74: "This solitary reflective awareness of the self which occurred previously, which is the unfoldment of the universe of the knowable, [now] exists in the aspect of the power of cognition."

    svātmapratyavamarśo yaḥ prāg abhūd ekavīrakaḥ//
    jñātavyaviśvonmeṣātmā jñānaśaktitayā sthitaḥ/
    (vol. 2, p. 85)
74. *TĀ*, 3, comm. (pp. 85-86).

"When the power of cognition awakes (*unmiṣanti*), it consists in the unfoldment (*unmeṣa*) of all the desired objects, [and it is] *u*."[75]

The divinities who appear at this stage are, unlike those who were in *ī*, fearsome, and they obstruct the path toward liberation.[76]

Ū

Like the power of will, that of cognition takes on two successive aspects according to how much it it disturbed (*kṣobhita*) or its objective aspect (*jñeyāṃśa*) is in evidence. Disturbance here, as with *i* and *ī*, refers to the movement prior to the manifestation which becomes more perceptible as the intent or impulse toward emanation emerges more distinctly in Śiva. Like *īśāna* in *icchā*, *ūnatā* rests in *unmeṣa*.[77] And like *i*, the phoneme *u* is twofold: short (*u*) and long (*ū*).

"When, as revelation becomes more marked, the objective aspect [of the power of cognition] sustains a great disturbance, then deficiency (*ūnatā*)[78] arises in pure consciousness."[79]

This *śloka* of the *TĀ* is commented upon by Jayaratha as follows:

> The aspect of what is to be known (or of objectivity, *jñeya*) expanding because it predominates over that of knowledge (or cognition, *jñāna*), there is then a perturbation, the support of the diversity of objectivity, that is, of all that is blue, pleasant

---

75. *PTV*, p. 168: *unmiṣanti tu jñānaśaktir īṣyamānasakalabhāvonmeṣamayī u iti.*
76. *TĀ*, 3, *śl.* 74-75 (and comm.):

iyaṃ parāparā devī ghorām yā mātṛmaṇḍalīm//74//
sṛjaty aviratam śuddhāśuddhamārgaikadīpikām/

"This supreme-nonsupreme Goddess continuously emits the circle of the fearsome Mothers, who alone light the pure-impure pathway."

77. *TS*, chap. 3 (p. 13).
78. In *ABS*, 16.47, the condition of *ū* is *ūṇarūpa.*
79. *jñeyāṃśah pronmiṣan kṣobham yadaiti balavattvataḥ/*
ūnatābhāsanaṃ saṃvinmātratve jāyate tadā//
TĀ 3.75-76 (vol. 2, p. 86).

and so forth. Then, due to this prevalence of the objective, an incompleteness (*apūrṇatva*), that is, a deficiency (*ūnatā*), of the pure cognitive aspect of cognition appears, contraction (*saṅkoca*) prevails. In this way is produced the sixth phoneme.[80]

Here now is how in the *PTV* Abhinava, in the cryptic style that he often employs, describes this stage:

> The absolute consciousness (*anuttarasaṃvid*), being awakened (*unmiṣattaiva*) since it is the animating principle of the awakening (or unfolding) of all that tends toward unfoldment, becomes deficient (*ūnībhūtā*). This is due to the contraction resulting from the fact that there begin to appear the outlines of differentiation in the totality of objects, though the latter appear after the [stage of] *unmeṣa* only: they are then still unmanifest, their condition being comparable to that of objectivity when it is held within the internal organ (*antaḥkaraṇa*). So the mass of all that exists, being taken into itself [by the supreme consciousness], is borne (*ūḍha*) [in that consciousness], the udder (*ūdha*) of the celestial Cow[81] that is the supreme Deity. The power of cognition thus expands in the most manifest manner (*susphuṭā prasṛtā*): it is *ū*.[82]

So, with the arising of *ū* a representation of the objective world begins to emerge within consciousness. To quote the *TĀ* 3.76-77:

> It is said that [when deficiency is] developed, the course of what is to be known begins to exist. This development consists in that

80. *jñānapekṣayā jñeyarūpo 'ṃśa udriktatvāt prasphuṭībhavan yadā kṣobhaṃ tattannīlasukhādyātmanā citrākāradhāritām eti tadā jñeyasyādhikyāt jñānasya jñānamātrarūpatāyām ūnatvasya apūrṇatvasya ābhāsanaṃ jāyate saṃkocādhigamo bhavet, iti ṣaṣṭhavarṇodayaḥ.* (Ibid., p. 87)
81. We saw previously that in the *Ṛg Veda* Word and Cow are interrelated (*RV* 3.55.1, or 8.100.10-11); cf. chap. 1, p. 23.
82. *PTV*, pp. 168-69: *unmiṣattaiva unmimiṣatām api antaḥprāṇasarvasvarūponmeṣottaraikarūpair api antaḥkaraṇavedyadeśīyāsphuṭaprāyabhedāṃśabhāsamānabhāvarāśibhiḥ saṃkocavaśena ūnībhūtānuttarasaṃvitsarvabhāvagarbhīkāreṇa anaṅgadhainavīrūpaparadevatāyā ūdhorūpā ūḍhasakalabhāvarāśiḥ susphuṭā prasṛtā jñānaśaktiḥ ū iti.*

the ocean of perceptions assumes a variety of forms. The yogins know that this is the seed of all that constitutes [the world of] duality.[83]

It goes without saying that the object of the power of cognition, on this level, is a purely mental, or internal, representation of the forms of the world that is later on to appear empirically. The universe emerges within Śiva's consciousness, at this level, as inseparable from his awareness thereof. We are on the plane of nondifferentiation. This ideal representation begins to be more clearly defined, and thus loses its pristine fullness, and this is why it is deficient (*ūna*). This is also why waves (*ūrmi*, a term used, in fact, for *ū* in *TS*, chap. 3, p. 13) arise in the ocean of consciousness. But as yet there is no actual objectivity. There is no form.[84] Form and world are there in seed-form.

The phoneme *ū*, indeed, is regarded as the seed of the process of the manifestation of the phonemes, that is, as being much more so than the rest of the vowels from *a* to *aḥ*, though all of them are, like Śiva, seeds (*bīja*) of the manifestation. "Truly, this phonematic awareness (*parāmarśa*), the sixth one, is the principal of those made of the supreme self-awareness [of the Lord. Therefore it is] from this one that, separately or fusing mutually, arise all the other [phonematic] awarenesses.[85]

This preeminent position of *ū* is due to its being taken, as it were, as symbolic of the first six phonemes, which are the initial—highest—stages of the Word, therefore those from which all the others derive (in this respect *PTV*, p. 224, 1.10-11: *ūkārāntāḥ tatprabhavatvād anyasya*: [the phonemes from *a*]

---

83. *rūḍhaṃ tajjñeyavargasya sthitiprārambha ucyate//76//*
rūḍhir eṣā vibhodhābdheś citrākāraparigrahaḥ/
idaṃ tadbhedasaṃdarbhabījaṃ cinvante yoginaḥ//77//

84. Thus Jayaratha's commentary upon *śl.* 76 (p. 88):
tatra anuttarānandayor śuddhasaṃvinmātrarūpatvāt tadapekṣayā bhedābhāvāt prameyavārtāpi nāstī/

85. *TĀ*, 3.77, comm.: *iha khalu etad eva paravimarśātmamukhyaṃ parāmarśaṣaṭkaṃ yataḥ parasparaṃ prameyeṇa vā saṃghaṭṭe sati nikhilaparāmarśodayaḥ.* (vol. 2, p. 88).

to *ū*, for [from these] arise the rest of [the phonemes].[86]

To conclude, here is how Abhinavagupta in the third chapter of the *TS* (p. 13) sums up the situation of the first six vowels: "The three first [phonetic] awarenesses (*parāmarśa*: *a*, *i*, *u*) being essentially on the side of the aspect of light [of consciousness] (*prakāśabhāgasāratvāt*), are solar (*sūryātmakam*). In the three other ones [*ā*, *ī*, *ū*] dominates delight (*āhlāda*),[87] which is essentially rest (*viśrānti*); they have, therefore, the nature of the moon. It is understood, however, that [in both cases] there is no aspect or element of action (*karmāṃśa*: that is, there is, on this plane, no objectivity, where normally action—*karma*, *kriyā*—prevails)." This active aspect of the energy will assert itself with the diphthongs, before which arise the four liquids.

Ṛ, Ṝ, Ḷ, Ḹ

The first six phonemes (*a*, *ā*, *i*, *ī*, *u*, *ū*) each conveniently provided the initial letter of a term (*anuttara*, *ānanda*, *icchā*, etc.) suitable to denote the aspects successively assumed by the energy, within Śiva, in order to initiate the process of manifestation. The four liquids, which are our present concern, are of no help for such a use: few—and in any case, no suitable—words begin with *ṛ*, and nearly none with *ṝ* and *ḷ*; as for *ḹ*, its existence is purely theoretical. Hence it was even more difficult to vindicate the presence of these four phonemes (which the *varṇasamāmnāya*, however, brings inevitably after *ū* and before the diphthongs) as stages of Śiva's inner evolution. As a result, intricate considerations, intermingling phonetics and cosmogony, are put forward in an attempt to demonstrate the necessity of inserting these four "sterile," "neuter," phonemes in the midst of the kinetic and vibrant creative movement of

86. Also *TĀ* 3.184 (p. 180): *svarāṇāṃ ṣaṭkam eveha mūlaṃ syād varṇasaṃtatau.* The next *śloka*s of the *TĀ* reduce indeed the six phonemes to the first three, the basic triad of the phonematic emanation consisting of the energies of consciousness, will, and awakening: *ataḥ ṣaṇṇāṃ trikaṃ sāraṃ cidiṣyunmeṣaṇātmakam* (*śl.* 192).

87. One may note that *ā-HLĀD* (in the causative) means to revive, to refresh, as well as to delight or gladden: the moon is essentially cool, refreshing.

consciousness, as it is bringing forth the universe within itself. Abhinavagupta solves the problem by seeing in *ṛ*, *ṝ*, *ḷ*, and *ḹ* a necessary stage for the initial impulse of consciousness (*icchā*), notably in its aspect of disturbance or stir (*kṣobha*). At that stage there must be a kind of pause in consciousness, which shines, then in four different forms, before it proceeds with its creative movement. In the *TĀ*, he interpolates between *śl.* 79-81 and 91-92 that describe these phonemes ten *śloka*s about the creative stir—*kṣobha, kṣobhana*—of consciousness, which is at once that stir proper, its cause (*kṣobhaka*) and its support (*kṣobhādhāra*). Abhinavagupta stresses how this *kṣobha* is essential for the emergence of manifestation.[88] Jayaratha, in his commentary (like Abhinavagupta himself in the *PTV*, p. 209), points out (pp. 94, 95, and 96) its sexual connotation also: an aspect of the creative process that we shall see again later (*infra*, pp. 281-82).

Here again, the power of will, the emanative impulse (*icchā-śakti*) predominates. We have seen that *icchā* assumes successively two aspects: quiescent and disturbed or stirred, corresponding to the two phonemes *i* and *ī*, depending on how clearly the object of its intentness, that is, manifestation, appears in it.

This twofold energy now associates with the sound *ra* or the sound *la*. Those are, it should be noted, the sounds *ra* and *la* (*ralayoḥ śrutimātram*) and not the phonemes (*varṇa*s) *ra* and *la*, semivowels that, in our system, are classified with consonants and are therefore not on the level of Śiva, but on that of the next categories (*tattva*s) of the emanation. Jayaratha, pointing to this, explains that the sound *ra* flashes

---

88. Cf. also *ŚSV* 2.7, comm. (p. 61), and *TS*, chap. 3 (pp. 13-14). As we said above (p. 249, n. 70), Abhinavagupta (*PTV*, p. 170) correlates the six vowels from *a* to *ū* with the movements of the first nondiscursive awareness of objectivity in the human being, prior to all discursive knowledge. *Ū* in this case is that moment where knowledge of an object, a vase for instance, arises as "a many-colored, self-luminous knowledge of the known." Next arises a kind of inner stir (*u*); then the free consciousness (*ī*), condensing, becomes bliss (*ā*) and finally is lost in rapturous wonder (*a*): this is the reverse movement of the—cosmic—process we are following here.

forth instantaneously like lightning, whereas a phoneme has a certain duration, and he adds that in Śiva there is no objectivity (whereas it is already there at the level of the phonemes *ra* and *la*).[89] Further, according to tradition and not only to the Trika, the phoneme *ra* (and the *bījamantra RAṂ*) is regarded as the seed of fire (*agnibīja*), and the phoneme *la* (and the *bījamantra LAṂ*) as the seed of earth (*pṛthivībīja*).[90] So, when the power of will, in its undisturbed form, flashes forth instantaneously like lightning, the phoneme *ṛ* will arise; and in its disturbed form, equally bright but comparatively more stable, *ṝ* will arise; then, when this twofold energy appears as stability or stillness (*sthairaya, niścalatā*), a state belonging to earth, *ḷ* and *ḹ* will arise.

The description of *ṛ* and *ḷ* as consisting of a consonantal and a vocalic element is to be found in traditional phonetics, whose conceptions are here translated in terms of metaphysics.[91]

Stability is immobility; earth is the last of the *tattva*s, where the movement of emanation comes to an end. If this stable point is reached, how can the emanative movement be carried on in Śiva? Jayaratha, for his part, writes that the object of the power of will (*iṣyamāna*), that is, that which objectivity will consist of, and the gradual emergence of which marks the inner evolution of Śiva toward emanation, is not to be found in *ṛ, ṝ, ḷ,* or *ḹ*, where there is only its shadow (*chāyamātreṇaiva*).[92] Further, *śloka* 80 of the *TĀ* mentions once again that the energy of revelation (*unmeṣa*) which precedes

---

89. *TĀ* 3.79, comm. (pp. 89-90), which refers to the *Mahābhāśya* to substantiate its view that *ṛ, ḷ* and *ra* and *la* are different types.

90. The *bīja*s of the other elements are *ya* (*yaṃ*), air; *va* (*vaṃ*), water; and *kṣa* (*kṣaṃ*), ether. Cf. chap. 6, p. 346, *TĀ* 11.20, comm. (vol. 7/2, p. 12), and *SvT* 4.103ff.

91. Cf. for instance *Atharva Prātiśākhya*, 1.37.39: *saṃpṛṣṭarephaṃ ṛvarṇam . . . salakāram ḷvarṇam.* It is to be noted however that Bhartṛhari (*VP* 4.148) holds that the vocalic element related to *ṛ* or *ḷ* is *a*. Similarly *ABS* 16.53 (vol. 1, p. 150) establishes that *ṛ* and *ḷ* arise from the conjunction of *a* with *r* and *l*. (Should this be paralleled with Grammont's definition of the English *r* vowel as a "kind of *a*"? Cf. J. Bloch, "La prononciation de R en sanskrit," *BEFEO* 44: 43-45.

92. *TĀ* 3.79, comm. (p. 90).

these four phonemes, is but the receptacle of objectivity, not its source, which lies in the previous form of energy: *icchā*. And regarding the actual manifestation of this objectivity, it will occur at a lower stage only, when the power of action (*kriyāśakti*) emerges.

Now, insofar as the object upon which the power of will is intent is already there, in this will, if only in its subtlest lineaments—and we have seen that this is actually the case between *i* and *u*—the emanative intentness retains its efficiency. But here nothing is left of that upon which the power of will is intent. Only its shadow (*chāyā*) remains, a rather unclear term[93] (for how do we differentiate between the shadow and the lineaments of objectivity?), yet denoting, at least in Jayaratha's mind, the absence of this objectivity as emanative efficiency. So here we would have but pure will devoid of creative potency, a point where the emanative energy has come to a kind of standstill.

This pause is consciousness at rest (*viśrānti*) within itself; now such a rest, in our system, is bliss (*ānanda*) and light (*prakāśa*). And indeed, according to *śloka* 81 of the *TĀ*, "This fourfold aspect of the power of will is called supreme ambrosia. Since no further disturbance can arise therein, it is not the seed of anything else."[94] This nectar of immortality, says Jayaratha, is the supreme *camatkāra*, arising from resting in one's own Self.[95] As to the disturbance (*kṣobha*), it is mentioned here because it is an attribute of the seed (*bīja*), whereas the womb (*yoni*) is the support of the disturbance: a traditional Indian concept. It is out of the union of seed and womb, and of the disturbance of the latter by the former, that everything arises. Now, vowels (from *a* to *aḥ*) are seeds. Śiva is the seed. Consonants (from *ka* to *kṣa*), Śakti, are wombs. Their union gives rise to the universe. If this is so, the phonemes *ṛ*, *ṝ*, *ḷ*, and *ḹ*,

93. It is also used by Abhinavagupta in *TS*, chap. 3 (p. 14).

94. *icchāśakter ataḥ prāhuś cāturūpyaṃ parāmṛtam/*
kṣobhāntarasyāsadbhāvān nedaṃ bījaṃ ca kasyacit// (vol. 2, p. 91).

95. Also *TĀ* 3.92 (p. 101): *ātmany eva ca viśrāntyā tat proktam amṛtātmakam:* "When [the energy] rests within itself, this is said to be the nectar of immortality" (or ambrosia).

phonetically sharing in both these categories of phonemes, should have, as may be assumed, a specific creative power. However, this is not so, but just the opposite. This is explained in the *TĀ* by saying that these four phonemes are not exactly seeds. Consequently they can neither be the cause nor the support of a disturbance.[96] So they are not creative. They are indeed called neuter (*napuṃsaka*) or sterile—literally "eunuch" (*ṣaṇḍha*)[97] phonemes.

In the *PTV* Abhinavagupta propounds another explanation of the case: "This group of four [phonemes] is called sterile, just like a seed that has been burned, because they participate in the nature of voidness and not because they do not at all possess the nature of seed. No [state], in fact, exists apart from that of the couple Śiva and Śakti, who are [respectively] seed and womb: there is no [third] state in addition to these two to be found in the *Mālinīvijayottaratantra* or in any other treatise. In the pleasures of this world, too, the same sort of rest, that is, of bliss, is to be found. This is why these [phonemes] are called the four ambrosiacal seeds".[98]

Here we meet again with one aspect of these four phonemes that we have already touched upon: *ṛ*, *ṝ*, *ḷ*, and *ḹ* are not only known as sterile but also as *amṛtavarṇa*: ambrosiacal phonemes. Ambrosia is, as we have seen, the enraptured wonderment of consciousness at rest within itself.[99] When no disturbance arises, then the pure, noncreative energy is at rest. Such a rest, as the

96. Ibid., *śl.* 91 (p. 100):

prakṛitaṃ brūmahe nedaṃ bījaṃ varṇacatuṣṭayam/
nāpi yonir yato naitat kṣobhādhāratvam ṛcchati//

97. In fact, *ṣaṇḍha* is also a grammatical term with the same meaning as *napuṃsaka*, that is, "neuter."

98. *PTV*, p. 174: *etac catuṣkaṃ śūnyarūpatānupraveśād dagdhabījam iva ṣaṇḍharūpaṃ bhaṇyate na tu sarvathā bījarūpatvābhāvāt, bījayonyātmakaśivaśaktyubhayātirekiṇaḥ kasyacid api abhāvāt, śrīpūrvādiśāstreṣu cānabhidhānāt laukikasukhādiṣu caivaṃvidhaiva viśrāntir ānandarūpeti, tad evāmṛtabījacatuṣkam ity uktam.*

99. *TĀ* 3.92: *ātmany eva ca viśrāntyā tat proktam amṛtātmakaṃ/* and Jayaratha, ibid., p. 101: *asya varṇacatuṣṭayasya prakṣobhakatvābhāvāt svātmamātraviśrāntyā paracamatkāramayatvam.*

"Since they rest within themselves, they are said to be of the nature of

PTV would have it, does not mean the incapacity for creation, since these four phonemes are endowed with the twofold nature necessary to any creation, but it means that here willpower wishes to keep its creative energy within itself and enjoy the bliss of the restful state thus achieved. Abhinavagupta's mention of worldly pleasures alludes to that brief moment of standstill in the spasm preceding the creative emission, a moment of utmost pleasure. It might equally be taken as an allusion to Tantric sexual practices, from which these metaphysical considerations may derive, and where the yogin achieves the highest bliss and the goal of his practice if he is able to retain his energy within, that is, to prevent the emission of semen.

We saw, finally, that the *PTV* ascribed the sterility of these phonemes to their having entered voidness. We should return now to this point. Abhinavagupta writes:

> With regard to this,[100] all that [will appear later and] is mixed up, combined and interrelated with others, must first assume a form —one might say void—and not perceptible by the senses: it is like the jumping of frogs.[101] But these things nevertheless continue to be made of the Absolute (*anuttara* = *a*) and of bliss (*ānanda* = *ā*), and they are indescribable since they are both the substratum of all forms of cognition and their ultimate point of rest. On the contrary, the stirring (*saṃrambha*) extending from the energy of will (*i*) to that of sovereignty (*ī*) can bear successivity and can thus spread out either within itself[102] or on the plane of

ambrosia." Jayaratha introduces this half-*śloka* as follows: "These four phonemes, when free of any disturbance, rest in themselves alone and consist therefore in supreme wonderment."

100. Regarding the power of activity and the nature of action, which consists of successive moments: its activity begins to operate from the phoneme *e*, which comes immediately after *ḹ*.

101. When hopping about, frogs shift from one point right to another, or rather they pass through a middle space which is like a void, a condition of invisibility. Similarly the power of action operating within the diphthongs *e*, and so on, but originating in the vowels from *ā* to *ū* (since the phonemes *e*, and so forth, are produced through combining *a* and *i*, etc.), moves from the vowels to diphthongs through the "void" of the phonemes *ṛ*, *ṝ*, *ḷ*, and *ḹ*.

102. This results in *ṛ*, *ṝ*, *ḷ*, and *ḹ*, which are nothing but the pure power of will.

anuttara and *ānanda* (*a* and *ā*).[103] When it spreads within its own body, which is void, it becomes luminous, igneous: *ṛ* and *ṝ*. For how can one deny that in these two phonemes the two vowels *i* and *ī* are present, associated with the sound of the letter *r*, the nature of which is brightness? This is said by the illustrious Puṣpadanta:[104] "This is also established by the similarity with the sound *ra.*"

In fact, when one wishes to enter in a stable aspect[105] of voidness, one [first] goes progressively through a state of luminous consciousness (*bhāsvararūpasaṃvitti*), then when one enters in a state of stability, the phonemes *ḷ* and *ḹ* appear, being accompanied by the sound of the letter *la* which is stability, a condition proper to the earth. Finally, sovereignty (*ī*) plunges[106] as long as possible and, surpassing then all forms of objectivity, reaches the condition of [total] voidness and stability, that is, the protracted state (*plutatvam*) of the syllable. This is in conformity with the rule: "there is no lengthened form of the phoneme *ḷ*."[107] Whilst for the phoneme *a* and the other [phonemes] the protracted form is only a lengthening of their long (*dīrgha*) form, [here, for *ḷ*,] in conformity with the rule quoted above, the long form [of the phoneme] is not to be taken account of. But this is enough!"[108]

---

103. Which associates *i* and *ī* with *a* and *ā*, and results in *e* and *ai.*
104. A grammarian of this name is mentioned by Jayantabhaṭṭa in the *Nyāyamañjarī.*
105. And no longer luminous.
106. *plutvā:* having plunged or blown up, that is, having assumed the most lengthened, or protracted form: *ḷ*. This deliberate ambiguity is meant to give the sentence a double reading, from the standpoint of phonetics as well as of the process of the energy itself.
107. There is only one short (*hrasva*) form of *ḷ*, having a value of one mora (*mātra*), and a protracted one (*pluta*) with the value of three morae; see *Kāśikā* 1.1.9. See chap. 3, n. 214
108. *PTV*, pp. 172-74: *tatra yad yad anyavyāmiśritasāṃkaryam anyasaṃbandhād eti tat tad anāmarśanīyaśūnyaprāyasvarūpākramaṇapuraḥsarīkāreṇa tathā bhavati—plavānām iva bhekādiḥ/ tatrānuttarānandātmakaṃ vapur na vyapasarati, avyapadeśarūpatvāt sarvajñāneṣu sarvādhāravṛttitvena paryavasyati paryantabhittirūpatvāt, api tu kramasahiṣṇutvāt saṃrambha icchaiveśanāntā svātmany anuttarānandapade ca prasaraṇakṣamā/ tataḥ saiva śūnyātmakaṃ svaṃ vapur avagāhamānā bhāsvaraṃ rūpaṃ tejomayam iva prathamaṃ gāhate ṛ-ṝ iti/ atra hi i-ī ity anugamo bhāsvararūparephaśrutyanugamaśca katham apahnūyatām/*

If the phonemes *ṛ*, *ṝ*, *ḷ*, and *ḹ* can be looked upon as "void," the reason is the same, seemingly, as their being regarded as rest and ambrosia: this is because the powers of will and sovereignty sink within themselves instead of moving toward manifestation. They shine there first because the energy is luminous and associated with the *bīja* of fire, *ra*; then as voidness expands, the quiescence associated with the *bīja* of earth, *la*, becomes prevalent. This state of complete vacuity is associated by Abhinavagupta later in the same text[109] with the deep sleep state, *suṣupti*—which, according to *ĪPV* 3.2.15, corresponds to consciousness as resting in voidness[110]—where breath is identified with the "great space" (*mahāvyoman*), the dwelling place of the third *brahman*, that is, the supreme deity as complete void (*paripūrṇaśūnya*). It is indeed well known that the Trika, the Śrīvidyā, and others sometimes describe the highest stages of the emanation as characterized by vacuity or void (*śūnya*), not, of course, as an ontological void—but quite on the contrary as consciousness, or energy per se, free of any trace of objectivity; and this is indeed how *ṛ*, *ṝ*, *ḷ*, and *ḹ* primarily appear.[111]

---

tathāha bhagavān puṣpadantaḥ raśrutisāmānyād vā siddham iti/ śūnye hi niścale rūpe anupravivikṣāyāṃ bhāsvararūpasaṃvittisopānākramaṇaṃ sthitam eva/ tato niścalarūpānupraveśāt pārthivarūpasatattvaniścalatātmakalakāraśrutyanugame ḷ-ḹ iti/ tathā ca paryante īśanarūpataiva samagrabhāvātmasvarūpollanghanena dīrghataraṃ plutvā niścalāṃ śūnyāṃ sattām etīti plutatvam eti "ḷvarṇasya dīrghā na santi" iti nyāyāt/ avarṇādīnāṃ tu dīrghasyaiva dīrghataratā plutatvaṃ, tac ca prāṅnītyā dīrghatvam eva pṛthag aparyeṣaṇīyam ity āstāṃ tāvat.

We have quoted and translated on p. 258 the six lines that follow this passage.

109. *PTV*, p. 228.

110. *tāvanmātra* (*jñeyaśūnyatā*) *stithau proktaṃ sauṣuptam* . . . (vol. 2, p. 260).

111. We have seen above (chap. 3, p. 95), that the sound energy, at its highest stages, from *vyāpinī* to *unmanā*, is sometimes also described as a void. This is also said in *VBh*, 127: In his commentary, Aghoraśiva quotes a *śloka* which defines *śūnya* as devoid of all stain and free of all *tattva*s and all objects of sense-knowledge (*ālambanadharma*). He also quotes a portion of the *Vimarśinīdīpikā* according to which the stage of *śūnya* is freedom, fullness, what is known as Śiva, that where all the *tattva*s are reabsorbed and whence they all arise:

A particular position of these phonemes in the process of the manifestation of the energies of Śiva is also pointed out in other portions of the *PTV* and the *TĀ* we have already mentioned.[112] There Śiva, through the flashing forth of the synthetic awareness of the supreme "I" (*ahaṃparāmarśasphuraṇāt*), appears first as manifesting his solar aspect with the twelve limitating energies (*kalā*s) of the phonemes from *a* to *visarga*, minus the *ṣaṇḍhavarṇa*s, then as revealing his lunar aspect, divided into sixteen *kalā*s, which makes it necessary to bring in the four phonemes, or *kalā*s, hitherto missing. The latter are known, as we have seen, as *amṛtavarṇa*s; now *amṛta*, the nectar or ambrosia, is also called *soma*, and *soma* is the moon. Through their arising Śiva is able to achieve the fullness of that energy which consists in the sixteen *kalā*s, together with his full nature, which is *soma-sūrya*, moon and sun, that is, the holder of the energies, Śiva, together with the aggregate of his energies, Śakti.[113] However, *ṛ*, *ṝ*, *ḷ*, and *ḹ*, at the same time, give rise, in Śiva, to a tendency toward limitation (this indeed is the purpose of the *kalā*s), which is the heralder of the limited manifestation to arise later. From this standpoint, then, the four liquids, in the arising of the differentiated manifestation, play an altogether positive part, which is rather different from that of the mere resting place, the voidness, that is, of a state of pure consciousness, that they assume in the system with which we are now dealing.[114]

But after this stage, evolution will be carried on with the diphthongs issued from the combination of the first six vowels, which we are now going to examine.

---

svatantraṃ paripūrṇaṃ ca śivākhyaṃ śūnyadhāma tat/
tattvāni yatra līyante yasmāt samudayanti ca//
(*VBh.*, pp. 110-11 of the KSTS edition). Maheśvarānanda, in the *Parimala* of the *MM*, 38, associates the *ṣaṇḍhavarṇa*s to the *melāpasiddha*, also associated with *suṣupti*.

112. Chap. 3, pp. 157-59.

113. Here too, for the Krama, there are two moments, first "emaciated" (*kṛśa*), then "full" (*pūrṇa*), of the awareness of the world.

114. *Soma* is indeed viewed as being more specifically the power of action which reveals in the undifferentiation of Śiva that which will give rise to the manifestation. Cf. Jayaratha *ad TĀ* 4.134 (vol. 3, p. 144) *kriyāśaktyātmā soma.*

E

The inner movement of Śiva toward emanation came to a kind of pause with the four "sterile" phonemes, which corresponded to the unalloyed power of will at rest within itself. For it is only through the combination, the union of two complementary elements or aspects that, in a system of thought which, like the Trika, is thoroughly permeated with sexual symbolism, manifestation can progress. The movement toward emanation will therefore continue with the next four phonemes, the diphthongs *e*, *ai*, *o*, and *au*, that are produced through the combination of the first six phonemes from *ā* to *u*.[115] (Of the five phonemes, says the *TĀ*, for the power of bliss, *ānanda*, *ā*, is held as inseparable from the Absolute, *anuttara*, *a*.)

"The five [vowels] precedingly described, all springing upwards, mixing and confounding with one another, take on different forms. The Absolute, supreme vibration, and bliss, moving up and rubbing and embracing will and unfoldment, assume the most diverse forms."[116] This diversity is that of the four diphthongs *e*, *ai*, *o*, and *au*.

"When the two [aspects of] consciousness, absolute and bliss, are fastened to the energy of will [there appears] what is called "triangle," embellished by the joy of emission."[117] This triangle is the phoneme *e*, which is known indeed as *trikoṇa*.

We find again here the considerations upon the written form of the phoneme we saw previously with *a*, for the letter *e* in *devanāgarī* is more or less triangular in shape (ए). *E* is

---

115. *ABS* 16.48-52 gives the four diphthongs as appearing before the liquids. It calls them *kūṭa*, a term it also applies to *kṣa*, of which it is a usual name. *Anuttarecchayogena hy edhamānaḥ sa e smṛtaḥ*/: "That which swells due to the junction of the Absolute and of will is called *e*."

116. *TĀ* 3.92-94 (p. 101-02):

itthaṃ prāg uditam yat tat pañcakaṃ tat parasparam//92//
ucchaladvividhākāram anyonyavyatimiśraṇāt/
yo 'nuttaraḥ paraḥ spando yaś canāndaḥ samucchalan//93//
tāv icchonmeṣasaṃghaṭṭād gacchato 'tivicitratām/

117. *TĀ* 3.94-95 (p. 103):

anuttarānandacitī icchāśaktau niyojite//94//
trikoṇam iti tat prāhur visargāmodasundaram/

called *trikoṇa* also because within it three powers are manifested: those of will and knowledge, which were already there, and that of action (*kriyāśakti*), which is here just emerging and which will bring about the—archetypal—manifestation of objectivity in Śiva. Each of these powers is regarded as forming one of the angles (*koṇa*) of the triangle.

Here is what Abhinavagupta writes in the *PTV*:

> When [the energies of] will and sovereignty enter into the body of [the energy of] bliss (*ā*) and in the abode of the Absolute (*a*) that precedes it and that never loses its own [transcendent] nature [one has, combined, the phonemes], *a* or *ā* and *i* or *ī*, [in this order and] not in the reverse, and, as has been said, [the conjunction of] the letters *a* and *i* give *e*. There is, however, a difference between the penetration [in bliss, *ā*] and the penetration in the abode of the Absolute (*a*), for the penetration in the stage of bliss [results in] a manifest state [of the phoneme], whereas the [phoneme] resulting from the union with the Absolute is, as compared with the other one, more subtle.[118]

Abhinava then quotes a passage of Patañjali's *Mahābhāṣya*,[119] saying that according to some *Sāma Veda* schools *e* and *o* are uttered as short syllables. Here again a fact of phonetics (and a Vedic conception!) is used to substantiate a metaphysical elaboration. From the standpoint of the manifestation of the power of activity, each of these four phonemes typifies a more manifest state of the energy: *asphuṭa* in *e*, *sphuṭa* in *ai*, *sphuṭatara* in *o*, and *sphuṭatama* in *au* (*TĀ* 3.96, comm., p. 106).[120]

So *e* is *a* or *ā* + *i* or *ī*.

---

118. *PTV*, pp. 174-75: *tad evam iccheśanaṃ cānandavapuṣi anuttarapara-dhāmani ca prāgbhāvini svarūpād apracyāviny anupraviśya a ā i ī iti e, na tu viparyaye, yathoktam avarṇa ivarṇe e iti/ anupraveśe cānuttara-padānupraveśe syād api kaścid viśeṣaḥ, ānandapadānupraveśe hi sphuṭatā/ anuttaradhāmasaṃbhede tu sūkṣmatā tadapekṣayā.*

119. *Mahābhāṣya*, 1.1,48.

120. Abhinavagupta refers also to the pronunciation of *e* and *o* in the *aṅga-mantras* and *vaktramantras* in the Śaiva tradition. On this point cf. the *SP1* (p. 144-45), where Hélène Brunner quotes Nirmalamaṇi's commentary upon Aghoraśiva's *Paddhati*, which distinguishes between

In a system where triads play a prominent role, this phoneme, owing to its triangular aspect, could not but hold an eminent position. Since it is produced either through the conjunction of the absolute power (*a*) and the power of bliss (*ā*) with the power of will (*i*) or that of sovereignty (*ī*), or through the conjunction of the three powers of will, cognition, and action, *e* appears as the synthetic seed of the energies which will bring forth the universe. It may also be regarded as synthesizing the three stages of speech: *paśyantī*, *madhyamā* and *vaikharī*,[121] which correspond to the powers of will, cognition, and action as dwelling, of course, in the Word at its highest level, *parā*, that level where *e* lies.

We have seen[122] that the Trika already brings in this notion of triad (so foundational in a system of thought named after this very notion) in the first phoneme, *a*, with regard to its written form in the *devanāgarī* script, and Abhinavagupta, in a passage of the *PTV*,[123] describes the great secret (*mahāguhya*)—for the revelation of which the Goddess approaches Śiva, and which is the Absolute, *a*—as being, among other things, the trigon (*trikoṇa*) of the energies, and so forth, all dwelling in the undifferentiated pure cognition.

Metaphysically and graphically triangular, *e* will often be referred to or invoked, in the Śaiva or Śākta traditions, whenever triads—energies, deities, and so forth—or a triangular figure are concerned, triads and triangles tending to blend into one. This is so, for instance, in the Śrīvidyā, where the central *cakra* of the *śrīcakra*, the *trikoṇa* or *madhyatrikoṇa*, produced by the division of the *bindu*, is also the phoneme *e*. (In this respect see *NṢA* 1.6, or, for instance, Naṭanānanda's commentary upon *KKV* 22-25, where in fact he quotes *TĀ* 3.94-95.) This triangle will evolve into all the other constituent *cakra*s of the *śrīcakra*, therefore into the whole cosmos. Similarly *e*,

---

the short (*hrasva*), long (*dīrgha*), and protracted (*pluta*) recitation of mantras: their *uccāra* rises according to the case either up to the *bhrūmadhya*, or to the *brahmarandhra*, or to the *dvādaśānta*.

121. *KKV*, *śl*. 22-24.

122. *Supra*, 241-43.

123. *PTV*, pp. 52-57.

for Abhinavagupta, is, right from the level of Śiva, the seed of the universe which arises through the conjunction of his three powers of will, cognition, and action. Owing again to its form, *e* is also associated with another energy, the energy of bliss, *ānanda* (*e* can indeed arise either from *a*, or *ā*, united with *i*): due to its being shaped like an inverted triangle, it takes on a very significant meaning for a Tantric or even simply an Indian mind, as conveyed by Jayaratha:[124] "By [the term] '*trikoṇa*' is indicated [or hinted at] the aspect of place of birth, in other words of the 'mouth of Yoginī' (*yoginīvaktra*) of this [phoneme]." The place in question, evidently, is the *yoni*, that is, both the maternal womb and the feminine sexual organ. "From this place," adds Jayaratha, "is born the supreme Energy, as has been said: 'When She comes forth, curved, out of the triangular seat' and: 'the triangle is called *bhaga* [that is: vulva], secret *maṇḍala*, abiding in the sky, its angles being will, cognition, and action while in its center evolves the *cincini* [sound]'."[125] "In ritual practice also," he says later on, "the place where the coming forth takes place is that of the highest bliss because of the discharge associated with it at the time of the bliss of emission."[126] Thus associated with triplicity and sexual symbolism,[127] *e* cannot fail to be of paramount importance in the Trika.[128]

---

124. *TĀ* 3.94, comm. (pp. 103-04).
125. For this sound, cf. chap. 3, p. 97, n. 31.
126. *trikoṇam ityanena yoginīvaktrāparaparyāyajanmādhārarūpatvam apy asya sūcitam/ tata eva hi parā śaktir udetīti bhāvaḥ, yad uktam:*
yad ullasati śṛṅgāṭapīṭhāt kuṭilarūpiṇī/
iti/ tathā:
trikoṇaṃ bhagam ity uktaṃ viyatsthaṃ guptamaṇḍalam/
icchājñānakriyākoṇaṃ tanmadhye ciñcinīkramam//
iti
. . . caryākrame 'pi visargasyānandaphalasya saṃbandhinā sphāreṇa parānandamayaṃ prasarasthānam, iti/ (vol. 2, p. 104).

See also *TĀ* 29.124-26 (vol. 2/2, p. 88-89).
127. For the sexual symbolism of the triangle, cf. G. Tucci, "Tracce di culto lunare in India," *R.S.O.* xiii (1929-30): 419-27, and J. J. Meyer, *Trilogie Altindischer Mächte und Feste der Vegetation*, vol. 3, pp. 133-294.
128. These are meanings also ascribed to it in other Tantric traditions. Thus in the *Jayākhya Saṃhitā* (6.37) and in the *ABS* (17.9), which calls it *tryaśra*, or triangle, and *jagadyoni*, or matrix of the universe.

Finally *e* appears as having a special role in the *mālinī:* Abhinava (*PTV*, p. 155) states that according to "the *Nityā* and other Tantras," *e*, the seed of delusion or distraction (*ekārātmakamohanabīja*), plays there a prominent role. But the passage is obscure. It seems to refer to *prastāras*, diagrams where phonemes are placed for the purpose of extracting (*uddhāra*) mantras, in some of which (in the case of the *mālinī*?) the letter *e* would be in a central position. According, however, to another interpretation (followed by R. Gnoli in his edition of the *PTV*, which he substantiates with Jayaratha's commentary on the *VMT*), this role would be assumed by *ai* and not *e*.

AI

Let us quote here the *TĀ* (3.94-95) and Jayaratha's commentary:

> The two energies—Absolute and Bliss—entering there in a state of growth, attain, by the conjunction of two triangles, the state of six-angled [phoneme].
>
> "When 'there,' that is, in the *e* triangle," says Jayaratha, "the Absolute (*a*) and bliss (*ā*) 'grow,' that is, are reinforced following the rule of *sandhi* [described by Pāṇini in *sūtra* 1.1.1: *vṛddhir-ādaic*: 'the phonemes *ai* and *au* are called *vṛddhi* ['increase(d)'], then, by the union of the Absolute and of bliss, both of which are triadic—since the former has the three energies Raudrī and so forth, and the latter is only an expansion of the former, there takes place a conjunction of the two triangles of *a* and *e*. The condition thus obtained is that of a six-angled or six-pointed figure; that is, there appears the form or nature (*rūpatā*) of the letter *ai*. This form [of the letter *ai*] does not appear in writing because it is extremely secret: one only draws a line above the letter *e*, which is thus doubled. In the practice[129] a six-angled *mudrā* is obtained when the triangle of the *siddha* and that of the *yoginī* interlock."[130]

---

129. This refers to practices of sexual yoga—hence our translation of *carya-krame* with "in the practice." The six-pointed *mudrā* is regarded as formed by the union of the yogin and his consort.

130. *TĀ* 3.95-6 (vol. 2, p. 105):

This passage quite aptly conveys what should be said about the phoneme *ai*, which is produced (this is phonetically true) by the addition of *a* or *ā* to *e*. Thanks to the "triangular" quality of *a*, due as we have seen[131] to its holding within itself the three energies: Raudrī, Ambikā, and Jyeṣṭhā—a quality that extends to *ā* insofar as *ā* is nothing but the expansion of *a*—its union with the triangle *e* results in a theoretical figure formed of two inverted triangles, that is, a six-pointed star.

In view of the symbolism of these triangles, *e* appears as *yoni* and *a* as *bīja* (it is *bīja*, seed, *par excellence*); hence *ai*, the figure thus formed, typifies, in an ordinary context, as indicated by Jayaratha, the sexual union of the yogin and his consort, such union being valued because it reproduces on the human level the archetypal union of Śiva and Śakti. In the cosmic context, the double *ai* triangle is precisely symbolic for the inseparable union of Śiva and Śakti in the undifferentiation of the principle. Jayaratha uses indeed, with respect to the ritual union of the yogin, the term *sampuṭa*, which not only designates the union but also the interlocking or "encasement," the total coincidence of Śiva and Śakti.

Ai is one of those phonemes graphically described in our texts. But such representation is purely theoretical. It is based indeed partly on script—for the triangle forming *e*—and partly on the number of energies supposedly present in the phoneme *a*, which transforms *e* into *ai*: a second energy triangle symbolically added to the previous one. This may look a somewhat hybrid elaboration, resulting from Abhinava's combining

---

anuttarānandaśaktī tatra rūḍhim upāgate//95//
trikoṇadvitvayogena vrajataḥ ṣaḍarasthitim/

tatra trikoṇe 'pi yadā anuttarānandau rūḍhim "vṛddhirecī" iti saṃdhikrameṇa prarohaṃ prāptau, tadā anuttarasya pūrvoktanītyā raudryādiśaktitrayamayatvena ānandasyāpi tatsphāramātrasāratvena trikoṇarūpatvāt akāraikāraḷakṣaṇatrikoṇadvayayogena, ṣaḍarāṃ ṣaṭkoṇāṃ sthitiṃ vrajataḥ aikārarūpatām avabhāsayata ityarthaḥ/ lipau punar evaṃrūpatvam atirahasyatvāt na pradarśyate—ityekārasyaiva dviguṇībhāvonmīlanāyopari rekhāvinyāsaḥ/ caryākrame 'pi hi siddhayoginītrikoṇadvayasaṃpuṭībhāvena ṣaḍaramudrāmayī sthitir jāyate, iti.

131. *Supra*, p. 242.

heterogeneous materials which he did not fully coordinate. But we may perhaps rather consider that here is one more case where two different sets of symbols relevant on two levels are skillfully combined within a symbolical elaboration uniting the most abstract, *paramaśiva*, to the most concrete, *pṛthivi*.

Although *ai* is produced by the addition of the energies of the Absolute and of bliss to the energies collected in *e*, it is regarded, because of its making a step further toward emanation, as containing more distinctly than in *e* the power of action.[132]

Finally let us note that in the Śrīvidyā *ai* (in the form of the *bīja AIṂ*) is particularly associated with the first part of the Śrīvidyā, the *vāgbhava*, and that Abhinavagupta quotes the *NṢA* (1.100) on this point in the *PTV* (p. 230). For the *LT*, too (26.12-25), *AIṂ* is the *vāgbhavabīja* and it is the womb of the universe (*jagadyoni*) as being formed of Viṣṇu (*a* and *ā*) associated with his energy (*i* and *ī*).

O-AU

A and *ā* now unite with *u* or *ū*, thereby producing a thirteenth phoneme, *o*. The first two phonemes, in this case, are considered as seeds and the other two as wombs. The unfolding (*unmeṣa*) and the deficiency (*ūnatā*) of consciousness proper to these phonemes representing a more advanced stage in the movement toward manifestation than will (*icchā*, *i*), and sovereignty (*īśāna*, *ī*), it is considered that in *o* the power of action is more manifest than in *ai*.[133] The other powers are also there, since they arise with the phonemes from *a* to *u*, all contained within those following them, but at this stage the emphasis is more especially placed on the power of action.

This active energy will be even more clearly in evidence at the next stage, *au*, which is much more important than this one with regard to the divine energy and to yoga as well,

132. *ABS* 16.51 states that the phoneme *ai* is known as *aiśvaryavān:* "endowed with power."

133. *ABS* 16.52 says that *o* is *ota*, "invoked," and that *au* is characterized by its potency, *aurjitya*: one must always find, for each phoneme, an epithet or a name beginning with this same phoneme.

and which is produced on the arising of a further phonematic awareness where *a* and *ā* unite with *o*. This is what the *TĀ* (3.96-97 and 103-05) says on this theme:

> These two [selfsame energies] unite with unfolding (*unmeṣa*: *u*). Then, being again in the same condition, they mutually cause the power of action to appear in its most manifest form. . . . This diversity of the reciprocal fusion of the energies is precisely what is called the supreme and manifest body (*vapuḥ*) of the energy of action. Since in this fourteenth stage (*dhāman*) the three energies are [equally] manifested, the Master has called it 'trident' in the *Pūrvaśāsana* (i.e., the *Mālinīvijayottaratantra*)."[134]

In *au* the powers of will and cognition are equally present in the clearest form. *Au* owes its importance precisely to the three powers of Śiva being there perfectly balanced in their full intensity. This is why *au* is called *triśūlabīja*, the seed that is the trident of Śiva's energies,[135] the trident typifying unity in triplicity. At this level, the three powers are absolutely pure, with no tinge of objectivity, because precisely of their being unified and because, says Jayaratha, this unity is the power of action free of all objectivity.[136]

---

134. *ta evonmeṣayoge 'pi punas tanmayātāṃ gate//96//*
kriyāśakteḥ sphuṭaṃ rūpam abhivyaṅktaḥ parasparam/ . . .
. . . svātmasaṃghaṭṭavaicitryaṃ śaktīnāṃ yat parasparam//103//
etad eva paraṃ prāhuḥ kriyāśakteḥ sphutaṃ vapuḥ/
asminścaturdeśe dhāmni sphuṭībhūtatriśaktike//104//
triśūlatvam ataḥ prāha śāstā śrīpūrvaśāsane/

135. *TĀ* 5.60, comm. (vol. 3, p. 365): *"śūlam" icchādiśaktitrayam aukāraś ca.* Cf. also *PTV*, p. 175: *tathā hy aukāra eva kriyāśaktiparispandaḥ parisamāpyate itīcchajñānayor atraivāntarbhāvāt triśūlarūpatvam asya ṣaḍardhaśāstre nirūpitam.*

"Thus, the subtle vibration of the power of activity arises and subsides in the phoneme *au*. Since the [powers of] will and cognition abide there [in the power of activity], it is said in the Trika teaching that it is of the nature of the Trident."

136. Cf. *TĀ* 3.107, comm., p. 114: "When the triad of energies of will, cognition, and action shine in essential fusion (*sāmarasya*) due to the energy of action, there is then nothing left that can be known: nothing onto which these energies may be directed may appear, because they

Au is also one of the three phonemes which make the *bījamantra SAUḤ*, dealt with, notably, in the *PTV*. There it stands for the fully unfolded energy. It is also the central portion of this *bīja*, that is, *au*, which, when this mantra pervades the universe, is associated with the cosmic sphere of energy (*śaktyaṇḍa*).[137]

The *Tantrāloka* further states that the yogin who is able to become fully immersed in this throbbing threefold energy attains that pure, spotless (*nirañjana*) state which is an unshakable state of perfection, freed from all impurity, and wherefrom he will never fall into a lower condition.[138]

Finally, one may note that, according to *TĀ* 3, *śl.* 109,[139]

---

annul each other mutually. . . . This mutual incompatibility of that on which these three energies may be directed results in the fact that nothing can be conditioned, 'colored,' by them. This is why it will be said later on (*śl.* 172): 'The Goddess Action is spotless (*nirañjanā*, lit., 'without ointment')."

137. Cf. *PS, śl.* 43-45, comm. (pp. 78-79 in L. Silburn's edition). This *vyāpti* is described in *MV* 4.25 (p. 23), a text quoted by Jayaratha, p. 124. Abhinavagupta, in the commentary upon *śl.* 29 of the *PT* (*PTV*, p. 265 and *PTlv*, pp. 21-22), mentions also *au* as the trident of energies, identifying it with Śiva as the seat (*āsana*) of the Goddess, that is, as being that upon which rests the emanative energy. However, the trident can also be that of the three goddesses, Parā, Parāparā, and Aparā, conceived of as united on the plane of total transcendence: it is viewed in this way in some practices, aiming, with the awakening of the *kuṇḍalinī* through a mantra, at reabsorbing the yogin and the whole cosmos into pure energy. On this last point, cf. A. Sanderson's study "Maṇḍala," *op. cit.* For *SAUḤ*, cf. ch. 7, pp. 417-22.

138. *TĀ* 3.108 (p. 115). There is in the *Netra Tantra*, 7.37-39 (vol. 1, pp. 168-70) a definition of the *nirañjana* state which underscores its unique quality: "The yogins, O fair one, who attain this state, become one with Him, the spotless, who is subtle, who holds within himself all the modalities, who is changeless, supreme, free of all objectivity, all-pervading, the perfect and peerless condition of the supreme Lord," a *śloka* which Kṣemarāja glosses with a variety of epithets stressing the complete freedom, the undifferentiation, the lordship, which is enjoyed by one who attains this state. *Nirañjana* is also a name of Śiva. Finally it is worth noting that *nirañjanā* (with a long *ā*) is the full moon, which is, as we have seen previously, the fullness of Śiva's energy (cf. chap. 3, p. 90).

139. Ibid., p. 115.

eight divinized energies—"Brahmī and the others"—may be associated with each of the eight phonemes from ṛ to *au.* Each phoneme is then successively taken as "that which expresses" (*vācaka*), as the phonetic seed, of each of the eight *devī*s, who are thus multiplied by eight and appear therefore sixty-four times. We have already encountered[140] these eight divinities who also preside—sometimes bearing other names—over the eight *varga*s. Why are they given here as associated with the phonemes from ṛ to *au*? Probably to have them arise right from the level of Śiva, and so they may be next projected into the emanation: according to the *ābhāsa* system of the Trika, everything must indeed have its existence first archetypally in Śiva, so that it can subsequently be reflected in the lower levels of the emanation. Let us add that together with an initial emergence in Śiva of these divinities, there is thus, at this same transcendental level, the paradigm of the number sixty-four, which in Tantrism is important: it is a *śākta* number, and it is notably, as we have seen,[141] that of the division of the phonemes when their morae are included.

Bindu[142]

The phoneme we shall now discuss, the *anusvāra*, is not a vowel (neither is the next one, the *visarga*). It is simply, as the name *anusvāra* indicates, a nasal sound, an "after-sound," a nasal utterance added to a vowel. Moreover, this phoneme, known as *bindu*, or "drop"—a term referring both to its written form: a dot above the vowel, and to what it symbolizes because of this form—does not, strictly speaking, correspond (neither does the *visarga*) to a movement toward emanation within Śiva. It is only a symbol for the undifferentiated unity of consciousness, the oneness of Śiva, the dimensionless point which however contains in seed-form all the worlds, the seed of the entire emanation. In other words, *bindu* is Śiva himself within whom fourteen different moments have been distin-

140. Chap. 3, p. 155.
141. Ibid., pp. 161-63.
142. For *bindu* in the manifestion of sound, cf. chap. 3, pp. 105ff.

guished, but who actually never ceases to be the undifferentiated point, the sole and radiating source of all energy, and who goes back, as it were, to the supreme plane before emitting the manifestation. Thus we have the fifteenth and sixteenth phonematic awarenesses (or the fifteenth and sixteenth *kalās*) that are *bindu* and *visarga.*

This is how Abhinavagupta describes the *bindu* in the *TS* (chap. 1, pp. 14-15): "Then, at the end of the power of action, all that was to be done and has been accomplished is about to enter into the Absolute, but, before doing so, it all exists as the *bindu* which is essentially knowledge (*vedana*) and pure light (*prakāśamātra*)" . . . "When [the energies of] will and cognition," he says in the *PTV*, "have increased because they have entered into the nature of the Absolute [*a*—which gives *e, ai, o, au*], they abandon this state of subtle vibration (*parispanda*) [which is, however] conditioned, and identify themselves with the *bindu* that is knowledge, associated with the *puruṣatattva*, pure consciousness having attained to undifferentiation. When they thus dissolve on the plane of the Absolute, [they become the *bindu*]: *aṃ.*"[143]

One could perhaps be clearer, even with regard to such a paradoxical condition as the *bindu*'s, which includes diversity while transcending it, and wherein also the supreme consciousness and the *puruṣa* seem to coincide. In the *TĀ*, where he deals more extensively with the *bindu*, Abhinavagupta is comparatively less obscure. After describing the effulgence of the first principle as being either solar, lunar, or fiery,[144] he continues: "This pure light, shining while these three luminous aspects (*dhāmatraya*) remain, is called *bindu* in the scriptures. It is regarded as Śiva's *bindu.*"[145] "This *bindu*," says Jayaratha

143. *PTV*, p. 176: *evam icchājñāne anuttarasvarūpānupraveśena prāptopacaye paścāt parityajya tathāvidhopādhiparispandasattām abhedasattārohanacinmayapuruṣatattvasatattvavedanā rūpabindumātrāvaśeṣeṇa vapuṣā tathānuttarapadalīne aṃ iti.*

144. These are the three aspects of knower, knowledge, and known, present in the preceding stages of the energy, and notably in *au* (referred to as "conditioning" the *parispanda* of the energies in the above quotation).

145. *TĀ* 3.133-34 (p. 136).

atra prakāśamātram yat sthite dhāmatraye sati//133//

in his commentary (ibid., pp. 136-37), "is the supreme knower, and has no connection whatever with the *bindu* (the *anusvāra*) of ordinary speech." Here the emphasis is placed on *bindu* as being pure consciousness, or knowledge, a character stressed by Abhinavagupta and Jayaratha as well when they term it *vindu* rather than *bindu*, using thus a term derived from the verbal root *VID*, to know.[146] "At this point, the energy of the Absolute, her body becoming fully manifest, assumes as a result from the turbidness of objectivity, the nature of *vindu*.[147] "This is," says Jayaratha (ibid., p. 117), "the autonomous knower in the very act of knowing. Its nature is light, supreme, indivisible (*avibhāgaḥ paraḥ prakāśaḥ*). He never loses anything from its original nature." Therefore it is the supreme itself, but as the holder of the seed of diversity.[148]

"This undivided light," Abhinava goes on saying, "[shining] when the energy of action is awakened, this luminous seat of sun, moon, and fire, such is for us the supreme *bindu*.[149] . . . This light exists in itself, totally free from the variety of things pleasant, unpleasant, and the like, from white, red, and so forth. As the Master[150] has said, 'This innate splendor that

---

uktaṃ bindutayā śāstre śivabindur asau mataḥ/

Dhāman, a term with a wealth of meanings and thus difficult to render, is at once light or glory, power as related to a function, "'form' as resulting from a function" (Renou). It also denotes, among other things, a self-luminous place (for instance, a star), a point where energy is manifested, "a holder, a container of numinous power" (Gonda). For this word, see J. Gonda's study, "The meaning of the Sanskrit term *dhāman*" (Amsterdam, 1967) and (mainly for the Vedic uses of the term) L. Renou, *EVP*: 1, p. 21; 8, p. 74; 9, p. 108.

146. *vettīti vinduḥ:* the word *bindu* is traditionally derived from *VID, v* and *b* being interchangeable.

147. *atrānuttaraśaktiḥ sā svaṃ vapuḥ prakaṭasthitam/*
kurvanty api jñeyakalākāluṣyād vindurūpiṇī//110//

148. *ABS*, 16, in which the *bindu* emerges before the phonemes, ascribes a similar role to *ma* which, for this text, is also *bindu*.

149. *TĀ*, 3.111

uditāyāṃ kriyāśaktau somasūryāgnidhāmani/
avibhāgaḥ prakāśo yaḥ sa vinduḥ paramo hi naḥ//111//

150. Kṛṣṇa probably, since these three lines remind us of *BhG* 15.6, a *śloka* already borrowed with a slight modification from *MundUp*. 2.2.11.

neither sun, moon, nor fire illumine, but without which the light of the sun, the moon, or the fire would not exist', that which thus shines is consciousness."[151] So the *bindu* brings together in its undifferentiated oneness all the triads that *sūrya*, *soma*, and *agni* (equivalent here to knower, knowledge, and known—*pramātṛ*, *pramāna*, and *prameya*) stand for, gathered in the supreme knower, totally autonomous and one, even though it holds within itself the entire universe: "Consciousness itself, while identifying, as a result of its freedom, with the known, is self-existent and utterly self-dependent."[152] Or again: "The knower is that stage of consciousness conveyed by the thought 'I am' (*aham asmi*) without any dependence on, or connection with means of approach to things that are to be known, and so forth. It is not unlike [the condition of] one who knows the scriptures."[153] A person who knows the scriptures, Jayaratha explains (ibid., p. 130), keeps them within himself (in his memory): they are thus part of him, and remain so even when he does not need to refer to them: this precisely is why he may be said to know them. Similarly the whole "known" —the totality of the cosmos—abides in the Self, for the supreme knower holds within himself all the aspects of knowledge.[154] This is an interesting comparison, especially to the point in a culture where tradition is mostly memorized and imparted by word of mouth; the *guru*, like Śiva—who is the supreme *guru*—holds everything within himself while being always free

---

151. *hlādataikṣṇyādi vaicitryaṃ sitaraktādikaṃ ca yat//114//*
svayaṃ tan nirapekṣo 'sau prakāśo gurur āha ca/
yan na sūryo na vā somo nāgnir bhāsate 'pi ca//115//
na cārkasomavahnīnām tat prakāśād vinā mahaḥ/
kim apy asti nijaṃ kiṃ tu saṃvid ittham prakāśate//116//

152. *TĀ* 123-24 (p. 127-28):

saṃvid eva vijñeyetādātmyād anapekṣiṇī//123//
svatantratvāt pramātoktā vicitro jñeyabhedataḥ/

153. *jñeyādyupāyasaṃdhātanirapekṣaiva saṃvidaḥ//125//*
sthitir mātāham asmīti jñātā śāstrajñavad yataḥ/

154. Later on (*śl.* 126.7), Abhinava states that unlike the limited knower, the true knower, that is, the Lord himself, has no need to refer to the known, since, although holding it within himself, he remains totally aloof from it.

of it. (This can also be taken as an interesting definition of traditional knowledge: something one has received and keeps rather than something one discovers.) Regarding the reference to "I am," it is no surprise that the *bindu*, which is *aṃ* and holds within itself the whole of what will be manifested (that is, phonetically, all the phonemes from *a* to *ha*), should be assimilated to *ahaṃ* (*a* + *ha* + *ṃ*), the absolute "I."[155]

One may note, incidentally, as regards symbolical phonetics, that here again (as with the liquids—cf. *supra*, p. 257) occurs the notion of shadow (*chāyā*). Abhinava, in effect, states that the bindu *aṃ* should not be confused with the nasal *ma*: "It is different from the letter *ma*: it is, as it were, only its shadow. The case [here] is similar to that of the letters *ra*, *la*, and *ha* in relation to the sterile phonemes and to the *visarga*."[156] Here again, a phonetical notation is used to distinguish between what is relevant to the manifest, to objectivity, and what is beyond it. Similarly, in the yogic practice of the *uccāra*, *bindu* is that through which one goes beyond the final nasal of a *bījamantra* and attains, through the subtle *kalā*s of *ardha-candra*, and so forth, the absolute, *unmanā*.

Regarding yoga, precisely, Abhinava quotes a now lost text, the *Tattvarakṣavidhāna*: "This *bindu* which abides in the lotus of the heart, immaculate, [the triad of] the human being, energy and Śiva, is to be known through the practice of divided absorption (*layabhedena*). It is," he adds, "a sound (*śabda*) in the nature of a subtle sound resonance (*nādātmaka*) present in all animate creatures and dwelling there, dividing between high and low [while] beyond all activity."[157] Jayaratha

155. This assimilation is also found in the Śrīvidyā; for instance in *KKV*, 3-7, for which the *bindu* is *ahaṃ*: *bindur ahaṃkārātmā*. Naṭanānanda comments on this term, saying that the union of *a* and *ha* in *bindu* is that of *prakāśa* and *vimarśa*. *Bindu* is thus the totality of consciousness.

156. *TĀ* 3.134-35 (p. 137):

makārād anya evāyaṃ tac cchāyāmātradhṛdyathā//134//
ralahāḥ ṣaṇṭhavaisargavarṇarūpatvasaṃsthitāḥ/

157. Ibid., 112-14 (p. 118-19):

tattvarakṣāvidhāne ca tad uktaṃ parameśinā/
hṛtpadmamaṇḍalāntaḥstho naraśaktiśivātmakaḥ//112//

is not very explicit on this practice of *layabheda*. The *TĀ*, however, probably alludes here to the role of the *bindu* (in a mantra) during some practice of "ascendant meditation" linked to the movements of the *kuṇḍalinī* as are often used in Tantrism, where the ascending and descending breaths, *prāṇa* and *apāna* (the "high" and the "low") unite, and then are stilled, in the *uccāra* that goes from the heart *cakra* up to the *dvādaśānta*. We may note, by the way, that here is found again what we saw in chapter 3: a subtle resonance, *nāda*, both cosmic and human, having the *bindu* for its essential nature or center.

Visarga

The movement of energy within Śiva, after having effected, with *bindu*, a return to its undifferentiated source, *a*, together with a concentration of the energies, will go on, but now it will be endowed with emitting force, acting both inward upon and within itself—that is, in Śiva—and outward toward the manifestation, the stages of which will be linked to the arising of the consonants following the *visarga* and heralded by it.

Bindu is a single dot. The *visarga* is written with two dots in both the *śāradā* and *devanāgarī* scripts. Its written aspect allows one therefore to view it as a division of *bindu* into two and therefore as a further step toward differentiation and toward manifestation. The word *visarga*, also, indicates in Indian grammar a release, an escape, of breath, after a vowel, at the end of a word, in lieu of *r* or *s*.[158] Since it indicates the emission of breath, this term was quite suitable to indicate, in a system of phonematic emanation, the emitting movement of Śiva which produces both the first sixteen phonemes within himself and, (to a certain extent) externally, all the phonemes

---

boddhavyo layabhedena vindur vimalatārakaḥ
yo 'sau nādātmakaḥ śabdaḥ sarvaprāṇiṣvavasthitaḥ//113//
adha ūrdhvavibhāgena niṣkriyeṇāvatiṣṭhate/

158. W. S. Allen (*Phonetics in Ancient India*, p. 51) suggests to "render it by 'off-glide,' as referring to the breathy transition from the vowel to silence."

from *ka* to *kṣa*. This emission is somewhat intricate, for it appears at several levels. What Abhinavagupta (with Jayaratha's commentary) writes on the subject in *TĀ*, third *āhnika*, is also complex. *Visarga* is dealt with rather extensively, first in *śl.* 136-47, where Abhinava considers the levels of the emission, and touches upon the meaning of *visarga* at the human level of aesthetic or sexual enjoyment. Several portions in the *PTV* deal also with the *visarga*. We will try to give here, on the basis of these two works, a picture as clear as possible of this phoneme, that is, in fact, of Śiva as emitting, and as the emission of, the manifestation, such as these are viewed by Abhinavagupta. His views will be met again, explicitly or implicitly, but never with so much elaboration, in the works of his disciple Kṣemarāja and in the authors (notably of the Śrīvidyā), who are intellectually linked with the Trika-Pratyabhijñā idealist tradition of *saṃvidadvaya*.

Abhinavagupta underlines from the very outset this Śaiva, exalted nature of the *visarga* (and of the *bindu* as well), when he says in the *TĀ* (135-36): "Just as the letter *i*, due to the shade of a fragment of the letter *ra* [changes into] another vowel, so *a*, when absorbing a fragment of *ma* and *ha*, while remaining a vowel [changes into] two different vowels. That inner desire for emitting [the manifestation], which has been [previously] called the supreme *kaulikī* [energy], is also that which, when disturbed[159] certainly [reaches] the emanative state."[160] So this is indeed the energy of the *akula*, of the Absolute, of the primordial *a* (*anuttaraprakāśātmana ādi-*

---

159. Jayaratha (ibid., p. 139) explains that such a disturbance of the *kaulikī* energy consists in its being intent on the [appearance of the] outside world: *bahiraunmukhyalakṣaṇam.*

160. *TĀ*, 135-37 (p. 138-39):

ikāra eva rephāṃśacchāyayānyo yathā svaraḥ//135//
tathaiva mahaleśādaḥ so 'nyo dvedhāsvaro 'pi san/
asyāntar visisṛkṣāsau yā proktā kaulikī parā//136//
saiva kṣobhavaśād eti visargātmakatāṃ dhruvam/

In the same way, *MMV* 1.890-1 (p. 82): "This supreme *kaulikī*, the highest energy, is [the energy] of the Absolute, *a*, *akula*, the supreme Bhairava. This is the *visarga* wherefrom this universe springs forth."

varṇasya: J., p. 139). This reflective awareness (*vimarśa*) intent on cosmic emission (*visisṛkṣā*) remains thus within the supreme knower (*antaḥpramatraikātmyena vartamānā*, ibid.). The movement within Śiva which brought about, out of *a*, the emergence of the various forms of energy, from the power of bliss, *ā*, to the power of activity, *au*, comes to an end with this flowing forth (*procchalantīṃ sthitim*), that is, says Jayaratha, the bursting forth of the countless forms of the manifestation arising through the successive phonematic awarenesses of Śiva which we have seen (*tat tat parāmarśāntaravaicitrya-rūpatayā parisphuraṇam*).

So *visarga* is not so much the origin, the emission, of the manifestation, as manifestation itself as dwelling in the principle: "Such is," says Abhinavagupta (*TĀ* 3.145), "the span or nature of the emission: its nature is to be made of everything it encompasses. So it is with the ocean, which is [nothing else] than the unending succession of its waves."[161] Even more explicit, Jayaratha (ibid., p. 147), says in his commentary that *visarga* cannot possibly be the cause of the manifestation, because in a causal relation there is duality, which at this level does not exist: the very nature of *visarga* is that of what is contained within it (*garbhīkṛta*). It consists of the infinitude of the appearing of the world (*anantābhāsamaya*). It is the primal and perennial act of the first principle, of the ever self-aware consciousness, which eternally emits and holds the cosmic manifestation: this view agrees totally with the system of the nonduality of consciousness, *saṃvidadvaya*, of the Trika. "The emittive state is the projection of the Self, in the Self, by the Self," *svātmanaḥ svātmani svātmakṣepo vaisargikī sthitiḥ*, says Abhinavagupta in a striking formula. He also states in the *PTV*: "The supreme Lord, as containing the universe and blissfully vomitting and devouring it, is the *visarga*, which, condensing, will come to assume the form of the letter *ha*, then under the action of all the variety of possible combinations

161. *TĀ* 3.145 (p. 147):

visarga eva tāvān yad ākṣiptaitāvad ātmakaḥ/
iyadrūpaṃ sāgarasya yad anantormisaṃtatiḥ//145//

[of phonemes], that of *kṣa.*"[162] Later on in the same work (p. 230), while commenting upon the term *tṛtiyaṃ brahma* of *PT*, *śl.* 9, he equates *visarga* with Bhairava[163] as identical to the whole series of *tattva*s whose movement within himself is that of the emanation which this supreme god projects as a kind of outpouring of his plentitude, such emitting state remaining, however, one and unadulterated by the multiplicity of phenomena.

This twofold aspect of *visarga* is outlined by Kṣemarāja in the *ŚSV*, where he states that the two *bindu*s forming the *visarga* correspond to a double emission, inward and outward, resulting from two self-awarenesses, one internal (*antarvimarśa*), revealing the universe as resting in the absolute, the other external (*bahirvimarśa*), producing the five groups of five consonants, from *ka* to *ma*, and the *tattva*s, from *pṛthivi* to *puruṣa.*[164] This division of the *visarga* is also described (though somewhat differently) in the *TĀ* (3.138), since it appears as going beyond the sixteen vowels or *kalā*s of Śiva, and forming a seventeenth which transcends and supports all the others.[165] Abhinava substantiates his view by quoting

---

162. *PTV*, p. 200: *etad viśvam antaḥsthitam ānandaśaktibharito vaman grasamānaś ca visarga eva parameśvaro ghanībhūya hakārātmatāṃ pratipadyānantasamyogavaicitryena kṣarūpatām apy eti.*

163. Bhairava, a fearsome form of Śiva, is the usual aspect of Śiva in the Bhairavāgamas. He stands more especially for the undivided supreme consciousness as relating with the cosmos which he emits and reabsorbs. On this point see L. Silburn's introduction to the *VBh*, p. 12, or P. E. Müller-Ortega, *The Triadic Heart of Śiva*, pp. 34-35, 144-45, and 177-78.

164. *ŚSV* 2.7, p. 62: *yugapad antarbahirvisarjanamayavindudvayātmānaṃ visargabhūmim uddarśitavatī/ ata eva antarvimarśanena anuttare eva etad viśvaṃ viśrāntaṃ darśayati, bahir vimarśena tu kādimāntam pañcakapañcakam a-i-u-ṛ-ḷśaktibhyaḥ puruṣāntaṃ samastaṃ prapañcayati.*

165. We have seen (*supra*, p. 234) that vowels are assimilated to the sixteen *kalā*s, or to the *tithi*s, "days" of the lunar fortnight, all of them making up a totality. The sixteenth, immortal, *kalā* is their source and background, just like the *visarga* here. Cf. also chap. 3, *supra*, p. 90. The sixteenth *kalā* may be regarded as extending further to form a seventeenth or even an eighteenth one. Similarly a thirty-seventh *tattva*, transcendent (and immanent), will sometimes be added to the thirty-six others and will be considered as the supreme, transcendent Godhead, Paramaśiva.

from an early work, the *Triśiraḥśāstra*,[166] according to which (and to Jayaratha, comm., pp. 141-44) the *visarga* is the ambrosial or immortal (*amṛtarūpiṇī*) seventeenth *kalā*, the supreme level where it is no longer the "half of *ha*" (*hārdha-kalā*, according to its usual definition), but half of this half, *hakārārdhārdha*, that is, the pure resonance underlying all phonemes as well as the entire manifestation, pure consciousness, immortal, and therefore higher even than the emission, which is the sixteenth *kalā*, the *visarga* which we have seen. These same *śloka*s of the *TĀ* (139-40) assimilate these two aspects of the *visarga* with the *kuṇḍalinī* (which reappears here—it is an all-pervading symbol). The first aspect is that of the quiescent *kuṇḍalinī*, turned within, "looking like a dormant snake," this is the *śaktikuṇḍalikā*, pure consciousness (*saṃvinmātrarūpā*), which does not emit. The second is the *prāṇakuṇḍalikā* aspect, which is in the nature of the cosmic "breath," and which emits. Thereafter she becomes quiescent once again. "She merges in the sky of Śiva" (*śivavyoman*), the supreme *brahman*. "The movements of emanation and of resorption," the *TĀ* concludes, "are nothing but the emission of the Lord."[167] That the *visarga* should not be considered as the emission and what lies beyond it only, but as the resorption as well clearly shows that the "emitting state" (*vaisargikī sthiti*) is ultimately the very state of that deity who emits and reabsorbs "itself, within itself, and by itself" the universe: it is the very cosmic pulsation of the deity. But at the same time, one must note that, to describe this perennial, infinite, cosmologic state, the image of the *kuṇḍalinī* is used, as connected with the phonemes, but even more as symbolizing the cosmic and human energy. All that takes place in the cosmos is naturally found reflected in human beings, but the *visarga* affords us precisely an instance where these macro-microcosmic analogies are more especially in evidence.

In a tradition permeated with such correlations and where, moreover, there is a constant symbolical handling of the

166. Also known as *Triśirobhairava* or *Triśiromata*, this text, frequently quoted in the *TĀ*, appears as a Kaula work. It is now lost. Cf. *HTSL*, p. 49.

167. *TĀ* 3.141: *visargamātraṃ nāthasya sṛṣṭisaṃhāravibhramāḥ*/

elements of language—*nomina numina*—the word *visarga*, which may indicate the emission of semen and not only of the cosmos, was bound to give rise to speculations about sexual matters. And all the more so since "sexo-yogic" practices held a significant place in the Kula tradition (linked as it was with the ancient Kāpālika background) into which Abhinavagupta was initiated. Such practices were in evidence in the early Tantras (quoted occasionally in the *TĀ*), where they may well have initiated certain cosmogonic speculations: at the beginning, often was the act. Although in the days of Abhinavagupta these ancient texts had already been reinterpreted to make them more acceptable,[168] these sexo-cosmic (if one may say so) practices were, however, still in use.[169] This is evidenced notably by the description of the secret ritual of the Kula in *TĀ*, chapter 29. This is also clear from Abhinava's statements about the *visarga* in the *PTV* and the *TĀ*.

On the one hand the *PTV* (especially pp. 46-48), distinguishing between three types of utterance for the *visarga*—normal, short, and very short (these last two forming the seventeenth and the eighteenth *kalā*s)—correlates them not only with the highest aesthetic enjoyment, but also with the ejaculation (*visarga*) of semen. Any form of enjoyment indeed is a stirring up of energy (*vīryakṣobha* and *vīrya* also means semen). This energy at its highest intensity appears as *visarga*, and this *visarga* in its supreme cosmic form is the energetic presence of the manifestation within the divine consciousness.

On the other hand, this *visarga*, as both emission and presence of that which is emitted within the heart of the (human) emitter, may also be a sound arising from sexual activity. "This same emission," says the *TĀ* (3.146-48ab), "consisting of an unmanifested energy portion of *ha* (*avyakta-*

168. Cf. above, chap. 2, p. 60-61.
169. They have in fact always survived. On this subject see for instance the *Yonitantra*, edited by J. A. Schoterman (New Delhi, Manohar 1980). On a rite still performed in Puri, see F. A. Marglin, *Wives of the God-King. The rituals of the Devadasis of Puri* (Delhi, Oxford U.P., 1985), chap. 8.

hakalā) is called *kāmatattva* in the *Kulagahvaratantra*,[170] [which says]: 'This unmanifested phoneme arising in the throat of the beloved, pure sound (*dhvani*), which cannot be controlled, which is neither an object for meditation nor for concentration, he who focuses his mind thereon at once gains control over the universe.'"[171] "This sound," Jayaratha explains (ibid., p. 150), "is self-existing. It is uncreated (*svayambhu*), spontaneous (*sahaja*), pure. It is the subtle, all-pervading, phonic vibration (*satatoditanāda*) through which reality expresses itself, the very essence of the vital and cosmic breath (*prāṇatattva*). So this is the Word in its most spontaneous and creative aspect. During sexual enjoyment," says Jayaratha (ibid.), "when, losing all self-control, the female plunges in the delight of love, her inner sense (*antaḥkaraṇa*) being henceforth unconnected to anything, this sound, although [eternal], arises in her throat, swells up and becomes perceptible . . . Although very subtle (*susūkṣma*), since it consists of 'unstruck' (*anāhata*) sound, it will evolve into the sound *hāhā*. . . . This, however, is not the perceptible *ha* sound," says Jayaratha (p. 151), "but *anackakalā*: a phonetic force without vocalic support, a mere emission of breath then. The *sādhaka* should focus on this *anāhata visarga* and conceive it as going back and forth with the rhythm of sexual union, from his eyes to those of his partner." Jayaratha then quotes: "'Those whose minds are overwhelmed by the emission in the midst of the most intense pleasure utter it continuously in the delight of

---

170. This text (called *Kulaguḥvara* by Abhinava and Jayaratha in the KSTS edition of the *TĀ*) appears as a Kaula work, now lost as it seems. *Gaḥvara* is a cave, a hidden place. According to Jayaratha (ibid., p. 167), *kula* is the Energy, *gaḥvara*: Śiva, *kulagaḥvara* being their union.

171. *ata eva visargo 'yam avyaktahakalātmakaḥ/*
kāmatattvam iti śrīmatkulaguhvara ucyate//146//
yat tad akṣaram avyakta kāntākaṇṭhe vyavasthitam/
dhvanirūpam anicchaṃ tu dhyānadhāraṇavarjitam//147//
tatra cittaṃ samādhāya vaśyed yugapaj jagat/

The *sādhaka*, as we know, is primarily a *bubhukṣu*, one who pursues power rather than liberation.

the union with a fair-limbed woman.' The masters of yoga, with their mind totally engrossed in that, attain to the supreme union."

Here we see how that which may have appeared as a purely abstract metaphysical construction, or as a gratuitous play with the Sanskrit phonemes, can also be experienced bodily, and it is not impossible that these speculative elaborations may have originated from such experiences. The emission of the *visarga*, this uncreated, spontaneous "breath" and its potency, can be experienced by a human being, or more accurately by the yogin in sexual union (hence its name *kāmatattva*[172]), a union that, precisely, involves the deepest impulses or instinct, and that, moreover, duplicates on the human level the creative divine union of Śiva and Śakti. We shall see another such elaboration regarding the sibilant *sa.*[173]

But let us return to the emission as giving rise to—and as being—the cosmic manifestation. The *visarga*, being a symbol for the Absolute, *anuttara*, as the emitter of the sixteen vowels of which Śiva consists and of the thirty-four consonants from *ka* to *kṣa* which arise subsequently, will produce all the categories (*tattva*s) of which the universe is comprised. As Jayaratha puts it: "It is nothing but the supreme Knower who, holding within himself the infinite number of worlds, and extending from the Absolute to *ha*, manifests through his inner and outer luminous throbbing his [threefold] nature: [that of the three cosmic states] of the human being, the energy, and Śiva."[174] So this supreme emission is the manifestation

---

172. That is, the principle, the reality, or the very nature of desire: "*kāma*," says Jayaratha, "is will (*icchā*), and its reality (*tattva*) is its fullness whose nature nothing can ever destroy."

"Desire," says Abhinavagupta (*MMV* 1.381, p. 28), is the very urge to appropriate [something], which is fulfilled through the use of covering: *kāmaṃ svīkartum icchaiva tad acchādanayogataḥ,* "he who desires controls the universe, hence the term 'desire principle'": *viśvam sādhayate kāmī kāmatattvam idam yataḥ.*

It is worth noting that this principle works through the "covering" of what is desired. On *ācchādana*, see *supra*, p. 206, n. 96.

173. *Infra*, p. 301-03.

174. *TĀ*, vol. 2, p. 209: *sa eva hi parapramātrekarūpa 'śeṣaviśvakrodīkāreṇa*

as archetypically contained in the Absolute: the fifty phonemes will therefore already be contained therein, "expressive of" the world. (Even their division in eighty-one *pada*s is there.[175]) This, however, does not in any way affect the perfect purity and oneness of the Absolute. This is why the *TĀ* says that the phonematic awarenesses (*parāmarśa*) which occur with each of these phonemes, even though being divided in fifty or more, correspond to one single self-reflective awareness (*vimarśa*) of Śiva. They do not, therefore, bring any differentiation in Śiva. This can be also understood by the fact that at this level, that to which the phonematic awareness (*parāmarśa*) is directed does not exist yet as differentiated objectivity. There are no phonemes yet, not even the energy of the phonemes (or the phonemes as energy), *mātṛkā*, but Bhairava alone regarded as consisting of the totality of sounds (*śabdarāśibhairava*), appearing thus as a result of a single act of awareness (*āmarśa*). Śiva, inasmuch as he is the awareness (*parāmarśa*) through which all the phonemes abide in him—not as articulated but simply in the form of "resonance" (*nāda*)—appears as the universal and omnipresent agent, "the father and mother" of the universe: father and mother because he generates it through his union with the Energy, from which he cannot be separated. He shines, says Jayaratha, as the emission of the Absolute where there is no duality. Thus the universe is present in Śiva, free of duality, as *ahaṃ*, the absolute "I." There Śiva and Śakti are united in perfect fusion (*sāmarasya*), the synthetic self-recognition (*parāmarśa*) of Śiva and the cosmic energy being totally fused into one. Such is the supreme emission, a state of utter plenitude where light (*prakāśa*) rests within itself and where the phonemes—and therefore the whole manifestation—are merged in the ultimate in the form of that energy which generates them (*śaktisvarūpiṇī*); this occurs through a single recognition (*parāmarśa*) common to Śiva and Śakti. This is how the *TĀ* puts it: "This outflowing whose nature is energy, begins with the Absolute (*a*) and ends with *ha*. [Thus] con-

---

anuttarahakārātmanā prasphurann antarbahīrūpatayā naraśaktiśivātmatām ābhāsayet.

175. *TĀ* 3.196-97 (pp. 189-90).

densing [within itself] the entire universe, it disappears into the Absolute."[176]

Commenting upon this *śloka*, Jayaratha (who refers on this occasion to Pāṇiṇi's definition of *pratyāhāra*, 1.1.7) adds that in the Absolute, *a*, there are all the phonemes from *a* to *sa* lying between *a* and *ha*, and that the whole of this disappears, rests (*nilīyate viśrāmayati*) in the Absolute, the supreme reality, pure undivided light issuing from the principle without, however, ever leaving it, so that the whole phonematic manifestation both goes back and rests there. "Thus," says Jayaratha, "arises the awareness of the absolute 'I' (*yenāhaṃ parāmarśo jāyate*), and thereby—because of the principle of condensation (*pratyāhāranityā*)—is also the undivided awareness of all the phonemes" (*sarveśam api varṇanaṃ parāmarśaḥ syāt*; ibid., p. 196).

It is therefore appropriate at this point to say a few words about *aham*.

Aham

Aham (which ought to be spelled *ahaṃ*, since it is *a* + *ha* + *bindu*), "the supreme great mantra (*paramahāmantra*) symbolizes the supreme emitting energy as holding within itself the entire manifestation. "The initial aspect of the awareness of

---

176. *TĀ* 3.204 (p. 196):

anuttarādyā prasṛtir hāntā śaktisvarūpiṇī//204//
pratyāhṛtāśeṣaviśvānuttare sā nilīyate/

Abhinava elaborates extensively on the *visarga* in the *PTV* (pp. 195-98, but this cannot be quoted here for lack of space), underscoring the presence of the emission in all the phonemes and vice versa. The *visarga*, which cannot be separated from the Absolute, *a*, extends down to *ha* and includes therefore all that lies between these two phonemes: this is the movement symbolized by *ahaṃ*, or rather it is the supreme ipseity (*ahantā*), where everything merges into the Absolute—it is "the light at rest within the Self," as the *APS* puts it (*infra*, p. 288, n. 181). From the Absolute and *ahaṃ* pervading all levels of existence, Abhinava infers that the phonemes are all implicitly present in each: the totality of the eternal Word is always present in essence within each moment of its empirical manifestation.

the supreme 'I'," says Kṣemarāja in the *ŚSV*, "is of the nature of the absolute *akula*."[177] "This being the emission of the energy," says Abhinavagupta in the *TĀ* (201-02), "will next, as Śiva's *bindu*, take within itself the infinity of the universe and thereby regain the condition of the Absolute."[178] "The synthetic awareness of the Omnipresent," he adds (*śl.* 203cd-04ab), "in the nonduality of Śiva and Śakti, that is, of the Absolute and the emission, is known, because of its complete fullness, as the 'I'." And again (*śl.* 205cd-08ab): "This entire universe dwells in the energy, the energy in the supreme Absolute, and the latter in the energy. This truly is the interlocking (or encasement: *saṃpuṭīkṛti*) by the Omnipresent. This is how the interlocking described in the Parātriṃśikā[179] is made. All this creation shines in consciousness (*saṃvittau*) and shines there, indeed, due to consciousness. These three [namely, consciousness, Energy, creation]; uniting and combining by pairs, are the unique and supreme form of Bhairava, the 'I'."[180]

---

177. *ŚSV* 2.7 (p. 60): *ahaṃvimarśaprathamakalā anuttarākulasvarūpā.* We saw previously (p. 239) that *akula* is the supreme Śiva. Cf. also *ŚSV* 2.3 (p. 50).

The cosmogonic role assigned to the pronoun (or more accurately to the exclamation) *aham* is not proper to the Trika. See, for instance, the following passage from *BĀUp* 1.4.1: "The Self alone existed in the beginning of this [creation] in the shape of the Puruṣa. Looking about, he saw no one else but himself. He first said: 'I am' (*aham asmīti*). Hence came the name 'I' (*aham*)." *so'ham asmītyagre vyāharat. Tato 'haṃnāmābhavat.* There the primordial being appears as somehow becoming aware of its existence by uttering "I," *aham*, and from this point, as assuming a creative role. Further on (5.5.4) the same Upaniṣad states that *aham* is the secret name of the god who creates: *tasyopaniṣad aham iti* (Cf. on this subject J. A. B. Van Buitenen, "Studies in Sāṃkhya," *J.A.O.S.* 11, vol. 77 (1957): 15ff.).

178. *TĀ* 3.201-02 (p. 193):

visarga eva śākto 'yaṃ śivabindutayā punaḥ//201//
garbhīkṛtānantaviśvaḥ śrayate 'nuttarātmatām/

179. *PT*, *śl.* 30. The prescriptions of the *PT* are, in fact, of a mainly ritual sort, but they are developed and interpreted metaphysically by Abhinava in his two commentaries (*PTV* and *PTLv*).

180. Ibid., 203-08 (pp. 195-98):

anuttaravisargātmaśivaśaktyadvayātmani//203//

This somewhat repetitive formulation clearly defines *aham*. As explained by Jayaratha (ibid., pp. 128-29), the energy, at this point, is the *hakalā*, the kinetic part of *ha*, that is, the *visarga*, the emission—which, as we have seen, is at once the emission proper and that which is emitted—and this *visarga* throbs within the supreme conscious energy: the Absolute. Thus the *visarga* is identical with the Absolute, "and therefrom it springs forth, and in this form too and through this sole consciousness does it shine there, that is, while being the universe, it rests within the Absolute, being of the nature thereof." Thus we can see how this notion of *ahaṃ* comes in to substantiate the metaphysics of the nonduality of consciousness: the universe, at the stage of the emission—which is the stage of its essential nature (from the standpoint of the absolute, it is nothing else but that)—is finally nothing but the conscious energy of the Absolute, of the Ultimate, eternally shining forth from *a* to *ha* and coming back to *ṃ;* and it is self-contained since in ultimate truth He alone really *is.*[181] We shall see again *ahaṃ* in connection with the mantras, both

---

parāmarśo nirbharatvād ahām ity ucyate vibhoḥ/ . . .
tad idaṃ viśvam antaḥstham śaktau sānuttare pare//205//
tat tasyām iti yat satyaṃ vibhunā saṃputīkṛtiḥ/
tena śrītriśikāśāstre śakteḥ saṃpuṭitākṛtiḥ//206//
saṃvittau bhāti yad viśvaṃ tatrāpi khalu saṃvidā/
tad etat tritayam dvandvayogāt saṅghātatāṃ gatam//207//
ekam eva paraṃ rūpaṃ bhairavasyāhamātmakam/

181. Regarding this nature of *aham* as summing up the whole manifestation as emitted by—and resting within—the Absolute, the following *pada* from Utpaladeva's *Ajaḍapramātṛsiddhi* is often quoted: *prakāśasyātma-viśrāntir ahaṃbhāvo hi kīrtitaḥ*, "the resting of the light [of consciousness] within itself is known as the condition of "I." The complete stanza 22 of the *APS* runs thus:

nārthavyavasthā prāṇādāvahaṃbhāvanirodhataḥ
prakāśasyātmaviśrāntir ahaṃbhāvo hi kīrtitaḥ

"For animate beings, and so forth, no object can exist when the condition of 'I' is suppressed and what is known as the condition of 'I' is the resting of the light [of consciousness] within itself." The maxim is often quoted in nondualist Śaiva works. One finds it, for instance, quoted and commented upon by Kṣemarāja in *ŚSV* 2.7 (p. 64), or by

as being itself a mantra and as the source from which all the other mantras derive their potency, since it is, as we have just said, the absolute itself in its aspects of universal cosmic energy.

But let us now return to the various aspects that may be assumed by the *visarga.* While being indeed fundamentally one and absolute, it can take different forms, since, even as the energy which it is in essence, it is to be found on the various planes of the manifestation. As the latter emerges, the energy gradually becomes debased, weakened, passing from the supreme (*parā*) to the supreme-nonsupreme (*parāparā*) and to the nonsupreme (*aparā*) stages, these three corresponding to the three cosmic states of Śiva, *śakti* and *nara.*[182] Similarly Śiva's emitting act may be considered as threefold: supreme (*paravisarga*), supreme-nonsupreme (*parāparavisarga*), and nonsupreme (*aparavisarga*) emission.

In this regard, Abhinava in *TĀ*, 3.208-10 states at first once again that the *visarga* is present at the human level, not only, as we just saw, in sexual activity, but also more generally in any movement of joy or bliss, and more especially in all

---

Abhinavagupta in the *PTV*, pp. 55 and 198, in the *TĀ* 3.203 and 222, in the *ĪPV* 1.1.1, and so forth.

In that same *Siddhi*, Utpaladeva states that the reflective awareness resulting in bringing objectivity into existence (or, in the case of an individual subject, in revealing to him the objective world) can only be fully achieved because it rests within its essence, where it is recognized as being nothing but *ahaṃ*:

idam ity asya vicchinnavimarśasya kṛtārthatā/
yā svasvarūpe viśrāntir vimarśaḥ so 'ham ity ayam// (*APS*, 15, p. 6).

This *śloka* is cited by Jayaratha in the commentary upon *TĀ* 5.82 (vol. 3, p. 392) and he sums it up as follows: "The synthetic awareness of the 'I' is that level where the reflective awareness of objectivity is to rest." (*idaṃvimarśaviśrāntidhāmani ahaṃparāmarśo viśrāntiṃ kuryāt*). Abhinavagupta cites it in *ĪPV* 1.5.11 also, at the end of an elaborate explanation of its meaning (vol. 1, p. 244).

182. For these three cosmic states, see *PTV*, pp. 73-81, where Abhinavagupta distinguishes the various apsects of the reality related to these three planes.

that is related to aesthetic enjoyment,[183] which, as is well known, is very near to mystical experience. Owing to the correspondence between the human and the cosmic planes, the "vibration" (*spanda*), the palpitating radiance (*sphurattā*), and the free act, all characteristic of the divine, are also found in the human being, and this partly explains why sense-pleasure or even any intense feeling agitates or stirs up (*kṣobha*) the energy, enables one to attain identification with undifferentiated universal consciousness[184] or, as Utpaladeva puts it in the *ĪPK*, to experience this high luminous throbbing reality which is in essence the very heart of the deity.[185]

At the cosmic level, the emission is of three types according to whether it occurs in difference (*bheda*), difference-nondifference (*bhedābheda*), or nondifference (*abheda*).

> "In the first [emission]," says Abhinavagupta (*TĀ*, 3.211-14), all that is to be emitted is to be effected in the fire of voidness: it is the [emission] of the individual soul (*āṇava*), called 'rest in

---

183. "This emitting energy (*visargaśakti*) of the Lord, says the *TĀ* 3.208-10 (p. 199-200), is present everywhere in the following manner: from her only come all the [inner] movements whose essence is bliss. When, indeed, one hears a melodious song, or perceives a perfume such as sandal, and so forth, the [ordinary] average state [of mind] disappears and one experiences in one's heart a vibration (*spanda*) that is none else than what is called energy of bliss (*ānandaśakti*): it is due to that [energy] that a human being is 'sensitive' (*sahṛdaya*)."

For the aesthetic experience according to Abhinavagupta (and notably on the notion of *sahṛdayatā*, aesthetic receptiveness, understanding or sensitivity), see the studies of R. Gnoli and of Masson and Pathwardan, cited in the bibliography.

184. On this point see the means of identification with the supreme, Bhairava, as expounded in *VBh*, from which Jayaratha cites here (p. 200) *sūtra* 73.

185. *ĪPK*, 1.5.18:

sā sphurattā mahāsattā deśakālāviśesiṇī/
saiṣā sāratayā proktā hṛdayaṃ parameṣṭinaḥ//
(*TĀ*, vol. 2, p. 201)

On the notion of "heart" according to Abhinavagupta, I refer the reader to Paul Müller-Ortega's study *The Triadic Heart of Śiva*, quoted previously, p. 280, n. 163.

empirical consciousness' (*cittaviśrānti*). Then, all things visible, audible, and so forth, tend to [be absorbed in] the consciousness of the self (*svasaṃvidi*): this [emission], where energy radiates (*śāktollāsa*), is named 'waking up of empirical consciousness' (*cittasambodha*). When then [what constitutes] objectivity, oriented in this way, fuses and unites, it is absorbed in its plenitude in Śiva where the limited mind is dissolved. All possibility for any kind of limitation as previously seen being now dissolved, one has the supreme emission, that of Śambhu (*visargaḥ śāmbhavaḥ paraḥ*), named 'dissolution of [empirical] consciousness' (*cittapralaya*)."[186]

This exposition of the threefold *visarga* is intended to stress its human aspect: the presence of the energy of consciousness right from the empirical level, together with the movement through which it is possible to ascend from this to the supreme level where individual consciousness (as well as all phonemes, in the same movement of fusion and dissolution) become finally merged in the complete fullness of Śiva's consciousness. Abhinavagupta, taking up the same exposition while quoting another text unknown to us, the *Tattvarakṣāvidhāna* (*TĀ* 3.215-19), and Jayaratha in his commentary thereon (ibid., pp. 203ff.), further state that the lowest emission being that where duality or difference prevails, it is "endowed with parts," *sakala*. It is "gross" (*sthūlavisarga*), and phonetically and metaphysically of the nature of the letter *ha* (*hakārātmā*). It is associated with the cosmic state of man, *nara*.

The second emission is *niṣkala*, "without parts," duality being there immersed in consciousness. Consciousness is regarded here as being awake: *cittasambodha*, for it is the

186. *TĀ*, 3.211-214 (pp. 201-02):

pūrvaṃ visṛjyasakalaṃ kartavyaṃ śūnyatānale/
cittaviśrāntisaṃjño 'yam āṇavas tad anantaram//211//
dṛṣṭaśrutādi tadvastupronmukhatvaṃ svasaṃvidi/
cittasambhodanāmoktaḥ śāktollāsabharātmakaḥ//212//
tatronmukhatvatadvastusaṅghaṭṭād vastuno hṛdi/
rūdheḥ pūrṇatayāveśān mitacittalayācchive//213//
prāgvad bhaviṣyad aunmukhyasaṃbhāvyamitatālayāt/
cittapralayanāmāsau visargaḥ śāmbhavaḥ paraḥ//214//

most perfect knowledge possible on this level. It pertains to the energy (*śakti*); it is subtle (*sūkṣma*). Rather than an emission this is an emitting intentness, a desire to emit: *visarjanīya*, a term which, for grammarians, denotes in fact the same phonetic element as the word *visarga*; but as it refers not so much to the emission of breath proper than to that which indicates it,[187] it is appropriate to give a seemingly phonetic justification to this philosophical description of the emission.

The highest emission, finally, consists of a human being merging into Śiva, the dissolving of empirical consciousness in the Self (*ātmanirvṛtaḥ*: Jayaratha, p. 219). Hence coming back to a lower plane is impossible. Here pure self- (or Self-) awareness radiates forth, says Jayaratha (*saṃvinmātratayā parisphuraṇam*, p. 204).

In the cosmogony, this threefold emission occurs the other way around and in timelessness, the supreme emission remaining eternally the starting place, the foundation, and the essence of all that appears. Thus from *visarga*, the emitting energy of the transcendent, *akula* (that is, from the sixteen vowels within Śiva), the rest of the phonematic emanation will be produced, and therefore the whole manifestation. The role of the *visarga*, in this process, consists in the emitting act of Śiva's energy only. This energy, in its threefold highest form as the powers of transcendent consciousness, will, and cognition—that is, as the three phonemes *a, i,* and *u*—will bring into existence, after *visarga*, all of the other phonemes,[188] according to a process we are now going to examine.

Last, the *visarga*, while being threefold, can also be regarded as fivefold.[189] For it exists, says Abhinavagupta[190] without, within, in the "heart," in *nāda*, and in the supreme

---

187. *Visarjanīya* is in fact the ancient name for the *visarga*. Cf. L. Renou, *Terminologie grammaticale du sanskrit*, *s.v. visarga*, or K. V. Abhyankar, *A Dictionary of Sanskrit Grammar*, *s.v. visarjanīya.*

188. *Śl.* 221 (p. 208-09).

189. *Śl.* 222 and commentary (pp. 208-11).

190. Abhinava quotes here (*śl.* 220-25) again the *Siddhayogeśvarīmata*, a text dating certainly from a fairly early period. As said previously, the Tantric metaphysico-linguistic speculations are surely ancient.

stage. This means, according to Jayaratha, that *visarga*, that is, the emitting energy, is also found in a human being, externally (at the sexual level) and internally (in the transformation of this energy through yoga, since that same energy (*ojas-vīrya*) produces sexuality, aesthetic enjoyment, and spiritual endeavor —*PTV*, pp. 46ff., *TĀ* 3.229ff., and Jayaratha, comm., ibid., pp. 219ff.). It is found in the "heart" also, that is, at the very source of the human or cosmic energy, or in *nāda*, that is, in the phonic energy, and finally at the supreme and transcendent level of pure consciousness, of the supreme Word.

These aspects and stages of *visarga* are assimilated by Abhinava—in the same passage (*śl.* 220-25) where he quotes from the *Siddhayogeśvarīmata*—to the creative movement of the *kuṇḍalinī*, the stages of whose progress upward are correlated by Jayaratha in his commentary[191] with the five centers of the subtle body: heart (*hṛd*), throat (*kaṇṭha*), forehead (*lalāṭa*), *brahmarandhra* (here called *śaktyanta*), and *dvādaśānta*, which shows that here also the cosmic process is also a human one, that the adept must experience to progress toward liberation.

From KA *to* KSA: *The Consonants*

Consonants (*vyañjana*), which are now to be produced, form a portion of the phonematic emanation distinctly subordinated to the first category, vowels. And indeed, the cosmic categories (*tattva*s) following Śiva, which arise from, are sustained by, and grounded in him, arise with the consonants. "Vowels are the original cause of all the phonemes.[192]

Consonants, says Jayaratha, are regarded as having no autonomous existence. Their very name, *vyañjana*, comes from their being considered but as an external manifestation (*vyakti*) of the energy of the vowels. Prior to their existence as such, consonants are deemed to exist potentially in the vowels. The

191. Ibid., pp. 210-11.

192. *svarā eva sarvavarṇānāṃ mūlakāraṇam*, quoted by Jayaratha, *TĀ* 3.184, comm. (p. 180).

latter are their life-force (*prāṇa*), a notion which happens (not by chance, surely) to be confirmed in a fact of phonetics: consonants, "which do not contain any vowels" (*anacka*)[193] cannot be uttered; they have to be supported by a vowel, which usually is *a*,[194] and *a* is *anuttara.* Phonetics can thus be used to confirm the metaphysical principle of the all-pervasiveness of the Absolute. "This collection of phonemes (consonants)," says Abhinavagupta in the *TĀ*, "consists first of all of vowels. When related to a perceptible manifestation [they are called] 'consonants' (manifestation, *vyañjana*), because asuredly vowels give them life." Jayaratha explains, "The collection of phonemes, before being produced, wholly consists of vowels, that is, resides in vowels in the form of energy. Otherwise it could not be produced through the agency of these associations and dissociations [such as encountered in connection with the sixteen vowels]. . . . This collection of phonemes thus produced exists only because vowels give it life; otherwise, not containing any vowel, [consonants] could not be uttered."[195]

This subordination of consonants to vowels is also in evidence from vowels being regarded as germs or seeds (*bīja*), which have a creative action, and consonants as wombs (*yoni*), with a purely passive role. "Sages have called [consonants] from *ka* to *ha* the support of agitation (or disturbance of power)," says *TĀ* (3.180). "Support of agitation," Jayaratha explains, means that they are wombs, according to what has been said: 'the womb consists of [the consonants] *ka*, and the others'."[196]

---

193. That is, possessing no *ac.* (The *pratyāhāra* in Pāṇini's grammar representing a vowel is *ac.*)
194. In Sanskrit the frequency of *a* is twice that of all the other vowels.
195. *TĀ* 3.183:

ittham yad varṇajātaṃ tat sarvaṃ svaramayam purā//
vyaktiyogād vyañjanaṃ tat svaraprāṇaṃ yataḥ kila/

comm.: . . . *"svaramayam": svarāṇām evāntaḥ śaktyātmanā rūpeṇāvasthitam, . . . anyathā hy eṣāṃ tattatsaṃyojanaviyojanenaivaṃrūpatāyābhivyaktir eva na bhavet, . . . abhivyaktam eva etad varṇajātaṃ svarānuprāṇitam eva bhavet, anyathā hi anackatayā asya uccāra eva na bhavet.*

196. *TĀ* 3.180 and comm. (vol. 2, p. 177):

Such a view is based upon an ancient notion (still alive) about the role of both sexes in procreation, where the male alone is supposed to play an active part (notwithstanding the female character of the energy): he lays the seed in the uterus, which plays the passive role of receptacle. And even so, these wombs are themselves but the outcome of a transformation—a shrinking or a coagulation (*śyānatā*)—of vowels. "The coagulation of vowels, those seeds having the nature of Śiva, brings about consonants, which are wombs and pertain to Śakti. Indeed only from the seed does the womb grow."[197] Just as Śiva cannot be separated from his energies, in the same way, Śiva's essence, inherent in vowels, permeates consonants; it gives them life, potency, and will enable them to give rise, through their combinations, to syllables, words, and sentences, and thereby to the entire manifestation. This same interrelation of inherence and subordination is expressed when vowels are said to be "that which expresses" (*vācaka*), and consonants "that which has to be expressed" (*vācya*).[198]

The metaphysical, cosmogonic, conception of Sanskrit consonants being such, it is to be noted however, that Indian grammarians, for their part, held views that, although not conflicting therewith, were closer to the phonetic facts such as we understand them: consonants are subordinated to vowels because they cannot by themselves form a syllable. To call them *vyañjana* was, moreover, to underscore their role as revealing

---

kādihāntam idaṃ prāhuḥ kṣobhadhārayatayā budhāḥ/

kṣobhadhāratayā iti—yonitayety arthaḥ, yad uktam: "kādibhiś ca smṛtā yoniḥ . . ."

197. *PTV*, p. 149: *śivātmakasvarabījarūpā śyānataiva śāktavyañjanayonibhāvo bījād eva yoneḥ prasaraṇāt.*

Cf. also *MVT* 3.10-12 (p. 15), which Abhinavagupta quotes in the *PTV*, p. 148. Also *SvT* 1.32, comm. (vol. 1, p. 38): "The nature of womb of consonants is due to the fact that they give rise to the universe": *jagatkāraṇatvād yonitā.*

198. *PTV*, p. 148: "The power of expressiveness (*vācakatvam*) belongs to vowels, which are seeds, and the state of that which has to be expressed (*vācyatvam*) to consonants, which are wombs, [these two groups] being respectively in the nature of Śiva and Śakti. Śiva is known as seed and Śakti as womb [says indeed the *MVT*]."

and defining the syllable, a role now acknowledged by linguistics. Sanskrit script, indeed, being syllabic, forms the simple or complex syllable with a single graphic sign in the form of the consonantic element to which is added—except for *a*—a vocalic sign: the written form clearly shows the informative nature of the consonant which, in language, as is well known, is more important than the vowel's, the latter's superiority being only of a metaphysical order. But it should be noted that the consonant assumes this importance in language and writing, that is, from the perspective of the phonematic emanation, on a lower level, which is in accordance with the principles: here again cosmogony and phonetics come together.

But while the sixteen phonemes of Śiva, as a whole, are seeds, three of them, however, are regarded as more important, for they give birth to the rest. These are the three vowels *a*, *i*, and *u*, connected with the powers of absolute consciousness (*anuttara*), of will (*icchā*), and awakening (*unmeṣa*) or cognition.[199] We shall see that to these three powers or phonemes are connected the twenty-five consonants, the four semi-vowels, the four spirants, and even, somehow, *kṣa*.

The five guttural consonants, from *ka* to *ṅa*, are regarded as arising from the "solidification," the "hardening" (*ghanatā*) of the phoneme *a*[200] or of the Absolute.[201] How five consonants are produced out of the single phoneme *a* can be explained, according to Jayaratha,[202] by the fact that the Absolute, notwithstanding its being comprised mainly of the energy of the supreme consciousness (*citśakti*), holds, however, within itself Śiva's five energies.[203] The principle that each

---

199. Cf. *supra*, p. 254, n. 86. "This triad is known as the supreme glory of Bhairava," adds *TĀ* 3.192: *tad eva tritayaṃ prāhur bhairavasya paraṃ mahaḥ.*

200. We shall here describe the phonematic awarenesses (*varṇaparāmarśa*) of the thirty-four consonants from *ka* to *kṣa*, without mentioning their corresponding *tattva*s since these correspondences differ depending upon the levels of the emanation, with which we shall deal in the next section of this chapter.

201. *PTV*, p. 182.

202. *TĀ* 3.149 (p. 152).

203. These are normally *cid*, *ānanda*, *icchā*, *jñāna*, and *kriyā*. But judging from the next *śloka*s (150-52) of the *TĀ*, they seem likely here to be

energy holds somehow in itself the other ones, will be held valid as well for the energies which give rise to the other groups of consonants and will explain why each group consists of five phonemes produced from a single vowel.

One might be tempted to explain this situation and the connection of the Absolute with the *tattva*s corresponding to the guttural consonants, by the fact that, in the emanation in *paśyantī*, those are the ones closest to Śiva. But the reason for this connection lies actually, and indeed more logically, in traditional grammar, for which *a* and *ā* are guttural.[204] Such is Abhinavagupta's approach in the *PTV* when he writes: "The hardening of the phoneme *a* results in the group [of the consonants beginning by] *ka* because [these consonants have, like *a*] the quality of gutturals."[205]

As we are going to see, the connection of the remaining consonants to various forms of energies is based similarly upon grammar,[206] the working of the energies which give rise to these consonants being but an ingenious justification on the metaphysical level of grammatical or phonetic notions.

The palatals, from *ca* to *ña*, come from *i* because, says Abhinavagupta, all these phonemes are palatal: *talavyatvāt*.[207] They arise, states the *TĀ*, from the power of will abiding in itself—corresponding to the phoneme *i*—but gradually emerging more and more distinctly (*TĀ* 3.151).

The cerebrals, from *ṭa* to *ṇa*, and the dental consonants, from *ta* to *na*, are also connected to the power of will, but in the form that it assumes in the phonemes *ṛ* and *ḷ*, that is, abiding in itself but connected either to a kind of sudden illumination (and this brings about *ṛ*) or, on the contrary, to stillness (and this brings about *ḷ*).[208] Indian phoneticians,

---

anuttara, *ānanda*, *icchā* (disturbed and undisturbed) and *unmeṣa*, which have been seen to act with the vowels from *a* to *ū* and for the liquids.

204. "*Kaṇṭhyo 'kāraḥ*". *Ṛk-Prātiśākhya*, 1.38.

205. *PTV*, p. 182, line 6: *akārasya ghanatā kavargaḥ kaṇṭhyatvāt*.

206. For the places of articulation allotted by traditional grammar to the phonemes of the Sanskrit alphabet, cf. Allen, *op. cit.*, pp. 48ff.

207. *PTV*, p. 183. Cf. *Pāṇinīyaśikṣā*, 17: *i-cu-ya-śās tālavyaḥ*.

208. Cf. *supra*, pp. 254-62. It might be unexpected that the "sterile" phonemes (*saṇḍha*) *ṛ* and *ḷ* should generate consonants; Abhinavagupta anticipated

indeed, classify the retroflex vowel *ṛ* with the cerebral consonants,[209] whereas the vowel *ḷ* is said to be dental.[210]

The labial consonants, from *pa* to *ma*, says the *TĀ*,[211] come from the power of awakening or unfolding (*unmeṣa*), that is, from the phoneme *u*, which is indeed regarded by Indian grammarians as labial (*oṣṭhya*).[212]

Jayaratha quotes in his commentary on the *TĀ* the two following *śloka*s, which sum up this emergence of the consonants.

"The second class [of phonemes] made of a fivefold energy is issued out of the Absolute. Then from [the power of] will, in its undisturbed form, connected with fire or earth, the two [groups comprising] eight [phonemes] beginning with *ṭa*, *pa*, and so on, are produced by the [power] of awakening. In this way are expounded the consonants."[213]

The four semivowels, *ya*, *ra*, *la*, and *va*, are, like the consonants, issued out of the vowels *i*, *ṛ*, *ḷ*, and *u*, through their junction with *a*. This results, as Jayaratha recalls,[214] from the rule laid down by Pāṇini (6.1.77): "*iko yaṇ aci*," that is, "semivowels (*y*, *v*, *r*, *l*) are the respective substitute for the vowels *i*/*ī*, *u*/*ū*, *ṛ*/*ṝ*, *ḷ*/*ḹ*, before a vowel."

---

and met this objection (*TĀ* 3.175-78, pp. 173-76), saying that actually it is the power of will (thus *i* or *ī*) permeating the sterile phonemes that produces the cerebral, dental, and so forth, consonants. But then, one may ask, why bring in *ṛ* or *ḷ* when *ī* was sufficient? This is simply because Indian phoneticians classified consonants together with these vowels; the former must need then connect with the latter.

209. *Pāṇinīyaśikṣā*, 17: *syūr mūrdhanyā ṛ-tu-ra-ṣāḥ, PTV*, p. 182, line 8: *ṛkārasya ṭavargo—mūrdhanyatvāt.*

210. Ibid. *ḷkārasya tavargo—dantyatvāt.*

211. *TĀ* 3.152 (p. 153).

212. *Pāṇinīyaśikṣā*, 17: *oṣṭhajā vupū, PTV*, p. 182: *ukārasya pavarga—auṣṭhyatvāt.*

213. *TĀ* 3.152, comm. (p. 154):

akulāt pañcaśaktyātmā dvitīyo varga utthitaḥ/
anārūṣitarūpāyā icchāyāś ca tataḥ paraḥ//
vahnikṣamājuṣas tasyāṣṭatādyaṃ ca dvayaṃ tataḥ/
pādir unmeṣato jāta iti sparśāḥ prakīrtitāḥ//

214. Ibid., 154-56, comm. (p. 157).

We have just seen, moreover, that *ya* is classified with *i* among the palatals, *ra* with *ṛ* among the cerebrals, and *la* with *ḷ* among the labials; as for *va*, it is regarded as a labio-dental, and is thereby classified with the "labial" vowel *u*. Abhinavagupta, in the *PTV*, puts it this way: "*Ya* and *śa* are connected with the [palatal consonants of the] *ca* group; *ra* and *ṣa* with the [cerebrals of the] *ṭa* group; *la* and *sa* with [the dentals of the] *ta* group; and *va* with the [dentals and labials of the] *ta* and *pa* groups."[215]

Translating phonetics in terms of metaphysics, the *TĀ* describes this emergence as follows: the power of will, whether disturbed or quiescent (i.e., the phoneme *i* or *ī*), turning toward the other power (the Absolute, *a*), gives rise to the semivowel *ya*. *I* or *ī* + *a* is indeed *ya*. This phoneme is held as the seed of wind (*vāyubīja*); and the junction between *icchā* and *anuttara* is considered as characterized by a swift movement, an attribute of the wind. *Ya* seems to be characterized by dessication.

When the power of will, *i*, is looked upon as touched by objectivity and characterized by light, peculiar to fire, that is, when the vowel *ṛ* is concerned, this results in the semivowel *ra*, which is, as we have seen, the seed of fire (*agnibīja*),[216] and therefore primarily in the nature of heat.

The same energy, characterized by stability, peculiar to earth, will produce the phoneme *la*, which is the seed of earth (*pṛthivībīja*) and whose salient feature therefore is immobility.

The semivowel *va*, lastly, is regarded as arising from the junction of the power of awakening, *unmeṣa*, *u*, with the Absolute, *a*. *U* + *a* is *va*. It pours out the emanation, says the *TĀ*, and this is commented by Jayaratha, who says that *va* is the seed of Varuṇa, and thereby has a cooling action, and makes things flourish (*āpyāyakāritva*).[217]

But if semivowels are looked upon as born from the conjunction of the powers of will and awakening with the Absolute or with bliss, the question may be raised as to why

215. *PTV*, p. 182: *yaśau cavargasyāntaḥ raṣau ṭavargasya, lasau tavargasya, vakāro 'pi tapavargayoḥ.*

216. *Supra*, p. 256.

217. *TĀ*, 156 and comm. (pp. 156-57). Varuṇa is linked with air and water.

they differ, metaphysically, from the diphthongs *e*, *ai*, *o*, and *au*, which are produced likewise. The *TĀ* meets this objection, saying that in the case of diphthongs, the Absolute predominates, the power of will being subordinated thereto: that in Śiva the Absolute should predominate is indeed a matter of course; and moreover, phonetically, *a* comes first in the formation of the phonemes *a* + *i* and so forth. With semivowels, on the contrary, the power of will predominates and the Absolute is subordinated—or more accurately seems to be so, for nothing can remove the Absolute from its preeminent position; phonetically, *i* (*ṛ* and *ḷ*) or *u*, here, do come first: *i* + *a* = *ya*, and so forth. This is how phonetics are transposed into metaphysics.[218]

Similarly, the term *antaḥsthā*, "standing between," applied to the semivowels in Sanskrit grammar referring to the place that they occupy in the alphabet, between the stops and the fricatives—or to their nature, which may appear as intermediate between that of vowels and of consonants, is also used for its own ends by the *TĀ* (3.158). The latter construes *antar* as "in" and explains the word *antaḥsthā* as meaning that these phonemes "stay with the powers of will, and the rest." But it also takes it as *anta*, "completion," semivowels being considered as, somehow, bringing *icchā* to completion, inasmuch as, Jayaratha explains (p. 159), born from a contact between *icchā* and *anuttara*, they remain united with the supreme knower (*pramātraikātmyena vartamānatvāt*). This interpretation may be held as supported by grammarians insofar as they view semivowels as substitutes for the vowels *i*, *u*, *ṛ*, and *ḷ*.

The three sibilants (*ūṣman*)[219] are connected with the three aspects of the power of will which correspond to the

---

218. We have already seen this type of argumentation exemplified in *TĀ* 3.160-61 (pp. 160-61), where a rule of *saṇḍhi* concerning the vowel *a* is translated and vindicated on the level of the powers of the Absolute *supra*, p. 246).

219. This term indicates, in fact, the fricatives, and applies to the three sibilants along with the aspirate *ha* and the *visarga*. Sanskrit grammarians have no particular term for sibilants; *kṣvedana*, sibilation, denotes a mispronouncing, an overstressed sibilation.

phonemes *i*, *ṛ*, or *ḷ*. As it is, they are classified by Indian phoneticians with these three phonemes.

The power of will, says the *TĀ*, when it is pure, undeveloped, that is, in the form of *i*, and covered up, coarsened (*rūṣita*) by that upon which the power is directed, that is, by a still altogether ideal objectivity, develops as a "vapor," or "steam" (*ūṣman*)—that is, as an expiration—which produces the palatal sibilant *śa*.

When subsequently its object predominates over the power of will, in a swift manner, that is, with the phoneme *ṛ*, the "vapor" thus produced will be the cerebral sibilant *ṣa*. Lastly, when the same energy is highly awakened and controlled by the same object but in a steady way, resulting in *ḷ*, then the dental sibilant *sa* is produced. This is why, Abhinavagupta concludes (*śl.* 165), "the entire universe shines within the letter *sa*."

There is, however, a particular aspect of the phoneme *sa*. It is indeed the first phoneme of the *bījamantra SAUḤ*, the "seed of the heart" (*hṛdayabīja*), which plays an important role in the Trika. This is the mantra dealt with in the *PT*, and Abhinavagupta discusses it at length in the *PTV*. Now *sa*, in *SAUḤ*, is supposed to "pervade" (√*VYĀP*) three of the four cosmic spheres (*aṇḍa*), and it is the "third *brahman*," that is, the Absolute. Besides, *sa*, like *ha* (and sometimes in conjunction with it) plays a part in the sexo-cosmic speculations of the Kula as a symbolic form of the Absolute that can be experienced. Then it is known as the "*sīt* sound" (*sītkāra*). "The yogins," says Abhinavagupta with regard to this sibilant, "call it *amṛta* and supreme glory (*paraṃ dhāma*). It [arises] at the beginning, subsidence, and cessation of the perturbation, in the sound *sīt*, in pleasure, in the perfection of existence (*sadbhāva*), in absorption (*samāveśa*), and in *samādhi*. It is known as the undivided supreme *brahman*."[220] *Sa*, the *TĀ* continues (*śl.* 170), is also

---

220. *TĀ* 3.162-67 (pp. 162-66):

icchā yā karmanā hīnā yā caiṣṭavyena rūṣitā//162//
śīghrasthairyaprabhinnena tridhā bhāvam upāgatā/

called in some Kula texts "reality of poison" (*viṣatattva*). There it is a sibilation, which arises, notably, in amorous enjoyment. Thus it is the counterpart of the *kāmatattva ha*, as we saw previously. Just like the latter, says indeed Jayaratha (p. 167), it is *anāhata* and *satatodita*, "unstruck" sound, eternal and utterly spontaneous, a pure phonic emission (that is, *s anacka*, unsupported by any vowel), directly surging from the Absolute, which the yogin experiments in ritual sexual union.[221] Jayaratha (ibid., p. 165) refers explicitly on this point to the *ādiyāga*, the sexual ritual described in *TĀ*, chapter 29. Abhinavagupta (*śl.* 170, p. 168) further states that the fullness, the actuality of desire (*kāmasya pūrṇatā tattvam*) arises in the unifying friction (*saṃghaṭṭa*, the connotations—notably sexual—of which term we have seen), and the ambrosial reality of poison (*viṣasya cāmṛtaṃ tattvam*), when the obfuscation of the limited knower is dispelled. *Ha* and *sa* become thus part of the symbolism involved in these sexual practices. These two

---

anunmiṣitam unmīlatpronmīlitam iti sthitam//163//
iṣyamānaṃ tridhaitasyāṃ tādrūpyasyāparicyuteḥ/
tad eva svoṣmaṇā svātmasvātantryapreraṇātmanā//164//
bahir bhāvya sphutaṃ kṣiptaṃ śa-ṣa-satritayaṃ sthitam/
tata eva sakāro 'smin sphutaṃ viśvaṃ prakāśate//165//
amṛtaṃ ca paraṃ dhāma yoginas tat pracakṣate/
kṣobhādyantavirāmeṣu tad eva ca parāmṛtam//166//
sītkārasukhasadbhāvasamāveśasamādhiṣu/
tadeva brahma param avibhaktaṃ pracakṣate//167//

221. *Sītkāra* reappears in some other texts, for instance the *Haṭhayogapradīpikā*, 54. This text, admittedly, is not concerned with sexual union, but when he says that the yogin, with *sīt*, "becomes in the image of the god of love": it surely does not mention Kāmadeva by chance: something of an older tradition certainly survives there. See also *TĀ* 5.142, and Jayaratha's commentary, vol. 3, pp. 456-57.

It will perhaps be noticed that the letter *s* is the initial letter of a number of terms denoting the experiences enumerated in *śl.* 167 above, as well as of such words as *sat*, *satya*, *saṃghaṭṭa*, *sāmarasya* . . . Is this a chance occurrence or is there some significant pattern here? Mystico-linguistic speculations easily become obsessive. R. Gnoli, however, was struck by these, shall we say: coincidences? and he devotes an interesting note at the end of his translation (p. 300) of the *PTV* to this subject. In addition, he draws an ingenious and striking comparison with a passage from the Russian poet and poetician W. Khlebnikov.

phonemes also appear as assimilated with the *ha* and *sa* of *haṃsa*,[222] that is, with the unbroken, automatic utterance of breath (itself similar to the cosmic *prāṇa*), with the removal of all individual type of limitation, and with rest in the supreme. Jayaratha (ibid., pp. 169-70) explains that this is a twofold state which arises precisely in the "unifying friction," at the time of the stirring up of energy, which is sexual enjoyment mutually shared. It also appears when, in this friction, all perception of duality vanishes and only the "ambrosial reality" remains, that is, at the moment of complete blossoming forth (which is obviously the moment of full sexual enjoyment, as well as that of the mystical experience of the Absolute).

The four fricatives, says also the *TĀ*, differ from the rest of the consonants in that they are not born of the union of *anuttara* with another energy: "born from their own heat, they are called hot (or vapor) by Bhairava, the Immaculate."[223] They come forth as a breathing of the supreme, that is, Jayaratha glosses, through their own free spontaneous brilliance (*svātantryalakṣaṇena svātmatejasā*).[224] Phonetically, indeed, fricatives are a breathing, which can be assigned to various places of articulation and can therefore be classified with different groups of consonants. They are, however, supported by the sole vowel *a*. They appear therefore as an especially direct emanation of the Absolute.

Of these four, however, the aspirate *ha* is held to be closest to the Absolute. As Jayaratha puts it: "The energy of the Transcendent is the *visarga*, of which *ha* is the shrunken, dried-up form (*āśyānaṃ rūpam*), and because of this [direct con-

---

222. Cf. *supra*, chap. 3, p. 140.

223. *TĀ* 3.179 (p. 176):

etadvarṇacatuṣkasya svoṣmanābhāsanāvaśāt/
uṣmeti kathitaṃ nāma bhairavenāmalātmanā//179//

224. *LT* 19.17-19 correlates the four fricatives with the four Vyūhas, Aniruddha, and so forth, thus ranking them close to the supreme level. *Kṣa* is Satyā, Viṣṇu's energy. *ASB* 16.83 calls them *caturbrahman*. For this text, *ha* is the body (*tanu*) of the primordial Vyūha, Vasudeva. The *kūṭa kṣa* (which is *satyābīja*) being added to the four fricatives, they constitute altogether the fivefold *brahman* (*pañcabrahman*).

nection with] the Absolute, it has the same place of articulation as the latter's."[225] This is an obvious example of effect and cause being inverted: on the contrary it is the Indian grammarians who first regarded *a* and *h* as gutturals: *kaṇṭhyāvahau.*[226]

To these forty-nine phonemes is added a fiftieth phonematic awareness, that of the compound phoneme *kṣa* or *kūṭabīja.* The latter is produced not by the vowels but through the bringing together (*pratyāhāra*) of two consonants, *ka* and *sa*, regarded as vivified (*anuprāṇita*), one by the Absolute, *a*, the other by the *visarga*, which is, as we have seen, the energy of *akula.*[227] So it appears as a symbol for the inseparable union of Śiva and the energy, the source of all the phonemes, whose series end with a symbol of that wherefrom they were issued.

The *PTV* devotes several pages (195-200) to *ha* and *kṣa.* It looks at them from a somewhat different perspective, stressing the return to the supreme level (connected indeed with the rising of the *kuṇḍalinī*: ibid., p. 200). It even states that *kṣa* stands for the phonic stir, the rubbing or friction of the womb, which is the energy of (as well as the partner in) the ritual union—*dūtyātmakaśāktayonisaṃghaṭṭa*). This energy withdraws thereafter in the unstruck sound and evolves into the *visarga*—this at the central level of *prāṇa*, of the *kuṇḍalinī*—until it finally comes to rest on the unchanging level of *anuttara.* So *kṣa* appears as that point from which all the phonemes, issued successively (although beyond time) out of *a*, start moving back to the Absolute. This is not surprising, since the whole series of phonematic awarenesses (*varṇaparāmarśa*), we have seen, results actually (as we have seen, too) from a single awareness or representation (*āmarśa*) of Śiva.

---

225. Ibid., comm., p. 176.

226. *Pāṇiniyaśikṣā*, 17.

227. *TĀ* 3.180 and comm. (p. 177-78). Cf. also Jayaratha's comm. on *MVT* 1.10 (pp. 13-14): *kṣa* is a form of the Goddess; *ka* is in essence *anuttara*, and *sa* is *visarga*; *kṣa* brings them together in *pratyāhāra*, that is, in including all the intermediate phonemes. This sums up therefore the entire manifestation.

The Levels and Stages of the Emanation

In the foregoing pages we have examined the series of phonematic awarenesses (*varṇaparāmarśa*) corresponding to consonants, describing only the play of energies with which they appear and mentioning the rules laid down by Indian phoneticians, of which this play of energies is a translation. But we did not say, as we did for the first sixteen phonemes and for Śiva, which were the *tattva*s appearing with each of these consonants. This is because such correspondences differ depending upon the levels of the emanation. As we said,[228] the emanation occurs first in Śiva, at the level of the supreme Word: this is the "great emanation" (*mahāsṛṣṭi*). It is then reflected in the energy: this is the supreme-nonsupreme level (*parāpara*) corresponding to *paśyantī* and *madhyamā*. At this level, from the standpoint of the phonemes, it has two different aspects: *mātṛkā* and *mālinī.* Last, the energy appears at the nonsupreme level (*apara*), that of *vaikharī*, where the lowest point of emanation is reached: it cannot go further down. Once entirely produced, the cosmos can only end in cosmic resorption, by returning to its divine source.

We have seen[229] that the *visarga*, the emitting act of Śiva, is looked upon as subject to a threefold division corresponding notably to these three levels of the manifestation. Abhinavagupta sums up in the *TĀ* this threefold emanation as follows: "When [the manifestation] has for its essence (*svabhāva*) a single act of consciousness (*ekāmarśa*), that is Bhairava, the mass or totality of sound (*śabdarāśi*). When it is joined to the shadow of what is touched by this act of consciousness (*āmṛśya*), the energy and the *mātṛkā* are produced. And when the latter encounters and fuses with *śabdarāśi*, the *mālinī* is produced, she of the mixed wombs."[230]

228. *Supra*, pp. 290-93.

229. Ibid.

230. *TĀ* 3.196-99ab (p. 191):

ekāmarśasvabhāvatve śabdarāśiḥ sa bhairavaḥ/
*āmṛśyacchāyayā yogāt saiva śaktiś ca mātṛkā//*198*//*
sā śabdarāśisaṃghaṭṭād bhinnayonis tu mālinī/

Mahāsṛṣṭi, *the "Great Emanation"*

As already mentioned on several occasions, the idea of emanation through manifestation and reflection (*ābhāsa, pratibimba*) entails necessarily the presence in Śiva of the archetype of the emanation. "The rule according to which what is not here may exist elsewhere,"[231] says Abhinavagupta, "cannot indeed be applied to the supreme Word." To him this "great emanation" (*mahāsṛṣṭi*) is of such vital importance that he describes it most extensively in *PTV*[232] and in *TĀ*, third *āhnika*. It is, indeed, the original pattern which will be reflected on the lower levels. It is "the great emanation whence spring forth the billions of creations that [pre-]exist within itself. This is the Absolute, which is said to be [the universal Self] whence all things arise."[233] In other words, this is the energy of the Absolute, *kula* or *akula*,[234] when it assumes the form of the emanation, *sṛṣṭirūpa*.[235] "Of these phonemes, the plane that has just been described is that of the supreme Word where they are in the form of pure consciousness, nonconventional, eternal, uncreated. . . . In effect, everything moving or unmoving abides [first] in a supreme and invariable form, the essence of pure power, in Consciousness: the Self of the venerable Lord Bhairava—as is shown by all that is to be perceived of the infinite diversity of the world manifested in Consciousness in a manner first indistinct, then progressively more distinct."[236]

The whole collection of the phonemes appearing in Śiva so as to give rise to the supreme manifestation is termed *śabdarāśi* or *śabdarāśibhairava:* the mass or totality of sounds, or

---

231. *PTV*, p. 102, line 10: *nahi tatra yan nāsti tat kvapyastīti nyāyam.*
232. Pp. 97-144.
233. Ibid., pp. 83-84.
234. For these terms, cf. *supra*, p. 000-00.
235. *PTV*, p. 99, first line.
236. *PTV*, pp. 102-03: *tathāpi amīṣāṃ varṇānāṃ parāvāgbhūmir iyam iha nirṇīyate, yatraiva eṣām asāmayikaṃ nityam akṛtrimaṃ saṃvinmayam eva rūpam . . . tathā hi yatkiṃcit caram acaraṃ ca tat pāramārthikena anapāyinā rūpeṇa vīryamātrasārātmanā tadudbhaviṣyadīṣadasphuṭatameṣadasphuṭatareṣadasphuṭādivastuśatamṛṣṭikālopalakṣyamāṇa tattadanantavaicitryaprathonnīyamānatathābhāvena saṃvidi bhagavanbhairavabhaṭṭārikātmani tiṣṭhatyeva.*

Bhairava[237] as consisting of the mass of sounds. Indeed it is the totality of sound, included eminently in the Word at the supreme level, the source and foundation of the sound manifestation.[238] As has been said regarding the *visarga* and *kṣa*,[239] there is here no differentiating awareness: while the fifty phonemes must result from fifty distinct phonematic awarenesses (*varṇa-parāmarśa*), they are, however, contained in a single act of consciousness (*āmarśa*) of the divine subjectivity in its pristine purity and unity, for at this level there is no objectivity upon which this act of consciousness could be directed.[240] Yet this is where manifestation emerges, and it is described, in the *PTV* or in the third *āhnika* of the *TĀ*, as if it were already made up of the various ontic levels (*tattva*s) that will constitute it once issued from Śiva and Śakti. What exists on this plane, however, is only their paradigm.[241] And this is evidenced by the following

---

237. Bhairava, among other characteristics, is Śiva in relation to the manifestation, or when he swallows it up: see, for instance, *PTV*, pp. 63-64, or *VBh*, *passim*.

The term *śabdarāśi* for the fifty phonemes from *a* to *kṣa* associated with or included in Śiva does not seem to be used outside some of the Kula-related śaiva traditions. One finds it in some Śrīvidyā and Krama works, in the Kubjikāmata, also three levels of phonematic emanation, uses the names of deities since the goddesses of the Word Parā, Parāparā and Aparā are deities" Śabdarāśibhairava (or Mātṛkābhairava) and Mālinī. The system of phonematic emanation, though different from the pantheon, cannot be entirely dissociated from it.

238. Cf. Kṣemarāja's commentary upon the Śiva Sūtras: *ŚSV* 2.3 (p. 50, lines 9-12): "Knowledge (*vidyā*) is that of the expansion of the highest, undifferentiated. [What is called here its] body means its own nature. He whose body is in the form of this knowledge [that is, whose own nature is the highest undifferentiated manifestation] is the Lord as the "mass of sounds," whose essence consists of a pulsating radiance, the nature of which is the reflective awareness of the fullness of the [absolute] 'I,' inseparable from the totality of the universe."

239. *Supra*, 284-85, 304.

240. *TĀ* 3.198 (p. 191): *ekāmarśasvabhāvatve śabdarāśiḥ sa bhairavaḥ/ . . . . . . ekaḥ—āmṛśyaśūnyatvān niḥsahāyaḥ, āmarśanam āmarśaḥ parāmarśakaḥ pramātā, tatsvabhāvatve pañcāśato 'pi varṇānāṃ saṃkalanayā "śabdarāśir iti bhairava" iti vyapadeśaḥ.*

241. About this arising of the *tattva*s within the principle, the following passage from the *PTV* may, for instance, be quoted:

significant peculiarity: the *tattva*s associated with phonemes are enumerated from earth, the final "gross element" up to Śakti, whereas emanation should of course occur the other way around. The reason for this, says Abhinavagupta in the *PTV*, is that the "great Emanation," projected outside Śiva or the supreme energy, is reflected in the supreme-nonsupreme energy, so that the latter, working like a mirror, makes the *tattva*s appear in a reversed order, revealing first the one which comes last in Śiva.[242] As we are going to see, indeed, only the order of the *tattva*s is reversed, not that of the phonemes.

So let us come now to this emanation:

Consonants: The five guttural consonants from *ka* to *ṅa* produce the five "gross elements" (*bhūta*), from earth to ether; the five palatals from *ca* to *ña*, the five subtle elements (*tanmātra*), from smell to hearing; the five cerebrals from *ṭa* to *ṇa* bring forth

---

But in the supreme consciousness, in the same measure as there is manifesting light (*bhāsā*), in the very same measure there is the reflective awareness of the activity of the world. Therefore all forms of existence appear there in complete undifferentiation as water in water or fire in fire, and not as a reflected image. . . . Thus [Bhairava] causes to shine that which is his own light, the expansion of the *tattva*s and of all the states of being, in unity with himself, being reflectively aware (*vimṛśati*) of all this and without his wonderment of it all ever being lessened. Thus this self-representation (*vimarśanam*) [of the cosmos], this appearing (*bhāsana*) that renders visibly present the trillions of billions of infinite creations and resorptions of the realm of *māyā*, is [in truth] identical with [himself].

PTV, pp. 133-34: *atra tu parasaṃvidi yathaiva bhāsā tathaiva vyavahāramayo 'pi vimarśaḥ/ tena jala iva jalaṃ jvālāyām iva jvālā sarvathā abhedamayā eva bhāvā bhāsante, na tu pratibimbakalpenāpi/ . . . tattvabhāvavikāsātmamayam ātmaikyenaiva svaprakāśaṃ prakāśayati, tathaiva ca vimṛśati, anapetatathācamatkāratve 'pi/ yac ca tat tathāvimarśanaṃ tat bhāvimāyīyānantasṛṣṭisaṃhāralakṣakoṭyarbudaparārdhasākṣātkāriṇi bhāsane bhavet tathārūpam eva bhavati.*

Cf. also same text, p. 208, from line 3 to last but one. Such a coincidence between manifestation and transcendent is also explained by the theory of *sampuṭa*, the "encasement," the perfect coincidence of the Absolute, Śiva, and the Energy as manifestation.

242. *PTV*, pp. 144-47.

the five organs of action (*karmendriya*), from the organ of locomotion to that of speech, as do the five dentals, from *ta* to *na* with regard to the five sense-organs (*buddhīndriya*), from smell to hearing; and the five labials, from *pa* to *ma*, with respect to the following *tattva*s: the inner sense (*manas*), the individual principle (*ahaṃkāra*), the intellect (*buddhi*), *prakṛti*, and *puruṣa*. Those are the twenty-five categories which correspond, for the Śaiva schools, to the impure (*aśuddha*) manifestation, that is, limited and subject to illusion and duality.

Jayaratha points out how this connection betwen full objectivity and consonants (*sparśa*) is only natural:[243] here we are in the domain of the senses, of what can be touched, *spṛṣṭa*. "They are called contacts (*sparśa*) because they can be touched by the senses," he says.[244] Contact (*sparśa*) does indeed differentiate consonants (*vyañjana*) from vowels and among them stops involve the highest degree of contact, or the most restricted opening of the organ (*karaṇa*) used to produce sound;[245] now, objective manifestation is subject to necessity or restraint (*niyati*); here again, phonetics give a basis to a cosmological construction.

Semivowels: The four semivowels, *ya*, *ra*, *la*, and *va*, give rise to the five *kañcuka*s and to *māyā*. The five "coats of armor" (*kañcuka*) are so called because like a body armor, they cover the Self and deprive it of its original freedom and extension. These are: *rāga*, attachment; *vidyā*, the limited knowledge, linked to discursive thought; *kalā*, the principle of determination —which correspond to the phonemes *ya*, *ra*, and *la*—together with *kāla*, time, and *niyati*, necessity, which are held as included in the three preceding ones.[246] *Māyā*, the principle of illusion, the root-cause of all that veils pure consciousness (and first of

---

243. *TĀ* 3.153 and comm. (p. 155).

244. *Indriyaiḥ spṛśyanta iti sparśāḥ*; ibid. p. 155, lines 14-15. The *sparśa*s are properly what we would call "stops." They were so called, it is said, because the *karaṇa* (the tip of the tongue) touches the place of articulation when they are pronounced. Cf. K. V. Abhyankar, *op. cit.*, p. 404, *sv. sparśa*.

245. *Atharva Prātiśākhya*, 1.29: *spṛṣṭaṃ sparṣānāṃ karaṇam.*

246. *PTV*, p. 199, lines 11-12.

all of the *kañcukas*), appears with *va.*

When outside of Śiva, all of these categories form the pure-impure (*śuddhāśuddha*) manifestation. They are called *dhāraṇa*, upholders, supports, because, says Abhinavagupta, playing upon the possible meanings of the term, they are upholders (*dhāraṇa*) of the manifestation and because they cause it to be upheld—that is, they "reveal as separate" all the objects of which it consists—and which are at the same time held in consciousness.[247] This twofold nature of the *dhāraṇas* is aptly attributed to them since they correspond to semivowels whose name, *antaḥstha*, evokes precisely a median, intermediate position. We have seen[248] that in the *TĀ* (3.158) this term is taken as evidence of the presence of semivowels in the powers of will and awakening. In the same way, Kṣemarāja, in the *ŚSV* (2.7),[249] justifies their appellation by the fact that these phonemes lie in the *puruṣa* (*antaḥpuṃbhūmau*), and are therefore subject to the limitation inherent to this cosmic level. They are called *dhāraṇa*, he adds, because they uphold the universe, insofar as they support the plane of the knower (*pramātṛbhūmidhāraṇena viśvadhāraṇāt*).

Fricatives and kṣa: These five phonemes correspond, according to the *PTV*, to *mahāmāyā* (*śa*), *śuddhavidyā* (*ṣa*), *īśvara* (*sa*), *sadāśiva* (*ha*), and *śakti* (*kṣa*). *Mahāmāyā* is not a *tattva.* It exists only at the supreme level of the "great emanation." This is the transcendental illusion, at a level where Śiva and the universe are still undifferentiated, and which includes within itself the power which will bring forth differentiation, and therefore *māyā tattva.*[250] *Mahāmāyā* is sometimes not included in

247. *PTV*, pp. 113-17. Similarly in *ABS* 16.86 (vol. 1, p. 155): "These phonemes are called *dhāraṇas* for they hold the universe—*viśvasya dhāratvāt.*" Alternative explanation in the *Lakṣmī Tantra* (19.13): *dhārayanti yato madhye puruṣaṃ dhāraṇāḥ smṛtāḥ* (p. 64).

248. *Supra*, p. 300.

249. *ŚSV*, p. 62, lines 7-9.

250. Cf. *TĀ* 9.150-52 and comm. (vol. 6, pp. 116ff): "The great illusion," Jayaratha writes, "is the first appearance of duality, the supreme vision [of the forthcoming universe] which appears when arises the first impulse toward external manifestation, but prior to the actual state

the description of the supreme emanation, and in such a case the four fricatives from *śa* to *ha* correspond to the *tattva*s from *śuddhavidyā* to *śakti*, and *kṣa* to *anāśritaśiva*.[251] Like *mahāmāyā* the latter is not a *tattva* but the outcome of a twofold division of Śiva, who, on the one hand, is the fullness of the Absolute, holding within himself the whole cosmos, and on the other, is comparatively lower owing to its moving further toward manifestation, a situation in which he does not perceive the cosmic totality dwelling within himself. Kṣemarāja defines *anāśritaśiva* as another name for Śiva when he has no perception of the [total and full] oneness of consciousness, a state of absolute void (*cidaikyākhyātimayānāśritaśivaparyāyaśūnyātiśūnyātmā*).

These five categories as a whole constitute what is known as *brahmapañcaka*[252] "because," Abhinava writes, "the greatness (*bṛhatva*) and expansion (*bṛṃhakatva*) of these *tattva*s are primarily due to their transcending differentiation and to their being the cause of the expansion of the *saṃsāra*."[253] We saw previously that the fricatives are regarded as a vapor emanating from the Absolute: their association with these

---

of differentiation": *bahirullilasiṣāmātratvena āsūtritaprāyatvāt vibhāgam aprāpto'ta eva ādyo yo bhedāvabhāsaḥ sā parā niśā mahatī māyetyarthaḥ.* Cf. also *PTV*, pp. 117-19, which justifies the existence of *mahāmāyā* by the hierarchy of knowers (*pramātṛ*). It is necessary, he says, that there be, between *māyā tattva*, the level of *pralayākala*s, and *śuddhavidyā tattva*, peculiar to the *vidyeśvara*s, a level for the *vijñānākala*s who, while deprived of pure knowledge, are not however trapped in the multiplicity of the empirical world.

Mahāmāyā is also found in dualistic Śaivism, but there the term has a different meaning: it is, for the Saiddhāntikas, the creative power of Śiva, who, in the form of *bindu*, brings forth the pure manifestation. Thus it is the primal cause of the whole manifestation and not, as for the Trika, merely the forerunner of *māyā*, a condition that is not antecedent to, but arising at the final stage of, the pure manifestation.

251. Abhinava, in the *PTV*, p. 199, mentions this conception, which is not that of the Trika, and where these five principles make up the fivefold *brahman*.

252. *PT*, *śl.* 7 (p. 98) and *PTV*, p. 119. For *ABS* 16.85, they make up *pañcabrahman*; the *LT* (19, 16-17), uses the term *brahmapañcaka* (p. 65).

253. *PTV*, p. 119.

higher *tattva*s is therefore quite natural. As we have seen, the *TĀ* deals in some details with the fricatives, and especially the dental sibilant *sa* which, along with *ha*, holds an outstanding position among consonants, which may be due, among other reasons, to the fact that when these phonemes are combined they form the *haṃsa*, a symbol for Śiva's phonic energy.[254]

As for *ha*, it is generally taken as symbolizing the energy, although it does not always correspond to the *śakti tattva.* But this is due to its being a "coagulated" form of the *visarga*, the energy of the Absolute, *akula.*

Finally, we must note that in the "great emanation," when *ha* does not correspond to the *śakti tattva*, it corresponds to *sadāśiva.* Now this is, normally, the level where arises *paśyantī*, the stage of speech following just after *parāvāc*, that is, pure energy: the energy on which is reflected the "great emanation."

Kṣa, finally, typifying the indissoluble union of Śiva and Śakti, is naturally associated either to the one or to the other (depending whether or not the transcendental illusion is taken into account) of these principles which, as is well known, cannot be separated.

Mātṛkā

"When [the phonic emanation] is made up of one single act of consciousness," says the *TĀ*,[255] "this is Bhairava, the Mass of Sounds; when this [mass of sounds] is touched by the shadow of the object of the act of consciousness, this [results in the arising of the phonemes in] the energy, the *mātṛkā.*"

This occurs at the level of the supreme-nonsupreme (*parāparā*) energy, that of *paśyantī.* Its characteristic feature, beyond the emergence of the first lineaments (*āṃśāṃśa*)[256] or of the shadow (*chāyā*) of objectivity, is above all the reflection (*pratibimba*): *mātṛkā* is a reflection in *paśyantī* of *śabdarāśi-*

---

254. Cf. above, chap. 3, pp. 140ff.

255. *TĀ* 3.198:

> *ekāmarśasvabhāvatve śabdarāśiḥ sa bhairavaḥ/*
> *āmṛśyacchāyayā yogāt saiva śaktiś ca mātṛkā* (p. 191).

256. *PTV*, p. 143, next to the last line: *bhedāsūtraṇātmāṃśāṃsollāsaḥ.*

bhairava, the emanation in *parāvāc*. Abhinavagupta states this very forcibly—if not very clearly—in the *PTV*:

> The Visionary, which is of the same nature as the venerable Parāparā [that is, of the supreme-nonsupreme Word] is the power proper to the supreme Energy, where, as in a mirror, the innate form or nature (*svarūpa*) of the venerable supreme [Word] is reflected in the manner of a reflected image. . . . [A reflected image, however, is both the identical and the reversed form of the original.] In the same way, the body of the venerable glorious supreme [Word] that, as has been said, contains in itself in its fullness successively all the *tattva*s starting with the earth, while, however, keeping in itself [in their original order] all the synthetic awarenesses [of the phonemes from *ka* to *kṣa*] that are, as was said, indestructible, supremely real, and so forth, casts the reflection of all this in the immaculate mirror of Parāparā, namely of *paśyantī*. This reflected image is made up of all the *tattva*s, earth, water, and so forth, identical in essence with Parā, together with the synthetic awarenesses of the phonemes *ka* and the rest, since these cannot admit of any change in their order, the whole being reflected in the mirror of *paśyantī*, of the same sort as the [supreme energy]. Then appears the reversal due to reflection, namely that that which in supreme consciousness is *śaktitattva*, is the *tattva* of earth (*pṛthivi*) on the plane of Parāparā, and conversely the *tattva* of earth becomes *śaktitattva*. So the phonemes *kṣa* and the rest [up to *ka*] correspond henceforth to [the *tattva*s] of earth and so forth [up to *śakti*]. The venerable Lord Bhairava, however, ever full, infinitely free, is not in any way inverted, for, as has often been said, nothing can transcend the [supreme] consciousness. In the awareness that is that of Parā the *tattva*s have no other nature than that of the synthetic awareness (*parāmarśaikatattvam*)[257] and this awareness is, in its ultimate nature the phonemes from *ka* to *kṣa*, made of energy (*śākta*), a plane where there is only nondifferentiation (*abhedaiva*). In Parāparā, as is the rule in a reflection, there is differentiation in nondifferentiation (*bhedābheda*). And this Parāparā who is also made of awareness (*parāmarśamayī*) and whose body is that of the garland of letters from *ka* to *kṣa*,

257. That is, they have no empirical existence; they exist as pure consciousness only.

sustains in herself the reflection of the *tattva*s that are higher than her in the venerable supreme [Word]. So, these *tattva*s abide, inverted in their order from top to bottom in these awarenesses of the phonemes from *ka* to *kṣa* (that are not submitted to *māyā*, and inaudible), since in any reflection that which is on the top in the original is on the bottom in the reflection. So there is no contradiction in the fact that [in *paśyantī*], from the standpoint of the purifiable, *kṣa* should correspond to the earth. But there also the order of the phonemes beginning with *ka* [remains], since the supreme plane cannot ever pass away."[258]

Indeed, although the "great emanation" is reflected in the supreme-nonsupreme energy (which results in reversing the order of the *tattva*s), phonemes are *not* reflected. Whether or not there is a move toward differentiation, as long as their original matrix suffers no disturbance, they remain in their regular, indestructible (*anapāyin*) order, for this stems from

---

258. *PTV*, pp. 144-46: *paśyantī ca parāparābhaṭṭārikāsatattvā paraśakter eva svātmaśaktir darpaṇakalpā yatra tatparābhaṭṭārikāsvarūpam eva cakāsti pratibimbavat . . . evaṃ ca paśyantīsatattvaparāparavimalamukurikāyāṃ tattattathāvidhoktakramapūṛṇapṛthivyāditattvasāmagrīnirbharam antas tathāvidhasahajākṛtrimapāramārthikānapāyikādiparāmarśakroḍīkāreṇaiva vartamānam api śrīparābhaṭṭārikāvapuḥ pratibimbam arpayat svarūpānyathātvāsahiṣṇukādiparāmarśānanyathābhāvenaiva tatparaikarūpaṃ parāmṛśyaṃ dharaṇyambhaḥprabhṛti tathollasadbhedasūtraṇatayā sajātīyāyāṃ vimalāyāṃ ca yāvat pratibimbayati tāvad dharāditattvānāṃ viparyāsa evopayāyate/ yat parasaṃvidi śaktitattvaṃ tad eva parāparātmani pṛthivītattvam, yat tu dharātattvaṃ tacchaktitattvam, iti kṣakārāt prabhṛti dharādīnāṃ sthitiḥ/ bhagavadbhairavabhaṭṭārakas tu sadā pūṛṇo 'nantasvatantra eva na viparyasyate jātucid api cidrūpātirekādyabhāvād ity uktaṃ bahuśaḥ/ parātmani parāmarśe parāmarśaikatattvāny eva tattvāni parāmarśaś ca kādikṣāntaśāktarūpaparāmartha iti tatra abheda eva/ parāparāyāṃ tu bhedābhedātmakatā pratibimbanyāyena/ sā ca parāparā parāmarśamayī kādikṣāntavarṇamālāśarīrā yāvat svordhvavyavasthitaparābhaṭṭārikānivisṭatattvapratibimbāni dhārayati tāvat teṣv evāmāyīyāśrautakādikṣāntaparamārthaparāmarśeṣūrdhvādharaviparyāsena tattvāni sampadyante ūrdhvabimbādharapratibimbādhāmasvabhāvamahimnā—iti tātparyam/ tataḥ pṛthivī kṣakāra ityādi ṣodhyarūpāpekṣayā na kiṃcid viruddham/ tatrāpi paradaśānapāyāt eṣa eva kādivarṇasaṃtānaḥ/*

the supreme,[259] and is the order of their enunciation by Śiva (which is that of the *varṇasamāmnāya*). It is, of course, Śiva, the Word at its highest level, who is here at work. It is the Word that casts the reflection (*pratibimbam arpayet*) of the *tattva*s of the manifestation in *parāvāc* into the next stage, that of the supreme-nonsupreme energy where differentiation, utterly absent at the level of Śiva, gradually arises. But since there exists no other energy than that of the Word, the energy acts as a—not at all passive—mirror "made of the Word." This mirror, or more accurately, this supreme-nonsupreme energy, says Abhinavagupta,[260] is constituted by the garland of phonemes from *ka* to *kṣa* (*kādikṣāntavarṇamālāśarīra*). Thus only the *tattva*s are reflected, and not the phonemes, since these form the phonematic energy upon which the consonants are reflected. This explains the inverted correspondences we have here, resulting in the first consonant *ka* henceforth corresponding to the *tattva* of *sadāśiva* or of *śakti.*

This is an original theory and peculiar, I believe, to Abhinava. It is not recorded in the Tantras and Abhinava himself expands it mostly in the *PTV*, which alone, at least as far as I know, gives the entire series of correlations between phonemes and categories of the manifestation. This is how the correlations are listed for *paśyantī*:

ka:	*sadāśiva*	*ṅa:*	*kalā*
kha:	*īśvara*	*ca:*	*vidyā*
ga:	*śuddhavidyā*	*cha:*	*rāga*
gha:	*māyā*	*ja:*	*niyati*
		jha:	*kāla*,

and so forth up to *kṣa*, earth.[261] One will note that here *sadāśiva* corresponds to *ka*. However, Abhinavagupta says on page 147

259. Ibid., p. 147, lines 3-4.
260. Ibid., p. 146, lines 11-12.
261. The correlations between phoneme and *tattva* such as given in *PTV*, pp. 152-54, with respect to the various stages of the emanation, are not always correct. They are emended in R. Gnoli's edition. It should be noted, however, that on p. 82 of his translation of this text, Gnoli

of the *PTV* that the furthest point (*paramakoṭī*) of *paśyantī* is *anāśritaśakti*.[262] Further, if *mātṛkā* is a reflection of *śabdarāśi*, should not the five *kañcuka*s here also correspond to three phonemes only? The correspondence between *ka* and *sadāśiva* seems, however, valid. This pattern is, in fact, symmetrical to that of the "great emanation" which, taking place in Śiva, ends with regard to consonants, with *śakti* or *anāśritaśiva*. Here, in the energy, that is, in the next lower *tattva*, it stops similarly at the next lower stage: *sadāśiva* or *anāśritaśakti*. We have thus a "great emanation" in *parā*, extending up to *śakti* (*kṣa*), with *anāśritaśiva* as a link, so to speak, with Śiva in which this emanation takes place; and, symmetrically, the emanation in *paśyantī*, *parāparā*, extending up to *sadāśiva* (*ka*), with *anāśritaśakti* as a link with the energy in which this emanation unfolds.[263]

There are now six phonemes instead of four corresponding to *māyā* and the *kañcuka*s: this is a necessity, however, if one wants to avoid having two extra consonants, and this is logical. It may be assumed in fact, that in the emanation in *parā, kalā* was listed with *māyā* and *niyati* with *rāga* only because there were no available phonemes for them: trying to relate cosmogony with grammar is not always an easy task. It may be also noted that the *PTV* does not mention vowels, and indeed rightly so, since we are no longer at the level of Śiva but of

---

gives a chart of the *varṇa-tattva* correspondences where, for *paśyantī*, he arranges the phonemes—but not the *tattva*s—in a reversed order. This of course is for the convenience of typography: the order of the phonemes, as Abhinava states repeatedly, cannot be reversed.

262. Like *anāśritaśiva*, this is not a *tattva* but an intermediate stage or the outcome of a logical twofold division of *śakti*. It is placed between *sadāśiva* and *śakti* and is, in fact, nothing but *śakti*, only viewed as especially oriented toward emanation.

263. In this respect one may refer to a *śloka* of *SvT* 10.1234-35 (vol. 5, p. 548), which Abhinavagupta quotes at the beginning of the exposition of the emanation in *paśyantī* (*PTV*, p. 144), and which describes the emanation as extending from earth to *sadāśiva*. The context wherefrom this *śloka* is taken is in fact quite different from the present, but Abhinavagupta, surely, did not quote it at this point without reason. For the dualist or nondualist nature of the *SvT*, cf. *supra*, chap. 2, p. 66, n. 86.

Śakti. Even so, however, these vowels must also be reflected as such on the level of energy, and not just as giving life to these consonants. It is in fact the "mass of sounds," the whole of *śabdarāśi*, that is reflected in the energy. If it were not so, manifestation would be incomplete and human beings would not be aware of vowels. A further proof of this is given in *madhyamā*, where all the phonemes are mixed up and form the *mālinī*. Kṣemarāja's commentary to *Śiva Sūtra* 1.4: "*jñānādhiṣṭhānaṃ mātṛkā*," describes indeed *mātṛkā* as the mother of the letters from *a* to *kṣa*: *ādikṣāntarūpā*. Other such passages could be cited if necessary.[264]

We shall not return here to what has been said previously[265] about the *mātṛkā*s—the phonemes as the mother-energy of all that gives its power to speech—nor to *paśyantī*, a stage which, being related to the power of will, represents more than any other the efficacy, the aspect of powerful force, of speech. What has been said about the supreme-nonsupreme emission (*parāparavisarga*)[266] or about the emission of energy (*śākta-visarga*) could be repeated for the emanation in *paśyantī*. This lies, like the former, at the junction of transcendence and immanence, on the *parāpara* plane, at a level where duality and nonduality coincide (*bhedābheda*), though here objectivity has hardly emerged and is still subordinated to the subjectivity, the "I-ness" of the principle. From this principle indeed springs the energy found here, but Śiva, or *parāvāc*, is transcendent,[267]

---

264. In most of the countless Tantric texts dealing with the phonemes of the *mātṛkā*, it is found primarily in a ritual context. It is mainly used for placing (*nyāsa*) over the body (or objects): *antarmātṛkānyāsa* or *bahirmātṛkānyāsa*. While we are describing here a cosmogonic theory, it should however be remembered that ritual is, for all Tantric texts (and their followers), the outstanding feature. It probably did exist prior to theory, or at least to its mystico-linguistic elaborations and, as evidenced by the present-day practice in Hinduism, it has survived them: most of the priests and their attendants in temples these days are unable to explain the rites they perform.

265. Chap. 3, p. 147ff.

266. *Supra*, p. 290-91.

267. Insofar, of course, as there is such a thing as transcendence in the Trika and as both terms may be opposed.

TABLE 5.1: Correspondences between phonemes and *tattva*s according to *śabdarāśi*, *mātṛkā*, and *mālinī* at the *parā*, *paśyantī*, and *madhyamā*—or Parā, Parāparā, and Aparā—levels.

Parā śabdarāśi		*Paśyantī mātṛkā*	*Madhyamā mālinī*		*Parā śabdarāśi*	
					KA	pṛthivī
					KHA	jala
					GA	tejas
					GHA	vāyu
					ṄA	ākāśa
					CA	gandha
					CHA	rasa
					JA	rūpa
					JHA	sparśa
					ÑA	śabda
A			NA		ṬA	pāda
Ā			Ṛ		ṬHA	upastha
I			Ṝ		ḌA	pāyu
Ī			Ḷ		ḌHA	pāṇi
U			Ḹ		ṆA	vāc
Ū			THA		TA	ghrāṇa
Ṛ			CA		THA	rasana
Ṝ		Śiva	DHA	Śiva	DA	cakṣus
Ḷ	Śiva	reflected	Ī	united	DHA	tvac
Ḹ	(Śakti)	in Śakti	ṆA	with	NA	śrotra
E			U	Śakti	PA	manas
AI			Ū		PHA	ahaṃkāra
O			BA		BA	buddhi
AU			KA		BHA	prakṛti
AṂ			KHA		MA	puruṣa
AḤ			GA		YA	rāga (niyati)
					RA	vidyā
					LA	kalā
					VA	māyā (kāla)
					ŚA	mahāmāyā or śuddhavidyā
					ṢA	śuddhavidyā or īśvara
					SA	īśvara or sadāśiva
					HA	sadāśiva or śakti
					KṢA	śakti or anāśritaśiva

TABLE 5.1 continued

	Paśyantī *mātṛkā*		*Madhyamā* *mālinī*
	sadāśiva or anāśritaśakti	GHA	sadāśiva
	īśvara	ṄA	īśvara
	śuddhavidyā	I	etc.
	māyā	A	↓
	kalā	VA	
	vidyā	BHA	
	rāga	YA	
	niyati	ḌA	
	kāla	ḌHA	
	puruṣa	ṬHA	
	prakṛti	JHA	
	buddhi	ÑA	
	ahaṃkāra	JA	
	manas	RA	
	śrotra	ṬA	
	tvac	PA	
	cakṣus	CHA	
REVERSING OF THE REFLECTION	rasana	LA	
	ghrāṇa	Ā	
	vāc	SA	
DIRECT REFLECTION	pāṇi	AḤ	
	pāyu	HA	
	upastha	ṢA	
	pāda	KṢA	
	śabda	MA	
	sparśa	ŚA	
	rūpa	AṂ	
	rasa	TA	↓
	gandha	E	
	ākāśa	AI	
	vāyu	O	
	tejas	AU	
	jala	DA	jala
	pṛthivī	PHA	pṛthivī

whereas *śakti* and *paśyantī* are immanent to the cosmos. *Mātṛkā* is the reflection of the phonematic archetype within this immanent energy; hence its essential role in providing manifestation with the efficient presence—for better or worse—of the powers of speech.

The same immanent and, as it were, usable character is also that of another form of phonematic emanation, which we shall now see, the *mālinī*, and it explains the important role given to it.

Mālinī

The manifestation of sound—and therefore of the universe—in the form of the fifty phonemes, before it takes the form of "letters, syllables, and words" of the language of human beings, that is, the level of "gross" speech, reaches a third level of the Word: *madhyamā.* There it assumes a form altogether different from the former two, which anticipates at least certain aspects of speech in *vaikharī.* This is the *mālinī,*[268] the energy in the form of the "garland of letters," a term indeed which may be applied as well to the *mātṛkā*, which is the primeval garland, *pūrvamālinī*, while that which appears in *madhyamā* is the *uttaramālinī*; but the term *mālinī* is hardly used to denote the *mātṛkā*, and usually indicates the *uttaramālinī.*

One of the earliest texts (probably not very early, however) known to me dealing with the *mālinī* is the *Kubjikāmata,*[269] where a mythic account is given of the birth of the form of the supreme Goddess called Mālinī and also (in chapter 4) of the extraction (*uddhāra*) by means of a diagram (*mālinīgahvara*)

---

268. *Mālinī* is a name of the Goddess, so called because she wears a garland (*mālā*), whether of fifty phonemes (*varṇamālā*), of human skulls, or whatever. For other meanings of the word *mālinī*, cf. Bhāskararāya's commentary on the *Lalitāsahasranāma, śl.* 146 (p. 114).

269. See *The Kubjikāmatatantra, Kulālikāmnāya Version*, critical edition by T. Goudriaan and J. A. Schoterman (Leiden, 1988). See also J. A. Schoterman's works cited in the bibliography: edition of the *ṢaṭSS*, and the article in *ZDMG*, suppl. 3.2 (1977). See also Dory Heilijgers's unpublished doctoral dissertation, *Kulamūlaratnapañcakāvatāra, parafrase met commentar* (Utrecht, 1983).

of the order of the fifty *akṣara*s of the same name. The *KmT* holds this series as the energetic female form of the phonemes, by contrast with *śabdarāśi*, which is male and associated with Śiva Bhairava. The *KmT* also describes practices such as *nyāsa* and so forth, connected with these arrangements of the Sanskrit letters. It is therefore possible that Abhinava's threefold system of phonematic emanation might have originated from the *KmT* or from other works of this same *Kaula* tradition, the *paścimāmnāya*.[270] But he has also borrowed, for the cosmic and ritual aspect of the *mālinī*, from another, comparatively early Trika text, the *MVT*. Jayaratha (*ad TĀ* 15.121-24, vol. 9, pp. 34-35) quotes, in connection with the *nyāsa* of the *mālinī* in *dīkṣā*, a long passage from the *Triśirobhairavatantra*, a work known to us only through quotations (especially Abhinava's, which are frequent in the *TĀ*), and which seems to belong to the Trika. All of these references, then, come from works pertaining to the Kaula tradition.[271] The particular feature of the *mālinī* is that its fifty constituent phonemes are not in the grammatical order, from *a* to *kṣa*; rather, vowels and consonants are mixed in what seems to be complete disorder, *na* being the first phoneme and *pha* the final one: the *mālinī* is *nādiphāntarūpa*.[272] One may wonder why Abhinavagupta included the *mālinī* in the phonematic emanation at the level of *madhyamā*

270. Cf. above, chap. 2, p. 62.

271. Abhinava mentions again the *mālinī* in *TĀ*, 29th *āhnika*, in connection with the Kaula ritual. The goddess *Mālinī* is sometimes called Pūrvāmnāyeśvarī, ruler of the Eastern or original *āmnāya* of the Kula. Since the Kubjikā tradition is connected with the Kula, the *mālinī* may be seen as a Kaula notion.

There is a *mālinīcakravinyāsa* in *Gorakṣasaṃhitā*, 7, which is related to the Kubjikā tradition. The *nyāsa* of *śabdarāśi* and *mālinī* is also described in *Agni Purāṇa*, 145.

272. Phonemes are arranged, in the *mālinī*, as follows:

na ṛ ṝ ḷ ḹ tha ca dha ī ṇa u ū ba ka kha ga gha ṅa i a va bha ya ḍa ḍha ṭha jha ña ja ra ṭa pa cha la ā sa aḥ ha ṣa kṣa ma śa aṃ ta e ai o au da pha.

There is (Schoterman, *ṢaṭS*, p. 217) at least one variant in this arrangement, where *tha* is placed after *na* and not between *ḹ* and *ca*.

vāc. Very likely, and primarily, it was because this ordering of letters was in use in the Kula tradition into which he had been initiated, where the *mālinī* was the phonematic pattern more specifically linked with the energy. But the presence of the *mālinī*, here, at the stage of the intermediate word, had the further advantage of revealing, before the appearance of the empirical, "gross" world, and right from the level of the energy, an order of the alphabet different from that of the grammar and prefiguring, as it were, what is found in language. We shall see, moreover, that its being associated with *madhyamā vāc* is fully justified by our authors, and that it plays an outstanding role with respect to the efficiency of the Word.

The *mālinī* is usually termed *bhinnayoni*,[273] that is, she where the wombs are intermixed, or disturbed, or else: where wombs (consonants) and seeds (vowels) are mixed up,[274] a term justified by the way the fifty phonemes are produced.

But while the phonemes arise in disorder, the *tattva*s, on the other hand, remain in the normal order of the emanation, from Śiva to earth. All of them are listed in the correspondences given by the *MV* or the *PTV*,[275] with the exception of that of *śakti*, which already was not found as such in *paśyantī* with regard to the *mātṛkā*, since in both cases *śakti* is not a discrete part, but the support of the phonematic emanation. *Śakti*, moreover, metaphysically, cannot be separated from Śiva. She abides phonetically in him, in the phonemes corresponding to him, that is, as previously, in the first sixteen: from *na* to *ga*, the presence of these phonemes being here of course no longer explained by their phonetic nature but by the whole system of the *mālinī*. The remaining thirty-four phonemes correspond to the thirty-four *tattva*s, from *sadāśiva* (*gha*) to earth (*pha*).[276]

---

273. For instance, *PTV*, pp. 121, 151, 155.

274. In this sense: Jayaratha, *TĀ* 3.199, comm. (p. 192, line 2): "mixed up, that is, where wombs, or consonants, are separated by seeds [vowels]."

275. *MV* 4.15-17 (p. 23); *PTV*, pp. 151 and 153.

276. It goes without saying that here, as in the two former stages, only the *tattva*s corresponding to the level of *madhyamā*, from *sadāśiva* to *śuddhavidyā*, are actually manifested. The rest, from *māyā* onward, are present as aspects of the energy only.

Abhinava (followed by Jayaratha in the case of the *TĀ*) presents the *mālinī* in two different, but not inconsistent, ways. According to the *PTV*, it evolves out of *śabdarāśi*, when the latter's reflection in *paśyantī* produces the *mātṛkā*:

> The venerable supreme [Word] at the very moment when she places her own reflected image in *paśyantī* in the manner that has been said, manifests herself on the plane of the Intermediate, not different in essence from her, a condition where wombs are mixed up [with seeds] which is that of the *mālinī* and where, due to the infinite forms resulting from the mixing up of wombs and seeds, she can assume a vast number of different aspects such as those of the *kulapuruṣa* and others. It is said indeed: "One must sacrifice to the Goddess, to Mālinī, in a shape where she is surrounded by innumerable goddesses and powers of Kula."[277]

"The blissful *mālinī*," Abhinava adds, (ibid., p. 151), "corresponds fundamentally and essentially to the stage of *madhyamā*, being in the nature of energy."[278] Thus the *mālinī* appears primarily as a highly efficacious energetic shuffling of *śabdarāśi*.

In the *TĀ*, on the other hand, Abhinavagupta states that the *mālinī* arises from the *saṃghaṭṭa*, from the unifying fusion

---

277. *Parābhaṭṭārikaiva hi proktanayena paśyantyāṃ pratibimbaṃ svakam arpayamāṇā tatsamakālam eva svātmatādātmyavyavasthitamadhya-madhāmni bhinnayonitām aśnuvānā tattadyonibījaparasparasaṃbheda-vaicitryasyānantyād asaṃkhyenaiva prakāreṇa tattatkulapuruṣādi-bhenenāparigaṇanabhedabhāginī māliny eva, yathoktam*

anantaiḥ kuladevais tu kulaśaktibhir eva ca/
mālinīṃ tu yajed devīm parivāritavigrahām// (*PTV*, p. 154.)

The *kulapuruṣa* mentioned here seems to be a particular arrangement of the phonemes found apparently in the Kula tradition. *TĀ*, 15.129-30, enumerating placings (*nyāsa*) to be performed during initiation, mentions the *mātṛkā* and above all the *mālinī*, which includes a phonematic classification called *kulaputtalikā*, resulting, according to Jayaratha (ibid., vol. 9, p. 68), from various perturbations (*kṣobha*) of seeds and wombs.

278. *evaṃ bhagavatī māliny eva mukhyapāramārthikamadhyamādhāma śaktisattvam.*

and friction of *śabdarāśi* and the *mātṛkā*, that is, actually from that of Śiva-Bhairava and Śakti: "When this [*mātṛkā*] rubs and fuses with *śabdarāśi*, one gets the *mālinī* where wombs are mixed up [with seeds]" and: "This [emitting energy] is called *śabdarāśi* and *mātṛkā*. She appears as *mālinī* when the perturbing and the perturbed [elements] interpenetrate. The *mālinī*, whose beauty is that of the emission due to the coming together of the seeds and the wombs, supreme Energy, is described as manifold" (or: as having the form of the universe).[279]

The *mālinī* appears thus (and even more in Jayaratha's commentary, *ad loc* pp. 191-92 and 222-23), as corresponding to a further step toward the manifestation of the universe, whose diversity and even divisions start now to emerge within the creative Word: this is what we saw previously (chap. 4, p. 209) in connection with the *madhyamā* stage of the Word, which is that of the *mālinī*.

Moreover, since everything arises out of the fusion of Śiva and Śakti, to imply that *mālinī* arises from the same act is, to some extent, to identify it with that act or at least to acknowledge it as highly efficient and powerful: *mālinī* is more than the phonetic energy of the universe, it is the very phonic energy which creates it. And in fact this is how it appears in the texts dealing therewith, where it seems more especially to be used (for instance, in *TĀ*, chap. 15) for the placings (*nyāsa*) which infuse the adept with divine power.

The two above-mentioned descriptions of the arising of the *mālinī* are not contradictory.[280] Indeed, to say as the *PTV* does, that the *mālinī* appears in *madhyamā* when *śabdarāśi*

---

279. *TĀ* 3.199 (p. 191): *sā śabdarāśisaṃghaṭṭād bhinnayonis tu mālinī/*
Ibid., 232-33 (pp. 221-23):

śabdarāśiḥ sa evokto mātṛkā sā ca kīrtitā/
kṣobhyakṣobhakāveśān mālinīṃ tāṃ pracakṣate//232//
bījayonisamāpattivisargodayasundarā/
mālinī hi parā śaktir nirṇītā viśvarūpinī//233//

280. Neither should they be taken as necessarily inconsistent with the description of the arising of the phonemes of the *mālinī* in the myth of the Goddess Mālinī of the Kubjikāmata.

In *TĀ* 15.131, Abhinava relates the *mālinī* with the Rudras and ascribes to it the power to grant both enjoyment and liberation: *mālinī*

projects its reflection in *paśyantī*, amounts to make such an arising dependent upon a conjunction (the projection of the reflection) of Śiva (*śabdarāśi*) and Śakti (*mātṛkā*); and a projection, even that of a reflection, is still a form of emission (*visarga*). As it is, in the *PTV* itself, *śabdarāśi* and *mātṛkā* are found to intervene explicitly. Abhinavagupta, in this text, taking the sixteen phonemes corresponding to Śiva in the *mālinī*, describes[281] a movement of energy and of sound evolving from the primordial resonance (*nāda*) associated with the first phoneme *a* down to the gross elements, then from the world of senses up to Sadāśiva; this is achieved by associating these phonemes to their corresponding *tattva*s, first in *parā*, and then in *paśyantī*. We have thus the initial stage of the *mālinī* interpreted in the light of the other two phonematic emanations, the aim being to show thereby that the *mālinī*, even more explicitly than the two former emanations, makes Śiva and the manifestation mutually inherent. The explanation is cleverly contrived, its interest being that it illuminates another movement of the energies in Śiva, then in the emission that follows. Admittedly, this is somewhat arbitrary, since the arrangement of the phonemes in the *mālinī* surely was not initially developed on the basis of the correspondences between the phonemes and the *tattva*s that are found in *śabdarāśi* and *mātṛkā*. The way in which Abhinavagupta combines these three systems is, however, helpful for him to expound the cosmic manifestation and the omnipresence of the Word. Indeed, he enumerates (pp. 152-54) all the phonemes of the *mālinī*, giving for each of them the three corresponding *tattva*s according to *śabdarāśi*, *mātṛkā*, and *mālinī*. He shows thus how the *tattva*s are included in each other, that is, in fact, how Śiva and the manifestation pervade each other, and also how fecund is the conjunction of consonants and vowels. "Thus," he concluded, "is now firmly established the principle that everything is in everything":[282] *ity evaṃ sarvasarvātmakatvaṃ nirvyūḍhaṃ bhavet* (ibid.,

---

mālitā rudrair dhārikā siddhimokṣayoḥ (vol. 9, p. 69).

He gives it a prominent role in the ritual resorption of the *adhvan*s in the *dīkṣā*.

281. *PTV*, pp. 151-52.

282. *sarvasarvātmakatā; PTV*, pp. 47, 66, 137, 139.

p. 154)—an important notion in *saṃvidadvaya.* Abhinava also shows in this way the movement of energy by which one passes from one phoneme (or one *tattva*) to another, and thereby how they are all vivified with the same cosmic energy. The symbolic values of each of the fifty phonemes are here quite central, as they make for the coherence of the system. Undoubtedly the *mālinī* is regarded as endowed with exceptional power and efficiency, derived from the union of Śiva and Śakti, whether it is regarded as born from this union or reproducing it within itself. Here is, in this respect, a significant passage of the *Tantrasāra*: "The glorious *mālinī* has indeed the nature of power par excellence and, being made of the mixing up of wombs and of seeds, she is [the Cow that] accomplishes all that one wishes. Her name is in conformity with her nature: she is associated with the energies of Rudra. As she gives fruits, she blossoms. She is the bee whose murmur brings to an end the coldness of the *saṃsāra.* She gives powers and liberation and, the phonemes *ra* and *la* being interchangeable, she is endowed with the power of giving and of taking away [the resorption of the cosmos]."[283]

So *mālinī* is indeed the highest energy as pervading the manifestation. This pervasion, admittedly, is normally brought

---

283. *TS*, 13, pp. 134-35: *mālinī hi bhagavatī mukhyaṃ śāktaṃ rūpaṃ bījayonisaṃghaṭṭena samastakāmadugham/ anvarthaṃ caitan nāma rudraśaktimālābhir yuktā phaleṣu puṣpitā saṃsāraśiśirasaṃhāranādabhramarī siddhimokṣadhāriṇī dānādānaśaktiyuktā iti ralayor ekatvasmṛteḥ.*

There is in *TĀ* 15.131-32 and comm. (vol. 9, pp. 69-70) an elucidation of the interpretations of the name *mālinī*, especially the one given in the last words of this passage: the term *mālinī* is broken up into *ma*, that is, negation and therefore resorption, and *alinī*, the bee. As for *ra* and *la*, they are taken out of the *l* of *mālinī* and construed in this way: *ra* as meaning to give and *la* to take back.

This passage of the *TS* merely restates what Abhinavagupta wrote in *TĀ*, 15th *āhnika*, where he indicates even more markedly (*śl.* 125) that if the *mālinī* is thus saturated with power, it is because of its being agitated by Śiva: "What power," he adds (*śl.* 126), "could not be derived from, and what deficiency could not be removed, through the arising of the emitting power created by the stirring up of seeds and wombs? . . ." (*TĀ* 15.120-38; vol. 9, pp. 62-73).

about through the mere working of the energies, an expression and a symbol of which being, as we have already seen, *aham*;[284] but the role of the *mālinī* is to give a further illustration of this principle, and, even more—since one achieves this pervasiveness through the mixing up of the phonemes—to give a greater impetus to the power resulting from the union of Śiva and Śakti, and to establish it more firmly in the universe. This is why it is said that the most efficient ritual assignations (*nyāsa*) and the most potent mantras are those made with the *mālinī*.[285] Because he has this in mind, Abhinavagupta incorporates in the *PTV* the exposition of the *mālinī* in that of *madhyamā*, whose salient features[286] are (1) the "covering up[287] of objectivity by pure subjectivity—the former being regarded as Śakti and the latter as Śiva—and, (2) the mutual inherence of that which expresses (*vācaka*) and that which has to be expressed (*vācya*). Vowels, related to Śiva, are identified with that which expresses, and consonants, related to Śakti, with that which has to be expressed. The *mālinī*, where consonants and vowels are mixed up, may therefore be regarded as consisting of their union; now "when seeds, or vowels, and wombs, or consonants, are mixed up, all the fruits are produced effortlessly."[288] Hence the efficiency of the *mālinī*.

The "Gross" Phonematic Emanation

"Then, on the plane of *māyā*," says Abhinavagupta in the *TS*,[289] "the divisions and differences becoming manifest participate in the māyic nature of the phonemes. These, having

---

284. *Supra*, pp. 286ff.
285. *PTV*, p. 151, quoted previously. Cf. also *TĀ* 15.135-38 (vol. 9, pp. 71-72), which quotes also *MVT*, 3.35-36.
286. Cf. *supra*, chap. 4, pp. 148-49.
287. *pracchādana*.
288. *PTV*, p. 149. The sentence is, in fact, an objection made to Abhinavagupta, but he points out that it is groundless, since it expresses a reality, if only because, finally, the Word is identical to consciousness, which is one and holds within itself the totality of things.
289. *māyāyāṃ punaḥ sphuṭībhūtabhedavibhāgā māyīyavarṇatāṃ bhajante, ye paśyantīmadhyamāvaikhariṣu vyāvahārikatvam āsādya bahīrūpatattvasvabhāvatāpattir paryantāḥ te ca māyīyā api śarīrakalpatvena yadā

gone through the states of *paśyanti*, *madhyamā*, and *vaikharī*, finally assume the nature of the external categories of manifestation. These [phonemes], however, though being of the nature of *māyā* and being so to say corporeal (*śarīrakalpatvena*), never cease to be reanimated, in accordance with what has been said, by the pure acts of awareness (*śuddhair parāmarśaiḥ*) that give them life. They become thus efficacious (*savīryā bhavanti*) and therefore are able to bestow enjoyment and liberation." Indeed, as we have seen (chap. 4, p. 218) in connection with *vaikharī*, the lower levels of speech always "rest" in those which arose before them, the whole manifestation being, from the standpoint of *saṃvidadvaya*, but the appearing of the supreme consciousness. Of the empirical stage of the phonemes, even as of the whole "corporeal" manifestation, there is, from such a viewpoint, little to say—except of course as concerns the use to be made of the things of this world for ritual purposes and for achieving supernatural power and liberation, such a use being one of the main traits of all Tantric traditions. In this respect, for Abhinavagupta, phonemes and mantras are made use of especially in the "ways" or "means" (*upāya*s) of energy and of the individual soul (*śāktopāya* and *āṇavopāya*) where, as we have seen and shall see again, not only phonemes and ritual utterances but ordinary speech and language as well, may be used as a means for attaining to divine consciousness: these kinds of practices, as we know, permeate Tantric Hinduism.

At the level of the manifestation the arising of "corporeal" phonemes will be accompanied by that of all the cosmic categories of the manifestation down to the earth *tattva*, no longer paradigmatically in Śiva alone, or at the level of the energy, but in the empirical reality, in the "impure" creation. This, the state of the world subject to duality, limitation, and error, begins to take shape from the *māyā tattva*, with the "coats of armor" (*kañcuka*s), and becomes firmly established with the "soul" (*puruṣa*). It is indeed to the *tattva*s from *puruṣa* to *pṛthivī*

---

dṛṣyante yadā ca teṣām uktanayair etaiḥ jīvitasthānīyaiḥ śuddhaiḥ parāmarśaiḥ pratyujjīvanaṃ kriyate tadā te savīryā bhavanti, te ca tādṛṣā bhogamokṣapradāḥ. (*TS*, ch. 3, pp. 18-19)

that correspond consonants (*sparśa*), which represent the most differentiated and the lowest form of the phonematic emanation: such was the case in the energy, with the *mātṛkā*, and it is still the case here, in *vaikharī*. But of course here as in the previous cases all the fifty phonemes are present. More than that (or rather less, as we are moving further and further from the fullness of the primary principle), we have now, since we are at the level of speech, the whole collection of letters, syllables, and words, of which human language is comprised.[290] The creative movement of the Word reaches its lowest point here. Abhinavagupta does not give any description of this. There is no process of image and reflection such as we saw earlier. It is the final phase of the condensation of the Word and, after the letters used by human beings, after words and language—and all perceptible sounds—the objective phenomenal manifestation is at last completed. It is, however, worth mentioning that, even as *ha* and *kṣa* marked, at the end of *śabdarāśi*, the return of the whole *parāmarśa* of the phonemes to its original fount—the Absolute—in a different way to be sure, and yet quite similarly in some respects, manifest speech retains the capacity to come back (and above all to take back) to its source.

In the next two chapters we are going to see, precisely, some of the notions on this theme, as are found in various Tantric works. With the sixfold path, the *ṣaḍadhvan*, we shall see at first yet another way to expound the emergence of the world out of the Word, but according to a system which is, perhaps, more commonly used as a way of purification, of return to the origin. Mantras, lastly, with which we shall close this work, are forms of speech, sometimes described as the origin of everything; but above all they are pervaded by an extra mundane force, which leads to omnipotence as well as to liberation through union with the source of the Word.

---

290. "*Vaikharī*," says Naṭānānanda in the comm. on *KKV*, 32 (p. 52), "consists of all the phonemes from *a* to *kṣa;* it is responsible for the unfolding of the whole universe and consists of the totality of sounds." Other such formulations could also be found elsewhere.

6

The Sixfold Course

The *ṣaḍadhvan*, the sixfold pathway or the six courses,[1] offers yet another picture of that cosmic evolution of the Word extending from the Godhead down to our world, a movement one can go back over by retracing the Word to its source. We shall find here the same hierarchies, principles, categories, mythic values, and material as before. Within this sixfold system, the arrangement of these various elements may differ from what we have seen. A greater or lesser importance may be given them (especially with respect to the divisions of the cosmos); they may operate differently (cosmogonically or for the liberation of the adept). In spite of such differences, however, they remain part and parcel of the same general pattern: we find the same mythical cosmos, the same conception of the universe and of the structure and place in the world of human beings. This cosmic and soteriological course is sixfold because it divides, on the side of the Word, into three ways: the ways of *varṇa*s, mantras, and *pada*s, and, on the objective side, into three further ones: the ways of *kalā*s, *tattva*s, and *bhuvana*s. This arrangement in two series of three reflects, at least as far as Kashmirian Śaivism is concerned, a hierarchical order going from the Word to the manifestation, from the highest to the lowest.

1. *Adhvan* is translated as "pathway" or "course" so as to emphasize that these are primarily ways or courses, that is, progressions toward a goal, a course to be followed, and not merely a path or way *per se* existing by itself even though it is not used. "These six are the six paths that lead to Brahman-experience" (Introduction to the *ŚT*, Tantrik Text edition, p. 15).

Surely, the *ṣaḍadhvan* pattern existed quite early, at least in some form, in the Śaivism of northwestern India. However, since its constituent parts do not always fit together perfectly, one may infer that it was not developed at first as a whole but, more likely, that it was built up combining materials from earlier cosmogonies.[2] It does not seem to have been actually systematized, in nondualist Śaivism, before the times of Abhinavagupta. But when dealing with it Abhinava relies on the *MVT* and the *Devyāyāmala*, as well as on the *SvT*, that is, on comparatively early texts (even though these cannot be dated). What will be discussed in this chapter is its exposition by Abhinavagupta and Kṣemarāja, and by the texts to which they refer.[3]

The *ṣaḍadhvan* is also found in dualistic Śaivism and in Pāñcarātra Vaiṣṇavism. In the Śaiva Āgamas, that is, before Abhinavagupta, its role is confined to *dīkṣā*, or initiation,[4] where the master uses these six courses to lead the disciple from the earth, where he lives, up to Śiva. The way in which these six ways are arranged—concurrently and included within each other, and not hierarchically—and are used, make it look like a borrowed system (as H. Brunner has noted), more or less ingeniously adapted to the Āgamas' own doctrines and practices.[5] Śrīkaṇṭha, a dualistic, probably Kashmirian author,

---

2. See also below, p. 356.
3. It goes without saying that other texts will also be mentioned occasionally. Thus I shall refer to the Śrīvidyā tradition, with Śivānanda and Vidyānanda (thirteenth century), and to the Krama in its later form, that is, Maheśvarānanda. The *Īśanaśivagurudevapaddhati* (part 3) also deals with the *ṣaḍadhvan* (in this order: *tattva, varṇa*, mantra, *bhuvana, pada, kalā*).
4. The *SvT* and the *TĀ* also deal with it in this connection (*SvT*, 4 and *TĀ*, 15, mostly).
5. See H. Brunner's very clear and thorough exposition and discussion of the āgamic *ṣaḍadhvan* in the Introduction (pp. xiii-xxii) of the *SP* 3, and the passages from that volume concerning the *adhvan*s. It is worth noting that in the Āgamas the two series of three ways are presented in a—logical—ascending or descending order of subtlety: *varṇa, mantra, pada* or *kalā, tattva, bhuvana*: if this is a borrowed system, it retains, however, some coherence, which is not always the case elsewhere (thus, *NT* 8.22-24, vol. 1, p. 188, and 22.19, vol. 2, p. 312).

V. Dviveda has published a study, *Vaiṣṇaveṣu taditareṣu cāgameṣu ṣaḍadhavanvimarśaḥ*, in *Tantrayātra* (Banaras: Ratna Publications, 1982),

gives a brief sketch of the *ṣaḍadhvan* in his *Ratnatraya*, *śloka* 85ff. It is also briefly described in Śrīkumāra's commentary on Bhojadeva's *Tattvaprakāśa* (1.5) (whose date is probably about the same as Abhinava's: the early eleventh century). In both cases the *ṣaḍadhvan*, considered according to the five *kalā*s, *nivṛtti*, and so on, derives from the *bindu*, which itself is in the nature of *śabdabrahman*: *pañcadhā bhidyate kalās tā binduvṛttayaḥ*, says Śrīkaṇṭha (*śl.* 85).[6]

In the Pāñcarātra, the *ṣaḍadhvan* might have existed from an early period, since it is found in *SātS*,[7] ch. 19 (*śl.* 126-59), dealing with *dīkṣā*. Here the *ṣaḍadhvan* is described as extending from the energy of *śabdabrahman* down to the phonemes (*varṇa*s), which are the Lord in his phonic form (*śabdamūrtir bhagavān*) and which evolve into the *kalā*s linked with Viṣṇu's six *guṇa*s. These evolve into *tattva*s, out of which mantras are issued, which produce the *pada*s, from which finally arise the *bhuvana*s. The six courses are given in the same order in *LT* (22.10-11), a later text. In both cases the order is, apparently, a cosmogonic—that is, emanative—one, which is logical enough, even though its exposition is linked with that of a resorptive process leading the adept from the empirical world to the Godhead; the latter perspective is, as we said above, a characteristic feature of the *ṣaḍadhvan*, the constituent parts of which (as we shall see) are usually envisaged as extending from the lowest to the highest: thus the first *kalā* is *nivṛtti*, phonemes extend from *kṣa* to *a*, and so forth.

Dealing with the means for liberation based upon time (*kālopāya*), Abhinava in *TS* (chap. 6, p. 47), sums up the *ṣaḍadhvan* in the following way: "The power of action [of Śiva

---

pp. 14-34. There is a good study of the nondualistic Kashmirian Śaivism system by Jun Takashima in his (unpublished) doctoral dissertation (Paris, 1990), on *La dīkṣā selon le Tantrāloka d'Abhinavagupta*, a substantial work summarized in "*Dīkṣā* in the Tantrāloka," in S. Visuvalingam (ed.), *Abhinavagupta and the Synthesis of Indian Cultures* (forthcoming).

6. Śrīkaṇṭha, *Ratnatraya*, pp. 35ff. *Tattvaprakāśa* (Trivandrum Sanskrit Series), pp. 33-42. Cf. Bibliography.

7. The *SātS* is one of the "Three Jewels" of the Pāñcarātra, that is, one of its basic texts. This is a comparatively early work, earlier than the tenth century (it is quoted by Utpaladeva).

engenders] on the one hand the way of time (*kālādhvan*), on the other, as the variety of forms, the way of space (*deśādhvan*). In the way of time are the *varṇa*s, mantras, and *pada*s, which are [respectively] supreme, subtle, and gross. Whereas in the way of space are the *kalā*s, *tattva*s, and *bhuvana*s." And in the *TĀ*: "In this respect, the manifestation of the [power of] action is called the way of time, a threefold way where appear clearly the phonemes, the mantras, and the *pada*s. What concerns the manifestation of forms is called the way of space, wherein dwell the three [divisions of] *kalā*s, *tattva*s, and worlds."[8]

The *SvT*, chap. 4, discusses the *ṣaḍadhvan* in connection with *dīkṣā*, from a ritual standpoint, without propounding any theory. Kṣemarāja, however, avails himself of this opportunity (in his commentary *ad* 4.97; vol. 2, pp. 50-53) to give a brief but clear and comprehensive description of the system as it may be conceived of in nondualistic Kashmirian Śaivism. The supreme Lord, he says, a dense mass of consciousness and bliss, in his absolute freedom, through the agency of this free energy (*svātantryaśakti*), *unmanā*—which, as we have seen,[9] is the highest stage of the sound energy—brings forth (*avabhāsayati*) on himself as substratum (*svabhittau*) all the aspects pertaining to "that which expresses" (*vācaka*) and "that which has to be expressed" (*vācya*), extending from the pure energy of Speech (*śūnya*) to earth, the lowest form in the manifestation. All this appearing is not, indeed, added unto him, since there is nothing apart from him. This appearing, when it is "that which expresses," shares in the Subject aspect, the "I-ness" of the Lord,[10] and it produces (in descending order of subtleness) the

---

8. *TĀ* 6.34-35; vol. 4, pp. 33-34:

tatra kriyābhāsanaṃ yat so 'adhvā kālādhva ucyate/
varṇamantrapadābhikyam atrāste 'dhvatrayaṃ sphuṭam//34//
yas tu mūrtyavabhāsāṃśaḥ sa deśādhvā nigadyate/
kalātattvapurābhikhyam antarbhūtam iha trayam//35//

Cf. also *TĀ* 11.1-92 (vol. 9/2, pp. 1-73), of which we shall quote several passages in the following pages.

9. Above, chap. 3 p. 95.
10. Insofar, says Kṣemarāja, as it participates in the aspect of knower of the world: *grāhakabhāgāvasthitam* (ibid., p. 51). Jayaratha *ad TĀ*

varṇas, mantras, and *padas*, the first corresponding to an awareness (*vimarśa*) free of duality, of differentiation, the second to difference-nondifference (*bhedābheda*), and the third to differentiated consciousness (*bheda*). In the same way the divine energy in the aspect of "that which has to be expressed" (*vācyarūpa*) is the energy known as *kalā* which, becoming increasingly differentiated and particularized, assumes the nature of the *tattvas* and then of the *bhuvanas*. So in the first case one goes from the supreme energy of the Word, the *mātṛkā*, the mother of everything, to the mantras, those forms of speech close to language but still pervaded by the supreme energy and oriented toward it, and then to the *padas*, the "words" which, as we shall see, are not actual words but mantras; but owing to their phonetic form and still more to their nature, they belong to the realm of differentiation, of duality. Similarly, in the way of space, the *kalās* are at once cosmic divisions and the Godhead's energy itself, dividing and fragmenting, which dividing and becoming condensed, produces the thirty-six *tattvas*, the ontic levels of the cosmos, then the *bhuvanas* (or *puras*), the "worlds," subdivisions of the cosmos, varied in number depending upon the texts, and extending from the divine worlds down to hells. As we have seen (*supra*, p. 333), Abhinava too (*TĀ* 6.34-35) distinguishes these two series, stating that the first one pertains to action (*kriyā*), the other one to form (*mūrti*—in the sense of thickening, hardening, which this term evokes).[11] It goes without saying, however, that in the case of the *adhvans* as in that of any cosmic manifestation, *vācya* cannot be separated from *vācaka*, since the latter is the basis, the foundation or essence of the former: both ways, in this respect, work, if not on parallel lines, strictly speaking, at least in a symmetrical *vācya-vācaka* interdependence.[12]

The following table can be made:

---

says: insofar as this abides in what belongs to the Knower, *pramātrāṃsāśrāyena.*

11. *Mūrti* is derived from the root *MŪRCH*: to thicken, to solidify.
12. Both being issued from the Godhead who is indissolubly *prakāśavimarśamaya*, these two ways are respectively *vimarśa* and *prakāśa.*

The Godhead's manifestative energy	*para*	*sūkṣma*	*sthūla*	MM. + Parimala
vācaka *kriyā* (*kalādhvan*)	*varṇa*	*mantra*	*pada*	*abhidāna* *vimarśa* Śakti *śabda*
vācya *mūrti* (*deśādhvan*)	*kalā*	*tattva*	*bhuvana*	*abhideya* *prakāśa* Śiva *artha*

In Abhinava's nondualistic perspective, nothing in this sixfold manifestation is ever separate or distinct from the supreme Śiva. The whole path, he says, cannot be separated from Bhairava. Ways are actually nothing but freely assumed modalities of the Godhead who, in the fullness of the light of consciousness, brings forth the universe through the action of his freedom and his outflowing being, which arouse him to the desire for producing within himself the forms of the limited objective world.[13] "When the Lord," he says in the same passage, keeps on producing differentiation through his energy, which is a form of his own free will, he nevertheless abides in himself, undivided, eternal, and quiescent."[14]

But the *ṣaḍadhvan*, while being the Godhead's pathway of cosmic creation, is also and above all a sixfold course leading back to the deity, that is, a way followed in meditation by the adept, and even more a practice of "purification" in *dīkṣā*, designed to place the disciple on the way toward liberation. Such is its primary meaning according to our texts. In the dualistic Āgamas (as mentioned above), the *ṣaḍadhvan* appears

13. *TĀ* 2.54 (vol. 7/2, p. 45): I give here both the meaning of the *śloka* and Jayaratha's interpretation of the same.

14. *TĀ* 2.41-42:

bhedaṃ visphārya visphārya śaktyā svacchandarūpayā//41//
svātmany abhinne bhagavān nityaṃ viśramayan sthitaḥ/

Jayaratha (ibid., *śl.* 59, comm. p. 49) repeats here that known and knowing cannot be separated: both arise together for there is no cognition

largely as six paths along which the master leads the disciple during *dīkṣā*, through mental and bodily identifications and "purifications," so as to take him back to Śiva. Though the Kashmirian nondualistic view results in a different view of the *adhvan*s and of how they operate, however these are still, *mutatis mutandis*, used much in the same way. Indeed the passages of chapter 4 of the *SvT* quoted above and those we shall see later deal with them in connection with *dīkṣā*, as does Abhinavagupta in the *TĀ*: the sixth *āhnika* is devoted to the "way of time," which is one of the *upāya*s, and chapters 8 to 11 look upon the *adhvan*s—in fact, not restricted to these six—as ways of salvation belonging to the *āṇavopāya*. So they serve a very significant purpose in *dīkṣā*. "For the dualists, this course is a means to move gradually to the desired plane of being, but for those who are awakened [it is thus called] because it is eaten up, for it is something that may be enjoyed," says Abhinavagupta.[15] This means that it is either a way to salvation or a reality to be "eaten up," absorbed, in order to become one with it. The *advaitin* identifies with it and internalizes it, so he can

---

which is not cognition of something, therefore which is not accompanied by the object to be known. This is why the path of the *kalā*s and so forth, arises at the same time as that of the *varṇa*s, mantras, and *pada*s.

Similarly, Maheśvarānanda writes in the *MM* (27): "There are six courses, half of which are characterized by objectivity and conscious light; the other half are in the nature of the Word and awareness. This is how Śiva shines forth and unfolds in the form of a couple":

yad adhvanāṃ ca ṣaṭkaṃ tatra prakāśārthalakṣanam ardham/
vimarśaśabdasvabhāvam ardham iti śivasya yāmalollāsaḥ//

These are, he adds in the *Parimala*, the two sides of the same reality which, in order to bring forth the universe, divide into two aspects, Śiva and Śakti, *prakāśa* and *vimarśa*; he compares them to the two sticks used for kindling fire by friction (*visargāraṇi*): it is both a creative and a fusioning friction that "emits" the fire. Maheśvarānanda quotes on this subject a stanza from Abhinava's *Paryantapañcāśikā*.

15. *TĀ* 6.30 (pp. 30-31, vol. 4):

adhvā krameṇa yātavye pade samprāptikāraṇam/
dvaitināṃ bhogyabhāvāt tu prabuddhānām yato 'dyate//30//

Adhvan is explained as derived from the root *AD*, to eat.

realize his deeper nature, that of the divine consciousness, both transcendent and immanent. However, in both cases the *ṣaḍadhvan* plays a central part in the progression of the disciple toward liberation.

This is also why Abhinava stresses the link between the *adhvan*s and *prāṇa*. "This whole course," he says, "is based upon the vital breath (*samasta evāyam adhvā prāṇe pratiṣṭhitaḥ*).[16] This fundamental connection with *prāṇa* is due to the fact that three of the six *adhvan*s form the "way of time" (*kālādhvan*), and time is linked to breath:[17] the practices of the conquest of time in the sixth *āhnika* of the *TĀ* are based upon this link. This is also due to the fact that the yogic-cum-ritualistic practices of *dīkṣā* involving the *adhvan*s for the purpose of liberation are linked with the movement and control of *prāṇa*, the subtle energy giving life to and pervading the cosmos and human beings alike: this energy, at its highest level, "abides in consciousness, beyond time—this is the Godhead's supreme energy, which is exalted as *Kālī*."[18] *Prāṇa*, however, is also present on a lower, more corporeal, plane, where it constitutes the subtle body—which is affected especially by *dīkṣā*. In *dīkṣā* all that has to do with "breath" plays an important role. *Prāṇa* ascends with the *kuṇḍalinī* up to the *dvādaśānta*. Abhinava thus states (*TĀ* 17.80-81, p. 160) that the master, in the course of initiation, should make the oblation by meditating on the way of time and that of space as abiding in *prāṇa*, the latter

---

16. *TĀ* 6.21 (vol. 4, p. 21) and ibid., *śl.* 5 (pp. 3-4): "This whole sixfold course, which will be described at great length, is based on nothing but *prāṇa* alone." Similarly *SvT* 4.241 (vol. 2, p. 156): *adhvaṣaṭkaṃ yathā prāṇe saṃsthitaṃ kathayāmi te.* I return to these practices later.

    Practices similar in many respects are to be found in the yogic ritual of the *triśūlamaṇḍala*, identified with the practitioner's body, as described by A. Sanderson in his already quoted study "Maṇḍala."

17. The other three *adhvan*s, belonging to space (*deśādhvan*) are also made use of in practices related to *prāṇa*. Indeed, time and space cannot be separated: Abhinava knew this as well as we do, and he takes this fact into account in his own way, here as elsewhere.

18. *TĀ* 6.7 (p. 6):

    kramākramātmā kālaś ca paraḥ saṃvidi vartate/
    kālī nāma parā śaktiḥ saiva devasya gīyate//7//

abiding in energy, and energy in consciousness, which is identical with Śiva:

> *prāṇasthaṃ deśakālādhvayugaṃ prāṇaṃ ca śaktigam /*
> *taṃ ca saṃvidgataṃ śuddhāṃ saṃvidaṃ śivarūpiṇīm //*[19]

Finally one may cite, for the soteriological use of the *ṣaḍadhvan*, *VBh*, *śloka* 56, which prescribes "to concentrate step by step on the whole universe in the form of *bhuvana*s and of the other ways, that is, upon the modalities extending from the gross to the subtle state, then to the supreme, until at last dissolution of thought [in pure consciousness] is achieved."[20] Here the *ṣaḍadhvan* affords a way for mystic contemplation to pass from the manifest and the diverse to the undifferentiated absolute, each stage of the way (where *vācaka* and *vācya* are connected) dissolving into the next (or, more accurately, ontologically, into the previous one), which "pervades" it (*vyāpaka*) and is its essence. This exactly fits with what we have already seen and, in fact, Aghoraśiva, when explaining this *śloka*, contents himself with quoting from *SvT* 4.95-97 and from Kṣemarāja's commentary on the same.

We now have to examine each of the constituent parts of the sixfold course, beginning with the highest one, the phonemes, or *varṇa*s.

Varṇa

The *varṇa*s are the fifty phonemes, which are usually given in the reverse order of grammar, from *kṣa* to *a:* since the sixfold

19. There is a similar teaching in *SvT* 4.242ff., where the sixfold course is described as abiding in *prāṇa* and extending from the feet to the head of the disciple, which means that it should thus be seen internally and meditated upon by the initiate. This *prāṇa*, as Kṣemarāja explains, is not ordinary breathing, but a subtle "breath" pervading the whole body: *samastadehavyāptisūkṣmaprāṇamātra evoddiṣṭo na tu prāṇacāraḥ* (ibid., p. 152). In this connection, Kṣemarāja quotes four lines from *paṭala*s 5, 13 and 10 of the *Vidyāpada* of *MatPār.*

20. *VBh*, KSTS ed., p. 46:

path is held primarily as a way to liberation, its order is normally that of the resorption (*saṃhārakrama*). These phonemes (if taken *sṛṣṭikrameṇa*) are produced by Śiva's active and nondual awareness[21] of the various forms of energy that give rise to the universe. These *varṇa*s, in short, are none but the "totality of sounds" (*śabdarāśi*) such as we have seen in the phonematic emanation. However, in his exposition in *TĀ*, 11.44ff., Abhinava refers to the *MVT*, and from another passage of the same (*TĀ*, 16.143-5, vol. 10, pp. 59-60) and Jayaratha's commentary thereon (ibid., p. 60), it appears that the phonemes of the *ṣaḍadhvan* can be "mixed up or unmixed" (*bhinnābhinnavarṇadvaye*). So they may also be made of the *mālinī*.[22] This may seem inconsistent with what was said before, in chapter 5, on the *mālinī* which we described then as appearing on a lower level than *śabdarāśi* and *mātṛkā*. The use of *mātṛkā* and *mālinī*, however, is here a ritual one: the *TĀ*, 16 mentions the *mālinī* for the placing (*nyāsa*) of phonemes.[23] Now, for purely ritual purposes both these series of letters may well be treated in the same way. We have already noted that the *ṣaḍadhvan* system, probably built from materials taken from various texts, is not always, even with Abhinavagupta, entirely consistent. However, it must also be added that Abhinava, in *TĀ* 16.332 (vol. 9, p. 166) quotes the *Siddhayogeśvarīmata* as saying that the supreme Goddess, Kālasaṃkarṣiṇī, is Parā, to which he identifies Mālinī and Mātṛkā, the perspective being, then, that of the cult.[24]

The path of the *varṇa*s, says Abhinavagupta, pertains to the Knower; it is pure cognition; it arises when all separateness (*audāsīnya*)[25] is left aside, as well as all agitation or disturbance

---

bhuvanādhvādirūpeṇa cintayet kramaśo 'khilam/
sthūlasūkṣmaparasthityā yāvad ante manolayaḥ//56//

21. They are, Kṣemarāja says, *abhedavimarśasāra* (*SvT* 4.96, comm.).
22. *TĀ* 16.144 (vol. 10, p. 59): *dvividho 'pi hi varṇānāṃ ṣaḍvidho bheda ucyate/* J's commentary: *mātṛkāmālinīgatatvena dvividho 'pi varṇānām yo bhedaḥ pratyekaṃ varṇapadamantravyāptyā ṣaḍvidha ucyate.*
23. *varṇādhvano 'tha vinyāsaḥ kathyate 'tra*
24. See chap. 5, p. 307, n. 237.
25. *audāsīnya/udāsīnatā* (from *ud* + *AS*: to be divided, set apart, hence not interested, indifferent), corresponds to a stage in cosmic revelation when the Godhead disregards, or is not aware of, his full plenitude.

(*prakṣobha*),[26] such definition emphasizing its aspect of pure transcendence and also of fullness. "When this way rests only in knowledge-transcending knower, knowledge and known," adds Abhinava, "then it shows itself as made up of phonemes (*varṇātmā*). The flow of these phonemes forms the basis of a form of consciousness made up of knowledge (*pramārūpam*). [The Godhead] is aware of them on the plane of consciousness proper to them by manifesting them insofar as this [consciousness] participates in the full extent of the objective world—even as far down as the earth—that appears together with it. These [phonemes] can name everything; they have an unlimited power whilst, however, experiencing the joy of resting in pure throbbing consciousness."[27] The purpose of this complex and somewhat cryptic phrase is to underline the twofold aspect of the phonemes:

---

26. *TĀ* 11.48-49 (vol. 7/2, p. 39):

audāsīnyaparityāge prakṣobhānavarohane/
varṇādhvā mātṛbhāge syāt pūrvaṃ yā kathitā pramā//48//
sa tu pūrṇasvarūpatvād avibhāgamayī yataḥ/

"That knowledge previously mentioned" (*pūrvaṃ yā kathitā pramā*) is probably the condition of pure consciousness, of the absolute "I" which is beyond the universe, while holding it within itself, as described in *TĀ*, tenth *āhnika* (*śl.* 264ff.). Abhinava returns to this in *śl.* 64-65, quoted below.

27. *TĀ* 11.62-65 (p. 61):

prameyamānamātṛṇāṃ yad rūpam uparisthitam//62//
pramātmā sthito 'dhvāyaṃ varṇātmā dṛśyatāṃ kila/
ucchalatsaṃvidāmātraviśrāntyāsvādayoginaḥ//63//
sarvābhidhānasāmarthyād aniyantritaśaktayaḥ/
sṛṣṭāḥ svātmasahotthe 'rthe dharāparyantabhāgini//64//
āmṛśantaḥ svacidbhūmau tāvato 'rthān abhedataḥ/
varṇaughās te pramārūpāṃ satyāṃ bibhrati saṃvidam//65//

In his commentary upon these *śloka*s, Jayaratha, referring to Bhartṛhari's definition of *paśyantī*—whch is, according to this text, that level of consciousness peculiar to the *varṇa*s—states that this collective whole of phonemes which, at this level, is free of duality since time, there, has not yet intervened, forms, on the plane of *śuddhāvidyā* (that of *paśyantī*), objectivity, that is, all the *tattva*s as arising within the supreme consciousness, not different from it. Their essence, he writes, is a synthetic awareness of objectivity as covered by the supreme "I-ness" as consciousness, as abiding in the absolute, and at the same time as the seed, the basis, of the manifestation; thus they bring about the transition from the absolute to the relative and, on the side of the Word, from the primal Word to the lower forms of speech, down to the level of language, thereby endowing it with efficacy.

Abhinavagupta, further in this same *āhnika* (ibid., 72ff.), stresses this vital role of phonemes at the level of the supreme Word as the foundation of the subsequent levels of speech. We have already quoted (*supra*, chap. 4, p. 184) *śl.* 66-71:

> 'Therefrom only,' he says, 'are produced the phonemes of the realm of *māyā*. The other phonemes, free from the conventions which give their efficacy to those of *māyā*, are considered as being knowledge itself. One whose knowledge is obstructed, who is stupid, will never be able to understand what other people say: grasping only the succession of [sounds, and not their meaning], he will repeat them like a parrot. For, to understand them one must have knowledge, which implies the possession of freedom. The one into whom this inner knowledge arises, together with the suppression of all obstacles that might appear, this one is a knower, able to master the multitude of the phonemes which go on to form sentences and so forth.'[28]

It is therefore quite clear that if the knower is endowed with the faculty of intelligent use of language, and thereby with

---

(that is, immersed therein): *ahantācchāditedantaparāmarśasāra*. Then they bring forth the universe. They are the basis of consciousness, of the supreme reality, which is that wherein abides (i.e., which is beyond) the triad of knower, knowledge, and known.

28. *TĀ* 11.72-76a, vol. 7/2, p. 57-59:

yata eva ca māyīyā varṇāḥ sūtiṃ vitenire/
ye ca māyīyavarṇeṣu vīryatvena nirūpitāḥ//72//
saṅketanirapekṣās te prameti parigṛhnatām/
tathā hi paravākyeṣu śruteṣvāvriyate nijā//73//
pramā yasya jaḍo 'sau no tatrārthe 'bhyeti mātṛtām/
śukavat sa paṭhaty eva paraṃ tatkramitaikabhāk//74//
svātantryalābhataḥ svākyapramālābhe tu boddhṛtā/
yasya hi svapramābodho vipakṣodbhedanigrahāt//75//
vākyādivarṇapuñje sve sa pramātā vaśībhavet

knowledge, this is due to his possessing the basic elements of speech that are the phonemes, and to his possessing also the higher levels of speech, *parā* and *paśyantī*. It is also due to their being dependent upon, and receiving their power from, "non-māyic" phonemes that these "māyic" phonemes possess an efficacy leading to cognition and, if their user wishes, to salvation. This efficacy of the *varṇa*s is one aspect of their role as *adhvan*. In practice, they will serve this purpose through the ritual and/or mystic realization (due to creative meditation, *bhāvanā*) of the *parāvāc* nature of the phonemes. Their role is thus similar to that which we saw in the previous chapter, except that the latter expounded the *śāmbhavopāya*, the precognitive intuition of the divine *icchā*, whereas here the level is that of *āṇavopāya*, that of the lower means, hence those *nyāsa*s on "breath" (*prāṇa*), the visualization of the *ādhāra*s in the body, and so forth, that are a necessary part of *dīkṣā*. Particulars on the subject can be found notably in *SvT*, fourth *paṭala*, where the *varṇādhvan* is integrated into "breath": consisting of sound (*śabdātmaka*), the *varṇa*s arise with *prāṇa* and are reabsorbed with it in Śiva (*śl.* 247-48).[29]

In the system of *adhvan*s, phonemes are associated with the other cosmic divisions. They are at first correlated with the thirty-six *tattva*s, the correspondences being the same as in *paśyantī* (since such is the level of this *adhvan*), from earth, *kṣa*, to *sadāśiva*, *ka*, and the vowels from *visarga* to *a* for Śiva/Śakti and, similarly, from *pha* to *cha* and from *ca* to *na*, in *madhyamā*, for the *mālinī*.[30] That phonemes should be associated with the *tattva*s is quite natural in a system of phonematic emanation. It is also obvious that but for such association, the *varṇa*s could

---

29. *prāṇa eva varṇādhva sthitaḥ*, says Kṣemarāja (ibid. p. 156).
30. "From *kṣa* onward each phoneme corresponds to one particular *tattva*, beginning from the earth, while to the supreme [principle], Śiva, are said [to correspond] the sixteen phonemes from the *visarga* onward" (*TĀ* 11.49-50, vol. 7/2, p. 40):

tata ekaikavarṇatvaṃ tattve tattve kṣam āditaḥ//41//
kṛtvā śaive pare proktāḥ ṣoḍasārṇā visargataḥ/

For the *mālinī*, cf. *MVT* 4.15-18.

not serve the purpose of the resorption of the universe, which is their primary role as an *adhvan*.

We shall see later how phonemes associate with the other cosmic divisions, and notably with the *kalā*s, with which they have a special affinity since *kalā*s are connected, like them, to the supreme (*para*) aspect of the *ṣaḍadhvan*: *varṇa*s and *kalā*s, as we have seen, arise at the same time in the supreme Godhead.

Mantra

The path of mantras (*mantrādhvan*) is the second (or the penultimate) of the "course of time" (*kālādhvan*). Mantras are a more evolved, lower, form of the energy of Speech than *varṇa*s—a subtle (*sūkṣma*) and no longer a supreme form, wherein a certain degree of differentiation can be discerned. They correspond, says Kṣemarāja, to an active, comparatively grosser, awareness, where there is at once duality and non-duality.[31]

According to Abhinavagupta, the course of mantras arises during resorption, when subsides that form of—disturbed (*kṣubdha*)—energy peculiar to the *pada*s, which belong to the means of cognition (*pramāṇa*). Mantras, however, are on the side of the knower: *pramātṛbhāgagataḥ* (J., ibid., p. 45): "When [Bhairava] appears in the form of the knower, he is known as the course of mantras:" *mātṛrūpastho mantrādhveti nirūpitaḥ*.[32] "Indeed, when all that is to be expressed is swallowed up by the active self-awareness of consciousness (*cidvimarśena grastā*), the latter, having relinquished that which belongs to the means of cognition—all that which is but the wild sport of the countless host of limited energies—and being intent on the act of thinking (*manana*) and of saving (*trāṇa*),[33] worthy as it is of the action

---

31. See Kṣemarāja's commentary *ad SvT* 4.96 (vol. 2, p. 96): *kiṃcit sthaulyena bhedābhedavimarśanātmakamantrarūpatām*.
32. "There is a twofold pulsation of consciousness: disturbed and undisturbed. The undisturbed, in this case, corresponds to the means of cognition and the path of *pada*s" (J.'s commentary, ibid., p. 47).
33. Traditional explanation of the word mantra. Cf. *infra*, chap. 7, p. 373.

and cognition of Śiva, it enters the course of mantras."[34] This course, higher than that of *pada*s, seems, however, closer to *pada*s than to *varṇa*s, judging from what the same Abhinavagupta said on the subject a few *śloka*s earlier: "It no doubt retains the nature of an active self-awareness (*vimarśātmārūpam*), for such is indeed its own nature [it being the very essence of the stage] of the means of cognition [to which belong the *pada*s], without, however, the disturbance [proper to the means of cognition]. This is why the teaching of the Trika[35] says that mantras and *pada*s are of one and the same nature—the only difference being that the nature [of the former] is disturbed and [the latter] beyond movement (*niḥspanda*)."[36] Abhinavagupta does not indicate at which level of the Word the *adhvan* of mantras is situated, but mantras as knowers are usually placed at the level of *śuddhāvidyā*, therefore of *paśyantī*—which, however, would situate this *adhvan* at the same level as *varṇa*s.[37] But these are details of little import: most important is what *mantrādhvan* consists of and its role in the cosmic manifestation, as well as in the resorption process of the cosmos, or in *dīkṣā*.

What does this course of mantras consist of? It does not, obviously, consist of the whole collection of mantras (in theory

---

34. *TĀ* 11.55b-57a (p. 40):

tathā hi cidvimarśena grastā vācyadaśā yadā//55//
śivajñānakriyāttamananatrāṇatparā/
aśeṣaśaktipaṭalīlīlāmpaṭyapāṭavāt//56//
cyutā mānamayād rūpāt saṃvin mantrādhvatāṃ gatā/

35. That is, says J. (ibid., p. 39), the *MVT* (*śrīpūrvaśāstre*).
36. *TĀ* 11.46-7 (p. 38):

tathāpi na vimarśātmarūpaṃ tyajati tena saḥ/
pramāṇātmavimarśātmā mānavat kṣobhabhāṅ na tu//46//
mantrāṇāṃ ca padānāṃ ca tenoktaṃ trikaśāsane/
abhinnam eva svaṃ rūpaṃ niḥspandakṣobhite param//47//

Niḥspanda does not mean motionless but beyond motion, while permeated by the vibrant energy of *spanda*. This is a latent, internalized *spanda*.

37. Cf. above, p. 342

seventy million in number!), but only of some of them, the list and form of which vary according to traditions and even, within the same sect, according to the texts, or rather according to the end, ritual or otherwise, to which they are put. (All these speculations, as one knows, occur in ritual as well as cosmological contexts).

Mantras (like *pada*s) are arranged, in the *adhvan*, according to the cosmic division of the *kalā*s, which, being the most all-inclusive, tends to be used as a frame for all the others. The particular correspondence established between mantras and the *kalā*s may appear somewhat inconsistent: here *varṇa*s would seem more appropriate, but they are traditionally linked to the *tattva*s, probably as a matter of number. Such lack of symmetry may be due, basically, to the fact that the synthetic system of the *adhvan*s brought together earlier, unrelated, classifications. As we shall see, *varṇa*s are also present in the *kalā*s, and mantras sometimes appear as being nothing else but those *varṇa*s.

Abhinavagupta in *TĀ* (11.51-53)[38] states that there are ten mantras divided amongst the five *kalā*s, from *nivṛtti* to *śāntātītā*. Actually those are in fact but the fifty *varṇa*s divided into ten groups, these being themselves (not equally) distributed amongst the five *kalā*s. To each phoneme is added the nasalization, *bindu*; they become thus as many *bījamantra*s or groups of *bīja*s. Thus we find *kṣam* in the *nivṛttikalā*, the following five mantras: *haṃsaṃṣaṃśaṃ*, *vaṃlaṃraṃyaṃ*, *maṃbhaṃbaṃphaṃpaṃ*, *naṃdhaṃdaṃthaṃtaṃ*, *ṇaṃḍhaṃḍaṃṭhaṃṭaṃ*, distributing into *varga*s, *pratilomyena*, the fricatives, the semi-vowels, and three groups of consonants, located in the *pratiṣṭhākalā*. Next come the two mantras *ñaṃjhaṃjaṃchaṃcaṃ* and *ṅaṃghaṃ*, for the *vidyākalā*; *gaṃkhaṃkaṃ* for the *śāntakalā*, and finally, a mantra consisting of the *visarga, bindu,* and the fourteen diphthongs and vowels from *au* to *a*, all with the *bindu* placed above them, for the *śāntyatītākalā* which, being cosmically situated at the level of Śiva/Śakti, has quite naturally as mantras the same sixteen *svara*s, with the *bindu*. According to

38. Vol. 7/2, pp. 41-42, referred to *infra*, p. 361.

the *MVT* 6.27-29, the same kind of distribution is used in a similar fashion for the fifty phonemes of the *mālinī*. There are thus two different series of "alphabetical" mantras.[39]

If we refer, however, to the distribution of mantras into the five *kalā*s as given in *SvT*, fourth *paṭala* (or in Kṣemarāja's commentary thereon), we find that there are still ten mantras, but quite different ones. Those are the mantras of Śiva-Bhairava's five faces (*vaktra*). They are known especially in the Āgamas as *brahmamantra*s: *sadyojāta*, *vāmadeva*, *aghora*, *tatpuruṣa*, and *īśāna*, each associated with one of Śiva's five *aṅgamantra*s: *hṛdaya*, *śiras*, *śikhā*, *kavaca*, and *astra*.[40] They are distributed as follows: *sadyojāta* and *hṛdaya* in the *nivṛttikalā*; *vāmadeva*, *śiras*, and *śikhā* in the *pratiṣṭhā*; *aghora* and *kavaca* in the *vidyā*; *tatpuruṣa* and *astra* in *śānta*; and *īśāna*, alone, in the *śāntātītākalā*. These mantras of ancient origin are referred to by their names in the *SvT* (and in the *TĀ*), but in rites they are, as a rule, used in the form of their monosyllabic *bīja*s;[41] now, these are also, according to tradition, the *bīja*s of the five elements: *sadyojāta* is *LAṂ* (earth), *vāmadeva*, *VAṂ* (water), *aghora*, *RAṂ* (fire), *tatpuruṣa*, *YAṂ* (air), and *īśāna*, *KṢAṂ*

39. Abhinava quotes this passage of the *MVT* in *TĀ* 16.144-46. It is a passage where he describes a *nyāsa* rite which, as we have said (*supra*, p. 327), is one of the main uses of the *mālinī*. We have seen that Mātṛkā and Mālinī are, for the *MVT*, the two main "alphabetical" deities (p. 307).

40. *Aṅgamantra*s are usually six in number, *netra*, the "eye" (or the eyes) being added to the other five. There are then eleven mantras, this figure being sometimes obtained by adding the *mūlamantra* of Śiva (whose *bīja* is *HAUṂ*) to the other ten, the *netra* being then omitted.

The *mantrādhvan*, in the Āgamas, consists of eleven—and not ten—mantras; cf. *SP*3.

On the interesting and scarcely known subject of the *aṅga*s, or the "limbs," that is, the parts of the *mūrti* of Śiva—but they are also his powers or else the parts of his mantra—see H. Brunner's study, "Les membres de Śiva," *Asiatische Studien/Etudes Asiatiques* XL.2 (1986): 89-132, which sheds light and provides much needed information on this difficult issue.

41. These mantras are usually given as *oṃ hṛdayāya namaḥ*, *oṃ śirase svāhā*, *oṃ śikhāyai vauṣaṭ*, *oṃ kavacāya huṃ*, and *oṃ astrāya phaṭ*. The *bīja*s noted above are, according to our texts, those used for *dīkṣā*, and so forth. They are not the *bīja*s used for the worship of Śiva, which differ by applying different vowels to one single consonantal base.

(ether). Abhinava states this at the beginning of *TĀ*, eleventh *āhnika* (*śl.* 8 to 31), where he correlates the five *kalā*s and the five elements which, in this perspective, are regarded as "pervading" (*vyāpaka*)[42] the whole cosmos. He notes—referring to the *Kalottarāgama* (therefore to a dualistic text)—that these five mantras are the "mantric body," *mantratanu*, of the five "faces" of Śiva.[43] The *SvT*, however, summing up the *ṣaḍadhvan* (4.198-200), following its description of the five *kalā*s as used in the course of *dīkṣā*, numbers eleven mantras: *mantrā ekadaśa jñeyāḥ*, which means that, like the Āgamas,[44] it includes either the *mūlamantra* or, rather, according to Kṣemarāja's commentary (ibid., p. 121-22), the sixth *aṅgamantra*, *netra*, which would be in the *śāntātītākalā*, not as a distinct mantra but merged with the *īśāna* mantra (which seems indeed, in this case, to be considered as the *mūlamantra*). One should bear in mind, however, that the exposition of the *SvT* is not of a theoretical or cosmological kind, but of a ritual one: it deals with the ritualistic, meditative, and yogic practices (linked with the movement of breath and the *kuṇḍalinī*) of *dīkṣā*. Therefore some of its elements may vary according to the particular requirements of rites.

The *SvT*, on the other hand, after showing how through ritual practice a link is created between *ṣaḍadhvan* and *prāṇa* (cf. above, p. 337)—the latter being on this occasion assimilated with *haṃsa*, the "median breath" (*madhyaprāṇa*) which rises or stops with the *kuṇḍalinī*—describes the movement of the *mantrādhvan* as divided in eleven stages: those of the *uccāra* of *OṂ—a,u,m*, *bindu*, *ardhacandra*, *nirodhikā*, *nāda*, *nādānta*,

---

42. For this term, cf. *supra* p. 103, n. 51.
43. *TĀ* 11.19-20 (vol. 7/2, p. 11-2):

śrīmatkalottāradau ca kathitaṃ bhūyasā tathā/
pañcaitāni tu tattvāni yair vyāptam akhilaṃ jagat//19//
pañcamantratanau tena sadyojātādi bhanyate/
īśānāntaṃ tatra tatra dharādigaganāntakam//20//

Cf. also *TĀ* 4.93. Here the five mantras appear as a means to infuse the whole manifestation in each of its elements: *sarvasarvātmakatā*.
44. Cf. *SP*3, introduction, p. xviii, and p. 244, n. 198.

śakti, *vyāpinī*, and *samanā*,[45] beyond which (therefore outside the *adhvan*) there is yet *unmanā*. It shows next (*śl.* 257-60) how yogins can associate the movement of *haṃsa*, the "unstruck" and eternal sound,[46] with the enunciation of the eleven stages of the *uccāra* of *OṂ*. To describe this movement of the eleven stages of the *mantrādhvan* as uninterrupted (*nitya*) means considering it as more than a ritual operation necessarily limited in time; it means considering it as one aspect of the "cosmo-theandric" structure of the universe. *SvT* chapter 4, however, is not concerned with cosmogony but with the ritual yoga of *dīkṣā*; a characteristic feature of the *SvT*, however, as of all the Tantric texts we are studying here, is to mix up these two levels, usually making it impossible to tell which served as a basis for the other: are such metaphysical speculations based on ritual and/or yogic practices, or is it the other way round?

But let us proceed with the *vācakādhvan*.

Pada

The third, lowest, aspect of the "expressing" (*vācaka*) half of the sixfold course is that of the *pada*s: *padādhvan*. I do not translate *pada*, for neither the term *word*, its most frequent sense, nor any other term, is able to convey the meanings of *pada* in the *ṣaḍadhvan*, where it may be a word, or a syllable, or a group of syllables, sometimes even a sentence. It would thus, in truth, not differ very much from a mantra, as we shall see. The term *pada* also means portion or division: this is rather how it appears here. From the grammarian's point of view,

---

45. *SvT* 4.254 (vol. 2, p. 159):

. . . . . . mantrādhvānaṃ nibodha me//253//
mantraikādaśikā yā tu sā ca haṃse vyavasthitā/
padaikādaśikā sa ca prāṇe carati nityaśaḥ//254//
akāraś ca ukāraś ca makāra bindur eva ca/
ardhacandro nirodhī ca nādo nādānta eva ca//255//
śaktiś ca vyāpinī caiva samanaikādasī smṛtā/

46. Which is why, notably, the *praṇava OṂ* is preceded by *ha anacka* = *h*: *hakāras tu smṛtaḥ prāṇaḥ* (*śl.* 257). On this point, cf. *SP*, 3, p. 380, n. 424, and infra, ch. 7, p. 404, n. 68.

pada is a word, but also, more generally, it is a unit made up of a letter or of letters and having a meaning.[47]

As we have seen (*supra*, pp. 332-35), the *padas* stand for the "gross" aspect of the *kālādhvan*, where there is an awareness of the differentiation.[48] While still related, like *varṇas* and mantras, to the knower aspect (*pramātṛbhāga*) of reality, *padas* belong, however, to a stage where reality, prior to its producing objectivity which hides, as it were, its higher nature, first generates within itself the modality of cognition or of its means (*pramāṇa*), preceding the appearing of objectivity to which it applies. "That aspect of the path which, while pertaining to the aspect of the knower, is in the nature of knowledge, is called *pada*, owing to [this path] being permeated by understanding, comprehension (*avagama*)," says Abhinavagupta in the *TĀ*.[49] This is a moment, Jayaratha explains (ibid., p. 37), when the knower experiences a disturbance, for he is directed toward external things[50]—either because from the objective world he

47. For the various meanings of *pada*, cf. L. Renou, *Terminologie Grammaticale du Sankrit* (pp. 193-95 and 445-47) or K. V. Abhyankar, *Dictionary of Sanskrit Grammar, s.v. pada.*

Pada is defined in the *Vājasaneyī Prātiśākhya* (3.1) as "[that which has a meaning" (*arthaḥ padam*), which is interpreted by Uvaṭa as "that by which an object or a sense is meant" (*gamyate 'rtho anena*), relating it thus to *padyate*. J. (*ad TĀ*, 11.44) refers precisely to this interpretation of the word *pada* to vindicate that this *adhvan* corresponds to the level of cognition. In the *ṣaḍadhvan*, the *padas* serve the purpose of bringing about objectivity, objects: *artha*.

48. Kṣem., *ad SvT* 4.96 (vol. 2, p. 51): *tato 'pi sthaulyena bhedavimarśāvagamakapadarūpatayā bhānti.*

49. *TĀ* 11.44 (vol. 7/2, p. 37):

yat pramāṇātmakaṃ rūpam adhvano mātṛbhāgagam/
padaṃ hy avagamātmatvasamāveśāt tad ucyate//

In this passage, Abhinava follows the *adhvans* from the lower stage: after the three aspects belonging to the "known," to the *deśādhvan*, the course, with the *padas*, becomes permeated with knowledge before going back to the knower. See also ibid., *śl.* 57: *pramāṇarūpatām etya prayāty adhvā padātmatām*, "When it takes on the nature of the means of cognition, the path enters the condition of *pada*."

50. *pramātrāṃśāśrayanena pramāṇātmakaṃ bāhirmukhyāt prakṣubdham adhvano rūpaṃ tat padam ucyate.*

goes back to interiority (in resorption, therefore in *dīkṣā*), or because, in the cosmogony, he becomes open to the exteriority he brings forth within himself. It is in this sense that in the *pada*s objectivity becomes known (*padyate jñāyate 'nenārthāḥ ity avagamātmakaṃ padam*).[51] As noted above (p. 344), there is not much difference between the course of *pada*s and that of mantras: the knower (*pramātṛ*) and the self-awareness (*vimarśa*) predominate in both cases, but in the course of *pada*s there are still found (or are appearing) thought-constructs, *kalpana*, and sequentiality (or temporality): *krama*, that is, elements belonging to duality. "When it takes on the nature of the means of cognition, the path enters the condition of the *pada*s. The agent of cognition, indeed, abides there, uniting with a number of phonemes. This union belongs to temporality, and even has the nature of discourse (*saṃjalpātmakam*).[52] It forms thus the very essence of discursive thought (*vikalpa*). There, all that belongs to experiencing (*bhoga*) becomes henceforth manifest. This is why our Master said that the course of *pada*s is of the nature of the means of cognition."[53] At this level appear the characteristic features—temporality and discursive thought—of language. We are thus indeed at the junction, as it were, of the plane of the "expressing" Word and of that of the objectivity which is "to be expressed." What is found in the *pada*s in this respect is not unlike what we have seen regarding the levels of the Word from

---

51. Ibid., p. 37.
52. In chapter 2 we translated *saṃjalpa* as "inner murmur." The term means also "talk," "conversation," the emphasis always being on the sequential, discursive aspect of speech.
53. *TĀ* 11.57b-59 (vol. 7/2, p. 47-48):

prāmāṇarūpatām etya prayāty adhvā padātmatām//57//
tathā hi mātur viśrāntir varṇān saṅghaṭya tān bahūn/
saṃghaṭṭanaṃ ca kramikaṃ saṃjalpātmakam eva tat//58//
vikalpasya svakaṃ rūpaṃ bhogāveśamayaṃ sphuṭam/
ataḥ pramāṇatārūpaṃ padam asmadgurur jagau//59//

Cf. *TĀ* 16.250: *vikalpa kilaḥ saṃjalpamayo yat sa vimarśakaḥ:* "discursive thought consists of discourse, and thereby is an activity of consciousness."

parā to *madhyamā*, where an inner expression (*antarabhilāpa*) arising in the supreme Word, in consciousness, gradually becomes more concrete and subject to temporality until it comes, together with discursive knowledge and thought, down to empirically expressed speech. But, since "knowledge cannot arise if it is deprived of an [objective] support," as Jayaratha states when commenting upon the passage from the *TĀ* with which we are presently dealing,[54] concurrently with knowledge there must appear (or exist) the object of cognition, *prameya*, namely that which makes the remaining portion of the *ṣaḍadhvan*: *kalās*, *tattvas*, and *bhuvanas*. Jayaratha states this expressly: the disturbance (*kṣobha*) peculiar to *padas* consists, for the knower, in experiencing objectivity—to experience it, *bhoga*, that is, to feel its pleasant or unpleasant quality. However, before we examine the three courses of objectivity, we must examine first what comprises the *padas*: as we shall see, they are variously described.

Regarding the ritual placing (*nyāsa*) of the *padas*, the *MVT* (6.18b), quoted by Abhinava (*TĀ* 16.233), says that these "are in this case of two types, according to whether they are divided into *vargas* or into *vidyās* (*padāni dvividhāny atra vargavidyāvibhedataḥ*). The division into *vargas*, mentioned by Abhinava in *TĀ* 11.51-53 is that of the groups or classes of the fifty phonemes of the *varṇasamāmnāya*. These are distributed between the five *kalās*, as was the case with the *varṇas*, from which these *padas*, these "words," hardly differ. Thus we have the *pada kṣa* in the *nivṛttikalā*; five *padas* in the *pratiṣṭhā*: *hasaṣaśa*, *valaraya*, and so on, up to *ṇaḍhaḍaṭhaṭa*; two *padas* in the *vidyākalā*: *ñajhajachaca* and *ṅagha*; one *pada* in the *śānta*: *gakhaka*; and finally one *pada* in the *śāntātītākalā*, consisting of the sixteen vowels from *visarga* to *a*. The *kalās* are arranged in ascending order, and the *padas*, similarly, consist of phonemes arranged from the final one to the initial. *Padas*, in this case, are "words" in that they can, formally, be treated as such: they can be given a termination or inflection—*vibhakty-*

54. *jñānaṃ na jāyate kiṃcid upastambhanavarjitam* (ibid., p. 49).

ānta, to quote the *Mahābhāṣya.*[55] But they do not convey any meaning (*artha*), or at least none but in the sense of *vācya*, the objective portion, "to be expressed," of the manifestation; so this is a metaphysical and not a grammatical interpretation of *pada*, although (as always!) based on grammatical notions. Insofar as they somehow appear as words, constituent parts of language, the *pada*s constitute a stage of the Word lower than the stage of mantras and lower still than the *varṇa*s. They nonetheless extend, as the latter, up to the highest *kalā*, that of Śiva, but all the *adhvan*s arise from, or lead to, the Supreme.

The other form of the *pada*s mentioned for the *nyāsa* by the *MVT* is that of the *vidyā*s—which, as one knows, are generally the mantras of the female deities. Here, these *vidyā*s are the mantras of the three goddesses, Parā, Parāparā, and Aparā, the main triad of the Trika.[56] Like the previous *pada*s, these *vidyā*s are divided and distributed between the constituent elements of the cosmos, in the present case, the *tattva*s. The *vidyā* of Parā is *SAUḤ.* It breaks up into *SA* for the *tattva*s from *prakṛti* to *māyā*, *AU* for those from *śuddhavidyā* to *sadāśiva*, and *visarga* for Śiva: the *pada*s, here, effect the pervasion, the *vyāpti*, of the cosmos by the *bījamantra SAUḤ* as it is described in *MVT* 4.25. The *vidyā* of Parāparā is a long mantra: it is a variant of the *vyomavyāpin* (which we shall see below) broken up into nineteen *pada*s of various length, distributed between the seven groups of *tattva*s, from the earth up to Śiva.[57] The *vidyā* of Aparā is *HRĪḤ HUṂ PHAṬ, PHAṬ*, pervading the *tattva*s from *pṛthivī* to *prakṛti*; *HUṂ*, those from *puruṣa* to *māyā*; and *HRĪḤ*, those from *śuddhavidyā* to *sadāśiva.* The *pada*s of Aparā, the lowest of the three goddesses, do not

55. Pāṇini's (1.4, 14) definition of the word (*pada*) is: "A form ending with [a termination included in the shortened utterance] *'sup'* or *'tin'*[is known as] *pada* ['inflected word']" (*suptiṇantaṃ padam*).

56. See A. Sanderson, "Maṇḍala," quoted above.

57. For their distribution, see *TĀ* 16.213-216a, where they are given as being used for the *nyāsa* of the *tattva*s (performed "following the flow of introversion"). Abhinava refers here also to *MVT* 4.18-23, which, however, gives the correspondences *tattva/pada* "following the flow of extraversion—or manifestion" (*sṛṣṭikrameṇa*): from Śiva (*oṃ*) to the earth (*phaṭ*).

extend up to Śiva, and are distributed (according to *MVT* 4.24), between the four cosmic spheres (*aṇḍa*), which do not extend beyond *sadāśiva*.[58]

Finally, there is another, probably more widespread, way of reckoning *padas*, where they are eighty-one in number. As one may remember,[59] that is the number of *padas* (in fact, of *ardhamātrās*, half moraes) into which the Sanskrit alphabet can be divided. It is also the number of the constituent squares of the *vastumaṇḍala*. Here it is the number of the constituent parts of the mantra *vyomavyāpin*, a formula which is held as important in āgamic Śaivism as well as in the texts with which we are dealing here. In dualistic Āgamas, the eighty-one *padas* are precisely those of this mantra, distributed into groups of one, eleven, twenty, twenty-one, and twenty-eight (that is, eighty-one altogether) between the five *kalās*, from *śāntātītā* to *nivṛtti*.[60] Maheśvarānanda gives the same mantra and the same distribution in the *Parimala* on the *MM* (27).

The *SvT* also counts eighty-one *padas* similarly distributed among the five *kalās*, but they are in fact entirely different ones. They consist of the nine following phonemes: *oṃ*, *ha*, *ra*, *kṣa*, *ma*, *la*, *va*, *ya*, and *ū*, considered as the respective *vācakas* of the *tattvas* of *śakti*, *sadāśiva*, *īśvara*, *śuddhāvidyā*, *māyā*, *kāla*, *kalā*, *niyati*, and *puruṣa*, and of the group of *tattvas* from *prakṛti* to *pṛthivī* (*SvT* 5.5-7, vol. 3, pp. 3-5), the whole of which encompasses the whole manifestation.[61] These nine phonemes are

---

58. Cf. chart, p. 358.
59. Cf. above, chap. 3, pp. 163-65.
60. The same indications are found in Śrīkaṇṭha's *Ratnatraya* (*śl.* 93ff., p. 38), as well as in Śrīkumāra (but with a somewhat different system) in his commentary upon the *Tattvaprakāśa*, where (pp. 39-41), he enumerates the words "which the *vyomavyāpin* consists of."

    There is also, in the Āgamas, a distribution into ninety-four *padas*. For the *vyomavyāpin* in the Āgamas, see the *SP*3, intro., p. xviii and pp. 240-43, where H. Brunner gives the sequence of the *vyomavyāpin* in full and describes how it is used. Cf. also *Rauravāgama*, 1, ch. 10 (vol. 1, p. 186), where the words of the *vyomavyāpin* are explained.
61. The *kañcukas* missing from this list: *vidyā* and *rāga*, are supposed to be included in those mentioned, and *OṂ* is supposed to stand for both Śiva and Śakti—Kṣemarāja (ibid., p. 7): *śaktir iti śaktitattvaṃ paramaśivarūpam*.

repeated nine times, but with the difference that, through cyclic permutations, the *pada oṃ* occupies the first place in the first group, then the second one in the second group, and so forth, and finally the last one in the ninth, so that the eighty-one *pada*s taken all together begin and end with the *praṇava oṃ*. This collective whole is called *vidyārāja*, the king of the *vidyā*s.[62] Starting and ending with *oṃ* and encompassing the cosmos, the course of *pada*s can thus be used to return to the Absolute, to "purify" the manifestation from the earth up to Śiva, and, simultaneously, to purify the disciple who receives the *dīkṣā*.

The *SvT*, moreover, describes the *pada*s of the *vidyārāja* as forming a diagram bringing together the nine groups of nine *pada*s, taking up successively their permutations. Therefore each group of nine *pada*s reads from the upper left angle, then downward, turning round, upward and back, counter-clockwise, finally reaching the center, the whole diagram being itself traversed in the same way, that is, *pratilomyena*. Since the square is oriented, one moves from North-East to North, to North-West, and so on, finally from the East toward the center; *oṃ*, skipping one place in each of the nine squares, indicates each time the proper direction. An adept following this course[63] will move with the center of each square or that of the whole diagram on his left, which is the opposite of the regular *pradakṣina*, such reversal being due, possibly, to the fact that the process here is that of resorption.[64] Here is the diagram as printed with the commentary on the *SvT* (vol. 2, p. 57):

62. The series of nine syllables that are used to make it up—*h, r, kṣ, m, l, v, y, ū*, and *oṃ*—if taken without the supporting vowels, appears as a variant of the *navātmamantra* of Bhairava: *RHKṢLVYŪṂ* (given, for instance, in *TĀ*, 30.11-16), which is to be found in the Kula-related traditions—cf., for instance, *YH* 3.102 and *Dī ad loc.*

63. Which is quite possible, since that is a very large *maṇḍala*.

64. A philosophical interpretation of this diagram will be found in C. Conio's study "Les diagrammes cosmogoniques selon le *Svacchandatantra*—perspectives philosophiques," in *Mantras et Diagrammes rituels dans l'Hindouisme*, pp. 99-113.

EAST

prakṛti *sadāśiva* *īśvara*

N.E. S.E.

OṂ	*HA*	*RA*	*Ū*	*OṂ*	*RA*	*Ū*	*HA*	*OṂ*
YA	*Ū*	*KṢA*	*YA*	*HA*	*KṢA*	*YA*	*RA*	*KṢA*
VA	*LA*	*MA*	*VA*	*LA*	*MA*	*VA*	*LA*	*MA*
Ū	*HA*	*RA*	*Ū*	*HA*	*RA*	*Ū*	*HA*	*RA*
OṂ	*YA*	*KṢA*	*YA*	*OṂ*	*KṢA*	*YA*	*KṢA*	*OṂ*
VA	*LA*	*MA*	*VA*	*LA*	*MA*	*VA*	*LA*	*MA*
Ū	*HA*	*RA*	*Ū*	*HA*	*RA*	*Ū*	*HA*	*RA*
YA	*VA*	*KṢA*	*YA*	*LA*	*KṢA*	*YA*	*MA*	*KṢA*
OṂ	*LA*	*MA*	*VA*	*OṂ*	*MA*	*VA*	*LA*	*OṂ*

NORTH *puruṣa* SOUTH *śuddha-vidyā*

N.W. S.W.

niyati *kāla* *māyā*

WEST

For ritual uses, this diagram, called Navanābhamaṇḍala, consists of nine eight-petalled lotuses placed, like the portions of the above diagram, in a square of the usual type for a *maṇḍala.* The *pada*s are written in the order seen above on the petals and at the center of each lotus. The *SvT* (5.19ff., vol. 3, p. 11ff.), describes, for the *padadīkṣā,* the drawing and worship of this *maṇḍala.* It should be 224 *aṅgula* in size:[65] 224 is, for this text, the number of the *bhuvana*s; and thus Kṣemarāja describes this diagram as a "reflection of the course of the worlds" (*bhuvanādhvapratibimbarūpam*; ibid., p. 11), underlining in this way the close relation of the course of *pada*s to that of the *bhuvana*s.

But now we must come to this second part of the sixfold course, that of *kalā*s, *tattva*s, and *bhuvana*s.

65. About 4.5 meters.

Kalā, Tattva, Bhuvana

In contrast with the three courses we have just seen, which constitute what is usually termed the *kālādhvan*, the "way of time," the next three constitute the so-called "way of space" or of extension (*deśādhvan*), a term which stresses its more manifest, more concrete character. While the first three belong to the "expressing" aspect (*vācaka*) of the Word and to *vimarśa*, these belong to *prakāśa*[66] and constitute the portion "to be expressed" (*vācya*) of the manifestation: the knowable, the objectivity (*prameya*), which the Word brings into existence—it being understood, however, that these *adhvan* nevertheless have a purely metaphysical, nonempirical nature. They form, as described by Abhinavagupta, a lower aspect[67] of the cosmos, at once subordinated and parallel to the other one. This symmetry, however, is rather artificial. It is likely, indeed, that the *kalā*s, *tattva*s, and *bhuvana*s were at first three different, unrelated, cosmic classifications, which were subsequently arranged in a comprehensive but not entirely consistent system.[68] It is all the less so since the three series of *kalā*s, *tattva*s, and *bhuvana*s are combined with the system of the four cosmic spheres (*aṇḍa*), and since they are correlated with other classifications—knowers (*pramātṛ*), modalities of consciousness, and so forth—and lastly, since the various deities or divinized energies of the Śaiva Tantras are added to them. The correlations between these three *adhvan*s and the other three, through the presence or "pervasion" (*vyāpti*) of phonemes, mantras and *pada*s, together with their subdivisions in the *kalā*s, *tattva*s, and *bhuvana*s, seems artificial as well. While the whole pattern, embracing the cosmos, looks quite impressive, its lack of homogeneity and consistency is obvious.

---

66. It has been pointed out above (p. 177, n. 31) that there is a link—which at first may seem paradoxical—between *artha* and *prakāśa*.
67. This is not so in dualistic Āgamas, where the way of "sound" (*śabdātmaka*) appears on the contrary as subordinated to the other one: cf. H. Brunner, *op. cit.*, p. xvii.
68. There was, as it seems, a "way of the worlds" (*bhuvanādhvan*) among the Lākulas, a group of Śaiva ascetics belonging to the Pāśupatas.

As we have already stated on different occasions, the elements we meet here—formulas, mental representations, and ritual or yogic practices—were surely at first used for ritualistic purposes only—mainly for the various *dīkṣā*—and then were later brought together and more or less organized into a comprehensive system. This system appears in its most perfected form in the *TĀ*, a work whose primary purpose indeed was to develop an abstract, general scheme combining in a reinterpreted way the metaphysics of the *ŚS* and the Pratyabhijñā with the rites, beliefs, pantheons and speculations of the early Tantras.

Kalā

In the eleventh *āhnika* of the *TĀ*, dealing more especially with the way of *kalā*s (*kalādhvan*), Abhinava defines the latter in three different ways. First, he says that each *kalā* brings together within itself a group of similar *tattva*s, differing from those of the other groups; such a definition is said to come from Śiva (*śāmbhava*). But, Abhinava adds, according to some (*kecid āhuḥ*), *kalā*s also differentiate owing to the predominance in each of a very subtle energy (*susūkṣmikā*), abiding in the *tattva*s that it brings together. Such is the case, for instance, with the sustaining, upholding (*dhārikā*) energy in the earth *tattva*. These two assumptions, he says, are not mutually exclusive. But, he adds, others say (*anye vadanti*) that a *kalā* is a conventional (*samayāśraya*) group yet quite valid because it was conceived by Śiva (*śivena kalpita*) as an aid to understanding *dīkṣā* and so forth (*dīkṣādau sukhasaṃgrahanārthaḥ*).[69] This is an interesting definition, for Abhinava thereby seems to accept that the main *raison d'être*, and probably (as we just said) the origin of the *adhvan* system, is to be found not so much in cosmological speculations as in ritual, even though this cosmic *kalā* pattern afforded subsequently a useful framework for cosmogonic descriptions, providing them with five great

---

69. *TĀ* 11.6 (vol. 7/2, p. 3-4):

anye vadanti dikṣādau sukhasaṃgrahaṇārthataḥ/
śivena kalpito vargaḥ kaleti samayāśrayaḥ//6//

The Sixfold Path According to the *Tantrāloka* and the *Mālinīvijayottaratantra*

kalā	*tattva*	*bhuvana*	*varṇa*		mantra		*pada*
			śabdarāśi	*mālinī*	(*śabdarāśi*)	(*mālinī*)	
śāntātītā	1 + 1: Śiva + Śakti	0	16: *aḥ* to *a*	16: *ga* to *na*	1: *aḥ* to *aṃ*	1: *gaṃ* to *naṃ*	1: *aḥ* to *a*
śāntā	3: *śuddhavidyā*, *īśvara*, *sadāśiva*	18	3: *ga*, *kha*, *ka*	3: *i*, *ṅa*, *gha*	1: *gaṃkhaṃ-kaṃ*	1: *iṃṅaṃghaṃ*	1: *gakhaka*
vidyā	7: from *puruṣa* to *māyā*	28	7: *ña* to *gha*	7: *ma* to *e*	2: *ñaṃjhaṃ-jaṃchaṃcaṃ*, *ṅaṃghaṃ*	2: *thaṃdhaṃ-* etc.	2: *ñajhaca*, *ṅagha*
pratiṣṭhā	23: water to *prakṛti*	56	23: *ha* to *ṭa*	23: *da* to *jha*	5: *haṃsaṃṣaṃ-śaṃ*, etc.	5: *daṃauṃoṃ-aiṃeṃ*, etc.	5: *hasaṣaśa*, *varalaya*, etc.
nivṛtti	1: earth	16	1: *kṣa*	1: *pha*	1: *kṣaṃ*	1: *phaṃ*	1: *kṣa*
5	36	118	50	50	10	10	10

The Sixfold Course According to *Svacchandatantra*, Fourth *paṭala*

kalā	*tattva*	*bhuvana*	*varṇa*	*mantra*		*pada*	cosmic spheres	*devatā*
nivṛtti	1: earth	108: from *kālāgni* to *vīrabhadra*	1: *kṣa*	2: *sadyojāta*, *hṛdaya*	*A*	28: from *oṃ* to *ū*	*pṛthivyaṇḍa*	Brahmā
pratiṣṭhā	23: water to *prakṛti*	65: *guhya* to *yoga*	23: *ha* to *ṭa*	3: *vāmadeva*, *śiras*, *śikhā*	*U*	21: from *ya* to *la*	*prakṛtyaṇḍa*	Viṣṇu
vidyā	7: *puruṣa* to *māyā*	27: 8: linked to *puruṣa* and *rāga* 9: to *niyati* and *vidyā* 3: to *kāla* & *kalā* 7: to *māyā*	7: *ña* to *gha*	2: *aghora*, *kavaca*	*M*	20: *ma* to *kṣa*	*māyāṇḍa*	Rudra
śāntā	3: *śuddhavidyā* to *sadāśiva*	17: 1: *śuddhavidyā* 15: for *īśvara* 1: for *sadāśiva*	3: *ga*, *kha*, *ka*	2: *tatpuruṣa* and *astra*	*ardhacandra* to *nādānta*	11: *ra* to *ha*	*śaktyaṇḍa*	Īśvara
śāntātītā	1 (+ 1): *śiva* / *śakti*	16: subtle *bhuvanas*	16: from *visarga* to *a*	1: *īśāna*	*śakti* to *samanā*	1: *oṃ*		Śiva
5	36	224	50	10	10	81	4	

divisions into which could fall all the other elements, related to the word or to objects, of which manifestation is comprised.

Thus the *kalā*s appear as bringing together not only the *bhuvana*s but also the *tattva*s, in different groups, each group having some common character due to its qualitative distribution in the cosmos. Five in number, they remind one of a conception already met with (and to which Abhinava returns in this same *āhnika* of the *TĀ*, *śl.* 15-19, referring to the *Kālottarāgama*) and according to which the five elements, earth, water, fire, air, and ether "pervade" the entire cosmos. The way of the *kalā*s can be brought alongside other fivefold divisions, notably those of the modalities of consciousness, as found for instance in *MVT*, chap. 2 (to which J. refers in his commentary on *TĀ*, 11); the *MVT*'s description, interestingly enough, is one of the earliest available of these cosmogonic-cum-ritual speculations.[70]

The *kalā*s, although being (as we have seen, *supra*, p. 334) Śiva's fragmenting energy itself and hence arising from the highest stage, are yet always enumerated starting from the lowest one, that is, following the course of return to the Godhead: this is in accordance with their primary function as pathways toward liberation. We shall therefore look at them in this order. This is how Abhinavagupta describes them at the beginning of *TĀ*, eleventh *āhnika:* "The *nivṛtti*[*kalā*] is that of the earth *tattva.* The *pratiṣṭhā* extends from water to *avyakta* (*prakṛti*). The *vidyā* extends to the [cosmic] dream (*māyā*), and the *śānta* up to *śakti*, thus making the four cosmic spheres (*aṇḍa*). *Śāntātītā* corresponds to the *śiva tattva.* The supreme Śiva is beyond the *kalā*s."[71] Let us take up each of these.

---

70. For the dualistic Āgamas, the five *kalā*s are "sections cut off in that very subtle stuff, the *bindu*" (H. Brunner), that is, in the matter of which the higher worlds are made; each *kalā* is identified with one of the five elements (earth, and so forth), which in this case are not *tattva*s in the usual sense, but *dhāraṇā*s, supports of the cosmos. Cf. *SP*3, intro., pp. xiv-xv, and the relevant passages in that book.

    The same is true, as we have seen, for the *Tattvaprakāśa* (*supra*, p. 332).

71. *TĀ* 11.8-9 (vol. 7/2, pp. 4-5):

nivṛttiḥ pṛthivītattve pratiṣṭhāvyaktagocare/
vidyā niśānte śāntā ca śaktyante 'ṇḍam idam catuḥ//8//
śāntātītā śive tattve kalātītaḥ paraḥ Śivaḥ/

The *nivṛttikalā*,[72] the *kalā* of "cessation," is so called presumably because with it the cosmic manifestation ceases to expand further or, as Jayaratha puts it, because it brings to an end this externalization of Śiva that is the manifestation, of which it constitutes the outermost limit (*parāṃ kāṣṭhāṃ bahir mukhatvān nivartakatvena kalayitrī nivṛtty ākhyā*). It corresponds indeed to the earth *tattva*, which arises last in the cosmogonic process.

*Kalā*s arise concurrently with phonemes (cf. above, p. 335), and the *nivṛttikalā* is correlated with the *varṇa* associated with earth: *kṣa* in the system of Śabdarāśi (it should be *pha* in that of the Mālinī—both series of phonemes, Mātṛkā/Śabdarāśi and Mālinī, should indeed be present in the *kalā*s). Abhinava places there but one mantra, *KṢAṂ*, and one *pada, kṣa*. The *SvT* (chap. 4 and 5), as we have seen, associates with it the two mantras *sadyojāta*, (whose *bīja* is indeed *LAṂ*, that of earth), and *hṛdaya* or, if one takes the *vidyārāja* with eighty-one *pada*s, twenty-eight of them from *oṃ* to *ū*.[73] Since the *kalā*s are all-inclusive, they hold, in addition to *tattva*s, the *bhuvana*s, which are here, according to the texts, 56 or 118 in number (cf. *infra*, p. 366). As concerns the cosmic spheres, *nivṛtti* is at the same level as the sphere of earth, *pṛthivyaṇḍa*.[74] Abhinava sums it up in this way: "One *pada*, one mantra, one phoneme, sixteen worlds, earth, [such is the] *nivṛtti*[*kalā*]" (*TĀ* 11.51a).

---

72. It should be noted that the names of the four *kalā*s: *nivṛtti, pratiṣṭhā, vidyā, śānti* (or *śāntā*), are those of the four *kalā*s of *tatpuruṣa* in the system of the thirty-eight *kalā*s of Sadāśiva of dualistic Āgamas. Cf. Raurāgama, ed. by N. R. Bhatt, vol. 1 (Pondicherry, 1961), chart p. 38. The thirty-eight *kalā*s, in this case, have nothing to do with the five *kalā*s of the *ṣaḍadhvan*.

73. In the Āgamas, the *pada*s alloted to this *kalā* are the last twenty-eight *pada*s of the mantra *vyomavyāpin*—cf. above, p. 000, n. 60, chart 7 of *SP*3. We have seen (*supra*, ibid.) that Maheśvarānanda (*MMP*) also reckons one phoneme, two mantras, and twenty-eight *pada*s in the *nivṛttikalā*.

74. *Aṇḍa*s, cosmic spheres, are, for Abhinavagupta, lower stages of the energy, which encompass and somehow generate the worlds (*bhuvana*s). He refers in this matter to the doctrine of the Āgamas, notably to the Raurāgama (cf. *TĀ*, 8). Thus *aṇḍa*s are not to be found at the highest level of the cosmic reality, except, of course (as in fact stated by Abhinavagupta, *TĀ* 11.14) insofar as the whole manifestation first abides in Śiva: the *aṇḍa*s dwell within him but they do not encompass him.

The second *kalā* is the *pratiṣṭhākalā*.[75] This energy is known as such, says Jayaratha (ibid., p. 3), because it brings about and supports the differentiating activity of the twenty-four *tattva*s, from that of water to *mūlaprakṛti* (*abādimūlāntaṃ tattvacatvarimśater api bhedavyavahāra eva pratiṣṭhānena kalayitrī pratiṣṭhākhyā śaktiḥ*).[76] There the *varṇa*s of *śabdarāśi* are the twenty-three phonemes from *ha* to *ṭa*. Abhinava places there five *bījamantra*s formed out of these twenty-three consonants as we have seen above (p. 349). The *SvT* places the three mantras *vāmadeva*, *śiras*, and *śikhā* there. The *pada*s are, for Abhinava, five in number, and derive from the same groups of phonemes, going from *hasaṣaśa*, *valaraya*, and so forth, to *ṇaḍhaḍaṭhaṭa*. For the *SvT* the *pada*s are twenty-one of the eighty-one *pada*s of the *vidyārāja* (or twenty-one *pada*s of the *vyomavyāpin*, in the Āgamas). The *pratiṣṭhākalā* includes the *tattva*s from water to *prakṛti*, and fifty-six *bhuvanas*.[77] It corresponds to the cosmic sphere (*aṇḍa*) of nature, *prakṛti*, which, includes the same *tattva*s.

The third *kalā* is the *vidyākalā*, that of cognition or wisdom. It is situated between pure manifestation (from *śuddhāvidyā* to Śiva) and impure manifestation issued from *māyā*. Jayaratha (*ad TĀ*, 11) sees there the stage of limited knowledge—this is indeed the level of the *kañcuka*s, the "coats of armor" that limit and enclose the knower. Yet it corresponds to a higher stage than the two former *kalā*s. The *varṇa*s of *śabdarāśi* are seven in number, from *ña* to *gha*. The mantras are either seven in number, from *ÑAṂ* to *GHAṂ*, or two, *aghora* and *kavaca*; and the *pada*s, analogously, will be either *ñajhajachaca* and *ṅagha*, or twenty-one of the eighty-one *pada*s of the *vidyārāja* (or, for the Āgamas, twenty *pada*s of the *vyomavyāpin*).[78] The *tattva*s

75. For Kṣemarāja (*SvT* 4.171, comm., vol. 2, p. 108), this *kalā* is known as such because it is there that abide (*pratitiṣṭhati*) all those *tattva*s that are the source of experiencing, that is, of the life of the senses. The *tattva*s, in this *kalā*, number twenty-three, not twenty-four.

76. Abhinava's brief summary of the *kalā*s (*śl.* 51-53) is elucidated by Jayaratha (ibid., pp. 42-45), who quotes there *MVT* 2.50-57, which the *TĀ* follows.

77. Cf. *SP*, 3, chart 7.

78. For Maheśvarānanda's *Parimala* (*MMP*), the *vidyākalā* is comprised of twenty *pada*s and two mantras, *śikhā* and *aghora*.

are the seven extending from *puruṣa* to *māyā*. The *bhuvana*s are twenty-seven (*SvT* and *MMP*) or twenty-eight (*TĀ*) in number.[79] The cosmic sphere is that of *māyā* (*māyāṇḍa*).

Next comes the *śāntakalā*, the "quiescent," for there it is that the stage of *māyā* becomes "tranquil" (*māyīyapadopaśamana*—J., ibid., p. 3), which means that this stage is transcended or, according to Abhinava (*TS*, chap. 10, pp. 109-10), that there the movement related to the *kañcuka*s subsides. With it are associated three *varṇa*s: *ga*, *kha*, *ka*, and (Abhinava) either three mantras: *GAṂ*, *KHAṂ*, *KAṂ*, or (SvT) both *tatpuruṣa* and *sadyojāta* (*kavaca* and *tatpuruṣa*: *MMP*) and one *pada*, *gakhaka*. This *kalā* embraces the three *tattva*s *śuddhāvidyā*, *īśvara*, and *sadāśiva*, and eighteen *bhuvana*s. It corresponds to the highest cosmic sphere, that of energy, *śaktyaṇḍa*.

Finally, the fifth and last (or first) *kalā* is the *śāntātītā* (or *śāntyatītā*), that which is "beyond the quiescent." It is the most all-inclusive, owing to its being the very energy of Śiva united with Śakti in her limiting, fragmenting action: *śaktir hi na śaktimato bhinnā bhavitum arhati*—"the energy cannot possibly be conceived of as divided from her Master (J. *ad TĀ* 11.53, p. 43). Here, then, the sixteen phonemes abide in Śiva, from *visarga* to *a* (or from *ga* to *na* with the Mālinī). Here again there is but one mantra and one *pada*, consisting (according to J.) of these same phonemes. Alternatively there may be placed the mantra *īśāna* or, in the case of the *vidyārāja*, the *OṂ* located at the center of the *maṇḍala* of eighty-one *pada*s. Whatever the selected form of *mantra* or *pada*, this is always the highest one, since we are here on the supreme stage of the *kalā*s.

Here, the only *tattva* is Śiva inseparably united with Śakti, and there are no more *bhuvana*s since one is beyond worlds. *SvT* 4.196 states, however, that this *kalā* should be meditated upon as still holding sixteen, "subtle," *bhuvana*s: *bhuvanāni tu sūkṣmāni śāntyatīte tu bhāvayet.* Those are actually *bhuvana*s which the adept has to visualize as associated with the *kalā*s, that is, in this case, with the ascending stages of the phonic energy of *OṂ*; the latter, as a mantra abiding in the *śāntyatītākalā*, is necessarily there in the complete form it has

79. Twenty-seven or twenty-eight in the Āgamas: *SP*3, chart 7.

in the yogic *uccāra*, which ends with the *kalā*s from *bindu* to *samanā*, these *kalā*s being accompanied by these "subtle" worlds. Here we are no longer in the realm of the cosmos but of the meditative visualization and of the *uccāra* of the *mūlamantra* by the recipient of *dīkṣā*, whose mind must merge with this *uccāra* in the supreme level of sound, and thereby become free from bondage, become totally pure; we have already said that this *paṭala* of the *SvT* considers the *adhvan*s from the sole perspective—both ritual and yogic—of *dīkṣā*.

Beyond the five *kalā*s there still is the supreme Śiva, that Lord who is, say *SvT* 4.197 and Kṣemarāja, absolutely free, a solid mass of consciousness and bliss, both transcendent and immanent to the universe. He who becomes one with him through the prescribed practices will not be reborn and will be liberated.[80] Abhinavagupta emphasizes the immanence of the Godhead: nothing is extraneous to Him. "All this course," he says, "does not extend outside Bhairava. It is through the latter's complete freedom that the *adhvan* appears as self-existent."[81] Yet the fact remains that it should be traversed, in *dīkṣā* notably, if liberation is to be achieved.

However, one may also follow the other two ways of the *deśādhvan*, those of the *tattva*s or of the *bhuvana*s.

Tattva

Less "subtle," less inclusive than the course of *kalā*s, the course of *tattva*s consists of the thirty-six "realities," that is, cosmic categories or ontic levels of the manifestation, as recorded

---

80. Ibid., vol. 2, p. 123: *śivasyordhve śivo jñeyo yatra yukto na jāyate*//197// comm.: *uttīrṇaśivatattvopari viśvottīrṇaviśvamayacidānandaghanasvacchandabhaṭṭārako yatra vakṣyamāṇayojanikākrameṇa yukto na jāyate mucyate ity ārthaḥ*.

81. *TĀ* 11.54 (vol. 7/2, p. 45):

so 'yaṃ samasta evādvā bhairavābhedavṛttimān/
tatsvātantryāt svatantratvaṃ aśnuvāno 'vabhāsate//54//

Śl. 55 and those following this stanza deal mainly with the *varṇādhvan* and with the nature of the Word as abiding in the supreme knower.

in the Tantras, notably in the Trika texts; Abhinavagupta, indeed, refers in this respect mainly to the *Siddhayogeśvarīmata* (*TĀ*, 9.7) and to the *MVT*.[82] Deriving the word *tattva* from the root *TAN*, to spread, he defines a *tattva* as that which brings together and is inherent to (*vyāpaka*) a collection of qualities or common elements: worlds, and so forth. He indeed classifies them into seven groups according to the hierarchy of knowers (*pramātṛ*) followed by the Trika, extending from Śiva, the Omniscient, down to the *sakala*s, the limited knowers subject to the triple *mala*.[83] As we just saw, the *tattva*s are also distributed, in their traditional order, among the five *kalā*s. Kṣemarāja[84] explains *tattva* as that which spreads (*tananāt tattvam*), that is, which brings forth the manifestation, and he states that, while relating to specific aspects of the manifestation, they are in a general sense, however, that which is the cause of its emergence: they are that wherefrom the modalities of the becoming originate; they are not these modalities proper. So they are energies emanated from and projected by the supreme consciousness upon itself—which is, for the Trika, the very definition of the cosmic manifestation.

Like the *SvT*, Abhinava emphasizes in the *TĀ* the relationship between *tattva*s and *prāṇa*, and especially with that particular *prāṇa* which, rising from the heart to the *dvādaśānta*, is measured out in thirty-six *aṅgula*, and which may be thus easily correlated with the *tattva*s. Meditative practices connected with the movement of breath therefore play an important part in the "purification," or resorption, of the course of *tattva*s. He who follows this pathway in *dīkṣā* will reach thereby the highest level of knowers: the extinction of all desire and repose within the Self.[85] This will be achieved, of course, through yogic-cum-

82. He also refers to the *vidyāpada* of the *Matpār* (ibid., *śl.* 6, p. 6).

83. This is the theme of *TĀ*, tenth *āhnika*. This doctrine is said to be the secret teaching peculiar to the Trika: *trikaśāstraikarahasyam* (ibid., *śl.* 1). It is indeed found notably in *MVT*, 2.

84. In the commentary on *SvT* 4.241-42 (vol. 2, p. 151).

85. *MVT* chap. 2 focuses on the *tattva*s and on that form of liberation that may be attained through them; this is achieved through various "penetrations" or absorptions (*samāveśa*), obtained and experienced

ritual and meditative practices making use of the elements of the way of the Word: *varṇa*s, mantras, or *pada*s. We have seen in effect that the fifty *varṇa*s are precisely the *vācaka*s of the *tattva*s.

Bhuvana

The lowest of the courses is that of the *bhuvana*s, the worlds, (also called *pura*: town, house, dwelling-place). Those are the different hells, earths, or heavens, or the purely spiritual realms, making up the whole manifestation looked at as consisting of various places for the soul to experience what it has earned for itself. The *TĀ*, dealing with them in its eighth *āhnika*, reckons—like the *MVT*—118 of them. But there are 224 *bhuvana*s in the *SvT* (and in a number of Āgamas as well),[86] while it is said in the same text (ibid., 10.3-4, vol. 5, p. 3) that they are in fact countless. All this varies widely.[87] They are distributed between the five *kalā*s, as we have seen. The course of *bhuvana*s, in view of their number, is the longest but probably the easiest one for the spiritually undeveloped.[88] Like the other *adhvan*s, it is traversed upwardly through successive dissolutions of the lower into the next higher, up to Śiva, a process always described as linked with the movement of *prāṇa* and the use of *varṇa*s, mantras, or *pada*s. No course, indeed, can be traversed without recourse to the efficacy of the Word—and this is in fact the only reason for our being concerned with them here.

---

by means of various processes usually belonging to the *āṇavopāya*. One finds there an exposition of the hierarchy of the seven knowers: *sakala*, *pralayākala*, *vijñānākala*, *mantra*, *mantreśa*, *mahāmantreśvara* and *Śiva/Śakti*, correlated with the five modalities of consciousness, from *jāgrat* to *turyātīta*.

86. See also Śrīkumāra's commentary on the *Tattvaprakāśa*.

87. It is noteworthy that the *bhuvanas* are generally presided over by Rudras, which bears evidence of the ancient, rudraic, origin of this cosmological classification.

88. It seems to be, with the *kalādhvan*, the most commonly used for *dīkṣā* in dualistic Śaivism. Cf. H. Brunner, *SP*3, intro., p. xvi.

To bring this chapter to a close, it would not be out of place to examine very briefly those practices by which the initiated adept travels along the six courses, up to Śiva,[89] their ultimate goal: in a *dīkṣā* the adept follows but one complete course. There is a wide range of practices depending upon traditions and also upon the texts, and of course upon the type of *dīkṣā* for which they are used, but they all have a bodily basis: a number of texts describe very clearly how the constituent elements of the *adhvan*s are distributed in the adept's body, and especially that the most inclusive of the divisions, that of the *kalā*s, wherein the others are distributed, divides his body, as it were, from head to foot, into portions corresponding homologously to cosmic divisions.[90] Moreover, these are practices linked with *prāṇa* (and therefore with the *kuṇḍalinī*), since it is the latter which gives life to the human body and to the cosmos alike. The cosmic elements to be "purified" with the help of the *adhvan*s are placed by *nyāsa* in "*prāṇa*" as much as in the human body. We will not attempt here to give even a sketchy account of the various yogic-cum-ritual practices involving the *adhvan*s, for this would take us too far. We have indeed said above, occasionally, how, according to the *TĀ* or the *SvT*, some of these *adhvan*s could operate, notably those more directly related to the Word. I shall therefore add here a few remarks only, referring the reader to the texts which are, if not always very clear, at least readily accessible.

The importance of *prāṇa* in the practice of the *adhvan*s is underlined by Abhinavagupta from the beginning of *TĀ*, sixth *āhnika*: the awakening, *udaya* (that is, the bringing into action, for soteriological purpose) of the *varṇa*s, mantras, and *pada*s, he says, (ibid., *śl.* 5),[91] takes place in the movement of voluntary, or spontaneous, breath." Furthermore, after saying that "the

---

89. Or up to Viṣṇu in the case of the *ṣaḍadhvan* of the Pāñcarātra and so forth.
90. This is especially in evidence in charts 3 and 4 of the *SP*3.
91. *TĀ* 6.5 (vol. 4, pp. 3-4):

adhvā samasta evāyaṃ ṣaḍvidho 'py ativistṛtaḥ//
yo vakṣyate sa ekatra prāṇe tāvat pratiṣṭhitaḥ//5//

single phoneme, consisting of pure sound, abiding in all the phonemes, is the unstruck sound, for nothing can stop it," that "this is the very reality of Bhairava, the essence of [all] conscious beings (*mātṛsadbhāva*),[92] the supreme Goddess, the one and only *akṣara*, wherein merges all that is moveable and immoveable,"[93] Abhinavagupta posits from the start the eternal and omnipresent nature of the supreme Word (*parāvāc*) or, more accurately here, of the initial phoneme *a*, the *anuttara*: any soteriological practice, in this system, as we can see once more, ends up in the union of the adept with the Word-Absolute (which, with respect to worship, is the supreme Goddess). But this can be achieved—at least in the *āṇavopāya*, which is the level of these *ṣaḍadhvan* practices—only through means involving a central role for *prāṇa*. Abhinavagupta then states the position occupied by the various phonemes in the respiratory breath according to whether their "awakening" is "supreme" (and then it is that of the forty-nine *varṇa*s from *a* to *ha*), or "subtle" (and then we have the eighty-one half-morae—which is the number of *pada*s, the practice of which belongs to the "gross" aspect of the Word). The awakening of the phonemes may indeed also be "gross," and in this case they abide in breath as the nine *varga*s. All these practices, briefly described in the *TĀ* (*śl.* 219-51), and which Jayaratha elucidates to some extent (ibid,. pp. 179-203), are based on the resorption of the phonemes and of their subdivisions into the movement of *prāṇa*, these phonetic fragments being themselves correlated with the spans

---

92. *Mātṛsadbhāva* is the name given in the *MVT* (ibid., 8.39-43) both to the supreme Goddess as somehow transcending Parā, Parāparā and Aparā, and to her mantra. Abhinava identifies Mātṛsadbhāva with Kālasaṃkarṣiṇī, the devourer of time, the supreme deity of the *Devyāyāmalatantra*. On this difficult point, cf. A. Sanderson, "Maṇḍala," esp. note, p. 194. According to the *MVT* the mantra of *Mātṛsadbhāva* is *HSKHPHREṂ*; see *infra*, p. 422, n. 110.

93. *TĀ* 6.217-18 (p. 178):

eko nadātmako varṇaḥ sarvavarṇāvibhāgavān/
so 'nastamitarūpatvād anāhata ihoditaḥ//217//
sa tu bhairarasadbhāvo mātṛsadbhāva eṣa saḥ/
parā saikākṣarā devī yatra līnaṃ carācaram//218//

of human and then of cosmic time: this leads to the resorption of time in the breath, and thereby, for the initiate, to the conquest of time and to liberation (and/or to the attainment of supernatural powers).

This practice leads to a realization mainly of a spiritual order, and seems to involve, besides the yogic control of respiration, almost only mental means.[94] *TĀ*, seventh *āhnika*, on the other hand, deals with the "deliberate" processes (*yatnaja*, involving self-effort), used for mantras and *a fortiori* for *pada*s, where also the movement of *prāṇa* comes into play, especially that of respiratory breath. Time, says Abhinavagupta, is based on *prāṇa*, and *prāṇa* pervades the entire body (*prāṇe pratiṣṭhitaḥ kālas tadāviṣṭa ca yat tanuḥ*, *śl.* 65b, vol. 4/2, p. 52). "All the cosmic emanations and resorptions," he says in conclusion, "abide in the awakening and the dissolution of that breath which moves through the body. They differ only insofar as there are differences in breath."[95] As we said above, *TĀ āhnika*s 8 to 11 deal with the *adhvan*s of the *bhuvana*s, *tattva*s, and *kalā*s, each being empowered by the resorption of a lower element into the next higher one, until there occurs the fusion in Śiva. The *adhvan*s are again found in *TĀ*, 15ff., dealing with *dīkṣā*, where the master places them in himself before proceeding to their installation in the disciple, where they are reabsorbed.[96]

The *SvT* also describes various methods to "purify" the

94. Of the same sort is the meditation of the *adhvan*s prescribed in chap. 12 of the *TĀ*, where the disciple must visualize his body as filled with all the *adhvan*s, with all the various forms of time and space implicit in them, with all the deities: "He who is pervaded by this [consciousness] is liberated" (*tadāviṣṭo vimucyate*) *TĀ* 12.6-8).

95. *TĀ* 7.70-71 (p. 56):

atra madhyamasaṃcāriprāṇodayalayāntare//70//
viśve sṛṣṭilayās te tu citrā vāyvantarakramāt/

96. *Adhvan*s may also be placed on the guru's hand—which then becomes the "hand of Śiva," *śivahasta*—and through its touch the disciple's body is infused with Śiva's cosmic force which saturates the hand.

Abhinava says in *TĀ* 16.164-68, that in view of the wide variety of mantras and pathways (*adhvan*s) that may be followed, there are up to 8,540 different forms of *dīkṣā* altogether, and later on (*śl.* 185-6), he adds that for the *MVT* their number extends to as many as 597,800!

*adhvan*s in *dīkṣā*. We cannot review these practices even sketchily, for this would amount to study the whole *dīkṣā* as described in this text that devotes over one thousand *śloka*s thereto. We have seen above (pp. 347-48) how the *mantrādhvan* can be reduced to the *uccāra* of *OṂ*. Regarding the *pada*s, Kṣemarāja, in his commentary on *śl.* 42-43a of the *SvT* (ibid., vol. 3, pp. 31-33) describes a *padadīkṣā* divided into nine grades based upon the nine groups of the *vidyārāja pada*s. With the first set of nine (*praṇavādy ukārāntam*), the two *kalā*s *nivṛtti* and *pratiṣṭhā*, the twenty-five *tattva*s from *pṛthivī* to *prakṛti*, and the first one hundred and sixty-four *bhuvana*s are purified. The phonemes from *kṣa* to *ṭa* associated with these *tattva*s, together with the five mantras corresponding to these two *kalā*s—*sadyojāta*, *hṛdaya*, *vāmadeva*, *śiras*, and *śikhā*—are also purified through the same process, owing to the principle that each form of energy abides within all the others, and that beneath all of them lies the supreme energy, so that, as we said above, any of the six *adhvan*s may lead one to liberation and entails at the same time the purification of the others. The process of the *padadīkṣā* proceeds with the second set of nine from the *vidyārāja*, for the *tattva*s of *puruṣa* and *rāga*, and so forth,[97] on to the last one, which takes everything back to Śiva.

Other *dīkṣā*s—of the thirty-six *tattva*s, of the nine *tattva*s, of the five or three *tattva*s (*ātma-*, *vidyā-*, and *śivatattva*)—are also expounded in this *paṭala* and elucidated by Kṣemarāja. Each according to its own process brings the *dīkṣita* from the earth to Śiva, the element bringing about the purification always being essentially of a phonic type: *varṇa*, mantra (mainly *OṂ* and its subdivisions), or *pada*s (of the *vidyārāja*). The mental representations (or at least their formulation, the utterance of the mantras of the ritual, *mantraprayoga*), through which the process is enacted by the master and his disciple, are accompanied by ritual placings over the body (*nyāsa*), suffusing it with the energy of the Word, since the body, too, just like the

97. This movement follows the course of the *vidyārāja*, whose diagram is given on p. 355.

mind, must be purified, must give way to a "divine body." In all this the element deemed to be effective is always the Word.[98]

In order to bring to a close our review on the Tantric word, we have now to deal with this Word in its most powerful form, that which, in any case, permeates Tantric and tantricized Hinduism: the mantras.

98. It may be worth noting that in the texts we have just examined, that is, with authors such as Abhinavagupta or Kṣemarāja, liberation is achieved—or seems so from a formal standpoint—on the completion of the rite of *dīkṣā*, where the action of the *ācārya* (and through him of Śiva, who bestows his grace) seems more important than what the adept himself is supposed to do. Only the *bubhukṣu*, the adept pursuing powers, seems to have to practice himself intricate ritual and meditative exercises. The *mumukṣu*, the follower of Svacchandabhairava in Kashmirian Śaivism, a *gṛhastha*, for whom Abhinava's and Kṣemarāja's works are first of all intended, did not have to submit to this. But in both cases—whether performed for or by the initiate if he is seeking powers—the rite retains its vital importance. And, except in the somewhat special case of the *śāmbhavopāya*, it is through ritual that the powers of the Word are brought into play.

On the position of the *mumukṣu* and the *bubhukṣu* in Kashmirian Śaivism, see A. Sanderson's studies, notably "Purity and Power," already cited, and "Meaning in Tantric Ritual," paper presented at the Colloquium on Ritual of the Section des Sciences Religieuses of the Ecole Pratique des Hautes Etudes, Paris, in 1986 (to be published in vol. 3 of A-M. Blondeau and K. Schipper (eds.) *Essais sur le Rituel.* Louvain-Paris, Peeters.

7

The Mantra

Mantras are relevant to our study for the same reason as the *ṣaḍadhvan*: inasmuch as they are a form of metaphysically (and ritualistically) creative and effective speech and, especially, a means to take their user to the source of speech: to its primordial level, which is the Godhead. This is how we shall consider them in this chapter. Our inquiry being thus restricted is all the more justified by the fact that the subject—too often treated in fanciful and misleading ways—has given rise in recent years to some substantial publications. A large volume, notably, recently published in the U.S., explores the subject almost exhaustively; it constitutes the latest research in this field, and deals especially with the notion of mantra according to some Kashmirian Śaiva works.[1] It would be pointless to consider here what has been said elsewhere, nor would it be useful to repeat here what I wrote on the subject in the early 1960s, in the first edition of this work. I shall therefore limit myself, in the following pages, to a few specific points of the "Kashmirian" theory of mantras, and to a few examples—also taken

1. Harvey P. Alper, ed., *Understanding Mantras*, (Albany: State University of New York Press, 1989), which includes, notably, an impressive "Working Bibliography for the Study of Mantras" (pp. 327-443); eighty-five pages of bibliography; and a study of the mantra according to Kṣemarāja's *ŚSV*. My own contribution to the volume is an overview entitled "Mantras, What are They?", where I attempt to clarify a few notions and to review some of the issues encountered when investigating mantras.

See also the volume *Mantras et diagrammes rituels dans l'hindouisme*, quoted previously. Cf. Bibliography.

from nondualistic Śaiva works—focusing on how they operate and serve as instruments and pathways leading back to the primordial Word. In so doing I shall leave aside some important points in the theory and practice of the *mantraśāstra*, some of them established since Vedic times, others peculiar to Tantric Hinduism. But to discuss them, even briefly, would require much more than one chapter. Therefore they will be ignored quite deliberately,[2] and I shall limit myself to what seems to me (whether I am right or wrong) more importantly relevant to the theme and general purpose of this book.

Definition and Characteristics of Mantras

With reference to its etymology, namely the root *MAN*, to think, and the suffix *tra*, used to make words denoting instruments or objects, the mantra is an instrument of thought. However, thought as associated with the mantra or as arising with its help in the mantrin, is no ordinary thought:[3] it is not the conceptual, discursive, differentiating form of thought (*vikalpa*) that accompanies empirical language. This is a more intense, more effective thought, a thought that is also one-pointed since it is connected with a concentrated form of speech, endowed with special potency and efficacy.

This is how the mantra is generally understood in Tantric texts, notably those with which we are dealing here. Such interpretation relates the suffix *tra* in the word mantra to the root *TRAI*, to save, which allows us to see in mantras a form of salvific thought. This is the idea conveyed in the oft-quoted formula: *mananaṃ sarvaveditvaṃ trāṇaṃ saṃsārasagarāt*/

2. For all these points, as well as the problems of the linguistic nature of mantras (of their being a special kind of language or not), the "meaning" they may have, the nature of their efficacy, their relationship with ritual, and so forth, one should refer to *Understanding Mantras* cited in the preceding note.
3. Cf. J. Gonda: "Etymologisch bedeutet *Mantra* ein Mittel oder Werkzeug zum Vollzug der Handlung *man*—'geistig erregt sein', d.h. 'im Sinne haben, wollen, beabsichtigen; erkennen, begreifen; gedenken'" (*Die Religionen Indiens*, 1, p. 22).

mananatrāṇadharmavān mantra ity abhidhīyate// "The mantra is so-called because it is in the nature of thought and deliverance. It is indeed all-knowing thought and release from transmigration." There are other similar formulas.[4] In the same way Jayaratha explains mantra in his commentary of the *TĀ* (3.225, vol. 2, p. 214): *mananaṃ sarvavetṛtvaṃ trāṇaṃ saṃsāry-anugrahaḥ*, "a thought which is omniscience, a liberation which is grace bestowed upon the transmigratory soul."

Admittedly, these two formulas cannot apply to all mantras, and even less to all the levels where mantras are found. They refer to their highest form, and especially to that notion elaborated—following, in particular, the *ŚS* (*ŚS* 2.1: *cittaṃ mantraḥ*)—by the Kashmirian nondualistic Śaiva authors. It should not be extended to all the mantras uttered in so many different rituals. Nonetheless, they convey the widespread, and in some respects always relevant, opinion that mantras are the most effective form (especially for emancipation) of the energy of the Word, by which they are always pervaded. If mantras are effective—and so are they acknowledged to be—this is because they are, in various degrees, but always eminently, in the nature of this supreme Word-Energy whose creative impulse we have examined in the foregoing chapters. Now, this energy cannot possibly be present to a higher degree than in the phonemes, the *varṇa*s, these constituent parts of mantras: *mantrāḥ varṇātmakāḥ sarve, varṇāḥ sarve śivātmakāḥ*, as it is often said,[5] or, to quote from the *Tantrasadbhāva* with Kṣemarāja in the *ŚSV* (2.3, p. 51): "all mantras consist of phonemes and their nature is that of energy, O dear One. Know, however, that this energy is the *mātṛkā*, whose nature is that of Śiva."[6] This is clearly to say that the nature of mantras is that of the energy of the phonemes, which is that of Śiva.

---

4. Thus in the *RT, śl.* 266 (p. 91).
5. Quoted notably by Abhinava (*PTV*, p. 235, *in fine*) and by J. (*ad TĀ* 12.24, vol. 7, part 2, p. 106), as taken from the *Sarvācāratantra.* Kṣemarāja (*PHr*, 12, comm.) quotes it as taken from the *Sarvavīratantra*: perhaps this is another name for the same text, which has not survived.
6. *sarve varṇātmakā mantrās te ca śaktyātmakāḥ priye/*
śaktis tu mātṛkā jñeyā sā ca jñeyā śivātmakā//

It may not be out of place to note here, incidentally, that while mantras are usually described as consisting of phonemes —even if those, in practice, cannot be pronounced—and more precisely of Sanskrit phonemes, we can, however, sometimes see mantras related to certain inarticulate sounds. Thus, Abhinavagupta in the *PTV* (p. 189) says: "The supreme Lord (viz., Śiva) Himself has explained that an unmanifest sound [but should this be taken as meaning "inarticulate"?] is generally somewhat like a mantra" (*pārameśvare 'pi avyaktadhvaner mukhyatayaiva prayāśo mantratvam*). We have seen above that the sounds *hāhā* and *sīt* are inarticulate, spontaneous, sounds arising from the deepest unconscious layers of the soul, and therefore close to the Absolute. We shall see later on that the subtle parts, the *kalā*s, of *bījamantra*s—all the inaudible and unutterable phonic vibration that follows the *bindu* in the *uccāra*—bring about the fusion of the mantra and of the mantrin's consciousness in the supreme Śiva. This, in fact, is not new: in the Brāhmaṇas already, the *anirukta* sound, indistinct speech, is related to the limitless and its force. The superiority of the unuttered over the uttered, as we also know, is an essential notion in Indian thought. This, notably, accounts for the traditionally acknowledged superiority of the silent mantra repetition (*japa*)[7] over the audible one.

---

7. On *japa*, cf. my study in the *BEFEO*, lxxvi, 1987, pp. 117-164.

Regarding the link between mantra and inarticulate sound, one may refer to the *ṣaṇḍhabhāṣā* of Buddhism, the "intentional language" or "twilight language", as it is sometimes called in English, which conceals a hidden, secret, meaning behind what the words actually say, its pregnant significance being due to its obscureness, to its departure from the norm of ordinary language. This aspect is probably also instrumental in the case of mantras insofar as they consist of meaningless syllables or obscure series of words or sounds, or in such mantric practices as *pallava*, *sampuṭī* and so forth, where words or syllables are uttered interpolated, inverted, in reverse order, and so forth. This can be compared with what Maheśvarānanda writes in the Parimala on *MM*, 71 (p. 186) where he justifies the use of Prākrit allowing for a greater richness of meaning due to its imprecision and resultant ambiguity.

On *ṣaṇḍhabhāṣā* see for instance G. R. Elder, "Problems of Language in Buddhist Tantra" in *History of Religions*, vol. 15/3, 1976, pp. 231-50.

Notwithstanding the above-mentioned formulas about the "Śaiva"—because "phonetic"—nature of mantras, one should note and underline the twofold nature, empirical and metempirical—trivial, as it were, and supreme—of mantras. One should not fail to emphasize this nature in a work such as this which, owing to its specific orientation, tends to put the emphasis on their highest aspect, that which has been especially stressed in the texts we are studying. One should remember, however, that in addition to this, mantras also have a more ordinary, more "worldly" (*laukika*) aspect: assuredly, they are forms of the supreme energy, but they are also formulas uttered by human beings. (And in fact, that is the form in which they pervade the life and religious practices of their users.) Indeed Abhinava points out that there are mantras on the various levels of the Word when he says in the *PTV* "Mantras are the Venerable [Energy] of the phonemes. They are in the nature of the world as well as of the supreme Lord, and so forth. They are thought and liberation. They consist of discursive thought as much as of pure consciousness."[8]

It is to be noted that in essence the mantra is always the pure energy of the Word, whether the mantrin is aware of this energy or not, and in this respect it is always at the highest level. But at the same time there are in fact countless numbers of mantras—seventy million according to the tradition!—all manner of syllables or formulas which, depending on their nature, are effective at various levels of the manifestation and which, moreover, exist at the level of the empirical world,

8. *PTV*, p. 243: *mantrā varṇabhattārakā laukikapārameśvarādirūpā manana-trāṇarūpā vikalpasaṃvinmayyāḥ.*

R. Gnoli in his edition of the *PTV* reads: *mananatrāṇarūpā avikalpa saṃvinmayāḥ*, which takes Abhinava as saying that mantras consist of nondiscursive consciousness (*essenziata di non-discorsiva Coscienza*; ibid., p. 156). This reading may seem more consistent with the spirit of the Sanskrit language. However, I wonder if the text of the KSTS edition, for which I have opted, is not more appropriate to emphasize the twofold nature of mantras, which Abhinava notes precisely here, without denying indeed that they are in essence nondiscursive pure consciousness. The main point of this passage, I feel, is to stress their twofold nature.

since they can be uttered at the *vaikharī*[9] level and can even be written down. Finally, there are, in every tradition, mantras which are in the form of meaningful sentences and which, therefore, appear as related to discursive thought. However, notwithstanding this apparent variety, mantras are always regarded as a form of speech differing from language in that, unlike language, they are not bound by "conventions" nor associated with objects, but on the contrary are oriented toward the very origin of the Word and of the energy. Therefore, instead of activating the ordinary mental process and drawing their utterer toward the world of differentiation, the mantra makes the user turn within, toward the primary, transcendental, source of all speech and therefore of all manifestation.

The emphasis will be placed here on mantras as leading toward the source of the Word, or as being a form of the Word close to the primordial source,[10] since (as with the *ṣaḍadhvan*) what I wish to deal with more specifically in this chapter is this aspect of return to the origin, without losing sight, however,

9. On this subject, cf. Rāmakaṇṭha's commentary on *SpK* 2.10-11 (pp. 80-84), where he explains how it happens that mantras have but a limited efficacy although their deeper nature is that of Śiva himself, who is omnipotent. We return to this text below, p. 389.

10. Abhinava underlines this aspect very frequently. Thus in the *TĀ* (5.140-41, vol. 3, pp. 454-55): "Even more," he says, "these phonic seeds concentrated [in a mantra], which have nothing to do with the conventions [of language] and which cause consciousness to vibrate, are means to reach the latter. The fullness found in these clusters of phonic seeds is due to the fact that they do not convey any [empirical] meaning, that they [consist of] a vibration of consciousness turning away from [the external world], that they are self-luminous and [associated with] the awakening or the suppression of breath."

kiṃ punaḥ samayāpekṣāṃ vinā ye bījapiṇḍakāḥ/
saṃvidaṃ spandayanty ete neyuḥ saṃvidupāyatām//140//
vācyābhāvād udāsīnasaṃvitspandāt svadhāmataḥ/
prāṇollāsanirodhābhyām bījapiṇḍeṣu pūrṇatā//141//

(Abhinava alludes here to the *bījamantras* *SAUḤ* and *piṇḍanātha*, hence his mentioning the movement of *prāṇa*. We shall return to this passage below, on p. 420.

of the other aspects: that is, of the wide variety, in form and purpose, of mantras in the Tantric lore. In Tantric Hinduism mantras are no longer what they usually were in the Veda: a verse or a group of verses—*ṛc, yajus, sāman*—even though that is sometimes what they are.[11] Rather, they consist of short sentences (often injunctions), words, and mostly syllables or groups of syllables or phonemes, usually devoid of any apparent meaning but having a value and a function, and especially having a stereotyped, fixed form, and a particular use. This symbolic value of the mantra and its conveying a particular "meaning"[12] —that is, its being charged with an intentionality—expressed through its fixed form are its basic features according to the texts we shall consider.

Because mantras are of so many forms a question may be raised: If they range from a sentence (or a group of sentences), to a syllable, a phoneme, or a sound, how do we distinguish those sentences, letters, or sounds that are actually mantras from those that are not? There is only one answer to this, namely

---

11. There are also long mantras in Tantric texts. For instance, we have seen in the preceding chapter the *vyomavyāpin.*
12. We cannot deal here with the oft-discussed problem of the meaning (or meaninglessness) of mantras. On this subject, see *Understanding Mantras* (notably J. F. Staal's article and my "reply" to it in the conclusion of that book).

    On the difference between Vedic and Tantric mantras a quote must be cited from what L. Renou wrote in "Le destin du Veda dans l'Inde" (*EVP*, 6, pp. 11-12):

    "Le *mantraśāstra*, la théorie (phonématique, ou plutôt transphonématique) des Formules, a bien pu s'inspirer d'un ancien **mantraśāstra* appliqué au Veda, mais il le dépasse ou le nie, en impliquant que le *mantra* tantrique n'a pas d'existence indépendante (pas davantage, du reste, d'existence liée à un rite précis), qu'il est la divinité par excellence, la manifestation phonique du divin, son impact créateur, sa *śakti*, qu'il met en oeuvre un complexe de dispositions, non seulement visuelles ou auditives, mais graphiques (diagraphiques), qu'il s'emplit d'un syllabisme ésotérique, comparable aux *anubandha* des Grammairiens. Bref il tend à se situer au-delà du langage, éventuellement jusqu'à la zone même du silence, alors que le *mantra* védique était plutôt en deça du langage, témoin d'une sémantique inachevée."

    This statement is, I believe, remarkably insightful and stimulating.

that a mantra is what is pronounced as such by the revealed tradition and the teaching of the masters: it is a formalized utterance declared to be a mantra, "revealed" by those texts and masters who are entitled to do so, that is, who are recognized as holding authority in this matter by the group to which they belong.[13] This being so, and considering the texts on which we focus in this work, were I to give a tentative definition of mantras such as is found in Tantric Hinduism, I would say that a mantra is a formula or a sound with a fixed and prescribed form, to be used according to certain rules and in prescribed circumstances, and empowered with a general or a specific efficacy acknowledged by the tradition wherein it is used. One might add that the mantra is said to be effective because it is looked upon as a form of the energy of the Word (*vākśakti*) and, more especially, as being (in a number of cases) the phonic form, endowed with a power that can be used effectively (in rites and according to the rules), of a deity or of an aspect of the deity.[14] In this respect, philosophically, a mantra is an aspect of the cosmic energy, and thereby it lies at a certain level of consciousness. (When stating this, however, I am perhaps implicitly opting for a conception of the mantra that is not accepted by all.) Just as there are infinite forms of energy, from the unlimited form of the supreme Word to the lowest ones, likewise there are countless numbers of mantras, high or low, dangerous or beneficial, endowed with limited or unlimited powers.

Mantras, thus understood, vary in their nature and degree of efficacy according to the level ascribed to them and to the way they are used, the same formula being indeed able to operate on several levels.[15] At the lowest (and most common) stage,

13. There are formal criteria for mantras: the use of the *jāti*s (*svāhā*, and so forth), of *bīja*s (and in their case, the presence of *bindu*), and so forth. A typology of mantras could thus be established. But I am not sure it would be useful except as an aid for classification.
14. For the various possible definitions of mantras, cf. *Understanding Mantras*. On this point and others, G. Gonda's study "The Indian Mantra," in *Oriens*, vol. 16, 1963, is still very much worth reading.
15. Such would be the case of the mantras known as *sādhāraṇa*, applicable to all, which can be used generally. According to Kṣemarāja's commentary

mantras are those particular formulas endowed with efficacy, producing an "effect," used in every circumstance of life and religion, and especially in the various forms of ritual and magic, of which they are a constituent part. In such cases, they are forms of empirical speech (although not necessarily of language), vocally or mentally uttered. But the mantra is also the phonic, "expressing" (*vācaka*), form of a deity, its subtle form, its essence, its efficient aspect,[16] the supernatural entity that is "to be expressed" (*vācya*) by the mantra being itself more or less high and powerful. (The mantra is not the same as the name of the deity, even though the latter, in some cases, notably in *japa*, can be used as a mantra.) Last, the mantra may be considered as a pure force or spiritual reality, even as one from the highest plane: as the Word-Energy or the supreme Godhead.[17] Such is the case with the *praṇava*: *OṂ*, *HAUṂ*, or any other, of *AHAṂ*, and so forth, of the mantra when considered to be the root-cause of everything or as identical with the supreme consciousness, a conception put forward in Kashmirian nondualistic Śaivism but also to be found elsewhere.

That there are different levels in (and different uses for) mantras is apparent, notably in the Trika system of *upāya*s, where mantras are considered and used differently depending upon the *upāya*. In *śāmbhavopāya*, where there should occur, an intuitive experience of the divine *icchā*, the precognitive impulse lying at the root of the emanative unfolding of the Word, the mantra is the formula gathering in itself the whole cosmos as present in the Lord: *AHAṂ*,[18] the power of which is

---

on the *NT* (16.22, vol. 2, p. 101), such is the case for the *mṛtyujit* or *netramantra*, for the *praṇava*, and all mantras that, being Śiva himself, are the *vācaka* of all that exists. The same is probably said in other traditions with respect to other *mūlamantra*s.

16. *devatāyāḥ śarīraṃ tu bījād utpadyate dhruvam.* "Verily, the body of the *devatā* arises from the *bīja*-phonic seed," says a *Yāmalatantra* quoted in *Principles of Tantra*, p. 610.

17. It goes without saying that the hierarchy of mantras—"higher" or "lower" forms—given here is that of the traditions I describe: I do not make it mine.

18. *TĀ* 3.200ff. We have seen *AHAṂ* in chap. 5, pp. 286ff. The cosmos as present in the absolute consciousness is also expressed by the "heart-*bīja*" *SAUḤ*, on which see below, pp. 417-22.

to be nondiscursively intuited. In *śāktopāya*, where a purification of the mind leads to the supreme realization, the creative and resorptive power of the mantra (*mantravīrya*) as embodying the cosmic *spanda* is realized through the mantras *SAUḤ* and *KHPHREṂ*.[19] In *āṇavopāya* a number of different mantras can be used as efficacious spiritual forces set at work through practices involving both the adept's body (yoga, *mudrā*, rites) and his mind. There are thus different approaches to mantra. But when a mantra is being used for spiritual ends, the mantric practice as it unfolds may carry both the adept and his mantra from one plane to another. Also, a mantra can be used to different ends—ends that, though different, are not necessarily incompatible. A characteristic of Hinduism is precisely that one passes easily from one plane to another, that liberation, supernatural powers, and even destructive magical abilities can not only be taught in the same text, but even be bestowed to an adept through the performance of one ritual only, the *pūjā* of the Goddess surrounded by her *āvaraṇadevatā*s, for instance. The mantras used in such a case necessarily function on different levels. One must therefore necessarily take into account the wide scope of this notion of mantra and always regard the mantra as a word of power existing and operating on all levels, from that of a person engaged in (even the lowest) activities of this world, pursuing material enjoyment or supernatural powers, to that of the liberated-while-living, and up to the level of Śiva, of the supreme Word, *parāvāc*, of the absolute and undifferentiated consciousness, the latter being always, indeed, that which ultimately endows mantras with life, power, and efficacy.[20]

We have already had a glimpse on the role mantras may have in the cosmogonies of the Word. Without going as far back as the Vedic Upaniṣads (cf. above, chap. 1), where *oṃ* is

---

19. Ibid.

20. We are not concerned here with the interesting question of the nature of the acknowledged efficacy of mantras (symbolic or otherwise). On this, cf. *Understanding Mantras* and F. Chenet's study "De l'efficience psychagogique des mantras et des yantras" in *Mantras et diagrammes rituels dans l'hindouisme.*

the primordial Word, identical with the Universe, the "supreme thing" upon which all words are based (ibid., pp. 14-19), we have seen in chapter 3 (p. 129) how the *kuṇḍalinī*, in the course of her cosmic rise, divides into five mantras (*sadyojāta* and so forth) prior to its producing the fifty phonemes. In the diagram of the *kāmakalā*, the *kuṇḍalinī* is the *bījā ĪṂ* at the center of the two coupled cosmic triangles, forming as it were the axis of the Goddess' body.[21] We have seen also that *haṃsa* (*supra*, pp. 140-42) is shown in the *SvT* as the original utterance, the vivifying breath dwelling in all living creatures, while also residing at the very source of the Word. Now, *haṃsa* is recited in the *ajapājapa* and as such it is a mantra.[22] To state that the cosmos originates from a mantra is only another way to assert the primary creative power of the Word (and more especially of the ritual word), a Vedic notion taken up and expanded by Tantrism into the vast body of the *mantraśāstra* that is the teaching of the Tantras.[23] In the Tantras, which usually do not engage in much theological or metaphysical abstractions, the cosmic role of mantras is primarily that of the formula of the main deity, its *mūlamantra.* The field is of a magico-religious sort, whether the text describes the mantras as bringing about vision or inducing possession (*āveśa*) or trance, or whether it simply proclaims, without further developments, the cosmogonic power of the mantra: the context is not at all a sophisticated one.[24] Kashmirian nondualistic Śaivism, on the other

21. *YHDī*, p. 132. It should be noted that this is both a visual and a phonic symbol, as is the *kuṇḍalinī* also. In the same *paṭala* of the *YH*, the cosmic evolution is described as related to the *śrīvidyā*, which, as well as the *śricakra*, is a symbol of the cosmic dynamism of the Goddess.
22. In *ABS*, chapter 16 (cf. above, chap. 4, p. 225) the state of the power of action about to create the phonemes is called *mantramayīm*, "consisting of mantra." On this subject one could also quote *NT* 21.59ff., as well as a number of Āgamas.
23. On the transition from Vedic to tantric mantras, cf. L. Renou in *EVP*, quoted above, p. 378, n. 12.
24. Very characteristic in this respect is the following passage from a modern work, *Principles of Tantra* (Madras, Ganesh & Co., 1952), edited by A. Avalon:
"At the beginning of the creation of the Universe, the luminous bud of

hand, notably in the Kula-related traditions, while still retaining a fund of ancient notions, developed a much more elaborate and refined theory of the mantra, of great interest as regards both the nature of the mantras and the foundation of their efficacy.

The Nature of Mantras

In the Trika's system of thought the essential nature of mantras is that of Word, as Śiva's energy. They are therefore in the nature of consciousness, since consciousness, divine energy, and Word are but different names or aspects of the same reality which is all this at once. (As we have seen in chapter 4, the four stages of the Word correspond to levels in the cosmic evolution of consciousness.) Such is the essential nature of the mantras in nondualistic Śaivism: it is not merely a self-operative formula endowed with an intrinsic or magical efficacy. To state that the mantra is the energy of the Word is to state that it is spiritual energy. It works to the extent that it shares in the energy of consciousness or of the supreme Word, and it can be used effectively by the adept to the extent that he takes hold of this spiritual and cosmic energy. This efficiency of mantras, *mantravīrya*, as it is called notably by Abhinavagupta (*PTV*, p. 188), owing to their being in the nature of Consciousness-Word, must be briefly studied here, at least in some of its aspects (for it is not possible to cover the whole subject), before proceeding with the soteriologic working of certain mantras.[25]

The *ŚS* sums up the nature of mantras in the two words of the first sūtra of chapter 2: *cittaṃ mantraḥ*, "the mantra is consciousness" or is an act of consciousness. "Consciousness,"

Mantras blossomed and created the fourteen worlds, which are the petals of its flowers. It is the fragrance of its pollen, which is existence, consciousness and bliss, which fills the three worlds with delight (p. 753)."

25. Being concerned with mantras as connected with that movement which leads back to the source of the Word, we shall see them here primarily in their soteriological or redemptive aspect. Whatever their role, however, mantras are regarded as efficacious because they come from and essentially abide in the divine Consciousness-Word.

Kṣemarāja explains in the *Vimarśinī*, "is that by which one cognizes (*cetyate*), one becomes aware of (*vimṛśyate*), the ultimate reality. It is that reflective awareness (*vimarśarūpam saṃvedanam*) of [mantras such as the] *prāsāda*, the *praṇava*,[26] and so forth, which are in the nature of the fullness of pulsating radiance. That by which one deliberates (*mantryate*) secretly, or contemplates inwardly, that by which one becomes aware of not being different or separate from the supreme Lord, is mantra." "The mantra," he further says, "is not a mere conglomerate of different syllables.[27] It is the very mind of the devotee who, through intense awareness of the deity of the mantra, acquires identity with that deity . . . As said in the *Tantrasadbhāva*: 'The life of mantras is she who is considered as the imperishable Energy. O fair One, without her they are fruitless like autumnal clouds.' Similarly in the *Śrīkaṇṭhīyasaṃhitā*: 'The mantra by itself, or the mantrin by himself, cannot be successful. Knowledge alone is the root of all this. Without it [i.e., without becoming aware of that energy which gives life to the mantras], one cannot be successful.'"[28]

---

26. The *prāsādamantra*, according to various Āgamas (as well as to the *SP*—cf. *SP*1), is *HAUṂ*, and so it is in the *KālikāPur* (59.56-57). (It should not be confused with the *parāprāsāda*—or *prāsādaparā*—*mantra* of the *Kulārṇavatantra*). According to the *LT*, it is *OṂ HAUṂ*.

    The *praṇava* is *OṂ*. It may also be *HAUṂ* (in the *SvT* for instance), or some other *mūlamantra*. The *Sārdhatriśatikalottarāgama*, ch. 19, gives eighteen different forms of the *prāsāda*.

27. In the *Anubhavanivedana* (Offering of the Innermost Experience), Abhinava says: "The mantra is that which appears to the mind and where one cannot distinguish any particular arrangement of the constituent letters" (*mantraḥ sa pratibhāti varṇacaraṇā yasmin na saṃlakṣyate*). That is, the mantra is something other than the mere addition of its constituent parts. The awareness of the mantra by the adept, also, must transcend all phonetic distinctions: thus awareness must be that of its spiritual essence only.

28. *ŚSV* 2.1 (pp. 47-48): *ceyate vimṛśyate anena paraṃ tattvam iti cittam/ pūrṇasphurattāsatattvaprāsādapraṇavādivimarśarūpaṃ saṃvedanam/ tad eva mantryate guptam antar abhedena vimṛśyate parameśvararūpam anena/ iti kṛtvā mantraḥ . . . atha ca mantradevatāvimarśaparatvena prāptatatsāmarasyam ārādhakacittam eva mantraḥ na tu vicitravarṇasaṃghaṭṭanāmātrakam/ . . . Śrītantrasadbhāva 'pi*

Sūtra 2.3 of the *ŚS* again touches upon the problem of the nature of mantras: "The secret of mantras is that being whose body is [pure] knowledge (*vidyāśarīrasattā mantrarahasyam*)." "This knowledge," Kṣemarāja comments, "is the unfolding of the supreme nonduality. [Its] body is its own nature or essence (*svarūpa*). That whose body is knowledge is the blissful One in the form of the totality of sounds (*bhagavān śabdarāśiḥ*), whose soul is the pulsating radiance, the awareness of the perfection of the absolute "I," consisting in the undivided totality of the universe. Such is the secret [that is, the deeper nature, the essence] of mantras." Then Kṣemarāja quotes the *Tantrasadbhāva*: "All mantras consist of phonemes, O dear One! and these are a form of the energy. This energy should be known as *mātṛkā*, which is to be known as being made of Śiva."[29] As we can see, the mantra is explained as the energy of the supreme Word, that of the phonemes as they emerge from Śiva where they are the totality of the reflective awareness of the Godhead and of His awareness of the universe as abiding within Himself.

That divine consciousness and the Word are identical, and thereby that mantras are in the form of Consciousness-Word is also underlined by Abhinavagupta in the *ĪPV* (1.5.14), where, commenting upon a *kārikā* that describes the pulsating supreme essence of reality as the "heart" of the supreme Lord,[30] he says

---

mantrāṇāṃ jīvabhūtā tu yā smṛtā śaktir avyayā/
tayā hīnā varārohe niṣphalāḥ śaradabhravat//
iti/ Śrīśrīkaṇṭhīyasaṃhitāyām
pṛthaṇ mantraḥ pṛthaṇ mantri na siddhyati kadācana/
jñānamūlam idaṃ sarvam anyathā naiva siddhyati//

29. *ŚSV*, pp. 50-51: *vidyā parādvayaprathā/ śarīraṃ svarūpam/ yasya sa vidyāśarīro bhagavān śabdarāśiḥ/ tasya yā sattā aśeṣaviśvābhedamayapūrṇāhaṃvimarśātmā sphurattā sā mantrāṇāṃ rahasyam upaniṣat/ yad uktaṃ śrītantrasadbhāve*

sarve varṇātmakā mantrās te ca śaktyātmakāḥ priye/
śaktis tu mātṛkā jñeyā sā ca jñeyā śivātmakā//

From this quotation (and the previous one) it is interesting to note that this notion of mantras as the energy of phonemes occurs even in one of the Trika's earlier Tantras.

30. *sa sphurattā mahāsattā deśakālāviśeṣiṇī/*
saiṣa sāratayā proktā hṛdayaṃ parameśthinaḥ//

that this heart is reflective awareness and the supreme mantra (*hṛdayaṃ vimarśarūpaṃ paramantrātmakam*). "The mantra," he says, "is the heart of everything [that is, the place where everything rests in the primary emitting energy]. It is in the nature of the free activity of consciousness, and the latter consists in the energy of the supreme Word. [It is said] indeed in the Āgamas that but for these [mantras] there would be neither words, nor objects, nor movement of consciousness."[31]

The Potency of Mantras: Mantravīrya

Such is therefore the source—Consciousness-Word—of the effective power of mantras. But the Word in its most intense form only could be considered as the source of the mantric potency. Therefore the authors with whom we are concerned here—following in this, probably, Abhinava—say that the source of the potency of mantras is to be found in another mantra, the *paramahāmantra AHAṂ*, that is, in the absolute "I," which, as we have already seen, is the fullness of the Godhead united with his energy, both transcendent and immanent (cf. Chapter 5, pp. 286-89). Enclosing in himself the full power of all the phonemes, from *a* to *ha*, of which mantras consist (and drawing them together in a single point of concentrated energy, the *bindu, ṃ*, its final letter), *AHAṂ* is not only the primordial and supreme mantra, *fons et origo*, of all the others, but even more the foundation of everything. Here, in a purely metaphysical perspective, the mantra is placed at the origin of the universe. "This energy [which creates the worlds]," says Abhinava at the beginning of the *PTV*, "abides first of all in the absolute consciousness beyond time and space, made

---

31. *sarvasya hi mantra eva hṛdayaṃ mantraś ca vimarśātmā vimarśanaṃ ca parāvācchaktimayam/ tata evoktaṃ na tair vinā bhavec chabdo nārtho nāpi citer gatiḥ . . . ity āgameṣu/* The same idea is found in the two following stanzas from the *Trikahṛdaya*, quoted by Abhinava in the *PTV* (p. 156): "This energy of the phonemes which is everywhere—in the divinized energies, in weapons, kings, rivers, living creatures, discs, tridents, lotuses, or stones—is also that which is found in mantras. If it disappears, they too disappear, and there is nothing left but [dead] letters."

of the supreme great mantra" (*sa ca śaktiḥ . . . prathamataraṃ paramahāmantramayām adeśakālakalitāyāṃ saṃvidi nirūḍhā . . .*).[32]

There is no need to repeat what has been said earlier about *ahaṃ*, that absolute and nondiscursive reflective awareness by the divine consciousness of its fullness and potency. But one should underline how authors such as Abhinavagupta, introducing the notion of *paramahāmantra* as the origin of the other mantras, place what constitutes the basis and the essential power of mantras on a primordial, foundational, supreme, plane. "This energy of the supreme Word (*parā vākśakti*), which is not different from the light of consciousness," says Kṣemarāja, in the *PHṛ*, "is in the nature of the supreme great mantra, eternally present and manifest. She is the active and living reflective awareness of the absolute 'I'."[33] And further: "In this condition of the absolute "I" lies the greatest efficient potency, for this is the stage from which all mantras arise and in which they abide. Owing to this sole force they can be used for one or another definite purpose. Thus the *SpK* say: 'having taken hold of this force [of the *spanda*], mantras become omniscient and able to perform their functions.'"[34]

In the fourth *āhnika* of the *TĀ*, concerning the *śāktopāya*, in connection with the two mantras *SAUḤ* and *KHPHREṂ*, saying once more (*śl.* 181) that the supreme consciousness is at once synthetic self-awareness (*parāmarśa*), spontaneous and eternal sound (*dhvani*), and vibration (*spanda*), Abhinava calls this consciousness "the great supreme heart (*paramaṃ hṛdayaṃ*

---

32. "Śiva," he adds later on (p. 45), "consists of the emission of the efficient power of the great mantra, which is in the nature of the supreme Word" (*śivo hi paravāṅmaya mahāmantravīryavisṛṣṭimayaḥ*).

33. *PHṛ*, p. 67: *citprakāśād avyatiriktā nityoditamahāmantrarūpā pūrṇāhaṃvimarśamayī yā iyaṃ parā vākśaktiḥ.* Also *PTV*, p. 55: *prakāśasya hi svābhāvikākṛtrimaparavāṅmantravīryacamatkārātma aham iti*: "that of which consists the wonder of the potency of the supreme mantra, the supreme, spontaneous and uncreated word of the light of consciousness, is *aham.*"

34. Ibid., p. 97: *eṣaiva ca ahantā sarvamantrāṇām udayaviśrāntisthānatvād etad balenaiva ca tattadarthakriyākāritvād mahati vīryabhūmiḥ/ tad uktaṃ tadākramya balaṃ mantrāḥ ity ādi.*

mahat), which, mantrically, takes the form of these two "heart-mantras," that of the emanation (*SAUḤ*) and that of the resorption. "This synthetic and intense reflective awareness (*parāmarśa*), uncreated and immaculate, peculiar to these [two mantras], is known, [the masters] say, as 'I.' It is the very light of light. It is the efficient power—in the nature of the heart—of all the mantras. But for it they would be lifeless, like a living being deprived of heart."[35]

Such is the source of the power acknowledged to be that of mantras, that which forms their essence, their inner being. It is nothing else, indeed, than the source of the cosmic manifestation which, for the Trika, is the source of consciousness or the Word: *saṃvid* or *paravāc*. But when looked at in their concreteness, as ritual formalized utterances, mantras are obviously far remote from this supreme stage. They are, no doubt, a higher form of speech than ordinary language and are associated, as a rule, to nondiscursive (*nirvikalpa*) thought. They are turned toward the Absolute and, through their intrinsic dynamism, embodied notably by the *bindu*[36] (with which most of the *bījamantra*s are provided), they lead toward the source of the Word. However, they are not the supreme Word itself. They are a way or a stage leading to it, provided that the mantrin is able to grasp and make use of their deeper nature.[37]

---

35. *TĀ* 4.192-93 (vol. 3, p. 224):

etad rūpaparāmarśam akṛtrimam anābilam/
aham ity āhur eṣaiva prakāśasya prakāśatā//192//
etad vīryaṃ hi sarveṣāṃ mantrāṇāṃ hṛdayātmakam/
vinānena jadas te syur jīvā iva vinā hṛdā//193//

36. Cf. *infra*, p. 394.

37. *Mantrasādhana*, the mantric ascesis, is meant for the adept to gain control over his mantra. *Mantrasādhana* is a ritual practice which, metaphysically, may be understood as a gradual penetration into the higher stages of the Word, up to the supreme stage. For this ritual practice, see H. Brunner's study, "Le *sādhaka*, personnage oublié du śivaisme du sud," *J.As*: 1975. Cf. also A. Padoux, "Contributions à l'étude du *mantraśāstra*, III: Le *japa*" *BEFEO*: 1987, quoted before.

In nondualistic Śaiva works the adept's realization of the deeper nature of his mantra is described in a more intellectual, mystical, fashion, and not exclusively in terms of ritual and religion.

Here we are faced with two problems, one concerning the nature of mantras, the other their empowering.

First, as concerns mantras, were they in every respect nothing but supreme Word and consciousness, they would have the same unlimited power as the Godhead: any mantra could achieve anything, and any adept capable of using it would arrive at omniscience and liberation. But this is not so: this is not the view of the various traditions, and mantras are different in value, power, and effects. Admittedly, some of them are held more especially as forms of the primordial energy of the Word. Such is the case with *AHAṂ* (when used as a mantra), and that also of *OṂ*, *SAUḤ*, or of the *mūlamantra*s of the various sects. However, the others share but in a more limited way—to a greater or lesser degree—in the energy of the Word. Their power varies notably according to the *devatā*s of which they are the *vācaka*s, depending on whether these are more or less powerful, that is, they are on a more or less elevated level in the hierarchy of the cosmos and of the planes of consciousness. This point is touched upon in the *SpK* 2.11, which says that mantras, vivified by the power of the *spanda*, the primal "vibration," operate in the same way as the sense organs of animate beings."[38] "As the sense organs," Rāmakaṇṭha explains in his commentary (pp. 80-84), "perform different functions while being part of the same living being, while belonging to the same individual consciousness, likewise mantras, although equally vivified, in essence, by the infinite power of the divine *spanda*, have each their particular role and field of activity." Rāmakaṇṭha adds that besides having their own inherent limitations, mantras are also limited in their action depending upon the mantrin: Mantras, he says, perform definite functions for adepts who are aware only of their limited self although they are, in their innermost soul, one with the supreme state (ibid., p. 82).

---

38. *tad ākramya balaṃ mantrāḥ sarvajñabalaśālinaḥ/*
pravartante 'dhikārāya karaṇānīva dehinām// (*SpK*., p. 80)

The "Empowering" of Mantras

This brings us to a second problem linked with the former —and to a further point of our study, that of the "empowering" of mantras, that is, how to bring them into play. For our authors, (Rāmakaṇṭha in the *Vivṛti* on the *SpK*, Kṣemarāja in the *SpN*, Abhinava in the *TĀ*), if the adept is able to rise to the highest level of consciousness, if, liberated-while-living, he has become one with the *spanda*, the "heart," the supreme Śiva, then he is possessed with this very divine energy and to him all mantras are equally able to achieve anything. Even more, "whatever word he utters with the desire to reach one goal or another, for him this word will be an effective mantra."[39] Can any word then be a mantra? Of course not, for the overwhelming majority of people. In fact, as we have seen, mantras are both formally and in their uses thoroughly codified forms of speech: they are rule-governed utterances. No mantra and therefore no mantric efficacy exists apart from these rules. But matters seem different with the liberated-while-living who, in every word, sees and experiences nothing but the supreme Word. This is expressed in *ŚS* 3.27: "The conversation [of the liberated-while-living] constitutes a mantric recitation," *kathā japaḥ*. That is also clearly stated by Abhinavagupta in *TĀ* 4.194: "One who has reached this uncreated heart, whatsoever he does, whatever he animates or thinks, all this is regarded as mantric recitation."[40] "The yogin whose mind abides in the synthetic awareness of the uncreated 'I'" (*akṛtakāhaṃparāmarśa viśrānto hi yogī*), Jayaratha comments (ibid., vol. 3, p. 227), "whatsoever his external activity, for him all this will be a *japa*, that is, it will shine forth like a mantra, because he abides continuously in the active awareness of the deity who is the Self (*svātmadevatā-vimarśānavaratāvartanātmatvena*) . . . this is why it has been said rightly that 'any word is *japa*.'" Jayaratha quotes here *ŚS* 3.27.

---

39. *yad yad vacanaṃ yena yenābhisaṃdhinā uccārayati tat tasyāmogha-mantratām āpadyate* (ibid., p. 84).

40. *akṛtrimaitaddhṛdayārūḍho yat kiṃcid ācaret/*
prāṇyād vā mṛśate vāpi sa sarvo 'sya japo mataḥ//

In this case it is quite clear that the mantra is no longer a fixed formalized utterance, but the supreme stage of the Word: what is described here is not the mantra as such, but that particular level of the Word which is the essential nature of mantras: this is quite a different matter. As we can see, when dealing with the nondualistic Śaiva theory of mantras, account must be taken of these two different meanings that the word *mantra* may assume. What is meant is either the mantra as is exists empirically and is used in practice, or else what the mantra is in the abstract or in essence—at the level of the supreme consciousness. This is why the question of the mantrin's level of consciousness is of paramount importance. First, because at the highest stage, the adept's consciousness will take him beyond the mantra, toward its source. Next, and more generally, because the mantra is effective only when uttered (and therefore also held in his consciousness) by a mantrin, and in this respect it cannot be separated from that consciousness.

Not all the texts deal with this subject—far from it. Those of nondualistic Śaivism, however, teach generally that there is a hierarchy of knowers (*pramātṛ*),[41] one of their levels being that of mantras; they therefore agree that mantras normally correspond to a certain level of consciousness (which, with respect to the Word, is usually that of *madhyamā*). In this hierarchy, *mantreśvara*s and *mahāmantreśvara*s stand for higher mantric levels of consciousness. Such a hierarchy appears as an autonomous system. In spite of this, the mind of the adept plays, for Abhinavagupta and Kṣemarāja, a primary role as far as mantras are concerned. According to them, a mantra cannot be separated from its user: while the mantra is consciousness, since the Word, for the Trika, is consciousness, it is also consciousness when used by the adept, who is himself a knower whose self is in essence identical to the supreme knower, Śiva—just like the mantras: *ete* (*mantrāḥ*) *śivadharminaḥ*, say the *SpK* 2.1.

---

41. This hierarchy of seven *pramātṛ*s (Śiva/Śakti, Mantramaheśvara, Mantreśvara, Mantra, Vijñānākala, Pralayākala, and Sakala) appears in the Trika as early as the *MVT*. See chap. 3, p. 104, note 54.

From such a perspective the mantra never acts by itself, autonomously, through some spontaneous action brought about by its mere utterance.[42] Utterance, to be sure, is necessary: it involves the movement of *prāṇa.* Proper pronunciation must also be ensured, whether the mantra is actually uttered or not (and even if it is unpronounceable). But the mantra is effective only to the extent that it has been assimilated by the adept's consciousness. This is what Kṣemarāja said in the above-quoted passage (p. 384) from the *ŚSV*: "[The mantra] is the very mind of the devotee who, through intent awareness of the mantra's *devatā*, realizes his identity with the latter." This formula clearly shows not only that the adept's consciousness and the mantra he practices are on the same level, but also that the mantra and the devotee's mind are identical. And this mental act by which the adept becomes one with the mantra and makes it effective, is *vimarśa*, a term used precisely to define the energy of consciousness which is supreme Word. Admittedly, this act of consciousness that is *vimarśa* may itself take place on different levels: the level of Śiva is different from that of a human being. Nonetheless the mantra, at all these different levels, is associated with the free activity, with the energy of consciousness, with an intense living awareness beyond all empirical thought-construct.[43]

---

42. The idea of mantra as a spiritual or vital energy (there is hardly any distinction between them in Tantrism) is not peculiar to nondualistic Śaivism: it is a very common notion. Mantras, it is generally agreed, are effective only insofar as this energy is present, working and awakened in them. The *mantrasaṃskāra*s (usually ten in number) serve precisely the purpose of arousing, energizing, or redirecting this energy. All these practices combine *prāṇa* and mantra: *japa* and *uccāra* cannot be separated from the movement (or the stilling, or, at least, presence) of *prāṇa*, vital energy.
43. "Discursive, dualistic, thought," says Abhinava in the *TĀ* (16.250-51, vol. 10, pp. 98-99), "verily, is discourse (*saṃjalpamaya*), but [in its deeper nature], it is awareness (*vimarśa*). But as this awareness is mantra, it is pure, free from any bondage, perpetual, and inseparable from the eternal and grace-bestowing Śiva. When uniting with this [mantra] even the master's discursive thought attains Śivahood."

This connection between the mantra and the mantrin's mind is also underlined in the *SpK* (2.11) when they say, following a passage we have just seen: "The mantras [pervaded by the power of the *spanda*], merging therein, become quiescent and spotless. Then, along with the devotee's mind, they achieve Śivahood."[44] Here mantras appear (and especially from Rāmakaṇṭha's commentary, p. 83) as capable of reabsorbing the adept's usually discursive thought into their own level of pure, nondiscursive awareness. To use a mantra means to be absorbed, possessed (*āveśa*) by it. The yogin's spiritual exertion for becoming one with the mantra's level of consciousness (through a kind of mental implosion of his own self into the highest consciousness) is essential. But that energy which pervades the yogin intent on achieving dissolution, which upholds him and wherein he merges ultimately, is not different from the energy of the mantra. Thus, while this exertion from the yogin may be held as essential, and necessary for making the mantra effective, it may be as well believed (perhaps even moreso)[45] that mantras do play the main part in this practice and take the yogin's mind into their own ascending movement of return to the source.

---

vikalpaḥ kila saṃjalpamayo yat sa vimarśakaḥ/
mantrātmāsau vimarśaś ca śuddho pāśavatātmakaḥ//250//
nityaś cānādivaradaśivābhedopakalpitaḥ/
tadyogād daiśikasyāpi vikalpaḥ śivatāṃ vrajet//251//

Throughout this passage (*śl.* 250-95), wherein Abhinava discusses the nature of mantras and their purpose (*prayojana*) in *dīkṣā*, he underlines their twofold nature: an ordinary one, that of a rule-governed utterance with specific, limited action, belonging to discursive dualistic thought, and another one, free of duality, that of the supreme consciousness with which the master must become one, so that he can transmit divine grace to his disciple.

44. *SpK* 2.11 (p. 80):

tatraiva saṃpralīyante śāntarūpā nirañjanāḥ/
sahārādhakacittena tenaite śivadharmiṇaḥ//

45. This, of course, is the view of the nondualistic Śaiva authors, not that of an observer objectively considering the mantric phenomenon.

Kṣemarāja also mentioned this point in his *Vimarśinī* on *ŚS* 2.2, *prayatnaḥ sādhakaḥ*: "The continued exertion [or endeavor] is that which brings about [that on which one is intent]." "That through which is experienced the nature of the mantra as previously defined [i.e., as *citta*, awareness]," he says, "is this spontaneous endeavor consisting of taking firm hold of the initial emergence of the desire to experience it.[46] This effort is effective because it brings about the identification of the mantrin with the deity of the mantra. As is said in the *Tantrasadbhāva*: 'O dear One! When a kite, in the sky, has spotted a prey, it swoops down upon it right away with natural impetuosity; even so the king of yogins should send out the *bindu*, his mind, as an arrow placed on a bow flies up powerfully from the outstretched bow. Even so, O fair One, flies the *bindu* with the ascending force of the mantric utterance (*uccāreṇa*).'"[47] This text aptly conveys the intensity of the spiritual exertion demanded by the practice of a mantra when used for other than purely ritual purposes, and the instrumental role of the mantrin's consciousness in its working. To be sure, one could point out that the mantra, as any magical formula, is "effective" only according to how much faith is put into it, and that the stronger the faith the more effective the mantra. (This is one of the reasons why *mantrasādhana* takes such a long time, as the *sādhaka*'s psyche must literally be permeated by his mantra.) But such is not the view, of course, of our authors, for whom there is an actual interaction between two spiritual powers: that of the mantra and that of the mantrin, the former being finally, for them, probably the most important.

---

46. One should note the emphasis on the initial emergence of awareness, the initial stir of desire, as an opening on reality.

47. *ŚSV* 2.2 (p. 49): *yathoktarūpasya mantrasya anusaṃdhitsāprathamonmeṣāvastambhaprayatanātmā akṛtako yaḥ prayatnaḥ sa eva sādhako mantrayitur mantradevatātādātmyapradaḥ/ tad uktam śrītantrasadbhāve*:

āmiṣaṃ tu yathā khasthaḥ saṃpaśyac śakuniḥ priye/
kṣipram ākarṣayed yadvad vegena sahajena tu//
tadvad eva hi yogīndro mano binduṃ vikarṣayet/
yathā śaro dhanuḥ saṃstho yatnenātāḍya dhāvati//
tathā bindur varārohe uccāreṇaiva dhāvati// iti.

That is indeed the view emphasized in Kṣemarāja's commentary upon the same *Spandakārikā*s: "Mantras," he says, "become spotless in that, after the accomplishment of their particular functions, they are freed from the impurities inherent in these functions. They become quiescent in the sense that they cease to be in the nature of formulas 'expressing' (*vācaka*) a deity. Then they attain to complete nonduality—they are dissolved—in the force that is *spanda*, never to return again to a lower state. They are henceforth freed of the impurities attendant on their former particular activities and they dissolve completely [in the *spanda*] along with the devotee's mind, that is, his wordly awareness."[48] The latter, in effect, "possessed" by the mantra[49] (that has the power to absorb it into the nondiscursive state which it embodies), vanishes and is replaced by the transwordly awareness of fusion with Śiva. The fusion of the mantra and the mantrin, Kṣemarāja adds, occurs also in *dīkṣā*, when the disciple receives a mantra from his master. The *spanda* therefore constitutes in every respect the basis, the substratum (*bhitti*) of the nature as of the functioning of mantras.

Finally, it may be interesting to quote from another work, of the later Krama, Maheśvarānanda's *MM*, of which stanza 49 takes up, from a spiritual and mystical standpoint, the traditional explanation of the word mantra as *mananatrāṇa-*

---

48. *SpN* 2.1-2 (p. 45-6): *tathā nirañjanāḥ kṛtakṛtyatvān nivṛttādhikāramalāḥ śāntaviśistavācakātmasvarūpās tatraiva spandātmike bale samyag abhedāpattyā prakarṣeṇāpunarāvṛttyā līyante adhikāramalān mucyante ādhārakacittena upāsakalokasaṃvedanena saha|*

49. According to Rāmakaṇṭha (*ad SpK* 2.11, p. 83), the mind of the *sādhaka*, freed of all impurities linked to some precise purpose, together with the purified mantra, becomes spontaneously possessed by it (*svābhāvikamantrāveśa*).

Mantrāveśa takes place in ritual context also. See, for instance *TĀ* 15.151-52, where the blindfolded disciple is suddenly shown the sacrificial ground "illuminated by the radiance of the mantra" and is then pervaded by this radiance; being thus possessed by the mantra (*tadāveśavaśād*), he is identified with it (*tanmayatāṃ prapadyate*). In this case, the disciple feels the intimate presence of the mantra (*mantrasaṃnidhim*) because he receives the grace of God (or of the guru): *śaktipātakṛtaḥ*.

rūpa. It reads thus: "Reflection (*manana*) upon one's own omnipresence, 'protection' (*trāṇa*) against the fear of one's limitations, an indescribable experience wherein all dichotomized thought is dissolved, such is the meaning of the word mantra."[50] Commenting upon this stanza in his *Parimala*, Maheśvarānanda stresses the role of that intuition linked to the spiritual energy that is to be experienced in one's own heart (*svahṛdaye*). He refers here to the *ŚS* and to Abhinavagupta, and quotes this *śloka* from the *Rājarājabhaṭṭārakatantra:* "The mantra does not consist of phonemes. It is not the ten-armed or five-faced body [of a deity]. It is the flashing forth of the subtle resonance [arising] at the starting-point of the intention [to utter it]."[51] This formulation, like the above, (see p. 394, n. 46) can be explained by the influence of Buddhist notions concerning the self-revelatory instant of all cognition which is free of all thought-construction. In nondualistic Śaivism also, the distinct, discursive perception of an object is held as occurring after an initial moment of nondiscursive all-inclusive apprehension, which is a grasping of the true nature of that thing, and therefore of the Absolute.

While—for those texts on which we focus here—the mantric practice involves the coalescence of the mantra's spiritual energy with the adept's consciousness, both flowing back toward the Godhead, such a fusion demands of course a special type of mental effort. It implies also practices which, in such a tantric context, are primarily of the yogic sort, that is, connected first of all with the movement of *prāṇa* and with the arousal of the *kuṇḍalinī* (the importance of which we have already seen in the previous chapters). We shall see briefly later on some aspects of these practices. First I would like to bring to the reader's attention some notions that intervene in such practices,

---

50. *MM*, 49 (p. 121):

mananamayī nijavibhave nijasaṅkoce bhaye trāṇamayī/
kavalitaviśvavikalpā anubhūtiḥ kāpi mantraśabdārthaḥ//

51. *MMP* (p. 122):

varṇātmako na mantro daśabhujadeho na pañcavadano 'pi/
saṅkalpapūrvakoṭau nādollāso bhaven mantraḥ//

notably those of *anusaṃdhāna*, of *smaraṇa* and, above all, of *uccāra*.

The term *anusaṃdhāna* may be translated as one-pointed attention mentally aiming at, or searching. "By one-pointed attention on the Great Lake," says the *ŚS*, 1.22, "one experiences the power of mantras."[52] This experience, explains Kṣemarāja (*ŚSV*, p. 44), consists of being incessantly inwardly aware of one's identity with it. It implies a concentrated, voluntary, one-pointed attention directed at the mantra the power of which is thus realized as none other than the supreme "I" shining as the totality of sounds and as identical with the inner self of the yogin.

More surprising as a means to become one with a mantra may seem remembrance or calling to mind (*smaraṇa, smṛti*), to which however a real importance is given as a practice helping to grasp the essence of a mantra. The role of *smaraṇa* is however justified by Abhinava's conception of memory. Remembrance or memory, for him, insofar as it enables one to bring back a moment from the past to the present time, is considered as evidence of the continuous existence of the oneness of consciousness: that of the individual subject who remembers, but that also of the divine consciousness assuming all forms, underlying every thought therefore of the supreme knower.[53] Thus Abhinavagupta, noticing that memory is unity in multiplicity, goes so far as to write in the *IPV*: "Thus, he who remembers is none other than the supreme Lord" (*evaṃ ca sa eva parameśvaraḥ smarati, IPV*, 1.4.1, vol. 1, p. 153). "Memory," he says in the *TĀ* (quoting the *Triśirobhairavatantra*), "a recalling to mind, is at the root of all the modalities of existence; verily its innermost nature is the mantra. It is that which allows the apprehension of the deeper nature of these modalities when they arise. Memory, [indeed], induces this nature. Coloring [or

52. *mahāhradānusaṃdhānān mantravīryānubhavaḥ.* Consciousness is like a lake in that it is still and holds the whole cosmos within itself, as a lake contains fish and so forth.

53. Substratum and continuity, the existence of which is asserted by Abhinava, in contrast with the Buddhist logicians who denied both. However, some Buddhists did admit, with *ālayavijñāna*, a causal continuum of *saṃsāra*.

taking hold of] all objective modalities, as it is present in the multiplicity of forms, it partakes of the innate nature of all things, it is consciousness in the highest sense [of this word], abiding in what has been manifested. Know that as such it is called supreme reality [or essence]."[54] Thus the outstanding role of memory, its eminent nature, coincides somehow with the preeminence of the mantra as supreme consciousness. They do not appear as distinct from each other: in both cases (as far as there are two cases), there seems to be a single movement of grasping the deeper, essential nature of everything, which is mantra and consciousness as well.[55]

Stressing *anusaṃdhāna* or *smaraṇa* is to place the emphasis on the mental and spiritual aspect of the mantra. It is to adopt an "intellectual" perspective, that indeed of Abhinava. Notwithstanding the above-mentioned quotation from the *Triśirobhairavatantra*, this is probably not the perspective of the earlier Tantric texts (hardly known at all, it is true), nor even that of Tantras in general. In fact, it is not even always Abhinava's perspective, whose *TĀ*, for instance, retains a number of *mantrayoga* practices and does not disregard ritual. Indeed, only in the *śāmbhavopāya* and in the *śāktopāya* does spiritual ascesis free itself from rites and all mental and bodily practices, which are foremost in the *aṇavopāya*, in the rites of *dīkṣā*, and

---

54. *TĀ* 5.137-39 (vol. 3, p. 450 and 452):

smṛtiś ca smaraṇaṃ pūrvaṃ sarvabhāveṣu vastutaḥ/
mantrasvarūpaṃ tadbhāvyasvarūpāpattiyojakam//137//
smṛtiḥ svarūpajanikā sarvabhāveṣu rañjikā/
anekākārarūpeṇa sarvatrāvasthitena tu//138//
svasvabhāvasya saṃprāptiḥ saṃvittiḥ paramārthataḥ/
vyaktiniṣṭhā tato viddhi sattā sā kīrtitā parā//139//

55. "Memory," Abhinava says in the *IPV* (1.4.1, vol. 1, p. 154), "when vivified by the mantra, and so forth, is like the miraculous jewel which can bestow all the supernatural powers," a sentence also quoted by Jayaratha (*ad TĀ* 5.136, vol. 3, p. 449) in support of the assertion that recalling to mind is the supreme efficient power of mantras: *mantrāṇāṃ paraṃ vīryam.*

In his commentary on *YH* 3.181 (p. 368, Dvivedi's edition: Delhi, 1988), Amṛtānanda explains *smaret*, in the *japa* of the *viṣuva* with the *śrīvidyā*, as *anusandhāna*, thus underscoring the similarity of these two mental processes.

so forth, described at great length throughout the *TĀ*.

These are all cases when the mantra must be put into practice through utterance, *uccāra(ṇa)*, basically a yogic performance. Here we can see once more that in Tantric traditions, theory and practice cannot be separated, and that practice is always both corporeal and mental: the mantra is used in *sādhana*, or during a rite, both of which involve the whole human being, made up inseparably of body and mind (to use a dichotomy which, though not Indian, is familiar). That the *uccāra* as utterance is necessary in mantric practice is obvious. Every mantra, indeed, even though being in essence consciousness, consists, in the form and substance of its expression, of at least theoretically pronounceable phonemes or sounds. It is a phonic energy that, quite naturally, manifests itself through an emission which, even when not vocal, still has, at least theoretically, the aspect of a phonetic process even though the latter remains a purely "inner" and abstract one.

We have already come across the term *uccāra* (or *uccāraṇa*), the primary meaning of which is to go upwards, to rise, to let some content issue out, hence the derived meaning of utterance or pronunciation of a letter (as an emission of sound resulting from the upward movement of the breath in the larynx). We have seen (above, p. 142), notably in connection with *haṃsa*, that the *uccāra* is not the actual pronunciation of a sound, but the conjunction of the phonic energy of the supreme Word, *haṃsa*, with the "breath" (*prāṇa*), that is, the vital energy, this being nothing other than the human and cosmic energy, the *kuṇḍalinī*. *Uccāra* is thus the creative, vital movement of the supreme energy.[56]

But the *uccāra* is also the utterance of a mantra, and as such it is no longer a spontaneous, cosmic phenomenon, but a voluntary, human one, where the movement of *prāṇa* is associated with mental concentration, *anusaṃdhāna* or *dhyāna*, and to remembrance, *smaraṇa*. Thus in the *TĀ* (5.43-72), the

56. The *uccāra* of *haṃsa* is described in various texts. It is usually called *ajapājapa*, on which one may refer to my study of *japa* in the *BEFEO*, 1987, where I describe this practice as expounded in the *Dakṣiṇamūrtisaṃhitā*.

uccāra of the *bījamantra SAUḤ* is a practice where creative mental concentration (*bhāvanā*) awakens and follows the movement of *prāṇa*, "the heart utterance" (*hṛdayoccāra, śl.* 52-53), taking the yogin up to the supreme stage. In that stage there occurs also a further *uccāra*, the nature of which is consciousness (*cidātmā*), and where a still greater bliss is experienced, such a bliss being in fact linked to sexo-yogic practices (*śl.* 70). There the *uccāra* appears as a fusion of the yogin's vital and spiritual energy with the source of the mantras' energy. The same chapter (*śl.* 131-32, p. 444) describes the *uccāra* as that wherein is uttered "a phoneme similar to an unarticulated utterance or sound" (*avyaktānukṛtaprāyo dhvanir varṇaḥ*), the "form" (*tanuḥ*) of which being that either of the *sṛṣṭibīja* or of the *saṃhārabīja* (i.e., *SAUḤ* or *KHPHREṂ*): by practicing this, the yogin attains to pure consciousness. Such an utterance seems in fact to be more in the nature of a state of consciousness, of a mental representation, than of an actual, empirically perceptible, utterance.[57] Abhinava adds, in fact, (*śl.* 133-34), that the utterance or the calling to mind of the *anacka* consonants, from *k* to *s*, induces various states of consciousness (*saṃvit*—explained in Jayaratha's gloss, p. 445, as experiences, *anubhāva*; Jayaratha adds that the calling to mind or the constant repetition of these phonemes leads one to experience the fusion into consciousness: *cidaikātmyam anubhavet*).

The *uccāra*, however, even in Abhinava's perspective, may consist in a perceptible utterance. It may take a form not unlike prayer (especially the "prayer of the heart" of Orthodox Christianity), since in this same chapter of the *TĀ* (*śl.* 135-36) he quotes the *VBh* (130), which states that "through unbroken recitation of the word *Bhairava* [one becomes] Śiva," (*bhairavaśabdasya saṃtatoccāraṇāc chivaḥ*). This is one of the relatively few cases in the texts that we are considering[58] where

---

57. The *uccāra*, insofar as it is linked with the "breath" (*prāṇa*), usually reaches its perfection when the *prāṇa* and *apāna* breaths join together in the *suṣumnā*, wherein they rise, then become still, "resting" in the Absolute: this is a kind of mystical experience, not a phonetic enunciation.

58. The practice becomes more frequent from the Indian Middle Ages onward, with the mystic saint-poets, from the fourteenth century to the present day. Cf. my study on *japa* in the *BEFEO* cited above.

the name of a deity—or, more accurately, the syllables of which this name consists, each with its own value, its own meaning[59]—is treated as a mantra. Commenting on this *śloka* of the *TĀ*, Jayaratha explains that the word *Bhairava* should be repeated while merging into the self of consciousness. Such *uccāra* consists of an intensive awareness of the mantra associated to the ascending movement of the *kuṇḍalinī* in the *suṣumnā*, from the heart up to the *dvādaśānta*, thanks to which one will attain union with Bhairava.[60]

Study of Four Mantras

To supplement our rather brief discussion of mantras, it may not be out of place to further explore how nondualistic Śaiva texts describe some particular mantras and the way they should be uttered or meditated. We cannot obviously make here an in-depth study of mantric practices in all their diversity: they are too many and too varied. Furthermore, they are described in a number of works dealing with rituals.[61] We shall limit ourselves to the study of four particular mantras because these are held as important ones in the texts studied in this book and because they may help in more concretely illustrating, or elucidating, the more general notions about mantras—notably as regards their salvific function, or the intuitive realization of the Godhead's cosmic game. Thus we shall see successively *OṂ*, the *netra* mantra (or *mṛtyujit*), the "heart *bīja*" *SAUḤ*, and

59. On this, see Śivopadhyāya's extensive commentary upon this *sūtra* of the *VBh* (pp. 113-16 of the *KSTS* edition).

60. *ātmavyāptigarbhīkāreṇa bhairaśabdasya paunaḥ puṇyena "uccāraṇāt" madhyadhāmni hṛdayād dvādaśāntaṃ yāvat parāmarśanāc chivo bhaved bhairavaikātmyam anubhavet* (*TĀ*, vol. 3, p. 448).

Ātmavyāpti, fusion or oneness with the "self of absolute consciousness", which is the vision of the essence, is generally thought of as occuring at the *samanā* level. Cf. *ŚSV* 3.7, quoting *SvT* 4.434 (p. 87).

61. For the Āgamic Śaiva ritual the most extensive and accessible source, as well as the most judiciously and thoroughly expounded and commented upon, is the *SP* in H. Brunner's edition, to which we have already referred the reader. For the utterance or the recitation of mantras, here again I refer to the collective work *Understanding Mantras*, H. Alper, ed. (Albany: SUNY Press, 1989) and to my study of *japa*, *BEFEO*, 1987.

the *piṇḍanātha* (or *mātṛsadbhāva*). *OṂ* will afford us the opportunity to ascertain what has been said of the mantra as a means to gain access to the primordial Word, since it will take us along the whole path leading from the world of empirical utterance to the transcendental origin of the Word. With the *netra* mantra, we shall see a bodily and mental practice of tantric *mantrayoga*, whereas with *SAUḤ* and the *piṇḍanātha* we shall emphasize the metaphysical (linked, however, with a mental practice) aspect of these formulas.[62] I shall add that these particular mantras are given as mere examples. Admittedly they are characteristic: they reflect a number of common conceptions and usages. But they do not stand as an absolute norm, as practices and notions to be met with unchanged under all circumstances. Here as elsewhere in India an overall unity in principles is expressed through a great diversity of practices and rules.

OṂ

It is only natural to begin with the *prāṇava OṂ* not only because we have considered it already (*supra*, chap. 1, 3 and 6) but also and primarily owing to the prominent place this hallowed syllable has always occupied since Vedic times, and which it still retains in the Tantric texts studied in the present book. This lends to the metaphysico-linguistic speculations on *OṂ* a somewhat paradigmatic character. The division of its *uccāra*, for instance, is also found with other *bījamantra*s (*HRĪṂ*, and so forth).

OṂ is often given as the original mantra (*mūlamantra*), the

---

62. It would have been interesting to see also the *śrīvidyā*, since it would have allowed us to look at an important Kula-related tradition, hardly touched upon in this book, though its doctrines and practices are of interest. But studying how this *vidyā* can be empowered would have been too long for this chapter. I gave a brief outline of the *japa* of the *śrīvidyā* according to the *YH* in a study published in the first volume of the *Tantric and Taoist Studies in Honor of R. A. Stein* (Brussels, 1981). There is a description of the so-called six *artha*s (that is, of interpretations and practices) of the *śrīvidyā* in the second *paṭala* of the *YH*: see my forthcoming translation of this text and its commentary by Amṛtānanda.

primordial seed (*ādibīja*),[63] as the mantra which more than any other symbolizes or embodies the supreme, transcendental, and attributeless (*niṣkala*) reality. Its being designated as *praṇava* (from *pra-ṇu*, to sound, to reverberate, to make a humming sound, derived from the root *NU*, to praise or command, but also to sound or shout) is explained by Kṣemarāja in the *Uddyota* of the *SvT*: *prakarṣeṇa nuyate paraṃ tattvam*, "that by which is eminently praised or expressed the supreme reality." "The *praṇava*," the *NT* says, "is the vital breath of animate beings present in all living creatures;"[64] and the *SvT*: "All that which, consisting of speech, [is extant] in this world, comes to be [only because it abides] in Śiva's knowledge [that is, his

---

63. According to the *LT* 52.20 (p. 219), it is because of their fusion with the fullness of the supreme "I-ness" (*pūrṇāhantasamāveśāt*) due to the presence of this primordial seed (*ādibījasamanvayāt*), that the totality of mantras (*mantraganaḥ*) becomes identified with Śrī, Viṣṇu's supreme energy.

The *prāṇava* is that which expresses the Lord, says the *YSū* 1.27: *tasya vācakaḥ praṇavaḥ*. And, referring both to the cosmic level and to the philosophy of knowledge, verses 9 and 10 of Bhartṛhari's *VP* (*Brahmakaṇḍa*) read:

"True knowledge, that known as "perfection," to that a single word gives access; it is wholly contained in the *praṇava*, which does not go against any opinion. From it [i.e. from the *praṇava*], the creator of the worlds, proceed various sciences together with their main and secondary annexes, through which the knowledge of [Brahman] and of the rites is achieved."

satyā viśuddhis tatroktā vidyaivaikapadāgamagā/
yuktā praṇavarūpeṇa sarvavādāvirodhinī//

vīdhātus tasya lokānām aṅgopāṅganibandhanāḥ/
vidyābhedāḥ pratāyante jñānasaṃskārahetavaḥ//

64. *NT* 22.14: *praṇavaḥ prāṇināṃ prāṇo jīvanaṃ sampratiṣṭhitam/* (vol. 2, p.309). Kṣemarāja's commentary on this passage (ibid., pp. 310-12) elaborates on the Tantra's assertions, attributing to *oṃ* all the characteristic features of the primordial energy of the Word, the source and basis of all that is in existence. "The *praṇava*," it says, "is that energy which gives life to creatures; it is the universal vivifying power; it is the generic *spanda*, the synthetic awareness, the 'unstruck' sound; it is none other than the initial move *abhyupagama*) [toward manifestation], the cause of all knowledge, action and objectivity," and so forth.

consciousness], and such knowledge abides therein [i.e., in the *praṇava*]."[65] We have seen above (p. 347) that the *ṣaḍadhvan*, according to the *SvT*, may be looked at as consisting of eleven subdivisions of *OṂ*. Similarly we shall see later (p. 410), according to the same text, the whole universe correlated with its fivefold division.

The mantra *OṂ* appears thus as a symbol of the supreme reality and as expressing (or corresponding to) the totality of the cosmos. Its meditative utterance, with its attendant practices of mental creation, is therefore for the adept a means to become identified with the stages of the process of cosmic resorption; thereby it is a way and a means to gain access to that reality, wherein the cosmos abides—an especially eminent means, since *OṂ is* primarily the supreme reality, Brahman, or for our texts, the transcendental supreme Śiva.[66]

The yogic meditative utterance (*uccāra*) of *OṂ* is described in several chapters of the *SvT* and in chapter 22 of the *NT*, both of them commented upon by Kṣemarāja.[67] While largely in agreement, these two descriptions differ on particular points (with variants even from chapter to chapter in the *SvT*; this can be explained by the fact that the *uccāra* of the mantra is regarded in those texts as an element in rites (above all, of various *dīkṣā*s) which differ from each other. Abhinava, I believe, does not describe it. The same *uccāra* of *OṂ* is found in the Āgamas also and in the ritual handbooks of dualistic Śaivism, for instance in the *SP*.[68] In all these cases, where (except for *NT*, 22) the ritual described is usually that of *dīkṣā*

---

65. *yat kiṃcid vāṅmayaṃ loke śivajñāne pratiṣṭhitam/ śivajñānaṃ ca tatrastham* . . . (vol. 3, p. 107).

66. In the texts of the Śrīvidyā, the *bīja* of the Goddess, *HRĪṂ*, plays a similar part, with the same divisions into *kalā* from *bindu* to *unmanā*. Cf. A. Padoux, "Un *japa* tantrique," quoted above, n. 62.

67. Kṣemarāja quotes *SvT*, 7 and alludes to the *uccāra* and to the phonic stage of *unmanā* in his *Vimarśinī ad ŚS* 3.5 (pp. 80-83).

68. Cf. *SP*3, pp. 380ff., where the *uccāra* is that of *HAUṂ* (or of *H*/*HA* + *OṂ*). Aghoraśivācārya's commentary on this passage refers to *SvT*, 4. On this point see charts 12-14 of *SP*3, which give, together with the location of the subtle body's centers, the chart of the *uccāra* of *OṂ*, according to three different texts, including the *SvT*.

(where the initiate must rise through the various levels of the universe, back to their divine origin), the human and cosmic aspects of this process cannot be separated: the stage of the phonic energy described as lying in tiers in the adept's body and which he experiences, are also cosmic planes. The movement leading back to the highest plane, the "transmental" (*unmanā*), is both human and cosmic. We have seen this phonic evolution in chapter 3, as following the movement of emanation, and then the movement of resorption in chapter 6: it is the same anthropocosmic return to the origin of the Word that is again found here.

So the adept must first utter the three, theoretically[69] constituent, phonemes of *OṂ*: *A*, *U*, and *MA*, all three supported and "pervaded" (*VYĀP*) by the energy of the ascendant breath, *haṃsa* (typified by the phoneme *ha anacka*),[70] an energy which flows, with *A*, from the heart *cakra* (*hṛd*—where the *kāraṇadevatā* is Brahmā), rises to the throat *cakra* (*kaṇṭha*—Viṣṇu) with *U*, and reaches the palate *cakra* (*tālu*—Rudra) with *MA*.[71] Next comes *bindu*, the nasal sound following the phoneme *MA*. As it continues and becomes more subtle, the *bindu* moves further upward through the two stages of *ardhacandra* and *nirodhinī*.[72] With *bindu*, the utterance is conceived of as located in the *ājñācakra*, between the eyebrows (*bhrūmadhya*); it corresponds to Īśvara. For the *NT* these stages from *A* to *bindu* make up the "gross" portion of the *uccāra*, as is underscored by the fact that these utterances are correlated with the "gross" elements, from earth to water. *Ardhacandra* and *nirodhinī*, located at the forehead level (*lalāta*), are not uttered in a *cakra* and do not correspond to any *kāraṇadevatā*, perhaps because they are held merely as moments of the phonic vibration as it proceeds from *bindu* to *nāda*. The latter, also situated at the forehead level, corresponds with Sadāśiva.[73] It ends with

69. In theory, since *OṂ* is always pronounced as *om*.

70. *hakāraḥ prāṇaśaktyātmā*: *SvT* 4.263 (vol. 2, p. 167).

71. *SvT* 4.263-64 (ibid.).

72. It is not necessary to repeat here what we said above, in chapter 3, on the symbolic values attached to these three stages of *uccāra*.

73. According to chart 12 of the *SP*3, *ardhacandra* and *nirodhinī*, located, like *nāda*, at the forehead level, correspond also to Sadāśiva.

nādānta, the "end of the *nāda*," which arises when the ascending thrust of the *uccāra* is entirely absorbed in the energy: this is the stage of *śakti*. The yogin, as it seems, here reaches the cosmic level of the *śakti tattva*, located between those of Sadāśiva and of Śiva. As *śakti* cannot, however, be separated from Śiva, the stage reached by the adept from *śakti* onward is that of Śiva. The moments of the utterance are then: (1) *śakti*, which is, as it were, the very phonic energy, the actual energy aspect of the Word;[74] (2) *vyāpinī*; the same energy as all-pervading, is that level of the Word immanent to the universe which generates all of its aspects; it is also called "great void," *mahāśūnya*; (3) in *samanā*, thereafter, the energy is also void (*śūnya*), though not indifferent to the manifestation, whose substratum it somehow constitutes (*sarvabhāvābhāvabhāsabhittikalpam*). However high the stage reached by the yogin, he is still regarded as not freed from the "endless net of bondage" (*pāśajālam anantakam*) wherein he is naturally caught.[75] Total liberation will occur only when, having relinquished all thought of bondage and perceiving his own essence, he becomes one with (or permeated by) the Self (*ātmavyāpti*).[76] Then he moves up to the ultimate stage of the undivided Self (*niṣkalam ātmatattvam*, according to *NT* 22.22), that of the "transmental" phonic energy, *unmanā*. This is the stage of absolute consciousness, of complete pervasion by and inherence in Śiva (*śivavyāpti*): the transcendental void (*śūnyātiśūnya*), beyond all appearing: *nirābhāsaṃ paraṃ tattvam anuttamam*, as the *NT* puts it. The ascending movement of the *uccāra* stops here, since the phonic energy of the mantra now dissolves in its transcendental, changeless source, beyond time and all possible utterance. As for the yogin, "attaining this *unmanā* energy, the pure light inseparable from the cosmic

---

74. *NT* 22.22 (vol. 2, p. 313) calls it *kuṇḍalinī*, thus underlining the link between the *uccāra* and the arousal of the *kuṇḍalinī*.

75. *SvT* 4.432 (vol. 2, p. 271). *NT* 22.48 includes the half-stanza: *samanāntaṃ varārohe pāśajālam anantakam*, and Kṣemarāja, in his commentary (ibid., p. 328), notes that the *kāraṇadevatā*s, from Brahmā to Śiva, reach up to *samanā*.

76. *pāśāvalokanaṃ tyaktvā svarūpālokanaṃ hi yat/ ātmavyāptir bhaved eṣa* (*SvT*, 4.434, p. 272).

totality [in Kṣemarāja's words], he becomes completely fused with the supreme Bhairava, the undivided mass of consciousness and bliss."[77]

It should be noted that the *SvT* (4.344-55, vol. 2, pp. 220ff.) gives the durations of the utterance, in moras (*mātra*), of the different stages of the *uccāra*. They range from one mora for *A* to $\frac{1}{64}$ of a mora for *vyāpinī*. Such instantaneous flashes of time cannot possibly correspond to actual utterances. They are indeed regarded as beyond the level of empirically pronounceable speech. Their briefness is probably meant to suggest the *uccāra*'s growing degrees of subtleness.[78] This unreal aspect of the *uccāra* appears also in the way it is located in the body of the adept. It is deemed to extend there from the heart *cakra* to the *brahmarandhra*, and then beyond, up to the *dvādaśānta*. The *SvT* (4.342-48) mentions the number of finger's breadths (*aṅgula*) between these centers, the whole span of which measures the bodily extension of this utterance. Now, while these particulars emphasize the corporeal aspect of this yogic operation, here again the dimensions given are inconsistent with human anatomy: the human body in this case is not the physical, concrete, body of the adept, but an imaginal or phantasmal one.

That this *uccāra* takes place in the body is due to its being in the nature of Kuṇḍalinīyoga, that is, of an operation at once corporeal and phonic (since one follows the fading out of a phonic—at least in theory—utterance), mental, spiritual as well as metaphysical, since the stages of the *uccāra* carry the adept from the level of empirical speech and of thought-constructs to the supreme stage of the transcendent Śiva. To each of these stages, always correlated with a particular spot in the subtle body, correspond also deities, elements, and cosmic

---

77. *yugapad aśeṣaviśvābhedaprakāśātmonmanāśaktyāśrayena śivaṃ vrajec chivānandaghanaparabhairavasamāpattiṃ śrayet* (*SvT* 4.261, comm., vol. 1, p. 166).

78. The same is found in the *YH* 1.29-34, where the *uccāra* of the *kalā*s of *HRĪṂ* ranges from half a mora for *bindu* (as here) to 1/256 of a mora for *samanā* (*unmanā* "having no definite form cannot be uttered"), which makes it even more unfit for actual utterance.

divisions. The human being in all its aspects, the universe, and the Godhead, all are involved: we have already encountered this "cosmotheandrism," though not expounded in such a thorough and striking way as here. The following chart brings together the elements of this *uccāra* according to the *SvT*:

UCCĀRA OF *OṂ*

	devatā	*tattva*	*cakra*, areas in the body	*aṅgula*	duration (morae)
unmanā	Paramaśiva		*dvādaśānta*		no duration
samanā	Śiva /	*śiva*			?
vyāpinī	Śakti		*śikhā*	12?	1/64
śakti	Śakti	*śakti*	*brahmarandhra*	1	1/32
nādānta					?
nāda	Sadāśiva	*sadāśiva*	from the forehead to the top of the head	11	1/16
nirodhinī					1/8
ardhacandra			forehead region		1/4
bindu	Īśvara	*īśvara* *śuddhavidyā*	eyebrows (*ājñā*)	2	1/2
MA	Rudra	*māyā*	palate	4	3
U	Viṣṇu	6 *tattva* (*puruṣa* to *kalā*)	throat	8	2
A (*H*)	Brahmā	24 *tattva* (earth to *prakṛti*)	heart	4	1

All of these correspondences are scattered through several portions of the *SvT*, which, depending upon the particular aspect of *dīkṣā* dealt with, underlines some specific point. They are given more systematically in *NT*, chapter 22. This text, dealing with the symbolism of the *netra* mantra, or *mṛtyujit*, *OṂ-JUṂ-SAḤ*, discusses (*śl.* 14-18, and 25-50) the *uccāra* of *OṂ*, and describes it as containing within itself the whole universe. Kṣemarāja's commentary gives further details, but no full clarification.

"The *praṇava*," says Kṣemarāja in an initial and interesting elaboration (*NT*, vol. 2, pp. 310-12), "is the vivifying breath of all living creatures" (cf. above, p. 403, n. 64). It is the primary universal vibration (*sāmānyaspanda*), which is an act of consciousness arising at the level of nonmanifest (*anāhata*) sound, and the first move toward that whence everything originates. Thus it is the animating background of the cosmos. Here we again meet the ancient notions (cf. *supra*, chapter 1, p. 14) equating *OṂ* with *brahman*. Dwelling in all beings, it animates their vital breath (*prāṇa*), wherein it divides up into its constituent parts. Originally abiding at the level of the supreme Word (*parāvāc*), it is both the origin of the cosmos and that which draws it together and takes it back to its source through the successive stages of the *ṣaḍadhvan*:[79] this is the twofold—creative and resorbing—movement of the Word, a recurrent theme throughout this study.

In *śl.* 19 through 50 of chapter 22, the *NT* enumerates the sequence of the six *adhvan*s, next that of the *kāraṇadevatā*s, and then gives the eleven stages of the *uccāra*, from *A* to *samanā*, which, still caught up in the chains of limitation (*pāśajāla*), belong to the universe that has to be transcended (*śl.* 21-22, and comm., pp. 313-14). Then one comes to the level of the Self (*ātmatattva*), which is *niṣkala* and pure energy, and which further extends to Śiva as associated with the appearing of the world (*sābhāsa*)—this is perhaps the level of Sadāśiva. There is still one more stage beyond that: the supreme reality

---

79. We have seen above, chapter 6, p. 347, that the *mantrādhvan* may consist of the eleven *kalā*s of the *uccāra* of *OṂ*, from *A* to *samanā*.

beyond all appearing (*nirābhāsaṃ paraṃ tattvam, śl.* 23). This ultimate transcendental stage seems to be that which is designated as "the seventh" (*saptamam*), thereby lying beyond the six *kāraṇadevatā*s. It arises when these stages are transcended, at the level where they are reabsorbed and rest in their primal unsurpassable receptacle: *ṣaṭtyāgāt saptamaṃ proktaṃ layam ālayam anuttamam* (*śl.* 23, p. 315).

Reviewing (*śl.* 25-50) these twelve moments of the *uccāra*, from *A* to *unmanā*, the *NT* gives the distribution of the sixty-five *kalā*s, those limiting energies or "parts" of the universe, between the *kalā*s[80] of *OṂ*, from *A* to *samanā* (situated on the level of energy, *śakti*). Beyond that, with *unmanā*, is the plane of Śiva who, in his plenitude, is however regarded as threefold: the pure *ātman*, inseparable from the energy, pure consciousness (*cinmātra*), transparent and spotless (*śl.* 51-52); the transcendental energy united with Śiva, *unmanā* (*śl.* 52); and finally Śiva himself, *nirābhāsa*, that is, utterly transcendent.

This system is lacking in clarity and coherence. The correspondences between the stages of the *uccāra* of *OṂ* and the divisions of the cosmos, while enumerated in details, do not form a well structured scheme. *Śl.* 25 through 47 give, for instance, the distribution of the sixty-eight *kalā*s between the stages of the *uccāra*, which are also correlated with the six *kāraṇadevatā*s and with Śiva's aspects and functions. These *śloka*s also ventilate the stages of *OṂ* in the adept's body. But they do not say clearly how are distributed, in the subtle body, the four *kalā*s, *A*, *U*, *MA*, and *bindu* (to which is added *nāda*), and the rest of the *kalā*s (*ardhacandra* and *nirodhinī* on the one hand, those of *nādānta* to *samanā* on the other). Admittedly, the general pattern of the system as well as its role in the soteriological function of *OṂ* are clear, but there is no coherence in details.[81] We see here what we have seen previously with the *ṣaḍadhvan*: classifications that are correlated

80. The *kalā*s, in this case, are the divisions of the phonic energy of the mantra *OṂ*, not the cosmic divisions or portions of Śiva.

81. There is a discussion of this distribution (and its inconsistencies), with a chart of the correspondences between *uccāra*, gods, elements, and so forth, in H. Brunner's study on the *NT*, p. 193.

but not entirely consistent, this being probably due, in both cases, to an (inadequate) bringing together of earlier systems.[82]

OṂ JUṂ SAḤ: The Netra Mantra

As we said before, the *mūlamantra* of the *NT* is that of the Eye (*netra*) of Śiva, also known as *mṛtyujit*, "conqueror of death." It consists of the three *bīja*s *OṂ*, *JUṂ*, and *SAḤ*. The speculations about *OṂ* of the *NT* that we have just seen deal in fact with the first of these three *bīja*s. This being so, one might be tempted to say that if *OṂ* is by itself enough to give its user Śivahood, *JUṂ* and *SAḤ* must be of little use. But the *NT* (22.15-18) explains that while *OṂ* "grasps the universe in its entirety," that is, draws it together and takes it to the plane of Śiva, *JUṂ* (understood as deriving from the verbal root *HU*, to sacrifice, to offer in oblation: *juhoti* in the present indicative) offers this universe, first brought together and purified, as an oblation into the fire of Śiva; while with *SAḤ*, ending with the *visarga ḥ* (we have seen its symbolism), Śiva (and therefore the adept) attains a state of plenitude: that is, that of the plenary oblation (*pūrṇahuti*), and above all that of the divine energy in its full power, embracing within itself the whole cosmos. This is the Tantric vision of plenitude where unto the fullness of the deity is added that of the divinized cosmos. Fusion in this fullness may be achieved through meditation of the mantra alone, provided the aspirant be a *jñānin* capable of such a spiritual exertion: this is prescribed in chapter 8 of the *NT* as supreme meditation (*paradhyāna*). Chapter 6, on the other

---

82. The sixth *paṭala* of the *SvT*, entited *Pañcapraṇavādhikāra*, considers a fivefold *japa* of *OṂ*. This *japa*, also associated with *haṃsa*, is made up of various divisions into five, leading to a sixth, transcendental, stage. The system is quite close to that examined here. They coincide to a large extent. It is therefore not necessary to discuss it here.

For the *pañcapraṇava*, cf. *TĀ* 8.328 and *SvT* 10.1133, where it appears as five Rudras. Cf. also *YH-Dī*, p. 80. In the *Kubjikāmata*, the term indicates the five *bīja*s: *AIṂ*, *ŚRĪṂ*, *HRĪṂ*, *PHREṂ*, and *KṢAUṂ*.

There is a very characteristic, very complex, example of Kuṇḍalinī-yoga associated with the *uccāra* of a mantra in the *japa* prescribed in the third *paṭala* of the *YH:* cf. above, p. 402, n. 62.

hand, describes a "gross" (*sthūla*) way of realization, consisting of a ritualistic worship of the mantra, through cult, oblations, and the use of *yantra*s and *mudrā*s: this is the common type of *mantrasādhana*,[83] accessible to the least gifted adepts, where the mantra is treated as a deity to whom are paid reverence and obeisance. There is, however, an intermediate practice also, the "subtle meditation" (*sūkṣmadhyāna*) of the *mṛtyujit*, of which I would like to give here a brief outline, for it is probably the most interesting of the three. Like the other two, and even more so, it is a distinctly tantric form of *mantrayoga*.[84]

Like any practice of this type, this "meditation" is based upon the yogic image of the body,[85] that is, on the structure of the "subtle body," which the adept visualizes with sufficient intensity to "see" it mentally and feel its presence in his physical body. This is a complex structure, since in addition to the *cakra*s, here six in number, there are also, tiered along the axis of the body, twelve "knots" (*granthi*) and sixteen "supports" (*ādhāra*), together with five "spaces" or "voids" (*vyoman*, *śūnya*), three "dwelling places" or "abodes" (*dhāman*) and three subtle centers "to be perceived" (*lakṣya*) in meditation.[86] From these centers radiate forth the *nāḍī*s, the "arteries" of the subtle body: ten principal and seventy-two thousand secondary (sometimes believed to be 35 million!); these are the channels through which the *prāṇa* moves and through which mantras infuse their energy, thus converting the yogin's (physical) body into a "divine body" (*dīvyadeha*), free of all

---

83. For the *mantrasādhana*, I refer again to H. Brunner's article "Le *sādhaka*, personnage oublié du śivaïsme du sud" (*JAs*: 1975), already mentioned.

84. A brief summary of this practice is given in H. Brunner's analysis of the *NT* (*BEFEO*, vol. 61, 1974) pp. 142-45. I refer to this study for those points which I shall overlook here. As Brunner notes, the *NT* is a rather obscure text and Kṣemarāja's *Uddyota* is not always very illuminating. It is possible, however, to describe this practice and bring out its characteristics and interest.

85. For this bodily image, with its centers and channels, see, for instance, the chart, p. 122, in A. Danielou, *Yoga, The Method of Reintegration* (New York: University Books, 1955). See also A. Sanderson, "Maṇḍala," for the "pervasion" of the body by the Triśūlamaṇḍala of the Trika.

86. For these centers, see H. Brunner, *op. cit.*, pp. 142-43.

affliction. The mantrins, in fact, more than liberation, want to gain supernatural powers. Even more than the practice of *OṂ*, that of the *mṛtyujit* consists of working on the image of the body, through *bhāvanā*, the intense creative meditation that causes to appear to the mind vivid images with which the meditator becomes identified.[87] The *NT* describes two forms of "subtle meditation"—that of the Tantras and that of the Kula[88]—differing in their particulars but based on the same conception of the subtle body and of its functions, on the same structure of the cosmos, and on the same stages in the utterance of the mantra. We shall describe briefly the second of these two meditations (*śl.* 16-52).

The adept must first mentally collect all his energy, that of the primordial cosmic "vibration" (*spanda*), in the *kanda*, the center of his subtle body located above the genitals (and whence, in theory, originate all the *nāḍī*s). Prior to this, however, the energy should have reached "down to *kālāgni*," that is, both to his toes and to the "world" (*bhuvana*) of Kālāgni, the world of the Fire of Time, the lowest of all. The whole body and cosmos are therefore involved right from the start in this process. Once collected there, the power (*vīrya*), which is vibrating energy (*śāktaspanda*), should be sent upward through the whole body; this ascent is induced and stimulated by successive expansions and contractions of the *mattagandha-sthāna*.[89] Then it rises through the *suṣumnā*, where it should

---

87. For the *bhāvanā*, see F. Chenet's papers in *"Mantras et diagrammes rituels dans l'hindouisme,"* and in *Numen*, vol. 34, fasc. 1 (1987).

The *NT* itself uses the term *bhāvanā* in chapter 8 only once or twice, but *bhāvanā* and *bhāvayet* are of frequent occurrence in Kṣemarāja's commentary.

88. On the Kula as a reform of the tantric cult of the *yoginī*s, see A. Sanderson, "Śaivism and the Tantric Traditions," in S. Sutherland *et al.*, eds. *The World's Religions* (London: Routledge, 1988), already quoted in this book (see chapter 2, p. 000, note 49).

89. "The place of exciting smell," this expression often indicates the sexual organs—thus *TĀ* 29.246, or *TĀ*, 3.170, comm. Here it refers to the "bulb" (*kanda*).

The *Haṭhayogapradīpikā*, 3.113, describes the *kanda* as enclosing the coiled-up *kuṇḍalinī*. The *NT* here (*śl.* 31-32) gives five equivalent

become still, permeating the sense organs (*kāraṇa*) of the adept. Thereafter, "rejecting all that belongs to *māyā* (i.e., to the senses), it moves up beyond the *kāraṇadevatās*, Brahmā, and so forth, and "pierces" the six *cakras*, the twelve *granthis*, the five *vyoman* or *śūnya*, all stages to be transcended, until it finally reaches the level of the supreme energy which, says Kṣemarāja (p. 162), is *unmanā*, the supreme reality (*paratattva*), Śiva. The piercing of the subtle body's centers is accomplished, the Tantra says (*śl.* 30), with the "spear of cognition" (*jñānaśūlena*), that is, says Kṣemarāja, "through the pulsating radiance of consciousness assuming the form of the mantra's efficient energy" (*mantravīryabhūtacitsphurattā*). Since this force, both of the mind and of the Word, is sent upward through contractions and expansions of the *kanda*, this appears as a mental and phonic process, based, however, on the physical (the physical body acting on the subtle centers). It is a process that, however paradoxical, is easily understandable in the visionary system of mental representations of *mantrayoga*. Those are mental pictures conjured up and superimposed in the body through *bhāvanā*, whilst yogic practices trigger the phenomena proper to the *kuṇḍalinī*, whose arousal, actually felt because intensely imagined, confirms the upward thrust of the mantra—and of consciousness—from the base of the spine to the top of the head. This ascent is also a passage from the empirical world to the divine level: we deal here with a set of facts and images where the mental, the phonic-phonetic, the physical, and the cosmic are thoroughly interwoven.

To return, however, to this process: in the *kanda* the yogin "finds" (*vindate*) the *khecarīmudrā*, that is, at this moment of the *uccāra*, he attains that form of energy through which one can "move in the sky of consciousness."[90] He must also probably

---

terms for *kanda*, including *janmasthāna* ("birthplace") and *mūlādhāra*. Its meaning is therefore not quite certain. However, it clearly refers to the genito-perineal region.

90. The *khecarīmudrā*, says Abhinava (*TĀ* 32.32-33; vol. 12, p. 333-34), enables the adept to arrive at the very root of the universe, the creative power inherent in all mantras. *Āhnika* 32 of the *TĀ* is devoted mainly to this *mudrā* and its variants. There, *mudrās* are defined both as a

assume the corporeal-cum-mystical attitude peculiar to this *mudrā*.[91] Thanks to the energy of *khecarī*, the mantra and the mind of the adept rise up to the *dvādaśānta*, where, as the "breaths" now come to a stop,[92] the adept's mind, pacified, pure, pervaded by the three undivided energies of Śiva (will, cognition, and action) merges into the supreme Godhead, the omnipresent, primal Energy, "the womb of all the gods and all the energies, that *yoni* wherein the whole universe is born," "wherein all the mantras gather together and become henceforth endowed with the power of salvation, the supreme abode, the birthplace of the cosmic energy" (*śl.* 40-42). At this point, the yogin must energize the *bindu*, the center between the eyebrows, and thereby cause an outpouring of the nectar or ambrosia, the *amṛta*[93] which, "like a tidal wave," first rises to the level of *brahman*, then flowing down again, goes from the *suṣumnā* through all the *nāḍī*s and fills the whole physical and subtle body of the practitioner (and also all the worlds, from *kālāgni* to Śiva). The *sādhaka* (through *bhāvanā*) is now immersed in, permeated by, this nectar, and thereby merged in Śiva. From then on he enjoys perfect health (*śl.* 50). He becomes immortal: he is *mṛtyujit*, "conqueror of death," and *kālajit*, "conqueror of time" (*śl.* 51-52): freed from all limitations, that of time and any other as well.

---

reflection or a reproduction of the appearance of the deity and as that from which the deity appears and therefore thanks to which the adept is united with (or possessed by) it. Cf. A. Padoux, "The Body in Tantric Ritual: The Case of the *Mudra*s," in T. Goudriaan, ed. *The Sanskrit Tradition and Tantrism* (Leiden: Brill, 1990).

91. Kṣemarāja's commentary (p. 169) describes the *mudrā* according to the *MVT* (chapter 7) as a yogic practice combining a bodily posture and the upward thrust of the *netramantra* through three *vyoman*s, "thanks to which the great yogin achieves the power to move through space."

    In the *ŚSV* 2.5 (p. 58), Kṣemarāja defines this *mudrā* as "the surging forth of the bliss of the self" (*svātmānandocchalatārūpā*) and "the essence of the supreme consciousness (*parasaṃvittisvarūpā*).

92. Both the ascendant and descendant breaths join together and become still at the "place of the center," *madhyadhāman*, the "central" point of the "breath," and the center of the soul.

93. The *amṛta* flows naturally from the *bindu*, since *bindu* is the moon: cf. *supra*, chapter 3, p. 109, n. 66.

What comes foremost in such a practice is evidently the bodily and mental practice of *kuṇḍalinīyoga*, with all the visionary system of mental representations and with the phantasmal manipulations of the body image it implies. The mantric and phonic element proper seems subordinated to the other elements. Nevertheless this is a practice of *mantrayoga*, and it is described as such by the *NT*. We are therefore still dealing here with the salvific power of mantras: it is the *mṛtyujit* that is deemed to have caused and brought about the return of the mantrin's consciousness to the supreme energy and its fusion in this energy, which is indissolubly consciousness and Word.

SAUḤ—Piṇḍanātha/Mātṛsadbhāva

What we shall now see, with *SAUḤ* and the *piṇḍanātha* (also called *mātṛsadbhāva*), is the symbolism, the role of a mantra, its condition as the "seed" (*bīja*) of the supreme Godhead rather than its practice and use. The soteriological use of these mantras, however, will not be overlooked. Indeed, the main *raison d'être* of a mantra is that it is an embodiment of the power of the Word that can be used by an initiated adept for practical, ritual, symbolical, or soteriological purposes. As it is, these two "mantras" are used to grasp intellectually (or rather to realize intuitively) the cosmic process as abiding within the Godhead, and through this realization, to impart liberation to the adept. The phonetic symbolism involved here is similar to that of the *varṇaparāmarśa* which we have seen. But it is gathered together, concentrated, as it were, in a monosyllable: the more secret, the more mysterious, the shorter[94] the mantra, the more effective it is. The passages dealing with these two mantras are also especially obscure and elliptic. They are to be found mostly in the *MVT*, the *TĀ*, and the *PT* and its

94. As we have already emphasized on several occasions, here and elsewhere, in Indian thought, the concise, the concentrated, is traditionally held as superior to the diluted, the discursive. On this point, cf. Charles Malamoud's remarks in *Le svādhyāya, Récitation personnelle du Veda*, pp. 84-89.

commentaries, especially Abhinava's *PTV*.[95] The importance given to these two mantras seems a particular trait of the Kula's Trika tradition.

SAUḤ

The *PT* describes this mantra thus: "United with the fourteenth [phoneme], O fair One, associated with the last [portion] of the Master of the *tithi*s, the third *brahman*, O fair-hipped Woman, is the heart of the Self of Bhairava."[96] The fourteenth phoneme is *AU*. The *tithi*s, the lunar days, are the sixteen "vowels" corresponding to Śiva in the phonematic emanation:[97] Śiva is therefore their Master and the "last" of them is the *visarga AḤ*. The "third brahman" indicates the letter *sa*, or more accurately, the sibilant *s anacka*.[98] Thus we have *S* + *AU* + *Ḥ* = *SAUḤ* which, for the *PT*, is the Godhead's

---

95. The *MVT* 3.52-54 gives *SAUḤ* as the mantra of the goddess Parā. *Śl.* 9ff. of the *PT*, and therefore a portion of Abhinava's commentaries (*PTV* and *PTLv*) on these stanzas concerns *SAUḤ*. The *TĀ*, 4.186-91 and 5.142-50 deals with *SAUḤ* and *piṇḍanātha*. *TĀ* 30.27-36 gives the forms *HSAUḤ*, *SHAUḤ*, and *SHSAUḤ*, which it attributes to the *Triśirobhairavatantra*. *TĀ* 30.45-53 deals with various forms of the *piṇḍanātha/mātṛsadbhāva*. They are also considered in a short text by Kṣemarāja, the *Parāpraveśikā*. (See also the *PS*, 1-42, where *SAUḤ* is the third part of Tripurabhairavi's mantra).

    On the subject of the heart and the heart-mantra, I refer the reader to P. E. Muller-Ortega's study of this theme, *The Triadic Heart of Śiva* (Albany: State University of New York Press, 1989), especially chapter 8, "The Heart as Mantra."

96. *caturdaśayutaṃ bhadre tithiśāntasamanvitam//9//*
    tritīyaṃ brahma suśroṇi hṛdayaṃ bhairavātmanaḥ/ (*PTV*, p. 218)

97. Cf. above, ch. 5, pp. 233ff.

98. Pp. 221-230 of the *PTV* comment upon the expression "third *brahman*," its various interpretations being explained by Abhinava as pointing to various aspects of the supreme reality. But in his commentary on *TĀ* (3.167, vol. 2, p. 166) Jayaratha states expressly that the "third *brahman*" is the letter *sa*: *tṛtīyaṃ brahma sakāraḥ*, relying in this on the *Bhagavad Gītā*, 17.23: *oṃ tat sad iti nirdeśo brahmaṇas trividhaḥ smṛtaḥ*: *sat* comes indeed third in this list, and the simple removing of the final *t* results in *sa*, which stands for *sat*. . . .

"seed of the heart" (*hṛdayabīja*), the heart-mantra holding within itself the totality of the cosmos. As it is said in stanza 24 of the same text: "Just as a big tree abides potentially in the banyan seed, even so this animate and inanimate world abides in the "seed of the heart."[99] Characteristically, Abhinava's commentary upon this *śloka* (*PTV*, pp. 258-60), stressing that the perfect knowledge of this heart alone, achieved through the *nirvāṇa-dīkṣā*, bestows liberation, does not differentiate between the Heart—that is, the dynamic center of the Godhead—and the *bījamantra*, which is its phonic form. Deity and mantra are one, and both are received through *dīkṣā*. But what the mantra stands for—the supreme reality that it *is*—is intuited by practice (bodily ritual placings, or *nyāsa*s, repetition, or *japa*, of the mantra, and imagining its presence in the body).

In the *TĀ* (4.186-89), Abhinava defines *SAUḤ* as follows: "Indeed, this being (*sat* = *S*) whose root is Brahmā and which is called the sphere of Māyā (*māyāṇḍa*) would not be said to exist if it did not enter into the [trident = *AU* of the three energies of] precognitive impulse, cognition, and action. For it is through entering into these three energies that it is emitted (or projected: *visṛjyate* = *visarga: Ḥ*) into the consciousness of Bhairava. Or it is emitted outside because of that. Thus the fact that these [constituent elements of the cosmos] exist (*sat* = *S*) actually results in their being in the nature of the three energies (*AU*) in the emission (*visarga* = *Ḥ*) that is projected outward by the supreme consciousness."[100] From this rather cryptic description of *SAUḤ* and from Jayaratha's commentary on it, it appears that *SAUḤ* is taken here by Abhinava as symbolizing first, from the perspective of resorption (*saṃhārakrameṇa*), the fact that the cosmos rests (*viśrāntiṃ yāyād*) in the self of the supreme

99. *yathā nyagrodhabījasthaḥ śaktirūpo mahādrumaḥ/*
tathā hṛdayabījasthaṃ jagad etac carācaram//24// (p. 258)

100. *tathā hi sad idaṃ brahmamūlaṃ māyāṇḍasamjñitam//186//*
icchājñānakriyārohaṃ vinā naiva sad ucyate/
tac chaktitritayārohād bhairavīye cidātmani//187//
visṛjyate hi tat tasmād bahir vātha visṛjyate/
evaṃ sadrūpataivaiṣāṃ satāṃ śaktitrayātmatām//188//
visargaṃ parabhodena samākṣipyaiva vartate/ (vol. 3, pp. 216-19)

knower, Bhairava, and then, from the perspective of emission (*sṛṣṭikrameṇa*), the projection outward of the cosmos by the creative process of the energies, a projection that takes place, however, in consciousness. To be more explicit: the span of creation, from the earth to *māyā*, is, in the mantra, taken in its essence as pure being (*sat* = *S*). It is then absorbed in the three energies of Śiva (*A U*), thanks to which it is imbued with consciousness (more specifically with the self-revelatory and free awareness called *vimarśa*), to be afterwards (but eternally, out of time) emitted (*Ḥ*) in consciousness. This description occurs in a passage about the power (or efficiency) of mantras, *mantravīrya*, where the supreme Godhead is described as intense self-awareness (*parāmarśa*), pulsating radiance (*spanda*), an ocean with innumerable waves, a full and palpitating all-inclusive reality, creating ceaselessly: all of which is symbolized by *SAUḤ*. With its three constituent phonemes we have the Absolute itself (*S*), the triad of Śiva's fundamental powers in their absolute fullness (*A U*), and finally the perennial surging forth (both internally and externally, but always within consciousness, the stuff the world is made of) of the Godhead's creative flow, the throbbing of the divine Heart (*Ḥ*). One understands easily, therefore, that to meditate on this mantra, to grasp its full meaning directly through an all-embracing intellectual intuition, is a liberating experience.

It is to be noted that this passage is from the fourth *āhnika* of the *TĀ*, which describes the "way of energy" (*śāktopāya*), where the liberating intuition through identification with a "truth" constantly perceived and contemplated in *dhyāna* and *bhāvanā* (thus through an assimilative internalization of a mentally-created notion) is *vikalpasaṃskāra*: a revelation through the purifying action of thought, without having recourse to rites or practices.[101] The fifth *āhnika*, on the other hand, which deals with the *āṇavopāya*, where rites and tantric *mantra*-

101. The mantras *SAUḤ* and *piṇḍanātha*, says the same passage, lead the adept to the realization of the potency of mantras (*mantravīrya*) as being identical with *ahaṃ*. This passage was quoted *supra*, p. 387-88, n. 35.

yoga practices hold a vital part, reveals a quite different use of the mantra.

This is to be found in a passage we have quoted above,[102] dealing with the nature of phonemes (*varṇatattva*), that is, with their creative and transformative power due to their being the Godhead himself. The mantras are described there as "luminous," "endowed with fullness" (*pūrṇatā*), and as linked either with the awakening or with the stilling of the vital airs (*prāṇa*). The passage emphasizes the power of mantras as related to (and due to) their nature of "nonconventional" pure word, of direct expression of the primordial vibration (*spanda*) of being. Abhinava goes on to say: "The initial awareness (*saṃvedana*) that may be experienced of the primary consciousness (*saṃvid*) present in pleasure, in amorous sighs (*sītkāra*), in pure being, in enjoyment, or in the equal [vision of things],[103] is a contact with consciousness at its supreme level (*anuttarasaṃvid*). Penetration into the three places (*dhāman*) that are the heart, the throat, and the lips in their total fulfillment, is the fourteenth [phoneme *au*] united and merged with [the former one. The adept,] absorbed in the mantric recitation (*japa*), while uttering the *visarga* (= *Ḥ*), now brings together the ways of the two *dvādaśānta* by uniting them with the heart. Thus this seed gives rise, inside the median channel of bliss, to a vibration which rises from the "bulb" to the heart, the throat, the palate, the upper *kauṇḍāli*, and then to the highest point."[104]

---

102. Cf. *supra*, p. 377.

103. *Sāmyam* is explained by Jayaratha (ibid., p. 457) as *rāgadveśādidvandvaparihāraḥ*: "the relinquishing of the pairs [of opposites such as] attachment, hatred, and so forth."

104. *sukhasītkārasatsamyaksāmyaprathamasaṃvidaḥ/*
saṃvedanaṃ hi prathamaṃ sparśo 'nuttarasaṃvidaḥ//142//
hṛtkaṇṭhyoṣṭhatridhāmāntarnitarāṃ pravikāsini/
caturdaśaḥ praveśo ye ekīkṛtatadātmakaḥ//143//
tato visargoccārāṃśe dvādaśāntatathāv ubhau/
hṛdayena sahaikadhyaṃ nayate japatatparaḥ//144//
kandahṛtkaṇṭhatālvagrakauṇḍilīprakriyāntataḥ/
ānandamadhyanāḍyantaḥ spandanaṃ bījam āvahet//145//
(*TĀ* 5.142-45, vol. 3, pp. 456-59).

These three cryptic *śloka*s can be explained as follows: the first phoneme of *SAUḤ* uttered with *sītkāra* is *S anacka*: we have seen[105] its symbolic values—notably sexual—as well as its particular closeness to consciousness. To utter *S* is therefore to come in touch with the highest level of consciousness. *AU*, next, the "trident of energies,"[106] is by implication the *triśūla* present in the body of the yogin who follows the Trika, extending from the base of the spine up to the *dvādaśānta*.

AU is also (and first of all, here) the three powers of Śiva united in their fullest intensity: when the adept utters this *AU*, it becomes present in his heart, wherefrom it rises up to his throat and to his lips, where it is uttered. The reason, however, why *AU* is said to go that way is that the diphthong *au* is defined by Indian grammarians as "gutturo-labial" *kaṇṭhoṣṭhya*, that is, produced both at the *kaṇṭha* (throat) and on the lips (*oṣṭha*). (*Mantrayoga* also models itself on grammar!) To complete the utterance of *SAUḤ*, the yogin finally emits the *visarga Ḥ*. For this he causes a vibratory movement to appear, that of the arousal of the *kuṇḍalinī*, who moves from the lower center of the "bulb" (*kanda*) up to the *dvādaśānta*, or more accurately, to the "two *dvādaśānta*s," those of Śiva and Śakti,[107] until she finally reaches the highest point. As Jayaratha writes, "So, starting from the 'bulb' and moving successively through the different centers up to the *dvādaśānta*, this seed of the creation (*sṛṣṭibīja* = *SAUḤ*) causes a vibration in the central channel, that is, it flashes forth as a direct awareness of the absolute consciousness (*anuttarasaṃvidāmarśātmanā prasphuret*," (ibid., p. 460). This practice of *mantrayoga* is also described by Abhinavagupta himself in this same *āhnika*, where in *śl.* 52 to 62 (vol. 3, pp. 356-65) he says that the yogin, by the *uccāra*, is to take the *prāṇa* straight up (this is the "method of the stick," *daṇḍa*) from the heart (*S*) to the top of the head where the three powers (*AU*) abide, then further on, where the *uccāra* (according to *TĀV*, p. 360), having gone through the

105. Cf. *supra*, chapter 5, p. 302.
106. For *au*, cf. above, chapter 5, pp. 271-72.
107. This seems to imply a movement of "breath" going from twelve fingerbreadths beyond the nose, to twelve fingerbreadths above the head.

stages of the utterance from *nāda* to *samanā*, merges with the cosmic vibration (*spanda*): this is the *visarga*, *Ḥ*. The latter is not, however, an emission or projection, but *spanda*: an unbroken succession of expansions and contractions, a cosmic pulsation where everything at once arises and is dissolved. "In this supreme Heart," he concludes, "where the great root (*S*), the trident (*AU*), and the *visarga* (*Ḥ*) become one, [the yogin,] uniting with the totality of the cosmic fullness, ultimately finds rest,"[108] that is, he realizes the complete fullness of the absolute divine 'I' which is, as we have already said,[109] according to the widely used formula of the *APS*, "light-consciousness resting within itself," (*prakāśasyātmaviśrāntir ahambhāvo hi kīrtitaḥ*).

Piṇḍanātha/Mātṛsadbhāva

While the mantra *SAUḤ* makes the adept realize the Godhead's creative and resorbing cosmic pulsation, what predominates there is, however, the Godhead's creative flow: the heart is the core of all life. But the Godhead also destroys the universe, or rather reabsorbs it after having brought it forth. And this occurs both eternally, beyond time—this is the *spanda* vibration—and cyclically, throughout the recurring cosmic periods of time, the *kalpas*. Also, as we have seen, the adept progresses toward liberation with the help of the salvific power of mantras, which leads toward the source of the universe: a movement parallel and homologous to that of the cosmic resorption. Hence the importance of another mantra, the counterpart on all these levels of the one we just saw: the "lord of the microcosm," *piṇḍanātha* (or *pañcapiṇḍanātha*), also called *mātṛsadbhāva* ("essence of the Mothers"[110]), which, by contrast with the *sṛṣṭibīja SAUḤ*, is the *saṃhārabīja* (or *saṃhārahṛdaya*), the seed (or heart) of the resorption. "The uncreated, unstained, aware-

108. *ekīkṛtamahāmūlaśūlavaisargike hṛdi//60//*
parasminn eti viśrāntiṃ sarvāpūraṇayogataḥ/ (*TĀ* 5.60-61, vol. 3, p. 364.)
109. Cf. *supra*, p. 288.
110. *Mātṛsadbhāva* was, for the Trika as expounded in the *Siddhayogeśvarīmata* and the *MVT*, the higher aspect of Parā, the supreme Goddess. Abhinava, quoting these texts in the *TĀ* (for instance, *TĀ* 15.533), calls

ness of these two mantras," says Abhinava in the *TĀ*, "is, according to the [Masters], that of the absolute 'I,' the light of all light. Verily, this is the power, the heart, of all mantras, without which they would be lifeless like animate creatures deprived of heart."[111] Source of the universe, heart of all reality, these two mantras are regarded as the origin of all the others and are therefore of paramount importance.[112]

Let us now consider this "heart of the resorption." Its most common form seems to be *KHPHREṂ*: this is the one given in the *TĀ* (4.189-91; 5.75-78; 30.45-46), which, of course, relies upon earlier texts, notably the *MVT*, 8.39-43, where it is described as the supreme essence of all the Mothers, or of all conscious beings: *sadbhāvaḥ paramo hy eṣa mātṛṇām.* It is, however, also given as *HSHPHREṂ.*[113] None of these formulas is pronounceable, but this is immaterial since the *uccāra*, as we have just seen with *SAUḤ*, is not so much an utterance as a mental representation of the mantra's phonic elements associated with the movement of *prāṇa*, and the use of their symbolic meaning. Thus the mantra *KHPHREṂ*, the very "essence of the Mothers," that is,

---

also this mantra Kālakarṣiṇī, since resorption is the destruction of time. He also, however, interprets the name Mātṛsadbhāva as "The Essence of [all] Conscious Beings," taking *mātṛ* as meaning *pramātṛ*, since Parā is for him the Absolute as pure consciousness; see *infra*, n. 117. (On these aspects of the Goddess, cf. A. Sanderson, "Śaivism and the Tantric Traditions," quoted above.)

111. *etadrūpaparāmarśam akṛtrimam anābilam/*
aham ity ahur eṣaiva prakāśasya prakāśatā//192//
etad vīryaṃ hi sarveṣāṃ mantrāṇāṃ hṛdayātmakam/
vinānena jadās te syur jīvā iva vinā hṛdā//193// (*TĀ* 4; vol. 3, p. 224)

112. One must remember, however, that in each system a *mūlamantra* can be placed above all the others and be regarded as the source of everything. In traditions where any word is in essence the supreme Word, any formula can be at the origin of all: it suffices to proclaim it as such and to build up, for its *uccāra*, the imaginary representation of the cosmic process this utterance will be deemed to foster and embody. The mantra, in such cases, is that of the supreme godhead of that tradition: here it is Parā.

113. In the *TĀ* 30.47-49 its form is *HSHRPHREṂ*. The form *HSKHPHREṂ* seems to be also sometimes acknowledged: it is given in the first stanza of the *Ṣaṭsāhasrasaṃhitā*, which calls this mantra *kulakūṭa* (ibid., chap. 37), the principal *bīja* of the Kula tradition, to which the Trika also belongs.

of the ruling divinities of the cosmos (and above all, of the supreme Goddess, since it is her mantra), helps the yogin to realize intuitively (and identify with) a cosmic process that no empirical utterance can express.

As was the case with *SAUḤ*, the *piṇḍanātha* is used in the *śāktopāya* and the *aṇavopāya*. This is what Abhinava says in the fourth *āhnika* of the *TĀ*: "This being (*sat*) [who appears] external[ly] is first dissolved in the fire of knowledge. What remains then is what is left of the awareness which is inner resonance. The condition of space being reached, by passing through the three energies, one attains to what is made of knowing, ultimately to dissolve in what is resorption."[114] These enigmatic *śloka*s should be understood as describing a movement of the mind that sees the world merged in the "sky" of consciousness (*KH*, because of *kha*, space, sky) in a resonance (*PH*), this merging taking place through the action of the fire of knowledge (*R*, since *ra* is *agnibīja*);[115] the world, through the action of the triad of Śiva's fundamental powers, *icchā*, *jñāna*, *kriyā* (*E*, since it is the *trikoṇabīja*),[116] is then being engulfed in the *bindu Ṃ*, since *bindu* is that point where the manifestation withdraws upon itself to return within the Godhead—all of which results in *KHPHREṂ*.[117]

---

114. *tat sad eva bahirūpaṃ prāgbodhāgnivilāpitam//189//*
antarnadatparāmarśāśeṣībhūtaṃ tato 'pi alam/
khātmatvam eva samprāptaṃ śaktitritayagocarāt//190//
vedanātmakatām etya saṃhārātmani līyate/ (*TĀ* 4.189-91, vol. 3, p. 220)

115. Cf. *supra*, chapter 5, p. 256.

116. Cf. ibid., p. 263-67.

117. In his commentary upon these two *śloka*s, Jayaratha (*TĀ*, vol. 3, pp. 220-23), gives a first explanation of the *piṇḍanātha* (p. 221), where the resorption of the cosmos is described as taking place in Kālasaṃkarṣiṇī. Then he gives a second explanation (p. 222) which, while describing the same movement of the return of the universe to its source, brings in prior to *kh* the *kūṭabīja kṣa*, which, he says, stands for the *saṃhārakuṇḍalī*. The mantra explained here is thus the "*pañcapiṇḍanātha* consisting of the phonemes from *ra* to *bindu*" (*evam ca rephādibindvantavarṇapañcakarūpatayā śrīpañcapiṇḍanātho 'yam ityāgamajñāḥ*), therefore, it seems: *RKṢKHEṂ*. Finally, J. quotes a text—from the Krama, presumably—describing the resorption of the cosmos through this *bīja* as associated with the *kuṇḍalinī*.

For the *āṇavopāya*, Abhinava mentions the *piṇḍanātha* in a passage of the fifth *āhnika* dealing with the penetration (*praveśa*) of the yogin into the supreme reality (*paratattva*). Such a yogin, withdrawn from the agitation of the world, no longer perceives the universe as different from himself, but as the sport of the divine consciousness, into which his own consciousness becomes merged. Thus he abides within the heart of the supreme reality. This is how the text puts it: "Having relinquished the wretched condition attendant on intentional action and attained to inactivity, which is in the nature of the inner as well as of the external void (*kharūpam* = *KH*), one should become established on the level of the blossoming (*phullam* = *PH*) *nāda* and then break open the inner side of consciousness, through which the wheel of cognition, of the senses, and of the breaths[118] can no longer be separated from the knowable. The latter is thus dissolved into what is called the fire (*vahninā* = *R*) of consciousness and, thus dissolved, merges into this triangle (*trikoṇa* = *E*), which is the fire of energy. The yogin, totally happy and appeased in the noble essence of the *bindu* (*Ṃ*), which is cognition, rests now in the seed of the resorption (*saṃhārabīja*) and acquires thus the very nature of the supreme."[119]

Although belonging to the *aṇavopāya*, this practice seems to consist essentially in a meditation where the yogin experiences the end of all urge to act in this world, the fusion with a subtle, inner phonic vibration, together with the realization that all

---

118. *saṃvidakṣamaruccakram*: here, once again, is the terminology (and vision) of the "wheel of energies" (*śakticakra*) of the Krama. For this, see L. Silburn, *Hymnes aux Kālī, La roue des énergies divines* (Paris: Institut de Civilisation Indienne, 1975).

119. *arthakriyārthitādainyaṃ tyaktvā bāhyāntarātmani/*
kharūpe nirvṛtaṃ prāpya phullāṃ nādadaśāṃ śrayet//75//
vaktram antas tayā samyak saṃvidaḥ pravikāsayet/
saṃvidakṣamaruccakraṃ jñeyābhinnaṃ tato bhavet//76//
tajjneyaṃ saṃvidākhyena vahninā pravilīyate/
vilīnaṃ tat trikoṇe 'smin śaktivahnau vilīyate//77//
tatra saṃvedanodarabindusattāsunivṛtaḥ/
saṃhārabījaviśrānto yogī paramayo bhavet//78// (*TĀ* 5.75-78; vol. 3, p. 383-87)

that belongs to the activity of the mind, of the senses, or of the vital breaths, is both inseparable from the objective world and immersed in consciousness, that is, divine energy itself. The yogin (at the level of *bindu*, therefore on the ultimate stage of the *piṇḍanātha*) finally comes to rest in this energy, being completely immersed, dissolved, in the supreme reality. Jayaratha's commentary upon these four *śloka*s (vol. 3, pp. 384-88) does not state those practices of *mantrayoga* through which the human being can experience this return of all that is to its one and only substratum of consciousness. The experience seems therefore to be essentially a spiritual one, the *piṇḍanātha*'s role being that of a guide to its successive intellectual stages. By "intellectual," however, I do not mean disembodied. There is nothing in these systems that is not both corporeal *and* mental. But, more specifically, the next *śloka*s (86 to 100) of this *āhnika*, referring to the *Triśirobhairava-tantra*, give some indications of how the *uccāra* of mantras should be conducted, that is, how the yogin is to raise the *prāṇa* upward in the central *nāḍī*, the *suṣumnā*, up to its highest level, and how to meditate, at this point, on the supreme reality. Now, these directions are probably valid for the practice of the *piṇḍa-nātha* according to this *upāya* also. Therefore, however 'subtle,' or spiritual, this practice may appear, it nonetheless surely belongs to tantric *mantrayoga*. Whatever the actual practice of the *piṇḍanātha* may consist of, however, it will bring back the adept to the source and origin of every word and of every thing.

Conclusion

The all-powerful activity of the Word, some aspects of which, (such as described more especially in the Kashmirian non-dualistic Śaiva texts) have been examined in the course of this study, have appeared as both human and cosmic, and as always associated with a twofold movement of expansion and contraction, with a kind of eternal pulsation that is the very life of the Word-Energy. In its highest aspect, it is the "vibration" (*spanda*) that is the essence of the Absolute. On a somewhat lower plane, it is the movement that brings forth and dissolves the worlds, the constant change and recurrence characteristic of every form of existence. But whatever the level, it is always the same pulsation. The Word, thus, which is creative autonomy, pure freedom, and which, in essence, never loses this pristine perfection, for it is the eternal origin (not the temporal beginning) of everything, becomes self-limited, brings the empirical world into existence, becomes the human language, a source of error and bondage. But the Word is also the source of liberation, since it is animated by a twofold movement; since the all-pervading reality is hidden to the ignorant, while the initiate is able to "recognize" it under the veil of "conventions"; and since he will be all the more successful in his attempt if he makes use of mantras, that is, of linguistic elements situated on the outer limit of language, and within which abide, condensed and supremely effective, all the powers of the Word, and especially its salvific potency.

But while Energy is Word, while everything occurs within and through the latter, we have noted that the movement of the

Word starts from—and returns to—a point where every word, every sound, fades out into silence. This we have seen with regard to the *kuṇḍalinī* as well as to *parāvāc*, to the phonematic emanation, to the sixfold course, or to the *uccāra* of mantras such as *OṂ*. Indeed, extolling *bījamantra*s, as Tantrism does, means to place at the highest level a form of the word "lying beyond language and reaching to the plane of silence."[1] The Word as extolled in the various Tantric schools is not that of explicit, diffuse, language. On the contrary, the further it is from ordinary language, from prolixity, the briefer, the nearer to silence, the higher it is. And indeed from silence does the Word arise. The transcendental stage, the Absolute, is this pure consciousness, still and unmoving (although alive), that is the origin of the Word, then of words and of the diversity of existence, whilst (in nondualistic thought) always inseparably united with them. Therefore, Tantric cosmogonies of the Word are, in fact, cosmogonies born of Silence. And indeed, as we have noted, the predominance of the invisible over the visible, of silence over speech, is one of the oldest Indian notions, a notion faithfully kept up in most Tantric traditions.

Thus a study devoted to the powers of the Word finally leads to accept the preeminence of Silence. But this is a silence pregnant with all the possibilities of the Word, and even of language. The unconditioned Absolute is, for nondualistic thought, pregnant with all the diversity that is to issue from it, that it dominates and transcends, underlies and pervades, without, however, being affected thereby. Thus, moving from language to its original levels, one ultimately arrives at its source, at silence: *OṂ* merges into the resonance, *nāda*, which in turn gradually dissolves in the pure light of consciousness, in the silence of the supreme and transcendent Godhead. But the latter is at the same time indissolubly united with the Word, which is its energy, and it is within and through this Word that all is accomplished: Energy, says Abhinavagupta

---

1. "Située hors du langage et éventuellement jusqu'à la zone du silence," L. Renou, *EVP*, 6, p. 12.

in the *PTV* (pp. 220-21), originates from the union of Śiva with this supreme Word, and the universe is nothing but a form assumed by the energy: it is the cosmic body born of the word of Bhairava.

Select Bibliography

This is not a complete bibliography of the subject. It includes those works or studies only that I have read or consulted for the purpose of this book, or which have had some influence on my views on some subject treated here.

I. Texts (and translations)

A. Veda, Brāhmaṇa, Upaniṣad

Aitareya Āraṇyaka. Calcutta, Bibliotheca India, 1876.

Aitareya Brāhmaṇa. Calcutta, Bibliotheca Indica, 1895.

The Aitareya and Kauṣītakī Brāhmaṇas of the Rig-Veda. A. Berriedale Keith, trans. Harvard Oriental Series. Cambridge: Harvard University Press, 1902.

Atharvavedasaṃhitā. R. Roth and W. D. Whitney, eds. Berlin, 1924.

The Atharvaveda, W. Dwight Whitney, trans. C. R. Lanman, ed. Cambridge: Harvard University Press, 1905. Revised edition by N. S. Singh, 2 vols., Delhi, 1987.

The Bṛhadārāṇyaka Upaniṣad, with the commentary of Śri Madhvāchārya. The Sacred Books of the Hindus. Allahabad: Dr. L. M. Basu, 1923.

Gopatha Brāhmaṇa, in *The Atharvaveda.* Bloomfield, ed. *Grundriss der Indo-Arischen Philologie und Alterstumkunde.* Strasbourg, 1899.

Jaiminīya Upaniṣad Brāhmaṇa (the *Jaiminīya* or *Talavakāra Upaniṣad Brāhmaṇa*). Hanns Oertel, trans. *JAOS* 16, 1894.

Kāthaka Saṃkalana (of the *Yajurveda*). Suryakanta: Lahore, 1943.

Kauṣītaki Brāhmaṇa, B. Lindner, ed., trans. Jena, 1887.

Mahānārāyaṇa Upaniṣad, édition critique avec une traduction française et en annexe la Prāṇāgnihotra Upaniṣad, J. Varenne, Paris: *Publications de l'Institut de Civilisation Indienne*, fasc. 11 & 13. 1960.

Maitrāyanī Saṃhitā (Die Saṃhitā der Maitrāyanīya-Śakha). 4 vols. *Hrsg. von* L. von Schroeder, Leipzig, 1881-1886. Repr.: 1970-1972.

Maitrāyanīya Upaniṣad. J. A. B. van Buitenen, trans. The Hague, 1962.

Pañcaviṃśa Brāhmaṇa. G. Caland, trans. Calcutta, 1931.

Ṛgveda Saṃhitā (The Sacred Hymns of the Brahmans). F. Max Muller, ed. London, 1890-1892. Repr.: Banaras, 1983.

Der Rig-Veda. 3 vols. Harvard Oriental Series. K. F. Geldner, trans. Cambridge: Harvard University Press, 1951.

Śatapatha Brāhmaṇa, A. Weber, ed. Berlin, 1855.

The *Śatapatha-Brāhmaṇa* according to the text of the Mādhyandina school. J. Eggeling, trans. 5 vols. Oxford, 1882-1900. Repr.: Delhi, 1978-1982.

Taittirīya Brāhmaṇa. H. Mahadeva Śastri, *et al.*, ed. 4 vols. Government Oriental Library Series. Mysore, 1900-02.

Taittirīya Saṃhitā (The Veda of the Black Yajus School). A. B. Keith, trans. 2 vols. Harvard Oriental Series. Cambridge: Harvard University Press, 1914.

The Thirteen Principal Upanishads. R. E. Hume, trans. London, 1931. Repr.: Delhi, 1983.

B. Grammar/Philosophy of Grammar/Darśana

Amarakośa. *Nāmaliṅgānuśāsanam* (with the commentary Amarakośodghāṭana of Bhaṭṭa Kṣīrasvāmin). Har Dutt Sharma, ed. Poona, 1941.

Bhartṛhari. *Vākyapadīya.* Banaras: Chowkhamba Sanskrit Series, 1937.

Nandikeśvara Kāśikā. *Upamaṇyukṛtaṭikasahitā.* Calcutta: Calcutta

Sanskrit Series, 1937.

Pāṇini. *Aṣṭādhyāyī*, Sriś Chandra Vasu, ed., trans. Allahabad, 1891. Repr.: Delhi, 1988.

———. *La grammaire de Pāṇini.* Renou, trans. Paris, 1954.

———. *Pāṇinīya Sikṣā.* A. Weber, ed., trans. "Indische Studien", 4. Leipzig: 1858.

———. *Atharvaprātiśākhya.* W. D. Whitney, ed., trans. *JAOS* 7, 1886.

———. *Ṛkprātiśākhya.* M. D. Shastri, ed., trans. Lahore, 1937.

———. *Shabara-Bhāṣya.* Ganganath Jha., trans. 4 vols. ("Gaekwad Oriental Series" nos., 66, 70, 73, 103). Baroda, 1933-45.

———. *Nyāyasūtra* (with the *Bhāṣya* of Vatsyāyana). Anandashram Sanskrit Series, no. 121). Poona, 1922.

Annambhaṭṭa. *Tarkasaṃgraha.* A. Foucher, trans. Paris, 1949.

Īśvarakṛṣṇa. *Sāṃkhya Kārikā.* (with the commentary of Gauḍapādācārya). Har Dutt Sharma, ed., trans. Poona Oriental Series, 1933.

Mādhavācārya. *Sarvadarśanasaṃgraha.* I. Vidyasāgara, ed. Calcutta: Bibliotheca Indica, 1853-58. Repr.: 1981.

Sarva-darśana-saṅgraha. E. B. Cowell & A. E. Gough, trans. London, 1882. Repr.: Banaras: Chowkhamba Sanskrit Series, 1961.

C. Yoga/ Yoga and sectarian Upaniṣads/ Purāṇas

Agnipurāṇa. Rajendralal Mitra, ed. 3 vols., Bibliotheca Indica. Calcutta, 1870-1879. Repr. 1985.

Pātañjalayogasūtrāṇi (*Vācaspatimiśraviracitaṭīkāsaṃvalitavyāsabhāṣyasametāni*). Poona: Anandashram Sanskrit Series, 1932.

The Yoga-System of Patañjali. J. H. Woods, trans. Harvard Oriental Series. Cambridge: Harvard University Press, 1927.

Gheraṇḍa Saṃhitā. Sriś Chandra Vasu, ed. and trans. Adyar, 1933.

Haṭhayogapradīpikā. Srinivasa Iyengar, trans. Adyar, 1949.

Kālikāpurāṇa. K. R. van Kooij, trans. *Worship of the Goddess according to the Kālikā-Purāṇa*, part I (Translation, introduction, and notes of chapters 54-69). Leiden, 1972.

Kaula and other Upaniṣads, with a commentary by Bhāskararāya. Tantrik Texts, vol. XI. Calcutta and London, 1922.

Ṣaṭcakranirūpaṇa and *Pādukāpañcaka.* A. Avalon, ed. and trans. *The Serpent Power, being the* Shat-chakra-nirūpaṇa *and* Pādukā-panchaka, *two works on Laya Yoga.* Madras, 1953.

The Śaiva Upaniṣads. Commentary by Śrī Upaniṣad-Brahma-Yogin. Adyar, 1950.

The Śaiva Upaniṣads. T. R. Srinivasa Iyengar, trans. Adyar, 1953.

The Śākta Upaniṣads. Commentary by Śrī Upaniṣad-Brahma-Yogin. Adyar, 1950.

The Śākta Upaniṣads. A. G. Krishna Warrier, trans. Adyar, 1967.

The Yoga Upaniṣads. Commentary by Śrī Upaniṣad-Brahma-Yogin. Adyar, 1920.

The Yoga Upaniṣads. T. R. Srinivasa Iyengar, trans. Adyar, 1952.

D. Nondualist Kashmirian works/Śrīvidyā

1. Nondualist Kashmirian works

Abbreviations

APS *Ajaḍapramātṛsiddhi* of Utpaladeva. See *Siddhitrayī.*

ĪPK *Īśvarapratyabhijñākārikā* and *Vṛtti* of Utpaladeva. Srinagar, 1921. KSTS no. 34—published with the *Siddhitrayī.*

ĪPV *Īśvarapratyabhijñāsūtravimarśinī* of Abhinavagupta. *Bhāskarī,* a commentary on the *Īśvarapratyabhijñāvimarśinī.* K. A. Subramanya Iyer and K. C. Pandey, eds. Vols. 1 & 2. Allahabad, 1938-1950.

Vol. 3: *Bhāskarī,* an English Translation of the *Īśvara Pratyabhijñā Vimarśinī* in the Light of the *Bhāskarī,* by K. C. Pandey. Lucknow, 1954. The Princess of Wales Saraswati Bhavana Series, no. 84.

ĪPVV *Īśvarapratyabhijñāvivṛtivimarśinī* of Abhinavagupta. 3 vols., Bombay, 1938-43. KSTS nos. 60, 62, 65. Repr.: Delhi, 1987.

Mahānayaprakāśa of Rājanaka Śitikaṇṭha. Bombay, 1918. KSTS, no. 21.

MM *Mahārthamañjarī* of Maheśvarānanda, with the auto-commentary *Parimala.* V. V. Dvivedi, ed. Banaras, 1972.

Yoga-tantra-granthamālā, vol. 5.

MVT *Mālinivijayottaratantra*. Bombay, 1922. KSTS, no. 37.

MVV *Mālinīvijayottaravārttika* of Abhinavagupta. Srinagar, 1921. KSTS, no. 31.

NT *Netratantra* with the commentary *Uddyota* by Kṣemarāja. 2 vols. Bombay, 1926-39. KSTS nos. 46, 61. New edition by V. V. Dvivedi: *Netratantram* (*Mṛtyuñjaya Bhaṭṭārakaḥ*) with commentary *Uddyota* by Kṣemarāja. Delhi: Parimal Publications, 1985.

PS *Paramārthasāra* of Abhinavagupta, with Yogarāja's *Vivṛti*. Bombay, 1916. KSTS no. 7.

Parāprāveśikā of Kṣemarāja. Srinagar, 1918. KSTS no. 15.

PTV *Parātriṃśikāvivaraṇa* of Abhinavagupta. Srinagar, 1918. KSTS no. 18.

Il commento di Abhinavagupta alla Parātriṃśikā (*Parātriṃśikātattva-vivaraṇam*). R. Gnoli, trans. Rome: ISMEO, 1985.

Abhinavagupta, A Trident of Wisdom. Translation of *Parātrīśikā-Vivaraṇa* by Jaideva Singh. Albany: State University of New York Press, 1989.

PTLv *Parātrīśikālaghuvṛtti* of Abhinavagupta. Srinagar, 1947. KSTS no. 68.

Parātrīśikātātparyadīpikā. Srinagar, 1947. KSTS, no. 74.

Parātrīśikāvivṛti of Lakṣmīrāma. Srinagar, 1947. KSTS no. 69.

PHṛ *Pratyabhijñāhṛdayam* by Kṣemarāja. Bombay, 1918. KSTS no 3.

Pratyabhijñāhṛdayam, Jaideva Singh, ed. and trans. Delhi: Motilal Banarsidass, 1963.

ST *Siddhitrayī* of Utpaladeva. Srinagar, 1921. KSTS no. 34.

ŚD *Śivadṛṣṭi* of Somānanda, with Utpaladeva's Vṛtti. Srinagar, 1934. KSTS no. 54.

ŚS *Śivasūtra* of Vasugupta, published with:

ŚSV *Śivasūtravimarśinī* by Kṣemarāja. Srinagar. KSTS no. 1.

Śivasūtras, The Yoga of Supreme Identity. Jaideva Singh, trans. Delhi: Motilal Banarsidass, 1979.

Śivasūtra con il commento di Kṣemarāja. R. Torella, trans.

Rome: Ubaldini, 1979.

ŚSvārt *Śivasūtra Vārttikam* by Bhāskara, published together with:
ŚSvr *Śivasūtra Vṛtti* by Kṣemarāja. Srinagar, 1913. KSTS nos. 4 and 5.

SvT *Svacchandatantra*, with Kṣemarāja's *Uddyota*. Bombay, 1921-1935. KSTS nos. 31, 38, 44, 48, 51, 53, and 56. Repr. in 4 vols. Delhi Saṃskṛt Gyan Saṃsthan, 1986.

SpK *Spandakārikāḥ Śrīrāmakaṇṭhācāryaviracitavṛttyupetāḥ*. Srinagar, 1913. KSTS no. 6.

Spandakārikāvṛtti of Kallaṭa. Srinagar: 1913. KSTS no. 5.

SpN *Spandakārikāḥ Kṣemarājakṛtanirṇayopetāḥ*. Srinagar: 1925. KSTS no. 42.

Spanda-Kārikās, The Divine Creative Pulsation. Jaideva Singh, trans. Delhi: Motilal Banarsidass, 1980.

SpS *Spandasaṃdoha* by Kṣemarāja. Srinagar, 1917. KSTS no. 16.

Stavacintāmaṇi by Bhaṭṭa Nārāyaṇa, with Kṣemarāja's commentary. Bombay, 1908. KSTS no. 10.

La Bhakti, Le Stavacintāmaṇi de Bhaṭṭanārāyaṇa, L. Silburn, trans. Paris: Ed. de Boccard, 1964.

TĀ *Tantrāloka* of Abhinavagupta with Rājānaka Jayaratha's commentary. 12 vols. Srinagar and Bombay, 1918-1938. KSTS nos. 3, 28, 30, 36, 35, 29, 41, 47, 59, 57, and 58. Repr. in 8 vols. Delhi: Motilal Banarsidass, 1987.

Luce delle Sacre Scritture, Tantrāloka of Abhinavagupta. R. Gnoli, trans. Torino: UTET, 1972.

TS *Tantrasāra* of Abhinavagupta. Bombay, 1918. KSTS no. 17.

Essenza dei Tantra, Tantrasāra of Abhinavagupta. R. Gnoli, trans. Torino: Boringhieri, 1960.

MV *Vāmakeśvarīmatam*, with Rājānaka Jayaratha's commentary. Srinagar, 1945. KSTS no. 66. See *Nityāṣoḍaśikārṇava*.

VS *Vātūlanāthasūtra*, with Anantaśaktipāda's *Vṛtti*. Bombay, 1923. KSTS no. 29.

VBh *Vijñānabhairava*, with Kshemarāja's and Shivopadhyāya's commentary. Bombay, 1918. KSTS no. 8.

Le *Vijñāna Bhairava*. L. Silburn, trans. Paris: Ed. de

Boccard, 1961.

Vijñānabhairava or Divine Consciousness. Jaideva Singh, trans. Delhi: Motilal Banarsidass, 1979.

2. *Śrīvidyā*

GT *Gandharvatantra*. R. C. Kak and H. B. Shastri, eds. Srinagar, 1934. KSTS no. 62. Repr. in *Tantrasaṅgraha*, vol. 3. See below.

JñT *Jñānārṇavatantram*. Poona, 1952. Anandashram Sanskrit Series no. 69.

KKV *Kāmakalāvilāsa* by Puṇyānandanātha, with Naṭanānandanātha's commentary. Arthur Avalon, ed. and trans. Madras: Ganesh & Co., 1953.

KT *Kularṇava Tantra*. A. Avalon, introd. Sanskrit text: *Tārānātha Vidyāratna*. Madras: Ganesh & Co., 1965.

LSN *Lalitasahasranāma*, with Bhāskararāya's *Saubhāgya-Bhāskara Bhāṣya*. Bombay: Nirnayasagar Press, 1935. Repr.: Delhi: Nāga Publishers, 1985.

Lalitasahasranāma, with Bhāskararāya's commentary. R. Anantakrishna Sastry, trans. Adyar, 1951.

NSA *Nityāṣoḍaśikārṇavaḥ Śivānandakṛtayā Ṛjuvimarśinyā Vidyānandakṛtayā Artharatnāvalyā ca samvalitaḥ. Sampādakaḥ: Śrīvrajavallabhadvivedaḥ*. Banaras: Vāranaseyam Saṃskṛt Mahāvidyālaya, 1968. *Yoga-Tantra-Granthamālā* no. 1. Published with Śivānanda's *Subhagodaya, Saubhāgyahṛdayastotra* and *Subhagodayavāsanā*, and Amṛtānanda's *Saubhāgyasudhodaya*.

NU *Nityotsava* of Umānandanātha, supplement to *Paraśurāmakalpa-sūtra*. Baroda: Oriental Institute, 1977. Gaekwad's Oriental Series no. 23.

Paraśurāmakalpasūtra, with Rāmeśvara's commentary. Baroda: Oriental Institute, 1950. Gaekwad's Oriental Series no. 22.

Saundaryalaharī (The Ocean of Beauty) by Śrī Saṅkara-Bhagavatpāda. S. Subrahmanya Sastri & and T. R. Srinivasa Iyengar, eds. and transls. Adyar, 1948.

Saundaryalaharī, with several commentaries. Madras:

Ganesh & Co., 1957.

TRT *Tantrārajatantra.* Lakshmaṇa Shastri, ed. Delhi: Motilal Banarsidass, 1981.

Varivasyārahasya of Śrī Bhāskararāya Makhin, with his own commentary. Subrahmanyya Sastri, ed. and trans. Adyar, 1948.

Śrividyārṇava Tantra of Shri Vidyāraṇya Yati. Ram Kumar Rai, ed. Banaras: Prachya Prakashan, 1986.

E. *Other Tantras and Tantric Compilations*/ Mantraśāstra

Kaulajñānanirṇaya and Some Minor Texts of the School of Matsyendranātha, P. C. Bagchi, ed. Calcutta, 1934. Calcutta Sanskrit Series no. 3.

Kramadīpikā. Ram Chandra Kak and Harabhaṭṭa Śāstri, eds. Srinagar, 1929. KSTS no. 67.

Kubjikāmatatantra, Kulalikāmnāya Version, T. Goudriaan and J. A. Schoterman, eds. Leiden, Brill, 1988.

Luptāgamasaṃgraha. Vrajvallabha Dvivedi, ed. 2 vols. Banaras: Sampurnanand Sanskrit Vishvavidyalaya, 1970-83. *Yoga-Tantra-Granthamālā* vols. 2 and 10.

MNT *Mahānirvāṇa Tantra:* The Great Liberation. A. Avalon, trans. Madras: Ganesh & Co., 1927. Repr.: Delhi: Motilal Banarsidass, 1977.

Mantramahodadhiḥ saṭīkaḥ. Bombay: Śrīvenkateśvara Steam Press, 1938.

PST *Prapañcasāratantram*, A. Avalon, ed. 2 vols. Calcutta, 1935. Tantrik Texts, vols. 18 & 19. Repr. in 1 vol. Calcutta: Asiatic Society, 1981.

Śaktisaṅgamatantra, B. Bhattacharyya, ed. 4 vols. Baroda: Oriental Institute, 1941. Gaekwad's Oriental Series vols. 91, 101, 104, and 166.

ŚT *Śāradātilakatantram.* A. Avalon, ed. 2 vols. Calcutta, 1933. Tantrik Texts vols. 16 and 17. Repr.: Delhi: Motilal Banarsidass, 1985.

Siddha-Siddhānta-Paddhati and Other Works of Nāth Yogis. Kalyani Mallik, ed. Poona: Oriental Bookhouse, 1954.

Tantrasāra of Kṛṣṇānanda, part 1. Banaras. Chowkhamba Sanskrit Series, 1938.

Tantrasaṅgraha. Gopinath Kaviraj, ed. 3 vols. Banaras: 1970-1979. *Yoga-Tantra-Granthamālā* vols. 3, 4, and 6.

F. *Dualist Śaivism/Śaivasiddhānta/Āgamas*

MatPār *Matangapārameśvarāgama:* all four *pāda*s in 2 vols. with Bhaṭṭa Rāmakaṇṭha's commentary. N. R. Bhatt, ed. Pondicherry: Institut Français d'Indologie, 1977, 1982.

Mṛg. *Śrī Mṛgendra Tantram* (*Vidyāpāda* and *Yogapāda*) with Nārāyaṇakaṇṭha's commentary. Bombay, 1930. KSTS no. 50.

Mṛg *Mṛgendrāgama* (*Kriyāpāda* and *Caryāpāda*). N. R. Bhatt, ed. Pondicherry: Institut Français d'Indologie, 1962.

Mṛgendrāgama, Bhaṭṭanārāyaṇakaṇṭha's *Vṛtti* and Aghoraśiva's *Dīpikā*. M. Hulin, trans. Pondicherry: Institut Français d'Indologie, 1980.

Mṛgendrāgama, Nārāyaṇakaṇṭha's *Vṛtti*. H. Brunner-Lachaux, trans. Pondicherry: Institut Français d'Indologie, 1985.

NK *Nādakārikā* of Rāmakaṇṭha, with Aghoraśiva's commentary.

RT *Ratnatraya* of Śrīkaṇṭha, with Rāmakaṇṭha's commentary. Published with the *Bhogakārikā, Mokṣakārikā* and *Paramokṣanirāsakārikā* in one vol. N. Kṛṣṇānandaśāstri, ed. Srīrangam, 1925.

Rau *Rauravāgama*. N. R. Bhatt, ed. 3 vols. Pondicherry: Institut Français d'Indologie, 1961, 1972, 1988.

SP1
SP2
SP3 *Somaśambhupaddhati*. H. Brunner-Lachaux, ed. and trans. 3 vols. (vol. 4 forthcoming). Pondicherry: Institut Français d'Indologie, 1963, 1968, and 1977.

Tattvaprakāśa of Śrī Bhojadeva, with Śrīkumāra's *Tatparyadīpikā*. Trivandrum: Government Press, 1920. Trivandrum Sanskrit Series no. 68.

G. *Pāñcarātra*

ABS *Ahirbudhnya Saṃhitā* of the *Pāñcarātrāgama*, M. D. Rāmānujācārya and F. O. Schrader, eds. 2 vols. Adyar, 1966.

JS *Jayākhyasaṃhitā.* E. Krishnamacharya, ed. Baroda: Oriental Institute, 1967. Gaekwad's Oriental Series, vol. 54.

LT *Lakṣmītantra,* a *Pāñcarātrāgama.* V. Krishnamacharya, ed. Adyar, 1959.

Lakṣmī Tantra, a *Pāñcarātra* text. S. Gupta, trans. Leiden: E. J. Brill, 1972.

Sanatkumārasaṃhitā, V. Krishnamacharya, ed. Adyar, 1969.

SātS *Sātvatasaṃhitā Alasiṅgabhaṭṭaviracitabhāṣyopetā.* V. V. Dviveda, ed. Banaras: Sampurnanand Sanskrit University, 1982. Library Rare Texts Publication Series no. 2.

II. Studies and Articles

A. General

S. N. Dasgupta. *A History of Indian Philosophy.* 5 vols. Cambridge: Cambridge University Press, 1951-1955.

J. Gonda. *Die Religionen Indiens.* 1. *Veda und Älterer Hinduismus.* 2. *Der Jüngere Hinduismus.* Stuttgart: Kohlhammer, 1960-1963.

W. Kirfel. *Symbolik des Hinduismus und des Jinismus.* Stuttgart: A. Hiersemann, 1959.

K. H. Potter, ed. *Encyclopedia of Indian Philosophies.* 1. *Bibliography.* 2. *Nyāya-Vaiśeṣika.* 3. *Advaita Vedānta.* 4. *Sāṃkhya.* Delhi: Motilal Banarsidass, 1970-1987.

L. Renou and J. Filliozat. *L'Inde Classique, Manuel des études indiennes.* 2 vols. Repr.: Paris: Adrien Maisonneuve, 1985.

B. Specific

K. V. Abhyankar. *A Dictionary of Sanskrit Grammar.* Baroda: Oriental Institute, 1961. Gaekwad's Oriental Series no. 134.

W. S. Allen. *Phonetics in Ancient India.* London: Oxford University Press, 1953. London Oriental Series vol. 1.

H. P. Alper. "Śiva and the Ubiquity of Consciousness: the Spaciousness of an Artful Yogi." *Journal of Indian Philosophy* 7 (1979) pp. 345-407.

H. P. Alper, ed. *Understanding Mantras.* Albany: State University of New York Press, 1989.

A. Avalon, ed. *Principles of Tantra* (The Tantratattva of Shrīyukta Shiva Chandra Vidyārnava Bhattacharya). Madras: Ganesh & Co., 1978.

P. C. Bagchi. *Studies in the Tantras*, part 1. Calcutta: University of Calcutta, 1939.

Agehananda Bharati. *The Tantric Tradition*. New York: Anchor Books, Doubleday & Co. 1970.

J. N. Banerjea. *Pauranic and Tantric Religion* (*Early Phase*). Calcutta: University of Calcutta, 1966.

A. Bergaigne. *La religion védique d'après les Hymnes du Rigveda*. 3 vols. Paris: F. Vieweg. 1878-1883.

R. G. Bhandarkar. *Vaiṣṇavism, Śaivism and Minor Religious Systems*. Strassburg, 1899. Grundriss der Indo-arischen Philologie und Altertumskund. 3.6.

S. Bhattacharji. *The Indian Theogony*. Cambridge: Cambridge University Press, 1970.

M. Biardeau. *Théorie de la connaissance et philosophie de la parole dans le brahmanisme classique*. Paris and The Hague: Mouton & Co., 1964.

———, *Etudes de Mythologie hindoue*, tome I, *Cosmogonies Puraniques*. Paris: Ecole Française d'Extrême-Orient, 1981.

———, *Etudes de Mythologies Hindoue, Vol. 4*. Paris: *BEFEO* 63, 1976.

———, *L'hindouisme, Anthropologie d'une civilisation*. Paris: Flammarion, 1981.

———, ed. *Autour de la Déesse hindoue*. Paris: Editions de l'EHESS 1981. *Puruṣārtha* 5.

J. Bloch. "La prononciation de *r* en sanskrit." *BEFEO* 44, 19.., pp. 43-45.

M. Bloomfield, *The Atharvaveda*. Strasbourg, 1899. Grundriss der indo-arischen Philologie und Altertumskunde 3.6.

H. Brunner. "Le *sādhaka*, personnage oublié du śivaïsme du sud." *JAs* 1975. pp. 411-443.

———, "Un chapitre du Sarvadarśanasaṅgraha: le *śaivadarśana*." In *Tantric and Taoist Studies in Honour of R. A. Stein*, vol. 1. Brussels: Institut Belge des Hautes Etudes Chinoises, 1981.

———, "Les membres de Śiva." *Asiatische Studien/Etudes Asiatiques*, 40.2, 1986, pp. 89-132.

J. A. B. van Buitenen. See L. Rocher, ed., 1988.

J. B. Carman and A. Marglin, eds. *Purity and Auspiciousness in Indian Society*. Leiden: E. J. Brill, 1985.

C. Chakravarty. *The Tantras, Studies on their Religion and Literature*. Calcutta: Punthi Pustak, 1963.

P. C. Chakravarti, *The linguistic Speculations of the Hindus*. Calcutta: University of Calcutta, 1933.

———, *The Philosophy of Sanskrit Grammar*. Calcutta: University of Calcutta, 1930.

S. Chattopadhyaya, *Evolution of Hindu Sects upto the Time of Śamkarācārya*. New Delhi: Munshiram Manoharlal, 1970.

Th. B. Coburn. *Devī Māhātmya: The Crystallization of the Goddess Tradition*. Delhi: Motilal Banarsidass, 1984.

V. Das. *Structure and Cognition. Aspects of Hindu Caste and Ritual*. Delhi: Oxford University Press, 1982.

C. G. Diehl. *Instrument and Purpose. Studies on Rites and Rituals in South India*. Lund: Gleerup, 1956.

V. V. Dvivedi. *Tantrayātrā*. Banaras, Ratna Publications, 1982.

L. Dumont. *Religion/Politics and History in India*. Paris: Mouton, 1970.

———, *Homo Hierarchicus*. Paris: Gallimard, 1966.

S. N. Eisenstadt, R. Kahane, and D. Shulman, eds. *Orthodoxy, Heterodoxy and Dissent in India*. Berlin and New York: Mouton, 1984.

M. Eliade. *Le Yoga, Immortalité et liberté*. Paris: Payot, 1968.

A. H. Ewing. "The Hindu conception of the functions of breath." *JAOS*, 22, 2nd part, 1901. pp. 249-308.

M. Falk. *Il mito psicologico nell'India Antica*. New ed. Milano: Adelfi, 1986.

———, "*Amāvāsya* in Mythical and Philosophical Thought." *Indian Historical Quarterly* 18, 1942. pp. 26-45.

———, and J. Przyluski. "Aspects d'une psycho-physiologie dans l'Inde et en Extrême-Orient." *BSOAS* 9.3, pp. 723-28.

J. Filliozat. "La force organique et la force cosmique dans la philosophie médicale de l'Inde et dans le Veda." *Revue Philosophique* 1933.

———. "Les āgama śivaïtes." Introduction to N. R. Bhatt's edition of the *Rauravāgama*. Pondicherry: Institut Français d'Indologie, 1961.

———, *La doctrine classique de la médecine indienne*. Repr. Paris: EFEO, 1975.

———, *Laghu-Prabandhāḥ, choix d'articles d'indologie*. Leiden: E. J. Brill, 1974.

R. Gnoli, *The Aesthetic Experience According to Abhinavagupta*. 3d Ed. Banaras, 1985. Chowkhamba Sanskrit Studies no. 62.

———, "Alcune techniche yoga nel scuola śaiva." *Riv. d. Studi Orientali* vol. 29, 1959, pp. 279-290.

———, "*Vāc*, il secondo capitolo della Śivadṛṣṭi di Somānanda." *Riv. d. Studi Orientali* vol. 34, 1959, pp. 5-75.

J. Gonda. "The Indian *mantra*." *Oriens* vol. 16, 1963.

———, *Change and Continuity in Indian Religion*. The Hague: Mouton, 1965.

———, *The Vision of the Vedic Poets*. The Hague: Mouton, 1963.

———. *Viṣṇuism and Śivaism, a Comparison*. London: Athlone Press, 1970.

———, *Notes on Name and the Name of God in Ancient India*. Amsterdam: North-Holland Publishing Co., 1970.

———, *Medieval Religious Literature in Sanskrit*. Wiesbaden: O. Harrassowitz, 1977. *A History of Indian Literature*, vol. 2, fasc. 1.

T. Goudriaan. *Māyā Divine and Human*. Delhi: Motilal Banarsidass, 1978.

———, *The Vīṇāśikhatantra, a Śaiva Tantra of the left current*.

Delhi: Motilal Banarsidass, 1985.

T. Goudriaan and S. Gupta. *Hindu Tantric and Śākta Literature*. Wiesbaden: O. Harrassowitz, 1981. *A History of Sanskrit Literature*, vol. 2, fasc. 2.

S. Gupta, D. J. Hoens, and T. Goudriaan. *Hindu Tantrism*. Leiden: E. J. Brill, 1979. *Handbuch der Orientalistik*, 2. Abt., 4. B., 2. Abs.

G. A. Grierson. "The śāradā alphabet." *JRAS* Oct. 1916, pp. 677-708.

G. W. Hauer. *Die Dhāraṇī im noerdlichen Buddhismus*. Stuttgart: Kohlhammer, 1927.

———, *Der Yoga, ein indischer Weg zum Selbst*. Stuttgart: Kohlhammer, 1958. Repr. Südergellersen: Verlag Bruno Martin, 1983.

R. C. Hazra. *Studies in the Puranic Records on Hindu Rites and Customs*. 2d ed., Delhi: Motilal Banarsidass, 1975.

M. Hulin. *Le principe de l'ego dans la pensée indienne classique: La notion d'ahaṃkāra*. Paris: Collège de France, 1978.

Gopinath Kaviraj. *Tantrik vāṅmay mẽ śāktadṛṣṭi*. Patna: Bihari Rastrabhāṣā Pariṣad, 1963.

———, *Tāntrik Sāhitya* (*Vivaraṇātmik Granthasūcī*).

S. Kramrisch. *The Hindu Temple*. 2 vols. Delhi: Motilal Banarsidass, 1976.

———, *Manifestations of Śiva*. Philadelphia: Museum of Art, 1981.

H. Lommel, "Anahita-Sarasvatī" in *Asiatica*, Festschrift Friedrich Weller. Leipzig: O. Harrassowitz, 1954, pp. 405-413.

H. Lüders. "Die Ṣoḍaśakalāvidyā" in *Philologica Indica*, pp. 509ff.

A. Macdonnell. *Vedic Mythology*. Strasbourg, 1897. *Grundriss der indo-arischen Philologie und Altertumskunde* 3.1.

Ch. Malamoud. *Le svādhyāya, Récitation personnelle du Veda*. Taittirīya-Āraṇyaka, livre II. Paris: Institut de Civilisation Indienne, 1977.

———, *Cuire le monde: Rite et pensée dans l'Inde ancienne*. Paris: La Découverte, 1989.

T. N. Madan. *Non-Renunciation*. Delhi: Oxford University Press, 1987.

T. N. Madan, ed. *Way of Life: King, Householder, Renouncer.* Delhi: Vikas, 1982.

M. Th. de Mallmann. *Enseignements iconographiques de l'Agni-Purāṇa.* Paris: PUF 1963.

A. Marglin. *Wives of the God-King.* Delhi: Oxford University Press, 1985.

J. L. Masson and M. V. Patwardhan. *Śāntarasa and Abhinavagupta's Theory of Aesthetics.* Poona: Bhandarkar Oriental Institute, 1969.

J. J. Meyer. *Trilogie altindischer Mächte und Feste der Vegetation.* 3 vols. Zurich and Leipzig, 1937.

P. M. Modi. *Akṣara, A Forgotten Chapter in the History of Indian Philosophy.* Baroda: State Press, 1932.

P. Mus. *Barabudur.* 2 vols. Paris and Hanoi, EFEO 1935.

J. Naudou. *Les Bouddhistes kaśmiriens au Moyen Age.* Paris: PUF 1968.

F. Nowotny. *Eine durch Miniaturen erläuterte Doctrina Mystica aus Srinagar.* The Hague: Mouton & Co., 1958. Indo-Iranian Monographs vol. 3.

B. Oguibenine. *Essais sur la culture védique et indo-européenne.* Pisa: Giardini, 1981.

———, *La Déesse Uṣas: Recherches sur le sacrifice de la parole dans le Ṛgveda.* Louvain: Peeters, 1988. Bibliothèque de l'Ecole des Hautes Etudes, Sciences Religieuses vol. 89.

A. Padoux. "Contributions à l'étude du *mantraśāstra.*" 1. La sélection des mantra-*mantroddhāra.* 2. *Nyāsa*, l'imposition rituelle des *mantra.* 3. Le *japa. BEFEO* 65, 1978; 67, 1980; 76, 1987: pp. 65-85; 59-102; 117-164.

———, "Un japa tantrique: Yoginīhṛdya." 3.170-190 in *Tantric and Taoist Studies in Honour of R. Stein*, vol. 1. M. Strickman, ed. Brussels: Institut Belge des Hautes Etudes Chinoises, 1981: pp. 141-154.

———, *"Vāmakeśvaratantrāntargataṃ yoginīhṛdayam" Ṛtam.* Lucknow: vols. 16-17. January 1984-July 1986: pp. 251-257.

———, "Un rituel hindou du rosaire (*Jayākhyasaṃhitā*, chap. 14)." *JAs* 225. 1987, pp. 115-129.

———, "Mantras, what are they?" in *Understanding Mantras*, H. P. Alper, ed. Albany, State University of New York Press, 1988.

———, ed. *Mantras et diagrammes rituels dans l'hindouisme*. Paris: Ed. du CNRS, 1986.

———, ed. *L'image divine. Culte et méditation dans l'hindouisme*. Paris: Ed. du CNRS, 1990.

K. C. Pandey. *Abhinavagupta, An Historical and Philosophical Study*. 2d edition Banaras: Chowkhamba Sanskrit Series Office, 1963.

R. C. Pandeya. *The Problem of Meaning in Indian Philosophy*. Delhi: Motilal Banarsidass, 1963.

P. H. Pott. *Yoga and Yantra*. Rodney Needham, trans. The Hague: Martinus Nijhoff, 1966.

N. Rastogi. *The Krama Tantricism of Kashmir*, vol. 1. Delhi: Motilal Banarsidass, 1979.

S. C. Ray. "Studies on the History of Religion in Ancient Kāśmīra." *Journal of the Bihar Research Society*, vol. 41, 1955 (pp. 178-99).

———, *Early History and Culture of Kashmir*. Calcutta: S. C. Ray, 1957.

L. Renou, "Connexion entre la grammaire et le rituel en sanskrit." *JAs* 1941-42: pp. 105-165.

———, "*Virāj*." *JAs* 240. pp. 141ff.

———, *Vocabulaire du rituel védique*. Paris: Klincksieck, 1954.

———, *Etudes Védiques et Paninéennes*, vols. 1ff., especially "Les pouvoirs de la Parole dans le Ṛgveda" (vol. 1, pp. 1-27) and "Le destin du Veda dans l'Inde" (vol. 6). Paris: de Boccard, 1955-1969.

———, *Etudes sur le vocabulaire du Ṛgveda*. Pondicherry: Institut Français d'Indologie, 1958.

———, *Terminologie grammaticale du sanskrit*. Paris: H. Champion, 1959.

———, *L'Inde fondamentale. Etudes d'indianisme réunies et présentées par* Ch. Malamoud. Paris: Hermann, 1978.

L. Renou & L. Silburn, "Sur la notion de *brahman*", *JAs*, 1949, pp. 7ff.

L. Rocher, *The Purāṇas.* Wiesbaden: O. Harrassowitz, 1986 *A History of Indian Literature* vol. 2, fasc. 3.

———, ed. *Studies in Indian Literature and Philosophy* (Collected Articles of J. A. B. van Buitenen). Delhi: Motilal Banarsidass, 1988.

D. S. Ruegg. *Contributions à l'histoire de la philosophie linguistique indienne.* Paris: de Boccard, 1959.

A. Sanderson. "Purity and Power among the Brahmans of Kashmir," *The Category of the Person,* M. Carrithers, St. Collins, and St. Lukes, eds. Cambridge: Cambridge University Press, 1985.

———, "Maṇḍala and the Āgamic Identity in the Trika of Kashmir." In *Mantras et diagrammes rituels dans l'hindouisme,* A. Padoux, ed. Paris: CNRS, 1986: pp. 169-207.

———, "Śaivism and the Tantric Tradition." In *The World's Religions,* S. Sutherland *et al.,* eds. London: Routledge & Kegan Paul, 1988; pp. 660-704.

———, "The vizualisation of the deities of the Trika." In *L'image divine, culte et méditation dans l'hindouisme,* A. Padoux, ed. Paris: CNRS, 1990.

K. M. Sarma. "Vāk before Bhartṛhari," *Poona Orientalist* 8, 1943: pp. 21-36.

J. Schoterman. ed. and trans. *The Ṣaṭsāhasra Saṃhitā, chapters 1-5.* Leiden: E. J. Brill, 1982.

F. O. Schrader. *Introduction to the Pāñcarātra and the Ahirbudhnya Saṃhitā.* Adyar, 1916.

R. Shamashastry. "The Origin of the Devanāgarī Alphabet." *Indian Antiquary,* vol. 35, 1906: pp. 253ff, 270ff. & 311ff.

L. Silburn. *Kuṇḍalinī; The Energy of the Depths.* Albany: State University of New York Press, 1988.

———, trans. *Hymnes de Abhinavagupta.* Paris: Institut de civilisation Indienne, 1970.

———, trans. *Hymnes aux Kālī: La roue des énergies divines.* Paris: Institut de Civilisation Indienne, 1975.

———, translations with introductions and notes, of *Paramārthasāra, Vātūlanātha Sūtra, Vijñānabhairava, Mahārthamañjarī.* etc.

Paris: de Boccard or Institut de Civilisation Indienne.

D. H. Smith. *A Descriptive Bibliography of the Printed Texts of the Pāñcarātrāgama.* 2 vols., Baroda: Oriental Institute, 1975-1980 Gaekwad's Oriental Series Nos. 158 and 168.

O. Straus. "Altindische Spekulationen über die Sprache und ihre Probleme." *ZDMG* 81 (1927): pp. 99-151.

P. Thieme. "*Brahman.*" *ZDMG* 102 (1952): pp. 91-129.

R. Torella. "Examples of the Influence of Sanskrit Grammar on Indian philosophy." *East and West* vol. 37 (December 1987): pp. 151-164.

R. S. Tripathi. *Kaśmīr Saivāgama mẽ vāk*, Vikramadityasimha Sanatanadharma Kalej Patrika, 1955.

G. Tucci. "Tracce di culto lunare in India." *Riv. d. Studi Orientali* 1919, vol. 12: pp. 419ff.

———, "Animadversiones Indicae." *JRASB* New Ser., vol. XXVI, 1930: pp. 215ff.

———, *The Theory and Practice of the Mandala.* London: Rider & Co., 1961.

V. Varadacharī. *Āgamas and South Indian Vaiṣṇavism.* Madras: M. Rangacharya Memorial Trust, 1982.

A. Weber. "Vāc und Logos." *Indische Studien* 9: Leipzig, 1865: pp. 473-480.

M. Winternitz. "Die Tantra und die Religion der Śākta." *Ostasiatische Zeitschrift* 4, 1915-16: pp. 153-163.

A. Wayman. *The Buddhist Tantras: Light on Indo-tibetan Esotericism.* London: Routledge & Kegan Paul, 1973.

H. Zimmer. *Kunstform und Yoga im indischen Kultbild.* Berlin, 1926. Repr. Frankfurt am Main: Suhrkamp Verlag, 1976.

Periodicals and Collections Quoted in Abbreviated Form

ABORI	*Annals of the Bhandarkar Oriental Research Institute*, Poona.
BEFEO	*Bulletin de l'Ecole Française d'Extrême-Orient*, Paris.
BSOAS	*Bulletin of the School of African and Oriental Studies*, London.
JAs	*Journal Asiatique*, Paris.
JAOS	*Journal of the American Oriental Society*, Boston.
IIJ	*Indo-Iranian Journal*, The Hague.
KSTS	Kaśmir Series of Texts and Studies, Srinagar.
WZKS	*Wiener Zeitschrift für die Kunde Südasiens*, Vienna.
ZDMG	*Zeitschrift der Deutschen Morgenländischen Gesellschaft*, Wiesbaden.

Index of Sanskrit Terms

A

a: the first phoneme, 127, 235-43, 259, 264, 268, 284-85, 288, 296-97
akatha: a triangle made of phonemes, 136
akula: the supreme godhead, 238-40, 278, 287, 292, 306. *See also anuttara*
akṣara: "imperishable", phoneme, syllable, 12-14, 16, 22, 147
akhyāti: the non-perception of the all-containing Absolute, 103, 191
agnibīja: the seed of fire (*RAṂ*), 242, 256, 299, 346
aṅgamantra: mantras of the 'limbs' or 'parts' (*aṅga*) of Śiva, 346-47
aṇu: the individual soul, 290. *See āṇavopāya*
aṇḍa: 'egg', a cosmic division, 301, 359, 361-63
adhisthātṛdevatā: presiding deity (of a class of phonemes, etc.), 155. *See* Brāhmī
adhvan: course or path. See *ṣaḍadhvan*
anacka: (consonant) without vowel, 283, 400, 417
anākhya: the Nameless, 131, 236
anāśritaśakti: Śakti 'unrelated [to anything]', 103, 191, 316
anāśritaśiva: Śiva unrelated [to anything]', 103, 311
anāhata (*nāda*/*śabda*), 'unstruck' (sound), 99-100, 117, 123, 141-42, 237, 283, 301
anuttara: the Absolute, 203, 230, 235ff., 244-46, 252, 260, 267, 284, 296, 401. *See also akula*
anunāsika: nasal phoneme, 108. *See also ardhacandra*
anusaṃdhāna: searching attention, intense awareness, 202, 397-99
anusvāra: 'after-sound', nasal utterance pronounced after a vowel, 105, 107, 118, 155, 230, 272, 274. *See also bindu*
antarabhilāpa: inner expression, 175, 179, 196
antarbhitti (or *bhitti*): surface or screen on which the cosmos is projected, 179
antaḥstha: 'standing between': the semi-vowels, 156, 226, 300, 309-10
abhilāpa: expression, enunciation, 175-76, 178-79, 184
abhyupagama: willing acceptance, assent, 247. *See also icchā*
amṛtabīja (or *amṛtavarṇa*): seed (or phoneme) of nectar or of immortality: 159, 258, 262, 301 (*sa*)
Ambikā: an energy, 116-18, 130, 268
arṇa: See varṇa
artha: thing, object, meaning, notion, 83, 115

parispanda: subtle vibration, 194, 250, 273
paśyantī: the Visionary (Word), 83, 102, 115, 133, 142-43, 157, 169, 188-204, 211, 232, 265, 312-13, 316-17, 340, 344
piṇḍanātha: the mantra *KHPHREṂ*, also called *mātṛsadbhāva*, 422-26
pūrṇam, pūrṇata: the All-containing, 256, 420
pṛthivībīja: the seed of earth, *LAM*, 256, 299
prakāśa: light, light of consciousness, 77, 78, 81, 86, 88, 110, 151, 174-75, 211, 239, 245, 254, 257, 274, 285-86
prakṣobha: stirring of energy, 249, 340. *See kṣobha*
pracchādana: covering, concealing by the 'I': *see ācchādana*
praṇava: the mantra *OṂ* (or *HAUṂ*), 142, 380, 402-04
pratibimba: reflection, reflected image, 80, 231, 234, 306, 312-15
pratibhā: insight, vision, illuminative intuition, 181, 187
pratisthā(kalā): one of the five cosmic *kalā*s, 358-89, 362
pratyabhijñā: recognition, 176
pratyavamarśa: reflexive representation or awareness, 175-78, 192, 197, 201, 247, 249
pratyāhāra: bringing together of several letters, 27, 286, 304
pramātṛ: agent of cognition, knower, 228, 272, 343, 349, 350, 365, 391; *pramāṇa:* medium or means of cognition, 275, 341, 343; *prameya:* object of cognition, 275, 351
pralayākala: 'those inert in dissolution', a category of *pramātṛ*, 104
prāṇa: flow of vital energy, respiratory breath, exhalation of breath, 24-26, 28, 83, 125, 136-38, 164, 207, 214, 217, 283, 294, 337-38, 347, 365-66, 367, 368, 392, 412
prāsādamantra: often *HAUṂ*, 384
pluta, pluti: protracted, protraction (to three *mātras*) of a phoneme, 163, 260, 265

B

bindu: dot, the fifteenth phoneme, 'drop' of energy, 19, 51, 83, 87, 98, 105-24, 126-27, 158, 214, 272-77, 287-88, 375, 388, 394, 405, 408, 415. *See also anusvāra*
bīja: seed, Śiva and the vowels, 41, 87, 154, 230-31, 257, 268; a division of *bindu*, 115-17, 131, 149, 158, 225-26, 265
brahman, 6, 8-9, 18, 22-25, 123, 281, 409; the third *brahman*, 301, 417
brahmapañcaka: the fivefold *brahman* (a group of five *tattva*s), 311
brahmamantra (or *pañcabrahman*): the five mantras *sadyojāta*, etc., 129, 227, 346
Brahmī (or Brāhmanī): one of the *adhisthātṛdevatā*s of the eight *varga*s, 155, 272
bhāvanā: creative meditation, self-creation through thought, 113, 205, 413-14, 419
bhinnayoni: said of the *mālinī* alphabetical order, 322-23
bhuvana: 'world': cosmic division—one of the *adhvan*s, 85, 128, 355, 363-64
bhuvanādhvan: one of the *adhvans*, made up of *buvana*s, 334, 356, 358-59, 363. *See also ṣaḍadhvan*
bhūtalipi: 'demon-writing', 149-50, 160

M

ma, 256
madhyamā: the Intermediate Word,

83, 115, 133, 143, 157, 196, 204-16, 265, 320-27
mantra, 4, 14, 18, 26, 49-50, 85, 94ff., 132, 160, 174, 185-86, 225, 286, 288-89, 343-48 (*mantrādhvan*), 372-426 (chap. 7); one of the *pramātṛ*, 104, 391
mantrakalā: the energy or power of mantras, 104
mantravīrya: the efficient power of mantras, 104, 174, 383, 419. *See also mantrakalā*
mantrādhvan: the course of the mantras, 343-48. *See also ṣaḍadhvan*
mantreśvara: lord of the mantras, 101-05, 391
mahāpaśyantī: the great *paśyantī*, 200-201
mahābindu, 112
mahāmāyā, 310-11
mahāsṛṣṭi, the great emanation, 231, 306-12. *See also śabdarāśi*
Mātṛkā: alphabet deity, 224
mātṛkā: 'mother' or 'little mother': the phonemes esp. as forms of energy, 29, 51, 132, 147-61, 285, 312-20, 339, 385
mātṛsadbhāva, see *piṇḍanātha*
mātrā: mora, prosodial unit of one instant, 19, 163, 260
māyā, 119, 121, 185, 216, 309, 327, 341, 418-19
Mālinī: alphabet deity, 224, 307
mālinī, 154, 156-57, 232, 267, 320-27, 339, 342, 346
mudrā: hand or body posture, trance-inducing posture, mystic attitude,, 47, 267
mūrdhanya: cerebral letters: the *ṭavarga* and the four retroflex: *see ṛ, ṝ, ḷ, ḹ*
mūlādhāra: the lowest of the bodily *cakras*, 125, 132-33, 135, 149, 151
mṛtyujit: the *netramantra OṂ JUṂ SAḤ*, 411-16

Y

ya (*ra, la, va*): semi-vowels, 298-99, 309-10. *See also antaḥstha*
YAṂ: seed of air, 346
yama: 'twin', one of a pair: transitional nasal sound, 161-62
yoni: womb: Śakti and the consonants, 154, 231, 257, 268, 294

R

RAṂ: seed of fire, 346. *See agnibīja*
rava: sound, humming, 114, 118, 122, 124
Rodhinī or Rundhanī: the Obstructive, an energy obstructing the path to *mokṣa*, 129
Raudrī: an energy, 116-18, 129, 130, 268. *See also* Jyeṣṭhā, Ambikā, Vāmā

L

LAṂ: seed of earth, 346, 361. *See also pṛthivībīja*

V

VAṂ: seed of water, 346
varga: group or class of phonemes, 129, 149, 154-55, 231, 272, 351
varṇa (or *arṇa*): phoneme, 51, 84, 85, 87, 99, 147, 162-65, 223-329 (chap. 5); *varṇādhvan:* the course of the *varṇas*, 338-343, 374; *see also ṣaḍadhvan*
varṇaparāmarśa: phonetic awareness, 228ff (chap. 5)
varṇasamāmnāya: the traditional collection of phonemes: the Sanskrit alphabet, 84, 154, 223, 230
vācaka/vācya: expressive/expressed, 50, 83, 98, 108, 154, 205-06, 209-12, 220, 295, 327, 333, 348

Ś

H